Food from your Garden

Food from your Garden

All you need to know to grow, cook and preserve your own fruit and vegetables

PUBLISHED BY THE READER'S DIGEST ASSOCIATION LIMITED · LONDON NEW YORK MONTREAL SYDNEY CAPE TOWN

FOOD FROM YOUR GARDEN

Edited and designed by The Reader's Digest Association Limited, London
First Edition Copyright © 1977
Reprinted with amendments 1985
The Reader's Digest Association Limited, 25 Berkeley Square, London W1X 6AB

Printed in Great Britain

Acknowledgments

Contributors and advisers
H. A. Baker, NDH
Kenneth A. Beckett
David C. Bland (*Southern Pullet Rearers*)
Lizzie Boyd
Audrey V. Brooks, B.Sc.
Arthur M. Dines
A. J. Halstead
K. M. Harris, B.Sc.
Roy Hay, MBE, VMH
D. B. Clay Jones, B.Sc.
Keith Mossman
National Federation of Women's Institutes

Olive A. Odell
Franklyn Perring, MA, Ph.D, FLS
David Pycraft, Dip. Hort. (Wisley)
Peter Russell, Dip. Hort. (Wisley)
Dr Joe Stubbs
Ben Turner
Brian Walkden
D. B. Wilkins, MA, MRCVS

Artists
Jeffery Matthews, MSIA *cover lettering*
Josephine Ranken (*The Garden Studio*) *cover illustration*

David Baxter (*The Garden Studio*)
Richard Bonson

Leonora Box (*Saxon Artists*)
Helen Cowcher
Patrick Cox (*The Garden Studio*)
Brian Delf
Colin Emberson
Shirley Felts
Ian Garrard (*Linden Artists*)
Tony Graham
Vana Haggerty
Nicolas H. T. Hall
Hayward and Martin
Richard Jacobs
Duncan Mil
Annabel Milne
Donald Myall (*The Garden Studio*)

Linda Nash
David Nockels
Charles Pickard
G. E. Robson
Ann Savage
Basil Smith (*Saxon Artists*)
Kathleen Smith, MSIA
Peter Stebbing
Venner Artists Ltd
Norman Weaver, FSIA (*Artists Partners Ltd*)
Michael J. Woods

Photographer
Philip Dowell

The publishers are grateful for help given by the following people and organisations:

A to Z Botanical Collection Ltd
Alcan Polyfoil Limited
Heather Angel
Ardea Photographics
British Egg Information Service
E. G. Burtt (*Assoc. of Bee Appliance Manufacturers*)
Craftsmen Potters Shop
Justin de Blank Provisions
Divertimenti
Samuel Dobie and Son Ltd
Barbara Dowell
East Malling Research Station
Brian Furner

Hills Industries Ltd
Humex Ltd
ICI Plant Protection Ltd
Robert Jackson and Co. Ltd
Long Ashton Research Station
Neville Marten
David Mellor
Ministry of Agriculture, Fisheries and Food
Murphy Chemical Ltd
Mushroom Growers' Association
National Institute of Agricultural Botany
National Society of Leisure Gardeners Ltd

National Vegetable Research Station
Natural History Photographic Agency
Potato Marketing Board
Prestige Ltd
Kathy Roche
Carolyn Russell
Suttons Seeds Ltd
Thompson and Morgan (Ipswich) Ltd
Tilemart Ltd
James Trehane and Sons Ltd
W. J. Unwin Ltd
Michael Warren, AIIP
Wedgwood & Gered

———◦———

Contents
of
Food
from your
Garden

——➤o◀——

BEFORE YOU START . . .
Essential facts about home food-growing.......8

A BASIC GUIDE TO
THE KITCHEN GARDEN
All about soil care and cultivation methods

Introduction 9
Re-planning your garden 10
Choosing and using garden tools 14
Soils and manures 15
Making your own compost 21
Digging and cultivating 22
Draining waterlogged soil 25
Planning the kitchen garden 26
Sowing seeds in the open 30
Sowing seeds under glass and indoors......... 32
Weeds and weedkillers 37
The fruit garden 40
Greenhouses, frames and cloches............... 48
Glossary of gardening terms 57

GROWING AND COOKING

An A-Z guide to 100 fruits,
vegetables and herbs

Introduction..61
Angelica to Watercress 62–276
Seasonal cooking:
    Spring and summer dishes 133
    Autumn and winter dishes.................... 205

A FOOD-GROWER'S CALENDAR

Twelve months of reminders for fruit and
    vegetable growers 277

PESTS AND DISEASES

How to identify and combat common
plant disorders

Introduction.. 281
Pests 282
Diseases 286
Chemical controls 292

HOME PRESERVING

Enjoying summer's plenty throughout the year

Introduction... 293
Freezing 294
Bottling 310
Jams 314
Jellies 320
Fruit cheeses and butters........................... 323
Syrups and juices...................................... 326
Pickles 328
Chutneys 335
Sauces, ketchups and relishes 339
Vinegars... 342
Drying.. 343
Salting.. 346
Preserving eggs 348

FOOD FROM THE COUNTRYSIDE

Fruits, greenfoods and fungi to pick and enjoy

Introduction... 349
Fruits and berries 350
Greenfoods 352
Mushrooms 354
Flowers... 356

MAKING YOUR OWN WINE

Delicious and inexpensive drinks from
garden produce

Introduction... 357
Equipment and methods 358
Recipes... 362

KEEPING POULTRY AND BEES

Producing eggs and honey in your own garden

Introduction... 365
Poultry 366
Bees 372

INDEX 375

Before you start . . .

The prospect of fresh, inexpensive fruit and vegetables from your own garden is obviously inviting. But is it realistic? The following comments are for all gardeners who would welcome a little reassurance before taking the plunge.

Is it worth it?
Lower housekeeping bills and a satisfying sense of achievement are assured if you grow part of your family's food. In addition, freshly picked vegetables and fruits have more flavour and a better texture than those sold in shops, and they are richer in vitamin C.

Even the smallest garden – with a vegetable plot of, say, 100–150 sq. ft – will provide salads and tomatoes for a family of four during many months of the year. With perhaps double this space, beans, onions, one or more kinds of fruit, and other money-saving crops can be added to the list.

To prove the point about money-saving, estimate your present weekly outlay on salads, vegetables and fruit – including tinned and frozen produce, and such items as pie fillings and vegetable soups. Even halving the sum should make a big difference to the family budget, and you can expect to do better than that if you have, say, 70–100 sq. yds for growing crops.

Remember that surplus produce – such as a glut of beans or apples – can be stored, or else processed in numerous ways.

You may even decide to venture further towards self-sufficiency by keeping poultry or bees.

Is it difficult?
No special skill or aptitude is needed if you follow the instructions in this book. It is essential, though, to have a reasonably well-drained plot that is open to the sun for a good part of the day. Clay soil need not be a hindrance. With the right treatment (see p. 15) it will often grow the finest crops of all.

But do not expect to get worthwhile results from poor, 'hungry' soil. Be generous with manure, compost and fertilisers – not forgetting lime, when necessary – and you will be surprised at your garden's bounty.

If you have tried before, and failed . .
Unless waterlogging or excessive shade was the cause, you probably made one of the following mistakes, all of them fairly common with beginners:

Failure to apply sufficient manure and fertilisers.
Sowing at the wrong times.
Growing crops too close together.
Failing to thin-out seedlings.
It could be worth trying again, this time following the instructions in the book.

When to begin
Autumn and winter are ideal times to make a start, because you will have time to dig and manure the plot, and to plant fruit trees and bushes, before spring sowings are due and the annual cycle of growth begins.

If you start in spring or summer, avoid trying to do everything at once. It is better to dig and manure a small area thoroughly, and sow a limited range of crops for the first season, rather than rush to get everything in on ill-prepared ground and run the risk of a disappointing harvest.

If space is a problem
As explained on p. 13, a surprising amount can be grown even on a sunny patio. However, if lack of space is a major drawback it is worth applying to your local council for an allotment.

The snag is that you may get no further than being put on a waiting list, because councils throughout the country are already trying to find plots for about 100,000 applicants.

However, the situation is much easier in some areas than in others, so it is well worth inquiring.

To give applicants a slightly better chance, some councils are splitting the traditional 300 sq. yd (250 sq. m.) allotment into two or more plots.

As an alternative to renting an allotment, consider taking over a garden belonging to an elderly or disabled neighbour. They would probably be delighted to see the plot cultivated, especially if given a share of the produce that you eventually harvest.

A BASIC GUIDE TO THE KITCHEN GARDEN

All about soil care and cultivation methods

Anybody can have green fingers; it is simply a matter of following straightforward instructions and applying common sense.

After all, it is in the natural order of things for seeds to germinate and for seedlings to develop into healthy, full-grown plants. All they need are the right conditions . . . This section of the book will help you to provide those conditions.

If there seems a lot to learn, take heart. There is certainly no need to read and remember every page before making a start in the garden. For instance, it

may be a year or two before there are fruit trees to prune or until you get the urge to buy a greenhouse for growing tender or out-of-season crops.

In the meantime, the main priority is to decide where to grow your fruit and vegetable crops, and then to set about improving and digging the soil ahead of the first sowings and plantings. The rest can follow as the need arises.

Technical terms are avoided as far as possible, but the glossary that begins on page 57 will help to resolve any doubts or queries that do occur.

Re-planning your garden

With careful planning, even a small garden can produce an abundance of fruit and vegetables.

The food-producing area should, however, harmonise with the rest of the garden, where children play and the whole family relaxes to enjoy the natural beauty you have helped to create.

Therefore, when re-planning a garden to give a greater emphasis to food growing, aim at making a happy marriage between the productive and the leisure areas. This can be achieved in a number of ways, as shown in the following pages.

Every garden presents problems arising from its shape, size or aspect, and every gardener must make his own choice of things to grow. These pages, therefore, will show you how to design a more productive and attractive garden to suit your individual needs and tastes.

Drawing up a plan

When planning a new garden, or redesigning one that is already established, first measure the plot and draw it to scale.

If you are re-planning an old garden, mark features such as paths and trees that might be incorporated in the new design.

Before sketching this design, list what you want to fit into the plan: greenhouse, frames, shed, compost bin, herb bed, the number and types of fruit trees and bushes and, possibly, bee hives or a poultry house.

Next, decide on the area that you are prepared to allot to growing vegetables.

If you plan to grow only salad vegetables, you can set aside a plot as small as 10 × 10 ft (3 × 3 m.) to gather regular supplies through the summer.

If, however, you want to make a significant contribution to the kitchen throughout the year, you must allow for a vegetable plot measuring at least 30 × 20 ft (9 × 6 m.), with an even larger area if you intend to grow main-crop as well as early potatoes.

Finding the right sites

Having listed the main items to be included in the garden, the next task is to fit them into the most suitable positions. You will probably have to amend your original rough sketch plan as you go along.

Vegetables Reserve an open site with plenty of sun and, if possible, sheltering walls or fences. Vegetables cannot be grown successfully within the rooting area of trees, or on a site that gets shade for much of the day (see also p. 26).

Paths In the vegetable garden, lay paths to such points as the tool shed, greenhouse, compost heap and garden frame. You will appreciate this part of your planning after heavy rain and when using the wheelbarrow.

Fruit When marking fruit trees and bushes on the plan, check with the planting distances recommended on p. 40. Make the most of garden space by siting cordons, espaliers or fan-trained trees on walls or fences.

Lawn This is the most variable part of the garden plan, as you can change the size to suit the area needed for fruit and vegetables. In a small garden you may even decide to do without a lawn and build a patio as your relaxing area.

Patio As with the lawn, the size can be altered as the plan develops.

Herb garden Ideally, plant herbs as near the kitchen as possible. You can grow the most popular types in a bed measuring about 6 × 6 ft (1.8 × 1.8 m.) or even smaller.

Flowers In a predominately food-producing garden, concentrate flowers in bold beds rather than dotting them in narrow strips.

Greenhouses Site the greenhouse where the light is best all the year round.

If possible, place it near the house to make it more accessible in bad weather. This will also make it easier and cheaper to lay water pipes and electric cables.

Set cold frames next to the greenhouse to save work when transferring seedlings from the house to the frame.

Compost bin Tuck the bin in a corner, but lay an approach path suitable for a barrow.

Shed If possible, site the shed within handy reach of both the house and the greenhouse.

Poultry house This should be sited as far as possible from any house – whether a neighbour's or your own.

Bee hives Site hives as far as possible from your own and neighbouring houses. Screen with a high fence or tall plants to force the bees high on their inward and outward journeys.

Getting the proportions right

Having decided on what you want in your garden, draw a rough sketch on your scale plan. Start with the lawn, making bold curves until the shape pleases you. This will give you an accurate idea of the amount of land remaining for growing fruit and vegetables.

If you have not left enough, 'swing the loop' – drawing curves inside the original line to reduce the size of the lawn and make a larger food-growing area.

In a formal garden with a rectangular lawn, work out the proportions on the plan in the same way. These methods can also be used for planning paved areas instead of a lawn.

ACHIEVING SCALE AND BALANCE

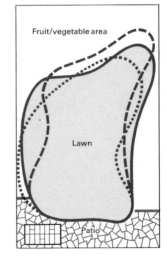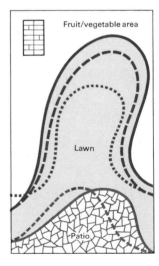

Whether you prefer curved, flowing lines or a more formal design, keep a balance between the proportions of the lawn and the overall shape of the garden – reducing the lawn's width, as well as its length, if necessary. Make trial sketches to find pleasing shapes for both lawn and patio that will leave sufficient space for growing food crops.

Where to grow fruit

If you plan to grow a free-standing fruit tree in the lawn – a bush, perhaps, or even a half-standard (see p. 41) – do not place it in the centre. Instead, plant the tree a little to one side.

The same principle applies when planting a group of soft-fruit bushes.

Try different positions on your plan so that the tree will be placed happily in the shape of the lawn and provide a focal point of interest. It may also help to conceal a shed or compost bin, or even a neighbouring building.

When planting a number of trees in a border with other plants, judge how they will fit into the general appearance of the garden when they mature into trees of different sizes. The nurseryman will be able to tell you what height and spread can be expected.

(For more detailed advice on planning a fruit garden, see p. 40.)

SITING FRUIT TREES AND BUSHES

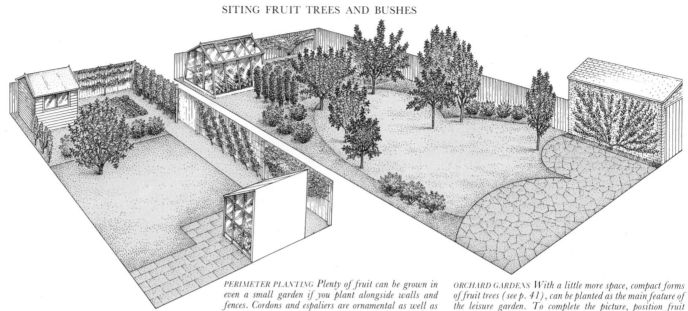

PERIMETER PLANTING Plenty of fruit can be grown in even a small garden if you plant alongside walls and fences. Cordons and espaliers are ornamental as well as productive. Fruit bushes make attractive edging subjects.

ORCHARD GARDENS With a little more space, compact forms of fruit trees (see p. 41), can be planted as the main feature of the leisure garden. To complete the picture, position fruit bushes to act as a foil to the trees.

Screening the vegetable plot

Even the most enthusiastic gardener may not wish to contemplate rows of vegetables while relaxing in a deck chair. If you decide to form a screen, this should blend in with the general shape of the lawn or patio, rather than form an obvious barrier.

Tall, flowering perennials or a rosemary hedge can make a summer screen. Soft-fruit bushes or trained fruit trees (see p. 41), make permanent screens.

Curve the path into the vegetable garden. This creates interest in what is on the other side but out of sight.

PRODUCTIVE SCREENS Several forms of screens are shown here, though in practice one may be sufficient. Each form can be productive – the pergola used to support a vine, the hedge formed of rosemary plants and the espalier bearing a crop of either apples or pears.

Vegetables as ornamental plants

In a small garden, one way to increase food production is to make a virtue of vegetables as ornamental features.

Cut beds of suitable size in a lawn near a path. Grow only one or two types of vegetables in each bed, so that the visual effect is stronger and the growing conditions can be varied to suit each sort.

Spaces may be left in paving to create similar beds; but on a patio, a raised bed (see p. 13) is more practical.

Sweet corn, tomatoes, herbs and salad vegetables can be grown in this manner.

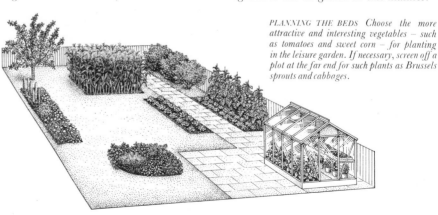

PLANNING THE BEDS Choose the more attractive and interesting vegetables – such as tomatoes and sweet corn – for planting in the leisure garden. If necessary, screen off a plot at the far end for such plants as Brussels sprouts and cabbages.

CHOOSING THE MOST SUITABLE TREES, BUSHES AND PLANTS FOR THE SITE

Making the plan work

Having drawn your scale plan, clear out unwanted growth or paths in an old garden, or dig over and level the ground of a new plot.

First lay the paths. To do this take measurements from the plan and drive in wooden pegs about 12 in. (305 mm.) apart to mark the edges of the paths. Make paths at least 2½ ft (760 mm.) wide.

The choice of material is an individual one. Concrete laid on a hardcore base is long-lasting and efficient, but dull in appearance; paving stones and bricks are attractive but expensive; gravel is attractive but gets carried into the house and must be treated against weeds.

Whatever path material you choose, make the patio at the same time, pegging out the shape first.

After laying paths and a patio, tackle the lawn. Dig the ground over, level, roll and rake it, then peg out the shape according to the plan. If sowing seeds – preferably in spring or autumn – follow the curves of the pegs, but allow a little seed to fall outside so that when growth is vigorous you can shape the edge neatly.

If turfing, bring the turves over the pegs. Remove the pegs and replace them over the identical spot on top. Cut the turf against the line of the pegs. Roll the lawn and fill in gaps between the turves with sifted soil.

Next plant fruit trees and bushes (see p. 42), site the greenhouse or shed, and dig over the vegetable garden.

The first growing season is already under way.

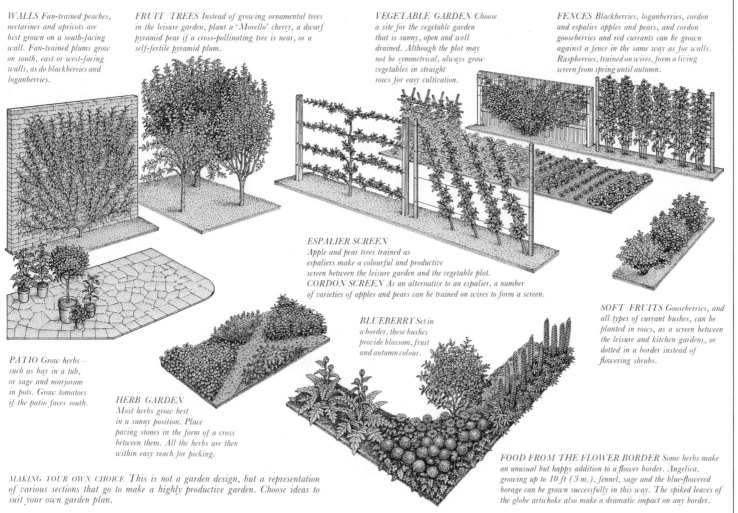

WALLS Fan-trained peaches, nectarines and apricots are best grown on a south-facing wall. Fan-trained plums grow on south, east or west-facing walls, as do blackberries and loganberries.

FRUIT TREES Instead of growing ornamental trees in the leisure garden, plant a 'Morello' cherry, a dwarf pyramid pear if a cross-pollinating tree is near, or a self-fertile pyramid plum.

VEGETABLE GARDEN Choose a site for the vegetable garden that is sunny, open and well drained. Although the plot may not be symmetrical, always grow vegetables in straight rows for easy cultivation.

FENCES Blackberries, loganberries, cordon and espalier apples and pears, and cordon gooseberries and red currants can be grown against a fence in the same way as for walls. Raspberries, trained on wires, form a living screen from spring until autumn.

ESPALIER SCREEN Apple and pear trees trained as espaliers make a colourful and productive screen between the leisure garden and the vegetable plot. CORDON SCREEN As an alternative to an espalier, a number of varieties of apples and pears can be trained on wires to form a screen.

SOFT FRUITS Gooseberries, and all types of currant bushes, can be planted in rows, as a screen between the leisure and kitchen gardens, or dotted in a border instead of flowering shrubs.

BLUEBERRY Set in a border, these bushes provide blossom, fruit and autumn colour.

PATIO Grow herbs – such as bay in a tub, or sage and marjoram in pots. Grow tomatoes if the patio faces south.

HERB GARDEN Most herbs grow best in a sunny position. Place paving stones in the form of a cross between them. All the herbs are then within easy reach for picking.

FOOD FROM THE FLOWER BORDER Some herbs make an unusual but happy addition to a flower border. Angelica, growing up to 10 ft (3 m.), fennel, sage and the blue-flowered borage can be grown successfully in this way. The spiked leaves of the globe artichoke also make a dramatic impact on any border.

MAKING YOUR OWN CHOICE This is not a garden design, but a representation of various sections that go to make a highly productive garden. Choose ideas to suit your own garden plan.

In large gardens of the past, sharply defined frontiers divided lawns and flower borders from the kitchen garden. In modern gardens such frontiers must be crossed if food production is to be increased.

Herbs, fruit trees and bushes provide not only worthwhile crops but can also add a beauty of their own.

Where a flowering tree is desirable, for example, plant a 'Morello' cherry. It will produce spring blossom, followed by excellent fruit for cooking and jam-making.

Grow fruit – such as apples, pears, peaches, apricots, red currants and gooseberries – on walls and fences, not only to save space, but also to make an attractive frame to the garden.

As the illustration above shows, some herbs and vegetables planted among flowers can add distinctive touches to a border as well as food and flavourings.

MAKING THE MOST OF LIMITED SPACE

In a small garden, even a paved area – such as a sunny patio or yard – can be used for a number of different crops. This generally means growing the plants in containers.

Make the most, too, of any wall or fence that faces between south and west. Blackberries and loganberries will thrive here – and occupy little space – or you may prefer to grow a fig, a grape vine or a fan-trained peach.

Pots, troughs and tubs Every garden centre offers a wide range of containers that are both attractive and practical.

Use clay or plastic pots and wooden troughs for tomatoes, peppers or aubergines. Placed near the house wall, which at night releases warmth stored during the day, the plants often do better than in the open garden. Daily watering is needed, together with free drain-age at the base of the container.

Bay trees remain popular subjects for tubs (for training, see p. 88), but a variety of culinary herbs can be grown instead. A substantial tub provides adequate space for a fig's root system and the sheltered position will help the embryo fruits to survive the winter.

PEAT BAGS The compost contains fertiliser to start the plants growing, but large plants need extra feeding as they mature.

POTS, TROUGHS AND TUBS Container-grown plants need good soil. Use John Innes No. 2 compost, or a peat compost.

STRAWBERRY POTS AND BARRELS *These containers are easy to net against birds and the fruits are kept clear of the ground.*

MAKING A RAISED BED If built against a wall, line the back with slates to avoid bridging the damp-proof course. Allow at least 12 in. (305 mm.) of soil.

Strawberry pots and barrels For an effective but functional focal point on a patio, grow strawberries in the type of tall, earthenware pot that incorporates planting pockets, or adapt an old barrel for the purpose. Cover the container with netting when the fruits form, and turn it every day or two to expose the plants to equal amounts of sunlight.

Peat bags Almost any type of vegetable can be grown in the peat bags sold by garden shops and centres. To ensure maximum return for your outlay, though, give first priority to high-cost crops such as tomatoes, peppers and aubergines.

Patio ideas The patio itself will contribute towards food production if you remove one or two paving slabs and form pockets of good soil for growing herbs. This idea is less practical if space is very limited, in which case herbs could form an edging between paving and lawn.

A raised bed, built with bricks or stone as a permanent feature on a patio, can be used for growing any of the plants suggested for containers. Free drainage is essential, so provide outlets at the base and lay a layer of rubble, topped with gravel, before filling with good soil.

SPECIAL CONTAINERS Pots wired to a board, an old chimney pot, hanging baskets and a window-box suggest the scope for imagination when choosing containers.

GROWING STRAWBERRIES IN A BARREL

Bore 2 in. (50 mm.) diameter holes about 12 in. (305 mm.) apart round the barrel, using a padsaw or a hole saw and staggering the holes. Bore ten $\frac{1}{2}$ in. (12 mm.) diameter holes in the bottom.

Stand the barrel on bricks to ensure good drainage.

Place an old drain-pipe in the centre of the barrel and fill it with gravel. Cover the base with rubble, then a layer of gravel, and fill the barrel with good garden soil.

Form a gravel core with a drain-pipe.

As filling proceeds, push plants through the holes from outside, firming soil over the roots. Withdraw the drain-pipe when the barrel is full, leaving the core of gravel as drainage.

Set additional plants in the surface soil.

Choosing and using garden tools

Only about half a dozen tools, and such essentials as a watering can and hose, are needed to grow vegetables and fruit for your family. Until you gain experience, avoid the more specialised gadgets displayed in garden shops.

Choose good-quality tools of a convenient size and weight. Compare different makes by handling as wide a variety as possible before buying. Because good tools will last for many years – some, perhaps, for a lifetime – it is false economy to buy cheap products of indifferent quality.

Tools you will need

The most useful tools and equipment for food growing are:

Spade At least one spade, with a blade measuring approximately 7 × 11 in. (180 × 280 mm.), is needed for digging. A border spade, with a blade about 6 × 9 in. (150 × 230 mm.), is a convenient alternative if you have heavy clay, and for digging holes for planting and for posts.

Though relatively expensive, stainless-steel blades are not liable to rust and the polished surface makes for easier digging on clay.

D-shaped handles made of polypropylene are stronger than those made of wood and are less likely to cause blisters. A flat tread will prevent damage to shoes and boots.

A semi-automatic spade, such as the Terrex, is an effective alternative – especially for gardeners with weak backs. This works by leverage instead of lifting and enables the soil to be turned over with a minimum of effort.

The knack of using a conventional spade lies in letting its weight do some of the work for you. A swinging, rhythmic movement when digging helps the blade to penetrate the soil.

Fork A four-tined fork is invaluable for breaking lumpy soil, for turning over a plot between crops and for lifting deep-rooted plants. It is also useful for shifting compost and garden rubbish. The overall tine measurements should be about the same as those of a digging spade, or a little larger.

Flat-tined forks are sold for potato lifting, but the normal square-tined digging fork is adequate for lifting garden crops.

Do not use a fork for levering out obstinate stumps or posts. Once bent, the tines are difficult to straighten and the tool becomes awkward to use.

Rake For levelling soil and preparing seed beds you will need a well-balanced rake with 10–14 teeth. One with a light head and a slender ash handle is the most suitable.

Test the tool's weight and balance, because you should support at least part of it with your lower hand rather than simply dragging the head through the soil. This ensures even penetration and makes it easier to level out ridges and hollows.

Hoes There are four main types of hoes:

Draw hoe. With the blade turned over roughly at right-angles to the handle, this tool is excellent for chopping out weeds on heavily infested ground, for forming drills (shallow furrows) when sowing seeds, and for drawing soil around such plants as potatoes and leeks.

Dutch hoe. The blade is almost in line with the handle and the tool is used with a pushing or prodding action. This hoe leaves the severed weeds uncovered by soil, making sure that they soon wilt and die.

Patent hoes. Hoes such as the Swoe and Saynor are improved forms of the Dutch hoe. They are good for routine hoeing but less suitable for clearing heavy weed growth.

Short-handled hoe. Also known as the onion hoe, this tool is like a miniature draw hoe and is ideal for working close to plants without damaging them. It is tiring to use unless you kneel.

Most gardeners develop their own technique for controlling weeds between rows of vegetable crops. It is best to hoe frequently – every week if possible – during the growing season – before the weeds develop beyond the seedling stage.

Row crops are easily hoed by first weeding between the plants in each row – by hand, or by working forwards with an onion hoe or a draw hoe – and then working backwards between the rows with a Dutch hoe. This allows close weeding between plants in the row but ensures that most of the

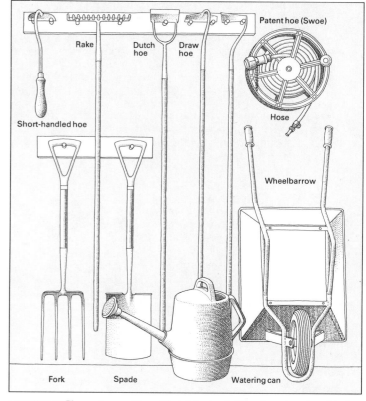

BASIC TOOLS FOR FOOD GROWING

LARGE TOOLS To save space, and prevent tools being knocked over, hang them clear of the floor on pegs or a rack. The storage shed or garage must be dry.

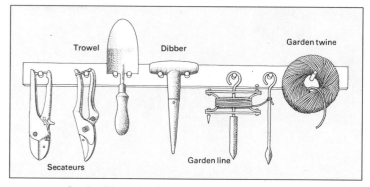

SMALL TOOLS In spite of the many gadgets available, the small selection of tools shown above will meet most needs in the vegetable garden and fruit garden.

severed weeds will be left uncovered and will not be pressed into the soil by your feet.

Using a patent hoe, such as the Swoe, the two operations can be combined.

Trowel Choose a sturdy tool with a long, not too broad blade. If you measure (and remember) the length of the blade, and of the whole tool, you will find these useful guides to spacing plants.

Dibber Though a trowel can be used instead, this tool is ideal for planting cabbages and other brassicas, leeks and lettuces. A steel-pointed dibber can be bought, or an old spade or fork handle shaped to a point.

After placing the plant in the dibber hole, stab the tool in a second time an inch or so away to firm the soil against the roots.

Garden line Though a length of string and two pegs will suffice for marking, a purpose-made reel and line save time and are easier to use. The line must be as long as your longest rows, and should preferably be of nylon.

Secateurs These essential aids to fruit pruning are also handy in the vegetable garden.

The basic choice lies between secateurs which have scissor-action blades, and those which have a single blade cutting against an anvil. Both are equally effective, provided they are kept rust-free and sharp.

Wheelbarrow A sturdy barrow, with as large a wheel as possible, is needed for moving soil, rubble and paving materials while garden-making, and for carrying compost, garden rubbish and crops that have been harvested.

Flimsy barrows, and some with low-slung bodies on two small wheels, are less suitable for shifting heavy weights.

Hose and watering can Sooner or later a hose will be needed on all but the smallest plots. Watering with a can is slow and tedious, and you are unlikely to give plants the thorough soaking they need during prolonged dry weather.

Whether or not you have a reel, coil the hose neatly during winter. Plastic hoses are intractable if they have been stored in a tangled heap. Tap connectors and extension pieces are easily attached if the hose is softened in hot water.

A 2 gallon (9 l.) can – plastic or metal, and with both a coarse and a fine rose – is essential for settling your plants into their bed, for applying liquid fertilisers and for occasional watering which does not call for a hose.

Caring for garden tools

Dry storage – first scraping damp soil from metal – ensures a long life for garden tools. Even better, oil or grease metal parts after removing the soil.

Keep hoe blades sharp by filing once or twice each season. Secure the head of the hoe in a vice, positioned so that you can sharpen the angled side of the blade.

Use a broad file and make sweeping strokes in one direction only – away from your body. Remove burrs on the other side with a few light strokes.

Powered cultivators

Although it is not worth buying a motor cultivator for the average suburban garden, in most areas these machines can be hired by the day. They provide an easy means of creating a kitchen garden.

Cultivators of all types have rotating tines that break the soil and, to some extent, turn it over. They will mix in a dressing of manure, and the depth of cultivation can be varied.

You may be offered the choice of a cultivator with power-driven wheels and tines or one with power drive to the tines only. Both are effective, but they have different characteristics.

A cultivator with power drive to both wheels and tines – the tines will be mounted at the rear, under a hood – is a little easier to use and tends to mince the soil finely. It is ideal for seed-bed preparation, but small models are less suitable for the initial breaking of heavy soil – especially as the depth of cultivation tends to be limited.

Although there are large, heavy machines of this type, suitable for all types of cultivating, they are seldom available for hire without an operator.

Cultivators which have power drive to the tines only – the tines being mounted under or in front of the engine – work on a different principle. They draw the machine forward as well as digging the soil, the rate of progress and depth of digging being determined by the gardener's handling of the machine.

The more substantial machines of this type are ideal for establishing a new kitchen garden. But beware of cultivating ground infested with perennial weeds, as chopping the roots into pieces makes eradication more difficult.

Soils and manures

More than any other factor, the quality of your soil will determine how successful you are in growing fruit and vegetables.

Fortunately, practically every type of land can be made to yield good crops. But to make the most of your garden you should first understand the nature of the soil you are dealing with.

Getting to know your soil

Soils fall into five general groups – clay, loam, sand, chalk and peat – but only a minority of gardens can be classified so distinctly. Most gardens have a mixture of soils, though often with one type predominating.

This guide will help you to identify your soil and cultivate it to the best advantage. Use it in conjunction with local knowledge gathered over the years by neighbours and garden societies.

To make your own classification, note first the reactions of the soil to extreme weather conditions, such as drought or prolonged heavy rain.

If puddles take hours, or even days, to disappear after heavy rain, and the soil bakes rock hard in a drought, you have a clay soil.

If water drains away fairly quickly after heavy rain but the ground stays unworkable for a day or two, you have a loam soil.

When water from even a heavy thunder shower drains away within minutes, your soil is probably light and sandy. In a drought, such soil must be constantly watered or heavily mulched.

However, if speedy drainage is combined with a surface that appears dusty white or grey during a drought, you have a chalky soil.

As well as classifying the soil in your garden, you should learn when to cultivate it and when to leave it alone. Cultivation on clay soil, in particular, needs careful timing.

Where a choice is possible, grow the crops best suited to your soil, and within any particular crop select the most suitable varieties. Grow long carrots, for example, on a light soil and stump-rooted varieties on heavy soil. Grow scab-resistant potatoes on chalk soil.

Bear in mind that whatever the type of soil in your garden, you will get out of it only as much as you put into it. To sustain and improve fertility, follow the manuring and fertilising programmes suggested on pp. 17–20.

Heavy or clay soils Soils of this type are the hardest to work because they are difficult to dig at any time and impossible to cultivate during rainy spells. Their growing season is shortened because spring sowing and planting must be delayed until the wet soil becomes warmer and drier.

However, clays have the advantages in summer of not drying out as quickly as sandy soils and, when well cultivated, they yield heavy crops of good quality.

On poorly cultivated land the exceedingly fine particles of clay – which are at least 1,000 times smaller than those of sand – clog together into a sticky mass when wet, and set hard when dry.

In these conditions roots have difficulty in extracting the mineral nutrients on which plants feed. However, clay contains these minerals in abundance and you can make them available to plants by improving the soil texture.

This can be achieved in two ways – by using bulky manures and by digging in the autumn with the aim of breaking down the soil by frost action. If the clay is acid, dressings of carbonate of lime also help in making the soil workable. This should not be applied, however, on the type of alkaline soil known as chalky boulder clay.

Every autumn or early winter dig in all available organic material, such as garden compost, well-rotted manure, leaf-mould or peat. As this continues to decay it opens up the texture of the soil and gives the roots a freer run. Weathered boiler ash and coarse sand also help.

When digging in autumn, leave large clods on the surface to be broken up by the action of frost. As the ground dries in spring – it should then look light brown – rake the surface to give a tilth fine enough for sowing seeds.

Every third year, after digging is completed, spread carbonate of lime on the surface at the rate of 8 oz. per square yard (250 g. per square metre). Do not work it into the soil, but allow it to wash in naturally.

If the soil drains so poorly that pools of water remain after the rain, it may be necessary to lay drainage pipes (see p. 25). This is an expensive remedy and it would be better first to see if the problem resolves itself after two or three years' cultivation.

Well-cultivated heavy soils are excellent for growing beans, brassicas, peas, potatoes (if given plenty of compost or peat), salad crops, spinach, most soft fruits and many tree fruits.

Medium or loam soils A balance of clay and sand makes these soils highly fertile and easy to work. They are usually dark and contain plenty of humus.

When moist, they feel neither gritty nor sticky. They break down to a good tilth when dry but they become lumpy if worked too soon after rain.

All types of vegetables and fruits can be grown on loam.

Light or sandy soils These soils are easy to work and they warm up quickly in spring, so making them valuable for growing early crops.

They are so porous, however, that soluble plant foods are constantly leached, or washed out of them. This leaching can be reduced by digging in garden compost or well-rotted manure. The humus formed also acts as a sponge to retain moisture.

To reduce loss from leaching, add compost or manure in late winter or early spring rather than digging it in before the main winter rains or snow have fallen.

Many crops on light soils have to be watered in summer, but you can reduce the frequency of watering by spreading a mulch of peat at least 3 in. (75 mm.) deep along the rows of plants.

Alternatively, crops can be mulched with spent hops, wood shavings, straw, bracken or black polythene. Always soak the ground well before laying the mulch. Before digging in wood shavings or straw, sprinkle on sulphate of ammonia at the rate of 2 oz. per square yard (60 g. per square metre).

Plants on sandy soils respond readily to general fertilisers. Give several small applications over the growing period rather than one heavy dressing.

Sandy soils are often deficient in potash, so supplement a general fertiliser by adding sulphate of potash at the rate of 1 oz. per square yard (30 g. per square metre), or use a tomato fertiliser, which has a high potash content.

Root crops, potatoes, onions, early cloche crops, outdoor tomatoes, asparagus and some of the less hardy tree fruits, such as peaches and apricots, can be grown successfully on well-cultivated light soils.

However, certain types of vegetables vary in their response to light soils: French beans, for example, generally crop better than runner beans, and New Zealand spinach better than summer spinach.

Chalk soils A thin layer of topsoil usually lies on chalk or limestone subsoils. Sometimes, as in parts of Kent and Sussex, the chalk is apparent in the greyish topsoil. The chalk will stick to your shoes in wet weather, but the surface seldom remains wet for more than a few hours.

These soils are strongly alkaline and seldom need liming. The main need is for organic manures.

Every autumn or early winter dig in all available garden compost or well-rotted manures. Peat, reinforced with dried poultry manure or fertilisers, can be used as an effective, if expensive, substitute.

In spring give a dressing of sulphate of ammonia or nitrate of soda at the rate of 2 oz. per square yard (60 g. per square metre) to overwintered crops such as spring cabbages and sprouting broccoli. These crops often look pale and sickly after a wet winter on chalk soils, but a nitrogenous fertiliser soon restores their colour and vigour.

Chalk soils dry out so quickly that in some seasons watering and mulching (see p. 36) may be necessary as early as May, or even April. Even so, well-established plants will show drought symptoms later than on a sandy soil, and early application of a mulch will ensure continued growth in all but the driest conditions.

Beds of black currants, raspberries and strawberries should, however, have a permanent mulch of peat or garden compost to a depth of 2–3 in. (50–75 mm.).

When well cultivated, this type of soil suits most vegetables except potatoes, which tend to do better in slightly acid conditions. To create more acidity, cover each tuber with a double handful of peat when planting.

Stone fruits, especially plums and gages, do well on chalk soils, but keep newly planted trees well watered during dry spells for the first year after planting.

Peat soils These are the least common garden soils. There are two completely different types: fen peats, which are probably the richest and most productive of all soils; and acid peats, which are sour, often waterlogged and extremely difficult to make productive.

The acid peats are found on and around moorland where decaying vegetation has accumulated over wet or impervious subsoil, or rock. They are acutely short of lime, and of essential nutrients.

Some form of drainage (see p. 25) may be needed to bring them under cultivation. Every autumn, dress with carbonate of lime at the rate of 8 oz. per square yard (250 g. per square metre).

Use a general fertiliser at the rate of 2 oz. per square yard (60 g. per square metre) during the growing season. Until the land improves, concentrate on crops known to do well on acid or neutral soils, such as blueberries and potatoes.

Fen soils, on the other hand, are easy to work and almost any crop will thrive in them.

Making a new garden or reviving an old one

Anybody who moves house must expect some surprises and a few problems when taking over the new garden.

The biggest gamble comes when moving into a newly built house, where the builder may have left the garden strewn with rubble and subsoil, or into an old town house where the soil is exhausted.

When getting a house built, arrange with the builder as early as possible for topsoil removed from foundation trenches to be placed in a mound and subsoil to be removed. Later, when creating the garden, spread the topsoil on the vegetable plot.

If you take over a new house which has already been completed, it may be necessary to make random trial diggings to determine the depth of topsoil and to see whether subsoil has been left on the surface.

If it is impossible to put things right by barrowing soil from one part of the garden to another, buy in a load of topsoil to provide an adequate depth for growing crops. A lawn may grow on a fairly shallow soil, but you will have little success with vegetables or fruit unless there is a minimum of 8–10 in. (200–255 mm.) of topsoil.

In the first few years dig as much rotted manure as possible into the vegetable plot. In the first season turn a large part over to potatoes, which by constant cultivation will help to clear the ground of weeds. Grow peas and beans, too, which add nitrogen to the soil, and quick-growing salad plants.

Thereafter, follow a rotational cropping plan (see pp. 26–27).

The soil in the neglected garden of an old town house is generally sour, with a high sulphur content. This is because rain brought down large amounts of sulphur in the time of open coal fires and belching factory chimneys.

It is better to treat such ground as subsoil rather than try to put new life into it. Dig it over and add manure or compost, lime and fertiliser dressings to improve fertility. Alternatively, spread a deep layer of good topsoil over the surface.

Since topsoil is expensive, treat a small part of the garden at a time rather than spreading the soil thinly over a larger area.

Feeding vegetables and fruit

Plants, like people, thrive on a balanced diet. Just as a well-planned meal contains proteins, carbohydrates and vitamins, a well-tended soil is rich in all the foods that plants need.

The chemical elements that are essential for healthy growth are taken up by the plants in two ways:

Carbon, hydrogen and oxygen are absorbed from both the atmosphere and the soil.

Other nutrients, dissolved in water, are taken up as a 'drink' by hairs growing near the tips of the roots. The three principal elements on which plant life depends – nitrogen, phosphorus and potassium – are absorbed in this way.

Nitrogen promotes the growth of leaves and stems. A nitrogen-rich soil is ideal for growing such plants as cabbages, celery, leeks, lettuces and onions. It soon gets washed out of the soil, however, and supplies must be renewed every year.

Phosphates are necessary for vigorous root development. They also play a part in the growth of plants and the production of flowers and seeds.

Root crops, such as carrots, parsnips, swedes and turnips, do best in a soil with a good phosphate content. Phosphates remain in the soil as a plant food for two or three years after application.

Potassium, or potash, is vital for maintaining growth and for providing plants with resistance to disease and adverse conditions.

It contributes to the building up of starches and sugars in vegetables, especially in potatoes, carrots, parsnips, beetroot and sweet corn. Potash is also needed by all soft fruits. It stays in the soil for two or three years after application.

As well as the three principal nutrients, plants need magnesium, sulphur, manganese, iron, boron, zinc, copper, chlorine and molybdenum. These are known as trace elements, because only minute quantities – or a trace – are taken up by plants.

Finally, plants and soils require differing amounts of calcium, or lime (see p. 19).

With the exception of lime, all the complex needs of a plant could be met by enriching the soil with farmyard manure, which consists of animal droppings mixed with straw or other litter.

The highly productive kitchen gardens of Victorian times received huge quantities of stable manure, and the natural processes of the soil, assisted by enough lime to keep it 'sweet', made it unnecessary for the gardener to worry about details of plant nutrition.

This simple method of maintaining fertility is no longer practicable for most gardeners, who must now rely on whatever organic material is available and on supplementing it with chemical fertilisers.

Organic manures are composed of decaying matter – plants that are decomposing or that have been digested by animals. In the soil they are converted into plant food by a teeming population of fungi and bacteria. Organic manures feed the soil and, through the soil's natural functions, the crop. They are slow-acting, and improve the structure of the soil and build up fertility from year to year.

Inorganic fertilisers feed crops more directly, supplying nutrients that a plant can absorb immediately. But they do nothing to improve the soil and may even deplete its reserves of organic material.

Aim to strike a balance, adding as much organic manure as you can find, and using fertilisers to remedy known deficiencies.

Organic manures

Two types of organic manures are used in the garden – for different reasons.

Bulky farmyard manures are dug in during the winter or are used as mulches in summer. Some are rich in plant foods while others have little immediate food value, but all add to the soil's humus content and improve its condition.

The second type of organic manure consists of processed materials, such as bonemeal and dried blood. These are concentrated foods, generally used as pre-sowing dressings or as top-dressings for growing crops. They add very little humus to the soil. Bulky manures include:

Garden compost Town gardeners may find that the compost heap (see p. 21) is their only source of bulky, organic material. However,

well-made compost can be twice as valuable as farmyard manure in its content of plant foods.

Stable and farmyard manures Horse manure is 'hot' – that is, it ferments rapidly – and for this reason was at one time widely used to form hot-beds for raising early crops. Nowadays, electric soil-warming cables (see p. 54) are more likely to be used instead.

It is one of the richest and driest manures, but often that sold by riding stables contains mainly urine-soaked straw and a few droppings; it decays rapidly into a disappointingly small heap.

Pig manure is slow to ferment and, when fresh, tends to be caustic and to burn the roots of young plants. It is best composted with straw and left for at least three months before use.

Cattle manure containing straw from the yards is wetter, and lower in nutrients, than horse manure. But it decomposes slowly into the soil, and is ideal for sandy soils.

Spent mushroom compost Mushrooms are grown commercially on a compost based mainly on horse manure. It is carefully prepared to produce a controlled temperature over a period as the crop matures.

When all the mushrooms have been harvested the compost is sold either in bulk by the cubic yard, or, more expensively, in pre-packed bags that can be carried in a car boot. This is a good garden manure or mulch, containing humus and plant foods. It also contains chalk, which makes it less suitable for soils that are already alkaline though it will probably not do much harm unless applied every year.

Deep litter poultry manure Partly rotted litter from poultry houses may be bought by the load from poultry farmers, but it is unsuitable for gardeners living in built-up areas. The manure is usually dry and dusty and must be composted before use.

It takes some weeks for the wood shavings or straw on which the manure is based to break down. During this time the heap may develop an offensive smell; so even in a country garden it should be placed as far away as possible from houses.

When composted, deep litter poultry manure is rich in nitrogen but deficient in potash and phosphates.

Leaf-mould Although leaves of all types can be composted, the best quality leaf-mould is made from oak and beech leaves.

Place alternate layers of leaves and soil, each about 2 in. (50 mm.) deep. A sprinkling of general fertiliser on each layer of leaves will assist decomposition. Do not make the heap more than 3 ft (1 m.) high. Turn it at two or three-month intervals.

The compost will be ready in about a year. Apply at the rate of 5–6 lb. per square yard (2.5–3 kg. per square metre).

Spent hops Large breweries sell their hop waste to fertiliser firms, who improve its nutrient content before selling it in bags as hop manure. It is excellent manure, but expensive to use in large quantities.

Some smaller breweries are prepared to sell the spent hops cheaply to local gardeners who provide their own transport. These untreated hops help to improve the physical condition of the soil, but they are low in plant nutrients. This can be remedied by using them in conjunction with a general fertiliser.

Other bulky manures, which can be obtained only in certain areas, include seaweed, municipal sewage sludge and wool shoddy.

Seaweed This is rich in plant foods, especially nitrogen and potash, and breaks down quickly into humus.

Stack for a month or two to allow rain to wash out most of the salt, then dig it in at the rate of about 12 lb. per square yard (5.5 kg. per square metre).

Sewage sludge This well-balanced manure, which is processed by some local councils, is generally inoffensive to handle.

Ask the council's Engineer's Department if it is available in your district.

Wool shoddy A traditional manure in parts of Yorkshire, shoddy is the waste from wool factories. Transport costs have now made it uneconomic to use at any distance from the factories.

Shoddy contains up to 14% nitrogen, which it releases slowly over about three years. Dig the manure in, without first decomposing it, at the rate of about 1 lb. per square yard (500 g. per square metre).

Among concentrated organic manures that are rich in plant nutrients but which add little or no humus to the soil are:

Dried poultry manure Being extremely rich in nitrogen, this manure is best used sparingly with bulky material such as peat. Also, use as a compost activator.

Bonemeal Animal bones, ground coarsely and sold as bonemeal, or ground more finely and sold as bone flour, provide a steady source of phosphates to the soil.

Bonemeal releases phosphates slowly over at least two years, while bone flour acts more quickly but loses its effect within a year.

Work in coarse bonemeal, therefore, at the rate of 4–6 oz. per square yard (120–180 g. per square metre) before planting fruit trees and bushes.

Before sowing or planting vegetables, rake in 4 oz. of bonemeal per square yard.

Hoof and horn This is the main source of nitrogen in John Innes potting composts. It releases nitrogen slowly over a long period but its cost is about double that of sulphate of ammonia or nitrate of soda, the two main inorganic sources of nitrogen.

Dried blood A quick-acting nitrogenous manure that can be used as a substitute for sulphate of ammonia or nitrate of soda. Use along a row of vegetables as a top-dressing at the rate of 1 oz. per yard run (30 g. per metre).

Fish meal Although an excellent plant food, fish meal is now scarce and expensive. It contains no potash, but generally manufacturers remedy the deficiency by adding sulphate of potash. This will be stated on the packet.

Before sowing, rake in fish meal at the rate of 3 oz. per square yard (90 g. per square metre).

Inorganic fertilisers

Chemical or 'artificial' fertilisers are divided into those classed as 'straight', each containing one or two of the three main nutrients, and those that are 'complete' or 'compound' and provide a balance of plant foods. Straight fertilisers include:

Sulphate of ammonia This nitrogenous fertiliser can be raked in before sowing at the rate of 1 oz. to the square yard (30 g. per square metre) or used as a top-dressing for growing crops, especially cabbages and related crops, and salads, at the same rate, or at $\frac{1}{2}$ oz. per yard run of the row (15 g. per metre).

The effects of using sulphate of ammonia can usually be seen within 10–14 days.

When used alone, sulphate of ammonia tends to make soils acid. It therefore works better on chalky or well-limed soils.

Best of all, use it with superphosphate and sulphate of potash to make up a compound fertiliser (see next column).

Nitrate of soda This quick-acting nitrogenous fertiliser is often used as a stimulant for growing crops, especially where plants have been checked by bad weather. Apply 1 oz. per square yard (30 g. per square metre).

Nitro-chalk Another nitrogenous fertiliser, Nitro-chalk is useful on acid soils because it does not make the ground sour. Use only as a top-dressing, at 1 oz. per square yard (30 g. per square metre).

Superphospate The most popular fertiliser for supplying readily available phosphates, it is usually raked or forked into the soil at sowing and planting times at the rate of 2–4 oz. per square yard (60–120 g. per square metre).

It is too slow-acting to be used as a top-dressing but it remains in the soil as a plant food for some years.

Sulphate of potash This is the most popular fertiliser for supplying potash, because it can be used safely on all plants. Apply it as a top-dressing at the rate of 1–2 oz. per square yard (30–60 g. per square metre) over the rooting area of fruit trees and bushes, and along rows of plants that will be in the ground for a long time.

It may be mixed with sulphate of ammonia and superphosphate to make a compound fertiliser (see below).

Muriate of potash More concentrated than sulphate of potash, this fertiliser may damage strawberries, red currants, gooseberries and tomatoes.

On other plants and bushes it can be applied as a top-dressing at the rate of 1–2 oz. per square yard (30–60 g. per square metre).

Compound fertilisers

Plants need a balance of nutrients. Proprietary compound fertilisers contain the three main nutrients – nitrogen, phosphate and potash – plus traces of minerals such as magnesium and iron. The rate of application of compound fertilisers is generally given on the bag or carton.

To make up a balanced fertiliser, mix thoroughly 4 lb. (2 kg.) sulphate of ammonia, 5 lb. (2.5 kg.) superphosphate and 2 lb. (1 kg.) sulphate of potash. For most purposes apply at 2 oz. per square yard (60 g. per square m.).

Liquid fertilisers

Concentrated compound fertilisers, sold in both solid and liquid form, must be diluted before use. They are easy to apply as a top-dressing and are quickly absorbed by plants.

Some liquid fertilisers are derived from seaweed and humus extracts; others are made solely from chemical elements.

They are mixed in various proportions to give a wide range of analyses to suit the needs of various plants and soils.

Foliar feeding

Plants take several days to make use of nutrients absorbed through their roots. However, if their leaves are sprayed with dilute solutions of fertilisers the process is accelerated.

Special fertilisers for foliar feeding are obtainable at garden centres and from horticultural suppliers. Some are based on soluble, inorganic fertilisers while other all-organic preparations have a seaweed base.

Foliar feeds should be regarded as a supplement to manures or fertilisers rather than as the sole means of feeding the crop. They are particularly useful, however, if the plants have a poor root system or during dry spells when the plants have difficulty in drawing nutrients from the soil.

Storing and using fertilisers

It is cheaper to buy fertilisers in bulk than in small quantities, but the saving will be lost if they are spoiled due to careless storage.

Store fertilisers in a dry place as they quickly absorb moisture from the atmosphere and become either a sticky mass or set into a solid block.

Do not store paper bags on concrete or against walls. It is best to keep fertilisers in plastic bags or in covered tins.

Do not apply more fertiliser than recommended. Measure roughly the area to be fed, then weigh the required amount of fertiliser on a kitchen scale. Halve the amount of fertiliser when farmyard manure or garden compost has been dug in.

A fortnight before sowing spread a general fertiliser evenly and hoe or rake it into the surface. Do not dig it in or it will soon wash down out of reach of the roots.

Do not scatter fertilisers along a seed drill as they may injure the germinating seedlings. Apply top-dressings along the sides of the rows and lightly hoe them in. Do not allow inorganic fertilisers – except the special foliar feeds – to touch the plant's foliage or it will be scorched.

In dry weather follow the application of fertilisers with a good watering because they cannot be absorbed by the plants until they are dissolved.

The condition of the soil and the weather also dictate the types of fertilisers to use.

A light, sandy soil, for example, needs more potash than heavier soils, especially in gardens where soft fruits are grown.

In districts with a heavy rainfall, nitrogenous fertilisers wash out quickly and should be replaced by regular top-dressings of sulphate of ammonia or nitrate of soda.

PLANT FOODS IN ORGANIC MANURES AND FERTILISERS

This table shows the approximate percentages of nitrogen, phosphate and potash available to plants in each of the principal manures and fertilisers. Fertiliser manufacturers give the actual percentages of nitrogen, phosphate and potash – in that order – on each packet. The percentages are given either with the chemical formulae – N for nitrogen, P_2O_5 for phosphate and K_2O for potassium – or alone as a sort of code.

In this case, the chemical content of National Growmore would be stated as 7-7-7; the content of nitrate of potash as 13-0-44.

FERTILISER	NITROGEN	PHOSPHATE	POTASH	FERTILISER	NITROGEN	PHOSPHATE	POTASH
Farmyard manure	0.25	0.25	0.25	Sulphate of ammonia	21	0	0
Coarse bonemeal	3.30	29	0	Nitrate of soda	16	0	0
Fine bonemeal	1.30	29	0.2	Nitro-chalk	15.5	0	0
Dried blood	9.5	0.8	0	Superphosphate	0	20	0
Hoof and horn	13	2	0	Sulphate of potash	0	0	49
Fish meal	9.5	8	0	Muriate of potash	0	0	60
National Growmore	7	7	7	Nitrate of potash	13	0	44

CORRECTING SOILS THAT ARE TOO ACID OR TOO CHALKY

Acidity and alkalinity are measured by what is known as the pH level, which runs from 0 to 14. Neutral is 7.

Readings higher than 7 show that the soil is alkaline; lower readings that it is acid.

Although most vegetables do best in a slightly acid soil with a pH level of about 6.5, some – including brassicas, beans, onions and asparagus – will still grow satisfactorily in fertile soils of pH 7. This level would not be ideal for potatoes or strawberries, which require slightly acid soil.

Most fruits require a neutral or slightly acid soil, though figs and grapes will tolerate conditions that are slightly alkaline.

Most soils can be treated to lessen extreme acidity. Use a soil-testing kit to find out the condition of your soil, and follow the instructions provided with it for the use of lime.

If the vegetable plot is over-acid, but you are not sure to what degree, adopt a cautious approach to avoid the possibility of over-liming. Apply a dressing of hydrated or 'garden' lime at the rate of 6 oz. per square yard (180 g. per square metre), or ground chalk or ground limestone at 8 oz. per square yard (250 g. per square metre) after digging in autumn or early winter.

Spread the lime on the surface and leave it to be washed in by rain. Do not dig it in, otherwise surface soil will remain untreated.

Clay soils are often, but not always, acid. A soil-testing kit will confirm if this is so.

Liming benefits an acid clay soil in two ways. It reduces the acidity and it also improves the soil structure by assisting the fine particles to collect into crumbs, which makes for quicker drainage and better rooting.

Over-liming, however, may reduce vegetable yields. Do not lime chalk soils; give only moderate dressings, where needed, to heavy soils over-laying a chalk or limestone subsoil.

Other heavy soils, as well as loams and acid, sandy soils, are almost sure to need routine liming as part of a crop-rotation programme (see pp. 26–27). Add this before growing cabbages, cauliflowers and other members of the brassica family.

Although acid soils can be corrected relatively easily, it is more difficult to make a limy soil neutral.

A method worth trying, when digging in autumn, is to mix 8 oz. (250 g.) of flowers of sulphur with a bucket of peat – preferably moss peat, which is acidic. Fork in a bucketful to the square yard. Forking in peat without the flowers of sulphur will also help.

A year after treating the soil, make another test. If there is an improvement, repeat the treatment.

If not, do not waste any more money on the relatively expensive flowers of sulphur.

Instead, build up the humus content of the soil with manure and peat. Use sulphate of ammonia when there is a need for a nitrogenous fertiliser.

Spotting the symptoms of mineral deficiencies

Discoloration or blemishing of leaves, stems or fruits may indicate a deficiency of a particular element or an imbalance of the plant foods in your soil. But it is often difficult to diagnose which element is lacking because deficiency symptoms are similar for a number of elements.

The chart is a guide to the most common symptoms. But before jumping to the conclusion that mineral deficiency is causing the trouble, check for an attack by a pest or disease (see pp. 281–92). This is the more likely cause if the soil has been well manured and given the recommended quantities of balanced fertilisers.

Do not give an overdose of fertiliser or lime to try to remedy a mineral deficiency. This is certain to upset the balance of minerals in the soil.

Instead, build up the soil's humus content by giving regular dressings of well-rotted farmyard manure or garden compost, and by applying the recommended amounts of fertiliser. A balance is best achieved by following the rotational cropping plan suggested on pp. 26–27.

Choose crops and varieties that do well on your type of soil – brassicas on limy soil, for example, and potatoes on slightly acid soil. Before planting apples on a limy soil, ask the nurseryman which varieties are most likely to succeed in your locality.

Although all plants require a balance of nutrients, the need for certain elements is greater in some plants than others.

The needs of particular crops are indicated in the chart.

SPOTTING THE SYMPTOMS OF MINERAL DEFICIENCY IN THE SOIL

ELEMENT	DEFICIENCY SYMPTOMS	SUSCEPTIBLE CROPS	TREATMENT
Nitrogen	Growth is poor; shoots are short; leaves are small and yellow, brassicas turn pink then orange. Fruits or tubers are small.	Black currants, brassicas and potatoes.	As a booster, top-dress with nitrate of soda, sulphate of ammonia or Nitro-chalk at the rate of 2 oz. per square yard (60 g. per square metre). As a more permanent cure, dig in all available garden compost or farmyard manure.
Phosphates	Root development and flower-bud formation are poor, and plants sometimes also show symptoms similar to that of nitrogen deficiency. Brown spots may appear on leaves, or edges may turn brown. Fruits have an acid flavour.	Beetroots, potatoes, swedes and turnips.	Before sowing or planting apply superphosphate at the rate of 1 oz. to the yard run (25 g. per metre), hoeing it in so that the roots will reach it quickly. Superphosphate is too slow-acting to use as a top-dressing. Alternatively, work in bonemeal or bone flour at 4 oz. per square yard (120 g. per square metre) before sowing or planting.
Potassium	Growth becomes stunted, and leaves turn a dull blue-green, with browning at the tips or at leaf margins or showing as blotches. Leaves of broad-leaved plants curl downwards. Fruits may drop while still immature.	Apples, cauliflower, currants, gooseberries, peas, potatoes and tomatoes.	Before sowing or planting, hoe in sulphate of potash at 2 oz. per square yard (60 g. per square metre) as a top-dressing. Apply at the same rate to the yard run. In January or February, give a top-dressing over the rooting area of fruit bushes and trees at the rate of 1–2 oz. per square yard. (30–60 g. per square metre).
Magnesium	Magnesium is a constituent of chlorophyll, the green colouring matter in leaves and stems. Any deficiency shows either as a loss of colour or as a mottling of red, orange, brown and purple tints. It may occur when a large amount of potash makes the magnesium inaccessible to the plants.	Apples, beetroots, brassicas, cherries and potatoes.	Spray the leaves as soon as the deficiency is suspected with a solution of magnesium sulphate (Epsom salts) at the rate of 8 oz. to 2½ gallons of water (250 g. to 12 litres), plus a few drops of detergent.
Manganese	A lack of manganese is often found in sandy and alkaline soils, and frequently occurs with iron deficiency. Chlorosis, where leaves go pale or change colour, begins generally on older leaves. On green peas the deficiency shows on the leaves as brown patches, and the seeds are hollow. On beetroots, the leaves have red-brown speckling.	Apples, beetroots, cherries and peas.	Spray plants with a solution of manganese sulphate at 2 oz. to 2½ gallons (50 g. to 12 l.) of water, plus a few drops of detergent. Alternatively, water the soil with a solution of 10 oz. manganese to 6 gallons of water (275 g. to 24 litres).
Iron	Chlorosis (loss of colour) occurs at the tips of young shoots and through the leaves, in the early stages, while the veins remain green. Eventually shoots die back. The condition usually occurs in limy soils, where the calcium carbonate prevents the plants or fruit trees from absorbing any iron that is naturally in the soil.	Apples and pears, particularly those on limy soils.	For a quick-acting, short-term measure, apply sequestered iron as a foliar spray. In January apply sequestered iron to the soil. Follow the manufacturer's instructions for the rate of application.
Boron	The roots of beetroots, swedes and turnips turn brown; brown cracks appear across the stalks of celery; apple cores become 'corky'; the growing points of plants die off.	Apples, beans, beetroots, brassicas, celery, grapes, pears, swedes and turnips.	Apply 1 oz. of borax to every 20 square yards of soil (30 g. per 17 square metres). Mix with light sand to ensure even distribution.
Molybdenum	Leaves, particularly of broccoli and cauliflowers, develop a disorder known as whiptail. Leaves become distorted and shrink back to the midrib, giving a tail-like appearance. On tomatoes, leaves become mottled and roll forward. Peas and beans show signs of nitrogen deficiency.	Beans, broccoli, cauliflowers, lettuce, peas and tomatoes.	Apply a solution of sodium molybdate at 1 oz. to 2 gallons (30 g. to 8 litres) to treat 10 square yards (8 square metres) of soil.

Making your own compost

When you make a compost heap, you are doing what nature does all the time – turning the remains of dead plants into food for yet more plants.

If the heap is well made, with a mixture of leaves and more fibrous material, conditions will be ideal for countless millions of micro-organisms to begin breaking down the waste into plant food.

It is best to make a compost heap directly on the soil, so that any excess water can drain away. Naturally, the soil beneath should be well drained.

The heap can be free-standing, but for neatness and convenience it is better to make it within a framework of wooden shutters or chicken netting. Alternatively, you can use a proprietary compost container.

Most garden waste is suitable – for instance, the tops of peas and beans, lettuces that have gone to seed, beetroot leaves, lawn mowings, dead flowers, leafy hedge clippings and annual weeds. To these can be added straw litter from rabbit hutches, and waste from the kitchen such as tea leaves, the outer leaves of vegetables and fruit skins.

Do not use perennial weeds, such as docks and nettles; woody material that will not decompose; or scraps of food that may attract vermin. Chop up hard roots and stems, such as those of cabbages, before adding them to the heap, and mix the material thoroughly.

To start a compost heap, spread a layer of garden waste about 9–12 in. (230–305 mm.) deep, water the material if it is dry, then cover this with a layer of animal manure about 2 in. (50 mm.) deep.

If no manure is available, use sulphate of ammonia as an accelerator, sprinkling it over the compost at the rate of ½ oz. per square yard (15 g. per square metre). Alternatively, use a proprietary activator.

Build a second 9–12 in. (230–305 mm.) layer of waste material and cover with manure. If sulphate of ammonia was used on the first layer, sprinkle the second layer with garden lime at the rate of 4 oz. per square yard (120 g. per square metre).

READY-MADE BIN

The circular Rotocrop bin has ventilated PVC walls and an inflatable weather cover. The manufacturers claim that it will make good compost in only a few weeks.

Continue building the heap, sprinkling lime on alternate layers if you use sulphate of ammonia as an activator. Never mix the two together.

If sufficient material is available, build the heap to a height of about 4 ft (1.2 m.), finishing with a layer of soil an inch or two deep. In most gardens there is rarely enough waste to make a heap of this height in one operation, so cover the top with polythene or sacking to keep in the heat until the next layer can be added.

Heat will build up rapidly at first but will die down after about a month, when the heap will have shrunk to about one-third its original size.

At this stage it is an advantage to turn the heap so that the outer material, which is slower to rot, can be placed on the inside of the new heap.

If you have compost bins of the type shown alongside, simply transfer the contents to the second bin. Mix the contents thoroughly as you do so, making sure that unrotted material is buried.

While the material is rotting, and also if the heap is to remain undisturbed for the winter, protect it by covering with polythene held down by bricks or stones, or tucked down between the compost and the rails of the bin.

Compost made in a proprietary bin is unlikely to need turning, and the cover will protect it from rain.

When ready, the compost should be moist, dark brown and of uniform consistency, with a smell resembling that of leaf-mould. In summer, composting may take only a month or two, but in winter it usually takes at least twice as long.

HOW TO MAKE COMPOST BINS

It is best to make a pair of bins, so that the contents of one are maturing while the other is being filled. To save money, use second-hand timber and vary the dimensions of the bins to suit the sizes you are able to obtain.

For a medium-size garden, dimensions of $3 \times 3 \times 3$ ft ($1 \times 1 \times 1$ m.) are satisfactory.

If you do not have a regular source of second-hand timber, ask local demolition merchants whether they have old floor boards for sale. (See Yellow Pages for telephone numbers.) Manufacturers of timber buildings often have offcuts.

To inhibit rot, soak the butts of the uprights in a non-toxic preservative, such as Cuprinol, for several days. Brush parts above ground liberally with preservative and repeat every two or three years.

Use galvanised nails for fastening. As the boards are secured *inside* the uprights, the timber – not the fastenings – takes the strain.

To make a bin, place the uprights for one of the side sections flat on the ground and nail the rails between them. The space between rails should be the same as the width of the rails.

Make the other side in the same way, then fasten the back rails between. Notch the back upper rail to the upper side rails.

Shallow notches in the removable front rails slot over the side rails, and prevent the uprights splaying under pressure from the compost. Secure the finished bins in position by sinking the base of each upright into the ground.

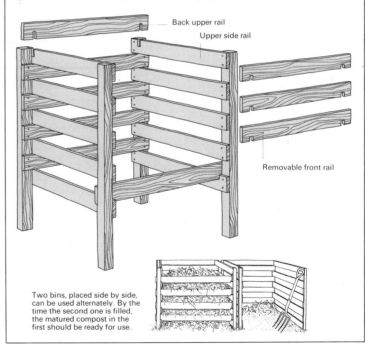

Back upper rail

Upper side rail

Removable front rail

Two bins, placed side by side, can be used alternately. By the time the second one is filled, the matured compost in the first should be ready for use.

Digging and cultivating

Thorough cultivations and good drainage help to provide the conditions in which crops will thrive. Tackled the right way, the work need not be as heavy as many beginners believe.

Why dig?

Digging is the first stage of preparing soil for cropping. In spite of experiments to find alternatives, it has remained standard practice because it does a number of essential things effectively.

Digging breaks up the top spit (spade-depth) of soil, leaving the surface in a semi-rough condition to be broken down by frost and rain into fine crumbs suitable for sowing and planting. It improves drainage, yet makes it easier for moisture to be drawn upwards to the plants' roots.

Digging also aerates the soil, providing suitable conditions for the bacteria that make soil nutrients available to plants. It provides an opportunity for working manure into the soil, for burying annual weeds and for removing deep-rooted perennials.

Is digging necessary?

Although practised by some gardeners, methods of cultivation which avoid digging are still not generally accepted by the majority. For the beginner taking over a garden for the first time, they are impracticable; nor, contrary to popular belief, are they especially labour-saving:

The essential feature of a 'no-digging' routine is that the soil, once cleared of perennial weeds, is kept covered with a layer of matured compost, adding at least 1 in. (25 mm.) a year. The action of bacteria and earthworms mixes this organic material with the soil, so that the upper 4–6 in. (100–150 mm.) becomes rich in humus and very fertile.

The surface remains well broken and easily worked, and the soil texture below is maintained by decaying vegetable matter and the presence of a large earthworm population.

Putting the theory into practice, however, may need more compost than the average garden can produce. In a new garden, where no compost will be available until a year after the first heap is started, it is out of the question.

To illustrate the scale of the problem, it is fair to assume that vegetable matter piled 12 in. (305 mm.) deep will, when rotted down, produce a 2–3 in. (50–75 mm.) layer of compost. Therefore, to estimate the amount of compost material you would have to collect for a full-scale 'no-dig' programme you must visualise your kitchen garden covered each year with, say, a 6 in. (150 mm.) layer of greenstuff, leaves, etc. This may be difficult to provide.

A further difficulty about giving up deep cultivation is the probable re-growth of perennial weeds. When left undisturbed they establish themselves and spread rapidly. Farmers who practise direct drilling, which is a 'no-ploughing' technique, control weeds by the use of herbicides on a scale that the private gardener would probably be unable or unwilling to imitate.

If you wish to experiment with 'no-digging' techniques, you are most likely to succeed on well-drained, weed-free soil. Mark out a small trial plot and treat it in this way for several seasons – assuming that you have compost to spare for the experiment.

This follows a principle that should be applied to most gardening innovations – to try out new methods and new varieties on a small scale, while relying on conventional ways and well-tried varieties until the new ones are shown to be better.

How to dig

If tackled sensibly, digging is neither as difficult nor as strenuous as many believe. Once the knack is acquired, digging a vegetable plot can be a satisfying and even relaxing occupation.

However, beginners should not attempt too much at first, even when the work seems to be going well and easily. An hour at a time is a reasonable limit until the spine and back muscles are attuned to the unaccustomed movements.

Types of digging

Normal digging consists of inverting the top spit of soil, and at the same time burying annual weeds (see p. 39), removing the roots of perennial weeds, and incorporating compost or manure if required.

This is known as single digging, and is adequate for most purposes. The alternative, which involves turning the soil two spits deep and is known as double digging, takes longer but in certain conditions gives better results.

Double digging is most worthwhile before growing deep-rooted crops, such as parsnips or runner beans, on land where the subsoil is compacted. But as a rule it is something to try once the basic technique of digging has been mastered.

Whichever method you choose, avoid digging when the soil is soggy or frozen.

Sandy, free-draining soils can be dug without difficulty at almost any time of year, except during a spell of freezing weather in winter, but late autumn is the best time to dig clay soils. They should not then be too wet, and winter frosts will crumble the soil into a fine tilth for sowing seeds in spring.

Single digging The method varies slightly, depending on whether you are digging bare soil or a plot covered with turf. Both are shown on the facing page.

Before burying or stacking turves, consider whether some of them could be used to renovate a worn area of lawn.

HOW TO HANDLE A SPADE

INSERTING With the shaft vertical, place your left foot on the tread (if you are right-handed) and push the blade down.

LIFTING With your left hand near the base of the shaft, tilt the shaft backwards and lift the blade just clear of the soil.

TURNING Tilt the blade to the right so that the spit of soil is inverted on the far side of the trench. Keep the trench open.

Single digging on bare ground

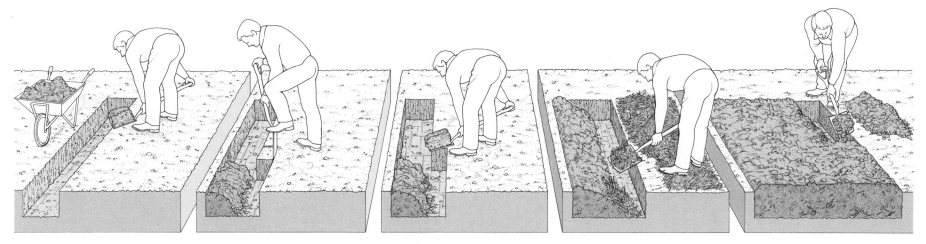

1 *Dig a trench across one of the narrower sides of the plot, moving the soil to the far end. Make the trench about 2–3 in. (50–75 mm.) wider from front to back than the blade of the spade, keeping the sides vertical.*

2 *In subsequent rows, make each spit spade-width and about 6 in. (150 mm.) from front to back. Stab the blade in at right-angles to mark the width, then push it in vertically in line with the trench.*

3 *Throw the soil well forward to maintain an open trench, keeping the near side vertical. Remove and burn perennial weeds. Dig in annual weeds, which will rot down and add humus to the soil.*

4 *If you are digging in manure or compost, scatter it over the sloping edge of the newly-turned soil so that it is evenly distributed when covered by the next row's digging. Do not leave any on the surface.*

5 *Continue digging in this way until you reach the final trench, filling this with soil removed from the first trench. Spread lime, if necessary, on the surface and allow it to be washed in by rain.*

Single digging on turf

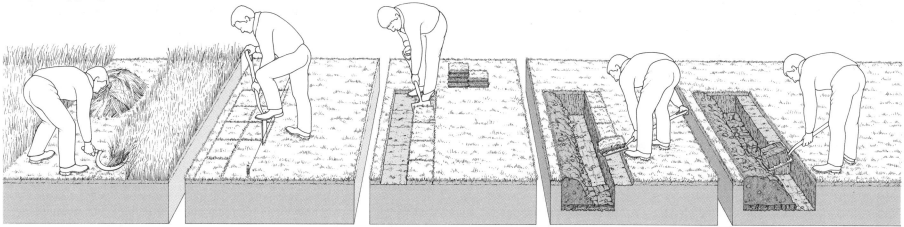

1 *When digging grassland or part of a lawn for vegetable growing, first cut the grass and remove any long growth. Decide whether to remove turves for growing elsewhere, to bury them or to stack them so that they rot.*

2 *If you want to use the grass elsewhere, lay a line and cut the turves with a turfing iron or spade into strips about 8 in. (200 mm.) wide, 1½ in. (40 mm.) thick and 12 in. (305 mm.) long.*

3 *Accurate cutting is less important if you are going to bury the turves or stack them to rot. Whatever you propose doing with them, remove the first two or three rows, then lift subsequent rows as digging proceeds.*

4 *To bury turves, lay them upside-down on the base of the trench and chop into several pieces. Keep the trench broad so that the edges of the turves do not turn upwards. Remove the roots of any perennial weeds.*

5 *Turn the next spit of soil on the inverted turves. Go along the trench, turning loose soil on the base onto the first spit to leave a flat surface for laying the next row of turves. Strip and invert these as before.*

Double digging on bare ground

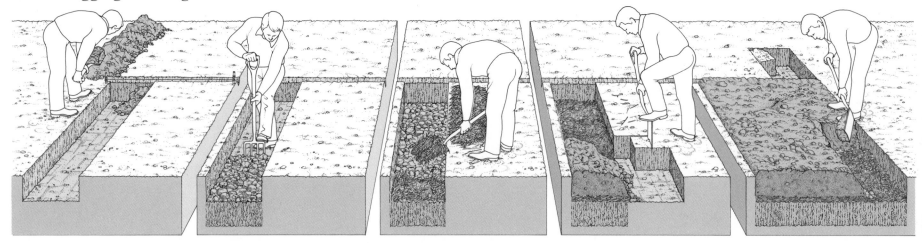

1 *To save barrowing large quantities of soil, divide the area in two with a line and chop a furrow along the mark. Place soil from the first trench just beyond the end of the adjacent section.*

2 *Dig the opening trench one spit deep and 18 in. (455 mm.) wide from front to back. Using a fork, break up the base another spit deep. Work backwards from one end of the trench to the other.*

3 *If you have manure to add while double digging, place this over the loosened base of the trench. The nutriments it contains will leach down into the loosened subsoil and aid root development.*

4 *Dig a second trench behind the first, placing the earth on the loosened subsoil. Three rows of digging will give a trench of similar width to the first. Fork over the floor of this new trench. Continue across the plot.*

5 *Fill the end trench with soil taken from the opening trench on the other half of the plot. Fill the final trench on this second side of the plot with the soil you removed when digging the original opening trench.*

Double digging on turf

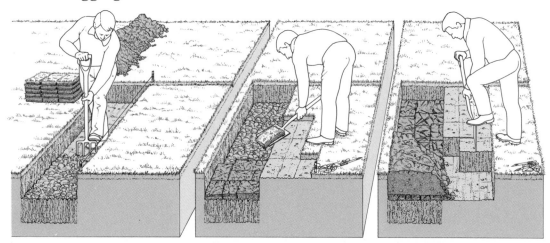

1 *After dividing the plot as above, use a line to mark an 18 in. (455 mm.) strip. Pare off and stack the turf, then dig out the top spit and fork over the base.*

2 *Pare the turf off the next 18 in. and place it upside-down on the loosened soil. Chop it into the soil, together with any manure, to assist decomposition.*

3 *Place the next spit of soil on top of the chopped turf and continue digging the plot trench by trench. Take care never to mix subsoil with topsoil.*

Double digging Digging the soil two spits deep allows roots to penetrate more deeply, releases fresh reserves of nutriments and improves drainage.

Even so, not many gardeners find time for double digging. If you decide to try it, experiment on part of the plot to judge whether the effect is worthwhile.

Spring cultivations

Final preparation of soil for sowing and planting will be straightforward if digging and manuring were completed by Christmas, or soon after. In the meantime it will have been crumbled by the action of frost, rain and drying winds.

Fortunately, suitable soil conditions generally coincide with the higher temperatures and longer days needed for germination of spring crops. However, the weather is not always in step with the calendar, so be guided by conditions in your garden, rather than the ideal sowing dates suggested elsewhere in this book or by seed merchants.

On clay soils, especially, you must wait until the soil is dry enough to be walked on without it sticking to your boots or shoes, or becoming compacted.

Immediately before sowing or planting, rake the top few inches to break the remaining lumps into a crumb-like structure.

For small seeds, such as lettuce and carrots, this needs to be as fine as possible. Larger seeds, such as broad beans and peas, will grow in slightly rougher conditions.

If the surface has been compacted by heavy rain it will need loosening with the tips of the fork tines before it can be raked. Do not disturb more than the top inch or two, and walk backwards to avoid treading on the loosened surface. Allow it to dry before giving the final raking.

If you were unable to dig during the winter, make as early a start as possible in the spring so that the soil has time to settle before crops are sown or planted.

A fork is better than a spade for this late digging as it will turn and break the soil in a single operation.

Although most spring cultivations are concentrated on the top inch or two of soil, deeper forking is a help before planting potatoes. This crop does best in a loose, open soil, even if it is somewhat rough and lumpy.

For this reason, fork over the potato plot well in advance of planting, breaking up the soil thoroughly to a depth of one spit.

Cultivating between crops

Land cleared of one crop in the middle of the season, and then planted with another, must be cultivated in between. A garden fork is the best tool and the depth of cultivation will depend on the condition of the soil.

After lifting early potatoes, for instance, the soil will need little more than levelling and raking. Where spring cabbages or some other long-standing crop has been grown it will be necessary to loosen and break up several inches of the top spit. In both cases allow as long as possible for the soil to settle before sowing or planting another crop, and then firm it additionally with your feet.

Draining waterlogged soil

No vegetables or fruits will thrive in soil that remains wet for much of the year. Their roots will be starved of oxygen and it will be difficult to carry out cultivation work at the correct time. Signs of waterlogging include persistent puddles after rain; algae and moss growing on the surface; and overwintered plants – such as sprouting broccoli – turning yellow and collapsing.

Sometimes, a badly drained garden can be improved in the course of digging; otherwise, it may be necessary to install underground drains before attempting to grow anything.

Improvement during digging is possible when the cause is a layer of impervious soil at about spade depth. This can occur naturally, due to what is termed an iron pan, or may be caused by continual ploughing or Rotavating at a constant depth.

One or two trial holes will show whether such a layer exists. Double digging (see facing page) is the ideal remedy, but there is a simpler alternative:

Choose a time when the soil is fairly dry, and dig it over to spade depth in the usual way (see p. 22). As you complete each row of digging, work along the bottom of the trench with a fork, driving it in to its full depth and levering it back so that the soil is lifted and fractured. A pick-axe or mattock may be needed to break the hardest type of iron pan.

Do not attempt to turn the layer of subsoil beneath the pan. Just push the fork in, move it until the soil begins to give, then withdraw it again.

A cure is more difficult if waterlogging occurs on heavy or low-lying land where there are insufficient outlets for the surplus water. The answer is to lay pipe drains, but this is worth attempting only when the trouble is really serious and if there is a ditch into which the pipes can empty.

Lacking a ditch, one solution is to construct a soakaway, although this will be of limited use during periods of prolonged and heavy rainfall – especially on a clay soil.

An alternative, for a very small area, is to make raised beds, for growing crops such as salads and tomatoes. Form the sides with bricks or stone blocks, and place a layer of rubble at the base.

If the problem is not extreme simply raise the overall level of the soil, using earth dug from drainage trenches at the side of the plot.

If you decide to lay pipe drains – also known as tiles – you can buy them from builders' merchants or agricultural merchants. For garden use, choose pipes with an interior diameter of 2 or 3 in. (50 or 75 mm.).

The best tool for digging deep, narrow trenches is a grafting spade with a narrow, slightly curved blade. It may be possible to borrow one from a builder; otherwise, use a narrow-bladed spade.

Lay the pipes with a slight fall towards the ditch or soakaway, with their ends about $\frac{1}{16}$ in. (2 mm.) apart so that water can enter from the surrounding soil. A drop of not less than 12 in. in 30 yds (305 mm. in 27 m.) is sufficient, but in planning the system allow for about 12 in. of soil or turf above the highest pipes.

If draining a large garden, for which a ditch outlet would be necessary, lay the pipes in a herringbone pattern, using 3 in. (75 mm.) diameter tiles for the main drains leading to the ditch, and 2 in. (50 mm.) tiles for the side drains. Space the side drains 30 ft (9 m.) apart, and position them so that their inner ends coincide with joints in the main drain. Cover the connections with pieces of slate or tile, and pack turf around them.

Before placing pipes in a trench, lay 1 in. (25 mm.) of gravel as a base. Place a further layer of gravel or small hardcore over them. Cover this with inverted turves or polythene sheeting.

THREE WAYS TO IMPROVE SOIL DRAINAGE

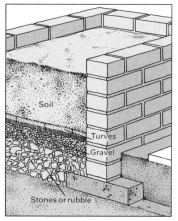

RAISED BED Make the bed 12–24 in. (305–610 mm.) high. Place stones on the base, followed by gravel and a layer of turves, then fill with good soil.

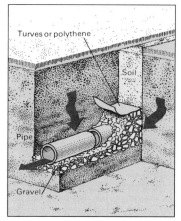

PIPES Whether leading to a ditch or a soakaway, lay the earthenware pipes on a gravel base. Cover with more gravel, then a layer of turves or polythene sheeting.

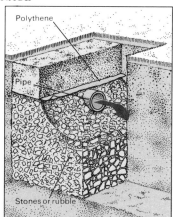

SOAKAWAY Make the pit as large as possible – at least a cubic yard – and fill with stones or hardcore. Before placing soil on top, cover with polythene.

Planning the kitchen garden

Deciding where to grow your vegetables can make the difference between success and failure. But once the site is chosen, you can use the same plot year after year.

Some of its features, such as a greenhouse, path or long-term crop, should be regarded as permanent; but most of the cropping area will need re-planning each season.

As explained on this page, crop rotation plays a key part in this annual allocation of space and the manuring programme that is linked with it.

Planning your vegetable plot

Vegetables grow best on land that gets plenty of sun and where the air moves freely. This is especially true of green crops, such as Brussels sprouts and cabbages, and also of swedes. So although shelter from north and north-east winds is an advantage, try to choose a part of the garden that is not hemmed in by trees or buildings.

However, all is not lost if the only available plot is in the shade for, say, half the day. The crops will not grow quite as well, but they can be helped by using cloches or a frame to provide a warmer start in spring.

You are unlikely to get worthwhile results if the site is in the shade for most of the day. It would be better to grow shade-tolerant plants, such as raspberries and blackberries, although even these will benefit from some sunshine.

Do not plant fruit trees in the vegetable plot. They create shade and also take nourishment and moisture needed by other crops.

This need for sunshine and air may help to determine the size and shape of the vegetable garden. You may decide, for instance, to have more than one plot, or to use an existing flower border for vegetables and choose shade-loving flowers and shrubs to grow in a part of the garden unsuitable for food crops.

A rectangle is the most convenient shape for a vegetable plot. In a small garden this will often be a single patch, with the crop rows running across the shorter dimension. In a larger garden, two or more beds, divided by paths, are preferable to a large square plot.

Beds can be of any convenient width, but it is worth remembering that the contents of seed packets are often based on the amount needed for a 30 ft (9 m.) row. This length is sufficient to give worthwhile yields of a variety of crops, and avoids the extra work of sowing a large number of short rows.

In practice, the best has often to be made of smaller or irregular-shaped beds. Where a bed is much narrower at one end than the other, use the shorter rows for successional crops, such as lettuces and radishes, with which it is better to make small sowings at intervals.

For most crops the direction of rows is not all-important, but east-west rows are definitely better for crops that are overwintered under cloches. In winter, the sun traverses a short arc from south-east to south-west, and if the side of the cloche row is exposed to the south it will gather more warmth than if the sunlight falls obliquely along it.

Rows that run from east to west are also marginally better in gardens exposed to strong westerly winds.

As well as making plans for the main growing area, you should consider the following points:

Permanent crops Set aside space for long-term crops, such as asparagus, globe artichokes and rhubarb. Once established, they will remain undisturbed for years and should be put where they will not interfere with the planning and rotation of annual crops.

Herbs (See also p. 28.) These are better grown near the house, in a sunny but sheltered position. If you have to grow them in the kitchen garden, set aside a small permanent patch where they will not interfere with crop rotation.

Paths A path in the vegetable garden need be no wider than $2\frac{1}{2}$ ft (760 mm.), but it should provide a firm surface for walking on and for wheeling a barrow.

Grass paths are the least satisfactory. Gravel or clinker paths are better, though a board or other edging should be fixed to keep the material in place, and at least an annual dose of weedkiller applied.

Best of all is concrete, either laid on site or in the form of paving slabs. The few weeds that will appear between the slabs are easily dealt with by watering simazine into the cracks.

Greenhouse and frame (See also pp. 48–54.) Ample light, a firm path and, if possible, a water supply, are the main considerations when deciding on a site. Do not place either under a tree.

Water supply A standpipe for a hose is not essential, but it saves the inconvenience and possible mess of using an indoor tap.

Crop rotation and planning

Even before digging the vegetable plot you should work out a rough cropping plan. This is because the vegetables will be grown in three groups, each requiring different soil treatment. The method is explained in detail on the facing page.

It is helpful to know why crops are grouped in this way and why the groups are moved to different parts of the plot each year. This system of growing vegetables is known as crop rotation.

One reason for rotating crops is that different plants need differing quantities of the various soil foods. If the same type of crop is grown continuously in the same soil, it will need special feeding to make up for the depletion of these nutrients.

Even more important is the fact that many crops suffer from soil-borne pests and diseases. However, infection is likely to become serious only when the host plant is grown in the same area of land year after year.

A third advantage of crop rotation is that manures and fertilisers can be used to greatest effect, and not given to crops that may not benefit from them.

Drawing a plan

Once the vegetable plot has been marked out and dug, you can make a fairly precise cropping plan for each of the three sections. Do this before ordering seeds. The easiest way is to make a plan on ruled paper, taking each square on the paper as a square foot – or any other convenient dimension.

For the correct crop spacings, refer to the At-a-Glance Guides (between pp. 62 and 276). When crops requiring different row widths are grown next to each other, leave a space equal to the difference between those widths.

For instance, rows of lettuces are sown 12 in. (305 mm.) apart; rows of French beans are sown 18 in. (455 mm.) apart. So leave about 15 in. (380 mm.) between a row of lettuces and a row of French beans.

Remember that some crops, such as leeks, can be grown on land where another crop has been harvested. Others, such as lettuces, may be grown as a quick catch-crop between slow-growing plants (see p. 28).

Allow space for a seed bed where you can raise plants of Brussels sprouts, cabbages and other brassicas.

Making the most of your vegetable garden

The smaller the vegetable plot, the greater the challenge to the gardener who wants to harvest crops throughout the year.

This aim can be achieved in

PLANNING A SMALL PLOT FOR HOME FOOD GROWING

THE RIGHT ASPECT Choose the most open part of your garden for vegetable growing. This is especially important for crops grown under cloches in winter and early spring, when shadows from trees and buildings are longest. Ample sun is also needed for tomatoes and other tender crops, such as sweet corn.

ROW DIRECTION Except in exposed gardens, where east-west rows are best, the main need is to plant rows at right-angles to the path. If planting east-west, site tall crops where they will not shade low-growing crops planted next to them.

'HUNGRY CROPS' AND SALADS (Group 1) As part of the crop rotation, plant about a third of the plot each year with any of the following crops: beans, celeriac, celery, leeks, lettuce, onions, peas, shallots, spinach, sweet corn and tomatoes. The first crops to be harvested can be followed by beetroot, carrots or a row or two of winter cabbage.

MANURE AND FERTILISERS Every season, dig in rotted manure or compost during the winter before planting crops in this group. In this way, each part of the plot will be manured every third year. If neither is obtainable, dig in peat and apply fertiliser in spring (see p. 18). Lime should not be needed on this section once a rotation is established.

GREENHOUSE AND FRAME (See also pp. 48–54.) Both need as much light as possible, especially during the spring. The greenhouse door should be alongside a path, and the frame placed nearby to save time when transferring plants. It is also helpful to have electricity and water near by.

PERMANENT CROPS Rhubarb, globe artichokes and asparagus will each occupy the ground for successive years, so place them where they will not interfere with crop rotation. Thorough soil preparation, adding plenty of manure or compost, is essential in each case.

BLACKBERRIES AND RASPBERRIES These two fruits will grow satisfactorily in partial shade. Cultivated blackberries provide heavy yields when trained against a fence or wall, yet take little or no space from the main vegetable area. Raspberries will do better in a separate bed. All soft fruit crops are semi-permanent, so grow them in a separate patch.

CLOCHES A position in full sun, with east-west rows, is needed for cloched crops in winter. When not in use, store polythene cloches away from daylight; stack glass cloches on end in a safe corner.

BRASSICAS (Group 2) Crops in this group are broccoli, Brussels sprouts, cabbages, cauliflowers and kale. Include a seed bed for raising plants.

MANURE AND FERTILISERS A dressing of fertiliser should be sufficient if this section was manured the previous season for pod-bearing crops and salads. However, dig in some manure if you are just starting to grow vegetables. A dressing of lime (see p. 19) is generally needed on all but chalky soils.

PATHS A firm, all-weather path, such as one made of concrete, is an asset both when growing and gathering vegetables. If you lay concrete, leave gaps for expansion every 10 ft (3 m.) and camber the surface. Lay paving slabs on sand. For a gravel or clinker path, fix timber or concrete edgings to keep the material in place.

SOFT FRUIT Currants, gooseberries, raspberries and strawberries are best grown in a plot of their own where they will not interfere with the rotation scheme. Since they are long-standing crops, thorough soil preparation is important. This includes getting rid of perennial weeds (see p. 37), which are difficult to eradicate after planting.

ROOT CROPS (Group 3) Potatoes and root crops should occupy about a third of the plot in a rotation scheme. Root crops include beetroot, carrots, parsnips, swedes and turnips. Crops harvested early can be followed by spinach and lettuce to make full use of the ground.

MANURE AND FERTILISERS Do not apply any manure before sowing root crops, except when growing potatoes in soil that is in poor heart. Avoid lime too, but give a dressing of fertiliser at sowing or planting time.

This scheme shows how a typical small plot can be laid out for food growing. Provided the basic principles are followed, it can be varied to suit the available space, the aspect of the garden and your family's taste in vegetables. If you are unable to keep exactly to the crop rotation scheme, at least remember to manure pod-bearers, tomatoes and other hungry feeders, to lime the brassica plot and to avoid planting root crops on freshly manured ground.

HOW THE PLOT CHANGES IN A THREE-YEAR CYCLE

FIRST YEAR In an established rotation, Group 1 ('hungry crops') is manured; Group 2 (brassicas) is given lime and fertiliser. On a new plot, plants in Group 2 would also benefit from manure.

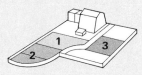

SECOND YEAR Although they have been moved to fresh sites, each group of plants is given a similar application of manure or fertiliser to the previous year. To make full use of plant foods it is important to move crops in the order shown.

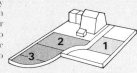

THIRD YEAR A further change of position completes the rotation cycle. Each group of crops will now have occupied each of the three sections of the plot, in the order shown. Fertility will actually increase year by year.

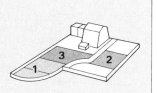

many ways, but the main point is not to allow any ground to lie idle. As soon as one crop is cleared, follow it with another. This is known as successional cropping and generally follows the sort of crop-rotation programme outlined on pp. 26 and 27.

Sometimes, however, there is a gap of a few weeks between the harvesting of one main crop and the planting of another. In such cases sow a catch-crop – generally a quick-growing salad vegetable that will be picked before the ground is ready for another main crop.

After Brussels sprouts have finished, for example, sow 'Tom Thumb' lettuces in March to crop just before the bed is needed for tomatoes in June.

Another form of intensive cultivation is inter-cropping – that is, growing quick-maturing vegetables, such as radishes, turnips or spring onions, between rows of slow-growing crops such as parsnips or Brussels sprouts.

Under certain conditions, some root crops may be sown closer together than is usually advised to produce a heavier crop. For instance, carrots may yield up to 50 roots per square foot by being sown thinly in drills 6 in. (150 mm.) wide and ½ in. (12 mm.) deep, instead of in traditional single rows.

When growing by this method, pull continuously as the roots become large enough to eat, so that those remaining have more space to develop.

In a few cases a slow-growing crop and a quick-maturing salad crop may be sown together in the same ground.

Parsley is notoriously slow to germinate, and it is often difficult to find the seedlings among the weeds, so at sowing time mix the seeds with those of radishes. The radishes, which will appear in only a few days, mark the row to make it easier to hoe the weeds. In pulling radishes you will also be starting to thin the parsley.

Radishes may also be sown in the rows with slow-germinating parsnips and, again, in the potato bed immediately after planting.

Extend the cropping period of a row of lettuces by sowing a mixture of varieties that mature at different times. Packets of carefully selected mixtures are available from seed merchants.

Successional crops

Some crops, such as sprouting broccoli, spring cabbage or early peas, are harvested at the height of the growing season. As soon as they are finished, prepare the ground for a successional crop, which may be quick-maturing for harvesting in the autumn, or slower-growing for winter and spring use.

Quick-maturing crops, such as lettuces, turnips, beetroots, peas and French beans, will not affect your rotation plan.

Those that are slower-growing – for instance, winter and spring cabbages, Brussels sprouts, sprouting broccoli and leeks – can be fitted into your rotation plan. For instance, the brassicas, which are in Group 2 in the plan (see p. 27), will be followed in the next season by either root crops in Group 3, or by a summer crop of peas, beans, tomatoes, sweet corn and other 'hungry crops' in Group 1.

Some examples of successional

sowings, month by month, are:
MAY–JUNE To follow winter cauliflowers, winter lettuces, spring cabbages: lettuces, marrows, ridge cucumbers, spinach, sweet corn or tomatoes.
JUNE–JULY To follow early potatoes (mid-June to early July): early varieties of carrots and peas, leeks, celery, swedes, spinach beet or salad onions.

To follow broad beans or early peas (early to mid-July): turnips, globe beetroot, early varieties of carrots, calabrese, autumn or winter cauliflower or sprouting broccoli.
JULY–AUGUST To follow secondearly potatoes, maincrop peas or dwarf beans: kale sown where it is to grow, spring cabbages (for transplanting, or to leave standing closely where sown for spring greens), lettuces, radishes, and before the end of July, a final planting of leeks.

As will be seen from this calendar, successional crops are sown or planted in the summer, when the ground is generally dry. A different form of soil preparation is necessary from that in spring.

Clear away the remains of the old crop and any weeds. Break up the top few inches of soil with a fork or hoe, but do not dig deeply. Deep digging will only accelerate loss of moisture from the soil.

On heavy land, where the soil has been trodden down, fork the top few inches into lumps and leave to dry thoroughly. Give a through soaking with water and leave for another day, when the clods will rake down to a fine tilth.

Dress the ground with a compound fertiliser at the rate of 2 oz. per square yard (60 g. per square metre), water the drills before

sowing and give a good soaking to the ground after planting.

Emergency sowings

If sowings of winter vegetables fail in the seed bed, make a direct sowing in the prepared bed before the second week in July.

Sow a pinch of seeds, spaced at the distance the brassicas would normally be planted. When the plants are about 2 in. (50 mm.) high, carefully remove weak seedlings to leave only the strongest in each batch.

How and where to grow herbs

Herbs are so useful in the kitchen that they merit a part of the garden to themselves – ideally, a sunny position near the kitchen door where they can be picked without bother.

This is not always possible, but herbs are so adaptable that they will thrive among flowers in a border, in pots on a patio, in a window-box, or in some cases in pots on an indoor window-sill. The soil or compost should be freedraining and fertile, but need not be especially rich.

Before planting an outside bed as part of the ornamental garden, draw up a plan that will make the most of contrasting leaf shapes and colours to give the plot an interesting appearance.

Take care to plant the taller herbs, such as angelica, dill, fennel and rosemary at the back; and smaller ones, such as chives, marjoram, parsley and thyme, near the front.

Some elaborate herb gardens have been laid out, including a chess-board design in which different herbs are planted in the 18

'black' squares, with paving or gravel filling the 'white' squares. But these are too troublesome for all but dedicated herb growers.

Such designs have the merit of placing all the herbs within easy reach for picking. The principle can be followed in a small garden by using paving stones in the shape of a cross.

The choice of herbs depends on taste, but no herb garden can be complete without chives, mint, parsley, sage and thyme.

After these, the herbs most likely to occur in recipes are bay, borage, dill, fennel, marjoram, rosemary, savory and tarragon.

But part of the interest in growing herbs is to try something different, so a larger bed can include angelica, balm, burnet, chervil, coriander and lovage.

Growing herbs in a flower border
Some herbs make an attractive addition to the flower border. Angelica, for example, can reach 10 ft (3 m.) high in rich, moist soil, and makes an impressive backdrop for other flowers.

Other herbs worth growing in the border are fennel – of which there are bronze and purple forms – with its feathery foliage; borage, which has star-shaped, blue flowers; and sage, with its grey leaves – sometimes variegated – and spikes of blue or white flowers.

Parsley and chives make an interesting and productive edging.

A herb garden on a patio All herbs, except perhaps the tall angelica, can be grown successfully in tubs, boxes or flower pots on a patio or in a town garden.

In some ways this is a more practical method of growing herbs than in the open garden, since the roots of invasive plants such as mint are kept in check. Pots containing chives, parsley, bush basil and marjoram can be brought indoors for winter.

Ensure good drainage by drilling holes in the bottom of boxes, and put a layer of rubble at the bottom of all containers. A potting compost, such as John Innes No. 1, will give more reliable results than ordinary garden soil.

Sow or plant as for herbs in the garden and keep the containers well watered, especially during periods of drought.

Every March or April remove 2–3 in. (50–75 mm.) of soil from the tops of tubs containing perennial herbs, such as bay, thyme or sage and replace this with fresh potting compost, and apply a liquid feed once a fortnight between May and September.

Growing in window-boxes Low-growing herbs, such as chives, parsley, pot marjoram and winter savory, can be planted in window-boxes in the same way as in containers on a patio.

If tall herbs, such as tarragon or fennel, are grown, pinch out the growing points regularly to restrict the size of the plant. Plant mint in a separate box or it will soon smother the other herbs.

Growing herbs indoors The kitchen window-sill may seem the most obvious and also convenient place to grow herbs indoors, but often it is the least successful.

A better place for an indoor herb garden is by a window or glass door in a room where there is plenty of light and also lower humidity.

Grow indoor herbs in John Innes potting compost No. 2, which is richer than the soil they need outside. Even then, do not expect them to be of the same quality as herbs grown in outdoor beds during the summer.

During February sow parsley, chervil and basil in separate pots. Let some of these plants grow on for early picking indoors, and plant out the remainder in the open in late May or early June.

Towards the end of September start potting up some of the perennial herbs that have been growing in the open during the summer. Sage, marjoram, chives and mint are among the most suitable.

Parsley can also be treated this way, but it is better to sow seed directly in a pot in June and bring it indoors in late September.

The size of the pot will depend on the size of the roots, but most will do well in 5–6 in. (130–150 mm.) pots.

Propagating herbs Most herbs, both annual and perennial, can be raised from seeds. Instructions for sowing are given for each type in the Growing and Cooking section, between pp. 62 and 276.

It is also possible to increase your stock of perennial herbs – or to replace old, straggly plants with new ones – by taking cuttings and setting them to root in pots containing equal parts (by volume) of peat and sand. Alternatively, root them in a seed compost.

Dipping the base of the prepared cuttings in hormone powder encourages rapid rooting.

You do not need a greenhouse to root cuttings but a garden frame is a great help. This is not only for the warmth it provides but also for the still, humid conditions inside the closed frame.

If you do not have a frame, cover the pot of cuttings with a plastic bag and secure this with a rubber band to retain moisture. Place it on a window-sill.

The sort of cutting to take depends on the type of herb you are propagating:

Nodal cuttings Herbs propagated by this method include hyssop and marjoram in April or May, and rosemary in July or August. However, hyssop and rosemary can also be propagated as heeled cuttings in late summer.

Remove the top 3–4 in. (75–100 mm.) of a main stem just below a leaf joint, or node. Pull off or cut away the lowest pair of leaves and pinch off the soft tip. Plant the cuttings firmly in a 3 in. pot of compost – several to a pot – water them and place in a frame.

The cuttings should root in from four to six weeks. When rooted, pot them individually in 3 in. pots of potting compost and grow them on in a ventilated frame.

Heeled cuttings Take this sort of cutting when propagating thyme in May or June, and bay or sage in late summer.

Cut off semi-ripened shoots from the parent plant, complete with a heel, or sliver of wood, from the main stem. To do this, make a slanting cut into the main stem just below the side-shoot joint, then make a similar cut above the joint to remove the shoot. A sharp knife is needed, so take care not to cut yourself.

Rooting and after-care is the same as for nodal cuttings.

A SIMPLE HERB BED

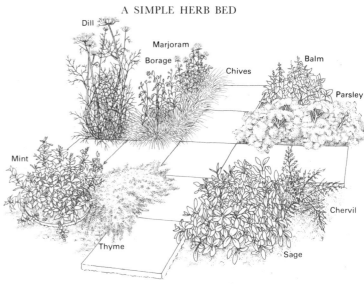

Paving stones, placed as a cross, allow easy picking and create four separate plots. Grow compact herbs as edging; plant taller ones, such as angelica or rosemary, behind.

NODAL CUTTINGS

1 After removing the shoot just below a leaf joint, pull away the lowest leaves.

2 Pinch off the soft tip, dip the base in hormone powder and insert in sandy compost.

HEELED CUTTINGS

1 Make an angled cut just below the shoot. Use a sharp knife or razor blade.

2 Make a second cut just above the shoot, which will then come away with the heel.

Sowing seeds in the open

Browsing through a colourful seed catalogue is one of the most satisfying pastimes for a gardener on a dull winter's day. It is also an essential job, because the choice of varieties to suit a particular garden and cropping plan will affect yields during the coming season.

Keep your cropping plan beside you when filling in the order form or making a list to take to a garden shop. You can then estimate the amounts you need and tick off each row as you order. This will also help you to avoid mistakes, such as ordering autumn-sown cabbages when your cropping plan calls for summer cabbages.

Order seeds as early as possible, otherwise you may find that some varieties are sold out.

Quantities and varieties

In many cases, a packet of seeds is sufficient for a row 30 ft (9 m.) long. However, this is only a rough estimate, since the amount of seeds in a packet varies and one gardener may sow with a heavier hand than another.

Often, a packet of a new variety contains fewer seeds than an established favourite. Even so, it will probably provide more plants than you need.

Choosing the varieties best suited to the soil and weather in your area is, to some extent, a matter of experience. Neighbours and local gardening clubs can suggest varieties that have proved reliable, though you may eventually find others that you think are of better quality.

Keep to the well-established varieties for the bulk of each crop, but every year try out a few that are different. In a small garden, try growing half a row of one variety and half a row of another, to compare results.

Recommended varieties for vegetables are given in the Growing and Cooking section, between pp. 62 and 276.

By all means experiment with varieties that are new on the market, but note that these seeds are generally dearer. So also are F1 hybrids, which are a cross of two distinct parent strains and produce plants of exceptional vigour – the 'F' standing for 'filial', and the 'I' for first cross.

Pelleted seeds Seeds sold in this form resemble small, grey ball-bearings. Each pellet, made of clay, contains one seed, so it is easy to place them evenly when sowing. Subsequently, thinning is easier.

Pelleted seeds are particularly worth-while for crops such as carrots and lettuces which are tedious to thin. For good results, the soil must contain the right amount of moisture (see facing page). This is not always easy to control.

Home-saved seeds In only a few cases is it advisable to save seeds from your own crops. Even where they can be saved, you should

consider whether the ground could not be used more profitably by immediately sowing or planting another type of vegetable to fit in with your cropping plan.

Most small seeds are not worth harvesting. Do not, for example, save seeds of the cabbage family, because cross-fertilisation takes place readily between these and other brassicas and may result in plants that are worthless.

Do not save seeds from F1 hybrids as they do not reproduce truly. True-to-type seeds can be obtained only from a crossing of the original parent varieties.

Peas and beans are the crops from which the gardener is most likely to be successful in taking his own seeds. If the space is not needed for another crop, pods may be left to ripen on the vine and the seeds shelled when dry.

Onions and leeks are worth saving, too – especially if you have a strain particularly suited to your area.

Spread out the seeds in a dry, airy place for a week before storing in envelopes. Write the name of each variety on the envelope.

Keep even small seeds, provided they are well-ripened, since they carry the genetic make-up of the parent plants and will still produce a normal crop. But do not save seeds from a crop with a large proportion of small or deformed pods, since this may indicate that the strain has deteriorated.

Sowing where plants are to grow

To germinate, a seed needs moisture, warmth and air. Therefore the soil must be damp, not too cold, and the seed must not be buried too deeply.

In spring, sow on land that has been dug in autumn or winter (see pp. 22–24) and manured or dressed with fertiliser, if necessary, to suit the crop to be grown.

Sow when the soil is dry enough to be walked on without it sticking to your boots. This is the best test for judging the time to sow.

Do not follow the calendar slavishly if conditions are unseasonably cold or wet. Plants sown a week or two later than the time suggested on the seed packet will still catch up.

If the ground is only slightly sticky, fork over the top 2 in. (50 mm.) so that the surface dries more quickly. When it is dry enough, firm the ground by treading, then rake to a fine, crumbly tilth.

To make a straight drill (furrow) for sowing the seeds, use a garden line if you have one, or push in pegs at each end of the row and tie string tightly between them. Straight rows make the most of available space and are easier to thin and hoe than rows sown haphazardly.

Take out the drill along the line with a draw hoe. Use a corner of the blade to make a narrow, V-shaped drill for small seeds, such as carrots and spinach, and the full width of the blade to make a wide, flat drill for peas and beans.

In both cases form the drill with a succession of smooth, separate motions rather than pulling the hoe along without a break. Make the drills $\frac{1}{4}$–$\frac{1}{2}$ in. (5–12 mm.) deep for the smallest seeds, such as carrots, turnips and lettuces; $\frac{1}{2}$–1 in. (12–25 mm.) deep for slightly larger seeds, such as spinach and beetroot; and about 2 in. (50 mm.) deep for the largest seeds, such as peas and beans.

SOWING SMALL SEEDS

1 Firm the soil by treading it evenly, then rake to a fine tilth. Remove large stones.

2 Using a taut line as a guide, scrape out a drill with the corner of a draw hoe blade.

3 With a few seeds in the palm of your hand, dribble them out evenly along the drill.

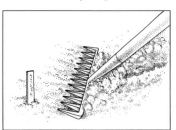

4 Use your feet or the back of the rake to replace the soil. Then firm it gently.

In each case, the shallower depths apply to spring sowings when the soil is warmer near the surface, and the deeper drills to the summer when seeds need to be in damp ground below the surface.

If in doubt, it is better to err on the shallow side. Sowing too deep is a common cause of failure, especially on heavy soils.

In summer, either water the ground thoroughly the day before sowing, or use a watering can without a rose to soak the bottom of the drill just before sowing.

Sow small seeds as thinly and evenly as possible by shaking a few at a time into the palm of your hand and letting them dribble between thumb and forefinger into the drill. Do not try to shake them directly from the packet, or the row will be uneven.

On light soils, cover the seeds by placing your feet on each side of the drill and shuffling the soil back. Alternatively, stand between the rows and pull the soil over the seeds with the back of the rake, then hold the rake vertical and tap the surface flat.

On heavy soils use only gentle pressure to firm the soil, otherwise it will become compacted and the seedlings may have difficulty in breaking through.

The best method of filling drills after sowing peas and beans is to stand between the rows, pulling the soil back with a draw hoe and then firming the surface with the blade of the hoe.

Before removing the marker line, insert a label identifying the vegetable and variety. An inscription in pencil – or, ideally, wax crayon – will withstand rain and mud until the plants mature.

In gardens where birds are a problem, tie black cotton (not thread) to sticks so that the strands criss-cross over the rows of seeds. Alternatively, fasten wire-netting or plastic-netting to canes just above soil level.

Sowing pelleted seeds

The soil for sowing pelleted seeds, either in a seed bed or in their permanent positions, must be kept moist without becoming sticky. If the ground dries out after sowing, the protective covering will not break up to allow the seed to germinate. If the ground is too wet, the coating will become treacly and stifle the seed.

Although pelleted seeds reduce the work of thinning, it would be unwise to take the risk of sowing single seeds at final thinning

SOWING PEAS AND BEANS

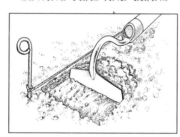

1 Use the whole blade of a draw hoe to form a broad drill. Keep the base flat.

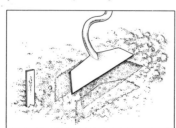

2 After sowing, replace the soil with the hoe. Firm evenly with the blade held flat.

distances. Instead, sow two pellets in each station and remove surplus seedlings later, if necessary.

Keep the soil moist by sprinkling until the seeds germinate, which will be about two days longer than the times given in the table on p. 32.

Sowing in a seed bed

Leeks and most members of the cabbage family (brassicas) are best raised in a seed bed and transplanted to their permanent positions. The plants tend to be 'leggy' if sown where they are to grow.

Relate the size of the bed to the size of your vegetable plot and the family taste for brassicas.

As a guide, nine rows, each containing 30 plants, can be raised in a bed measuring 5 × 5 ft (1.5 × 1.5 m.).

The vegetables in such a bed might comprise: two rows of leeks, and one row each of summer cabbages, autumn cabbages, savoys, Brussels sprouts, cauliflowers, broccoli and either sprouting broccoli or kale. This selection would provide greenstuff for most of the year.

Choose a piece of fertile ground and prepare the bed as for growing from seeds in the open – that is, digging during the autumn or winter, treading the ground when the soil is suitably dry in spring, and raking to a fine tilth.

In such a small area there is no need to use a line and hoe to make the drills. Instead, form the drills on light soils by pressing a rake handle about ½ in. (12 mm.) into the surface. On heavy soils, use the rake handle as a guide and scratch the drill with a draw hoe.

Space the rows 6 in. (150 mm.) apart, labelling each row as you

go. This is particularly important in a seed bed because, when young, the various brassicas look similar.

Birds may be troublesome, pecking out the brassica seedlings as they emerge, so cover the bed with netting stretched over pegs.

Sowing under cloches

Some crops can be harvested earlier if they are given a start under cloches. Sowing times can be advanced by two or three weeks for vegetables such as carrots, French beans and lettuces.

Prepare the ground as for sowing in the open and place the cloches in position two weeks before sowing to warm up the soil.

Distances between rows will be governed by the height and width of the cloches. As the seedlings grow they will need headroom, so do not sow too near the edges.

Surface soil dries quickly under cloches, though usually there should be no difficulty if it was sufficiently moist at sowing time. During hot weather it may be necessary to water the soil before the seedlings appear.

During damp weather scatter pellets to control slugs.

Causes of failure

The complete or partial failure of a sowing is rarely due to the quality of the seed. If the seeds do not come up, you probably have time to re-sow, but first make sure that the crop has failed.

Check with the germination times shown on p. 32.

There are several common reasons for failure, and these may be identified if the seeds are large enough to be dug up and examined.

Soil too cold The seed will be soft and decaying, with no sign of a shoot. This occurs in hardy crops sown too early in spring, and in tender crops, such as marrows, sown too early in April or May.

Delay first sowings of hardy crops until growth is evident in weeds and overwintered crops, and the soil feels warm to the touch after the sun has been on it.

Take local advice and do not be misled by sowing dates based on latitude. Spring in parts of East Anglia, for example, is often colder than further north.

Soil too dry The seed will be hard and appear much as it came out of the packet. In dry weather always soak the ground before sowing, and water at three-day intervals until seedlings emerge.

Fungus diseases Seeds are liable to attack by spores of a soil-borne fungus, and in this case will rot and may be hard to find. This is more common in heavy soils than in light ones.

Before sowing, treat the seeds with a fungicidal dressing, obtainable from garden shops. Some, such as Murphy's Combined Seed Dressing, also contain insecticides.

Peas and beans are particularly susceptible to these rotting-off troubles, but germination can be greatly improved by shaking the seeds with fungicide in the packet. Be careful not to inhale the dust.

Slug damage Occasionally, slugs may clear seedlings as they emerge. Sprinkle slug pellets over the bed immediately after sowing.

Mice Peas sown under cloches in autumn or early spring are the most likely target of mice. Set traps under the cloches, or use bait obtainable from garden shops.

Thinning seedlings It may seem a paradox of gardening that seeds must be sown thickly enough to ensure a full row, then thinned out to give the plants room to mature. Thinning, however, is vital, otherwise seedlings become weak and spindly as they compete with each other for food and light.

Thin in three stages, starting as soon as the seedlings are large enough to handle, first to 1 in. (25 mm.) apart, then to 2 in. (50 mm.) and finally to the distance recommended for each vegetable (see pp. 82–276).

Pelleted seeds, sown in pairs at their final spacings, only need thinning to a single seedling at each station.

Thin when the soil is damp to reduce root disturbance to the plants that are left. Put thinnings on the compost heap as they may attract pests if left between the rows – especially in the case of carrot thinnings.

At the second thinning, some of the plants removed – such as carrots, turnips and beet – may be used in the kitchen.

At the third thinning, check that only a single plant is left at each station. Sometimes a second plant may be missed, and this will be more difficult to remove later.

Plants in the seed bed need to be thinned only once before transplanting.

Germination times – and age limits for seeds

To minimise risks at sowing time, use only fresh seeds. Every seed packet carries the year of packing and an assurance that the contents comply with legal standards of germination.

The use of fresh seeds is particularly important with parsnips, whose seeds have a notoriously poor germination.

Other seeds may be sown safely a year after purchase if they have been stored in a dry, cool place. Some, indeed, have a much longer life, as the table below shows.

To avoid disappointment and the need to re-sow, test a sample of old seeds indoors a few weeks before they are due to be sown.

Count 20 seeds and sow them in a small container of moist seed compost. Place the container in a plastic bag and leave in a warm place, such as an airing cupboard, for the number of days shown in the column of germination times below. If 16–18 seeds germinate, the rest are worth sowing in the garden.

Sowing seeds under glass and indoors

Most vegetable seeds are sown directly in the ground, but there are two major groups that are sown in pots or trays – either in a frame or a greenhouse, or indoors.

One group comprises vegetables such as French and runner beans, which can be given an early start under glass and then planted outdoors when the danger of frost is past. They will mature several weeks earlier than crops sown outdoors.

In the other group are the seeds of more tender plants that need relatively high temperatures to germinate. These include aubergines, cucumbers, melons, peppers and tomatoes. The plants may be grown in a greenhouse or, like beans, moved outside when all danger of frost is past.

Plants of both groups are very easy to grow if you have an electrically heated propagator which produces the right temperature and humidity.

The propagator may be used in a greenhouse, so saving fuel costs because the rest of the greenhouse need not be heated, or it may be placed on a sunny window-sill in the house.

If you have no greenhouse or propagator, you can get seeds of hardy plants to germinate on a window-sill, but it is essential to pay attention to sowing times and to provide plenty of light to make sure that the seedlings are sturdy.

Seeds that need a fairly high temperature to germinate, such as cucumbers and melons, can be started in an airing cupboard, but again the timing must be right so that subsequent growth of the seedlings is not checked at any stage. (Sowing times for each type of vegetable will be found in Growing and Cooking, pp. 82–276.)

Risks of a check are minimised if you use a garden frame or cloches (pp. 53–56) for hardening off, or acclimatising, plants before they are put in their positions in the garden. If you have neither, you will need to carry the plants outside on mild days and bring them in at night.

It is a waste of effort to sow seeds so early that seedlings either grow too spindly indoors to be of any use, or die in the cold outside. If sown too late they may not have time to mature, and the fruits to ripen, before autumn.

Always use fresh, sterilised compost, which can be bought from garden shops. Garden soil contains weed seeds and, possibly, fungal spores that will infect seedlings. Most garden soils have the wrong texture for use in pots and boxes, and will become caked and compacted after a short time.

Sowing and potting composts

The composts used for sowing and potting are different from the compost made from decaying

USEFUL FACTS ABOUT VEGETABLE SEEDS

VEGETABLE	AVERAGE LIFE OF SEEDS (years)	AVERAGE DAYS TO GERMINATION (open ground)	AVERAGE TIME TO MATURE FROM SOWING (weeks)	VEGETABLE	AVERAGE LIFE OF SEEDS (years)	AVERAGE DAYS TO GERMINATION (open ground)	AVERAGE TIME TO MATURE FROM SOWING (weeks)
Beans, Broad	2	21	20–26	Leeks	2	14	29–34
Beans, French	2	14	9+	Lettuces	3	7	9–13
Beans, Runner	2	14	13+				
Beetroots	3	13	9–13	Marrows	3	7	9–13
Broccoli	3	8	39–50	Onions	2	14	21–30
Brussels sprouts	3	8	26–31				
				Parsnips	2	17	21–30
Cabbages, Early	3	8	17+	Peas	3	10	11–17
Cabbages, Late	3	8	21+				
Carrots	3	16	11–14	Radishes	3	6	3–6
Cauliflowers	3	8	13–17	Salsify	2	12	19–24
Celeriac	2	8 (indoors)	26–30	Summer spinach	2	11	7–13
Celery	2	8 (indoors)	26–30	New Zealand spinach	2	11	10–12
Chicory	3	9	17–21	Swedes	3	8	21+
Cucumbers	3	9	10–13	Sweet corn	3	9	17+
Kale	3	8	29+	Tomatoes	5	7 (indoors)	14+
Kohl-rabi	3	7	11–14	Turnips	3	8	7–12

vegetable matter in the garden.

Commercial seed and potting composts are formulated to give plants everything, except water, that they need for rapid growth. They have been sterilised to kill weed seeds and fungal spores, and are made of free-draining material that encourages root action and does not become waterlogged.

These composts are of two kinds – those based on loam and those with a peat base.

Loam-based composts The best-known of these are the John Innes range, available in four grades:

Seed compost, for sowing seeds; No. 1 potting compost, for seedlings moved from seed compost; No. 2, for potting on the plants; and No. 3, for growing plants such as tomatoes and aubergines to maturity.

John Innes is not a brand name. The formulae for the composts were evolved after long experiments at the John Innes Horticultural Institute, and anybody can make them up and sell them. The composts contain varying mixtures of sterilised loam, peat, sand and plant food to meet the needs of the plants at each stage of development.

Loam-based composts give a long-lasting supply of plant foods. Their disadvantage is that their principal ingredient is loam, and suitable types are now in short supply. As a result, some mixes of so-called John Innes compost are inferior. Ideally, the loam should come from the top spit of well-established pasture.

Soil-less composts These proprietary products, such as Levington compost, are based on peat to which plant foods have been added. They are light, clean to handle and uniform in quality. But plants left in them for more than two or three months need regular feeding with a general-purpose fertiliser.

Soil-less composts are sold in plastic bags and normally contain the right amount of moisture for sowing or planting. A compost will retain this moisture if the bag is resealed after only part of it is used.

Compost can be seen to have dried out when the surface is pale instead of dark brown.

When this occurs in the bag, tip out the contents, spread them thinly, water through a fine rose, and mix well before using or returning to the bag.

Where drying out occurs in a pot, immerse to the rim in water until air bubbles cease to rise from the compost. Treat seedlings growing in a tray by repeated light waterings from a fine rose.

Seed pans and plant pots

Plastic pans, pots and trays are all suitable for seed sowing. They can be washed easily after use and they do not harbour disease spores, which is always a risk with wooden seed boxes.

Indoors, any shape of container can be used, but in the greenhouse rectangular trays and pans are the most practical as they do not waste space on the staging. To save compost, use the smallest container that will provide you with sufficient seedlings.

More than one variety can be sown in the same container, provided the divisions between them are clearly marked and each variety is labelled. The easiest way to do this is to write the names of

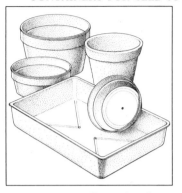

RIGID CONTAINERS Pots and seed pans made from clay or plastic are reusable.

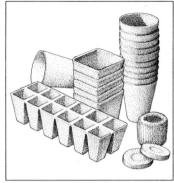

PEAT POTS Both the pot and its contents are planted in the bed, avoiding any check.

the varieties on plastic labels and use these as the division markers.

Plant pots are available in sizes from 2 in. (50 mm.) to about 18 in. (455 mm.), the measurements referring to the inside rim diameters. The most useful sizes are 3 in. (75 mm.), for growing on seedlings, 4½ in. (115 mm.) for potting on when the roots fill the first pot, and 8–10 in. (200–255 mm.) for plants grown to maturity.

Plastic pots are light, easy to clean and cheaper than clay pots. The rate of evaporation from the compost is slower, allowing less-frequent watering.

However, clay pots give excellent results, so do not discard them in favour of plastic pots. Always soak new clay pots, or any that have been stored indoors for some time, in water for an hour before using. Without soaking they will absorb too much moisture from the compost.

Peat pots are used differently from those made of plastic or clay. At planting time the pot is put straight into the ground with the plant in it. The compressed peat disintegrates and the roots grow through without any check.

Peat pots must be very damp when planted and the soil must be well watered if it is at all dry, otherwise, the peat will form a hard case and the roots will not be able to break through.

For the thrifty gardener, plastic yoghourt or cream cartons make excellent small plant pots.

Pots can be eliminated altogether by the use of soil blocks. These are lumps of loam-based compost in which seeds can be sown or seedlings planted. They maintain their cohesion long enough for the plants to reach planting-out size.

Another form of block is made from peat. Perhaps the most widely used is the Jiffy 7 – a large disc of highly compressed peat which contains plant foods and is enclosed in a fine-mesh net. When soaked in water it swells to a cylindrical block about 1½ in. (40 mm.) high on which a single seed is

sown, or a seedling or cutting planted.

Soil blocks and peat blocks are ideal for sowing large seeds, such as those of cucumbers, and for raising seedlings on a window-sill.

Germination temperatures

Hardy vegetables, such as lettuces, need a minimum temperature of 5–7°C (41–45°F) to germinate. Tomatoes and marrows require 10–13°C (50–55°F), cucumbers 21°C (70°F) and aubergines 18°C (64°F).

These higher temperatures are attainable in a propagator, and can be achieved in the greenhouse with a little ingenuity. If the heater is placed under the staging, and a polythene tent erected over the seed pans, an adequate and fairly steady temperature can be maintained.

Even without a heater you can still raise many plants in a greenhouse. It simply means that you

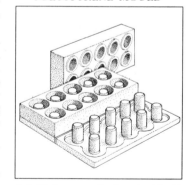

Soil blocks are easily formed with this reusable kit. Before sowing seeds or pricking out seedlings, firm the compost in the cavities by pressing downwards with the solid polystyrene sections. To remove the blocks for planting out, place the hollow section over the solid sections and press downwards.

will have to sow later, thus losing some of the advantage of protected sowing.

For instance, tomatoes can be sown in February – if you can provide moderate heat for germination. Without heat, sowing must be delayed until late March or April.

Sowing in a garden frame can begin at the same time as in a cold greenhouse. Conserve warmth as much as possible, ventilating at mid-day on warm days and covering with sacks or other material on cold nights. A soil-heating cable may be installed in a frame (see p. 54), in which case sowing times are as for a heated greenhouse.

Sowing in pans and trays

Fill the container to the rim with seed compost and press it down with the bottom of a similar container until it is $\frac{1}{2}$ in. (12 mm.) below the rim.

Sprinkle the seeds very thinly and evenly, spacing larger seeds, such as tomatoes, and pelleted seeds at least $\frac{1}{2}$ in. apart.

Cover the seeds with $\frac{1}{8}$ in. (3 mm.) of compost and firm the surface evenly. Water lightly, preferably using a fine rose that projects the spray upwards.

Use a crayon or felt-tipped pen to write the name of the variety and the date of sowing on the side of the tray or on a label.

If you are germinating the seeds in a greenhouse, but without a propagator, cover the container with a sheet of glass to conserve moisture and place a piece of brown paper or card over the top.

If growing on a window-sill, place each tray or pot in a polythene bag, tying it tightly at the top to conserve moisture but

SOWING SEEDS IN A PAN

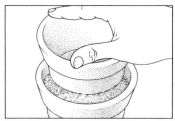

1 Fill the pan evenly with compost, then firm it with the base of another pan. If you wish, divide it with a seed label.

2 Sow the seeds thinly on the compost. If the pan is divided, sow two different species to avoid possible confusion.

3 Cover the seeds with a thin layer of compost. Label with the name of the variety and the sowing date.

4 Water the pan gently with a fine rose or with a sprayer. Do not flood the compost as the seeds may float to the surface.

enclosing as much air as possible.

Remove the covering as soon as the first shoots emerge. If left in the dark they can become drawn and worthless in 24 hours.

In a greenhouse propagator, remove the tray as soon as the seedlings break the surface. Place the seedlings where they will get both warmth and light.

Sowing in pots

Seeds of marrows, cucumbers, melons and sweet corn are best sown in potting compost in 3 in. (75 mm.) plastic, clay or peat pots and grown on without disturbance until their final planting.

Sow two seeds $\frac{1}{2}$ in. (12 mm.) apart and $\frac{1}{2}$ in. deep in the centre of the pot, inserting the seeds of marrows, melons and cucumbers on edge. Keep covered with glass and brown paper until they germinate.

In most cases two seedlings appear. Remove the weaker one.

French and runner beans can be given a good start by sowing them in moist peat in plastic cream cartons, in which drainage holes have been punched. Put five or six seeds $\frac{3}{4}$ in. (20 mm.) deep in each carton. Seal them in a plastic bag and put the containers in an airing cupboard for a few days until the seeds germinate.

Pricking out

Just as seedlings outdoors need thinning, so must those in trays be given room to develop. Do this by spacing them out in other trays or planting them singly in pots. Make this move, known as 'pricking out', as soon as the seedlings are large enough to handle and before they become tall and intertwined.

Fill the trays or pots with John

Innes No. 1 potting compost or a soil-less compost to within $\frac{1}{2}$ in. (12 mm.) of the rim when made firm and level.

Lift each seedling with the point of a plastic plant label, holding it by a leaf and not by the stem. Use a pencil or stick to make a hole in the compost and plant the seedling with its stem covered to just below the seed leaves – the leaves that appear first as the seedling breaks the surface.

Space lettuces and other small plants $1\frac{1}{2}$ in. (40 mm.) apart. Allow $2\frac{1}{2}$ in. (65 mm.) between tomatoes if pricked out into trays, though it is better to prick them out individually into 3 in. (75 mm.) pots.

Water the seedlings and keep them out of direct sunlight for two

PRICKING OUT

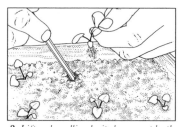

1 Use a seed label to ease the seedlings out of the compost. Loosen them carefully, otherwise the roots will be broken.

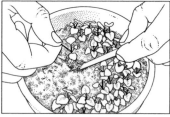

2 Lift each seedling by its leaves, not by the stem. Use a pencil or thin stick to plant it, burying it up to the seed leaves.

days, then place them close to the glass to encourage sturdy, short-jointed growth. Water regularly and shade the glass during sunny weather.

Hardening off

Plants raised in a greenhouse or indoors must be acclimatised before being planted outdoors.

Ideally, place them in a garden frame or under cloches a week or so before planting out. At first, leave frame lights or cloches open only during the day. A few days later, give some ventilation at night and, finally, leave the protection off altogether.

If a frame or a cloche is not available, stand the plants in a porch or verandah by day and take them in for the first few nights.

Remember that plants in small containers exposed to sun and wind need more frequent watering than when under cover.

Sowing seeds in a propagator

Propagators promote the ideal conditions for seeds to germinate: constant warmth and humidity. They help in producing crops which can be harvested days, or even weeks, earlier, while similar produce in the shops is still expensive.

The simplest consists of a seed tray with a snugly-fitting, plastic dome. This type is placed either above a greenhouse heater or in a warm spot indoors.

Most propagators, however, are electrically heated, some by low voltage cables set in sand, others by a warming panel on which the domed seed tray is placed.

After the initial outlay, an

PROPAGATORS FOR RAISING SEEDLINGS

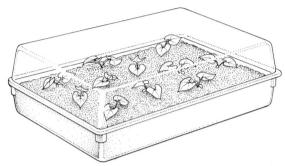

UNHEATED Used indoors, this simple type of container promotes humidity and fairly stable conditions for raising seedlings. But unless placed close to a stove or radiator it may not be warm enough for seeds of tender plants to germinate.

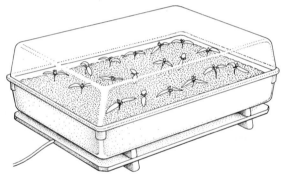

SOIL HEATING An electric element warms·the compost and provides ideal conditions for germination and root development. Some simple types are heated with a light bulb. Suitable for use indoors or in a greenhouse.

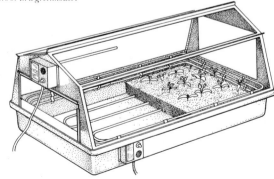

SOIL AND AIR HEATING Some large propagators have warming cables above and below soil level. As ventilation is adjustable, plants can remain until well established. However, it would hardly be justified unless also used for ornamental subjects.

electric propagator costs only a few pence a week to run. A small version suitable for a window-sill consumes merely 16 watts and a large greenhouse type, measuring 36 × 20 in. (1 m. × 510 mm.), only 40 watts.

Transplanting vegetables

When transplanting vegetables to their permanent positions after raising them under glass or in a seed bed, choose plants that are stocky, sturdy and well hardened off (see p. 34).

Check that the soil is moist and firm, and allow time for it to settle after digging.

If possible, wait for mild, still, damp weather. Unless the plants are given protection, they may be stunted by strong winds or hot sunshine.

Planting tender crops Courgettes, cucumbers, marrows, melons and tomatoes are among plants that will not grow when the soil and the air are cold, so timing is crucial when planting outdoors.

In the south, wait until the second or third week in May if these plants are to be protected by cloches, or until the end of May or early June if planted in the open. In the north, allow at least an extra week or two in both cases.

If the soil is dry, water it thoroughly the day before planting. Water the plants an hour or two before moving them, taking particular care that peat pots get a thorough soaking.

Marrows, cucumbers and melons may suffer a severe check if their roots are disturbed. For this reason they are often grown in peat pots, which can be planted directly in the soil.

If the plants have been raised in plastic or clay pots, tap them out carefully. Hold the pot upside-down in the palm of your hand, with the plant projecting downwards between your fingers. Tap the rim of the pot smartly against a solid object, such as a trowel, so that the plant slides out with the soil-ball intact.

Use a trowel to make a hole in the soil about 1 in. (25 mm.) wider than the peat pot or soil-ball. Set the plant in the hole and draw soil round it, firming with the back of the trowel or with your fingers.

Give enough water to help the soil to settle.

Transplanting from a seed bed

Move hardy plants, such as Brussels sprouts, from the seed bed to their permanent positions when about 4 in. (100 mm.) high. The plants should have short stems and spreading leaves. Make sure also that each has an inner growing point of undeveloped leaves.

During a dry spell, water the seed bed thoroughly the day before planting. At the same time, water the planting site.

Use either a trowel or a dibber to make the planting holes.

Lift the plants with a trowel and set each in a hole, planting it slightly deeper than it was in the seed bed. Make sure there is no cavity below the roots.

Firm each plant by pushing the trowel or dibber into the ground alongside and levering the soil firmly against the roots. Water the plants in.

To test if you are planting firmly, hold a leaf between finger and thumb and pull. If the leaf tears, the plant is firm enough; but

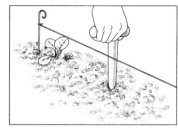

1 Using a line to ensure straight rows, make the holes with a trowel or dibber.

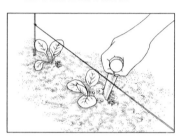

2 After planting, insert the tool alongside and press the soil against the roots.

3 Firm planting is vital. When pulled, a leaf should tear but the plant stay firm.

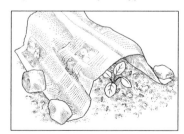

4 In hot weather, shade the plants for a few days with newspaper or black polythene.

if you pull the plant out of the ground, re-plant it more firmly and test the other plants.

If you are planting more than one row, stagger the plants in adjacent rows to give them more room to grow.

When planting during hot spells, give shade by placing newspaper over the plants for two or three days to help them to get established. Use bricks or stones to keep the paper in place.

Alternatively, if you have polythene tunnel cloches (see p. 55), use the wire supports and cover them with black polythene. To save time the polythene can be fastened to the wire with clothes pegs.

Birds sometimes pull brassica plants out of the ground after planting. Net the bed if you are not covering the plants with newspaper or black polythene.

After planting brassicas and lettuces, scatter slug pellets over the ground. Sprinkle bromophos or diazinon granules around stems of brassica plants as a precaution against cabbage root fly.

Keep the soil moist, and spray the plants each evening until they are established.

Buying plants

Generally, it is better to grow your own plants from seed rather than buy the plants from a nursery. You get a better choice of varieties and you are able to produce the plants just at the time you are ready to set them out.

However, if something goes wrong with your own sowing you will have to buy plants. These are the points you should then look for:

Buy sturdy plants with short stems and deep green leaves, indicating that they have been well hardened off.

Choose pots or trays that are already well watered.

Check whether varieties – especially tomatoes – are suitable for indoor or outside planting, and choose to suit your needs.

Mulching and watering

Soil is a natural reservoir. The more thoroughly it is cultivated, and the more decayed organic material (called humus) it contains, the greater its capacity to store water.

Apart from surplus rainwater which drains away, soil loses moisture in two ways: by direct evaporation from the surface, and through the action of plants, which take up water in their roots and transpire it through their leaves.

In hot, dry spells the moisture content of soil needs to be supplemented by watering, but it can also be conserved by mulching – that is, by placing a barrier between moisture-holding soil and the air. A mulch can be a layer of peat, polythene, garden compost or well-rotted manure.

Frequent hoeing is also of benefit. Without hoeing, and especially if trodden and compacted when wet, the surface remains dark in colour and may feel moist during dry weather. This is because moisture is being drawn to the surface, where it will be lost by evaporation. Later, the surface will bake hard and crack, increasing the loss of moisture.

This is less likely to happen if you hoe regularly, leaving a fine, surface up to 1 in. (25 mm.) deep.

The beneficial effect of hoeing can be increased by adding another moisture-retaining layer – peat, garden compost or manure – along both sides of rows of crops to a depth of 2–3 in. (50–75 mm.).

Mulch soft-fruit bushes and canes in April while the soil is still moist. Begin mulching annual crops of vegetables when they are a few inches high. If the ground is dry, water thoroughly before applying the mulch.

Mulches of organic material, such as manure or compost, are valuable because they ultimately add to the humus content of the soil. But black polythene makes an effective mulch for some crops – especially for strawberries and bush tomatoes, as it prevents the fruits resting on the soil.

Before laying polythene, ensure that the soil is moist and scatter slug pellets along each side of the row. Cover each edge of the polythene with soil to keep the sheets in position.

You can lay separate strips about 12 in. (305 mm.) wide on each side of a row of plants, or cut slits in a broader sheet to match the positions of plants.

Watering When using a hose or can, water the ground thoroughly, giving at least 5 gallons per square yard (23 l. per square metre). If you give too little, water will not reach the roots even though the top layer appears wet. If you continue to apply small amounts, the roots may be drawn up to the moist surface and will suffer even more if this dries out.

Some plants – for example, cucumbers, marrows, melons, pumpkins, runner beans and tomatoes are gross drinkers. They show distress very quickly if they do not have sufficient moisture.

Regular watering is essential during long, dry spells. Spasmodic watering can cause poor setting of the flowers of some crops and ripening fruits may split.

Water in the evening so that the plants get the benefit during the night. Water applied early on hot, sunny days will evaporate before it can reach the roots.

Harvesting and storing vegetables

Harvesting is one of the most satisfying jobs in the garden, the time when a gardener gets his reward for months of toil. But, like other stages of food growing, harvesting has its pitfalls. Much of the earlier effort can be wasted by failing to gather vegetables until they are past their best.

Make the most of the advantage you have over commercial growers by picking vegetables while they are young, tender and full of goodness and flavour – and only a few minutes before they are to be cooked or preserved. Check plants daily at times when crops are maturing quickly.

Pick French and runner beans before the seeds start swelling, or they will be tough and stringy and the plants will stop producing.

Pick peas when the pods are smooth and bright green. If only a few peas or beans are ready, keep picking frequently and put the pods in the refrigerator until you have sufficient to make a meal.

Pick perpetual spinach and sea kale beet regularly to discourage them from going to seed.

Storing vegetables Many summer-grown vegetables can be preserved by freezing (p. 294), bottling (p. 309), or salting (p. 346). Others, such as marrows, onions, potatoes and root vegetables can be stored for winter use in an airy, frost-free place such as a garage or shed.

Ensure that doors and windows fit well and, in a severe winter, give additional protection with sacking, straw or layers of newspaper.

Do not put sacks or containers directly on the floor and do not lean them against walls.

Store only undamaged and healthy vegetables, and inspect them regularly.

In the past it was often recommended that potatoes and root vegetables should be stored in an earth clamp outdoors, but few gardeners today grow enough to make this worthwhile.

Clamps are in any case an inconvenient method of storage as they may have to be opened in wet weather.

Instead, keep long-rooted beetroot, carrots and celeriac in boxes of damp sand or peat to prevent them shrivelling. Before storing, twist off the leaves of beetroot by hand and trim the foliage of carrots and celeriac with a knife.

Leave potatoes to dry on the ground before storing them in large, unsealed paper bags or hessian sacks. Potatoes in store need air but not light so it is inadvisable to store them in polythene bags.

Place the sacks on upturned boxes to keep them off the ground.

Either hang onions, shallots and garlic in nets, or tie them to lengths of rope. Store marrows and pumpkins in nets hanging from a beam or the shed roof. Leave parsnips, swedes and leeks in the soil until they are needed, as they will withstand frost.

Weeds and weedkillers

If weeds are not controlled they will at first compete with vegetables for plant foods and water, and may later overrun the crop altogether. However, their abundant presence does at least show that the soil is fertile.

There are three ways of getting rid of weeds: the hard way, by pulling them up by hand; the relatively expensive way, by drenching them with chemical weedkiller; and the simple way, by hoeing when they first appear.

Hoe regularly – at least weekly between April and July. A few minutes of regular attention are more effective than hours spent in clearing a badly overgrown plot.

In showery weather, rake up the weeds so that they do not get a chance to re-establish themselves, and put them on the compost heap. In dry weather, uprooted weeds may be left between the rows, as they will soon die.

The choice of hoe depends partly on the task and partly on the personal preference and needs of the gardener (see p. 14).

There are four main types: the draw hoe, which is especially useful for earthing-up potatoes; the Dutch hoe, which is ideal for destroying weeds between rows of vegetables; various types of patent hoes, which are mostly improved forms of the Dutch hoe; and the short-handled, or onion, hoe, which is excellent for accurate weeding close to plants.

Whatever type of hoe you use, make the most of hot, dry days – when uprooted weeds wilt and die almost immediately – and leave the surface loose and crumbly.

However carefully you use a hoe, some weeding will still have to be done by hand among close-growing plants, such as peas. Deal with the weeds when they are small, because if left too long their removal will disturb the roots of the vegetables.

Even in a well-tended garden, deep-rooted perennial weeds may get a hold among permanent crops such as asparagus, or among summer vegetables at holiday time. Get rid of them by easing the soil away with a trowel so that enough of the roots are exposed to pull them out cleanly by hand.

Such hand weeding is necessary where perennial weeds grow through a mulch.

Weeding a seed bed In a seed bed, vegetable seeds and weed seeds have exactly the same conditions for germination. The seedlings may therefore, emerge at about the same time, and may confront the gardener with a bewildering green carpet in which vegetables are hard to distinguish from weeds.

Anticipate this problem at sowing time by inserting small canes at the ends of each row. When growth is about 1 in. (25 mm.) high, tie string between the canes, so marking the seed row, and hoe to within 1 in. on each side.

Hand weed when the vegetables are clearly distinguishable, and thin them at the same time.

When sowing slow-germinating parsnip seeds, sprinkle radish seeds along the drill. The quick-germinating radishes will mark the row for weeding, and also provide a crop by the time the parsnips need to be thinned.

When sowing brassicas (plants in the cabbage family), onions, swedes and turnips, the bed can be treated with propachlor to inhibit the germination of weed seeds.

Using chemical weedkillers

Chemical weedkillers are most effective in clearing paths, waste ground and the soil beneath fruit trees and bushes. Their use is more limited in the vegetable garden. Here, periodic digging and regular hoeing keep down both perennial and annual weeds. Nevertheless, for the gardener with little spare time, or who wants to return from holiday to a weed-free garden, chemical weedkillers have a part to play. There are three types:

Total weedkillers, which destroy all plants and grasses.

Selective weedkillers, which kill weeds without harming the crop.

Pre-emergence weedkillers, which, on cleared ground, prevent weed seeds from germinating.

Total weedkillers

Simazine is especially useful for pathways, which it will keep weed-free for up to 12 months. The chemical remains in suspension in the top layer of the soil, and for this reason it can also be used as a selective weedkiller between soft fruit bushes whose roots are deeper than this.

It is sold under the trade names of Weedex and Boots Path Weed Control.

Simazine is mixed with diquat and paraquat in Pathclear; with aminotriazole in Super Weedex; and with MCPA and aminotriazole in Kilweed. The advantage of these mixtures is that they kill perennial as well as annual weeds.

Sodium chlorate is another total weedkiller, but it is liable to move sideways in the soil, killing any plants with which it comes into contact. There is a fire risk unless a brand containing a fire suppressant is used.

Grow nothing on treated soil for at least eight months. Do not put weeds killed by sodium chlorate on the compost heap; and do not use the chemical over tree roots. It is sold as ICI Sodium Chlorate and Liquisafened Chlorate.

Paraquat and diquat (sold as Weedol) are total weedkillers, in the sense that they kill all green plant tissue. But as both chemicals are inactivated by contact with the soil, they can be used selectively by applying them to the weed foliage while keeping them off the cultivated plants.

This is easily done with a Weedol applicator, or by using a sprinkler bar on a watering can.

The best of recent total weedkillers is glyphosate (sold as Tumbleweed). Sprayed on to the leaves, it moves to all parts of the plant, killing as it goes. If applied with care, it can be used to weed between vegetables and ornamentals.

Selective weedkillers

Dalapon kills annual and perennial grasses, including twitch and couch. It may be used under fruit trees and bushes and in asparagus beds. It is sold as Battle's Dalapon and Synchemicals Dalapon.

2,4,5-T is a powerful selective weedkiller for use on nettles, thistles, briars and woody or shrubby weeds. It does not kill grass.

It can also be applied by spot treatment – that is, dabbing weed leaves with a brush dipped in the chemical.

Do not use it close to tomatoes or store it in a greenhouse where tomatoes are growing. Do not put the dead weeds on a compost heap. It is sold as Nettlekiller and Brushwood Killer.

Other widely used selective weedkillers include mecoprop (Clovotox, Supertox) and 2, 4-D (Dicotox). Dichlobenil (Casoron G) can be used selectively in established perennial crops, but has little selectivity when applied to annual crops.

Pre-emergence weedkiller

Propachlor inhibits the germination of weed seeds for about six

---

WARNING

Store weedkillers out of the reach of children.

Never put liquid weedkillers in containers where they may be mistaken for something else. Read the makers' instructions and carry them out carefully.

Do not use weedkillers in a high wind.

Keep the outlet of the can or spray close to the weeds being treated.

Wash out sprays and watering cans thoroughly after use.

weeks, giving plants a better start. Unfortunately, it may be used only on a limited range of crops.

Propachlor may be applied immediately after sowing leeks, onions and brassicas, including turnips and swedes, and after planting brassicas. It is sold as Ramrod.

Identifying garden weeds

Both annual and perennial weeds are relatively easy to control in ground that is cultivated regularly. But sometimes a gardener takes over a neglected plot or faces an invasion by a seemingly indestructible perennial weed from a neighbour's garden.

Among the hardest of these intruders to eradicate are perennials that multiply by rhizomes – creeping underground stems that spread out from the parent plant and throw up fresh shoots to form a new plant.

The most diligent gardener might believe that he has cleared an area by digging, only to find the following spring that small pieces that he missed are throwing up new vigorous shoots.

For this reason it is important to be able to recognise weeds so that the most effective treatment can be given to destroy them. These illustrations show some of the most common weeds found in vegetable gardens or under fruit bushes and trees.

Recommended chemical treatment is given for the control of each perennial weed. Use paraquat/diquat (Weedol) if you want to use a chemical weedkiller for annual weeds. But remember that hoeing costs nothing and can be just as effective if done frequently during the spring and summer.

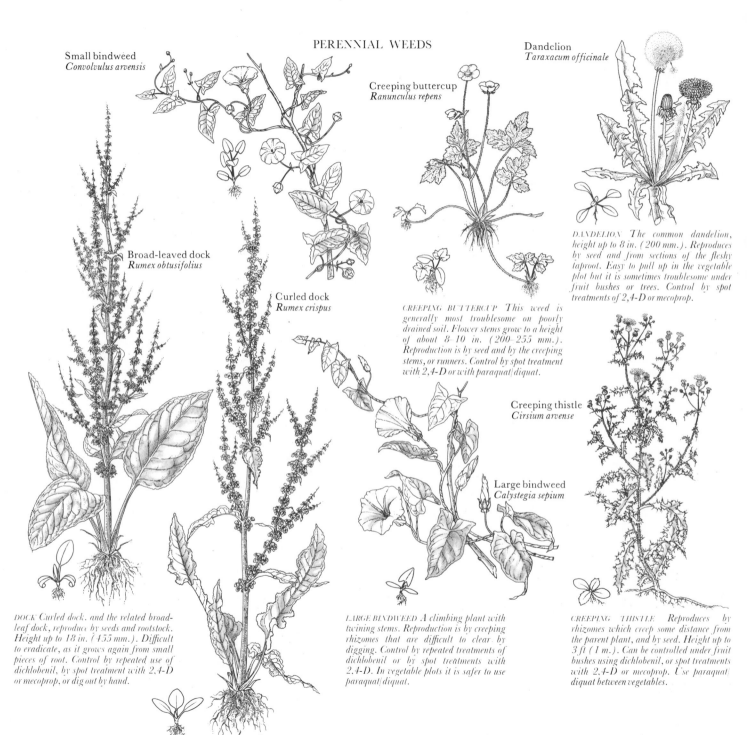

PERENNIAL WEEDS

Small bindweed
Convolvulus arvensis

Broad-leaved dock
Rumex obtusifolius

Curled dock
Rumex crispus

Creeping buttercup
Ranunculus repens

Dandelion
Taraxacum officinale

Creeping thistle
Cirsium arvense

Large bindweed
Calystegia sepium

DANDELION The common dandelion, height up to 8 in. (200 mm.). Reproduces by seed and from sections of the fleshy taproot. Easy to pull up in the vegetable plot but it is sometimes troublesome under fruit bushes or trees. Control by spot treatments of 2,4-D or mecoprop.

CREEPING BUTTERCUP This weed is generally most troublesome on poorly drained soil. Flower stems grow to a height of about 8–10 in. (200–255 mm.). Reproduction is by seed and by the creeping stems, or runners. Control by spot treatment with 2,4-D or with paraquat/diquat.

DOCK Curled dock, and the related broad-leaf dock, reproduce by seeds and rootstock. Height up to 18 in. (455 mm.). Difficult to eradicate, as it grows again from small pieces of root. Control by repeated use of dichlobenil, by spot treatment with 2,4-D or mecoprop, or dig out by hand.

LARGE BINDWEED A climbing plant with twining stems. Reproduction is by creeping rhizomes that are difficult to clear by digging. Control by repeated treatments of dichlobenil or by spot treatments with 2,4-D. In vegetable plots it is safer to use paraquat/diquat.

CREEPING THISTLE Reproduces by rhizomes which creep some distance from the parent plant, and by seed. Height up to 3 ft (1 m.). Can be controlled under fruit bushes using dichlobenil, or spot treatments with 2,4-D or mecoprop. Use paraquat/diquat between vegetables.

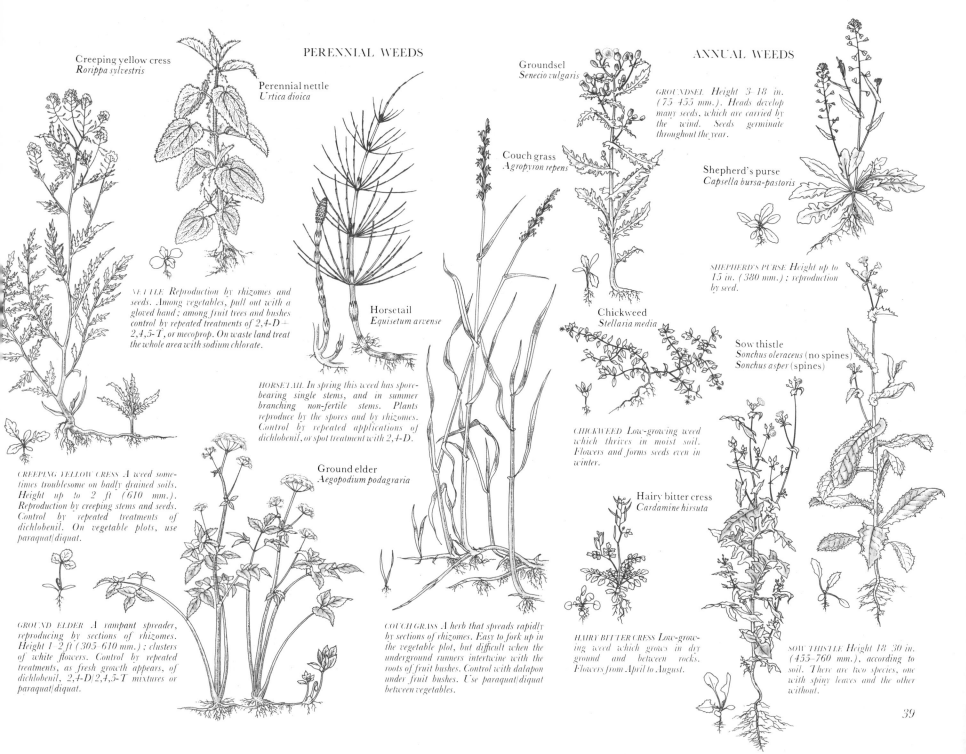

Creeping yellow cress
Rorippa sylvestris

Perennial nettle
Urtica dioica

PERENNIAL WEEDS

Groundsel
Senecio vulgaris

ANNUAL WEEDS

GROUNDSEL Height 3–18 in. (75–455 mm.). Heads develop many seeds, which are carried by the wind. Seeds germinate throughout the year.

Couch grass
Agropyron repens

Shepherd's purse
Capsella bursa-pastoris

NETTLE Reproduction by rhizomes and seeds. Among vegetables, pull out with a gloved hand; among fruit trees and bushes control by repeated treatments of 2,4-D + 2,4,5-T, or mecoprop. On waste land treat the whole area with sodium chlorate.

Horsetail
Equisetum arvense

SHEPHERD'S PURSE Height up to 15 in. (380 mm.); reproduction by seed.

Chickweed
Stellaria media

HORSETAIL In spring this weed has spore-bearing single stems, and in summer branching non-fertile stems. Plants reproduce by the spores and by rhizomes. Control by repeated applications of dichlobenil, or spot treatment with 2,4-D.

Sow thistle
Sonchus oleraceus (no spines)
Sonchus asper (spines)

CHICKWEED Low-growing weed which thrives in moist soil. Flowers and forms seeds even in winter.

CREEPING YELLOW CRESS A weed some-times troublesome on badly drained soils. Height up to 2 ft (610 mm.). Reproduction by creeping stems and seeds. Control by repeated treatments of dichlobenil. On vegetable plots, use paraquat/diquat.

Ground elder
Aegopodium podagraria

Hairy bitter cress
Cardamine hirsuta

GROUND ELDER A rampant spreader, reproducing by sections of rhizomes. Height 1–2 ft (305–610 mm.); clusters of white flowers. Control by repeated treatments, as fresh growth appears, of dichlobenil, 2,4-D/2,4,5-T mixtures or paraquat/diquat.

COUCH GRASS A herb that spreads rapidly by sections of rhizomes. Easy to fork up in the vegetable plot, but difficult when the underground runners intertwine with the roots of fruit bushes. Control with dalapon under fruit bushes. Use paraquat/diquat between vegetables.

HAIRY BITTER CRESS Low-grow-ing weed which grows in dry ground and between rocks. Flowers from April to August.

SOW THISTLE Height 18–30 in. (455–760 mm.), according to soil. There are two species, one with spiny leaves and the other without.

39

The fruit garden

Few home gardeners nowadays have space for an orchard. Fruit bushes, and certainly fruit trees, have to be fitted in as best they can, often at the expense of ornamental plants or part of the vegetable plot.

Fortunately, fruit trees can be attractive as well as useful. Trained as cordons, espaliers or fans, they also make effective screens and, to save space, they can be grown in these forms against walls and fences.

Planning a fruit garden

Even a small garden can yield heavy crops of a variety of fruits. But think ahead before you plant, since fruit trees and bushes may be in the ground for from six to 50 years.

Often the choice of what to grow is governed not only by the family's tastes, but by the amount of space available.

When making your plans, bear in mind the area a tree will occupy at maturity, not at the time of planting. Use the chart on this page as a guide to planting distances. In the early years, grow salad crops between trees and bushes to make the best possible use of the ground.

You will also have to decide, again according to taste and available space, on a balance between soft fruits and top fruits, which include apples, apricots, cherries, peaches and nectarines, pears, and plums and gages.

Soft fruits, produced on bushes, canes or low-growing plants, include black, red and white currants, gooseberries, loganberries and strawberries. They bear crops sooner after planting than top fruits and, generally, give a better return for the area of land that they occupy.

Top fruit trees, however, eventually produce heavy yields in good seasons. If you have a surplus, this can be put in store, or bottled or frozen.

Drawing up a plan

To help decide what fruits to grow, and where best to plant them, draw up a plan in the manner suggested for an overall garden design (see p. 10).

Make a list of fruits in order of preference by your family. Fit these into the plan, estimating how many trees and bushes you need under the reference for each fruit (see Growing and Cooking, pp. 62–276), and checking planting distances against the chart on the right.

Avoid planting fruit trees in the vegetable garden itself, where they will shade other plants and complicate your cropping plans. If soft fruit bushes or canes are to be planted in this area, form a block at one side of the vegetable plot so that they do not interfere with rotation of crops.

Choose a sunny wall or fence for a fan-trained apricot, peach or nectarine. If you have additional wall space, place cordons or espaliers of apples and pears, and cordons of gooseberries and red or white currants, against it. Alternatively, trees and bushes trained to these forms make excellent screens.

Decide on the fruits to grow as feature trees by the lawn or at the back of flower beds. Apples, pears and acid cherries are probably the best for this purpose, though plum on dwarfing stock would be suitable for a large garden.

In all cases choose a self-fertile variety when planting trees in isolation.

Lastly, fit soft fruit bushes, canes and plants into your plan. You will probably find that you do not have room for some of the fruits at the bottom of your list of preferences, but do not be tempted to plant too closely to squeeze them in.

Choose varieties to suit your taste, locality and the site you have chosen.

Do not, for example, choose a 'Bramley's Seedling' apple if you have only a small garden as it grows too vigorously and will occupy too much space. Choose instead, one of the recommended culinary apples and check with the nurseryman that it has been grafted on dwarfing stock.

USEFUL FACTS ABOUT FRUIT TREES AND BUSHES

FRUIT	FORM OR VARIETY	DISTANCE BETWEEN TREES AND BUSHES	BEST AGE TO PLANT (YEARS)	TIME UNTIL CROPPING (YEARS)	EXPECTED LIFE (YEARS)
Apples	Bush	12–20 ft (3.6–6 m.)	2–3	2–4	30–50
	Dwarf pyramid	5–6 ft (1.5–1.8 m.)	2–3	2–4	30–50
	Cordon	2½–3 ft (760 mm.–1 m.)	2–3	2–4	30–50
Apricots	Fan-trained	12–15 ft (3.6–4.5 m.)	3	2–3	15–20
Blackberries	'Himalaya Giant'	12–15 ft (3.6–4.5 m.)	1–2	1–2	10–12
	Other varieties	8–12 ft (2.5–3.6 m.)	1–2	1–2	10–12
Cherries	'Morello'	15–20 ft (4.5–6 m.)	2	4–5	30–50
Currants	Black	5–6 ft (1.5–1.8 m.)	2	2	12–15
Currants	Red and white, bush	5 ft (1.5 m.)	2	1–2	15
	Single cordon	15 in. (380 mm.)	2	1–2	15
Gooseberries	Bush	5 ft (1.5 m.)	2–3	1–2	10–15
	Single cordon	15 in. (380 mm.)	2–3	1–2	8–12
	Triple cordon	3 ft (1 m.)	2–3	1–2	8–12
Loganberries		12 ft (3.6 m.)	1	2	10
Peaches	Bush or fan-trained	12–15 ft (3.6–4.5 m.)	1–3	3–4	15–30
Pears	Bush	12–15 ft (3.6–4.5 m.)	3–4	2–4	40–60
	Dwarf pyramid	4–5 ft (1.2–1.5 m.)	2–3	2–4	40–60
	Cordon	2½–3 ft (760 mm.–1 m.)	2–3	2–3	40–60
Plums	Bush	12–15 ft (3.6–4.5 m.)	2–3	2–4	30–50
	Pyramid	10–12 ft (3–3.6 m.)	3	3	30–50
Raspberries		18 in. (455 mm.) 6 ft (1.8 m.) between rows	1	1	6–10

CHOOSING TREE FORMS TO SUIT YOUR GARDEN

The traditional orchard tree, known as standard or half standard, is too large for most modern gardens, but there are other forms and sizes to suit small gardens. These include bush, dwarf pyramid, cordon, espalier and fan-trained trees.

The largest of these is the bush, with a height and spread of 8–18 ft (2.6–5.8 m.). The size varies according to the type of fruit and, with apples and pears, to the vigour of the rootstock on which the tree has been grafted.

Shoots (called scions) of varieties of apples are grafted on to the roots (also called the rootstock, or stock) of wild apples, and pears on to those of quince. The various types of rootstock have a predictable effect on the eventual size of the tree and how it will crop.

When buying apple or pear trees, therefore, check with the nurseryman that they are on suitable dwarfing stock.

Apples, pears, peaches (in a few favourable areas), plums and acid cherries can be grown as bush trees.

In a more restricted garden, apples and pears are better grown as dwarf pyramids which, because of the dwarfing stock on which each variety is grafted and the method of pruning employed (see p. 66), will grow to only 7 ft (2.1 m.), with a spread of about 4 ft (1.2 m.).

Most economical in terms of space is the cordon, which consists of a main stem with short, fruiting spurs. It is grown obliquely against a wall, or in the open, and is supported by posts and wires.

Apples and pears can be grown by this method. Although the yield per tree is small, a row of cordons, set only 2½–3 ft (760 mm.–1 m.) apart, is very productive for the space occupied.

Another advantage is that a number of varieties can be grown in a comparatively small space.

Apples and pears can also be grown as espaliers, which carry fruit on a number of tiers, or horizontal branches. An espalier can be planted against a wall or fence, or trained on wires supported by posts to form a screen between the leisure garden and the vegetable plot.

Espaliers can even be grown as a form of ornamental and productive fence to surround an entire garden – an ideal solution for many new estates where only post-and-wire fences are provided.

A fan-trained tree is the best form for growing peaches, nectarines or apricots against a sunny wall.

In a very small garden where there is room for only one tree, you could grow a 'family tree' on which three varieties of apples, or three varieties of pears, are grafted on to a single stock.

This means that the selected varieties pollinate each other and give a succession of fruit over an extended season.

Check that dwarfing stock has been used, or the tree may grow so large that it defeats the original purpose of saving space.

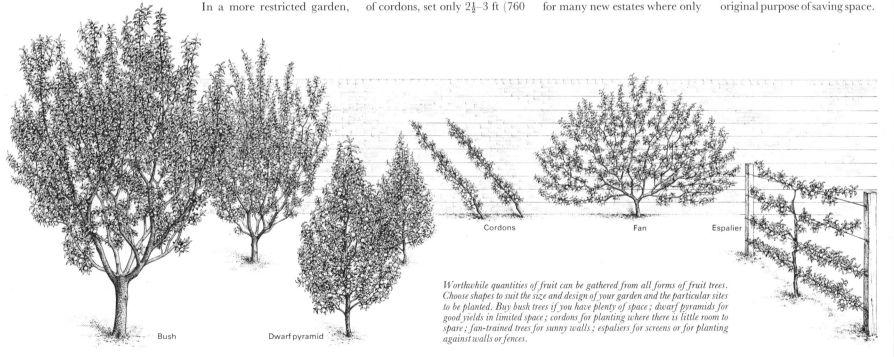

Bush   Dwarf pyramid   Cordons   Fan   Espalier

Worthwhile quantities of fruit can be gathered from all forms of fruit trees. Choose shapes to suit the size and design of your garden and the particular sites to be planted. Buy bush trees if you have plenty of space; dwarf pyramids for good yields in limited space; cordons for planting where there is little room to spare; fan-trained trees for sunny walls; espaliers for screens or for planting against walls or fences.

HEELING IN

Provided the ground is neither frozen nor too wet, trees or bushes can be set in a trench – with their roots well covered – until you are ready to plant them.

Buying and planting fruit trees

Plant fruit trees and bushes while they are dormant – from about the end of October or early November to just before growth begins again in March. The earlier they are planted the better.

It is essential that the ground should not be waterlogged or frozen.

When ordering, insist on two or three-year-old trees for bush, cordon and dwarf pyramid forms of apples and pears. Do not buy maidens or one-year-old trees, since you would then have to do the initial shaping, which is best left to a nurseryman.

Obtain espaliers with two tiers, or sets of horizontal branches, and fan trees with four ribs. Buy currant bushes at two or three years' old and cane fruits at one year old.

Preparing for planting

Prepare the ground according to the individual needs of each type of fruit. (See Growing and Cooking, pp. 62–276.)

Do not take the bushes or trees out of their wrapping if they are delivered at a time when the weather and ground are unsuitable for planting.

Keep them instead in a cool but frost-proof shed or garage.

The day before planting, unpack the trees or bushes and, if the roots are dry, soak them in water for 12–24 hours.

Heeling in

If the ground is suitable but you have not time to plant the trees in their permanent positions, unwrap them and heel them in – that is, lay them close together in a trench, lightly firming soil over their roots.

Place trees at an angle, away from the prevailing wind.

They may be left like this for several weeks.

Supporting

For bush trees and dwarf pyramids, drive a short stake into the planting hole before putting the tree in position. Tie the tree to the stake with strong string, wrapping sacking round the stem; or use adjustable ties, which can be bought at garden shops.

Before planting a fan-trained tree against a wall or fence, fix horizontal support wires with vine eyes, sold by garden shops. Stretch the wire tightly, preferably with straining bolts.

Plant with the stem about 9 in. (230 mm.) from the wall, leaning the stem slightly towards the wall. This will allow plenty of room for subsequent growth.

Before planting cordons and espaliers against a wall or fence, fix the support wires as for a fan-trained tree but space the lowest 2½ ft (760 mm.) above the ground, with 2 ft (610 mm.) intervals between this and subsequent wires.

When growing cordons or espaliers in the open, sink stout posts at 9 ft (2.7 m.) intervals to carry the support wires. Treat the posts with wood preservative – or, better still, buy them pressure treated – and sink them at least 2 ft (610 mm.) in the ground, leaving 7 ft (2.1 m.) above ground.

Brace each post with a 7 ft length of wood, setting it at an angle with about 2 ft in the ground. Use straining bolts to make the wire taut, and adjust these later if necessary.

Erect similar supports for raspberries (see p. 246), but the posts need be only 5½ ft (1.7 m.) above the ground for most varieties, and

SECURING TREES TO SUPPORTING STAKES

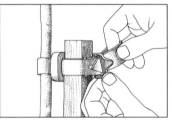

*ADJUSTABLE TIE **This is the best method. Slacken the tie as the trunk swells.***

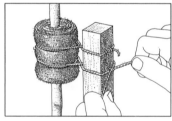

*TWINE AND SACKING **Wrap sacking round the trunk to prevent damage to the bark.***

SUPPORTING WIRES

*VINE EYES **For a secure fixing, drill holes and screw the eyes into wall plugs.***

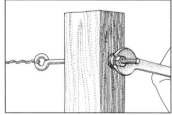

*STRAINING BOLTS **Turning the nut tightens the wire and prevents subsequent sagging.***

PLANTING FRUIT TREES

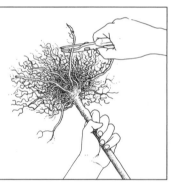

1 Trim dead or damaged roots with a pair of secateurs. Shorten over-long roots.

2 Make the hole large enough for the roots. Add compost if the soil is poor.

4 Lay a batten across the hole to check the height of the union above soil level.

5 Fork well-broken soil over the roots, shaking the stem to make the soil settle.

6½ ft (2 m.) for vigorous varieties, such as 'Malling Jewel'.

Set the bottom wire 2½ ft (760 mm.) above the ground, with the middle and top wires at 18 in. (455 mm.) intervals.

Planting

Before planting, use a pair of secateurs to cut back damaged roots to the undamaged part and shorten long roots.

Hold the tree upright on the planting site with its roots spread out on the ground. This will

3 Loosen the base of the hole with a fork, mixing in the compost if this was added.

6 Firm the soil with your feet. Replace the rest of the soil, then firm again.

indicate the size of the hole needed. Dig the hole deeply enough for the tree to be planted at its previous depth, as indicated by the soil mark on the stem.

Fork the soil at the bottom to improve drainage, adding well-rotted compost if the soil is poor. For bush and pyramid trees, drive in the stake.

Stand the tree about 4 in. (100 mm.) from the stake – or 9 in. (230 mm.) from the wall – spread out the roots and sift in fine soil. Shake the stem vigorously up and down to ensure that soil settles between the roots. Firm the soil carefully with your feet.

Plant cordons with the stems leaning towards the north, if possible, so that they receive maximum light. Allow 8 ft (2.5 m.) between the base of the last cordon in a row and the end of the wires or wall.

With all forms of tree, ensure that the union between the stock and scion is at least 4 in. (100 mm.) above soil level after planting, otherwise the scion may form its own roots.

This union shows as a knob-like projection.

Fruit bushes are planted in much the same way, except that a supporting stake is unnecessary. Plant them at the same depth as they were in the nursery, as shown by the soil mark on the stem.

After planting

The roots of trees and bushes are often disturbed by frost in the winter after planting. Check every week or so and firm any cracked ground with your feet.

Water the ground copiously during dry spells throughout the year after planting.

Pruning fruit trees and bushes

Pruning is a bogey that frightens many beginners. The bogey can be laid, however, by understanding a few simple principles.

In the first few years of the life of a tree or bush, the aim is to create the desired shape: to encourage the tiers, or horizontal branches of an espalier, for example, or produce the open-centre 'goblet' form of a bush tree.

After the framework of the main branches has been established, often about the fourth year after planting, the aim is to keep a balance between new growth and fruit production.

These aims are achieved in different ways and at different times of the year, according to the type and form of the fruit tree or bush. The calendar on p. 45 will act as a reminder of when to prune, while detailed pruning instructions are given for each fruit between pp. 62 and 276.

Hard pruning usually results in strong growth. A shoot that is cut back severely will quickly produce vigorous leaf-bearing shoots which become non-fruiting stems.

This is the aim in the early stages, when building up the formative framework of the tree, but it is a disadvantage when the aim is to produce fruit buds.

To achieve this, prune lightly or not at all.

If a tree has been neglected, spread the pruning over three years so that the shock of heavy pruning is lessened.

First take out diseased wood and branches that cross or rub against each other. In the case of a bush tree, the final stage is to remove branches in the centre.

Carry out this pruning at a time to suit the particular type of fruit.

Tools for pruning and lopping

A sharp pruning knife can be used surely and cleanly by a nursery-man or an experienced gardener.

In the hands of a beginner, however, it may cause more harm than good by tearing the bark or making jagged cuts which can let in disease.

An inexperienced pruner should use secateurs. There are two types:

Parrot-bill, which have curving blades and a scissors-like action. Modern pruners are a variant of this design.

Anvil secateurs, which have a thick edge, or anvil, against which a single blade does the cutting.

The two types are equally effective and choice is entirely a matter of preference by the gardener. Both can be used to prune stems up to ½ in. (12 mm.) in diameter. Do not try to cut stems thicker than this or the blade and joint may suffer permanent damage.

For stems up to about 1½ in. (40 mm.) in diameter use either a pruning saw or a heavy-duty lopper, which has sturdy, secateur-like blades and long handles to give extra leverage.

For branches over 1½ in., use only a pruning saw.

Get cutting blades sharpened every year or two, according to how much they are used. This is a job best done by a professional grinder or the cutting edge may be damaged.

Oil tools carefully after use before putting them away.

PRUNING TOOLS

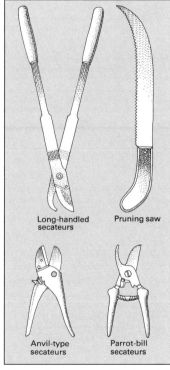

Long-handled secateurs

Pruning saw

Anvil-type secateurs

Parrot-bill secateurs

Many gardeners manage with only a single pair of secateurs. A saw and long-handled pruners are needed mainly for renovating neglected trees or for drastic surgery.

UNDERSTANDING THE TERMS USED IN PRUNING

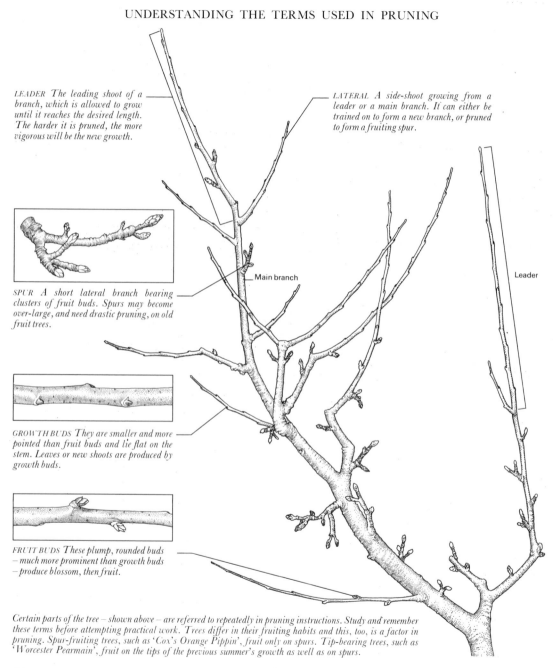

LEADER The leading shoot of a branch, which is allowed to grow until it reaches the desired length. The harder it is pruned, the more vigorous will be the new growth.

LATERAL A side-shoot growing from a leader or a main branch. It can either be trained on to form a new branch, or pruned to form a fruiting spur.

SPUR A short lateral branch bearing clusters of fruit buds. Spurs may become over-large, and need drastic pruning, on old fruit trees.

Main branch

Leader

GROWTH BUDS They are smaller and more pointed than fruit buds and lie flat on the stem. Leaves or new shoots are produced by growth buds.

FRUIT BUDS These plump, rounded buds – much more prominent than growth buds – produce blossom, then fruit.

Certain parts of the tree – shown above – are referred to repeatedly in pruning instructions. Study and remember these terms before attempting practical work. Trees differ in their fruiting habits and this, too, is a factor in pruning. Spur-fruiting trees, such as 'Cox's Orange Pippin', fruit only on spurs. Tip-bearing trees, such as 'Worcester Pearmain', fruit on the tips of the previous summer's growth as well as on spurs.

How to prune

When pruning for new growth, cut just above a healthy growth bud, pointing in the direction the new shoot is to grow.

Start the cut opposite to, and level with, the base of the bud and slant it upwards to finish just over the bud. Cut cleanly, using a steady pressure, so that the blade does the work. Do not twist the secateurs, otherwise the cut may have a ragged edge.

When pruning to remove an unwanted shoot, make the cut flush with the bark of the major branch from which it was growing, leaving no stub.

Lopping When removing a large branch, first cut it about 9 in. (230 mm.) from the trunk. Saw from the bottom until a quarter of the way through, then complete the cut from the top. Finally, remove the 9 in. stub close to the bark of the trunk.

This method reduces the risk of the wood and the bark splitting.

Always paint large wounds with a sealing compound to prevent the entry of disease spores.

NOTCHING

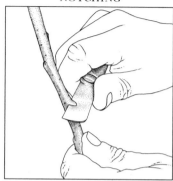

To encourage a growth bud to develop, use a sharp knife to make a shallow notch in the bark immediately above the bud.

Notching It is sometimes necessary to stimulate the growth of dormant buds after pruning. For instance, this may be helpful when training espaliers, in order to stimulate the two buds that will develop into the next tier. This is less likely to be needed with vigorous varieties.

This encouragement to growth is given by notching the bark just above the bud. Use a sharp knife for the purpose.

WHERE TO MAKE PRUNING CUTS

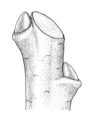  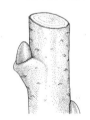

Correct cut, cleanly made and close to the bud.

Cut is too close to the bud, which may be damaged.

Cut is too far from the bud. The stub will die and may harbour disease.

Make each pruning cut just above a growth bud – but not too close to it – so that the new shoot develops without a stub of dead wood beyond it.

REMOVING BRANCHES

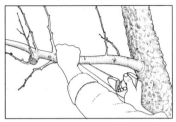

1 Make the first cut 9 in. (230 mm.) from the trunk. Saw from the underside, cutting about a quarter of the way through.

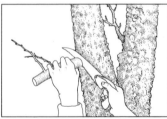

2 Complete the cut from the top of the branch. Cutting in two stages prevents the wood and bark splitting as the branch falls.

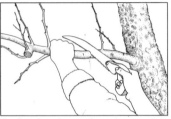

3 Remove the remaining stub in the same way, sawing first from the underside and then completing the cut from above.

4 Pare away any rough edges with a sharp knife. Paint the cut with wound-sealing paint to prevent disease spores entering.

MONTH-BY-MONTH PRUNING REMINDERS

Timing is a vital factor in pruning fruit trees and bushes. Follow this guide, because correct pruning is essential to keep a balance between fruit production and the growth of new wood. Some trees may also be put at risk of infection by being pruned at the wrong time of year. Detailed instructions are given between pp. 62 and 276.

JANUARY
Prune **apples** and **pears** (bush and half-standard); also **gooseberries** and **red** and **white currants**, if not completed earlier. Cut back newly planted **blackberry**, **loganberry** and **raspberry** canes.

FEBRUARY
Start the programme of rubbing out and pinching back **apricots**, **peaches** and **nectarines** after growth begins late in the month. Prune **apples** and **pears** (bush and half-standard), if not completed earlier; also cut back autumn-fruiting raspberries to within a few inches of the ground.

MARCH
Cut back newly planted autumn-fruiting **raspberry** canes. Prune **gooseberries**, and **red** and **white currants**, if not done in winter, and bush **plums**.

APRIL
Prune pyramid **plums** during the formative period, for four or five years after planting. Pinch back unwanted growth buds on **peaches**.

MAY
De-shoot wall-trained **peaches** and **nectarines**. Shorten leaders of mature **apple** and **pear** trees grown as cordons, dwarf pyramids or espaliers.

JUNE
Prune **gooseberries** and bush and cordon **white currants** at the end of the month. Remove shoots growing towards or away from a wall from fan-trained **cherries** and **plums**. Pinch out young growth of **figs**.

JULY
Summer-prune cordon, espalier and dwarf pyramid **apple** and **pear** trees, and pyramid **plums**, at the end of the month if new growth is mature. Cut out **raspberry** canes that have fruited.

AUGUST
Cut out **raspberry** canes after fruiting. Prune trained forms of **apples** and **pears**, if not done in July, and acid **cherries**, **damsons** and **plums** after fruiting. Cut out the shoots of **peaches** and **nectarines** that have fruited.

SEPTEMBER
Prune **black currants**, **damsons**, **plums**, and wall-trained **peaches** and **nectarines** after fruiting. Cut down **blackberry** and **loganberry** canes that have fruited. Cut back shoots of sweet **cherries** that were pinched back in June.

OCTOBER
Prune, if not already done, **black**, **red** and **white currants**, **blackberries**, **gooseberries** and **loganberries**. If there is a likelihood of bullfinch attacks, delay pruning of red and white currants and gooseberries until March.

NOVEMBER
Prune established bush and half-standard **apple** and **pear** trees. After planting, cut back **red** and **white currant** and **gooseberry** bushes, and **apple** and **pear** trees. Prune dwarf pyramid, cordon and espalier **apple** and **pear** trees for three or four years after planting.

DECEMBER
Complete any pruning advised for November. Do not, however, prune during hard frosts.

Protecting fruit from birds

Having lavished months of care and devotion upon your fruit bushes, nothing is more exasperating than to see birds gorging themselves on your just-ripening crops.

The problem is on the increase, since less soft fruit is grown nowadays than a few years ago.

It is of little use to erect scarecrows, or sticks bearing rattling lengths of silver foil. Within a short time, the birds will get used to them and the deterrent effect will be lost.

One measure worth taking is to place pans of water near the bushes in hot weather. There is no doubt that thirst adds to the birds' determination to get at the fruit. But the only real protection is some kind of netting enclosure.

Temporary protection

If you have only a few canes or plants, it is hardly worth building a permanent fruit cage around them. Protect them instead with a cheaper, temporary structure which can be easily removed at the end of the fruiting season.

This is most economically achieved by using $\frac{1}{2}-\frac{3}{4}$ in. (12–20 mm.) plastic netting supported on stakes or canes. To prevent the mesh tearing, cover the tops of the sticks with inverted jam-jars or fish-paste pots, choosing jars to suit the diameter of the posts.

Even when firmly seated in the soil, the sticks should be long enough to support the netting well above the tops of the plants or bushes you wish to protect. Allow for the plants growing taller during the season.

Insert the canes or stakes in the ground no more than 4 ft (1.2 m.) apart, and put the jam-jars on top. Peg the netting along one side of the plants, then carry the other edge up and over the stakes. Pull the netting taut so that it rides clear of the top of the plants, and peg it down firmly all round – including an overhang at each end of the structure.

Firm pegging is particularly

TEMPORARY CAGE

1 Insert canes on each side of the plants and place glass jars on top. Fasten the netting on one side and pull it over.

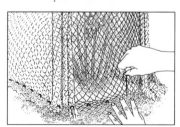

2 Use pegs made of wire or wood to anchor the edges of the netting. Alternatively, secure the netting with stones or bricks.

important, since blackbirds and thrushes generally look for an entrance at ground level.

Protecting wall fruit

Loganberries and blackberries, as well as peaches, nectarines, apricots and other fruits grown against a fence or wall, also require protection.

This is best provided by fixing a 2 × 1 in. (50 × 25 mm.) batten along the wall above the tops of the fruit trees or canes.

Stud the upper edge of the batten with small nails spaced not more than 6 in. (150 mm.) apart and hook the upper edge of the netting on to them. Bring the lower edge forward and pass it over stakes set in the ground in front of the trees or canes.

These forward supports need only be high enough to keep the netting clear of the fruit when pulled taut and pegged down at the front and ends.

Remove the netting as soon as the fruits are harvested.

Protecting strawberries

These succulent fruits are a favourite target for almost every bird in the neighbourhood, and you have little hope of keeping many for yourself unless you protect the plants.

Many gardeners simply spread nets over them, but this is quite useless. The birds sit on the mesh and peck the berries through it as it sinks beneath their weight. In addition, some fruits always grow through the mesh and it is difficult to avoid pulling them off when lifting the net during picking.

The answer is to construct a temporary fruit cage by placing jar-capped canes around the perimeter of the bed and drawing the net tightly over them. A height of 2 ft (610 mm.) is sufficient, but if the bed is a wide one it may be necessary to install one or more intermediate rows of supports to prevent the net sagging on to the strawberry plants.

Permanent enclosures

The ideal, though rather more expensive, way of protecting your soft fruit against birds is by constructing a permanent fruit cage. Its size depends on how much space you are prepared to allocate to soft-fruit growing; but an area of, say, 20 × 15 ft (6 × 4.5 m.) or more, would probably justify the building of a permanent enclosure – perhaps against a wall.

To make the best use of it, plant your bushes or canes as close together as you can without overcrowding. Expense can also be saved by using plastic or nylon mesh for the walls of the cage rather than the more traditional wire netting.

Support the netting on posts spaced no more than 6 ft (1.8 m.) apart. In order to give plenty of headroom, the tops of the posts should be 6 ft from the ground, but allow an additional 2 ft (610 mm.) to give a firm footing in the soil.

Long life for the cage is assured by using 2 × 2 in. (50 × 50 mm.) pressure-treated timber for intermediate posts, with 3 × 2 in. (75 × 50 mm.) braced posts at the corners. Alternatively, use metal piping. Link the tops of the posts with heavy-duty wire – 12–14 s.w.g. – stretched taut.

Further wires stretched from side to side across the cage should be enough to keep the roof netting from sagging unless the cage is wider than 18 ft (5.4 m.), when an additional row of supports up the centre is advisable.

Lay plastic or nylon netting over the roof and take it down the sides to the ground. Fix the net to the posts with brass hooks and peg the bottom firmly to the ground, or secure with bricks or large stones.

If there is a risk of bullfinches stripping the dormant fruit buds during the winter, leave the netting up throughout the year. Shake snow off as necessary, otherwise a heavy accumulation may cause the entire structure to collapse or be distorted.

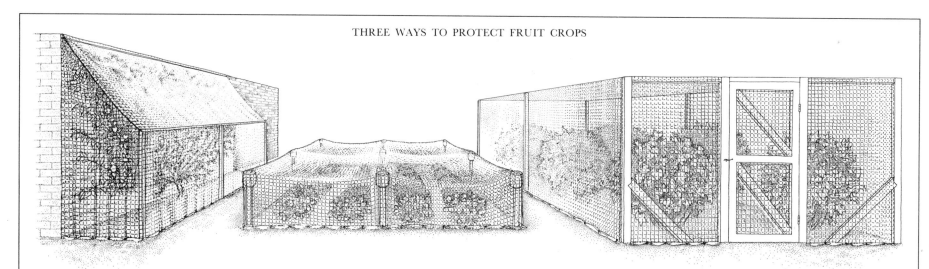

THREE WAYS TO PROTECT FRUIT CROPS

WALL CAGE Secure the upper edge of the netting to a wall batten and pass it over a frame of posts and battens set in the ground in front of the fruit. These keep the netting clear of the branches and allow space for picking the fruit. Fill in the ends with separate pieces of netting.

STRAWBERRY NET It is useless to lay the netting directly on the plants. Instead, unless the strawberries are grown in a true fruit cage, support netting on jar-topped canes 12 in. (305 mm.) higher than the plants. Peg the sides and ends to the ground to keep birds out.

PERMANENT ENCLOSURE Using pressure-treated timber for corner posts and intermediate supports, and with wire stapled to their tops, a simple, inexpensive framework can be made for supporting lightweight netting with $\frac{1}{2}$–$\frac{3}{4}$ in. (12–20 mm.) mesh. Make a doorway for easy access.

Raising your own fruit bushes

The grafting techniques needed for propagating top fruits, such as apples and pears, are beyond the scope of most amateur gardeners. But even a beginner can increase his stock of soft fruits.

This can be done in three ways:

Cuttings Pieces of new growth are cut into lengths and inserted in the soil to root. Gooseberries, and all three types of currants, can be propagated by this method.

Tip layering To increase blackberries and loganberries, bend over the tips of young canes and cover with soil. This induces the tip to root and new canes to spring up at the point of layering.

Root division Raspberry canes push out underground suckers which become the new canes. These new plants can be severed from the parent and planted in a permanent position.

Black currants

Take cuttings of straight, firm stems of black currants in early October. Trim back with a pair of secateurs any soft growth at the top to just above a bud. Cut at the base below a bud, leaving a cutting 8 in. (200 mm.) long. Remove any leaves, but leave all the buds.

Take out a trench in well-cultivated soil, making one side vertical by pushing the spade straight down. Stand the cuttings 6 in. (150 mm.) apart against the straight wall, with not more than three buds showing above the surface. Buds in the ground will produce new basal shoots.

Fill in the trench carefully, firming the soil round the cuttings with your hand or by treading. If the soil is heavy, sprinkle a little coarse sand round the cuttings as you fill in.

Inspect the cuttings every few weeks, and firm soil cracked by frost.

Black currants root easily, and about nine out of ten should show growth in the spring.

If growth is good during the summer, move the bushes to their permanent positions in the autumn. If it is poor, leave the cuttings in the trench and, during the winter, cut all shoots to a few inches above ground level to promote vigorous growth in the next season.

Gooseberries

A gooseberry bush is grown on a single stem, or 'leg', and this requires a different preparation from that given to black-currant cuttings.

In October, remove well-ripened shoots about 12 in. (305 mm.) long and rub off all but the top three or four buds from each. These will eventually grow into the main branches.

Bury the cutting to a little over half its length, leaving an exposed stem with the buds at the top. Treat afterwards as for black currants. Results, however, are unlikely to be as good.

Red and white currants

In mid-October, prepare cuttings, 10–15 in. (255–380 mm.) long in the same way as for gooseberries.

Cut off any unripened wood, which is generally no more than 1 in. (25 mm.) long at the growing tip. Cut just above a bud. No trimming is necessary, however, if the cutting is brown at the tip.

Trim the lower end to just below a bud, and rub off all but the four or five buds at the top. These will eventually form the branches. Dip the lower end of each cutting in hormone rooting powder.

Set cuttings 6 in. (150 mm.) apart in a trench, with the top 5 in. (130 mm.) above soil level.

Cuttings of red and white currants root readily and they can be planted in their permanent positions in the following autumn.

Raspberries

During the growing season, raspberry plants produce new canes at the base of the parent plant, and other canes, called suckers, that spring directly from the roots that spread out beneath the soil.

Those at the base are trained as fruiting canes for the following season, while suckers are generally destroyed by hoeing or by applying herbicides.

You can, however, increase your stock by allowing the sucker canes to grow and using the strongest of these as new plants.

In November, lift the suckers with a fork and sever them from the parent cane with secateurs. Lift them carefully with their roots intact and re-plant immediately. Grow these new canes only from healthy parent stock.

Always buy raspberry canes which are certified to be virus free. You can safely take new plants from them for the next two or three years, but you might risk spreading virus disease to take them after that.

Blackberries and loganberries

The easiest method of raising plants of blackberries and loganberries is to 'layer' the tips of young shoots so that they root in the soil.

Between mid-July and early

PROPAGATING RASPBERRIES

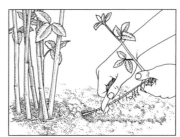

1 In November, ease strong suckers out of the ground with a fork. Use a knife to sever the sucker from the parent plants.

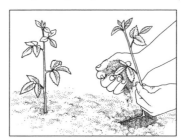

2 Plant the suckers at once in their new positions. Prune each stem to a bud about 12 in. (305 mm.) above soil level.

September – though not before it has developed fully – bend down a shoot that has formed during the season. Mark this spot and make a vertical cut about 4 in. (100 mm.) deep, with a spade or trowel.

On the side nearest the cane, and about 12 in. (305 mm.) from the first cut, make another cut at an angle of 45° so that the two join. Lift out the soil, lay the tip of the cane against the vertical side and replace the soil, firming it in.

Alternatively, simply dig out a circular hole with a trowel, but in this case take extra care to anchor the tip securely.

The tip will root within a few weeks and a shoot will spring up from the ground. In November, sever the new plant from the parent by cutting about 12 in. (305 mm.) from the base. Transfer the plant to its permanent position the following April.

Peaches

Although stones and pips from tree fruits may germinate well, they will not reproduce truly. You might, for example, sow hundreds of apple seeds and grow the trees to the fruiting stage, to discover that only one or two are worth keeping.

The chances of getting good fruiting trees are much higher than this in the case of a peach. Nectarine stones usually, if not always, produce peaches.

In early autumn, set a stone in a pot of potting compost. Seal the pot in a polythene bag and put in a cool spot – about 10°C (50°F).

When a shoot appears put the pot in a sunny window. It can be moved to the garden when 6 in. (150 mm.) high and planted in its permanent position when a year old.

Greenhouses, frames and cloches

A greenhouse helps to lengthen the gardening year, turning late winter into spring and coaxing summer to linger into autumn.

For this reason alone, a greenhouse is worth having. For a gardener keen on growing food, it is also a sound investment. The initial cost can be returned in a few years by the savings on plants raised from seed, and by harvesting vegetables when they are at their most expensive in the shops.

As a greenhouse is a long-term investment, give some thought to the type and size best suited to your needs and pocket.

How big a greenhouse?

If you want to grow vegetables, such as early lettuces, tomatoes, cucumbers, sweet peppers and aubergines, as well as raising seedlings, a glazed greenhouse measuring about 10×8 ft (3×2.5 m.) is ideal.

If you cannot afford this, either buy a similar-size house made of polythene (see p. 51) or purchase a smaller glazed house and use it mainly for raising early plants and for growing a summer crop of tomatoes.

When deciding on the size, consider the cost of heating if you plan to grow plants much earlier than their normal season. The larger the area of glass, the more expensive the house will be to heat.

Types of greenhouses

Although greenhouses are made in many shapes and sizes, there are four main types:

Vertical-sided Free-standing buildings with a span roof and vertical side walls – or walls set at only a slight angle – are the most popular type of garden greenhouse. Some have timber cladding up to the staging, or are designed to be built on low brick walls, but for food growing buy one with the glass extending to the ground on at least one side. This will enable you to plant tomatoes, melons or cucumbers directly in the greenhouse border.

Dutch light Large panes and angled side walls admit the maximum amount of light. Houses of this type are ideal for growing plants directly in the soil because the glass extends to the ground.

Temporary staging can be put up in late winter and spring for trays of seedlings, and removed in summer to make space for growing plants in the ground.

Lean-to As its name implies, this type of greenhouse is erected against a wall of a building, preferably facing south where it will get most sunlight. It is warmer than a free-standing house, and it is sometimes possible to heat it by an extension of the household central heating.

The approval of the local authority is needed if the greenhouse is to be erected against the wall of a house.

Circular Although it is of unconventional appearance, a house of this shape has many advantages. Light is let in evenly and little floor space is wasted because the gardener, working in the centre, can reach all the plants without having to walk up a path.

The flow of air is controlled by ventilators at ground level and an adjustable dome at the top.

Wood or metal?

The choice of cedar wood or an aluminium-framed greenhouse is

MINIATURE LEAN-TO GREENHOUSES

The combination of rising costs and small gardens has created the need for a really small greenhouse. The mini-greenhouse is basically a garden frame, turned on end, to form a small lean-to against a house or garage wall.

Sliding doors give access to shelves that can be placed at any height. The gardener works from outside the house – a disadvantage in bad weather.

Though of limited value for growing food crops, the mini would nevertheless suit a gardener with restricted space, or a flat-dweller who could erect it on a sunny patio. It is ideal for raising seedlings, and the wall against which it is sited will help to retain day-time warmth for dispersal during the night.

Rather like a vertical garden frame, a mini-greenhouse can be a good choice where space is severely restricted.

CHOOSING A GREENHOUSE TO SUIT YOUR NEEDS

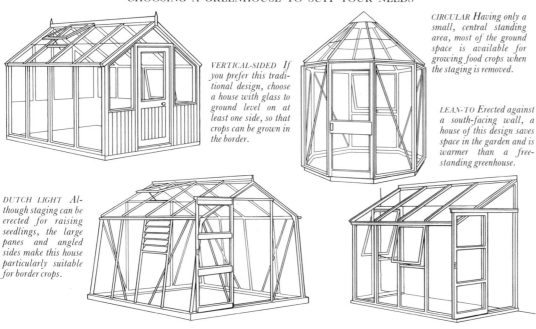

VERTICAL-SIDED If you prefer this traditional design, choose a house with glass to ground level on at least one side, so that crops can be grown in the border.

CIRCULAR Having only a small, central standing area, most of the ground space is available for growing food crops when the staging is removed.

LEAN-TO Erected against a south-facing wall, a house of this design saves space in the garden and is warmer than a free-standing greenhouse.

DUTCH LIGHT Although staging can be erected for raising seedlings, the large panes and angled sides make this house particularly suitable for border crops.

again a personal one. Cedar blends more happily into the garden background, and needs to be treated with a wood preservative only every two or three years.

Wooden greenhouses are generally delivered in pre-fabricated sections. The two sides, two gable ends and two roof sections are easily bolted together, but the glazing may take a day or two to complete.

Here the aluminium greenhouses have an advantage, because the panes can be clipped into place in a few hours.

Another advantage of the aluminium type is that it needs no maintenance.

Siting a greenhouse

Choose a position where the greenhouse catches the most sunlight, especially in late winter and early spring when seedlings are beginning to grow.

Avoid low-lying ground, which may get waterlogged or become a frost pocket. Choose, if possible, a position sheltered from cold winds.

Ideally, the greenhouse should be as near the house as possible to make it more convenient to lay electricity and water supplies. Wherever the site, lay a path leading to the door of the greenhouse.

Opinion is divided on whether a north-south or east-west alignment is preferable, but it does not matter a great deal. In a small garden the site itself will probably dictate which way it must go, but try to position the door on a side away from icy winds.

If the site is near a fence or wall, allow space all round for maintenance and glazing.

A greenhouse of any type needs a firm base for support and anchorage.

A base of old railway sleepers, laid on firm soil, is sufficient for the smallest sizes, but the best foundation is a course of bricks laid on a concrete strip.

Exact measurements are given in the manufacturer's instructions. When making the site, check that the corners are perfect right-angles by measuring diagonally between them. Provided facing sides are of equal length, the diagonal measurements should be identical.

For the concrete foundations dig out a trench 6–8 in. (150–200 mm.) wide and 4 in. (100 mm.) deep. Place a spirit level on a long, straight batten to check that the concrete is level. Place ½ in. (12 mm.) diameter rag-bolts – two or three on each side and end – in positions where they will correspond with the base frame of the greenhouse.

Lay the brick course a week later, if necessary cutting bricks to ensure that the mortar joints correspond with the rag-bolt positions. When erecting the house, drill holes for the bolts in the base frame and secure with nuts. Place a strip of damp-proof course or roofing felt between the bricks and a timber frame.

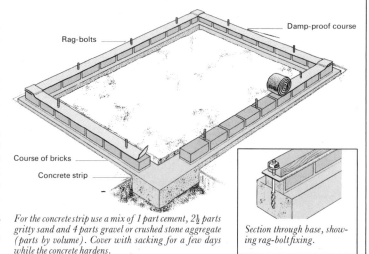

For the concrete strip use a mix of 1 part cement, 2½ parts gritty sand and 4 parts gravel or crushed stone aggregate (parts by volume). Cover with sacking for a few days while the concrete hardens.

Section through base, showing rag-bolt fixing.

Greenhouse management

Correct ventilation, watering and temperature control are necessary for success with greenhouse crops.

Ventilation Fungus diseases flourish in a warm, stagnant atmosphere. At least two roof ventilators, as well as one or more at a lower level, are needed to ensure an adequate air flow in hot weather. If necessary, the door can be propped open, or an opening hatch fitted in the lower half of a wooden door. An electric fan heater, with the heating element switched off, is also an efficient method of keeping the air flowing.

The guesswork and constant attention can be relieved by installing automatic ventilation. There are two kinds:

One is a vent opener which is sensitive to temperature changes and automatically opens or closes the ventilator. The other is an electric extractor fan which is thermostatically controlled to provide a continuous gentle movement of air and also to reduce condensation.

These fans are easy to install and cheap to run but, of course, they need a mains supply.

Watering A regular supply of water is essential at all stages of plant growth, but watering by hand is not always possible.

There are two methods of automatic watering which not only save a good deal of work, but also result in better plants.

The first, capillary irrigation, works on the principle that if a pot plant rests on a bed of wet sand the compost in the pot will soak up sufficient water to keep the plant healthy.

A number of capillary systems are available. In one, mains water is taken from a plastic tank fitted with a ball-valve. The water runs into a trough on one side of the staging and is drawn by a glass-fibre wick into the sand tray. In another system pots are placed on a highly absorbent mat, which again takes water from a mains-supplied trough.

Capillary watering is suitable only for seedlings and for plants small enough to be grown on the greenhouse staging.

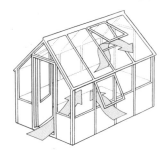

FREE-FLOWING Air enters through a low-level ventilator and is warmed by circulation in the greenhouse. This causes it to rise to the roof ventilator, where it leaves the house.

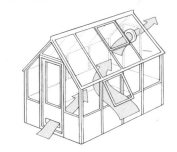

CONTROLLED FLOW Fan ventilation has a similar effect to fixed ventilators; but a thermostat starts the fan only when the temperature rises above a pre-set level.

IRRIGATION AIDS

TRICKLE Nozzles in the supply pipe drip water or liquid fertiliser around the plants at a pre-determined and adjustable rate.

CAPILLARY Plants draw their water from sand or an absorbent mat, kept moist by a cistern or an inverted drum or bottle.

An entirely different system – suitable for plants of all sizes – is trickle irrigation, in which a pipe is laid near the plants and drip nozzles release a steady supply of water. Liquid fertiliser can be added so that plants are watered and fed at the same time.

Temperature control

A gardener faces a challenge in trying to keep a greenhouse warm enough for seedlings to thrive in spring, and cool enough to prevent plants from getting scorched in a summer heatwave.

The biggest problem with artificial heating is the cost. Happily, vegetables and fruits do not need such high temperatures as ornamental plants, and worthwhile crops can be grown even in an unheated greenhouse. If you are trying to economise, wait until February or early March before making your first sowings.

The only time when fairly high temperatures are needed is when sowing seeds of some tender vegetables. But even then there is no need to heat the whole house. Either use an electric propagator for raising the seedlings, or put the greenhouse heater under the staging and erect a polythene canopy over the top to trap the warmth.

A saving on heating bills can also be made by insulating the greenhouse in winter and early spring with a light-gauge polythene lining. Kits, including fixing clips or suckers, are available from horticultural suppliers for various sizes of greenhouses. The linings are claimed to save 20% on heating costs.

If you decide to warm the whole greenhouse – and you can then enjoy a variety of crops while shop prices are very high – the choice of heaters is wide.

Gas Designed to burn mains gas, this relatively new type of heater has accurate temperature controls and costs less to run than most other forms of heating. But the initial outlay for the heater and for having it installed may be high, especially if the greenhouse is some distance from the house.

Gas heaters can be adapted for

GREENHOUSE HEATERS

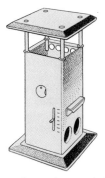

GAS Automatic control; economical to run. But mains installation may be costly.

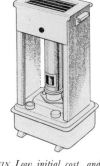

PARAFFIN Low initial cost, and portable. Few models have automatic control.

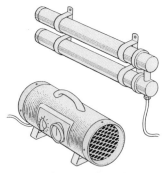

ELECTRIC Automatic, but costly to run. Needs professionally installed mains supply.

bottled gas, but running costs are higher than with mains gas.

Paraffin Portable paraffin heaters give reasonable frost protection, but they have limitations as the sole source of heating. Water vapour produced during combustion creates excessive condensation unless some ventilation is provided all the time.

Running costs are lower than for electricity but higher than mains gas. Only one or two types of paraffin heaters have automatic temperature control.

Electricity This is the dearest form of heating, but no other system is as versatile. When a supply has been connected to the greenhouse,

---

GREENHOUSE SHADING

Greenhouse plants must be protected from direct sunlight in the height of summer, and seedlings need shade even on a bright spring day.

Ideally, shading should be on the outside of the roof, an inch or two above the glass. Slatted wooden blinds that can be rolled up and down are the most efficient, but they are expensive.

Less costly alternatives are adjustable green plastic blinds inside the house, sheets of green polythene for clipping to the inside bars of the roof, and fine-mesh plastic netting that also allows air to circulate.

At one time gardeners sprayed the glass with a mixture of limewash and milk. Unfortunately, this left plants in the gloom during a cloudy spell. This disadvantage has been overcome by a spray now available from horticultural suppliers which turns opaque in bright sunlight but becomes more transparent on dull days.

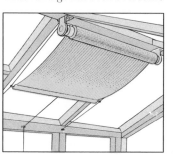

INTERIOR BLIND Roller blinds of PVC sheeting are effective. Ideally, support each side of the blind with a wire runner.

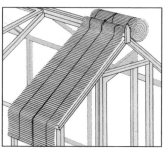

EXTERIOR BLIND May be made of plastic or wooden slats, or cane. Extra effective because the glass is kept cool.

equipment other than heaters can be used – such as a propagator, lighting and a fan extractor. Employ a qualified electrician for the wiring.

There are two main forms of electrical heaters: tubular and fan. Tubular heaters are fixed to the sides or floor of the greenhouse, and take up little room. Fan heaters move the air more vigorously, as well as raising the temperature. With all forms of heating it is useful to hang a maximum-minimum thermometer in the greenhouse, to inform you how the system is behaving when you are not there.

Staging

Manufacturers supply staging – slatted benching – to fit their houses. Alternatively, make it yourself using 50×50 mm. timber for the legs, and 50×25 mm. timber for the top framework. Nail 50×12 mm. battens to the frame to form the slatted bench.

Cross-bracing (50×25 mm.) between the legs and upper frame will keep the structure steady, provided the legs are placed on bricks or stone slabs.

STAGING

Sturdy construction, with diagonal cross-bracing, is needed to withstand the weight of pots, moist compost and plants.

Greenhouse hygiene

A greenhouse provides ideal conditions for plant growth, but these can be just as encouraging to pests and diseases.

Inspect plants daily during the growing season and apply the appropriate spray if the trouble is easily diagnosed. (See the pest and disease entries for each crop in the Growing and Cooking section between pp. 61 and 276; also pp. 281–92.)

Both pests and diseases can be controlled by fumigation, a process known as 'smoking'. Pesticidal smoke bombs control all insect pests, while fungicidal bombs prevent fungus diseases such as botrytis and mildew.

The advantage of these bombs is that the cloud of microscopic particles they emit penetrates to every part of a plant and to every crevice in the greenhouse.

Most smokes are harmless to food crops, but read the instructions carefully because some are lethal to plants such as melons and cucumbers.

Choose calm, warm weather, but do not fumigate in bright sunshine. Close the ventilators, block any gaps, and light the first bomb at the far end of the greenhouse. Working backwards towards the door, light any additional bombs as quickly as possible. Close the door firmly and lock it or put a notice on it.

The next day, open the door wide, wait for a few minutes then open the ventilators.

In late autumn, when growth has stopped, wash down the interior with disinfectant.

Before sowing in late winter, clean the glass inside and out to let in as much light as possible.

DECIDING WHETHER TO BUY A POLYTHENE GREENHOUSE

For the gardener who concentrates on food growing, a polythene greenhouse has one big advantage over a glazed greenhouse – the lower initial cost.

A polythene house 20×10 ft (6×3 m.), for example, may cost only half as much as a glazed house measuring 10×6 ft (3×1.8 m.). Using polythene, you can therefore put a substantial part of your vegetable plot under cover for a relatively small outlay.

This would suit a gardener with plenty of space, but one with a small plot should consider whether a small greenhouse used principally for raising seedlings might be more practical.

A polythene greenhouse consists of a framework of tubular steel hoops covered by special horticultural polythene. The hoops are driven directly into the soil or into tubes set in the ground.

Foundations are unnecessary and the house can be erected and dismantled quickly. This gives it a mobility that can be exploited in a crop-rotation plan.

The greenhouse can be used, for example, for growing tomatoes on one part of the plot one year and moved to another part where the tomatoes are to be grown the following year.

In late winter and spring, seedlings can be raised in pots or trays on a trestle table or on staging sold by the greenhouse manufacturers.

A polythene greenhouse may have certain disadvantages, however. The chief of these is condensation, producing a high humidity which can cause a number of plant disorders. This problem varies with the make and design, so choose a greenhouse with ventilators on the door and the far gable.

Heating, combined with good ventilation, will also reduce condensation, but the choice of heater is important. Natural gas or paraffin heaters only exacerbate the problem.

An electric heater is better, and the ideal is an electric fan heater which drives warm air to all parts of the greenhouse. In summer, the fan can be switched on without the heating element to keep the air moving.

A second drawback with polythene is that it is not as efficient as glass in keeping out frost. During frosty spells, therefore, shut the ventilators during the afternoon to increase the humidity. Condensation will then act as an insulator and slightly reduce the loss of heat.

A third disadvantage is that the polythene needs replacing at least every two to four years and this regular expense must be balanced against the initial cost of the greenhouse.

Polythene used in most greenhouse kits is treated with an ultra-violet light inhibitor to slow down deterioration caused by sunlight. If you decide to make a greenhouse of your own, ask the supplier for this material.

Wind is also a problem with a polythene greenhouse, not so much for wear and tear as for the loss of heat.

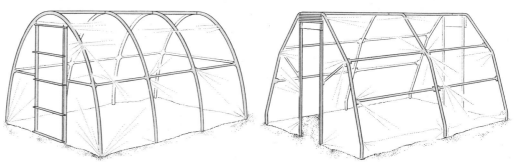

POLYTHENE GREENHOUSES The shape of a plastic greenhouse is less important than its ventilation arrangements. Check that these provide a free flow of air to minimise condensation. Some types have double skins for improved insulation and heat retention.

Making the most of your greenhouse

To get maximum value out of your greenhouse, aim to have crops at various stages for at least ten months of the year. The table alongside will help you to decide what to grow and when to make the sowings.

The growing programme can be divided into two periods. During the first, from January to May, make sowings of crops that will continue to maturity in the greenhouse, and of others that will eventually be transplanted in the open.

During the second, overlapping period – from March to October – grow a selection of plants, such as tomatoes, in pots or in the greenhouse border. These are marked with an asterisk in the table.*

During the summer, growing space will be almost doubled if you dismantle the staging and store it elsewhere. Do this in late May, when the last of the tender young plants are moved outdoors.

YOUR GREENHOUSE IN SPRING AND SUMMER

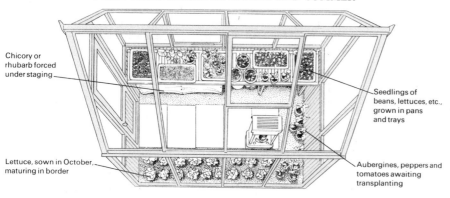

Chicory or rhubarb forced under staging

Seedlings of beans, lettuces, etc., grown in pans and trays

Lettuce, sown in October, maturing in border

Aubergines, peppers and tomatoes awaiting transplanting

SPRING Winter-sown lettuces are now ready for cutting. Seedlings of both outdoor and greenhouse crops are at various stages of development on the bench, ready for transplanting as soon as conditions are suitable.

Shading or blinds in position during hot, sunny weather

Staging removed. Border now planted with aubergines, peppers or other greenhouse crops

Tomatoes in border, replacing winter lettuce

Full ventilation during hot weather

Cucumbers or melons at end of greenhouse, where temperature and humidity tend to be highest

SUMMER With the staging now stored in a shed or garage, one end and both sides of the greenhouse are available for summer crops such as tomatoes, sweet peppers, aubergines, melons and cucumbers.

GROWING FOOD CROPS IN A GREENHOUSE

VEGETABLE OR FRUIT	TIME TO SOW	MINIMUM TEMPERATURE	REMARKS
Aubergines	*February	18°C (64°F)	Grow on at a minimum temperature of 16°C (61°F)
Broad beans	January–February	Unheated greenhouse	Plant out in March
French beans	Late March–early April	Unheated greenhouse	Transplant to cloches early May
	Mid-April	Unheated greenhouse	Plant outside end of May
Runner beans	Early April	Unheated greenhouse	Transplant to cloches mid-May
	Mid-April	Unheated greenhouse	Harden off and plant outdoors end of May
Cauliflowers	January–February	10°C (50°F)	Harden off in March and plant out
Chicory	Force roots November–March	7–16°C (45–61°F)	
Cucumbers	*Frame varieties: late February	21°C (70°F)	Grow in greenhouse. Minimum night temperature: 16°C (61°F)
Lettuces	August	Unheated greenhouse	Transplant to greenhouse border
	October–February	10–12°C (50–54°F)	Transplant to greenhouse border. Min. 10°C (50°F)
Marrows and courgettes	Early May	Unheated greenhouse	Harden off and plant out end of May
Melons	*Casabas: March–April	16°C (61°F)	Grow on in greenhouse
	Cantaloupes: mid-April	16°C (61°F)	Transplant to frames or cloches from mid-May
Pumpkins	Late April–early May	18–21°C (64–70°F)	Harden off and plant out late May–early June
Rhubarb	Force under staging, November–March	7–16°C (45–61°F)	
Sweet corn	April	Unheated greenhouse	Harden off and plant out in late May
Sweet peppers	*March	16–18°C (61–64°F)	Grow in the greenhouse with minimum night temperature of 7°C (45°F), or harden off in April and plant out at end of May
Tomatoes	*January	15°C (59°F)	Grow on in heated greenhouse
	*Late March	15°C (59°F)	Grow on in unheated greenhouse
	March–April	15°C (59°F)	Harden off and plant in open late May–early June

Growing crops in frames

The small area covered by a garden frame is often the most intensively cultivated part of a vegetable plot. By careful planning, a succession of food crops can be grown in a frame throughout the year.

If you have a greenhouse, or if you plan to germinate seeds indoors, the frame is also an essential halfway house in which to harden off, or acclimatise, plants before they go to their permanent positions outdoors.

With good management, the frame should never be empty. For instance, during the winter it can be used for protecting cauliflower plants that will be set outside in early spring, or for lettuces to heart up in the frame in early April when they are expensive in the shops.

Seeds of onions and lettuces can be sown in January, two months earlier than in open ground.

After the onions and lettuces are planted out, their places can be taken in April by French and runner beans. These, in turn, will be planted in the open, to be replaced by cucumbers or melons that will grow in the frame during the summer.

When harvesting is complete, the time has come to restart the cycle and sow cauliflowers and lettuces to overwinter in the frame.

By laying electric soil-warming and air-warming cables, the frame becomes a miniature greenhouse and the gardener's scope is widened even further.

Types of frames

Garden frames are obtainable in a wide variety of sizes and materials. There are four main types: wooden frames with glass tops (called lights); aluminium frames with glass or PVC lights; frames made of galvanised steel, with a similar light; and frames made completely of transparent plastic.

Each type has its advantages and disadvantages.

Wooden frames Fitted with glass lights, these are the most efficient in conserving heat. Most are made from cedar, which has natural resistance to rot and insect attacks. On many, the lights slide easily backwards or forwards on runners to provide ventilation and give access to the plants.

These frames last for many years but they are slightly more expensive than those made from aluminium, galvanised iron or plastic.

Aluminium frames Can be fitted with glass or acrylic lights. Acrylic is cheaper and a better buy in a garden where children play ball games. The advantage of aluminium frames is their lightness, which makes them easy to move from one part of the garden to another, and the fact that they need no maintenance.

Galvanised-iron frames About the same price as aluminium and, although a little heavier, they too can be moved easily from one place to another.

Plastic frames In addition to being the cheapest, they let in the most light. They lose heat quickly at night, however. This makes them of more use in the shorter, warmer nights of spring than in the winter.

D-I-Y frames A simple, home-made frame can be constructed from odd pieces of wood, some chicken wire and a sheet of heavy-gauge polythene. A practical size is about 3 ft (1 m.) square with the back wall 16 in. (405 mm.) high and the front 12 in. (305 mm.) high.

Staple the chicken wire tautly to the top and fix the polythene over this with drawing pins. The wire will prevent the polythene from sagging under the weight of rain water.

For access to the plants, simply lift the frame to one side.

Siting and management

Choose a sunny position, preferably sheltered from cold winds. If the frame has a single, sloping light, face this towards the south.

Prepare the ground thoroughly some weeks before planting by digging in well-rotted manure or compost at the rate of a bucketful to the square yard. Just before planting, rake into the top a general fertiliser at 3 oz. per square yard (90 g. per square metre), together with about half a bucketful of moist peat.

The manure and the peat will ensure that the ground is suitably moist for overwintering crops, which should not be watered until they start to develop in spring.

During late winter and early spring conserve heat in aluminium or galvanised-iron frames either by lining the inside walls with polystyrene sheeting or tiles, or by drawing up soil round the outside.

During frosts, cover the light of any type of frame with sacking or some similar material, removing this during the day. In warm spells open the light to let in air, and close it again in the evening.

Scatter slug pellets in the frame after sowing and planting, and make regular inspections for other pests while plants are growing.

Growing in heated frames

If you cannot afford either the money or the space for a greenhouse, a heated frame provides a worthwhile alternative. Use it in conjunction with an unheated frame or cloches, where plants will

TWO TYPES OF GARDEN FRAMES

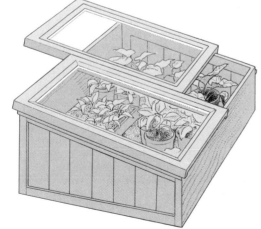

TIMBER FRAME The wood, which helps to conserve warmth, needs treating with preservative every year or two. Most timber frames have sliding lights, but some are hinged.

METAL FRAME Construction may be of aluminium or steel, and the sides metal-clad or glazed. Glass sides are ideal for spring and summer crops, but are colder in winter.

be hardened off before being put in their permanent positions.

Soil-warming cables laid under the surface will hasten early crops and give the right conditions for sowing at least a month earlier than in the open.

However, soil-warming does not provide full protection against frost. On cold nights cover the frame light with sacking, layers of newspaper or some other insulating material.

Alternatively, install air-warming cables on the inside walls of the frame, supplementing those warming the soil, to give frost protection.

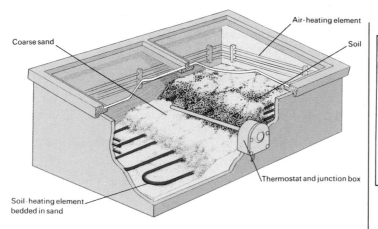

HEATED FRAME Soil-warming cables laid in sand are combined here with above-ground air-warming cables. Manufacturers supply installation instructions.

Growing crops under cloches

Gardeners discovered many years ago that a plant could be forced into early growth by protecting it with a glass cover. Eventually, a Frenchman, whose name has not gone into the history books, evolved a practical and efficient shape for forcing individual plants. It was a bell-shaped glass dome and it became known as a cloche, meaning bell.

The name has persisted to the present day, although cloches are no longer bell-shaped and they now protect whole rows instead of individual plants. The final change from the original concept has come about in recent years when glass, because of its cost, has largely been replaced by rigid plastic or polythene.

Since most vegetables are grown in straight rows, a number of cloches set in a line, with the ends closed to exclude draughts, are ideal for producing early crops and for protecting tender plants.

Generally, sowing and planting are possible about a fortnight earlier than in the open.

This early start, resulting in earlier harvesting, makes it possible for more than one crop to

be grown on the same ground in a season.

As an example of a cropping programme lettuces, sown in October, may be cut in April, to be followed by early-fruiting dwarf tomatoes. These in turn, may be succeeded by spring cabbages planted in the open. The cloches, meanwhile, are transferred to another part of the plot to restart the cycle.

This mobility enables a gardener to use a cropping technique whereby cloches are moved from one row to another as the season progresses.

Early carrots, for example, may be given a good start by being covered in March and April. They then go on to mature in the open and the cloches are moved in mid-May to enable newly planted tomatoes to become established. Three to four weeks later the cloches are again moved, this time to protect heat-loving plants, such as aubergines and peppers, for the rest of the summer or until they are too tall.

Types of cloches

Cloches are obtainable in a variety of sizes, shapes and materials.

Costs, naturally, are related to the size of the cloche, so it is prudent to decide what crops you intend growing under cloches before buying them.

If, for example, you plan to grow only early lettuces, a cloche 12 in. (305 mm.) wide and 9 in. (230 mm.) high is adequate. For growing melons to the fruiting stage, however, you will need cloches about 18 in. (455 mm.) wide and 12 in. high.

Measure the row, then buy the required number of cloches to

A YEAR'S CROPPING PROGRAMME FOR A COLD FRAME

VEGETABLE OR FRUIT	TIME TO SOW	HARDEN OFF	REMARKS
French beans	Late March–early April		Plant under cloches early May
	Mid-April		Plant in open end of May
Runner beans	Mid-April		Plant in open end of May
Carrots	March		Grow to maturity in frame
Cauliflowers	Late September–early October		Plant out late March–early April
	January (heated frame)	Early March	Plant out mid-March
Cucumbers	May (frame varieties)		Set out one plant in each frame
		May (ridge varieties)	Plant outdoors early June
Lettuces	August: 'Emerald' or 'Kwiek'. Sow outdoors	September (plant in frame)	Cut November–December
	October: 'May Queen'. Sow in frame		Cut March–April
Marrows	Early May		Plant outdoors end of May
Melons	Late April–early May (indoors)		Plant in frame mid-May
Onions	January: maincrop varieties		Plant out in April
Pumpkins	April–May (indoors)	May	Plant out early June
Radishes	January–February		Pick regularly as they mature
Sweet corn	April	Mid-May	Plant out late May
Tomatoes	Late March–early April (indoors)	May	Plant under cloches mid-May; plant outdoors late May–early June

TYPES OF CLOCHES

MOULDED PLASTIC Easy to use, but some types are expensive. Check expected life span.

NOVOLUX Simple and long-lasting. Corrugated PVC is secured in wire hoops.

TUNNEL Takes a little longer than others to erect. Inexpensive, and easy access.

TENT (GLASS) Patent clips enable odd panes to be used. Restricted height and width.

BARN (GLASS) Four panes are secured in a wire frame. Good protection, but costly.

form unbroken protection over it. Remember to buy two end panels, as the cloche is not fully effective until these are placed in position.

Each type of material used for cloches has advantages and disadvantages.

Solid plastic cloches are cheaper than those made of glass but, initially, are dearer than polythene. They have a greater life expectancy than glass, which is easily broken, or polythene which must be replaced every few years.

Plastic cloches can be made of corrugated PVC, polypropylene, clear polystyrene or a number of proprietary materials.

Makers have taken advantage of the flexibility and lightness of the plastic. Some cloches, for example, are 6 ft (1.8 m.) long, a size that would be excessively heavy and cumbersome to handle in glass. Only three of these cloches are needed to cover a row 18 ft (5.5 m.) long, so simplifying the task of moving them from crop to crop.

Widths of cloches vary from 7½ in. (190 mm.) for growing seedlings, to 2½ ft (760 mm.), in which two or three rows of vegetables can be grown to maturity.

Heights vary from 4 in. (100 mm.), for seedlings, to 15 in. (380 mm.), for fully grown plants such as bush tomatoes.

Solid plastic cloches are available with straight sides, or curved into hooped tunnels. Both designs are equally effective, but some straight-sided models have the added refinement of ventilation flaps to reduce condensation and get air flowing. Condensation in solid plastic cloches is not, however, as serious as in polythene tunnels.

Polythene cloches are obtainable either as separate units, which are then put end to end, or as a complete tunnel cloche made from a length of polythene draped over wire hoops.

Polythene is obtainable in various gauges, or thicknesses. The thinnest, 150 gauge, is the cheapest form of cloche material but it will last only a year or two. Heavy-duty polythene, 500 gauge, is more expensive but it will last three or four years with reasonable care.

Polythene treated with an ultra-violet inhibitor to slow down deterioration is now available from horticultural suppliers. This lasts longer than untreated material.

Condensation is a problem with polythene. It can provide conditions for the spread of fungal diseases, so it is important to ventilate the cloches to clear the condensation and to get air circulating.

As polythene is light and unbreakable it has a big advantage over glass when being moved from one crop to another. Its lightness can be a disadvantage, however, in areas subject to high winds. If gales are forecast, anchor individual cloches with bricks, or form an inverted 'V' over them with canes driven into the ground. Tunnel cloches are satisfactorily anchored by their method of construction.

Glass cloches have proved their worth for many years, but the cost of glass and delivery have made them an expensive investment.

Many gardening centres now carry only a restricted stock, while firms that sell by mail order advertise only the wire supports and it is necessary to buy the glass from a local glazier. If you feel it is still worthwhile, order horticultural glass, which is cheaper than window glass.

Inevitable breakages also add to costs, but glass has some advantages over rigid plastic and polythene. When kept clean, glass cloches let in the maximum amount of light, and on cold, clear nights they retain heat better than polythene. Ventilation is good and on exposed, windy sites

---

CONSTRUCTING AND USING TUNNEL CLOCHES

The cheapest form of cloche is a 'tunnel' made from a series of galvanised hoops pressed firmly into the ground and covered with a sheet of light-gauge polythene. A second hoop holds the polythene in place.

Kits containing hoops and about 35 ft (10.5 m.) of 150-gauge polythene are obtainable from garden shops and centres. The hoops will last for many years, but the polythene deteriorates in sunlight and needs to be replaced with new sheeting every year or two.

The tunnels can be put in place or moved from row to row in a matter of minutes.

There is no need to move the cloches to gain access for sowing or planting, or to provide ventilation. Simply slide back one side of the polythene cover.

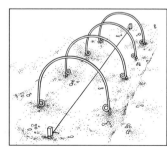

1 Insert the supporting wire hoops 3 ft (1 m.) apart, using a garden line as a guide to ensure a straight row.

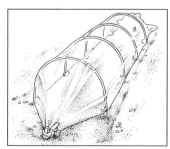

2 Knot one end of the cover to a peg inserted 2 ft (610 mm.) beyond an end hoop. Draw the cover over the hoops.

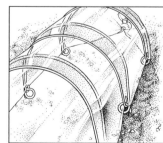

3 Secure the other end of the cover. Tension the cover by clipping the outer hoops on to loops in the supporting hoops.

their weight makes them more secure than lighter materials.

There are three types of glass cloches – the tent, low barn and high barn.

A tent cloche consists of two sheets of glass about 24 × 12 in. (610 × 305 mm.) fixed at the top by a galvanised-iron clip to form a pitched roof or tent.

Tent cloches are useful for raising seedlings or for single rows of crops such as lettuces, carrots and beetroots.

Barn cloches have four panes of glass, two forming sides and two the pitched roof. A low barn cloche is 2 ft (610 mm.) long and 12 in. (305 mm.) high. With a width of about 2 ft, it is possible to grow a central row of lettuces and outer rows of carrots or beetroot. The lettuces will be harvested first, leaving the other crops to mature.

A high barn cloche is as wide and long as a low barn but the height is about 19 in. (480 mm.). A row of high barn cloches is useful for getting plants such as tomatoes, peppers and aubergines to a fairly advanced stage before protection is no longer necessary in high summer.

Growing under cloches

If possible, prepare the ground at least a month before sowing or planting to give the soil time to settle. Dig in well-rotted manure or compost at the rate of a bucketful to the yard run.

About a fortnight before sowing or planting, rake into the surface soil a dressing of general fertiliser at about 2 oz. (50 g.) to the yard run. Mark a row with a line, leave this in position, and cover the row with the cloches to warm up the soil. Secure the end panels with two canes driven into the ground.

The cloches must be removed at sowing or planting time and the purpose of leaving the line is to centre the row where the plants will get most headroom.

After sowing or planting, scatter slug pellets and replace the cloches in exactly the same position as when the ground was being warmed.

Sow small seeds about $\frac{1}{4}$ in. (5 mm.) deeper than in the open because the surface dries during the warming-up period. Do not water until the seeds germinate. Water the soil after setting out young plants, however.

After that, cultivation is the same as for growing in the open. Although the surface soil may look dry, a few inches down it will have about the same moisture content as the uncovered soil alongside. Capillary attraction ensures that water reaches the plants' roots.

Although any type of cloche provides artificially benign growing conditions, you may need to take action when there are sudden changes in the weather.

If spring days are unusually warm, open up some continuous cloches or slide back the polythene of a tunnel cloche, to allow air to circulate. Replace or close the cloches an hour before sunset.

If late spring frosts are forecast, cover tender plants, such as tomatoes, with four or five sheets of newspaper in the evening and remove them in the morning.

A week before moving cloches from one row to another, harden off, or acclimatise, the protected plants that are about to be left in the open. To do this, leave off some cloches during the day and replace them in the evening.

Fruit under cloches

Melons and strawberries are the only fruit grown under cloches, but the results are usually highly successful.

Cloches serve a dual purpose when covering strawberries (see p. 263). They make it unnecessary to net against bird attacks and, if put in position in November, will provide an earlier crop than outside, generally in May. Any type of cloches may be used.

GROWING CROPS UNDER CLOCHES

SOIL PREPARATION Dig the soil several weeks before sowing, so that it settles. Rake in fertiliser a fortnight before sowing.

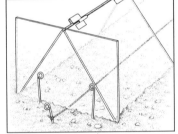

WARMING THE SOIL A fortnight before sowing, place cloches centrally over a garden line. Close each end of row with glass.

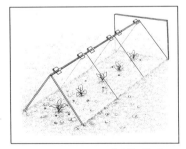

PLANTING – AND AFTER Set the plants, or sow seeds, along the line and replace cloches. Scatter slug pellets on ground.

FROST PRECAUTION On clear evenings in April or May place layers of newspaper over the glass. Remove next morning.

PROGRAMME FOR SOWING AND PLANTING UNDER CLOCHES

VEGETABLE OR FRUIT	TIME TO SOW *Only in heat	TIME TO PLANT UNDER CLOCHES	TIME UNDER CLOCHES
Aubergines	*March	May	May–September
Broad beans	In the North, January–February		In the North, January–April
French beans	March–April		March–May
Runner beans	April	April–early May	April–May
Carrots	March		March–April
Lettuces	August October January–February	September	September December October–April January–May
Marrows	*March–April	April–May	April–May
Melons	*Mid-April	Mid-May	May–September
Onions	January		January–March
Peas	October January–February		October–April
Peppers	*March	March–April	March–September
Radishes	October January–March		October–March
Strawberries		November–May	
Sweet corn	April	May	April–May
Tomatoes	*March	April–May	April–May
Turnips	February		February–May

Glossary of gardening terms

The language of gardening is often confusing to beginners. This glossary includes terms used in growing fruits, herbs and vegetables, with cross-references to other sections where methods are explained in greater detail.

Acid soil: see **pH level.**

Alkaline soil: see **pH level.**

Annual A plant that germinates, grows, produces seeds and dies in a single season. Lettuces and radishes are annuals. So are a number of herbs, including borage, chervil and dill.
Half-hardy annuals, such as sweet corn, cannot withstand frost.
Hardy annuals, which include many varieties of lettuce, are unharmed by frost.
Tender annuals, such as aubergines, do best when grown under glass throughout the season, though some succeed in a sheltered spot outdoors during a warm summer.
(See also Biennial and Perennial.)

B

Bastard trenching: see **Double digging.**

Biennial A plant that requires two seasons to complete its life cycle.
Cabbages and other members of the cabbage family are biennials because they do not as a rule produce flowers and form seeds until their second year, though the crop is normally harvested before this occurs.
Biennial bearing is a term used for fruit trees, especially apples, that tend to carry substantial crops only in alternate years.

Blanching Some vegetables are more delicately flavoured and tender if light is excluded from their stems during the later stages of growth. Chicory and seakale are examples of crops that benefit from blanching.
Another form of blanching – immersion in boiling water – is used to prepare vegetables for freezing.

Bleeding An excessive amount of sap may be lost if a tree or fruit bush is pruned too drastically, or if pruning is delayed until the sap is rising in spring. Bleeding, as it is called, is thought to weaken the tree. For this reason, spread the restoration of neglected trees over a three-year period.
The term is also used for the loss of juice that occurs when beetroots are lifted carelessly, damaging the skin, or if the tops are cut off close to the roots (see pp. 98–99) after harvesting.

Bletting The over-ripening process needed for medlars after harvesting the fruits in October or November. Pick the fruits on a dry day and lay them, eyes downwards, in trays, for three or four weeks until they soften.

Bolting Premature running to seed. Lettuces, particularly, are liable to bolt during hot, dry weather within a few days of the hearts forming. To reduce the risk, avoid checks in the plants' growth and keep the ground well watered. After April, sow lettuces where they are to grow, so avoiding a transplanting check.
If bolting occurs frequently, choose varieties that are slow to run to seed. 'All the Year Round' and 'Webb's Wonderful' are suitable lettuces.
The beetroot 'Boltardy' is resistant to bolting.

Brassicas Plants belonging to the cabbage family. These include Brussels sprouts, cabbages, cauliflowers, kale, swedes and turnips.

Broadcasting Method of sowing seeds by scattering them over an area of ground instead of sowing in straight drills. Though useful for lawns and annual flowers, few vegetables are sown in this way because it is difficult to thin the seedlings to ensure even spacing.

Buds An undeveloped growing point on a shoot, from which leaves or flowers develop. When pruning fruit trees it is necessary to distinguish between fruit buds and growth buds.
Fruit buds, which bear blossom and then fruits, are the fatter and rounder of the two – usually on short, gnarled twigs known as spurs.
Growth buds, from which leaves or a shoot will grow, are more pointed and often flattened.
Pruning cuts are often made just above an outward-pointing growth bud. This maintains the open form of the tree.

Bush A form of fruit tree – not a soft-fruit bush – that has a trunk 2–2½ ft (610–760 mm.) high beneath the lowest branches. The name is deceptive, however, since bush trees may have a height and spread of 12 ft (3.6 m.).

C

Catch-crop A quick-maturing crop grown in the interval between harvesting one crop and sowing or planting another. Lettuces, kohl-rabi, radishes and turnips make good catch-crops (see p. 28).

Clamp A form of outdoor storage for potatoes and root crops. The crop is protected from frost and rain by placing it as a conical or ridge-shaped heap and covering with straw and soil. A straw-filled gap at the top of the earth covering provides ventilation.
Clamps are used mainly for farm crops. In a garden, there is seldom sufficient produce to form a large enough heap. Repeated opening is inconvenient, especially in wet weather, and may damage the crop unless carried out with great care.

Clove A segment, or single bulb, in a cluster of garlic or shallots. Each clove will grow into a new plant if put in the soil the year after harvesting.

Compost A term with two meanings:
Garden compost is decomposed vegetable matter. Well-made compost (see p. 21) adds humus and plant foods to the soil and is an alternative to farmyard manure (see p. 17).
Seed and potting compost is the growing medium used in pots and seed boxes for raising seedlings and for growing plants. It may have a soil base, or consist principally of peat (see pp. 32–33).

Cordon A fruit tree trained as a single stem and pruned to carry only fruit-bearing spurs. A row of cordons makes an attractive and productive screen in a small garden, or the trees may be planted alongside a wall.

Crop rotation A cropping scheme devised to avoid growing the same types of vegetables on the same land in consecutive years. This prevents a build-up of pests and diseases associated with particular crops, and enables the best use to be made of manures and fertilisers (see pp. 26–27).

Cultivar A cultivated variety of a plant, as distinct from a naturally occurring botanical variety.

Curd The central flower head of a cauliflower or broccoli plant.

Cutting A piece of bud, leaf, root or stem removed from a plant and grown on to form a new plant (see p. 29). Plants raised by this vegetative form of propagation are exact replicas of the parent plant, whereas those raised from seed may not be. Several types of soft fruits can be propagated by cuttings (see p. 47), and also some perennial herbs (see p. 29).

Damping down Watering or spraying the floor and staging of a greenhouse in hot weather – which helps to increase the humidity and reduce the temperature. Damping down is particularly beneficial to cucumbers and other moisture-loving plants. However, avoid increasing humidity when the air temperature is low. A combination of cold and damp is fatal to many plants, especially to seedlings.

Deciduous A term used to describe trees and other woody plants that shed their leaves annually. All garden fruit trees and bushes are deciduous.

Disbudding In the fruit garden, buds on young shoots are sometimes removed, or pinched out, as an aid to shaping the tree. This is known as disbudding.

For instance, on wall-trained trees it is necessary to prevent shoots growing straight towards, or away from, the wall. The only buds left on the vertical trunk of an espalier are those needed to provide shoots that will form the horizontal tiers.

Division A method of separating a mature plant into smaller plants, each complete with roots and growth buds. Rhubarb is among

the few food plants propagated by this method, which is widely used for ornamental herbaceous plants.

Dormant Fruit trees and bushes are said to be dormant during the late autumn and winter when the leaves have fallen and growth is at a standstill.

Double digging A method of cultivating the soil two spits deep, instead of the normal spade depth. Its purpose is to break up the subsoil and so improve drainage and encourage vigorous root action.

Double digging is also known as bastard trenching (see p. 24).

Drawn Description of plants, especially seedlings, that have become weak and spindly due to overcrowding or insufficient light. Thin seedlings out, or prick them out (see p. 34), before this happens.

In a greenhouse, keep young plants close to the glass, where they get maximum light.

Drill A straight, shallow furrow, generally formed with a draw hoe, in which seeds are sown. For most small seeds a depth of ¼–½ in. (5–12 mm.) is satisfactory, but about 2 in. (50 mm.) is needed for peas and beans (see p. 30).

Dwarf pyramid A compact form of fruit tree, suitable for small gardens, with branches beginning about 15 in. (380 mm.) above the ground. With correct pruning the branches get progressively shorter towards the top, giving a tree 7–10 ft (2.1–3 m.) high and with a spread of about 3–6 ft (1–1.8 m.) (see p. 41).

Earthing up The practice of drawing soil round plants to exclude light from stems or tubers, or to reduce wind damage. Potatoes will turn green, due to the production of chlorophyll, unless earthed up before the tubers develop. The same process is needed to blanch the stems of leeks and celery, and earthing up gives extra support to the tall stems of Jerusalem artichokes.

Espalier A form of trained fruit tree with horizontal tiers extending on either side of the vertical trunk. There are usually three to five tiers, and the trees may be grown as a screen or against a wall (see p. 41).

Evergreen Description of trees and shrubs that retain their leaves throughout the year. Bay, rosemary and winter savory are among the few evergreen plants in the food garden.

Eye The undeveloped, slightly sunken growth buds on potato tubers are called eyes. Each will produce a shoot, so large seed potatoes may be cut in two provided each section has one or more eyes. When putting potatoes to sprout in January (see p. 240) set them with the eyes uppermost.

Family tree A fruit tree on which the scions (shoots) of more than one variety have been grafted.

Generally, three varieties of apples or pears are grown on a single bush-type tree. For good pollination, varieties are chosen for simultaneous flowering.

Fan trained A form of training, especially popular for growing peaches, in which the branches of a fruit tree are spaced like the ribs of a fan. A framework of supporting wires is needed. Fan-trained trees are often grown against walls (see p. 41).

Feather A dispensable lateral shoot left on a young fruit tree to help strengthen the future trunk.

Fertilisation The process whereby the male and female reproductive cells fuse. Without fertilisation, which is brought about by the transference of pollen from a male to a female flower, plants will not develop beyond the flowering stage to produce seeds and fruits.

Foliar feeding A method of applying fertilisers by watering a nutrient solution on to a plant's leaves. The fertiliser is absorbed very quickly, so this is a good method of giving weakly plants a rapid boost. Foliar feeds are sold in proprietary packs (see p. 19).

Forcing A method of stimulating growth in advance of the normal season. This may be done by excluding light and, sometimes, by providing warm conditions. Chicory, rhubarb and seakale are among crops that are often forced. Instructions on forcing are given, where appropriate, in the Growing and Cooking section between pp. 61 and 276.

Genus A group of closely related plant species. The genus *Allium*, for instance, includes chives, onions and shallots. The next group up the scale is the family, which consists of more than one genus.

Good heart A descriptive term applied to land that is in a fertile condition. It implies that both the physical structure and supply of plant foods are satisfactory, ensuring that a variety of crops will thrive.

Grafting A method of vegetative propagation by which parts of two plants are joined to make a permanent union. Grafting is used extensively in the production of fruit trees, especially apples and pears, as trees raised from seeds may not come true to type. Peach trees are a notable exception.

Instead, a cutting (called a scion) is taken from a tree of the required variety and grafted on to the rootstock (or stock) of a second tree – not necessarily of the same type.

The vigour and growth habit of the resultant tree are determined by the choice of rootstock, and a variety of stocks have been standardised and classified.

Grafting is normally left to the nurseryman. When buying a fruit tree, tell the nurseryman the form in which you want to grow it (see p. 41) so that he can provide a tree on a suitable rootstock.

Examples of tree forms are bush, cordon, fan-trained trees, dwarf pyramids and espaliers.

Half-hardy annual: see **Annual.**

Hardy annual: see **Annual.**

Haulm The stems of certain vegetable plants – particularly those with lax or straggling stems, such as peas, potatoes and runner beans.

Heeling in A term to describe temporary planting, especially of fruit trees and bushes, if permanent planting has to be delayed. The trees or bushes are set in a trench, with their roots well covered to prevent drying out. If set at an angle, away from the prevailing wind, they are less likely to be blown over (see p. 42).

Herbaceous Term used to describe perennial plants that produce non-woody growth which dies back in autumn. Globe artichokes are herbaceous plants.

Hybrid A plant that has resulted from crossing two different species, distinct forms of the same species or two species of different genera.
 F1 hybrids – noted for their exceptional vigour and uniformity – result from the careful selection and inbreeding of two different parent strains. When the desirable qualities of each are established, the plants are cross-pollinated to combine their best characteristics. Seeds from F1 hybrids do not come true to type.

Hydroponics A method of growing plants in a nutrient solution, without soil. Although practised commercially, it has at present only limited applications for amateur food-growers.

Inorganic: see **Organic.**

Intercropping Growing a quick-maturing crop between the rows of another crop that develops more slowly. As for catch-crops, some of the best plants for this purpose are lettuces, kohl-rabi, radishes and turnips (see p. 28).

Lateral shoot A shoot growing from a leader or a main branch (see p. 44).

Layering Method of vegetative propagation by which a stem attached to a plant is partially buried in the soil and so induced to form a root and, eventually, produce a separate plant. Though used fairly extensively for ornamental plants, tip layering (see p. 101) is the main application in the food garden.

Leader The shoot at the end of a main stem or branch (see p. 44).

Maiden tree A tree in its first year after grafting. Generally, it has a single stem. Those with a number of side-shoots are sometimes called feathered maidens. Maiden trees are not recommended for unskilled gardeners, as training will not have been started. Trees bought when between two and four years old will have been partly trained.

Mulching Placing a layer of compost or manure round growing plants – or mulching, as this is called – conserves moisture and suppresses weeds. Sheets of black polythene or a covering of damp peat may also be used for the same purpose.
 Avoid laying a mulch too early in spring before the soil has had time to warm up (see p. 36).

Natural drop Fruit trees often set more fruits than they are capable of carrying to maturity. This accounts for the dropping of surplus fruits from the tree while they are still small – during June in the case of apples. The terms 'natural drop' and 'June drop' are synonymous.

Node The joint on a stem from which leaves arise. Sometimes there may also be an axillary bud in the joint, which will develop into a shoot.

Organic Term applied to any compound derived from living organisms. In gardening, the term is used principally for fertilisers of animal or vegetable origin, such as bonemeal or seaweed.

Inorganic fertilisers, for example sulphate of ammonia or super-phosphate, are derived from mineral deposits (see p. 18).

Overwintering Helping plants to survive the colder months by providing protection. For example, overwintering in a frame or under cloches is required for some autumn-sown lettuce varieties.

Pan A hard layer that exists in some soils, often as a result of continual cultivation at the same depth. Some sandy soils have a naturally occurring hard layer called an iron pan. A pan impedes drainage and inhibits root development. The remedy lies in deeper cultivation, generally by means of double digging (see p. 24).

Perennial A plant that lives and flowers for more than two seasons. The term is generally restricted to herbaceous plants, which die down each winter, but it also applies to trees and shrubs.

pH level A scale of values against which soil acidity or alkalinity is measured. The neutral point on the scale is pH 7.0. Readings above this denote an alkaline soil; below it the soil is acid (see p. 19).

Pollination The transference of pollen from a male flower to a female flower, which is necessary for fertilisation and the production of seeds or fruits. In the open, pollen is carried mainly by the wind and by insects, especially bees. Under glass, it may be necessary to transfer pollen by hand – using cottonwool or a brush – for certain crops, including melons.

Pricking out The transfer of seedlings from a pot or seed pan to another container where they will have more space to grow. Sometimes, as for cucumbers or marrows, each seedling is pricked out into a separate small pot. For plants such as lettuces or celery, which make more compact growth and will not be harmed by further root disturbance, the seedlings are spaced out in a tray (see p. 34).

Propagation The reproduction or increase of plants. Propagation takes two forms: seminal, or sexual – reproduction by seed; and vegetative – reproduction by cuttings, division, grafting or layering. Plants reproduced by seed are entirely new growths, and may differ from the parents. Those reproduced vegetatively are a multiplication of the same plant, and so are identical.

Pruning The process of training and restricting the growth of a tree or shrub to attain a desired shape and to promote flowering and fruiting (see p. 43).

Ring culture Method of growing plants – principally greenhouse tomatoes – in bottomless containers (rings) placed on a base of fine aggregate. The aggregate lies in a polythene-lined trench, so isolating the plants' roots from the soil and avoiding the risk of soil-borne diseases. The aggregate is watered daily, and liquid fertiliser applied weekly once the first fruits set (see pp. 272–3).

Rootstock Plant with a vigorous root action – often a wild species – used for grafting fruit trees. (See Grafting, p. 58.)

Runner A rooting stem that grows horizontally at ground level. Strawberries propagate themselves by runners, though for rapid and reliable rooting it helps to peg the runners to the soil, or to compost-filled pots sunk into the soil (see pp. 264–5).

Scion A bud or shoot taken from a tree for grafting on to a selected rootstock. (See Grafting, p. 58.)

Seed leaves Term used for the first leaves, which botanists call cotyledons, produced by a germinating seed. They are often different from subsequent leaves in shape and texture. These later leaves are sometimes called true leaves or rough leaves.

Self-fertile Plants with flowers that can be fertilised by other flowers on the same plant. Some plums, for instance, are self-fertile. But most apples require pollination by another apple tree.

Self-seeding Term applied to plants that shed seeds readily. The seeds then germinate in the surrounding soil.

Set A term with two horticultural meanings:
(a) Shallots, potatoes and small onion bulbs used for planting are called sets.
(b) Flowers and fruit blossom which have been fertilised as a result of pollination are said to have set.

Soil warming A method of promoting plant growth by laying insulated electric cables beneath the soil in frames (see p. 53).

Species Closely related plants belonging to the same genus. For instance, the genus *Brassica* includes the species *Brassica rapa* (turnip) and *Brassica oleracea* (cabbage).

Spit A single spade depth of soil – about 10–12 in. (255–305 mm.). Normal digging is one spit deep. Double digging (see p. 24) also involves forking up the spit below, to assist root development.

Spur A short lateral branch bearing clusters of fruit buds. Most apple trees produce all their fruits on spurs.
Tip-bearing varieties produce about half their crop on spurs, the rest on the tips of shoots.

Standard Fruit tree with a trunk 6–7 ft (1.8–2.1 m.) high beneath the first branches. A half-standard has a 3–4 ft (1–1.2 m.) trunk. Though extensively planted in old gardens and orchards, both forms are too large for today's smaller gardens.

Stock : see **Rootstock.**

Stopping Pinching out the tip of a shoot or main stem. Sometimes, as with a cucumber or melon, the object is to encourage formation of fruit-bearing side-shoots. Outdoor tomato plants are stopped after four fruit trusses have formed, because this is the maximum number likely to ripen before autumn.

Subsoil The relatively infertile soil that lies beneath the upper, cultivated layer. Its depth varies, but it can be identified by its marked difference in texture and colour from the topsoil.
Sometimes the subsoil is of a completely different type – perhaps clay or gravel under loam – but in all cases avoid mixing it with the topsoil.

Sucker A shoot arising from the base of a plant or from roots below ground. Raspberries, for instance, produce many suckers, which are often a foot or more from the parent plant's stem. On grafted trees or bushes suckers grow from the rootstock and are therefore valueless for the production of flowers or fruits.

Tap-root A long root which extends vertically downwards with few or no branches. Many vegetables, including root crops and brassicas (members of the cabbage family), have tap-roots. Although no harm is done by breaking the tap-roots of such crops as cabbages and cauliflowers when transplanting, it is essential not to disturb those of root crops, such as carrots and turnips, which

eventually form the edible part of the crop. They are therefore sown where they are to grow.

Tender annual : see **Annual.**

Tendril The thin, curling out-growths by which certain climbing plants cling to supports.

Thinning A term with two horti-cultural meanings:
(a) Removing surplus seedlings to allow those that remain suf-ficient space to develop. Prompt thinning of vegetable crops (see p. 32) is essential for sturdy growth.
(b) Removing surplus fruits from trees that are carrying more than they can bear without quality being impaired.

Tile drains A name sometimes given to the earthenware pipes laid to improve land drainage.

Tilth The crumb-like structure of surface soil required when sowing seeds or setting out small plants. The quality of the tilth – a fine structure is ideal – is determined partly by the amount of organic material in the soil and partly by carrying out the necessary cultiva-tion (see p. 30) when it is neither excessively wet or dry.

Tip bearing The habit of some fruit trees, such as 'Worcester Pearmain' apples, of carrying a proportion of their crop on the tips of shoots.

Topsoil The upper layer of fertile soil, which has a different colour and texture from the relatively sterile soil beneath. Avoid mixing the two layers when digging or planting.

Trace elements Chemical elements which are essential for healthy plant growth but are present in the soil only in minute quantities. Boron, copper, iron, manganese, molybdenum and zinc are among the more important trace elements.

Transplanting Moving young plants from pots or a seed bed to their permanent growing posi-tions. This two-stage growing technique is used for many vege-tables including most green crops (see p. 35).

Trenching A method of digging three spits deep to improve drain-age and assist root penetration. Although occasionally practised in the past, it is seldom done today because of the work involved.

Variety Naturally occurring vari-ations within a species of plants are called varieties. Those which arise in cultivation are called cultivars. However, because the former term is more familiar to most gardeners, the fruits and vegetables named throughout this book are listed as varieties.

Wilting Flagging, or drooping, of plants – generally due to lack of moisture. Wilting may also be caused by pests, such as cabbage root fly, attacking the roots, or by fungal diseases affecting the water-conducting tissues in the stem.

GROWING AND COOKING

An A–Z guide to 100 fruits, vegetables and herbs

No book on gardening can provide a rigid formula for success. Part of the fascination of food growing is that the gardener must make his own judgments about the state of the soil and the progress of the seasons.

The times given here for such routine tasks as sowing, planting and pruning are based upon an 'average' year in the south of England. In such a season, gardeners living in the Midlands, northern East Anglia and south-west Scotland would begin planting about a week later; those in the north of England and most of Scotland a week later still; while those in the northern Highlands and on the east coast of Scotland might have to wait for as much as a month after work had started in the south.

At the other end of the summer, autumn tasks should be undertaken earlier in colder parts of the country.

However, chilly springs can occur anywhere. If the weather is unusually cold, delay spring work until warmer days arrive. Be prepared for an early autumn to curtail the harvesting period of late-summer crops.

VARIETIES Although those listed provide a good representative range, by studying seed catalogues each year you may discover new varieties that are particularly suited to your garden.

RECIPES Unless stated otherwise, all the recipes are based upon four servings. Use either imperial or metric measures throughout, not a combination of the two. The measures are not exact conversions.

Alfalfa:
see **Sprouting seeds**

Angelica

This flowering herb makes an imposing display at the back of a herb garden or flower bed, especially if it reaches its full height of 7–10 ft (2.1–3m.).

The plant has always been surrounded by superstition and credited with having magical and medicinal powers. It takes its name from the Archangel Michael – partly because it was thought to bloom each year on May 8, the day he is said to have appeared in a vision in the 14th century to say that the herb would cure the plague.

Angelica is a biennial that dies after it has produced seeds. However, if the stems are cut back before they flower it can be kept alive for several years.

The young stems and side-growths can be candied, the stems and leaves may be cooked with apples and rhubarb, while infused leaves – fresh or dry – make a refreshing drink.

Planning the crop

Angelica does best in deep, rich, moist soil in a sunny or partly shaded position. Dig the soil during the winter before sowing.

How much to grow One or two plants will provide enough angelica for the family, but an extra plant can be grown if you want to save your own seed for next year's plants.

How to grow angelica

Sow purchased seeds in March or April, ½ in. (12 mm.) deep in groups of three or four and about 3 ft (1 m.) apart, in the positions where they are to grow. As the seedlings develop, remove all but the strongest in each group.

Alternatively, sow the seeds in a seed bed and transplant the seedlings to their final positions in late autumn or the following March. The plants may not be as large as those grown, without transplanting, where they were sown.

If you keep seeds from one of your own plants, sow them as soon as ripe, and not later than September.

Pests and diseases APHIDS (p. 282) are the pests most likely to occur on angelica.

It is generally disease-free.

Harvesting the stems, roots and leaves

For drying (see p. 343), pick the leaves before flowering, while they are still a fresh green.

If roots are to be cooked, use them in their first autumn before they become woody.

Angelica is not suitable for freezing. 🙠🙢

AT-A-GLANCE TIMETABLE FOR ANGELICA

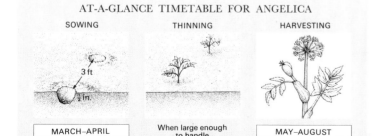

SOWING — 3 ft — ½ in. — MARCH–APRIL

THINNING — When large enough to handle

HARVESTING — MAY–AUGUST

Cooking with angelica

Add slices of raw, peeled stems to salads. Stems and leaves give a novel flavour to stewed fruits, such as apple or rhubarb, or to fruit pies.

Cook the roots as a vegetable, following the method given for Hamburg parsley (p. 223).

Apples

'Cox's Orange Pippin'

'Bramley's Seedling'

The apple is one of the oldest fruits known to man, and also one of the most widely cultivated. Originally growing wild in Europe and the Near East, it thrives inland throughout the British Isles.

However, apples do not grow well in coastal areas exposed to salt-laden winds, and in the north there is a greater risk of blossom being destroyed by spring frosts. This applies also in local frost pockets, in gardens in valleys or at the base of slopes where the temperature may be much lower than near by.

The earliest apples are ready for picking and eating in August; the latest can be stored for eating until

Bush tree

Dwarf pyramid

as late as the following April/May.

Although many of the apple trees planted in long-established gardens require a good deal of space, trained and dwarf forms can now be grown in even the smallest town garden.

It is also possible to buy 'family trees', in which three or four varieties are grafted on a single rootstock to provide a succession of fruits (see p. 41).

Planning the crop

Apple trees do best in an open, sunny, but sheltered site. They will grow in most soils, except those that are waterlogged or have a high lime content. The ideal is a slightly acid soil that does not dry out in summer.

In late September or early October, prepare the site where the trees are to grow. Fork into the soil well-rotted manure or compost at the rate of a bucketful to the square yard, and apply a general fertiliser at the rate of 3 oz. per square yard (90 g. per square metre).

How many trees to grow Many gardeners are content to make do with the apple trees that they take

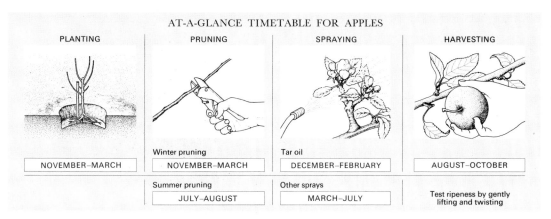

AT-A-GLANCE TIMETABLE FOR APPLES

PLANTING	PRUNING	SPRAYING	HARVESTING
NOVEMBER–MARCH	Winter pruning NOVEMBER–MARCH	Tar oil DECEMBER–FEBRUARY	AUGUST–OCTOBER
	Summer pruning JULY–AUGUST	Other sprays MARCH–JULY	Test ripeness by gently lifting and twisting

over when they move to a new home. But those who plant afresh have the opportunity to select the trees best suited to the site.

Bush trees, planted 12–20 ft (3.6–6 m.) apart, are a good choice where space is plentiful. One well-grown bush tree may produce 200 lb. (91 kg.) or more of fruit, according to the variety, with an average of 80–100 lb. (36–45 kg.).

Where space is more restricted, dwarf-pyramid trees, planted 5–6 ft (1.5–1.8 m.) apart, are more suitable. One tree may produce 15 lb. (7 kg.) or more of apples,

with an average yield of 8–10 lb. (4–5 kg.).

An espalier with a spread of 10–15 ft (3–4.5 m.) would be ideal for growing against a fence or wall in full sun or with a little shade. If preferred, it could be grown in the open and trained on wires (see p. 64).

Single-stemmed cordons, trained on wires (see p. 64) and planted 2½–3 ft (760 mm.–1 m.) apart, with 6 ft (1.8 m.) between rows, would enable a gardener to grow a number of varieties on a very small plot. Each fully established cordon may yield 10 lb.

(5 kg.) or more of fruit, with an average of 3–5 lb. (1.5–2.5 kg.).

Varieties The varieties listed on pp. 70–71 are commonly available in this country. When buying trees it is advisable to tell the nurseryman what position and type of soil they will be planted in, for only then can he recommend the best available variety.

Because most apple trees cannot pollinate themselves, it is necessary to plant at least two trees that will blossom at the same time. Varieties with overlapping blossoming periods are listed A, B, etc.,

on pp. 70–71. For instance, 'Discovery' and 'Merton Knave' will cross-pollinate satisfactorily.

A few varieties, including 'Bramley's Seedling', are such poor pollinators that a third tree is needed to fertilise the tree chosen as a pollinator.

An additional tree is unnecessary, however, if you buy a 'family tree', as the varieties will have been selected for simultaneous flowering.

How to grow apple trees

The best time for planting (see p. 42) is during frost-free weather between early November and late March.

Dig a hole of sufficient size to take the roots when they are well spread out. When planting a bush tree, first hammer in a supporting stake and plant the tree close against it. With all forms of tree, make sure that the union between the stock and the scion (see p. 41) is at least 4 in. (100 mm.) above soil level.

In the first growing season water copiously during dry spells. For the first two or three springs after planting, mulch around the trees with manure or compost to help retain moisture in the soil.

Every January, apply 1 oz. of sulphate of potash per square yard (30 g. per square metre). Every third year, add 2 oz. (60 g.) of superphosphate to that dressing.

In March, give a dressing of sulphate of ammonia. For cooking apples, and for any tree growing in a lawn, use 2 oz. per square yard. For all others, 1 oz. should be sufficient.

Sprinkle all these dressings thinly over an area a little larger than the spread of the branches.

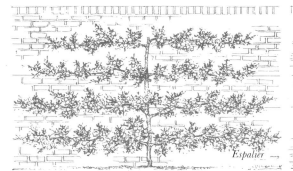

Espalier

Fan-trained

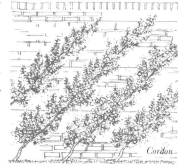

Cordon

Training and pruning (see also p. 43). During the first four years of a tree's life the aim should be to create a strong framework of branches.

The way they are trained and pruned will depend on the shape of tree required.

Apple trees can be bought as one-year-old maidens which have only a single stem. These are then pruned each winter to create the desired shape.

A beginner, however, would do better to buy older trees that have already been partly trained by a nurseryman. Bush trees, cordons and trees that are to be trained on as dwarf pyramids can be bought when two or three years old, and espaliers up to four years old.

Do not, however, take a further short cut and buy trees that are five or six years old, as they rarely re-establish themselves.

Training a cordon

After planting a cordon apple tree (see p. 42) no pruning is necessary except for tip-bearing varieties. Shorten the leader of these by a quarter.

Thereafter, all pruning is done in summer by what is known as the modified Lorette system. This is also the most effective method for other restricted forms.

Modified Lorette system Prune when the new summer growth matures – that is, when the shoots are at least 9 in. (230 mm.) long, the leaves are dark and the base is woody.

Cut back shoots from the main stem to three leaves beyond the basal cluster. Prune shoots from existing laterals or spurs to one leaf beyond the basal cluster. Delay pruning laterals less than 9 in. (230 mm.) long until they grow to the necessary length.

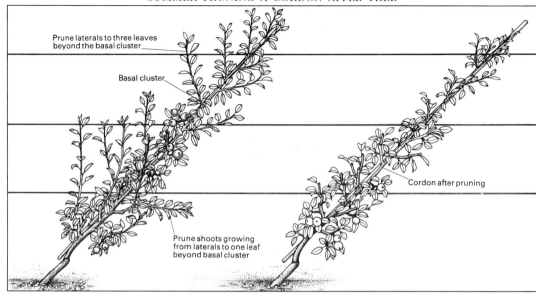

SUMMER PRUNING A CORDON APPLE TREE

Prune laterals to three leaves beyond the basal cluster

Basal cluster

Cordon after pruning

Prune shoots growing from laterals to one leaf beyond basal cluster

SUMMER TRAINING Prune cordons in summer when new growth matures – usually in mid-July in southern England, but later in the north. Cut back laterals growing from the main stem to three leaves from the basal cluster (where growth began in the spring) and cut back shoots from existing laterals or spurs to one leaf. This method is also suitable for espaliers and dwarf pyramids.

Training an espalier

A gardener who wants to grow an espalier, but has little pruning experience, should buy a three-year-old tree. This will have two tiers, or horizontal branches, already trained by a nurseryman. Annual pruning is carried out in two stages:

Winter pruning is needed in the early years to produce additional tiers, if required, and to thin overcrowded spurs later.

Summer pruning is the same as for cordons, using the modified Lorette system (see above).

Forming new tiers After planting (see p. 42) and tying the branches to the support wires, cut back the main stem to a bud about 2 in. (50 mm.) above the wire that will support the next tier above.

When growth begins select two good buds below the cut, on opposite sides of the stem, to grow into side branches. Rub out any buds between these three.

Tie a cane vertically to the support wires. As the centre shoot grows, tie it to the cane.

Fasten two more canes to the wires on each side of the first cane, setting them at an angle of 45 degrees. Tie the side-shoots to these as they grow.

If one grows more vigorously than the other, lower the angle of the cane and raise the cane of the other to a more vertical position.

In the following winter remove the side canes, lower the branches and tie them to the wire supports.

Repeat this process each year until the desired number of tiers is established. When forming the top tier, cut back the main stem to two side buds, leaving no upper bud.

Do not prune vigorous leaders on the tiers until they have reached the desired length. If growth is weak, however, cut back the previous summer's growth by a quarter to one-third. Cut in winter to a bud pointing along the support wire.

When the tiers have reached the desired length, cut back the previous year's growth to $\frac{1}{2}$ in. (12 mm.) in May. Repeat this treatment each May. Otherwise, only summer pruning by the modified Lorette system is necessary.

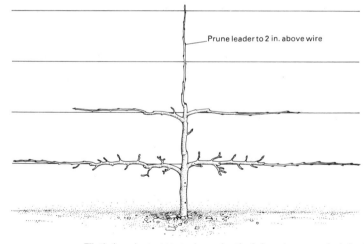

Prune leader to 2 in. above wire

AFTER PLANTING Tie the branches to support wires and cut back the main stem to a bud about 2 in. (50 mm.) above the wire that will support the next tier of horizontal branches.

Sometimes, secondary growth occurs after the summer pruning. In September or early October cut these shoots back to one bud on well-ripened wood.

When a cordon grows beyond the top support wire, untie it and re-fasten it at a more acute angle. Do not lower it to less than 35 degrees from the horizontal.

Lower neighbouring cordons so that they remain parallel.

When the cordon reaches its final height, cut back new growth on the leader to ½ in. (12 mm.) in May. Cut above a bud and repeat the operation each May.

As the tree gets older, thin overcrowded spurs while dormant during the winter.

SPRING TREATMENT

MAY PRUNING Once the main stem is fully grown, prune new growth on the leader to ½ in. (12 mm.). Repeat each year.

AUTUMN TREATMENT

SEPTEMBER PRUNING Cut back any secondary growth from the summer pruning to one bud on well-ripened wood.

Pruning a neglected cordon

Start to improve the shape of the tree in winter, first sawing back some of the thicker vertical branches to within 1–2 in. (25–50 mm.) of the main stem.

Cut long spurs back according to their thickness – the heaviest ones the hardest. Spread this pruning over two or three years.

During the following summer, prune by the modified Lorette system (see p. 64) – removing some of the growth completely.

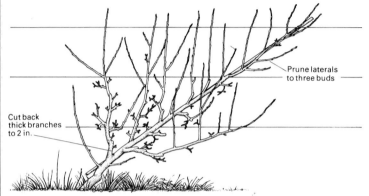

Prune laterals to three buds

Cut back thick branches to 2 in.

Spread pruning of a neglected cordon over several years, establishing the shape of the tree in winter but carrying out more detailed pruning in summer.

CONTROLLING THE LENGTH OF AN ESTABLISHED CORDON

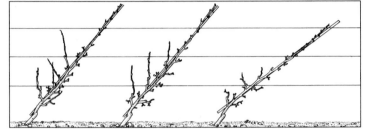

CHANGING THE ANGLE When a cordon grows beyond the top wire, untie the stem in winter, lower it by about 5 degrees and re-tie. Lower it a further 5 degrees a year later. Thereafter, control a leader's length by cutting back new growth to ½ in. (12 mm.) every May.

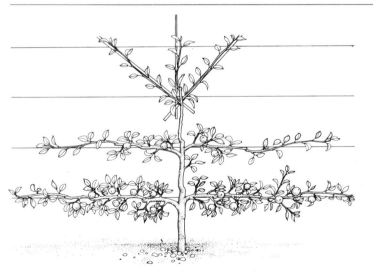

THE NEXT SUMMER As growth begins select two buds, one pointing left and one right, below the cut made at planting. As these shoots grow, tie them to canes set at an angle of 45 degrees.

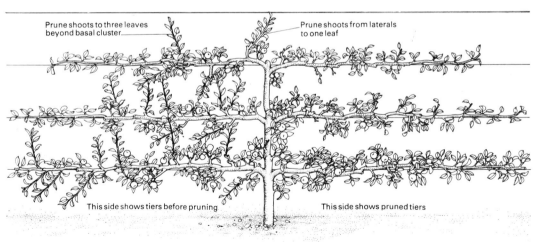

Prune shoots to three leaves beyond basal cluster

Prune shoots from laterals to one leaf

This side shows tiers before pruning

This side shows pruned tiers

AN ESTABLISHED TREE When the tiers have reached the desired length, cut back the previous year's growth to ½ in. (12 mm.) each May. In late July or August, prune shoots from tiers to three leaves from the basal cluster, and shoots from laterals to one leaf.

Training a dwarf pyramid

A dwarf pyramid is trained to a shape similar to that of a Christmas tree.

After planting a two-year-old tree (see p. 42), shorten the central leader to leave about 9 in. (230 mm.) of growth made the previous summer. To keep the leader straight, cut back to a bud pointing in the opposite direction from that chosen when the tree was pruned the previous winter.

Shorten branch leaders to about 7 in. (180 mm.), cutting back to an outward-pointing bud.

In late July or early August in the south, but later in the north, prune by the modified Lorette system (see p. 64). In addition, shorten mature new growth on branch leaders, but not the central leader, to five or six leaves above the basal cluster of leaves.

Each winter, shorten the central leader by the method used at planting time. Restrict the growth of the tree when it has reached a height of about 7 ft (2.1 m.) by cutting back by half the previous summer's growth on the central leader in May.

Each subsequent May shorten the previous summer's growth to $\frac{1}{2}$ in. (12 mm.).

Branch leaders can also be shortened in May if they are crowding a neighbouring tree.

Shaping and pruning a bush apple tree

After planting a two-year-old bush apple tree (see p. 42), shorten branch leaders by about half to two-thirds so that the tips of the branches are roughly level. Prune to an outward-facing bud.

In the following summer a number of lateral shoots will have grown from the branches. In the next winter choose some of these to form more branches. These should all point upwards and outwards.

As a general rule, prune them back to an outward-facing bud. The branches of some varieties, however, have a slightly drooping habit, and these are sometimes best pruned back to an inward-facing bud.

TRAINING AND PRUNING A DWARF PYRAMID

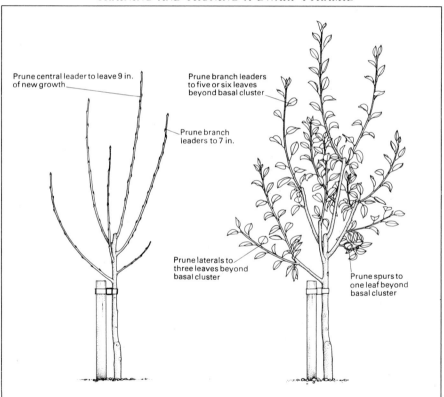

Prune central leader to leave 9 in. of new growth

Prune branch leaders to five or six leaves beyond basal cluster

Prune branch leaders to 7 in.

Prune laterals to three leaves beyond basal cluster

Prune spurs to one leaf beyond basal cluster

AFTER PLANTING Prune the central leader to a bud on the opposite side to that chosen during the previous winter, leaving 9 in. (230 mm.) of new growth. Shorten each of the branch leaders to 7 in. (180 mm.).

SUMMER PRUNING Shorten mature growth on branch leaders to five or six leaves above the basal cluster. At the same time, prune laterals in the same way as that advised for cordons on the previous page.

TRAINING AND PRUNING A BUSH APPLE TREE

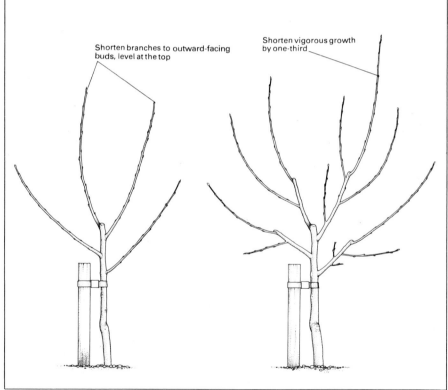

Shorten branches to outward-facing buds, level at the top

Shorten vigorous growth by one-third

AFTER PLANTING When pruning a bush tree, aim to achieve a goblet shape – open in the centre. Shorten branches by about a half to two-thirds to outward-facing buds so that their tips are level.

THE NEXT WINTER Choose well-placed shoots as new branches and prune these back to outward-facing buds. Shorten vigorous growth by one-third, the rest by half. The tips of branch leaders should be about level.

Shorten new growth by one-third if it is vigorous, and by half if it is weaker. After pruning, the tips of the branch leaders should be at least 18 in. (455 mm.) from their nearest neighbour and more or less level with each other.

Laterals not chosen to form main branches should be cut back to four buds from the base to form future fruiting spurs. Laterals crowding the centre can either be shortened or removed.

This pruning establishes the basic shape of the tree, although it may be necessary to carry out a little more formative pruning for the next two or three years.

Subsequent pruning of a bush tree depends on whether it is a spur-bearer or a tip-bearer.

A spur-bearer, such as 'Cox's Orange Pippin' or 'Grenadier', carries all of the fruit on spurs.

A tip-bearer, such as 'Worcester Pearmain' or 'Bramley's Seedling', bears fruit both on spurs and at the tips of shoots – the propor-tion differing with each variety.

Pruning a spur-forming bush apple tree

There are many methods of prun-ing an established spur-forming bush tree, but the easiest for the beginner is what is known as the regulated system. By this method the centre of the tree is kept open by light pruning each winter.

First, cut out dead and diseased wood and either remove shoots that cross or crowd each other, or shorten them so that they no longer cross.

Shorten in the same way any shoots competing with the branch leaders.

In the early years only, shorten branch leaders by cutting away a quarter of the previous season's growth if the leaders are vigorous, but by only one-third if they are weaker.

The regulated system encour-ages heavy cropping, but this in turn may cause the size of the fruits to become smaller as the tree gets older. If this happens, cut out some of the fruiting laterals and thin or remove some of the fruiting spurs during the winter.

Pruning a tip-bearing bush apple tree

Tip-bearing apple trees, such as 'Bramley's Seedling' and 'Worcester Pearmain', produce much of their fruit on the tips of shoots formed in the previous year, and some on spurs. The proportion

TRAINING AN ESTABLISHED SPUR-FORMING BUSH TREE

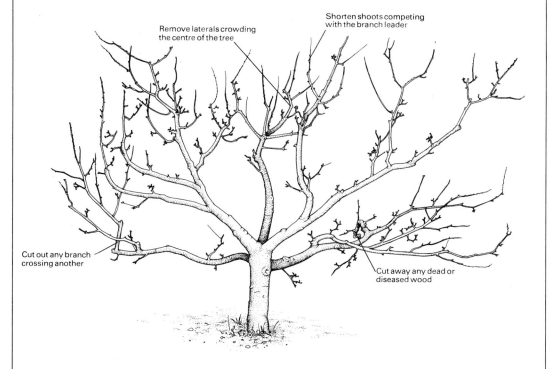

WINTER PRUNING Keep the centre of an established bush tree open, either by cutting out shoots that cross or crowd each other or by shortening them to one or two buds to form fruiting spurs. Remove dead and diseased wood and shorten shoots competing with branch leaders. In the first three or four years after planting, cut back vigorous branch leaders by a quarter of the new growth.

PRUNING A TIP-BEARING TREE

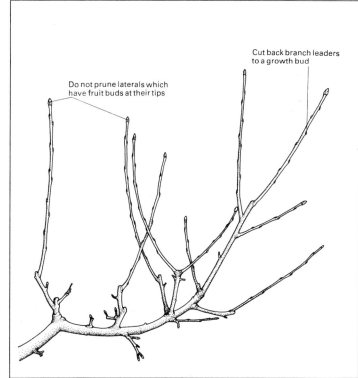

WINTER PRUNING Apple trees that produce much of their fruits on the tips of shoots generally require less pruning than varieties that fruit only on spurs. Cut back branch leaders to a growth bud. Leave unpruned laterals with fruit buds at their tips.

differs with each variety. Those that are mainly tip-bearing require comparatively little pruning. Prune others by the regulated system.

Every winter, cut back branch leaders to a growth bud to induce lower buds to break and form more tip-bearing shoots. Leave laterals with fruit buds at their tips unpruned, or much potential fruit will be lost.

Where, however, growth is crowded, thin by cutting out some of the previous summer's growth to three or four buds.

Restoring a neglected tree

An apple tree that has been neglected for some years can sometimes be brought back to fruitfulness by a systematic programme of pruning, fertilising and spraying against pests and diseases.

Neglected trees generally fall into two categories – those that are too vigorous and produce fruit well out of reach, and those that have weak growth and produce only small fruits.

With both kinds of tree, cut out dead and broken wood and treat cankers (p. 286). Protect all major pruning cuts with tree paint to prevent re-infection.

Pruning an over-vigorous tree

If a tree has grown too tall, cut it back gradually over three or four winters to reduce the shock of severe pruning.

This pruning method, known as 'de-horning', involves cutting out branches to open up the centre of the tree, and reducing the height of others to make fruit-picking easier.

First cut back high branches in the centre to the main trunk.

Prune back outer, tall-growing branches to a lower branch. Lightly thin out smaller laterals and young growth.

When pruning is complete, after three or four years, the main branches should be well spaced out, with the tips at least 2 ft (610 mm.) apart horizontally, and 3 ft (1 m.) apart vertically.

Space small laterals 18 in. (455 mm.) apart, and fruiting spurs 9–12 in. (230–305 mm.) apart.

Pruning a weak tree

If a tree has weak growth, the aim is to improve the size of the fruit and to encourage new growth.

In winter, reduce the length of long spur systems. This will cut out some fruit buds, so that those that remain will produce larger fruits.

Cut out the weakest spurs and leave, as far as possible, spurs carrying the plumpest fruit buds.

Thinning the crop

Bearing a heavy crop puts a strain upon a tree that might result in a harvest of poor-quality fruits.

Start to thin a heavy crop in early June, before the natural drop that occurs later in the month.

Use a pair of scissors to cut through the stalk, or hold the stalk between two fingers and press the apple away with the thumb.

First remove badly shaped fruits, then wait until after the natural drop before making a final thinning.

Heavy thinning is seldom necessary on cordons, espaliers and dwarf trees. On large bush trees, however, the fruit should be spaced out. Thin dessert varieties 4–6 in. (100–150 mm.) apart, and large cooking varieties 6–9 in. (150–230 mm.) apart.

All cooking and most dessert varieties can be reduced to singles, but some dessert varieties, such as

---

BRINGING A NEGLECTED TREE BACK TO FRUITFULNESS

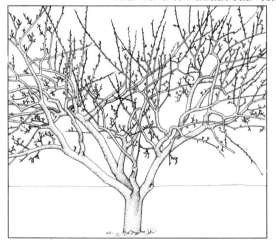

BEFORE PRUNING A neglected tree is worth saving if it has a sound, healthy framework of branches. During the dormant period cut out dead and broken wood, and branches crossing each other.

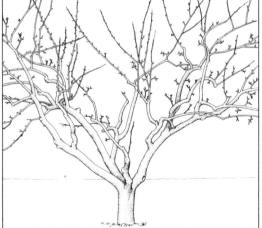

AFTER PRUNING The tree, after it has been pruned, should be open in the centre with branches spaced out. Protect pruning cuts with tree paint, treat for canker and spray against pests and diseases.

THINNING THE APPLE CROP

FIRST THINNING In early June start thinning a heavy crop by removing badly shaped fruits, either by cutting the stalk with a pair of scissors or by pressing off with your thumb. Before the end of the month there will be a natural fall of fruit – the 'June drop' – and the principal thinning of surplus fruits should be left until after this.

SECOND THINNING After the June drop, make a second thinning if the fruits are still overcrowded. The amount will depend on the type and variety of apple but, generally, thin dessert varieties to 4–6 in. (100–150 mm.) and cookers to 6–9 in. (150–230 mm.).

'Ellison's Orange', grow very large if left as singles.

At the second thinning remove blemished and mis-shapen fruits and also the large king, or crown, apple which grows in the centre.

However, the fruits on some varieties, such as 'Golden Delicious', grow on long stalks, and the king apple retains its shape. In this case it need not be cut out.

Pests and diseases APHIDS (p. 282), grubs of the CODLING MOTH (p. 283) and caterpillars of the WINTER MOTH (p. 285) are among the most troublesome pests, but apples may also be attacked by APPLE SAWFLY (p. 282), CAPSID BUGS (p. 282), FRUIT TREE RED

SPIDER MITES (p. 283), TORTRIX MOTHS (p. 285) and WOOLLY APHID (p. 285).

The chief diseases and disorders are APPLE CANKER (p. 286), BITTER PIT (p. 286), BROWN ROT (p. 286), FIRE BLIGHT (p. 288), HONEY FUNGUS (p. 288), MAGNESIUM DEFICIENCY (p. 288), PAPERY BARK (p. 289), POWDERY MILDEW (p. 289), SCAB (p. 290) and SILVER LEAF (p. 290).

Harvesting and storing

To test whether an apple is ready for picking, place the palm of your hand beneath it and give a simultaneous lift and gentle twist. It should part easily from the spur.

Eat early varieties as soon as

possible after picking, as they will not keep more than a few weeks.

Handle carefully later varieties intended for storing.

Keep the apples in a frost-proof garage or spare room where the temperature is stable but cool.

The apples can be wrapped in specially oiled paper, stacked on fibre trays or kept in clear, plastic bags with the tops unsealed or the sides perforated.

See also bottling (p. 309); chutneys (p. 335); drying (p. 343); freezing (p. 294); fruit cheeses and butters (p. 323); jams (p. 314); jellies (p. 320); pickles (p. 328); sauces, ketchups and relishes (p. 339) and wine-making (p. 357).

Spraying programme for apple trees

It is important to use the correct sprays at the right time to control the various pests and diseases that ruin fruits and affect the size of the apple crop. The timing is based mainly on the stage of bud development.

A systematic spraying programme will deal with the most common pests and diseases, while other, rarer, outbreaks can be dealt with if and when they should occur (see pp. 281–92).

Do not spray when the blossom is fully open, as this is when bees and other pollinating insects are most active.

Over-spraying can do more

harm than good by killing beneficial insects; so keep to the spraying programme and follow the manufacturer's instructions.

Every third year in the dormant period, between December and February, apply tar-oil wash to control aphids, scale insects and apple suckers.

If groups of minute, red eggs of the fruit tree red spider are numerous, spray with DNOC-petroleum wash in February.

The main spraying programme begins at bud-burst in March and continues, with only a break when the blossom is fully open – and pollination is taking place – until about the middle of July (see below).

WAYS OF STORING APPLES

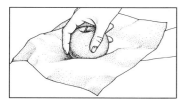

1 Late varieties of apples will keep for several months if wrapped individually in oiled paper, which is obtainable from horticultural suppliers or from garden centres.

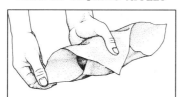

2 Place the apple in the centre of the wrap, fold two opposite corners over the apple and fold the remaining corners. Handle carefully so that the fruit is not bruised.

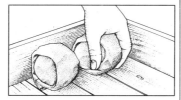

3 Place the fruit in a tray with the folds downwards. Store in a cellar, or a frost-proof garage or garden shed, with an even temperature – about 4°C (40°F) is ideal.

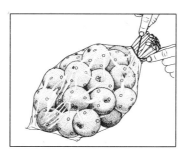

Apples may also be stored on fibre trays, which can be bought or are often given away by greengrocers. The advantage of this method is that trays can be stacked on top of each other, so saving space, and can be inspected easily. Store as for individually wrapped apples.

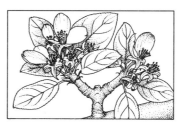

Apples can be stored in plastic bags, but first make a number of ventilation holes in them or else leave the tops loose.

SPRAYS TO USE IN SPRING AND SUMMER

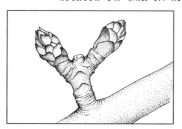

BUD-BURST TO GREEN CLUSTER (MARCH-APRIL) Control caterpillars and aphids with fenitrothion, scab and mildew with captan plus dinocap.

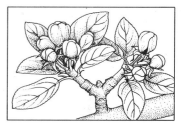

PINK BUD (LATE APRIL) Spray with captan plus dinocap, or with thiophanate-methyl or benomyl to control scab and mildew. Spray with dimethoate against sawfly.

PETAL-FALL (LATE MAY-JUNE) Repeat fungicide spray every 14 days. Apply dimethoate or HCH against sawfly and woolly aphids.

POST-BLOSSOM (MID-JUNE) Spray with fenitrothion or permethrin against codling-moth caterpillars. Repeat in mid-July. Repeat fungicides until the end of June.

APPLE VARIETIES

Varieties in the same pollination group (A, B or C) – for example, 'Discovery' and 'Merton Knave' – blossom at about the same time and will cross-pollinate satisfactorily.

Early apples

'George Cave' *(dessert)*
Pick: early August
Use: early to end August
Pollination group: A

Sweet, aromatic flavour; regular cropper; suitable for the north; spur-forming and tip-bearer.

'Grenadier' *(cooker)*
Pick: early August to early September
Use: August to September
Pollination group: B

Firm flesh; acid flavour; regular cropper; suitable for the north; spur-forming.

'Merton Knave'
(dessert)
Pick: end August
Use: August to September
Pollination group: B

Crisp, white flesh; sweet; good flavour; regular cropper; spur-forming.

'Discovery' *(dessert)*
Pick: mid to end August
Use: mid-August to September
Pollination group: B

Crisp, sweet and juicy; some scab resistance; spur-forming.

Mid-season apples

'James Grieve' *(dessert)*
Pick: early September
Use: September to October
Pollination group: B

Tender, juicy, excellent flavour; hardy and reliable but prone to canker; spur-forming.

'Worcester Pearmain' *(dessert)*
Pick: early September
Use: September to October
Pollination group: B

Crisp and sweet; hardy, reliable cropper; resistant to mildew; tip-bearer.

'Laxton's Fortune' *(dessert)*
Pick: mid-September
Use: late September to October
Pollination group: B

Sweet, rich flavour; some resistance to scab; hardy; tends to bear biennially; spur-forming.

'Ellison's Orange' *(dessert)*
Pick: mid-September
Use: September to October
Pollination group: C

Sweet, aromatic flavour; tends to bear biennially; suitable for the north; spur-forming.

'St Edmund's Russet' *(dessert)*
Pick: mid-September
Use: mid-September to October
Pollination group: A

Very fine flavour but fruits inclined to be small; compact growth; spur-forming.

'Lord Lambourne' *(dessert)*
Pick: late September
Use: October
Pollination group: A

Crisp, moderately sweet; some resistance to scab; hardy; spur-forming.

'Egremont Russet' *(dessert)*
Pick: late September
Use: October to December
Pollination group: A

Sweet, nutty; some resistance to scab; best russet for the garden; spur-forming; upright growth.

'Sunset' *(dessert)*
Pick: end September
Use: October to December
Pollination group: B

Crisp, excellent flavour; compact growth; attractive blossom; hardy; spur-forming.

'Kidd's Orange Red'
(dessert)
Pick: early October
Use: November to January
Pollination group: B

Crisp and sweet, with very good flavour; reliable cropper; spur-forming.

'Cox's Orange Pippin' *(dessert)*
Pick: early October
Use: November to December
Pollination group: B

Excellent flavour but needs good cultural treatment; susceptible to scab, mildew and canker; spur-forming.

Late apples

'Idared' *(dessert)*
Pick: mid to end October
Use: December to April
Pollination group: A

Crisp, juicy; recommended for its keeping qualities; regular cropper; hardy; spur-forming.

'Orlean's Reinette' *(dessert)*
Pick: late October
Use: November to February
Pollination group: C

Crisp, yellow flesh with sweet, rich flavour; may shrivel in store; spur-forming; vigorous growth.

'Spartan' *(dessert)*
Pick: early October
Use: November to January
Pollination group: B

Crisp flesh with juicy, wine-like flavour; prone to canker; hardy; spur-forming.

'Golden Delicious' *(dessert)*
Pick: mid-October
Use: November to January
Pollination group: C

Crisp, sweet and juicy; easy to grow; reliable cropper; hardy; spur-forming.

'Lane's Prince Albert' *(cooker)*
Pick: early October
Use: December to March
Pollination group: C

Crisp flesh; acid; regular cropper; compact habit; grows well in a garden; hardy; spur-forming.

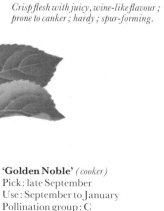

'Golden Noble' *(cooker)*
Pick: late September
Use: September to January
Pollination group: C

Tender, yellow flesh; acid; an excellent cooker; recommended for the garden; spur-forming.

'Howgate Wonder' *(cooker)*
Pick: early October
Use: October to January
Pollination group: C

Large, crisp fruits; regular cropper; suitable for the north; spur-forming.

'Bramley's Seedling' *(cooker)*
Pick: early October
Use: November to February
Pollination group: B (must be grown with two other varieties in group B)

Our best cooker, but suitable for the garden only when grafted on to dwarfing stock; spur-forming and tip-bearer.

71

Preparing & cooking apples

Both dessert and cooking apples can be used for cooking, although soft dessert apples – especially those that ripen in summer and early autumn – are best eaten fresh, as they tend to lose both texture and flavour when cooked. But firm dessert apples are excellent – on their own or with cooking apples – in pie fillings, in fruit and green salads, in cakes and in fruit fools.

Both sorts can be made into purées – sweet or savoury – to be used in sauces, soups, and fillings for baked and steamed puddings. Apple rings make attractive garnishes for salads, game or poultry in cider or Calvados sauces. Fried in butter, they go well with grilled bacon and pork. Goose, duck and pork can be stuffed with sharp apples; the acid in the apples offsets the fattiness of the meat.

Whole apples, cored but unpeeled, can be filled with a variety of stuffings. Cut in half, and peeled and roasted round a joint of pork for the last 20 minutes, they can be filled with red-currant or quince jelly and served instead of the usual apple sauce.

To ' prevent apples turning brown after peeling, either drop them into a bowl of cold water mixed with lemon juice, or brush apple slices and rings with fresh lemon juice.

DANISH APPLE CAKE

1½ lb. (750 g.) cooking apples
3 oz. (75 g.) caster sugar
4 oz. (125 g.) white breadcrumbs
2 oz. (50 g.) butter
½ pint (300 ml.) whipped cream
Red-currant jelly

COOKING TIME: 20 minutes

Peel, core and chop the apples. Cook with very little water for 10–15 minutes, or until tender, and rub through a coarse sieve to make a purée. Sweeten to taste with sugar. Mix the breadcrumbs with 2 oz. (50 g.) sugar and fry over a gentle heat in the butter until golden and crisp, stirring frequently to avoid burning.

Arrange the apple purée and breadcrumb mixture in a serving bowl, beginning with breadcrumbs and finishing with apple. Smooth the surface and cover with just over half the whipped cream. Pipe the remaining cream on top in a lattice pattern, and dot with jelly.
Serving Serve either warm or cold.
Variation Substitute brown breadcrumbs for the white, and flavour the apple purée with vanilla sugar. Layer the purée with the crisp, almost caramelised breadcrumbs and the jelly, finishing with breadcrumbs and smoothing the cream on top.
Photograph on pages 214–15.

APPLE SNOW

1 lb. (500 g.) cooking apples
3 tablespoons lemon juice
3 oz. (75 g.) sugar
2 oz. (50 g.) ratafia biscuits
White wine
2 egg whites
1½ teaspoons powdered gelatine
Garnish : grated chocolate

COOKING TIME: 10 minutes
CHILLING TIME: 1 hour

Peel and core the apples, cut them into chunks and put in a pan with the lemon juice and 2 tablespoons of water. Simmer gently until the apples have softened and thickened to a purée. Leave to cool, then drain off any excess liquid and sweeten to taste with sugar.

Put the ratafia biscuits in a glass dish, with enough white wine to cover and soak them.

Whisk the egg whites until stiff, then fold them thoroughly into the cooled apple purée. Dissolve the gelatine in 2 tablespoons of water and stir into the mixture. Spoon this over the ratafia biscuits and leave to chill and set in the refrigerator.
Serving Just before serving, decorate the top with a layer of dark, coarsely grated chocolate.

APPLES WITH MERINGUE

1½ lb. (750 g.) cooking or dessert apples
1–2 oz. (25–50 g.) melted butter
Sugar
1 teaspoon ground cinnamon
3 eggs, separated

COOKING TIME: 35 minutes
OVEN TEMPERATURE: 150°C (300°F) – gas mark 2

Peel, core and slice the apples; put in a pan with a little water and cook until tender. Rub the apples through a coarse sieve or blend lightly in a liquidiser; stir in just over half the butter, sweeten to taste with sugar and add the cinnamon.

Beat in the egg yolks, one by one, and spoon the mixture into an ovenproof serving dish brushed with the remaining melted butter. Whisk the egg whites stiff with sugar and spread evenly over the apples.

Set on the centre shelf of the oven, and bake until the meringue has set and is light brown.
Serving Serve lukewarm, with a jug of cream if liked.
Variation Fold a few roughly chopped hazel nuts into the apple purée, or flavour with ground cloves instead of cinnamon.

APPLE CRUMBLE

1½ lb. (750 g.) cooking apples
6 oz. (175 g.) demerara or caster sugar
2 teaspoons ground ginger
2 tablespoons orange juice
6 oz. (175 g.) flour
3 oz. (75 g.) butter

COOKING TIME: 40 minutes
OVEN TEMPERATURE: 190°C (375°F) – gas mark 5

Peel and core the apples and cut them into slices ½ in. (12 mm.) thick. Arrange the apples in a buttered ovenproof dish and sprinkle half the sugar and ground ginger over them. Add the orange juice.

Sift the flour into a bowl, cut up the butter and rub it into the flour until the mixture resembles breadcrumbs. Blend in the remaining sugar and ginger and lay the mixture over the apples, pressing it down well. Bake the apple crumble in the oven for 40 minutes or until the topping is crisp and golden-brown.
Serving Serve apple crumble either warm or cold, with a jug of fresh cream, whipped cream or vanilla ice cream.

BAKED APPLE DUMPLINGS

4 medium-size apples
4 oz. (100 g.) jam (black-currant,
* quince or ginger marmalade)*
4 oz. (100 g.) flour
1 teaspoon baking powder
2 oz. (50 g.) butter
1 tablespoon sugar
1 egg

COOKING TIME: 20–30 minutes
OVEN TEMPERATURE: 200°C (400°F)
– gas mark 6

Sift the flour and baking powder, rub in the butter until the mixture resembles breadcrumbs, then add the sugar and knead the dough with enough cold water to make it smooth and elastic. It should on no account be sticky. Roll the dough out on a floured surface and cut it into four circles around a saucer or plate, each large enough to envelop an apple.

Peel the apples and remove the cores. Set an apple in the centre of each pastry round, fill the cavities with jam or marmalade and draw the pastry up over the sides and top.

Seal the edges by pinching them and set the dumplings on a baking tray, seams down. Brush with the lightly beaten egg and sprinkle with a little extra sugar. Bake in the oven for 20–30 minutes.
Serving These dumplings are best served hot, either with custard or with a syrup or honey sauce.

MARZIPAN APPLES

4 large, even-size cooking apples
Juice of 1 lemon
2 oz. (50 g.) melted butter
4 oz. (100 g.) marzipan
1 dessertspoon brandy or rum
12 blanched, roughly chopped almonds
5 fl. oz. (150 ml.) whipped cream
12 cocktail cherries

COOKING TIME: 20–25 minutes
OVEN TEMPERATURE: 200°C (400°F)
– gas mark 6

Peel the apples and cut out the cores. Brush first with lemon juice, then with melted butter – inside and out – and arrange in a buttered, ovenproof dish. Knead the marzipan with the brandy until pliable, stuff most of it into the apple centres and lay the remainder over the top of the apples.

Sprinkle with the chopped almonds and bake in the centre of the oven for 20–25 minutes, or until the marzipan is golden.
Serving Serve the apples warm, with a separate bowl of whipped cream, blended with the chopped cocktail cherries.
Photograph on pages 136–7.

APPLE PUFFS

1 lb. (500 g.) cooking apples
2 oz. (50 g.) caster sugar
12 oz. (350 g.) prepared puff pastry
1 egg
Lump sugar

COOKING TIME: 30 minutes
OVEN TEMPERATURE: 220°C (425°F) –
gas mark 7; 190°C (375°F) – gas
mark 5

Roll out the prepared puff pastry to a rectangular shape, about 12 × 8 in. (305 × 200 mm.). Peel the apples, cut them into quarters and remove the cores, then cut each quarter into thin slices.

Lay the apples over half of the pastry, overlapping them slightly. Sprinkle with the sugar and brush all the edges with the lightly beaten egg. Fold the pastry over the apples and seal the edges by pinching them firmly.

Set the pastry on a moistened baking tray. Make four or five slits in the pastry for the steam to escape, brush all over with beaten egg, decorate with the pastry trimmings and sprinkle the top with a few crushed sugar lumps. Bake in a hot oven for 10 minutes; then reduce the temperature and continue baking for another 20 minutes, or until risen and golden.
Serving Leave the cake to cool. Serve it, cut crossways into slices, with a jug of cream.
Photograph on pages 214–15.

APPLE SALAD

4 dessert apples
Juice of 1 lemon
½ lb. (250 g.) kale
6 tablespoons oil
3 tablespoons lemon juice
1 teaspoon French mustard
Salt, pepper and caster sugar
Garnish : 2 hard-boiled eggs

Wash and dry the apples, cut them into quarters and remove the cores. Dice the apples, place them in a bowl and sprinkle with lemon juice to prevent discoloration.

Wash the kale and strip the leaves from the midribs, blanch in boiling water for 1 minute, then refresh at once under cold running water. Drain thoroughly before chopping it finely with a sharp knife. Blend the chopped kale into the diced apples.

Make a dressing from the oil, lemon juice and mustard, seasoning to taste with salt, pepper and sugar. Pour the dressing over the apples and kale, mixing it thoroughly.
Serving Garnish with slices or quarters of hard-boiled eggs and serve on its own as a winter salad, or with cold roast pork.
Photograph on page 216.

DUTCH APPLE PIE

1 lb. (500 g.) cooking apples
Grated rind of 1 lemon
1 oz. (25 g.) ground almonds
2 oz. (50 g.) currants
4 whole cloves
3 oz. (75 g.) demerara sugar
½ lb. (250 g.) shortcrust pastry
Glacé icing

COOKING TIME: 40 minutes
OVEN TEMPERATURE: 200°C (400°F) –
gas mark 6

Peel and core the apples, cut them in half and then into fairly thick slices. Sprinkle them with the grated lemon rind. Mix the ground almonds, currants and cloves with the sugar, blending thoroughly.

Arrange the apple slices in layers in a pie dish, and cover each layer with part of the sugar mixture. Finish with a layer of apples and pour 3 tablespoons of cold water over the top.

Cover the pie dish with the rolled-out pastry, brush the top with a little milk and decorate with cut-outs from the pastry trimmings. Bake in the oven for 35 minutes, remove, and brush the top with glacé icing made by mixing icing sugar and cold water to give a spreading consistency. Return the pie to the oven for 5 minutes, or until the glaze has set.
Serving This dish is best served lukewarm, accompanied with a jug of cream.
Photograph on pages 136–7.

Continued . . .

Apple recipes (continued)

BAKED APPLES

4 large cooking apples
2 oz. (50 g.) butter
2 oz. (50 g.) soft brown sugar
1 teaspoon ground cinnamon
Grated rind of ½ lemon
1 oz. (25 g.) seedless raisins
2 tablespoons caster sugar

COOKING TIME: 30–45 minutes
OVEN TEMPERATURE: 180°C (350°F)
– gas mark 4

Wash and dry the apples and remove the cores. Cut through the skin round the middle of each apple to prevent it bursting during cooking, and set in a buttered ovenproof dish.

Cream the butter and brown sugar until light and fluffy, beat in the cinnamon, lemon rind and raisins, and stuff this mixture into the apple cavities. Dissolve the caster sugar in 6 fl. oz. (175 ml.) of hot water and pour into the dish.

Bake in the oven for 30–45 minutes, or until tender but not mushy. Baste occasionally with the juices.
Serving Arrange the baked apples on individual plates, spoon over a little of the cooking juice and serve at once, perhaps with a jug of fresh cream or a bowl of caramel sauce.

APPLE CHARLOTTE

1½ lb. (750 g.) cooking apples
2 oz. (50 g.) butter
1 lemon
3–4 oz. (75–100 g.) sugar
2 oz. (50 g.) sultanas
Slices of buttered, white bread

COOKING TIME: 40 minutes
OVEN TEMPERATURE: 200°C (400°F)
– gas mark 6

Peel and core the apples and cut them into small chunks. Melt the butter in a pan, add the apples, grated rind and juice of the lemon and simmer over a gentle heat for about 10 minutes, until the mixture becomes pulpy. Stir often to prevent burning.

Remove from the heat and beat to a smooth purée. Add the sugar and sultanas.

Butter the base and sides of an ovenproof dish and line with thin slices of buttered bread. Spoon in the apple purée and then top completely with more buttered bread. Bake in the oven for about 30 minutes, or until the top is brown and crisp.
Serving Turn the apple charlotte out, upside-down, on to a plate. Sprinkle with sugar and serve at once, accompanied with a jug of cream or custard sauce.

Apples, Crab

Although grown mainly as ornamental trees, many species of wild apples, and their cultivated varieties, are valuable for making preserves and wine.

They need little pruning, and so are less trouble to grow than dessert and cooking apples. Some crabs are too large to warrant space in small gardens, but many are grown on dwarfing stock and one of these planted in a lawn will provide blossom in late spring and colourful fruits in September for making into jellies, pickles and wine.

Planning the crop

Crab apples will grow in any fertile, well-drained soil. A dressing of rotted manure or compost will help the tree to get started, but no feeding is needed subsequently.

Choose a variety on the most suitable stock to suit the site. Crab apples can be grown as standards (see p. 40) which have spreads of up to 25 ft (7.5 m.), so check the size of varieties offered by the nursery.

Crab apples are generally self-fertile, so only one tree need be grown to provide fruit. Even a dwarf tree will yield about 20 lb. (10 kg.) when established.

Varieties The following have medium-size or large fruits, which are borne in profusion and are suitable for making jelly or wine:

'Dartmouth': a broad tree; crimson fruits; flowers late May.

'John Downie': drooping habit; orange-scarlet, conical fruits; flowers late May. The finest variety for making jelly.

'Red Sentinal': medium-size tree; red fruits; flowers early May.

'Veitch's Scarlet': oval, scarlet fruits; deep pink blossom in May.

How to grow crab apples

Plant during autumn or winter (see p. 42), and secure the tree to a stake for a few years until well rooted. Keep the soil well watered if the weather is dry in the spring following planting.

Pruning No regular pruning is needed except to remove dead, diseased or crossing branches. Do this during the winter.

Pests and diseases As for cultivated apples (see p. 69).

Harvesting

The apples ripen in September and October. Although fruits of some varieties will stay on the tree all winter, they are better picked and used at once.

See also jellies (p. 320); pickles (p. 328) and wine-making (p. 357).

AT-A-GLANCE TIMETABLE FOR CRAB APPLES

PLANTING	PRUNING	HARVESTING
OCTOBER–FEBRUARY	Prune dead or crossed branches if necessary	SEPT–OCT

Apricots

The apricot, a native of China, is believed to have been first grown in this country by the gardener of Henry VIII in the 16th century.

Its name is partly derived from the Latin 'praecox', meaning 'precocious' – a reference to its early flowering.

This early blossoming, generally in February when there are few insects about to assist pollination, makes the apricot relatively difficult to grow in this country.

Fan-trained bush apricot.

North of the Trent, apricot trees cannot produce fruit except under glass, which is not practicable or economic in most gardens. In the south, however, they can be grown successfully as fan trees against a south-facing wall in a sheltered position.

In some well-sheltered gardens the apricot can be grown as a bush, but fan-training on the side of a house or a wall is more reliable.

Planning the crop

Apricot trees grow best in a well-drained, limy loam. If the soil is heavy, place a layer of rubble at the bottom of the hole before planting and spread lime at the rate of 2 oz. per square yard (60 g. per square metre) in late autumn or winter each year.

How many trees to grow Few gardens have space for more than one tree, since, when established, a fan on a wall 8 ft (2.5 m.) high will have a spread of at least 12 ft (3.6 m.) and a bush a spread of 10–15 ft (3–4.5 m.).

Varieties The following are in the order in which they ripen:

'Early Moorpark': ripens mid-July; small fruits with orange flesh; good flavour; tree vigorous and spreading.

'Hemskerke': ripens early August; fruits 2 in. (50 mm.) in diameter; sweet, rich flavour; tree large and spreading.

'Breda': ripens middle of August; orange flesh; sweet, rich flavour; vigorous grower.

'Moorpark'; ripens middle to late August; orange flesh; heavy cropper; the most popular variety.

How to grow apricots

Plant two or three-year-old trees, which might fruit when they are four years old. They can be planted (see p. 42) at any time from November to March.

To form the framework of the tree, train as for peaches (see p. 226) but prune in early spring as growth begins. Once the framework is established, prune fans in the same way as plums (see p. 237); train bush trees as for sour cherries (see p. 128).

Each winter, apply as a top-dressing 3 oz. of bonemeal and 1 oz. of sulphate of potash per square yard (90 g. and 30 g. per square metre) over the rooting area, which is equivalent to the spread of the tree. Every third year, omit the bonemeal but spread a 3 in. (75 mm.) layer of rotted compost or manure instead.

Apricots sometimes blossom as early as February, so protect the tree from frosts by covering with a double thickness of 1 in. (25 mm.) nylon mesh or plastic netting.

Because of this early blossoming, when few insects are about, it is worth using a camel-hair brush to transfer pollen from one flower to another and so ensure that the fruits set.

Never allow a tree to bear too heavy a crop. In April or May, thin the growing fruits to about 4 in. (100 mm.).

In June apply 1 oz. of sulphate of ammonia per square yard (30 g. per square metre). Water thoroughly during dry spells.

Pests and diseases Common pests of apricots are APHIDS (p. 282), CATERPILLARS (p. 282), GLASS-HOUSE RED SPIDER MITES (p. 283) and SCALE INSECTS (p. 285).

DIE-BACK (p. 287) is the most likely disease.

Harvesting and storing

Apricots soften some time before they are fully ripe. Leave them on the tree for as long as possible to ripen, which will be from late July to late August, according to variety. When ripe they are well coloured and part easily from the tree.

The fruits will keep for about a month if they are stored in a cool, well-ventilated place.

See also bottling (p. 309); chutneys (p. 335); drying (p. 343); freezing (p. 294); jams (p. 314); pickles (p. 328) and syrups and juices (p. 326). 🌿🌿

AT-A-GLANCE TIMETABLE FOR APRICOTS

PLANTING	PRUNING	HARVESTING
NOVEMBER–MARCH	MARCH	JULY–AUGUST

Recipes on next page

Preparing & cooking apricots

Fresh, just-ripe apricots are excellent as dessert fruits – on their own or with cream, ice cream or rich custard. Once the fruits become over-ripe, the flesh tends to be mealy and is then best used for purées and sauces.

To prepare and cook apricots, wipe them carefully with a damp cloth – they bruise easily – cut in half along the indentation on the skin, and twist the two halves apart. Remove the stone with the tip of a knife.

Poach apricots for about 8 minutes in a sugar syrup or wine. Flavour with – for example – vanilla, ginger, or a sweet liqueur.

Poached or puréed apricots also make good pie and flan fillings. Apricot sauce goes well with steamed sweet puddings and ice creams, and apricot glaze is traditionally used beneath almond paste on iced Christmas and wedding cakes.

Finely chopped fresh apricots, mixed with diced celery, butter, breadcrumbs and eggs, make a perfect stuffing for rich meats.

APRICOT MOUSSE

1 lb. (500 g.) apricots
3 oz. (75 g.) caster sugar
3 teaspoons powdered gelatine
Juice of ½ lemon
3 beaten egg whites
7 fl. oz. (200 ml.) whipped cream

COOKING TIME: 15 minutes
CHILLING TIME: 1–2 hours

Wash the apricots, cut in half and remove the stones. Put the apricots in a pan with enough cold water to cover, bring to the boil and cook over a low heat until quite soft. Rub the apricots through a coarse sieve and flavour the purée to taste with sugar. Set aside to cool.

Dissolve the gelatine in the strained lemon juice and a little water, and beat into the apricot purée. Continue whisking until the mixture begins to thicken, then fold in the stiffly beaten egg whites and two-thirds of the whipped cream. Spoon into a serving bowl and leave to chill in the refrigerator.

Serving Decorate the apricot mousse with piped whipped cream and serve with sponge fingers.

Variation Fold a little finely grated lemon rind into the whipped cream. Blend six blanched, coarsely chopped almonds into the apricot purée.

APRICOT SOUFFLÉ

1 lb. (500 g.) apricots
3 oz. (75 g.) caster sugar
2 oz. (50 g.) butter
2 oz. (50 g.) flour
½ pint (300 ml.) milk
Grated rind of ½ lemon
3 eggs

COOKING TIME: 1¼ hours
OVEN TEMPERATURE: 180°C (350°F) – gas mark 4

Prepare a 6 in. (150 mm.) straight-sided soufflé dish by buttering it thoroughly and sprinkling the base and sides with caster sugar. Wash and halve the apricots, and remove the stones.

Put the apricots in a pan with just enough cold water to prevent them burning. Simmer them over a gentle heat until soft and pulpy, stirring often. Rub the apricots through a sieve and measure the purée, which should be ½ pint (300 ml.) and fairly thick. If necessary, reduce it to a thick consistency by boiling it again, stirring all the time. Sweeten to taste with sugar and set aside to cool.

Make a thick white sauce from the butter, flour and milk, and stir in the finely grated lemon rind. Cool the sauce slightly, then fold in the apricot purée, blending it thoroughly. Separate the eggs and beat in the yolks, one at a time. Whisk the whites until stiff, fold them into the apricot mixture – using a metal spoon – and pour into the soufflé dish.

Set the soufflé dish in a pan of hot water and bake in the centre of a pre-heated oven for about 1 hour, or until firm.

Serving Remove from the oven, sprinkle the top of the soufflé lightly with sugar and serve at once.

APRICOT PASTY

10 oz. (275 g.) apricots
Sugar
6 oz. (175 g.) flour
1 teaspoon baking powder
3 oz. (75 g.) butter
1½ oz. (40 g.) caster sugar
2–3 tablespoons milk
1 beaten egg

COOKING TIME: 15–20 minutes
OVEN TEMPERATURE: 220°C (425°F) – gas mark 7

Cook the apricots in the minimum of water until tender, then drain and rub through a coarse sieve. If necessary, heat the purée until fairly thick; sweeten to taste with sugar.

Sift the flour and baking powder, rub in the butter until the mixture resembles breadcrumbs, add the sugar and gather the dough with milk until it is smooth and comes away cleanly from the bowl. Knead lightly and roll out thinly on a floured board.

Set on a greased baking tray and spread the apricot purée down the centre, leaving 2 in. (50 mm.) clear on each side. Fold over the short pastry ends, and slit the pastry on either side of the filling, at an angle of 45 degrees, and at 1 in. (25 mm.) intervals. Fold these strips over the filling so that they meet in the middle; brush with beaten egg and sprinkle with a little granulated sugar and almond nibs.

Bake in the centre of a pre-heated oven for 15 minutes, or until golden-brown.

MAKING THE PASTY

1 *When placing the dough leave 2 in. (50 mm.) uncovered on each of the longer sides.*

2 *Fold the ends over. Make angled slits in the dough on each side of the filling.*

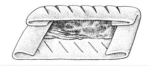

3 *Fold the sides of the pasty to the centre so that they meet over the filling.*

4 *Brush the dough with beaten egg. Sprinkle with sugar and almond nibs.*

APRICOT COMPÔTE

1 lb. (500 g.) apricots
3 oz. (75 g.) sugar
2 tablespoons Kirsch
Garnish : apricot kernels

COOKING TIME: 15 minutes

Wash the apricots, cut them in half and remove the stones. Put the sugar in a pan with ½ pint (300 ml.) cold water and bring to the boil, stirring until the sugar has dissolved. Add the apricots to this syrup, bring back to the boil, then simmer gently for about 10 minutes, or until the apricots are tender but not pulpy.

Lift the apricots into a serving dish, increase the heat and continue cooking the syrup until it has reduced and thickened. Stir the Kirsch into the syrup and pour the liquid over the apricots. Set aside to cool.
Serving While the compôte is cooling, crack about a dozen of the apricot stones, extract the kernels and blanch them for 5 minutes in boiling water. Before serving, decorate the compôte with the split kernels, or with blanched split almonds. A jug of cream is an optional extra.
Photograph on pages 214–15.

APRICOT FLAN

¾ lb. (375 g.) ripe apricots
3 oz. (75 g.) sugar
Rind and juice of ½ lemon
1 teaspoon powdered gelatine
7–8 in. (180–200 mm.) flan case
5 fl. oz. (150 ml.) whipped cream

COOKING TIME: 15 minutes
CHILLING TIME: 3 hours

Wash and wipe the apricots, cut in half and remove the stones. Put the sugar with ½ pint (300 ml.) cold water in a pan and bring to the boil over a low heat, stirring until the sugar has dissolved. Add the apricots, lemon juice and the thinly peeled rind, and cook over a gentle heat for about 10 minutes. Lift out the apricots and leave to cool.

Strain the syrup, return to a clean pan and reduce by about half through rapid boiling; cool slightly, then add the gelatine dissolved in a little water.

Spoon a little of the syrup into the flan case and let it set; arrange the apricot halves over the syrup, rounded sides up, pour over the remaining syrup and leave to set and chill in the refrigerator.
Serving Decorate the flan with piped cream, or serve the cream separately in a bowl.
Variation Set the apricots, hollow sides up, on the syrup and put a whole blanched almond in each half. Pipe with cream.
Photograph on pages 142–3.

Artichokes, Globe

History has not recorded the name of the adventurous gourmet who discovered that the base of the flower scales of the thistle-like globe artichoke – and also the base of the flowers themselves – could be eaten. But, whoever it was, he put into his debt generations of gourmets to come. The delicate yet unmistakable taste makes artichokes one of the most prized of garden vegetables.

They are, moreover, an asset in the ornamental garden, for their silvery-grey leaves provide a perfect foil for summer flowers. For this reason, they are often to be found in herbaceous borders.

Planning the crop

Globe artichokes need an open sunny position where the soil is rich and well drained.

Except in the south of England, however, the plant will not always survive the winter and it is best to grow it in a sheltered, but sunny, part of the garden.

In the winter before planting, dig in some well-rotted compost, manure or similar organic substance (see p. 17) and leave the ground rough until the spring. Then rake the soil to a fine tilth and spread on 3 oz. of general fertiliser per square yard (90 g. per square metre).

How many to grow Each mature artichoke can be expected to yield up to six heads, so the number grown will depend partly on its popularity in the household, partly on the space available. Place them 3 ft (1 m.) apart in each direction.

Varieties The three or four varieties available differ mainly in their degree of hardiness:
‘Grand Camus de Bretagne’: large heads; full flavour; most suitable for southern counties.
‘Green Globe’: suitable only for southern counties; less flavour than the French varieties.
‘Gros Vert de Laon’: perhaps the best-flavoured artichoke; suitable only for southern counties.
‘Purple Globe’: a hardier variety, suitable for the north; similar quality to ‘Green Globe’.

How to grow globe artichokes

Artichokes will continue to grow and flower for up to six years, but the heads tend to be smaller, and sometimes tougher, after the third and fourth years. Try, therefore, to

HARVESTING THE HEADS

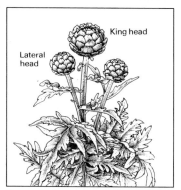

Remove the largest bud, or king head, first, then the smaller heads on lateral shoots.

replace a few each year so that you always have new plants maturing and some old ones dying down.

To start a crop, buy young plants or suckers in April, and plant them in well-manured soil to the same depth as they were in the nursery bed or pot. In May, apply a liberal mulch of manure or compost around the plants.

The new plants will provide some heads by August or September, but it is better to encourage growth in the first year by removing the buds as soon as they appear. Your patience will be rewarded by larger heads in subsequent seasons.

In their second and third years, allow each plant to develop only four to six stems. Leave the flower on the main stem – called the king head – and several others at the end of lateral shoots. Nip off any extra buds on side-shoots to ensure a good crop.

In November, cut the main stems down almost to ground level, draw the surrounding soil around them and cover the soil with a layer of straw. Enclose this with wire netting and cover with a sheet of polythene.

In dry periods, especially when the plants are growing strongly, make sure that they are well watered.

Raising new plants In April or November, select strong shoots about 9 in. (230 mm.) high on plants that are at least three years old. Cut vertically alongside each shoot, using a spade or sharp knife and retaining part of the rootstock beneath it.

Discard the rest of the plant after removing the shoots.

Shoots removed in April can be planted out immediately in their permanent positions.

If you remove shoots in November, pot them in potting compost and keep in a cold frame during the winter. The following spring, plant them out in their permanent positions.

Pests and diseases Artichokes are generally free from pests, although in damp conditions SLUGS AND

RAISING NEW PLANTS FROM OLD STOCK

DIVIDING Use a spade or a sharp knife to remove strong shoots in April or November, each with a piece of rootstock attached.

TRANSPLANTING Plant the shoots 3 ft (1 m.) apart in each direction. If removed in November, overwinter them in a cold frame.

SNAILS (p. 285) may sometimes be a problem.

The major disease is PETAL BLIGHT (p. 289).

Harvesting and preserving

Mature plants should produce ripe heads in June or July. Pick the heads, starting with the king head, when they are still green and tightly wrapped.

The flower heads on the lateral shoots are best picked when about the size of a hen's egg.

Use secateurs to cut off the heads, then cut back each stem to about half its original length. See also freezing (p. 294).

PRODUCING CHARDS

Before finally discarding a three or four-year-old plant, its blanched shoots, called chards, can be eaten. After harvesting the heads, cut back the foliage and allow fresh shoots to grow to a height of 2 ft (610 mm.).

Blanch by enclosing in a collar of black polythene or brown paper. When blanched, eat raw or cooked, like celery.

COVERING FOR WINTER

Protect with straw, enclosing this with netting and covering with plastic.

AT-A-GLANCE TIMETABLE FOR GLOBE ARTICHOKES

PLANTING	MULCHING	DISBUDDING (1st YEAR)	HARVESTING	CUTTING BACK	DIVIDING
APRIL	MAY	AUGUST–SEPTEMBER	JUNE–JULY	NOVEMBER	NOVEMBER or APRIL
FIRST YEAR OF PLANTING			SECOND AND THIRD YEARS		

Preparing & cooking globe artichokes

The artichoke head, at the top of a tough stalk, is composed of stiff scales, or bracts, closely compressed round a shallow base known as the heart or fond. A thick cluster of silky hairs – the choke – is embedded in the fond. The edible parts of a globe artichoke are the fleshy, half-moon shape at the base of each scale, and the fond.

Preparation To prepare an artichoke for cooking, trim the stalk level with the base of the head, cut off any damaged outer scales and slice off the top of the head. Trim the points of the remaining scales with scissors; wash well and stand them upside-down to drain.

Rub all cut surfaces with lemon to prevent discoloration.

The choke can be removed before or after cooking. Spread the outer scales apart and pull out the small inner scales until the choke is revealed. With a teaspoon, scrape off the hairs adhering to the fond. If the fond only is to be used, remove all the outer scales before discarding the choke, and rub the fond with lemon.

Cooking Fill a large pan with water to which salt and 2 tablespoons of lemon juice have been added. Bring to the boil; add the artichokes and boil, uncovered, for 40–50 minutes or until tender – when a scale can easily be pulled away.

Drain thoroughly, upside-down.

Serving Serve boiled artichokes as a first course, either hot with melted butter or Hollandaise sauce, or cold with a French dressing – using vinegar or lemon juice – mayonnaise or tartare sauce.

PREPARING FOR COOKING

Hairy choke

Fleshy part of scale

Fond

Parts of an artichoke, showing how the flower scales are joined to the fond at the base.

Use sharp scissors to trim the points off the flower scales.

Remove the hairy choke from the fond by scraping with a teaspoon.

ARTICHOKES IN GARLIC DRESSING

6 small globe artichokes
1 lemon
6 tablespoons olive oil
6 tablespoons lemon juice
2 garlic cloves, crushed
1 teaspoon fresh chopped marjoram
Salt and pepper

COOKING TIME: 25 minutes

For this appetiser, use small, immature artichokes. Trim the stalks level, slice off the undeveloped tops and cut each artichoke into four. Remove the small chokes and drop the quarters into a bowl of cold water to which the juice of 1 lemon has been added.

Blend the oil, lemon juice, garlic and marjoram, and season with salt and pepper. Add the drained artichoke quarters, turning them in the marinade until evenly coated. Transfer to a heavy-based pan, cover with a tight-fitting lid and cook over gentle heat for 25 minutes.

Shake the pan carefully from time to time and, if necessary, add a little more oil and lemon juice. Remove the lid for the last 5 minutes.

Serving Arrange four artichoke quarters on each serving plate and spoon over the warm marinade. Serve with toast fingers and provide finger bowls. Provide a plate for the discarded leaves.

ARTICHOKES VINAIGRETTE

4 globe artichokes
1 tablespoon lemon juice
Salt
French dressing

COOKING TIME: 40–45 minutes

Wash the artichokes thoroughly, trim the stalks level with the base and peel off any ragged scales. Cut off the top ½ in. (12 mm.) of each artichoke, and snip off the points of the other scales with scissors. Brush the cut surfaces with lemon juice.

Bring a large pan of lightly salted water to the boil, then add the artichokes. Cover and cook for 40–45 minutes, depending on size, until a scale can easily be pulled off. Drain the artichokes upside-down.

Pull the scales apart and remove the small inner scales until the central choke of fine hairy filaments is reached; remove this with a teaspoon.

Serving Arrange the cooled artichokes on plates and pour the dressing into a sauceboat; set a finger bowl at each plate.

The French dressing is poured into and round the artichoke; and as each scale is pulled off, the fleshy base is dipped into the dressing and eaten.

The heart, or fond, which is the tastiest part of the artichoke, is eaten with a knife and fork.

Variation Serve the artichokes hot with melted butter or a Hollandaise sauce.

ARTICHOKES WITH CURRY MAYONNAISE

4 globe artichokes
Salt
2 tablespoons lemon juice
5 fl. oz. (150 ml.) mayonnaise
2 teaspoons curry powder
8 oz. (250 g.) peeled shrimps
Garnish: fresh dill

COOKING TIME: 40–45 minutes

Prepare and cook the artichokes as for Artichokes vinaigrette. Remove all the scales and chokes until only the fonds or hearts are left. Leave to cool.

Stir lemon juice and the curry powder into the mayonnaise, and pipe this round the edges of the artichoke fonds. Arrange the shrimps inside the mayonnaise.

Serving Arrange the artichoke fonds on individual plates, garnish with small sprigs of dill and serve with fingers of hot buttered toast.

Variations Top the artichoke fonds with raw sliced mushrooms, marinated in a garlic dressing, or offer a bowl of tartare sauce. Alternatively, cover the fonds with chopped hard-boiled eggs mixed with drained, shredded tuna fish, and spoon over a dressing made from hard-boiled egg yolks, crushed garlic, oil, lemon juice, salt, pepper and finely chopped fresh dill.

Photograph on page 144.

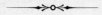

Continued . . .

Globe artichoke recipes (continued)

COLD STUFFED ARTICHOKES

4 artichokes
1 tablespoon lemon juice
Salt and pepper
6 oz. (175 g.) cooked lobster meat
3 oz. (75 g.) cooked asparagus tips
(optional)
6 tablespoons olive oil
2 tablespoons white wine vinegar
1 dessertspoon finely chopped tarragon
Paprika

COOKING TIME: 40–45 minutes
CHILLING TIME: 30 minutes

Prepare and cook the artichokes as described under Artichokes vinaigrette. Leave them upside-down to drain and cool, then carefully pull the scales apart and remove the complete choke. Pull out some of the smaller, inner scales to make a fairly large cavity.

While the artichokes are cooling, dice the lobster meat and cut the cooked and cooled asparagus tips, if used, into 1 in. (25 mm.) pieces. Blend the lobster and asparagus; leave them to marinate and chill in a dressing made from the olive oil, vinegar and tarragon, seasoned to taste with salt and pepper. Do not chill the artichokes, as they lose flavour when exposed to extreme cold.
Serving Stuff the artichokes with the lobster and asparagus mixture, spoon a little of the dressing over them, and dust the tops lightly with paprika. Serve as a first course.

ARTICHOKE QUICHE

6–8 globe artichokes
6 oz. (175 g.) shortcrust pastry
8 oz. (250 g.) finely chopped onions
$\frac{1}{4}$ teaspoon chopped dill or chervil
1 tablespoon sherry
2 egg yolks
$\frac{1}{2}$ pint (300 ml.) thick white sauce
Salt and pepper

COOKING TIME: 30–40 minutes
OVEN TEMPERATURE: 200°C (400°F) – gas mark 6

Prepare and cook the artichokes as for Artichokes vinaigrette; drain and cool. Remove and discard all scales and the chokes, and cut the fonds into $\frac{1}{2}$ in. (12 mm.) slices.

Meanwhile, make up the pastry from 6 oz. (175 g.) flour and use it to line a 7–8 in. (180–200 mm.) flan ring set on a baking sheet. Arrange the sliced artichokes and onions over the base, and sprinkle with dill or chervil. Beat the sherry and egg yolks into the cooled white sauce, season to taste with salt and pepper, and spoon over the flan filling. Bake in the oven for about 30 minutes, covering the flan with buttered greaseproof paper if the top browns too quickly.
Serving Serve hot as a first course, garnished with small sprigs of dill or chervil. Or serve with an accompanying green salad for a light luncheon dish.
Variation Use 8 oz. (250 g.) pastry and bake as a covered pie, brushed with egg and milk.

Artichokes, Jerusalem

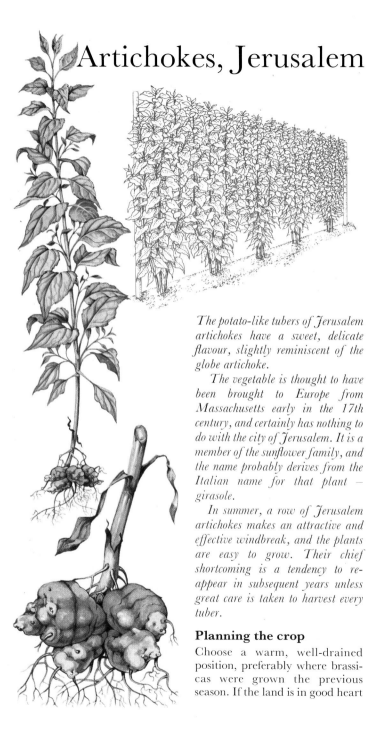

The potato-like tubers of Jerusalem artichokes have a sweet, delicate flavour, slightly reminiscent of the globe artichoke.

The vegetable is thought to have been brought to Europe from Massachusetts early in the 17th century, and certainly has nothing to do with the city of Jerusalem. It is a member of the sunflower family, and the name probably derives from the Italian name for that plant – girasole.

In summer, a row of Jerusalem artichokes makes an attractive and effective windbreak, and the plants are easy to grow. Their chief shortcoming is a tendency to re-appear in subsequent years unless great care is taken to harvest every tuber.

Planning the crop

Choose a warm, well-drained position, preferably where brassicas were grown the previous season. If the land is in good heart it is unnecessary to add manure; otherwise, to produce large tubers enrich the soil with well-rotted manure or compost in the autumn or winter before planting.

How many to grow Each seed tuber should yield 3 lb. (1.5 kg.) – that is, 42 lb. (19 kg.) per 20 ft (6 m.) row.

Varieties The small knobbly tubers that used to be grown have been superseded by two improved varieties. 'Fuseau' and 'New White' are both smooth-skinned and have more flavour than earlier kinds.

How to grow Jerusalem artichokes

In February or March, use a draw hoe to make a furrow 5 in. (130 mm.) deep and plant the tubers 18 in. (455 mm.) apart in the bottom of the furrow.

Alternatively, plant the tubers individually at this depth with a trowel.

Allow 3 ft (1 m.) between rows.

When you cover the tubers, leave a ridge about 2 in. (50 mm.) high over their tops. Spread a dressing of general fertiliser along this at 2 oz. per square yard (60 g. per square metre) and hoe it into the surface.

When the stalks of the plants are 6 in. (150 mm.) high, draw up another 1 in. (25 mm.) of soil. Repeat this every two weeks or so until there is a 6 in. ridge.

At this stage, drive a 6 ft (1.8 m.) stake or cane 2 ft (610 mm.) into the ground at each end of the row. Run wires between the stakes and tie the plants with soft string as they grow, so that wind will not rock them and expose the tubers.

STAGES IN RIDGING AND STAKING

FIRST RIDGING Use a hoe to start forming a shallow ridge along the row of plants when they are about 6 in. (150 mm.) high. Remove weeds at the same time.

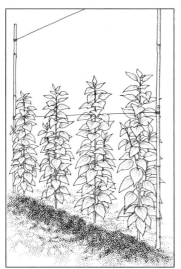

FOLLOW-UP RIDGING Continue drawing soil round the plants every two weeks or so until the ridge is about 6 in. (150 mm.) high.

SUPPORTING THE PLANTS Insert a cane or stake at each end of the row. Secure two wires between, and tie the plants to these.

Pests and diseases Jerusalem artichokes may be attacked by CUTWORMS (p. 283), ROOT APHIDS (p. 285) and SWIFT MOTH (p. 285).

Their principal ailment is SCLEROTINIA DISEASE (p. 290).

Harvesting and storing

The tubers will be ready for lifting by the end of October, when the top growth begins to turn brown. Cut the stems back to within 12 in. (305 mm.) of the ground.

The tubers may be left in the ground until needed during the winter, the cut stems serving as a guide to their position. When harvesting, make sure to dig up even the smallest tubers to prevent re-growth.

AT-A-GLANCE TIMETABLE FOR JERUSALEM ARTICHOKES

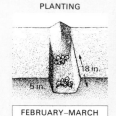
PLANTING
18 in.
5 in.
FEBRUARY–MARCH

RIDGING
6 in.
When plants reach 6 in. start earthing up

HARVESTING
FROM OCTOBER

Preparing & cooking Jerusalem artichokes

Prepare and cook Jerusalem artichokes in the same way as potatoes; but, as the creamy-white flesh discolours quickly, add lemon juice to the water in which they are rinsed and cooked.

Scrub the tubers under running cold water and peel thinly with a stainless-steel knife or potato peeler.

Cook in boiling salted water, with lemon juice, for 20–30 minutes, depending on size. Drain, and serve tossed in melted butter.

Par-boiled Jerusalem artichokes may also be sautéed in butter or cut into slices and deep-fried in hot oil. They can be roasted round a joint for 30 minutes, used for soups and stews, and served with various-flavoured sauces.

ARTICHOKES WITH ONIONS

1 lb. (500 g.) Jerusalem artichokes
4 tablespoons white wine vinegar
½ pint (300 ml.) milk
Beurre manié: 1 oz. (25 g.) butter, 1 oz. (25 g.) flour
Salt and pepper
Garnish: two thinly sliced onions

COOKING TIME: 15–20 minutes

Scrub the artichokes with a brush, put in a pan and cover with cold water and vinegar. Bring to the boil and cook for 5 minutes. Drain and peel the artichokes and cut into uniform chunks. Return to the pan, add the milk and bring to the boil over a gentle heat; simmer for 10–15 minutes, until tender.

Knead the butter and flour for the beurre manié and add to the milk in small knobs, whisking all the time until the milk thickens. Season to taste with salt and pepper.
Serving Pour into a serving dish and garnish with the onions, fried in butter.

SAUTÉ ARTICHOKES

1 lb. (500 g.) Jerusalem artichokes
1 tablespoon lemon juice
2 oz. (50 g.) butter
Salt and pepper
Tabasco sauce
2 tablespoons chopped parsley

COOKING TIME: 20 minutes

Peel or scrape the artichokes, dropping them into a bowl of cold water and lemon juice. Cut them into quarters or even slices, and put in a pan of boiling, lightly salted water. Cover, cook gently for 10 minutes, then drain.

Melt the butter in a pan, add the artichokes, and sauté gently until well-coated with the butter and lightly browned. Season with salt, pepper and a few drops of tabasco. Stir in the parsley.
Serving Spoon into a dish and serve with roast meat or poultry.

CREAMED ARTICHOKE SOUP

1 lb. (500 g.) Jerusalem artichokes
Juice of 1 lemon
1 small sliced onion
2 sticks of chopped celery
1 oz. (25 g.) butter
6 parsley stalks
2 pints (1 l.) chicken stock
Salt and pepper
½ pint (300 ml.) milk (optional)
5 fl. oz. (150 ml.) double cream
Garnish: whipped cream and chopped parsley

COOKING TIME: 35–40 minutes

Peel the artichokes and drop them into a bowl of cold water with the lemon juice to prevent them going brown. Cut into ½ in. (12 mm.) chunks, drain and wipe dry.

Sauté the onion, celery and artichokes in the butter until soft, but without becoming coloured. Add the parsley and stock, and bring to the boil. Season with salt and pepper; cover and simmer gently until the vegetables are tender, which will take about 20 minutes. Remove the parsley, rub the soup through a sieve or blend in a liquidiser.

Re-heat the soup, correcting the seasoning and adding milk to give the required consistency. Stir in the cream and heat the soup through without boiling.
Serving Serve in soup bowls, topped with a little whipped cream and chopped parsley.

Asparagus

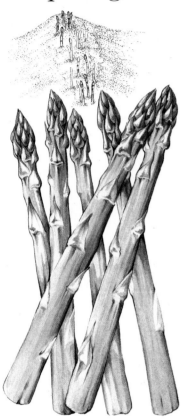

Asparagus, prized for the delicate flavour of its young shoots, is a luxury if you have to buy it. In some respects it is even a luxury to grow at home, because it has a cropping season of only six weeks and, being a perennial, it takes up space all the year round.

However, gardeners who relish its flavour may find this acceptable.

Planning the crop

Asparagus does best in a fairly open position that is sheltered from wind. It needs a rich, well-drained soil, so the initial preparation of the bed is vital to success for years to come.

In the autumn before planting, dig a bed 4 ft (1.2 m.) wide to accommodate two rows. Dig well-rotted manure or compost into the topsoil at the rate of a bucketful to the square yard. Lighten heavy soil by adding sharp, gritty sand.

If the soil tends to become sticky or waterlogged, make a raised bed enclosed by railway sleepers, stones or breeze blocks.

The following spring, rake the bed level and work in 4 oz. of general fertiliser per square yard (120 g. per square metre).

How much to grow Six mature plants – those more than four years old – should yield one average helping of spears a week during the six-week season.

Varieties The main distinction is between purple-tinged and white-tinged types.

'Connovers Colossal': purple-tinged; plump shoots; very tender tips.

'Martha Washington' and 'Mary Washington': purple-tinged; both are outstanding for size and quality.

'Purple Argenteuil': purple-tinged; large tips of fine texture.

'White Cap': white-tinged; ready slightly earlier than purple-tinged varieties.

How to grow asparagus

Asparagus can be grown from seed (see facing page); but for quicker results, buy plants that are one or two years old. Do not try to transplant roots older than this.

One-year-old crowns are best, but they will not yield spears large enough to eat for two years.

Plant in early April in the south, and about two weeks later in the north of England and in Scotland.

Use a spade to make trenches 8 in. (200 mm.) deep, 3 ft (1 m.) apart, and wide enough to take the plants' roots when spread out flat. Replace about 2 in. (50 mm.) of soil to give a domed base.

Remove the plants from their packing and set them 18 in. (455 mm.) apart in the trenches. Spread out their roots, and cover as quickly as possible with soil.

Cover the trenches with 3 in. (75 mm.) of soil, and firm the surface. Allow the trenches to fill up gradually by drawing soil from the sides as hoeing proceeds during the summer. By October the bed should be level.

For the first two years, lightly hoe to keep down weeds. Water thoroughly in dry spells. In late October or early November, when the stems turn yellow, cut down the ferns to within 1 in. (25 mm.) of the soil and mulch with well-rotted manure or compost.

Each spring, dress the rows with a general fertiliser at the rate of 2 oz. per square yard (60 g. per square metre). Follow this routine of organic manuring in the autumn, and fertiliser application in the spring.

In the third spring after planting, decide whether to grow in ridges – a method that will produce longer, blanched spears – or on the flat, where the stems will be shorter but may be cut earlier.

To make ridges, draw up the soil to a height of 5 in. (130 mm.) just

PLANTING ASPARAGUS CROWNS

1 Place the crowns at 18 in. (455 mm.) intervals on the rounded base of the trench. To prevent drying out, place sacking over them until you are ready to cover with soil.
2 Cover the roots with 3 in. (75 mm.) of fine
soil, firming this afterwards. Leave the remaining soil at the sides of the trench.
3 Fill the trench gradually while the plants are growing during the summer, drawing in the remaining soil while hoeing.

AT-A-GLANCE TIMETABLE FOR ASPARAGUS

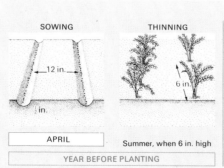

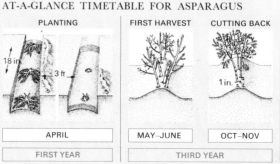
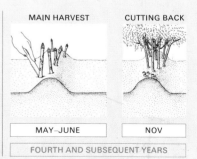

SOWING	THINNING	PLANTING	FIRST HARVEST	CUTTING BACK	MAIN HARVEST	CUTTING BACK
APRIL	Summer, when 6 in. high	APRIL	MAY–JUNE	OCT–NOV	MAY–JUNE	NOV
YEAR BEFORE PLANTING		FIRST YEAR	THIRD YEAR		FOURTH AND SUBSEQUENT YEARS	

CUTTING THE FERNS

In late October or November, cut down the yellowing foliage to 1–2 in. (25–50 mm.).

before the crop is ready to be cut. Level out the ridge in autumn.

On the flat, leave the soil as it is.

When the bed is established, cut back the foliage to 6 in. (150 mm.) from the ground when it changes colour each autumn, and burn it.

Raising new plants

Asparagus can be raised from seed instead of buying plants, but it will take an extra year to produce spears for cutting.

In April, soak the seeds overnight in lukewarm water and sow in drills ½ in. (12 mm.) deep and 12 in. (305 mm.) apart. When the seedlings are about 6 in. (150 mm.) high, thin out until they are 6 in. apart.

Water them generously during the summer and plant out in their permanent bed during the following April.

Pests and diseases The pests most likely to occur are ASPARAGUS BEETLE (p. 282), CUTWORMS (p. 283), SLUGS AND SNAILS (p. 285).

The principal diseases and disorders of asparagus are FROST DAMAGE (p. 288) and VIOLET ROOT ROT (p. 291).

Harvesting and storing

Do not harvest shoots grown from one-year-old crowns during the first two seasons. In the third year take only one or two spears from each plant.

In subsequent years, harvest for only six weeks, allowing subsequent shoots to grow into ferns. If the plants are encouraged to grow in this way, the bed should continue to produce good crops for up to 20 years.

Harvest the ripe spears when their tips are about 4 in. (100 mm.) above the soil. Use either a special asparagus cutter or a serrated knife, cutting the base of the spear up to 4 in. (100 mm.) below soil level.

If not used immediately, stand the spears in iced water for a few hours, then wrap and store in the refrigerator until they are needed. In this way it is possible to cut a number of spears daily, saving them until you have enough for a meal. This is better than allowing them to become too large.

See also freezing (p. 294). 🖎🖎

HARVESTING

Use a sharp, serrated knife to cut the spears up to 4 in. (100 mm.) below soil level.

Preparing & cooking asparagus

Few vegetables can compare in flavour with tender, home-grown asparagus. In their prime the small heads, or spears, should be tightly compressed; the stems, whether green or white, moist and glistening. The slightest trace of brown on the cut edge indicates that the asparagus is past its best, and is beginning to lose its succulence.

BOILED ASPARAGUS

Wash the asparagus carefully so as not to damage the tender tips. Trim the woody parts from the bases of the stems. Green stems need only washing, but white stems have a bitter and hard skin which must be peeled off, always from the tip downwards.

Trim the spears so that they are of uniform length, and tie in small bundles with fine string or cotton tape. Stand the bundles upright in a pan of boiling salted water for 10–12 minutes, depending on the thickness. Keep the asparagus tips above the water level so that they cook in the rising steam.

This delectable vegetable is served hot or cold as a first course, as an accompanying vegetable, and in veal and chicken fricassées. It is used in soups and sauces, in salads, soufflés and gratins, and in cream fillings for pies and vol-au-vents.

ASPARAGUS SOUFFLÉ

1 lb. (500 g.) asparagus
Salt and pepper
¾ pint (450 ml.) thick white sauce
4 eggs, separated
Pinch of baking powder

COOKING TIME: 1 hour (approx.)
OVEN TEMPERATURE: 180°C (350°F) – gas mark 4

Wash the asparagus carefully, and scrape them lightly from the tips downwards. Cut off the lower part of the spears just above the beginning of the woody parts, and trim the spears to even lengths. Set the trimmings and woody parts aside.

Tie the asparagus spears in small bundles with soft tape and stand them upright in a pan of lightly salted, boiling water, with the tips protruding above the water level. Add the trimmings and stem sections; cover with a lid, or with foil if the pan is not deep enough for the asparagus. Simmer for about 15 minutes, or until the tips are tender.

Lift out the bundles and leave to drain in a colander. Continue cooking the trimmings for a further 15 minutes and use, with the water, for soup.

Beat the egg yolks, one at a time, into the cool white sauce. Cut the asparagus into 1 in. (25 mm.) pieces and fold into the sauce. Whisk the egg whites with the baking powder until stiff, and fold gently into the

sauce. Spoon into a buttered, straight-sided soufflé dish, set in a pan of hot water, and bake in the oven for 35–40 minutes – or until well risen and golden.
Serving Serve at once, straight from the oven, with melted butter or a Hollandaise sauce.
Variation Use half the amount of asparagus, and replace the other half with peeled chopped prawns or diced cooked chicken.

ASPARAGUS À LA FLAMANDE

1 lb. (500 g.) cooked asparagus
3 hard-boiled eggs
Parsley sprigs
4 oz. (100 g.) melted butter
Garnish: grated nutmeg, finely chopped parsley or chervil

Arrange the drained, warm asparagus on individual serving plates and decorate each with a few slices of hard-boiled egg and two small parsley sprigs. Chop the remaining eggs finely and put in a small bowl; arrange the finely chopped herbs in a second bowl, and grated nutmeg in a third.
Serving At the table, each person mixes his own dressing of melted butter, chopped eggs, herbs and nutmeg in which to dip the asparagus. Serve with crisp, warm French bread.

Continued …

Asparagus recipes (continued)

ASPARAGUS SOUP

Asparagus stems
2 pints (1 l.) asparagus water
2 oz. (50 g.) butter
1 finely chopped onion
1 heaped tablespoon flour
1 pint (600 ml.) milk (approx.)
Salt and pepper
5 fl. oz. (150 ml.) cream
Garnish: finely chopped parsley

COOKING TIME: 25–30 minutes

Measure 2 pints (1 l.) of the water in which asparagus has been cooked (see Asparagus soufflé). Melt the butter in a large pan, and cook the onion over a gentle heat until it is soft but not coloured.

Stir in the flour and mix thoroughly. Gradually add the asparagus water and the stem sections, discarding the trimmings. Bring to the boil and simmer for 10 minutes, stirring occasionally. Blend the soup in a liquidiser, then strain through a sieve to get rid of any woody bits of asparagus. Return to the pan and add milk to give the desired soup consistency; season with salt and pepper. Stir in the cream, heat through, but do not let it reach boiling point.
Serving Garnish with parsley.
Variations Float a few shelled shrimps on the soup, or serve with tiny puff-pastry crescents.

ASPARAGUS SALAD

1 lb. (500 g.) cooked asparagus
3–4 oz. (75–100 g.) sugar
2 tablespoons boiling water
1 teaspoon pickling spice
4 fl. oz. (125 ml.) white wine
  vinegar
Garnish: finely chopped chervil

CHILLING TIME: 30 minutes

Cut the cooked, drained asparagus spears into 2 in. (50 mm.) lengths and put in a shallow serving dish. Melt the sugar in the boiling water, add the spice and bring to the boil – stirring until the sugar has dissolved. Stir in the vinegar, and strain this marinade over the asparagus. Chill in the refrigerator for about 30 minutes.
Serving Sprinkle with chervil and serve the salad with cold white meat, poultry or poached salmon.
Variations Mix the asparagus pieces with left-over cold chicken and sliced raw mushrooms. Fold into a lemon-flavoured mayonnaise, thinned down with a little cream.

Alternatively, serve the cooked asparagus spears whole as a first course, either warm with melted butter, Hollandaise or Mornay sauce, or cold with oil-vinaigrette or a herb-flavoured mayonnaise.
Photograph on page 144.

Asparagus peas

The asparagus pea is confusingly named, because it is neither asparagus nor even a true culinary pea. Nevertheless, it is a member of the pea family, and takes its name from the asparagus-like flavour of the pods, which are cooked whole.

It is also known as the 'winged pea' because of the four wavy flanges, or wings, on the pod.

Planning the crop

Asparagus peas grow best in well-drained, fertile soil in a sunny position.

The plant is half-hardy and therefore vulnerable to frost.

In the autumn or winter before sowing, prepare the bed by digging in some well-rotted manure or compost. Before sowing, dress the soil with a general fertiliser at 2 oz. per square yard (60 g. per square metre).

How much to grow A 20 ft (6 m.) row will provide regular pickings for a family of four during August. There is only one species of asparagus pea.

Growing asparagus peas

In the south, sow the seeds in the second week of May, 8 in. (200 mm.) apart in drills 2 in. (50 mm.) deep. The drills should be 18 in. (455 mm.) apart.

Sow two seeds in each station and remove the weaker one if both germinate.

In the north, sow the seeds 1 in. (25 mm.) deep in pots of seed compost in a greenhouse or frame, or on a sunny window-sill indoors, at the end of April, and plant out 8 in. (200 mm.) apart in early June when the danger of frost is past.

In each case a second sowing can be made a few weeks later to give a succession. Support the plants with twiggy sticks.

Pests and diseases Asparagus peas may suffer from the same pests as peas (see p. 233), but they are generally disease-free.

Harvesting and storing

Pick the pods when they are only 1–1½ in. (25–40 mm.) long. If they are allowed to grow longer, they become stringy and lose their delicate flavour.

Go over the plants daily, because regular picking will help to maintain supplies.

Cooking asparagus peas

Use the pods as soon as possible after picking, topping and tailing them as for young French beans. Cook the prepared peas in the minimum of boiling salted water for about 5 minutes. Drain and toss in melted butter, and sprinkle with chopped parsley, dill, marjoram or basil. Grated nutmeg and ginger also combine well with asparagus peas.

AT-A-GLANCE TIMETABLE FOR ASPARAGUS PEAS

SOWING (SOUTH)	SOWING (NORTH)	HARVESTING
2nd WEEK IN MAY	LATE APRIL	JULY–AUGUST
Sow outdoors and thin when necessary	Sow in pots. Plant out in early June	When pods are 1 – 1½ in. long

Aubergines

Also known as the egg plant because of its smooth skin and ovoid shape, the aubergine is a native of tropical Asia, though extensively cultivated elsewhere. For this reason, in the British Isles it is most likely to succeed when grown in a greenhouse.

Only in a long, hot summer, when planted against a south-facing wall, is it possible to grow it successfully outdoors. In this case it helps to give the plants a sheltered start under frames or cloches after raising the seedlings in a greenhouse or indoors.

A sunny patio also provides reasonable conditions for growing aubergines outdoors – either in pots or in the bags of compost sold by garden shops.

Planning the crop

In a greenhouse, grow aubergines in 7 in. (180 mm.) pots or plant them in the border. If grown outdoors, choose a position that is open to the sun for most of the day. They require well-drained soil, liberally dressed with manure.

How many to grow The space available in the greenhouse will generally determine the number of plants to be grown. Space the pots about 18 in. (455 mm.) apart, and allow a similar space between outdoor plants.

Indoors, you can expect up to about 12 fruits on each plant. Outdoors, up to four.

Varieties Two varieties are commonly grown:

'Blanche Longue de la Chine': good-sized fruits with a white outer skin.

'Early Long Purple': large, long fruits of fine flavour.

How to grow aubergines

For growing in a greenhouse or outdoors, sow the aubergines in seed compost in February (see p. 33). The temperature needs to be 18°C (64°F), so place the seed pan in a propagator or close to the heat source in the greenhouse.

When large enough to handle, prick the plants out singly into 3 in. (75 mm.) pots of John Innes No. 1 compost or a soil-less potting compost. Grow them on in a temperature of about 16°C (61°F).

If the plants are to be grown indoors, transfer them to 7 in. (180 mm.) pots of John Innes No. 2 compost when they are 4–6 in. (100–150 mm.) tall. Alternatively, plant them in the border.

Harden off outdoor plants during May (see p. 34), and plant them at the end of the month, spacing them 18 in. (455 mm.) apart. Protect with a cloche or frame until they are well established. For growing on a patio, plant in 7 in. (180 mm.) pots or in plastic bags filled with compost.

When the plants are about 9 in. (230 mm.) high, pinch out the tops to encourage them to bush.

On indoor plants, allow up to three fruits to form on each of the three or four lateral branches that will develop. Outdoors, pinch out the tips of each branch once a fruit has formed on it, leaving three leaves beyond the fruit.

Indoors and out, remove side-shoots that form on laterals.

Water generously and give weekly feeds of liquid manure once the fruits are visible. Spray the leaves with water regularly to keep down red spider mites.

Pests and diseases APHIDS (p. 282) and GLASSHOUSE RED SPIDER MITES (p. 283) are the pests most likely to affect aubergines. The plants are generally disease-free.

Harvesting

Aubergines are ripe when their colour becomes an overall black-purple or ivory-white, depending on variety, which will be between July and October for greenhouse crops and a month or more later outdoors. Handle the fruits carefully and remove by snipping the stems with scissors.

Aubergines can be kept for about a fortnight after harvesting. See also freezing (p. 294).

Recipes on next page

STOPPING AND PINCHING OUT

STOPPING Remove the growing point of each plant when it is 9 in. (230 mm.) high. This encourages side-branches to develop.

PINCHING OUT Outdoors, allow only one fruit to develop on each branch by pinching out the tip three leaves beyond the fruit.

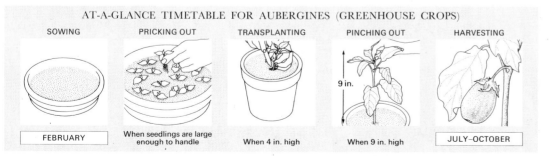

AT-A-GLANCE TIMETABLE FOR AUBERGINES (GREENHOUSE CROPS)

SOWING	PRICKING OUT	TRANSPLANTING	PINCHING OUT	HARVESTING
FEBRUARY	When seedlings are large enough to handle	When 4 in. high	9 in. — When 9 in. high	JULY–OCTOBER

Preparing & cooking aubergines

This vegetable is usually cooked in oil to be served as an accompanying vegetable, or stuffed with a variety of fillings and baked. The oblong or round fruits keep fresh for longer than most other vegetables, especially if they are stored in the salad basket of a refrigerator.

To prepare aubergines, wipe them clean with a damp cloth and trim off both ends. They may be peeled or left unpeeled, and for plain cooking are then cut crossways into thin slices. Sprinkle the slices with salt, and leave to stand for 30 minutes to draw out the bitter juices.

Rinse in cold water and dry thoroughly. Fry in butter or oil until golden-brown.

Drain on absorbent kitchen paper and serve with either grilled or roast meat.

Chopped basil or marjoram go well with fried aubergine slices, or they may be sprinkled with black pepper, ground ginger or paprika.

AUBERGINE SALAD

2 large aubergines
Salt and pepper
1 garlic clove, crushed
2 tablespoons lemon juice
1 tablespoon garlic vinegar
1 teaspoon fresh chopped marjoram or basil
6 tablespoons salad oil
Garnish : grated lemon peel

COOKING TIME: 10 minutes
CHILLING TIME: 2 hours

Peel the aubergines thinly and cut into narrow slices. Blanch for 5 minutes in boiling salted water; drain and leave to cool, then dry and arrange in a salad bowl. Mix the garlic with the lemon juice and vinegar, add the marjoram and season with salt and pepper. Gradually blend in the oil, and pour this dressing over the aubergines, turning until well coated. Chill in the refrigerator.
Serving Sprinkle the salad with finely grated lemon peel. Serve as a side salad, or as a first course with hot buttered toast.
Variation Serve the aubergine slices in a yoghourt or soured-cream dressing. Garnish with chopped parsley or halved, stoned black olives.

--◆◇◆--

AUBERGINES À LA GRECQUE

2 aubergines
½ pint (300 ml.) dry cider
3 tablespoons sugar
3 tablespoons olive oil
6 coriander seeds
Juice of ½ lemon
1 small bay leaf
2 tablespoons tomato paste
1 bouquet garni
Salt and black pepper
Garnish : chopped basil

COOKING TIME: 25 minutes
CHILLING TIME: 2 hours

Peel the aubergines, and dice them into 1 in. (25 mm.) cubes. Put all the remaining ingredients with ½ pint (300 ml.) water into a pan, seasoning with salt and black pepper. Bring this sauce to the boil, add the diced aubergines and bring back to the boil.

Simmer the aubergines for 15 minutes; until they are tender but still intact. Lift them into a dish with a perforated spoon, and boil the sauce rapidly until it has reduced by a quarter. Strain the sauce over the aubergines, allow to cool, then chill in the refrigerator for 2 hours.
Serving Spoon the aubergines and the sauce into deep plates. Sprinkle with chopped basil and serve as a first course.
Photograph on pages 210–11.

--◆◇◆--

MOUSSAKA

4 aubergines
Salt and pepper
1 large, finely chopped onion
4–6 tablespoons olive oil
1 lb. (500 g.) lean minced beef or lamb
2 teaspoons tomato purée
5 fl. oz. (150 ml.) beef stock
1 oz. (25 g.) butter
1 oz. (25 g.) flour
½ pint (300 ml.) milk
1 egg

COOKING TIME: 1½ hours
OVEN TEMPERATURE: 180°C (350°F) – gas mark 4

Peel the aubergines and cut crossways into narrow slices. Arrange in a single layer on a dish, sprinkle with salt and leave for 30 minutes.

Fry the onion in 1 tablespoon of the oil until soft; add the meat and continue cooking, stirring all the time, until brown and thoroughly sealed. Stir in the tomato purée and stock, and season to taste with salt and pepper. Bring to the boil, cover with a lid and simmer for about 30 minutes, until most of the liquid has been absorbed.

Drain the aubergine slices, rinse thoroughly and pat dry with absorbent paper. Fry the slices in the remaining oil until golden, then drain well on paper.

Arrange a layer of aubergine slices in a buttered ovenproof dish and cover with a layer of meat. Continue with these layers, finishing with aubergines.

Make a white sauce from the butter, flour and milk; season with salt and pepper. Remove from the heat and beat in the egg. Spoon the sauce over the aubergines and bake in the centre of a warm oven for 35–40 minutes.
Serving Serve straight from the dish as a meal on its own, perhaps accompanied with a green or tomato salad.
Variation Cover the moussaka with 2 eggs beaten with 4 tablespoons of plain yoghourt and 2 tablespoons of flour, instead of with the white sauce. Sprinkle with grated Parmesan cheese and dot with butter.

--◆◇◆--

TRIMMING AND CUTTING AUBERGINES

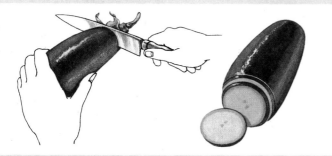

After removing each end of the fruit (left) cut crossways into thin slices.

Balm

The lemon-scented balm, a hardy perennial, has been credited with curing stomach ailments, improving the memory, healing wounds, and even of being a source of everlasting life.

Nowadays, however, it is generally grown for the more realistic purpose of flavouring salads, soups, sauces and cold drinks.

Balm is a good herb to grow near fruit trees, because it attracts bees which help pollination.

Planning the crop

The plant has tubular white flowers, and it might be worth dotting one or two plants in a perennial border. If you do, bear in mind that it is a fairly tall, bushy plant – up to 4 ft (1.2 m.) high, and with a spread of 18 in. (455 mm.) – and so needs ample space.

It tolerates light shade and thrives in most average soils.

How much to grow Bearing in mind its substantial size, even a single plant should be sufficient.

How to grow balm

Sow the seeds ½ in. (12 mm.) deep in late April or early May where the plants are to grow. Thin the seedlings to 18 in. (455 mm.) apart.

Keep the plants well watered during their first summer, and pick the leaves sparingly until they are well established.

In subsequent years, cut the stems back to about 6 in. (150 mm.) from the ground each June to encourage the growth of new shoots. Each October, cut them back to just above ground level. In exposed places, cover the roots with straw for the winter.

Raising new plants Divide in October, and plant pieces of root with three or four buds.

Pests and diseases Balm is usually trouble-free.

Harvesting and storing

Gather the leaves and young shoots throughout the summer for immediate use. For drying (see p. 343), pick leaves before the plant starts to flower in June and July.

See also freezing (p. 294).

Cooking with balm

Use the lemon-scented leaves, finely chopped, in salad dressings, or as flavourings for white sauces to accompany fish, such as plaice and sole.

Finely chopped leaves can be used as a substitute for grated lemon peel in sweets, cakes, sauces, mayonnaise and fresh-fruit salads.

Rub chicken portions for grilling with bruised leaves, or use the chopped leaves as a stuffing.

Basil

Basil, an annual herb, is used to give a clove-like flavour to soups, sauces and salads. The chopped leaves go particularly well with tomatoes.

The herb is related to balm, and in common with other plants in this family it is attractive to bees. It is a good idea, therefore, to grow it near plants that require pollinating.

There are two species – sweet basil, and the compact bush basil. Both can be grown from seed, either from indoor sowings during early March or from outdoor sowings made during May.

Planning the crop

Basil needs a warm, sheltered site and grows best in well-drained, fertile soil. If the only available site is exposed, protect the plants with a tall cloche or a plastic tent. This is in any case advisable in the north of Britain.

How much to grow Four plants of either type should provide plenty of fresh leaves from July to September, as well as sufficient dried leaves for use in the winter.

Two pots of bush basil will provide ample fresh leaves in winter.

Varieties Sweet basil grows to a height of 2–3 ft (610 mm.–1 m.), with a spread of 12 in. (305 mm.). Bush basil grows to a height of 6–12 in. (150–305 mm.), and is suitable for growing in a pot indoors or in a greenhouse, as well as outdoors.

AT-A-GLANCE TIMETABLE FOR BALM

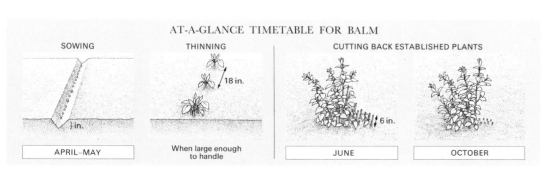

SOWING — ½ in. — APRIL–MAY

THINNING — 18 in. — When large enough to handle

CUTTING BACK ESTABLISHED PLANTS — 6 in. — JUNE — OCTOBER

AT-A-GLANCE TIMETABLE FOR BASIL

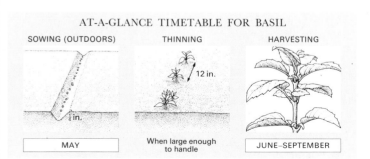

SOWING (OUTDOORS) — ½ in. — MAY

THINNING — 12 in. — When large enough to handle

HARVESTING — JUNE–SEPTEMBER

How to grow basil

For early plants, sow the seeds of sweet basil in March at a temperature of 13°C (55°F) in a pot or pan of seed compost (see p. 33). Prick out the seedlings into potting compost when they are large enough to handle.

Harden off the plants in mid-May (see p. 34), and plant them out 12 in. (305 mm.) apart at the end of the month. Keep the soil moist until the plants are well established.

Raise seedlings of bush basil for growing in pots in the same way, and transfer them to 5 in. (130 mm.) pots of John Innes No. 2 compost.

Basil seed may also be sown outside in May in the position where the plants are to grow. Sow in a drill $\frac{1}{4}$ in. (5 mm.) deep, and thin out the seedlings to give a spacing of 12 in. (305 mm.) between plants.

The seedlings can be transplanted, if preferred, but they will then receive a growth check which will delay development.

Water the plants during dry spells, and pinch out the flower buds at an early stage to promote the growth of leaves.

Pests and diseases Basil is usually trouble-free.

Harvesting and storing

If the leaves are needed for immediate use, pick them as required until the first autumn frosts. To harvest larger numbers of leaves at a single picking, for drying or freezing, cut the plants down once or twice to encourage fresh young growth.

See drying (p. 343) and freezing (p. 294).

Cooking with basil

Traditionally, this herb is used in the preparation of tomato dishes. The fresh young leaves are added, shredded, to salads; also to garnishing butters and to white sauces served with fish or poultry.

Basil leaves are used in savoury and sweet omelettes, added to soups as flavouring or garnish, and form the basis for the Italian *pesto*, a thick sauce of pounded basil, garlic, salt and oil, cheese and pine nuts, served with pasta dishes.

SWEET BASIL OMELETTE

A few sprigs of basil leaves
2 dessertspoons caster sugar
2 eggs, separated
Butter
Lemon juice

Pound the cleaned basil leaves with half the sugar to a smooth paste. Beat the egg yolks and the remaining sugar, and beat the whites fairly stiff. Fold the whites carefully into the beaten yolks and pour the mixture into a hot, buttered omelette pan.

Cook over a low heat until the mixture is just set, but still fluffy and slightly moist. Slide the omelette on to a serving plate and sprinkle with the sugared basil and a little lemon juice.

Bay

The sweet bay, or bay laurel, is grown for its aromatic leaves, which are used to flavour fish dishes, soups and sauces. Although native to countries around the Mediterranean, the bay survives as a hardy shrub in all but the harshest of British winters. If protected from cold north and east winds, it will flourish even in coastal areas.

The bay can be allowed to grow to its natural height of 20 ft (6 m.) or more, or grown in a tub and its growth restricted by pruning.

A single shrub, even when dwarfed by pruning, should provide more than enough leaves for a family throughout the year.

How to grow a bay

The bay grows well in any ordinary garden soil in a sunny, sheltered position. No pruning is needed for unrestricted trees grown in the open garden.

In a tub, use John Innes No. 3 compost. Plant in March or April.

When growing in a tub, you can plant either a shrub already trained by a nurseryman or buy a young plant and train it yourself. Nursery-trained shrubs are comparatively expensive, and there is also satisfaction to be had from training your own bay.

If you decide to do so, you have the choice of maintaining the shrub's natural shape, or of growing it with a bare stem beneath a ball-shaped head of leaves.

When young, the natural growth form of a bay tree is roughly pyramidal. To maintain this shape in a compact form, trim all actively growing shoots in late summer to maintain the desired outline. This usually means cutting them back by half.

The method of training a ball-headed standard tree is shown in the illustrations.

AT-A-GLANCE TIMETABLE FOR BAY

PLANTING	PRUNING	CUTTINGS

MARCH–APRIL	SUMMER	AUGUST–SEPTEMBER

1 The first step in training a bay tree is to remove the leading-shoot's tip when 4–5 ft (1.2–1.5 m.) high. Meanwhile, keep lateral shoots growing from the stem pinched back to two or three leaves.

2 The following summer, cut back the new shoots which will have formed at the top of the stem to 6 in. (150 mm.). These will in due course form the main head. Prune lower laterals to three leaves.

3 A year later, trim the head shoots to four or five leaves. Remove all the lower shoots. Thereafter, prune the head of the tree annually to maintain the ball shape.

Raising new plants In August or September take 4 in. (100 mm.) cuttings of lateral shoots, with a heel (see p. 29), and insert them in equal parts of peat and sand in a cold frame. In April, set the rooted cuttings in 3½ in. (90 mm.) pots of potting compost, and in the following October set the plants out in a nursery bed with other young plants or in their final positions.

If you plant them in a nursery bed, allow them to grow for a further 18 months before planting out the strongest in their permanent positions or in a tub, in March or April.

Pests and diseases The stems and undersides of leaves may be attacked by SCALE INSECTS (p. 285).

Bay is generally disease-free.

Harvesting and storing

Once the shrub is established, pick the leaves as required at any time of the year.

See also drying (p. 343).

Cooking with bay

Bay leaves are invaluable in cooking. The highly aromatic leaves are used freshly dried, to flavour marinades, pickles, stocks and sauces, casseroles, pâtés and terrines. Milk custards and puddings are greatly improved by the addition of a partly dried bay leaf, but the foremost use is in the classic bouquet garni.

Beans, Adzuki:
see **Sprouting seeds**

Beans, Broad

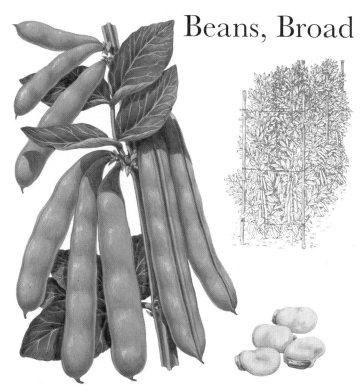

The broad bean is said to have been brought to Britain by the Romans, and it is known to have been an important crop during the Middle Ages. Its flavour is best when the bean is no larger than a 5p piece and before the pods become tough.

Field-grown beans sold by greengrocers are often twice this size, and the bean may then have a leathery skin.

The tops of the plants provide a bonus, as they can be picked and cooked like spinach.

Planning the crop

Broad beans thrive in fertile, well-drained soil that has had a dressing of manure. In general, spring-sown beans do best in medium to heavy soil; autumn-sown beans are more likely to thrive in lighter soil.

If you think the soil may be too heavy, work some coarse sand or peat into the top 6 in. (150 mm.) of soil just before sowing.

How much to grow A double row 20 ft (6 m.) long will provide about 40 lb. (18 kg.) of broad beans.

Varieties There are two classes of broad bean – longpods and Windsors – which further divide into green and white types. Green-seeded beans are the better choice for freezing.

Longpods have kidney-shaped seeds in pods which can be as long as 14 in. (355 mm.). Windsors produce round seeds in short, broad pods. The longpod varieties are hardier, and are therefore more suitable for autumn sowing, but the Windsors are sweeter.

Recommended longpod varieties include:

'Aquadulce', the best variety for autumn sowing, 'Dreadnought' and 'Exhibition Longpod'.

'Midget' is a dwarf variety, growing to only 12–15 in. (305–380 mm.). All the above are white-seeded.

Recommended Windsors include 'Imperial White Windsor' and 'Unrivalled Green Windsor' – with, respectively, white and green seeds.

How to grow broad beans

Except in the north of Britain, sow in November for an early crop, and March or April for the main crop.

Set the seeds 6 in. (150 mm.) apart and 1½–2 in. (40–50 mm.) deep in a double row, with 9 in. (230 mm.) between the rows. If more than one double row is sown,

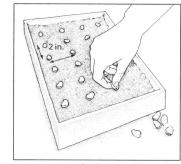

SOWING IN A SEED TRAY

Set the seeds 2 in. (50 mm.) apart each way and 1 in. (25 mm.) from the tray's edge. Average-size trays will take 24–28 seeds.

space each pair of rows 2½ ft (760 mm.) apart.

Always sow a few extra seeds in a clump at the end of the rows, to provide replacement plants for any that do not germinate or develop satisfactorily.

Sowing indoors In the north, particularly where the garden is exposed, it is not worth while trying to sow beans outdoors at the end of the year. Instead, sow in January or February in a cold greenhouse or frame, and plant

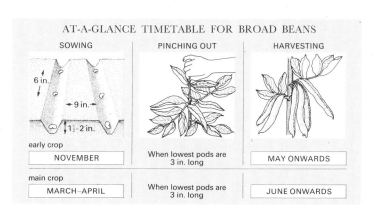

AT-A-GLANCE TIMETABLE FOR BROAD BEANS

SOWING	PINCHING OUT	HARVESTING
early crop **NOVEMBER**	When lowest pods are 3 in. long	**MAY ONWARDS**
main crop **MARCH–APRIL**	When lowest pods are 3 in. long	**JUNE ONWARDS**

out in March. Sow the main crop in April or May.

When sowing in a cold frame or greenhouse, set the seeds 2 in. (50 mm.) apart in both directions in trays of seed compost. Cover with a 1 in. (25 mm.) layer of compost and place a sheet of glass and a newspaper over the box.

Remove the glass and paper when germination begins, after about two weeks. Plant the beans out in their final position 6 in. (150 mm.) apart in a double row, with 9 in. (230 mm.) between the rows – in April.

In an exposed garden the beans need support. Insert 3 ft (1 m.) high stakes or canes along both sides of the row, and tie string at a suitable height all round. Hoe the rows regularly to keep down the weeds, and give plenty of water during dry weather.

SUPPORTING THE PLANTS

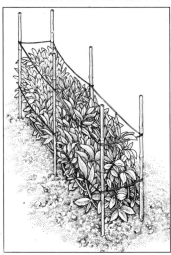

In exposed gardens support tall varieties by tying string to a double row of canes. Two strands will give adequate support.

PINCHING OUT THE TOPS

For larger pods, and to reduce trouble from blackfly, pinch out the growing point when the lowest pods are 3 in. (75 mm.) long.

When the lowest pods are 3 in. (75 mm.) long, pinch out the plant's growing points. This encourages pod growth and development, and removes the part of the plant most likely to harbour the bean's greatest natural enemy – black bean aphid, or blackfly.

Pests and diseases The principal pests of broad beans are BEAN SEED FLY (p. 282), BLACK BEAN APHID (p. 282) and SLUGS AND SNAILS (p. 285).

Diseases that may affect the crop are CHOCOLATE SPOT (p. 287) and FOOT ROT (p. 288).

Harvesting and storing

The earliest crops are ready in May. Start to pick them when the pods are no more than 2 in. (50 mm.) long, and cook them whole. In all other cases pick the beans as they are required, feeling the pods to get an idea of the size of the beans inside.

See also freezing (p. 294).

Preparing & cooking broad beans

Young beans, no thicker than a finger and 3 in. (75 mm.) long, are the most delicious. They are cooked in their pods. Larger broad beans must be shelled before cooking, and served as an accompanying hot vegetable or in a salad.

Mature beans, which tend to be floury, should also be shelled and, after boiling, the outer tough skin of the beans should be removed and the inner flesh mashed to a purée with butter and seasoning.

BROAD BEAN SALAD

½ lb. (250 g.) shelled broad beans
½ lb. (250 g.) shelled green peas
2 shallots
6 tablespoons olive oil
2 tablespoons garlic vinegar
Salt and pepper
1 clove garlic (optional)
Garnish: fresh basil

COOKING TIME: 15 minutes

Cook the broad beans and peas until tender, drain and leave to cool. Put in a serving bowl and mix with the finely chopped shallots.

Make a dressing from the oil, vinegar, salt, pepper and crushed garlic.
Serving Dress the bean and pea salad just before serving, turning it in the marinade until well coated. Sprinkle with roughly chopped basil leaves.

BROAD BEAN SOUP

1 lb. (500 g.) mature broad beans
4 oz. (100 g.) potatoes
3 carrots
1 parsnip
Bouquet garni
2 pints (1 l.) white stock
Salt, pepper and sugar
1 oz. (25 g.) butter
Garnish: leeks

COOKING TIME: 40 minutes

Shell the beans, put in a pan of lightly salted, boiling water and cook until just tender. Drain, and remove the outer skins.

Put the beans into a large pan with the peeled and chopped potatoes, the scraped, diced carrots and the peeled, chopped parsnip. Add the bouquet garni and stock; bring to the boil over gentle heat and simmer until all the vegetables are tender. Discard the bouquet garni. Remove from the heat, cool slightly, then blend in a liquidiser to a smooth purée.

Return the bean purée to the pan and, if necessary, thin down with a little milk. Season to taste with salt, pepper and sugar, and stir in the butter.
Serving Heat through, pour into individual soup bowls and top with the finely chopped leeks.
Variation Stir in 5 fl. oz. (150 ml.) double cream and heat through, without boiling. Serve with crisp bread croûtons instead of leeks.

BROAD BEANS WITH BUTTER

1 lb. (500 g.) young broad beans
Salt and pepper
4 oz. (100 g.) butter
Juice of ½ lemon
1 dessertspoon chopped basil or parsley

COOKING TIME: 15 minutes

Wash the young beans, then top and tail them and put in a pan of lightly salted, boiling water. Bring back to the boil and cook, covered, until they are tender, which will take 10–15 minutes.

Drain thoroughly, melt the butter in a pan and toss the beans until they are evenly coated. Sprinkle with freshly ground pepper and lemon juice.

Alternatively, melt the butter, stir in the lemon juice and serve separately.
Serving Serve buttered beans garnished with the finely chopped basil or parsley, or blend the herbs into the melted butter and lemon juice and serve in a sauce boat.
Variation Arrange the hot beans in a dish and spoon a little soured cream over them.
Photograph on pages 134–5.

Beans, French

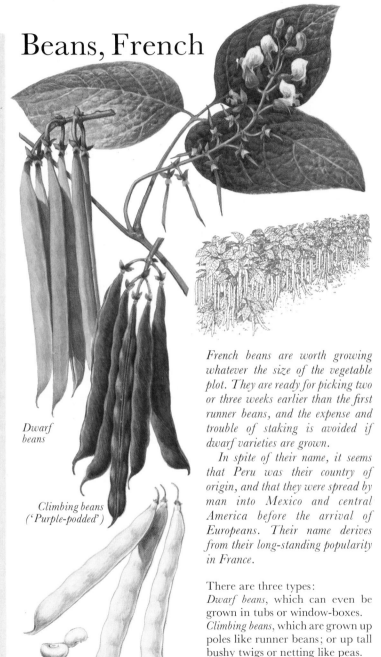

CREAMED BROAD BEANS AND BACON

1 lb. (500 g.) shelled broad beans
3 rashers streaky bacon
2 tablespoons plain flour
½ oz. (15 g.) butter
Salt and pepper
2½ fl. oz. (75 ml.) double cream
Garnish: chopped parsley

COOKING TIME: 20 minutes

Put the shelled beans in a pan of lightly salted, boiling water. Cover with a lid and cook for about 15 minutes, or until tender.

Meanwhile, remove the rind and gristle from the bacon, chop the flesh into small pieces and fry, without any extra fat, until crisp. Stir the flour into the bacon in the pan and cook for a few minutes; add the butter and gradually stir in part of the bean liquid. Stir continuously until the sauce is smooth and has the required consistency.

Season to taste with salt and freshly ground pepper.

Drain the beans thoroughly, fold into the sauce and heat through. Remove the pan from the heat and stir in the cream.
Serving Spoon at once into a serving dish and sprinkle the finely chopped parsley on top.
Variation Cook the beans as already described. Make a parsley sauce and stir in a good pat of butter. Dress the cooked, hot beans with this sauce.

Dwarf beans

Climbing beans ('Purple-podded')

Haricot beans

French beans are worth growing whatever the size of the vegetable plot. They are ready for picking two or three weeks earlier than the first runner beans, and the expense and trouble of staking is avoided if dwarf varieties are grown.

In spite of their name, it seems that Peru was their country of origin, and that they were spread by man into Mexico and central America before the arrival of Europeans. Their name derives from their long-standing popularity in France.

There are three types:
Dwarf beans, which can even be grown in tubs or window-boxes.
Climbing beans, which are grown up poles like runner beans; or up tall bushy twigs or netting like peas.
Haricot beans, which are dried beans taken from the pods of French beans that have been left to mature on the plant. There are some varieties better suited for use in this way, though all may be eaten green if preferred.

The three types need the same growing conditions and general cultivation.

Planning the crop

French beans thrive in light, well-drained soil in a sunny position. It is helpful, though not essential, to choose a sheltered site, as they are rather vulnerable to wind damage.

Dig the ground in the autumn before sowing, adding well-rotted manure or compost at the rate of a bucketful per square yard.

How many to grow A double row of dwarf beans 30 ft (9 m.) long may yield about 20 lb. (10 kg.) of beans. A similar row of climbing beans should yield double that amount.

A 30 ft (9 m.) row of haricot beans will provide a number of pickings of fresh beans, and a winter's supply of dried beans.

Varieties Among the most successful dwarf beans are:
'Canadian Wonder': heavy cropper; long, flat pods.

'Cordon': entirely stringless variety; pods remain tender for a long time.
'Earligreen': ready a week earlier than most other varieties; can also be used as a haricot.
'Flair': prolific and disease-resistant; especially good for freezing.
'Tendergreen': round, fleshy, juicy pods; heavy cropper; stringless; good freezer.
'The Prince': long-podded; a good exhibition variety.

Varieties of climbing French beans include:
'Blue Lake White Seeded': consistent cropper; good flavour.
'Purple-podded Climbing': pods turn green when cooked; heavy cropper.

Varieties grown mainly as haricots include: 'Comtesse de Chambord': heavy cropper; short pods.
'Granada': larger pods than 'Comtesse de Chambord'; excellent flavour whether eaten green or dried.

How to grow French beans

By sowing in succession, fresh beans can be picked from late June to October. French beans are not hardy, so to be sure of success do not sow outdoors until a week or so

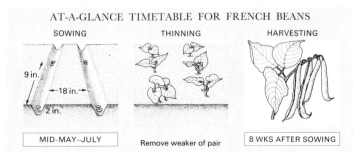

AT-A-GLANCE TIMETABLE FOR FRENCH BEANS

SOWING — 9 in. — 18 in. — 2 in. — MID-MAY–JULY

THINNING — Remove weaker of pair

HARVESTING — 8 WKS AFTER SOWING

before the risk of frost has passed – until about mid-May in the south and towards the end of the month in the north.

However, sowing a week or two earlier may, with luck, yield an earlier crop. If a late frost kills the seedlings, a fresh sowing can be made. Successional sowings may in any case be made until early July.

Sow the seeds 2 in. (50 mm.) deep, with the rows spaced 18 in. (455 mm.) apart. Set the seeds in pairs, 9 in. (230 mm.) apart, and remove the weaker of the two if both germinate.

When sowing, a drill may be formed with a draw hoe to the required depth, or the beans may be planted with a trowel. In each case, allow about 1 in. (25 mm.) between the seeds in each pair so that removing one does not disturb the roots of the other.

An earlier crop can be grown if you have a greenhouse, frame or cloches.

To raise early plants in a greenhouse or frame, sow the seeds in boxes of seed compost. Sow in late March or early April if the plants are to be set out under cloches; in mid-April if they are to be planted direct into open ground. They should germinate without artificial heat.

To plant under cloches, transfer the plants from the boxes in early May. Delay planting in the open until towards the end of May (early June in the north) and harden the plants off first (see p. 34). Plant the beans 9 in. (230 mm.) apart in rows spaced 18 in. (455 mm.) apart.

French beans also may be sown under cloches in mid-April, at the spacings advised for unprotected sowings, and the cloches left in position until the beans outgrow them.

Give support to climbing beans when they are about 4 in. (100 mm.) high.

Pests and diseases Common pests of French beans are BEAN SEED FLY (p. 282), BLACK BEAN APHID (p. 282) and SLUGS AND SNAILS (p. 285).

Diseases most likely to occur are ANTHRACNOSE (p. 286), FOOT ROT (p. 288) and HALO BLIGHT (p. 288).

Harvesting and storing

Dwarf beans start to crop within eight weeks of sowing, and many produce pods for up to eight weeks after that. The more they are picked, the more they produce – so look over the plants every day or two and remove pods while they are young and tender.

If they are left too long, the pods become stringy and the plants stop producing.

To make sure that you do not pull the whole plant out when harvesting, hold the stem with one hand and pull the pods downwards with the other.

Whether cooked immediately or preserved, French beans should be used as soon as possible after gathering.

To dry haricot beans, leave the pods on the plants until they have ripened and turned white, which will be in September or October. Choose a dry day to pull up the plants whole, and hang them in a dry, airy place.

When the pods feel crisp and dry, shell the beans and spread them out on trays to dry thoroughly. Store in jars.

Preparing & cooking French and haricot beans

French beans These are at their best when young and before the seeds begin to show through the pods. They are the perfect summer vegetable with roast meats, poultry and many fish dishes, and are as good hot or cold.

French beans are in most cases interchangeable with runner beans, which mature later. They are excellent in salads and are also used in pickles.

Haricot beans The pods are not usually harvested until the beans have dried in the early autumn, but they can also be picked while they are green.

Cook fresh haricot beans in a well-flavoured stock for about 25–40 minutes, until they are tender. Drain, and serve with butter and chopped parsley.

Alternatively, leave them to cool, then dress them with oil-vinaigrette and serve as a salad.

The cooked beans may also be made into a purée, and enriched with butter and cream.

Dried beans contain a large amount of the chemical lectin, a poison which can cause severe stomach upsets. Lectin is destroyed by thorough boiling. When using any recipe containing dried beans, make sure that after soaking and draining, the beans are put in a pan with fresh cold water, and boiled for 10 minutes. The beans can then be used normally.

Remove the pan from the heat, cover with a lid and leave to steep for 1 hour before draining and cooking.

FRENCH BEANS PROVENÇALE

1 lb. (500 g.) French beans
3–4 garlic cloves
1 egg yolk
Salt and pepper
5 fl. oz. (150 ml.) olive oil
1 tablespoon lemon juice

COOKING TIME: 7 minutes

In this dish, beans are served with the classic sauce known as aïoli, which is really a garlic-flavoured mayonnaise that can also be used with other cooked vegetables, such as broccoli and carrots, or with cold salads.

Begin by preparing the sauce. Peel the garlic cloves and pound to a paste in a mortar, add the egg yolk and a pinch of salt and beat thoroughly until creamy. Beat in the oil, drop by drop as when making mayonnaise, beating vigorously until the sauce thickens. Season to taste with salt, pepper and lemon juice.

Top, tail and wash the beans. Put them in a pan of boiling, lightly salted water and cook for about 7 minutes, or until just tender. Drain thoroughly.

Serving Arrange the hot beans in a dish, and either spoon the aïoli sauce over them or serve this separately. Serve the beans with any kind of roast meat, hot or cold.

CHEESY FRENCH BEANS

1 lb. (500 g.) French beans
2 tablespoons oil
1 garlic clove
Salt
3 oz. (75 g.) Cheddar or Cheshire cheese
Paprika
2 tomatoes

COOKING TIME: 30 minutes
OVEN TEMPERATURE: 190°C (375°F) – gas mark 5

Wash, top and tail the beans. Put in a pan of boiling, lightly salted water and cook for 5–7 minutes. Drain, then refresh in cold water.

Brush an ovenproof dish with a little oil, cut the garlic in half and rub over the dish. Lay the well-drained beans in the dish, brush them liberally with oil and sprinkle with salt.

Slice the cheese thinly and lay over the beans, sprinkle with paprika and top with tomato slices. Cook near the top of the oven for about 20 minutes, or until the cheese has melted.

Serving Serve on its own with hot garlic bread, or as a light supper dish with boiled cold ham or gammon.

Variation Young courgettes, cut in half lengthways, may be used instead of French beans.

BEANS AND TOMATOES

1 lb. (500 g.) French beans
4 tomatoes
3 tablespoons oil
1 large, finely chopped onion
Juice of 1 lemon
2 tablespoons tomato purée
Salt and pepper

COOKING TIME: 20 minutes

Wash, top and tail the beans. Skin the tomatoes, cut them in half, scoop out the seeds with a teaspoon and chop the flesh roughly.

Heat the oil in a heavy-based frying pan and cook the onion until soft and transparent – about 5 minutes. Add the beans and tomato pulp, the lemon juice and tomato purée; season with salt and pepper and mix all the ingredients thoroughly.

Cover with a lid and simmer over gentle heat for about 15 minutes, or until the beans are tender. Stir occasionally to prevent sticking, and if necessary add a little tomato juice.
Serving The beans are best served cold, with roast meat or poultry, but may also be served hot.
Variation If served cold, garnish with thin slices of raw onion and sprinkle with freshly chopped tarragon.

BEANS WITH HERBS

1 lb. (500 g.) French beans
3–4 tablespoons oil
1 finely chopped onion
1 garlic clove
1 chopped carrot
2 tablespoons brown stock
1 dessertspoon each of finely chopped
*   parsley, tarragon or chives, chervil*
*   and spring onions*
1 teaspoon of chopped marjoram
Salt and sugar

COOKING TIME: 20 minutes

Wash, top and tail the beans, and cut in half. Heat the oil in a heavy-based pan and cook the onion, crushed garlic and carrot for about 5 minutes, or until the onion is golden.

Add the beans, stock and all the finely chopped herbs; mix thoroughly, cover with a lid and simmer gently for 15 minutes, or until the beans are tender. Stir occasionally, and add a little more stock if the mixture begins to dry out. Season to taste with salt and sugar.
Serving This makes a light dish on its own, served with small, new, buttered potatoes sprinkled with parsley or chives.
Variation For a more substantial version, add ½ lb. (250 g.) of cooked, diced ham to the beans for the last 5 minutes of cooking.
Photograph on pages 140–1.

HARICOT BEAN SALAD

½ lb. (250 g.) green haricot beans
1 onion
1 carrot
1 bouquet garni
Salt and pepper
1–2 tinned pimentos
2 oz. (50 g.) black or green olives
5 tablespoons olive oil
1 tablespoon white wine vinegar
2 tablespoons chopped parsley, chervil
*   or chives*
1 garlic clove

COOKING TIME: 1–1¼ hours
CHILLING TIME: 1 hour

Peel and roughly chop the onion and carrot. Put them in a pan with 2 pints (1 l.) of cold water, the bouquet garni and a good seasoning of salt and freshly ground pepper. Bring to the boil, then simmer this stock for 25 minutes before adding the haricot beans. Continue simmering for 25–30 minutes.

Drain, and leave to cool.

Put the drained beans in a serving bowl and mix with the drained, diced pimento and the olives. Make a dressing from the olive oil and vinegar, seasoning well with salt and pepper and adding the finely chopped herbs and the crushed garlic.

Turn the beans in the dressing, then chill for 1 hour.
Serving This salad may be served with any type of meat, or with wholemeal bread it makes an unusual hors-d'oeuvre.
Photograph on page 216.

HARICOT BEAN CASSEROLE

1 lb. (500 g.) soaked, dried, boiled
*   haricot beans*
2 onions
4 cloves
2 carrots
2–3 sticks of celery
½ lb. (250 g.) belly pork or green
*   bacon*
2–3 tablespoons oil
1 tablespoon tomato paste
½ lb. (250 g.) tomatoes
1 tablespoon golden syrup
Salt and pepper

COOKING TIME: 4–4½ hours
OVEN TEMPERATURE: 150°C (300°F)
–gas mark 2

Put the soaked, boiled beans in a large pan. Add one peeled onion stuck with the cloves, the peeled and roughly chopped carrots and celery, and enough cold water to cover. Bring to the boil and simmer over gentle heat for about 30 minutes, or until the skins burst. Drain the beans and set the cooking liquid aside.

Heat the oil in a pan and fry the remaining chopped onion for about 5 minutes, or until golden. Add the diced pork or bacon and fry until browned and sealed.

Stir in the tomato paste, the skinned and roughly chopped tomatoes, the syrup and about ½ pint (300 ml.) of the strained cooking liquid. Season to taste.

Arrange the beans in an ovenproof dish, pour over them the contents of the pan and cover with a tight-fitting lid. Bake in the oven for 3½ hours, topping up with the bean liquid as necessary.

Remove the lid for the last 30 minutes of cooking, when the sauce should have reduced to a thick consistency.
Serving This makes a hearty winter casserole served straight from the dish, with triangles of toast.

HARICOT BEANS AND BACON

1 lb. (500 g.) dried haricot beans
1 pint (600 ml.) ham or chicken stock
1 bouquet garni
4 rashers streaky bacon
1 oz. (25 g.) butter
Salt and cayenne pepper
Garnish : chopped parsley, basil or
*   marjoram*

COOKING TIME: 30 minutes

After soaking the beans, boil them for 10 minutes, then drain and put in a pan with enough cold stock to cover. Add the bouquet garni, but no salt, and bring to the boil. Simmer for 30 minutes, or until the skins burst. Drain thoroughly and keep warm.

Meanwhile, cut the rashers crossways into strips and fry in the butter until crisp.
Serving Spoon the beans into a dish, sprinkle with salt and cayenne and pour the bacon and fat over them. Toss the beans well and garnish with finely chopped herbs.

Beans, Runner

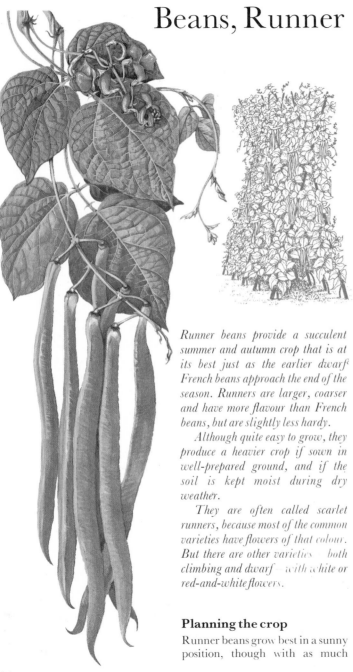

Runner beans provide a succulent summer and autumn crop that is at its best just as the earlier dwarf French beans approach the end of the season. Runners are larger, coarser and have more flavour than French beans, but are slightly less hardy.

Although quite easy to grow, they produce a heavier crop if sown in well-prepared ground, and if the soil is kept moist during dry weather.

They are often called scarlet runners, because most of the common varieties have flowers of that colour. But there are other varieties – both climbing and dwarf – with white or red-and-white flowers.

Planning the crop

Runner beans grow best in a sunny position, though with as much shelter as possible to encourage the insects needed to pollinate the flowers. They will grow in most garden soils, but do best in rich, well-drained ground. Runner beans need a deep, well-manured bed to allow maximum root development.

A month or two before sowing, dig a trench 18 in. (455 mm.) wide where you plan to sow the crop.

Remove the top spit of soil and fork a generous dressing of rotted compost or manure – at least a bucketful per square yard – into the 6 in. (150 mm.) of soil beneath. Replace the topsoil, first marking the centre of each end of the trench so that you will know where to sow. Any surplus soil can be banked along each side of the trench, where it will help to retain water.

If you plan to grow the beans in a circle, bury the manure accordingly and mark the site with pegs.

How much to grow A 20 ft (6 m.) double row of climbing runners, grown on well-manured ground, should produce up to 80 lb. (36 kg.) of beans between July and October.

The yield will be considerably lighter if the plants are dwarfed by pinching out their tips.

Varieties 'Enorma': an improved strain of 'Prizewinner'; long pods of fine flavour.

'Fry': white flowers; heavy crop of stringless pods; flowers set well in dry summer.

'Kelvedon Marvel': the earliest of all varieties; can be grown as a bush by pinching out the tips.

'Streamline': very heavy, reliable cropper; thick, fleshy pods.

'Yardstick': exhibition-length pods; good for freezing.

How to grow runner beans

In the south, sow runner beans outdoors about the middle of May – or a week or two earlier if you are prepared to sow again should a late frost kill the plants. Under cloches, sowing can be advanced to the second half of April.

For an even earlier crop, raise the seedlings indoors (see p. 32), or in a frame or greenhouse, by sowing in boxes of seed compost about the middle of April. After hardening the plants off (see p. 34), plant them out towards the end of May. If you are to plant the beans out under cloches, sow in early April.

In the north, delay these sowings and plantings for a week or two.

To grow plants up poles or canes, push the supports into the ground in two rows about 18 in. (455 mm.) apart. Set the poles in facing pairs, with 12 in. (305 mm.) between adjacent supports, and insert them at an angle so that each pair of poles crosses at about the halfway mark.

This is rather lower than the crossing point usually recommended, but ensures that pods on the upper parts of the plants, where growth is thickest, hang outwards and are easily seen. Tie additional poles horizontally at the crossing point to brace the structure.

Runner beans can also be supported by netting – plastic, string or wire – and in this case should be grown in single rows about 2½ ft (760 mm.) apart. Staple the netting to 2×2 in. (50×50 mm.) timber uprights, spaced about 3 ft (1 m.) apart along the row, with a strand of heavy-gauge wire along the top.

Yet another way of growing runner beans is in the form of a maypole. Insert an 8 ft (2.5 m.) stake in the centre of each circle, and attach strings from the top of the stake to pegs hammered into the soil about 2 ft (610 mm.) from its base. Allow 2 ft between pegs,

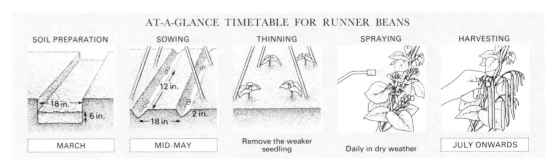

AT-A-GLANCE TIMETABLE FOR RUNNER BEANS

SOIL PREPARATION	SOWING	THINNING	SPRAYING	HARVESTING
18 in., 6 in.	12 in., 18 in., 2 in.	Remove the weaker seedling	Daily in dry weather	
MARCH	MID-MAY			JULY ONWARDS

SUPPORTS FOR RUNNER BEANS

CROSSED POLES Canes or rustic poles are equally suitable. Tie to a horizontal pole at the points where opposing poles cross.

NETTING Mesh of plastic, string or wire, supported by strong posts, is easy to erect and will last for years if stored carefully.

WIGWAM STRUCTURES These, and also maypole supports, make attractive garden features from mid-summer onwards.

and tie the strings in a half bow so that they are easy to undo if they become slack and need tightening.

Canes can be used instead of the strings, if preferred, and the centre post omitted. Tie their tops together, wigwam-fashion.

Sowing the seeds Whichever method of support is chosen, sow two seeds 2 in. (50 mm.) deep beneath the foot of each pole or string, or at 12 in. (305 mm.) spacings along the netting, and remove the weaker of the pair if both germinate. Use surplus seedlings to fill gaps where neither seed germinates.

Alternatively, sow only one seed in each position, but sow a few extra at the end of each row for filling gaps.

Immediately after sowing or planting out, scatter slug pellets over the bed.

Watering and spraying Frequent watering is needed to keep runner beans growing during dry spells,

and it is important not to let the soil dry out completely once the flowers appear. A thick mulch of compost or lawn mowings, applied when the ground is wet, helps to retain soil moisture.

While the plants are flowering, spray them daily with water during dry weather – preferably in the evening. When they reach the tops of the poles or netting, pinch out the growing tips to encourage the formation of side-shoots and to prevent the heads of the plants developing into a tangled mass.

PINCHING OUT THE TIPS

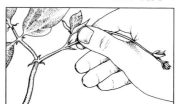

Remove the growing point of each plant when it reaches the top of the pole. This encourages flowering side-shoots to form.

After the crop has been harvested, cut down the stems but leave the roots in the ground as they add nitrogen to the soil.

Pests and diseases Runner beans may be attacked by BEAN SEED FLY (p. 282), BLACK BEAN APHID (p. 282) and SLUGS AND SNAILS (p. 285).

The most likely diseases are CHOCOLATE SPOT (p. 287) and FOOT ROT (p. 288).

Harvesting and storing

Pick the beans while they are still young and tender, before the seeds begin to swell in the pods. The more they are picked, the more the plants will produce. For this reason, always remove large beans that have been overlooked.

When pods cannot be used immediately, stand them in a cool place with the ends of their stems in shallow water.

See also drying (p. 343); freezing (p. 294) and salting (p. 346).

Preparing & cooking runner beans

Maturing shortly after French beans, runner beans may be used for the same recipes.

To prepare runner beans for cooking, wash them thoroughly, cut off the tops and tails and peel off any stringy edges. Chop the beans into diagonal lengths, no shorter than 1½–2 in. (40–50 mm.). Discard any discoloured or damaged parts.

Cook in a small amount of boiling, lightly salted water for 5–7 minutes. Drain thoroughly in a colander, and serve at once with a pat of butter.

SWEET-AND-SOUR BEANS

1 lb. (500 g.) runner beans
Salt and pepper
4 rashers streaky bacon
1 tablespoon white wine vinegar
1 tablespoon soft brown sugar

COOKING TIME: 15 minutes

Put the prepared beans in a pan of boiling, lightly salted water; cover, and simmer for about 7 minutes.

Meanwhile, remove rind and gristle and cut the bacon crossways into narrow strips. Fry without any extra fat until the bacon pieces are crisp. Lift them out with a perforated spoon and keep warm.

Stir the vinegar and sugar into the bacon fat, add the drained beans and stir to coat them

evenly with the sweet-and-sour mixture.
Serving Spoon the beans and liquid into a dish, sprinkle with the bacon pieces and serve with roast pork or boiled ham.

BEANS IN CREAM SAUCE

1 lb. (500 g.) runner beans
Salt and pepper
1½ tablespoons butter
2 tablespoons flour
5 fl. oz. (150 ml.) chicken stock
5 fl. oz. (150 ml.) cream
2 hard-boiled eggs
1 tablespoon chopped chives

COOKING TIME: 15 minutes

Cook the prepared beans in a pan of boiling, lightly salted water for 7 minutes, or until tender. Drain in a colander and keep warm.

Meanwhile, melt the butter in a pan, stir in the flour and cook through for a few minutes. Gradually add the stock and cream, stirring all the time until the sauce is smooth and free from lumps. Season to taste with salt and pepper.

Chop the eggs finely, add them to the sauce together with the chives, then fold in the drained beans and heat through.
Serving Spoon into a dish and serve with roast or grilled meat, or with fried or grilled fish.

Continued ...

Runner-bean recipes (continued)

BEANS AU GRATIN

1 lb. (500 g.) runner beans
4 oz. (125 g.) button mushrooms
2 oz. (50 g.) butter
5 fl. oz. (150 ml.) soured cream
Salt and pepper
2 tablespoons finely chopped parsley
2 oz. (50 g.) fresh white bread-
  crumbs

COOKING TIME: 25 minutes
OVEN TEMPERATURE: 180°C (350°F)
– gas mark 4

Top, tail and string the beans; wash and cut them into 1 in. (25 mm.) pieces. Put them in a pan of boiling, lightly salted water and cook for 5 minutes. Drain through a colander.

Trim the mushrooms, peeling off any ragged edges and wiping them with a cloth dipped in a little milk. Cut the mushrooms into slices and fry lightly in half the butter. Mix the drained beans with the mushrooms in a bowl.

Season the soured cream with salt and pepper, fold in the parsley and spoon this dressing over the beans and mushrooms, blending thoroughly. Spoon the mixture into a buttered ovenproof dish.

Melt the remaining butter in a pan, add the breadcrumbs and fry them lightly until they have absorbed all the butter. Spread the crumbs over the bean and mushroom mixture and bake in the oven for 20 minutes, or until the topping has crisped.

Serving This casserole can be served as a light meal on its own, or with grilled or fried sausages and bacon.

—————◦————

BAKED BEANS AND MUSHROOMS

1 lb. (500 g.) runner beans
½ lb. (250 g.) button mushrooms
2 oz. (50 g.) butter
3 eggs
5 fl. oz. (150 ml.) double cream
Salt and pepper
1 teaspoon freshly chopped basil

COOKING TIME: 25 minutes
OVEN TEMPERATURE: 180°C (350°F)
– gas mark 4

Prepare the beans and slice them into 2 in. (50 mm.) pieces; cook in boiling salted water for 5 minutes and drain thoroughly in a colander.

Meanwhile, trim the stalks and any ragged edges off the mushrooms; wipe clean and slice thickly. Fry for a few minutes in butter. Butter an ovenproof dish and lay the drained beans over the base; top with mushrooms.

Beat the eggs with the cream, salt, pepper and basil and pour into the dish. Bake in the oven for 20 minutes or until the topping is set and golden-brown.

Serving This is a light lunch or supper dish on its own, needing nothing with it except hot, crusty bread.

Photograph on pages 206–7.

Beans, Soya

Soya beans are twice as rich in protein as any other vegetable, and contain more even than prime steak. They have been one of the most important sources of protein in the Far East for thousands of years.

Since the Second World War, the United States has increased its production of soya beans six-fold – partly for the manufacture of textured vegetable protein, which resembles meat.

The crop has proved difficult to grow in Britain, but the introduction of the variety 'Fiskeby V' gives a greater chance of success.

In the kitchen, the versatile soya can be cooked whole as green beans, shelled like broad beans, or used dried like haricot beans.

Planning the crop

A warm site is more important than the state of the soil. In a good summer, soya beans may yield twice as heavily as in a cool season, so help to create the warmest possible conditions by choosing a sunny, sheltered site.

Prepare the ground in the autumn or winter before sowing by digging in well-rotted manure or compost at the rate of a bucketful per square yard.

On heavy soils, leave the ground rough for the frost to break down. On all but the most alkaline soils, give a top-dressing of carbonate of lime at the rate of 8 oz. per square yard (240 g. per square metre) during the winter, leaving this on the surface of the soil.

Before sowing, rake in general fertiliser at the rate of 2 oz. per square yard (60 g. per square metre).

How much to grow The yield will vary considerably, depending on the weather, but two or three rows, each 20 ft (6 m.) long, will provide a family with regular pickings of fresh pods in August and September, as well as dried beans for winter use.

If part of the crop is sown in mid-June, picking will be spread

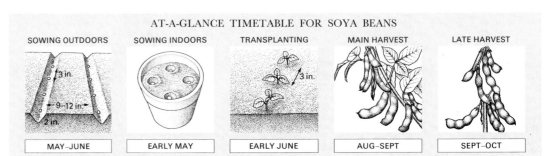

AT-A-GLANCE TIMETABLE FOR SOYA BEANS

SOWING OUTDOORS	SOWING INDOORS	TRANSPLANTING	MAIN HARVEST	LATE HARVEST
MAY–JUNE	EARLY MAY	EARLY JUNE	AUG–SEPT	SEPT–OCT

over a longer period than from a single sowing in May.

Variety The only variety readily available is 'Fiskeby V', which grows to a height of 12–30 in. (305–760 mm.). It carries up to 40 pods per plant in a good summer, but has only half that height and yield in a poor season.

How to grow soya beans

Sow in the open in the middle of May in the south, but not before the end of May in the north. If preferred, sow half the crop in June to extend the harvest. In light soil, sow in drills about 2 in. (50 mm.) deep; in heavy soil, make the drills only 1 in. (25 mm.) deep.

Place the seeds 3 in. (75 mm.) apart. Allow 9–12 in. (230–305 mm.) between rows. This close sowing is acceptable because soya plants form only a single stem, instead of branching like French beans.

Cover the rows with netting or cotton to protect them from birds. The seedlings will appear about three weeks after sowing, depending on the temperature and the amount of moisture in the soil.

Alternatively, sow the seeds in 3 in. (75 mm.) pots of seed compost – four to a pot indoors or in a cold frame – during the second week of May. Set them out singly in their final positions, 3 in. (75 mm.) apart, in the first week of June. Water the plants in, and make sure that they do not dry out during the first few days while they are forming new roots.

Sowing in pots prevents the seeds from being eaten by mice and wood pigeons, although the plants get off to a slower start than those sown where they will grow.

The plants will grow from 12–30 in. (305–760 mm.) high, depending on the season, and need supporting with twiggy sticks to keep them upright.

Pests and diseases BEAN SEED FLY (p. 282), BLACK BEAN APHID (p. 282) and SLUGS AND SNAILS (p. 285) are the most likely pests.

Soya beans are generally disease-free.

Harvesting and storing

Soya beans may be picked at two stages – first, for eating fresh, either shelled or cooked in the pod, and later for drying and storing.

In August or September, pick the pods while they are still green but when the seeds inside can be seen and felt. Usually, the pods on a plant are ready at the same time, and it may be more convenient to cut the stem at the base and remove the pods in the kitchen.

As the season progresses, the pods look more cream-coloured and the foliage takes on autumn tints. Shelled beans can still be cooked at this stage, but not the whole pod.

By the time the seeds are ripe the foliage will have died away. Pull up the plants, complete with their roots, tie them together and hang them in an airy place such as a shed or garage to complete the drying off.

Shell them when the pods are absolutely dry, and store the beans in tins or bags for use as needed.

They can be cooked like other dried beans.

Bean sprouts:
see **Sprouting seeds**

Preparing & cooking soya beans

The young green pods, in the immature stage when the beans are just showing through, may be cooked and served like mange-tout peas with butter and chopped herbs. After the immature stage, green soya beans must be shelled like broad beans.

This is rather more difficult than with other beans. In order to open the pods, first blanch them for 5 minutes in boiling, lightly salted water. Drain the beans in a colander, let them cool slightly, then break them in half so that the beans can be squeezed out of the pods.

Put the shelled beans in a pan of boiling, lightly salted water, bring back to the boil, cover with a lid and simmer for 10–15 minutes, or until they are tender but not mealy. Drain, and serve tossed in butter and chopped parsley.

Like other pulses, dried soya beans should be soaked in cold water overnight or for at least 4 hours. After soaking, drain the beans, cover with fresh cold water and boil rapidly for 10 minutes (see haricot beans, p. 92). Cover with a lid and simmer for 35–40 minutes.

Season with salt and pepper and coat with melted butter or a white sauce. Alternatively, mash the beans to a purée and cream with butter or milk, or use as a basis for a thick soup or as a savoury pie filling.

SOYA BEAN SALAD

½ lb. (250 g.) dried, soaked soya beans
1 onion
1 bouquet garni
Salt and pepper
2 tablespoons chopped parsley
3 shallots
3–4 sticks celery
5 tablespoons olive oil
1 tablespoon tarragon vinegar
1 teaspoon French mustard
½ tablespoon caster sugar

COOKING TIME: 3 hours (approx.)
OVEN TEMPERATURE: 140°C (275°F) – gas mark 1
CHILLING TIME: 1 hour

Rinse the soaked beans and boil them rapidly for 10 minutes. Drain and put them in a large ovenproof dish, with the peeled and quartered onion, the bouquet garni and a sprinkling of salt and freshly ground pepper. Pour over enough water to cover the beans completely; cover with a lid and bake in the oven for 3 hours, or until quite tender but not mushy.

Top up with water, as necessary, to prevent the beans from drying out.

Drain the baked beans through a colander and discard the onion and the bouquet garni. Arrange the beans in a deep bowl and blend with the parsley, the peeled and finely chopped shallots and the diced celery. Make a dressing from the oil, vinegar, mustard and sugar, seasoning with salt and pepper. Pour the dressing over the beans, blend thoroughly and chill in the refrigerator for about 1 hour.

Serving This is a satisfying winter salad to serve for lunch with boiled bacon or gammon.

BUTTERED GREEN SOYA BEANS

2 lb. (1 kg.) green soya beans
Salt and pepper
2 oz. (50 g.) butter
2 dessertspoons lemon juice
Garnish: 1 tablespoon chopped parsley or dill

COOKING TIME: 25 minutes

Put the shelled beans in a pan with enough boiling salted water to cover, and half the butter. Bring to the boil, cover with a lid and simmer for 15–20 minutes, or until just tender. Drain the beans and arrange in a serving dish.

Serving Toss the beans in the remaining melted butter and season with freshly ground white pepper. Sprinkle with finely chopped parsley or dill and serve with roast or grilled meat.

Variations Toss the cooked beans in soured cream, or garnish with crumbled, crisp-fried bacon. The cooked beans may also be left to cool and then added to a mixed green salad.

Beetroot

Globe beetroot

Long-rooted beetroot

These sweet-tasting roots, which have been popular in Britain since Tudor times and were known to the Romans, will succeed in most gardens that are fertile and not waterlogged.

There are two main types of beetroot. Globe varieties are generally grown for eating freshly boiled in summer and autumn; long-rooted kinds are more suitable as a main crop for harvesting in the autumn and storing for winter use.

Planning the crop

Like most vegetables, beetroot need an open, sunny site. Although they do best on a light, sandy loam they can be grown on heavier soil if this is suitably prepared. Dig the plot in the autumn or early winter before sowing and, if the soil is heavy, fork in sedge peat at the rate of a bucketful per square yard.

Do not grow beetroot on freshly manured ground or they will tend to divide into small, forked roots.

Before sowing, rake in a dressing of general fertiliser at 2 oz. per square yard (60 g. per square metre).

How many to grow A 20 ft (6 m.) row should produce about 25 lb. (12 kg.) of globe beetroot, or 45 lb. (21.5 kg.) of a long-rooted variety for winter use.

Varieties Recommended globe-rooted varieties:

'Boltardy': fine-textured, deep red root; highly resistant to bolting; can be sown earlier than most varieties.

'Crimson Globe': can be sown for succession from late April to July to give roots for winter use.

'Detroit': sweet, crisp flesh.

'Golden Ball': golden-yellow flesh of excellent flavour.

Recommended intermediate and long-rooted varieties:

'Cheltenham Green-top': very long roots that store well into spring.

'Covent Garden': deep red roots of medium length.

'Housewives' Choice': cylindrical roots of medium length; fine taste and texture.

How to grow beetroot

In sheltered positions in the south, sow bolt-resisting varieties from mid-March onwards. In the north, sowing should be delayed until mid-April. For a succession of roots in summer and autumn, sow globe varieties from April to July.

Sow long-rooted varieties in late May for winter storage.

For globe varieties draw the drills 12 in. (305 mm.) apart; for long-rooted varieties allow 18 in. (455 mm.) between rows. In both cases the drills should be about ¾ in. (20 mm.) deep.

A beetroot 'seed' is a fused cluster of from one to four separate seeds. As these will germinate as a group, sow sparingly to make subsequent thinning easier.

Space the seed clusters of globe varieties about 2 in. (50 mm.) apart. In the case of long-rooted maincrop varieties, sow two clusters every 8 in. (200 mm.) along the drill, later thinning to a single seedling.

When the seedlings of globe varieties are about 1 in. (25 mm.) high, remove the weakest from each group to leave a row of single seedlings spaced about 2 in. (50 mm.) apart.

When the roots are about half the size of a golf ball, start thinning so that the roots left to grow on are at 4 in. (100 mm.) spacings. The roots you remove can be boiled as a delicious summer vegetable.

Pull the rest of the crop as needed, but do not let any grow above cricket-ball size or they will become woody and will also tend to lose their flavour.

Pests and diseases BLACK BEAN APHID (p. 282) may give beetroot trouble.

Diseases and disorders that sometimes affect beetroot crops include BORON DEFICIENCY (p. 286), DAMPING OFF (p. 287), LEAF SPOT (p. 288) and VIOLET ROOT ROT (p. 291).

Harvesting and storing

Pull globe beetroot by hand as they are needed. Once out of the ground, hold the base of the leaves with one hand and twist off the remainder with the other. Cutting the leaf stems, or twisting them off too close to the root, results in 'bleeding'.

Lift long-rooted beetroot in November by putting a fork alongside the row and easing the soil so that the roots can be pulled out without damage. After twisting off the tops, store the roots in boxes of sand or peat in a frost-proof shed or garage.

See also chutneys (p. 335); freezing (p. 294); pickles (p. 328) and wine-making (p. 357).

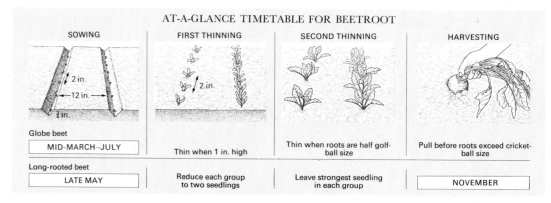

AT-A-GLANCE TIMETABLE FOR BEETROOT

SOWING	FIRST THINNING	SECOND THINNING	HARVESTING
2 in. / 12 in. / 1 in.	2 in.		
Globe beet MID-MARCH–JULY	Thin when 1 in. high	Thin when roots are half golf-ball size	Pull before roots exceed cricket-ball size
Long-rooted beet LATE MAY	Reduce each group to two seedlings	Leave strongest seedling in each group	NOVEMBER

HARVESTING AND STORING

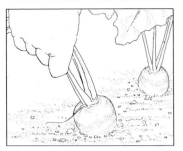

LIFTING Pull globe beetroot by hand; lift long-rooted types with a fork, taking care not to damage the roots.

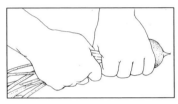

TOPPING Screw off the foliage, leaving the leaf stalks attached to the root so that 'bleeding' does not occur.

STORING Pack maincrop roots in a box containing sand, earth or peat. The material should be slightly damp.

Cover each layer of roots before placing the next, finishing with sand.

Preparing & cooking beetroot

At its best when pulled young, before the flesh becomes stringy, this root vegetable is chiefly used cold – either freshly cooked or pickled – in salads.

To cook beetroot, trim the leaf stalks 1–2 in. (25–50 mm.) above the root and leave the tapering root on. Cutting into the beetroot, or bruising the skin while washing it, will result in 'bleeding'.

Boil in salted water for 1–2 hours, depending on size. Refresh in cold water and rub off the skin.

QUICK BORSCH

1 lb. (500 g.) cooked beetroot
2 pints (1 l.) good beef bouillon (approx.)
1 large onion
Salt, pepper and sugar
2–3 pickled gherkins
3 tablespoons lemon juice
5 fl. oz. (150 ml.) soured cream
Garnish: 2 hard-boiled eggs

CHILLING TIME: 1 hour

Cut the tops and root ends off the cooked beetroot. Peel and grate, on the coarse side of a grater, into a large bowl. Alternatively, chop the roots finely.

Peel and finely grate the onion and stir into the beetroot, together with the finely chopped gherkins.

Stir the cooled bouillon into the beetroot – at this stage the soup may be blended in the liquidiser, or left chunky as it is – followed by the soured cream. Season to taste with lemon juice, salt, pepper and sugar. Chill for at least 1 hour.

Serving Chop the hard-boiled eggs finely, and sprinkle on the top of the soup just before serving. Serve borsch ice-cold.

Variation Pickled beetroot may also be used for this soup, and the pickling liquid can replace part of the bouillon.

Photograph on page 144.

BEETROOT & SOURED CREAM SALAD

3–4 beetroot
2 large dessert apples
5 fl. oz. (150 ml.) soured cream
Lemon juice
Salt and pepper
2½ fl. oz. (75 ml.) whipped cream

CHILLING TIME: 30 minutes

Peel the uncooked beetroot and grate coarsely. Peel and core the apples, grate and mix with the beetroot. Fold in the soured cream and season to taste with lemon juice, salt and pepper. Fold in the whipped cream and chill lightly in the refrigerator.

Serving A little sugar may be added if liked, but the salad should, ideally, be fairly sharp. Spoon into a dish and serve with cold roast pork.

RUSSIAN SALAD

3–4 boiled beetroot
4 boiled new potatoes
½ cucumber
1 pickled gherkin
2 hard-boiled eggs
6 tablespoons olive oil
2 tablespoons white wine vinegar
Salt and pepper
½ teaspoon dry mustard
Garnish: 1 hard-boiled egg; chopped dill, fennel or parsley

CHILLING TIME: 1 hour

Dice the beetroot, potatoes, cucumber and gherkin; mix thoroughly and add the roughly chopped eggs. Make a dressing from the oil, vinegar, salt, pepper and mustard; pour the dressing over the diced vegetables, turning well to coat them evenly. Chill for 1 hour in the refrigerator.

Serving Arrange in a bowl and sprinkle with finely chopped hard-boiled egg and dill.

Variation Replace the cucumber and gherkin with one large chopped onion and one large chopped apple.

BEETROOT STEAKS

2 lb. (1 kg.) beetroot
2–3 tablespoons seasoned flour
2 oz. (50 g.) butter
Garnish: 3–4 finely sliced onions

COOKING TIME: 1 hour, 10 minutes (approx.)

Trim the leaf stalks, but do not remove the roots. Wash the beetroot carefully without damaging the skin. Boil in lightly salted water until just tender, which will take about 1–1½ hours, depending on size. Drain in a colander and leave under cold running water until the roots are cold.

Rub off the skins and cut the beetroot into 1 in. (25 mm.) thick slices. Use the small end slices in a salad and coat the larger, central slices in seasoned flour.

Melt the butter in a pan and fry the beetroot slices for about 6 minutes until they are brown on both sides, turning once.

Serving Arrange on a dish and garnish with the onion – fried crisp and brown in a little butter – and small new potatoes.

Variation Coat the beetroot steaks in beaten egg and breadcrumbs, and pass through the beaten egg again. Leave in the refrigerator for 15–30 minutes to set the coating before frying as above.

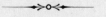

Blackberries

There are few fruits more prolific and easy to grow than blackberries. Suitable for any moisture-retaining, well-drained soil, and for growing in all parts of the country, they are ideal for training against a wall or fence. Here, they will yield a worthwhile crop without taking much space from other plants.

However, as with other fruit, soil preparation and some training are necessary for really good yields.

Blackberries fruit from late July to September, according to the variety. The best fruits are borne on shoots that developed during the previous season. The cultivated varieties produce larger and tastier fruits than wild plants.

Blackberries are self-fertile, so it is possible to grow only a single plant if this is all you have space for.

Planning the crop

Grow blackberries where they will be in the sun for at least part of the day. Although they will produce fruit in any soil, they do best in one that is slightly acid. Limy soil should be enriched with compost or peat, which will also help to retain moisture during dry weather.

How many bushes to grow Three bushes will provide plenty of berries for the average family.

Varieties The following will provide berries from late July into September:

'Bedford Giant': ripens late July to early August; medium to strong growth up to 8 ft (2.5 m.) in length; large fruits; good cropper. Plant 10–12 ft (3–3.6 m.) apart.

'Himalaya Giant': ripens from the middle to the end of August; extremely strong-growing, thorny canes; large, good-flavoured fruits; heavy cropper. Plant 12–15 ft (3.6–4.5 m.) apart. Unsuitable for small gardens.

'Oregon Thornless': ripens middle to end of August; canes 6–8 ft (1.8–2.5 m.) long, of moderate vigour; medium size, juicy, good-flavoured fruits. Plant 8–10 ft (2.5–3 m.) apart.

'John Innes': ripens August to September; vigorous canes up to 8 ft (2.5 m.) long; fruits large and sweet; good cropper. Plant 10 ft (3 m.) apart.

How to grow blackberries

November is the best month for planting, but any time from then until March is suitable. When planting the canes, spread the roots before covering them. After planting, firm the soil with your feet. Cut back each cane to 9 in. (230 mm.) above the ground, cutting just above a bud.

If you are training the canes up posts, insert a 9 ft (2.7 m.) high post for each, sinking it 2 ft (610 mm.) into the ground. Use 3 × 3 in. (75 × 75 mm.) sawn wood, or 3 in. diameter poles.

As new shoots grow from the base of the cut-back canes, tie them to one side of the post. The following season, tie new growth to the other side.

Separating the current season's wood from that of the previous year in this way helps to prevent disease from spreading.

To train blackberries on wires, which is more satisfactory than growing on posts, strain the wires between posts or secure them to walls with vine eyes. Use 10–12

To help prevent disease spreading, train the shoots of successive years to alternate sides of the root base. Here, last year's canes, which are now bearing fruit, were trained to the left. Current year's growth, which will fruit next year, is trained to the right. Each autumn, cut back to ground level the canes that have just fruited, leaving only the current season's growth tied to the wires. Space these evenly to allow as much light and air as possible between them.

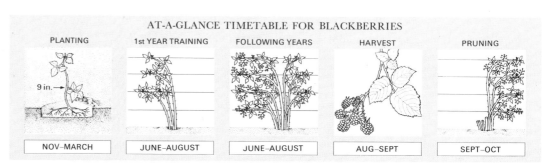

AT-A-GLANCE TIMETABLE FOR BLACKBERRIES

PLANTING	1st YEAR TRAINING	FOLLOWING YEARS	HARVEST	PRUNING
9 in. →				
NOV–MARCH	JUNE–AUGUST	JUNE–AUGUST	AUG–SEPT	SEPT–OCT

gauge wires, setting them 12 in. (305 mm.) apart up to a height of 6 ft (1.8 m.).

There are two methods of training the canes. One is to tie the fruiting canes to the wires in a 'fan shape and lead the new canes up the centre and along the top wire. Tie them temporarily to the wire. Alternatively, one season's canes can be pulled over to one side and tied, and the following season's canes trained to the other side. The latter is the simpler method.

Feed the canes in spring with 2 oz. of general fertiliser per square yard (60 g. per square metre). Watering is necessary only during dry periods in summer.

After the season's fruit has been gathered, cut down the fruiting canes to soil level. If the canes have been fan-trained, untie the new growths attached temporarily to the top wire and use them to replace the cut-out fruiting shoots.

Raising new plants Layering the tips of shoots is the easiest method of increasing your stock of blackberry canes.

Between July and September, bend down a shoot that has formed during the current season and plant its tip firmly in a 4 in. (100 mm.) deep hole dug with a trowel.

The tip will have rooted by early November, when the young plant can be severed from its parent. Cut just above a bud. Remove the plant from the ground the following April and plant it in its permanent position.

Pests and diseases RASPBERRY BEETLE (p. 285) is the most troublesome pest.

CANE BLIGHT (p. 287), CANE SPOT (p. 287), CHLOROSIS (p. 287),

RAISING A NEW PLANT

PLANTING In late summer, bend down the tip of a young shoot and bury it firmly in a hole 4 in. (100 mm.) deep. If necessary, secure the stem with bent wire.

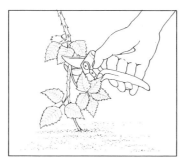

SEVERING In November, by which time the tip will have rooted, sever it from the parent plant. Transplant the following April.

CROWN GALL (p. 287), GREY MOULD (p. 288), HONEY FUNGUS (p. 288) and VIRUS DISEASES (p. 291) are the chief diseases and disorders.

Harvesting and storing

Blackberries deteriorate quickly after picking unless they are frozen.

See also bottling (p. 309); chutneys (p. 335); freezing (p. 294); jams (p. 314); jellies (p. 320); pickles (p. 328); sauces, ketchups and relishes (p. 339); syrups and juices (p. 326) and wine-making (p. 357).

Preparing & cooking blackberries

These large juicy berries are seldom served as a dessert on their own, although folded into natural yoghurt they make a refreshing cold sweet. They associate well with sharp cooking apples, and are used mainly in this combination as pie fillings and for fruit puddings, in jams and in jellies.

The berries bruise easily and should be handled and washed as little as possible.

BLACKBERRY YOGHOURT SHAKE

½ lb. (250 g.) blackberries
Caster sugar
1 pint (600 ml.) natural yoghourt

CHILLING TIME: 30 minutes

Pick over the blackberries, hull and rinse them if necessary, and drain thoroughly. Put the blackberries in the liquidiser and blend until quite smooth, then strain the mixture through a sieve to get rid of the pips.

Sweeten the blackberry mixture to taste with sugar, and gradually blend in the yoghourt to an even mixture. Pour into glasses and chill in the refrigerater for 30 minutes, or serve at once with the addition of a couple of ice cubes.
Serving Blackberry shake makes a refreshing summer drink on a hot day, especially for children.
Variations As a health drink,

ground wheat germs may be sprinkled on top. Alternatively, mix a small glass of liqueur or sweet sherry into the shake before serving.

BLACKBERRY COMPÔTE

1 lb. (500 g.) blackberries
1 pint (600 ml.) water
4 tablespoons cornflour
5 oz. (150 g.) sugar
Vanilla
Garnish : almond flakes

COOKING TIME: 15 minutes
CHILLING TIME: 2 hours

Bring the cleaned berries and the water to the boil and simmer for about 15 minutes, or until the berries are soft and squashy. Blend the cornflour smooth with a few tablespoons of cold water, add a little of the hot juice and return to the pan.

Continue cooking, stirring all the time, until the mixture thickens. Remove from the heat and add sugar and vanilla to taste. Pour into a serving bowl, and sprinkle the top with caster sugar to prevent a skin forming. Chill in the refrigerator.
Serving Decorate with tiny flakes of blanched almonds and serve with a jug of cream.
Variation Rub the cooked berries through a sieve.

Re-heat the blackberry juice and purée before adding the cornflour and sugar.

BLACKBERRY AND APPLE PIE

¾ lb. (375 g.) blackberries
¾ lb. (375 g.) cooking apples
3 oz. (75 g.) sugar
½ lb. (250 g.) sweet shortcrust pastry
Milk

COOKING TIME: 35 minutes
OVEN TEMPERATURE: 200°C (400°F) – gas mark 6

Prepare the blackberries, and peel, core and roughly chop the apples. Set a pie funnel in a pie dish and fill the dish with the mixed berries and apples, sprinkling with the sugar. Add 2 tablespoons of water.

Cover the pie dish with the rolled-out pastry, made from ½ lb. (250 g.) flour. Seal the edges and decorate the top with pastry trimmings. Brush with milk and dust with sugar. Bake in the oven for about 35 minutes and cover the pie with moistened greaseproof paper if the pastry browns too quickly.
Serving Serve warm or cold with a jug of cream or custard sauce.
Variations Replace the water with lemon juice, or mix 1 teaspoon of grated lemon or 1 dessertspoon of freshly chopped mint with the sugar.
Photograph on pages 208–9.

Continued . . .

Blackberry recipes (continued)

BLACKBERRY MOUSSE

1 lb. (500 g.) blackberries
3 whole eggs
2 egg yolks
4 oz. (100 g.) caster sugar
3 teaspoons powdered gelatine
3 tablespoons water
½ pint (300 ml.) double cream
Garnish: toasted almond flakes

CHILLING TIME: 2–3 hours

Hull and wash the blackberries carefully; set eight aside for decoration and put the remainder in a pan. Simmer gently for 5 minutes or until soft, then rub the berries through a sieve to make a purée, which should measure about ½ pint (300 ml.).

Put the eggs, egg yolks and sugar in a bowl and set over a pan of hot water. Beat until thick and fluffy. Remove from the hot water, set in a basin of chilled water and continue whisking until the mixture is cool.

Dissolve the gelatine in the water, stir into the blackberry purée and then whisk into the egg mixture. Whip the cream lightly, and fold into the blackberries when they begin to set. Spoon into a serving dish and leave to set in the refrigerator.

Serving Decorate with the reserved blackberries and sprinkle the top with toasted almond flakes.

Variation Sweeten the blackberry purée to taste, and layer in tall glasses with a thick, rich custard. Decorate with a whorl of piped cream and a whole berry.
Photograph on pages 136–7.

BLACKBERRY FOOL

¾ lb. (375 g.) blackberries
Caster sugar
1–2 tablespoons lemon juice
½ pint (300 ml.) whipping cream

COOKING TIME: 5 minutes
CHILLING TIME: 1 hour

Hull, rinse and drain the blackberries. Set 12 berries aside and put the remainder in a pan. Simmer over low heat for about 5 minutes, or until the berries have softened and the juices are running.

Rub the blackberries through a sieve to make a purée. Sweeten to taste with sugar and sharpen with lemon juice. Leave to cool.

Whip the cream until it holds its shape, then fold it thoroughly into the cooled blackberry purée. Spoon the mixture into tall glasses and chill in the refrigerator for about 1 hour.
Serving Decorate each glass with the reserved blackberries just before serving, accompanied with tiny macaroons.
Variation Replace half the cream with a rich custard sauce.

Blueberries

This bushy plant (Vaccinium corymbosum), also known as the highbush blueberry, originates in America but is related to our native wild bilberry, whortleberry or blaeberry (V. myrtillus), which has smaller fruits.

The plants are sometimes grown for their ornamental value.

Planning the crop

In the wild, the berries grow in acid, moorland soil. In the garden they need a moist, peaty, very acid soil and an open, sunny position.

A few weeks before planting, prepare the ground by digging a hole about 3–4 ft (1–1.2 m.) square. Break up the subsoil with a fork, but be careful not to bring it

to the surface. Mix an equal amount (by volume) of dampened peat with the topsoil, and fill in the hole so that the ground has time to settle before planting.

Do not manure the ground.

How many to grow Bushes may grow to 6 ft (1.8 m.) high with a spread of up to 4 ft (1.2 m.). Each bush will produce 5–10 lb. (2.5–5 kg.) of fruit, depending on the weather and soil conditions. Plant at least two bushes, preferably different varieties, to ensure good pollination.

Varieties Most of the following, except 'Jersey', have good autumn colour, so they could be planted among ornamental shrubs:

'Blue Crop': vigorous; grows to a height of 5 ft (1.5 m.) with a 5 ft spread; large sweet berries; reliable cropper.

'Earliblue': grows to a height of 4½ ft (1.4 m.) with a 5 ft (1.5 m.) spread; large berries ripening from mid-July.

'Herbert': a branching bush, 4 ft (1.2 m.) high and with a 4½ ft (1.4 m.) spread; heavy clusters of fine-flavoured berries.

'Jersey': strong growth, up to 6 ft (1.8 m.) high and with a 6 ft spread; long sprays of large fruit; most reliable cropper.

How to grow blueberries

Plant bushes in the prepared ground 5 ft (1.5 m.) apart at any time from November to March.

After planting, mulch to a depth of 5 in. (130 mm.) with peat or, if available, sawdust. Commercial growers have found that sawdust gives more successful results than peat, although the reason is not known.

AT-A-GLANCE TIMETABLE FOR BLUEBERRIES

PLANTING	PRUNING	HARVESTING

NOVEMBER–MARCH	NOVEMBER–MARCH	JULY–SEPTEMBER

Each March, apply a general fertiliser at the rate of 2 oz. per square yard (60 g. per square metre). At the end of April apply sulphate of ammonia at the rate of 1 oz. per square yard (30 g. per square metre).

Except for removing stems lying on the ground, pruning is unnecessary until the third winter.

Pruning Each winter, from the third winter onwards, cut back old, dry stems either to the ground or to a vigorous new shoot close to the ground.

Blueberries, which fruit on the tips of the previous season's growth, first produce side-shoots soon after flowering in spring, then in July vigorous growths push up from the base of the bush.

The aim should be to encourage this renewed growth. Hard pruning in winter will result in larger, earlier fruit.

Pests and diseases These plants are generally trouble-free.

Harvesting and storing
Pick the berries from mid-July to September as they ripen. Go over the bushes a number of times.

See also chutneys (p. 335); freezing (p. 294); jams (p. 314); jellies (p. 320) and wine-making (p. 357).

RAISING NEW BLUEBERRY BUSHES

LAYERING Select one or two long shoots in September, and cut a tongue in each where it can be bent to touch the ground (left). Peg down with bent wires. Sever the plant and set it in its permanent position when well rooted, after one or two years.

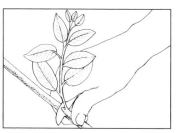

CUTTINGS Take cuttings of semi-ripe shoots, with a heel of old wood (left), in late June. Remove the soft tip, dip the heel in rooting powder, and plant in equal parts (by volume) of peat and sand in a cold frame. Spray frequently with water until rooted.

Preparing & cooking blueberries

Blueberries, and our native bilberries, are used chiefly for jams and jellies; but cleaned, and with the stalks and blossom ends removed, they may also be eaten fresh as dessert berries.

AMERICAN BLUEBERRY PANCAKES

½ lb. (250 g.) blueberries
1 egg
½ pint (300 ml.) milk
1 tablespoon caster sugar
¼ teaspoon salt
4–5 oz. (125–150 g.) plain flour
Grated rind of ½ lemon
Fat for frying

COOKING TIME: 25 minutes (approx.)

Clean the blueberries; wash, and drain in a colander.

Beat the egg with the milk, sugar and salt until well blended; sift the flour into a bowl and gradually stir in the egg-and-milk mixture. Beat until smooth and free from lumps; flavour to taste with the finely grated lemon rind. Leave the batter to rest for 30 minutes.

Stir the batter thoroughly, adding a little more milk if necessary. Fold in the berries.

Heat a heavy-based frying pan, melt just enough fat to gloss over the surface and pour in a ladle of the batter.

Turn the pancake when golden-brown on the underside (after about 1 minute), and cook on the other side.

Serving Warm honey or melted butter, with a bowl of sugar, are traditional accompaniments.

BLUEBERRY CHEESECAKE

¾ lb. (375 g.) blueberries
Juice and grated rind of 1 lemon
10 oz. (275 g.) caster sugar
½ lb. (250 g.) digestive biscuits
5 oz. (150 g.) melted butter
½ lb. (250 g.) cottage cheese
4 oz. (125 g.) cream cheese
2 eggs
½ oz. (15 g.) powdered gelatine
5 fl. oz. (150 ml.) double cream

COOKING TIME: 10 minutes
CHILLING TIME: 4 hours

Prepare the blueberries; put in a pan with a few tablespoons of water, 2 teaspoons lemon juice and 6 oz. (175 g.) of sugar. Simmer until the sugar has dissolved. Set aside to cool.

Crush the biscuits; put in a bowl with melted butter and blend evenly. Spread the mixture over the base and sides of a flan ring. Chill for 2 hours.

Rub the cottage cheese through a coarse sieve, and blend with the softened cream cheese and lemon rind.

Separate the eggs; beat the yolks with half the remaining sugar and a pinch of salt until creamy. Whisk in the gelatine,

dissolved in 3 tablespoons of water and mixed with the strained lemon juice.

Blend the mixture into the cheese, and fold in the egg whites – beaten until stiff with the remaining sugar. Whisk the cream lightly and fold in.

Spoon this mixture into the biscuit crust. Chill for 2 hours.
Serving Spread the blueberry compôte over the cheese filling and serve with a jug of cream.
Photograph on pages 208–9.

BERRY BRULÉE

½ lb. (250 g.) blueberries
3 oz. (75 g.) caster sugar
1½ level teaspoons arrowroot
5 fl. oz. (150 ml.) soured cream
Soft brown sugar

COOKING TIME: 10 minutes

Clean and rinse the berries. Put in a pan with about 6 tablespoons of water and simmer until tender. Sweeten to taste with caster sugar, stirring until it has dissolved. Blend the arrowroot with water, stir into the berries and bring gently to the boil, stirring all the time.

Leave the berries to cool before spooning them into small, flameproof, ramekin dishes; cover with a layer of soured cream and sprinkle with brown sugar. Set under a hot grill for a few minutes.
Serving Serve at once, with sponge fingers or shortbread.

Borage

The young leaves of borage, an annual herb, are used to flavour salads and wine cups. When bruised or shredded, the leaves taste like cucumber.

The flowers can also be used to garnish salads.

The plant, which grows 1½–3 ft (455 mm.–1 m.) high, and has a similar spread, carries bright blue, star-shaped flowers from June to September. It is therefore suitable for planting near the front or centre of a flower border, or in clumps at the top of a sunny bank, as well as in the herb garden.

Borage, like balm, is attractive to bees.

Planning the crop

Borage will grow in almost any type of soil, but it does best in well-drained ground in a sunny position.

How many to grow About six plants will provide plenty of leaves throughout the summer.

How to grow borage

Sow the seeds in April in the positions where they are to grow, setting them ½ in. (12 mm.) deep and 12 in. (305 mm.) apart, in groups of three. Remove the weakest seedlings, leaving the strongest to grow on unchecked.

Borage seeds germinate readily and the seedlings grow rapidly, making this one of the easiest herbs to grow. Borage also seeds itself freely, so in subsequent years you should be able to get all the plants you need by transplanting self-sown seedlings.

Transplant the seedlings before they develop their rough leaves, otherwise they tend to wilt and may either die or receive a severe check.

Pests and diseases This herb is sometimes attacked by APHIDS (p. 282), but it is generally free of disease.

Harvesting and storing

Borage plants make extremely rapid growth, and the young leaves are ready for picking in about eight weeks after sowing.

Borage can be dried for winter use (see p. 343), but this is more difficult than with many other herbs because the leaves tend to turn black if the ventilation is inadequate or the temperature too high. However, they may be frozen (see p. 294). 🌿🌿

Cooking with borage

Besides being used in salads, the flowers and leaves are also added to claret and other wine cups, to which they bring a cucumber-like coolness. Tea made from freshly chopped leaves is refreshing, and the flowers can be candied and used for cake and sweet decorations.

Boysenberry:
see **Loganberries**

Broad beans:
see **Beans, Broad**

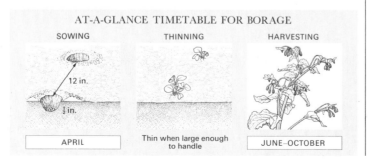

AT-A-GLANCE TIMETABLE FOR BORAGE

SOWING	THINNING	HARVESTING
12 in. / ½ in.	Thin when large enough to handle	
APRIL		JUNE–OCTOBER

Broccoli, Sprouting

A gardener who aims to gather fresh vegetables all the year round should include sprouting broccoli in his cropping plan.

Its purple or white heads help to fill a lean period in late winter and early spring, when Brussels sprouts have almost finished and the spring-cabbage season has yet to begin.

Sprouting broccoli does not produce a single, large head in the same way as a cauliflower. Instead, it grows spears – many small heads about 1–2 in. (25–50 mm.) across – which are cut with a length of stem and cooked in a bunch. As the spears are cut, so more develop over a period of four to six weeks.

A distinct type of sprouting broccoli is the less hardy calabrese, which produces larger, green heads in the autumn. It will not stand the winter, so do not sow for spring use.

Calabrese

Planning the crop

Sprouting broccoli and calabrese grow best in fertile, loamy soil in a sunny position. It is helpful, but not essential, to choose a site sheltered from winter winds for sprouting broccoli. Failing this, they may need supporting.

If the soil has not been manured for a previous crop, dig in well-rotted manure or compost during the autumn or winter before planting.

In spring, give all soils, unless already alkaline, a top-dressing of carbonate of lime at 4 oz. per square yard (120 g. per square metre). A fortnight before setting out the plants, hoe in a dressing of general fertiliser at 3 oz. per square yard (90 g. per square metre).

How many to grow Sprouting broccoli occupy a good deal of space – about 2 ft (610 mm.) between plants – for as long as eight months of the year. These two factors will determine how many can be grown in the space available.

Ten plants in a row 20 ft (6 m.) long should yield at least 15 lb. (7 kg.) of spears.

Varieties 'Express Corona' (calabrese): ready August-September; heavy cropper.

'Italian Sprouting' (calabrese): ready from September onwards; fine flavour.

'Early Purple Sprouting': ready March-April; very hardy.

'Early White Sprouting': ready February-March, similar to purple varieties, except in flavour.

How to grow calabrese and sprouting broccoli

Sow calabrese seeds in March, and those of sprouting broccoli in April, in drills ½ in. (12 mm.) deep in a seed bed. Allow 12 in. (305 mm.) between drills. Thin the seedlings to 2 in. (50 mm.) apart.

When they are about 4 in. (100 mm.) high, plant them in their permanent positions. For calabrese, allow 20 in. (510 mm.) between plants and 2 ft (610 mm.) between rows. Space sprouting-broccoli plants 2 ft apart, with 2½ ft (760 mm.) between rows. Firm well with your feet.

Keep weeds down with a hoe, and water thoroughly during dry spells.

Sprouting-broccoli plants may get rocked by winter winds, which loosens their roots. Drive stakes in on each side of the row, and tie strings between the stakes to support the plants.

Pests and diseases Pests that may occur include APHIDS (p. 282), CABBAGE ROOT FLY (p. 282), CABBAGE WHITEFLY (p. 282), CATERPILLARS (p. 282) and FLEA BEETLE (p. 283).

CLUB ROOT (p. 287) and WHIP-TAIL (p. 291) are the most likely diseases.

Harvesting and storing

Cut the heads of calabrese with about 1 in. (25 mm.) of stalk in late summer and early autumn when the flower buds are green and tightly closed. After the main head is cut, side-shoots will grow and further heads will be produced.

When harvesting sprouting broccoli, cut about 4–6 in. (100–150 mm.) of stem and cook this with the heads. Cut back to a point just above a pair of side-shoots, which will then produce fresh spears.

Calabrese and sprouting broccoli can be frozen (see p. 294).

Cooking sprouting broccoli

White, green and purple-sprouting broccoli are related to the cauliflower, but in flavour they are more reminiscent of asparagus. The fresh spears, on brittle stalks, may in fact be cooked and served in the same way as most asparagus dishes. Calabrese can be cooked whole.

To prepare broccoli, wash the spears carefully in cold water, strip off the leaves and trim off any tough parts from the base of the stalks. Cook in boiling, lightly salted water for no more than 12 minutes, and drain thoroughly before coating with melted butter.

BROCCOLI AU GRATIN

1 lb. (500 g.) broccoli spears or a head of calabrese
Salt and pepper
½ pint (300 ml.) white sauce
2 oz. (50 g.) butter
3 tablespoons white breadcrumbs

COOKING TIME: 15 minutes

Put the prepared broccoli spears in a pan of boiling salted water. Bring back to the boil and simmer, covered, until the spears are just tender. Drain thoroughly and arrange in a shallow flameproof dish.

Spoon the white sauce over the broccoli. Melt most of the butter in a pan, and mix in the breadcrumbs until the butter has been absorbed.

Sprinkle the breadcrumbs over the sauce and dot with the remaining butter. Set under a hot grill for a few minutes.
Serving With chicken or ham.
Variation Replace the breadcrumbs with grated cheese, fold half into the sauce and sprinkle the rest on top. Grill until bubbling.
Photograph on pages 134–5.

BROCCOLI VINAIGRETTE

12–16 broccoli spears or a head of calabrese
6 tablespoons olive oil
2 tablespoons white wine vinegar
1 teaspoon finely chopped fennel
Salt and pepper
Garnish: fresh fennel

COOKING TIME: 7 minutes
CHILLING TIME: 2 hours

Wash the broccoli spears carefully, trim the stalks and remove any leaves. Put in boiling salted water and simmer for 5–7 minutes. Drain in a colander and cool slightly.

Make up a dressing from the oil, vinegar, fennel, salt and pepper. Arrange the broccoli in a flat dish, pour over the dressing and chill for 2 hours.
Serving Set three or four spears on each plate, garnish with a sprig of fennel and serve with brown bread and butter.
Photograph on pages 138–9.

Continued . . .

AT-A-GLANCE TIMETABLE FOR SPROUTING BROCCOLI AND CALABRESE

SOWING	THINNING	TRANSPLANTING	HARVESTING

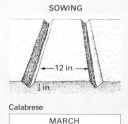

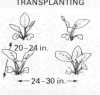

Calabrese	When seedlings are large enough to handle	Move when plants are about 4 in. high	AUGUST–OCTOBER
MARCH			
Sprouting broccoli	When seedlings are large enough to handle	Move when plants are about 4 in. high	MARCH–MAY
APRIL			

Sprouting-broccoli recipes (continued)

BROCCOLI WITH ALMONDS

1 lb. (500 g.) broccoli spears
Salt
2 oz. (50 g.) butter
2 oz. (50 g.) flaked almonds
Juice of ½ lemon

COOKING TIME: 10 minutes

Trim the stalks of the broccoli spears and remove the leaves. **Wash** the spears in cold water. **Put** the broccoli in a pan with a small amount of boiling, lightly salted water. Bring back to the boil and simmer for about 7 minutes, or until just tender.

Meanwhile, melt the butter in a pan, add the flaked almonds, sprinkle them with salt and fry over low heat until golden-brown. Stir in the lemon juice.

Drain the broccoli thoroughly through a colander, arrange in a serving dish and pour the browned butter and almonds over them.
Serving This makes an ideal vegetable dish with grilled fish, such as trout or mackerel, and with delicate meats such as veal.
Variation Cover the broccoli spears with a Hollandaise sauce, and serve as a vegetable dish or as a first course.

BROCCOLI CHEESE PUFFS

16 broccoli spears
½ lb. (250 g.) puff pastry
2 oz. (50 g.) firm Cheddar cheese
Salt and pepper
1 egg

COOKING TIME: 20 minutes
OVEN TEMPERATURE: 220°C (425°F) – gas mark 7

Carefully wash the broccoli spears and trim the stalks short. Put in a pan of boiling, lightly salted water. Simmer for about 5 minutes or until just tender, then drain through a colander.

Roll out the pastry thinly and cut into eight equal-size squares with 4 in. (100 mm.) sides. Cut the cheese into four slices and trim them a little narrower than the pastry squares; cut in half.

Lay a slice of cheese over half of each pastry square, arrange two broccoli spears on top and sprinkle with salt and pepper. Beat the egg and brush over the pastry edges. Fold over the pastry and seal the edges firmly.

Set the pastry parcels on a damp baking sheet, make three slits in each and brush the top with egg. Bake in the centre of the oven for about 20 minutes, or until risen and golden.
Serving Serve hot or cold, either as an appetiser or as a snack with a green salad.
Variation Turn the broccoli in a thick cheese sauce and enclose with the puff pastry.

Brussels sprouts

It is thought that Brussels sprouts, a descendant of the wild cabbage, were first grown in Belgium.

This hardy vegetable is rich in vitamin C, and will provide a crop during autumn and winter if both early and late varieties are planted. However, if you have a freezer it may be easier to make a single sowing of either type and freeze surplus sprouts to extend their period of use.

Brussels sprouts occupy a fair amount of space over a longer period (about eight months) than most crops. For this reason they may not be a wise choice for very small gardens, and in any case they do better in rather more open conditions than those provided by the average fenced-in suburban plot.

Planning the crop

Sprouts grow well only in fertile soil that has an adequate lime content.

Dig the following season's Brussels-sprouts bed during the winter, so that it has ample time to settle. Ideally, it should have been well manured for a previous crop; otherwise, add compost or manure when you dig. Afterwards, spread lime on the surface (see p. 19).

How many to grow Each 10 ft (3 m.) row of plants should yield about 16 lb. (7.5 kg.) of sprouts.

Varieties The introduction of F1 hybrid varieties (see p. 30) has greatly improved the quality and yield of Brussels sprouts. Only the best of the ordinary varieties give

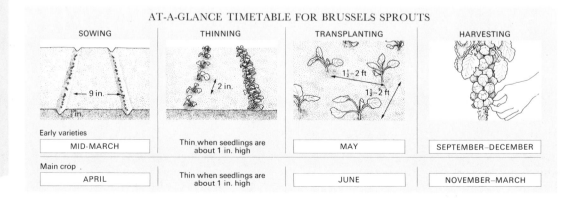

AT-A-GLANCE TIMETABLE FOR BRUSSELS SPROUTS

SOWING	THINNING	TRANSPLANTING	HARVESTING
← 9 in. → / 1 in.	↕ 2 in.	1½–2 ft / 1½–2 ft	
Early varieties	Thin when seedlings are about 1 in. high		
MID-MARCH		MAY	SEPTEMBER–DECEMBER
Main crop	Thin when seedlings are about 1 in. high		
APRIL		JUNE	NOVEMBER–MARCH

equal results. Following is a selection from the many varieties of both types currently offered by leading seed firms:

'Citadel' (F1): a heavy cropper; matures from December onwards.

'Early Dwarf': ideal for small gardens; the 18 in. (455 mm.) plants carry a good crop from October onwards.

'Fasolt' (F1): ready from November to February; freezes well.

'New Year': large, dark green sprouts; matures from December to February.

'Peer Gynt' (F1): matures from October onwards; freezes well.

How to grow Brussels sprouts

Although very early sprouts can be obtained by sowing under glass, these will mature at a time when plenty of summer vegetables are still available. Outdoor sowings will meet most needs.

Make the first sowings of early varieties in mid-March in a sheltered seed bed. Sow the seeds $\frac{1}{2}$ in. (12 mm.) deep in drills 9 in. (230 mm.) apart, thinning the seedlings to at least 2 in. (50 mm.) apart when they are about 1 in. (25 mm.) high.

Early varieties will be ready for harvesting between September and December.

Sow maincrop varieties in April, with similar spacings to early varieties. They will mature between November and March.

When plants of both early and maincrop sowings are about six weeks old, and 4–6 in. (100–150 mm.) tall, transplant them into their final bed, first dressing this with 3 oz. of superphosphate and 1 oz. of sulphate of potash per square yard (90 g. and 30 g. per square metre) or with 2 oz. per square yard (60 g. per square metre) of a general fertiliser.

Select only strong, healthy-looking plants, making sure that each has a growing point, and plant them firmly $1\frac{1}{2}$–2 ft (455–610 mm.) apart – the closer spacing for dwarf varieties – in rows the same distance apart.

The best way to plant is with a dibber, first making the planting hole with the tool and then, after planting, stabbing it in again close to the plant to firm the soil against it. If you use a trowel, firm the soil afterwards with your heel.

Sprinkle bromophos around the base of each plant as a protection against cabbage root fly.

Water the plants freely during dry weather.

Stake large plants that are exposed to wind.

Pests and diseases The pests most likely to affect Brussels sprouts are APHIDS (p. 282), CABBAGE ROOT FLY (p. 282), CABBAGE WHITEFLY (p. 282), CATERPILLARS (p. 282) and FLEA BEETLE (p. 283).

Diseases and disorders include CLUB ROOT (p. 287), LEAF SPOT (p. 288) and SPRAY DAMAGE (p. 291).

Harvesting and storing

The best time to pick sprouts is when they are small and nut-like; they then provide crisper eating. Harvesting after a slight frost also ensures a good flavour.

Pick the lower sprouts first. Sprouts at the top of the plant can be encouraged to swell by removing the cabbage-like head, which can be cooked as a separate vegetable.

See also freezing (p. 294).

Preparing & cooking Brussels sprouts

Pick the sprouts when they are not much larger than walnuts, and with their leaves still tight and firm. Old Brussels sprouts with loose leaves are practically tasteless.

Pick the sprouts just before cooking, peel off any ragged outer leaves, trim the base and cut an 'X' across it. Wash the prepared sprouts in cold water.

Cook in the minimum of boiling salted water for 8–10 minutes. The cooked sprouts should still be slightly chewy, not watery and squashy. Drain and serve.

The flavour is even better retained by boiling the sprouts for only 5 minutes, and then braising them with thinly sliced onions in a little butter, stock and seasoning for another 5 minutes.

BRUSSELS SPROUTS SOUP

2 lb. (1 kg.) Brussels sprouts
$\frac{1}{2}$ lb. (250 g.) sliced potatoes
1 sliced onion
2 oz. (50 g.) butter
$1\frac{1}{2}$ pints (850 ml.) rich stock
$\frac{1}{2}$ pint (300 ml.) milk
Salt, pepper, ground nutmeg
5 fl. oz. (150 ml.) cream

COOKING TIME: 35–40 minutes

Sauté the potatoes and onion in the butter for 10 minutes over gentle heat, until they have absorbed the butter. Toss the sprouts with the potatoes and onion and transfer to a large pan with the stock and milk. Bring to the boil, cover with a lid and simmer for 20 minutes. Season with salt and pepper.

Rub the soup through a sieve, or blend in a liquidiser. Season with nutmeg, add the cream and re-heat the soup without letting it boil.

Serving Pour into soup bowls and serve with crisp bread croûtons.

Variation Serve the soup chilled, stirring in the cream at the last minute.

Photograph on page 216.

BRUSSELS SPROUTS WITH NUTMEG

1 lb. (500 g.) Brussels sprouts
2 oz. (50 g.) melted butter
1 dessertspoon soft brown sugar
1 teaspoon freshly grated nutmeg

COOKING TIME: 10 minutes

Peel and wash the sprouts, make an 'X' in the base of each and cook in boiling salted water until just tender, which will take about 7–8 minutes.

Drain the sprouts thoroughly, dry off in the pan over a gentle heat and pour the melted butter over them. Toss to coat the sprouts evenly, add the sugar and toss again.

Serving Spoon into a serving dish and dust generously with grated nutmeg.

BRUSSELS SPROUTS AND PORK

1 lb. (500 g.) Brussels sprouts
4 pork steaks or lean chops
2 oz. (50 g.) butter
2 cooking apples
Salt and pepper
Juice of 1 lemon
1 tablespoon soft brown sugar

COOKING TIME: 1 hour
OVEN TEMPERATURE: 160°C (325°F) – gas mark 3

Clean and prepare the sprouts. Blanch in boiling, lightly salted water for 2 minutes, drain through a colander and leave to cool.

Meanwhile, flatten the pork steaks and trim away excess fat if chops are used; brown in butter over a good heat to seal both sides. Lift out the steaks.

Brown the sprouts lightly in the butter, then remove from the pan. Peel and core the apples and cut into slices.

Arrange the pork steaks and sprouts in a shallow, buttered, ovenproof dish, sprinkle with salt and pepper and cover with the apple slices. Spoon over the lemon juice and sprinkle with brown sugar.

Cover with a lid or foil and cook in the oven for about 45 minutes. Remove the lid for the last 10 minutes.

Serving Take straight from the oven to the table, and serve with creamed or sauté potatoes.

Continued . . .

Brussels-sprouts recipes (continued)

SPROUTS IN THE BASKET

¾ lb. (375 g.) Brussels sprouts
1 oz. (25 g.) butter
1 oz. (25 g.) flour
½ pint (300 ml.) milk
Salt and pepper
Ground nutmeg
1 lb. (500 g.) sausage meat
Bacon fat or dripping

COOKING TIME: 20 minutes
OVEN TEMPERATURE: 200°C (400°F)
– gas mark 6

Choose small, immature sprouts for this dish. Trim away outer damaged leaves, wash the sprouts and put in a pan with the minimum amount of boiling, lightly salted water.

Simmer gently for about 7 minutes, or until they are just tender. Drain thoroughly and reserve the water.

Make a white coating sauce from the butter, flour and milk and, if necessary, thin to the required consistency with the reserved water. The sauce should be fairly thick. Season to taste with salt, pepper and nutmeg, and fold in the sprouts. Heat through, stirring constantly.

Meanwhile, divide the sausage meat into eight equal portions and shape them into flat rounds. Brush eight round tartlet tins with melted butter on the outside and cover them with the sausage meat. Set them in a baking tin, covered side up, add a little melted fat and roast in the oven for about 20 minutes, or until brown and crisp.

Baste occasionally with the pan juices. Ease the baked sausage-meat shells from the tins, turn them upside-down and fill with the Brussels-sprouts mixture.

Serving These baskets make a complete meal served with buttered or mashed potatoes.

———>o<———

BRUSSELS SPROUTS WITH CHESTNUTS

¾ lb. (375 g.) Brussels sprouts
2 oz. (50 g.) butter
6 oz. (175 g.) chestnuts
Pepper

COOKING TIME: 15 minutes

Prepare and wash the sprouts; put them in a pan with a little boiling, lightly salted water. Boil for 5–7 minutes, drain thoroughly and keep warm.

Melt the butter in a pan and add the cooked, peeled chestnuts. Tinned chestnuts may be used, but they should be unsweetened. Sauté for 5 minutes, then add the sprouts and toss with the chestnuts until evenly coated. Sprinkle with freshly ground pepper.

Serving The dish is a traditional accompaniment to roast turkey at Christmas.

Photograph on pages 212–13.

———>o<———

BRUSSELS SPROUTS WITH MUSHROOMS

1 lb. (500 g.) Brussels sprouts
½ lb. (250 g.) potatoes
1 grated onion
3 oz. (75 g.) butter
Milk
5 fl. oz. (150 ml.) double cream
Salt and pepper
½ lb. (250 g.) button mushrooms

COOKING TIME: 30 minutes

Peel the sprouts and potatoes; cut up the potatoes and put to boil in a pan of unsalted water. Add the sprouts and grated onion for the last 7 minutes of cooking time. Drain thoroughly and mash the vegetables to a purée by rubbing them through a sieve or blending in a liquidiser.

Re-heat the purée, adding 2 oz. (50 g.) of butter, 2 tablespoons of cream, and sufficient milk to give the consistency of creamed potatoes. Season to taste with salt and pepper.

Meanwhile, sauté the sliced mushrooms in the remaining butter until golden-brown, pour the cream over them and continue cooking over a gentle heat until the cream sauce has thickened slightly. Season with salt.

Serving Spoon the purée into a dish, pour over the creamed mushrooms and serve with cold roast chicken or ham.

Burnet

The cucumber flavour of burnet – or salad burnet as it is often called – makes it a useful addition to soups, sauces, butters and salads. The plant is a hardy perennial and grows wild in Britain on downland. Here it has for centuries provided grazing for sheep throughout the year, although the wild plants are stunted compared with those grown in gardens.

Burnet has been grown in herb gardens since Roman times, and in this country was once valued for a variety of medicinal properties – real or imaginary. It was also planted between paving slabs, along with such herbs as thyme and chamomile, for the pleasant scent that it gives when trodden on.

Planning the crop

Burnet grows best in light, well-drained soil in a sunny position. There is no need to add manure or compost, but a dressing of lime is valuable on all but chalky soils.

How much to grow The plants grow to a height of 1½–2½ ft (455–760 mm.) if allowed to flower, with a spread of 9–12 in. (230–305 mm.). One or two plants should provide sufficient leaves.

How to grow burnet

Sow the seeds outdoors in a drill ½ in. (12 mm.) deep during March or April. When the seedlings are about 2 in. (50 mm.) high, transfer them to their permanent positions, at 12 in. (305 mm.) spacings.

Keep the soil moist until the plants are well established, and

AT-A-GLANCE TIMETABLE FOR BURNET

SOWING	TRANSPLANTING	HARVESTING
½ in.	12 in.	
MARCH–APRIL	When seedlings are 2 in. high	Pick leaves while young and tender

hoe frequently to kill weed seed-lings until the plants have grown sufficiently to smother them.

To encourage the growth of young leaves, which are the best for using in the kitchen, cut back the flowering stems as they develop during the summer.

Raising new plants Lift estab-lished plants with a fork during the autumn or spring; if possible, divide them into smaller, rooted pieces and re-plant at once in their permanent positions.

However, the plants tend to form tap-roots, and in this case it may be impossible to divide them into rooted pieces. If this happens, insert small, unrooted divisions in sandy soil in a cold frame and keep them shaded until rooted.

Pests and diseases The plants are generally trouble-free.

Harvesting and storing

Pick the leaves while they are still young and tender, before the plants flower. They can be used fresh, or may be frozen (see p. 294) for winter use. 🌶🌶

Cooking with burnet

Mix the finely chopped leaves into salad dressings, or sprinkle them over the salad itself.

The leaves may also be added to mayonnaise, butter garnishes, and to white sauces served with egg, fish and vegetable dishes.

With their slight taste and smell of cucumber, which is strongest when the leaves are bruised, they can also be used as a garnish for iced drinks.

Cabbages

Savoy cabbage

Summer cabbage

Winter cabbage

Spring cabbage

Red cabbage

The cabbage is generally regarded as the most boring of vegetables and has even lent its name as a term of contempt for a stolid, unadventurous person. But if grown and cooked properly, it is a tasty food and one rich in nourishment.

It is also hardy and easy to grow, and if different varieties are planted it will provide a succession of crops throughout the year.

In shape, cabbage heads, or hearts, may be round, conical or drumhead (round, with a flattened top); in colour they range from dark and light green to pink and purple.

Spring cabbages have bright green, loose-leaved heads and are in season during April and May. The small varieties may be cut early, in March, before they mature – when they are known as spring greens.

Summer cabbages have larger, more compact heads. They are ready during August and September.

Autumn and winter cabbages, which have solid heads like the summer varieties, are ready for cutting from October to February.

Savoy cabbages are round-headed, with crisp, crinkled leaves. They are very hardy and easy to grow, and with successional sowings will provide a crop of fresh green vegetables from September right through the winter to May.

Red cabbages, which are often grown for pickling, have solid heads of crisp leaves. They are another good autumn and winter crop.

Planning the crop

Cabbages need a sunny, open site in well-drained, alkaline soil. This

109

applies to both the seed bed, in which they are raised, and to the main growing site.

When cabbages follow pod-bearing crops and salads in a crop rotation (see pp. 26–27), the plot should not require manure or compost, but apply a general fertiliser at planting time. If you are growing vegetables for the first time, and therefore establishing a rotation, dig in a dressing of manure or compost during the previous winter.

Whether or not manure is needed, spread lime on the surface after digging (see p. 19) unless the soil is chalky or has recently been limed. If you omitted to apply lime after digging, rake it into the surface of the soil at planting time.

How much to grow A 10 ft (3 m.) row will yield about 10 lb. (5 kg.) of spring cabbages, 14 lb. (6.5 kg.) of summer cabbages or 12 lb. (5.5 kg.) of autumn, winter, savoy or red cabbages.

Varieties Summer cabbages with round heads:
'Emerald Cross' (F1 hybrid): large cabbage with solid heart.
'Golden Acre': early; medium-size; good flavour.
'Market Topper' (F1 hybrid): large, firm hearts; slow to bolt.
'Primo': early, dwarf, compact.
'Velocity': solid heart; quick to mature.
Summer cabbages with pointed heads:
'Greyhound': medium-size, with few outer leaves.
'Hispi' (F1 hybrid): large, solid, crisp heads.
Autumn and winter cabbages:
'Christmas Drumhead': dwarf and compact; very hardy.

'Hidena' (F1 hybrid): hard, oval-shaped head; good flavour.
'Ice Queen' (F1 hybrid): uniform cropper; hard heads.
'January King': very hardy; suitable for the north.
Savoy cabbages:
'Best of All': early; extra large.
'Ormskirk Late': large; very hardy.
Spring cabbages:
'April': crops heavily; firm hearts.
'Early Market': early, reliable and hardy.
'Golden Acre Springtide': neat, pointed hearts.
'Offenham Flower of Spring': very hardy; large, conical heads; can also be sown in spring.
'Wheeler's Imperial': earlier than most; very hardy.
Red cabbages:
'Blood Red': matures early; pickles well.

'Niggy': a compact, space-saving cabbage.

How to grow cabbages

Cabbages of all types are raised in a seed bed and then transplanted to the positions where they will grow and mature.

In both cases the ground should first have been dug and a dressing of lime applied if necessary (see p. 19). Before sowing or planting, tread the bed firm and rake it to a fine tilth. Apply a general fertiliser at 2 oz. per square yard (60 g. per square metre) to the main bed.

Summer cabbages Sow seeds in early April in a prepared seed bed, at the same depth and distances as for spring cabbages.

Thin overcrowded seedlings, and transplant those that are left to their permanent bed in late May or early June, setting them 18 in.

(455 mm.) apart in rows the same distance apart. Plant very firmly.

Hoe the bed regularly during summer, and make sure it never dries out.

Autumn and winter cabbages Sow seeds in April or May in a prepared seed bed, as for spring and summer cabbages. For a regular supply of cabbages throughout the winter months, sow two or more batches during these two months.

Transplant the seedlings to a permanent bed between May and July. Set them 18 in. (455 mm.) apart in rows 2 ft (610 mm.) apart. Keep the bed weed-free by regular hoeing until late autumn, and water freely during dry spells.

Savoy cabbages Sow the seeds in a prepared bed in the same way as for other cabbages. Seeds sown in April will produce a crop from

September to December; those sown in May will provide cabbages from January to March; a July sowing will give a crop the following April and May.

Transplant the seedlings to the permanent bed six weeks after sowing. Plant them 18 in. (455 mm.) apart, and leave 2 ft (610 mm.) between rows.

Hoe the bed regularly and ensure that it never dries out.

Spring cabbages Draw drills $\frac{1}{4}$ in. (5 mm.) deep and 6 in. (150 mm.) apart, in a prepared seed bed, during the first fortnight of August (late July in the north). Sow the seeds thinly in the drills.

It is important to sow spring cabbages at the correct time. If sown too early, the plants may grow too large to withstand a hard winter; if too late, they will not have sufficient time to develop beyond the seedling stage before the days become shorter and colder.

Ensure that the bed does not dry out, and thin overcrowded seedlings to 2 in. (50 mm.) apart.

Six weeks after sowing, transplant the seedlings to their permanent bed. Space plants required for use as spring greens 12 in. (305 mm.) apart. Allow 15 in. (380 mm.) between those that will be left to form hearts.

In both cases, leave 18 in. (455 mm.) between rows.

After planting, firm the soil around the young cabbages with the dibber or with your heel. Apply bromophos or diazinon granules to safeguard against cabbage root fly, then water the plants.

Keep the plot weed-free by hoeing. In March, dress the soil

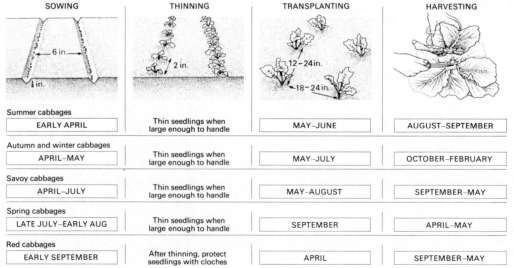

AT-A-GLANCE TIMETABLE FOR CABBAGES

	SOWING	THINNING	TRANSPLANTING	HARVESTING
Summer cabbages	EARLY APRIL	Thin seedlings when large enough to handle	MAY–JUNE	AUGUST–SEPTEMBER
Autumn and winter cabbages	APRIL–MAY	Thin seedlings when large enough to handle	MAY–JULY	OCTOBER–FEBRUARY
Savoy cabbages	APRIL–JULY	Thin seedlings when large enough to handle	MAY–AUGUST	SEPTEMBER–MAY
Spring cabbages	LATE JULY–EARLY AUG	Thin seedlings when large enough to handle	SEPTEMBER	APRIL–MAY
Red cabbages	EARLY SEPTEMBER	After thinning, protect seedlings with cloches	APRIL	SEPTEMBER–MAY

with ½ oz. of nitrate of soda per square yard (15 g. per square metre) and hoe into the surface.

Red cabbages Sow the seeds in early September, in the same way as for other cabbages. Leave the seedlings in the seed bed throughout the autumn and winter, protecting them with cloches during severe weather.

Transplant the young cabbages into their permanent bed in April, setting them 2 ft (610 mm.) apart in rows the same distance apart. Remove weeds regularly with a hoe, and water during dry spells.

Pests and diseases Cabbages are subject to the same pests as other brassica crops, namely APHIDS (p. 282), CABBAGE ROOT FLY (p. 282), CABBAGE WHITEFLY (p. 282), CATERPILLARS (p. 282) and FLEA BEETLE (p. 283).

Diseases and disorders include CLUB ROOT (p. 287), DAMPING OFF (p. 287), DOWNY MILDEW (p. 288), LEAF SPOT (p. 288), SPRAY DAMAGE (p. 291) and WIRE STEM (p. 291).

Harvesting and storing

Cut cabbages when their heads are firm and fleshy. Savoy cabbages are best eaten after a slight frost, which brings out their flavour.

Dig up and burn cabbage stumps after the crop is over. They will take a long time to rot if placed on the compost heap.

If the land is not needed immediately for another crop, however, a few stumps may be left in the ground to provide a further crop of greens. The clusters of leaves which will sprout from the stems should be cut and eaten while they are still tender.

See also freezing (p. 294).

Preparing & cooking cabbages

Although the cabbage has for centuries been a widely grown vegetable, it has suffered from incorrect, prolonged boiling, resulting in a tasteless, soggy mass and a pervading smell.

Prepare cabbages for cooking by removing the outer coarse leaves, cutting into quarters and cutting out the hard centre core and the base. Wash thoroughly and drain, and cook either in wedges or shredded. Use the minimum of boiling, lightly salted water – just enough to prevent sticking.

Cook shredded cabbage for 5–7 minutes; wedges for about 12 minutes. Drain thoroughly and toss in butter and freshly ground pepper.

Red cabbages, which are usually braised with butter, vinegar and sugar, require longer cooking.

Green-leaved and white-leaved cabbages, apart from their use as a separate vegetable, will also improve soups and stews; white and red cabbages will provide crisp winter salads; red cabbages are also frequently pickled, as are white cabbages for sauerkraut.

BRAISED SAVOY CABBAGE

1½ lb. (750 g.) savoy cabbage
6 oz. (175 g.) streaky bacon rashers
1 large onion
Salt, pepper, allspice

COOKING TIME: 20 minutes

Prepare the cabbage and shred it finely. Put in a pan of boiling, lightly salted water and cook for 5 minutes. Drain thoroughly.

Remove the rind and gristle from the bacon, chop crossways into narrow strips and put in a heavy-based pan. Fry the bacon until crisp, and the fat begins to run, then add the finely chopped onion and cook until soft.

Add the drained cabbage, stirring continuously until well coated; season to taste with salt, pepper and allspice, and heat through.
Serving Spoon into a serving dish and serve at once with roast or boiled pork.
Variation Braise the parboiled cabbage in dripping and white stock; season with nutmeg, marjoram or thyme, and thicken the cooking liquid with arrowroot.

COLESLAW WITH ROQUEFORT DRESSING

1 small white cabbage
2–3 carrots
2 dessert apples
Juice of 1 lemon
6 tablespoons olive oil
2 tablespoons white wine vinegar
1 teaspoon French mustard
Salt and pepper
2 oz. (50 g.) Roquefort cheese
1 teaspoon celery seeds

Remove the outer leaves from the cabbage, cut it into quarters, wash and drain, remove the centre stalks and shred the remainder finely. Peel or scrape the carrots and grate them coarsely. Wash the apples, but do not peel. Instead, quarter them and remove the cores, then dice them. Put these ingredients in a bowl, add the lemon juice and toss well.

For the dressing, whisk or shake together the oil, vinegar and mustard and season with salt and freshly ground pepper. Mash the Roquefort cheese soft with a fork, then gradually beat in the oil-and-vinegar dressing, beating until smooth and thoroughly combined. Pour the dressing over the salad ingredients and mix well.
Serving Mix this salad just before serving.

Serve it on its own, with crusty bread, or as a side salad.
Photograph on pages 138–9.

CREAMED CABBAGE

1 small green or white cabbage
1 large onion
2 oz. (50 g.) bacon fat or dripping
Salt and ground cardamom
5 fl. oz. (150 ml.) cream

COOKING TIME: 30 minutes
OVEN TEMPERATURE: 180°C (350°F) – gas mark 4

Remove the outer leaves from the cabbage, cut it into quarters and rinse under cold running water. Remove the tough stalk and shred each quarter coarsely. Peel and grate the onion.

Melt the bacon fat in a pan and fry the onion lightly for about 2 minutes, add the shredded cabbage and continue frying lightly until thoroughly coated with the fat. Season to taste with salt and cardamom.

Spoon the cabbage and onion into a lightly buttered ovenproof dish, pour the cream over it, cover with a lid and bake in the lower half of the oven for about 25 minutes.
Serving Creamed cabbage goes well with roast veal, pork and boiled ham.
Variation Shred and cook the cabbage as usual. Drain, and fold into a seasoned white sauce made with half milk and half cream.

Continued . . .

Cabbage recipes (continued)

CURRIED CABBAGE

*2 lb. (1 kg.) white or green winter
  cabbage*
*¾ pint (450 ml.) bouillon or white
  wine*
1 garlic clove
1 small onion stuck with 6 cloves
2 bay leaves
2 oz. (50 g.) butter
1 tablespoon curry powder
4 tablespoons flour
Salt, pepper, paprika

COOKING TIME: 25–30 minutes

Prepare the cabbage and shred it
finely. Put in a pan with the
bouillon, the garlic cut in half,
the onion and the bay leaves.
Bring to the boil and simmer for
about 8 minutes. Drain
thoroughly in a colander,
discarding the garlic, onion and
bay leaves, and set the cooking
liquid aside.

Melt the butter in a pan, stir in
the curry powder and cook for
2 minutes. Add the flour, stirring
until well combined. Gradually
stir in the reserved liquid to make
a thick sauce; boil for a few
minutes, then fold in the drained
cabbage and heat through.
Season to taste with salt, pepper
and paprika.
Serving This is an excellent
vegetable dish with grilled pork
chops, roast lamb or pork.
Variation Stir tomato purée to
taste into the sauce before adding
the cabbage.
Photograph on pages 134–5.

STUFFED CABBAGE

1 medium-size white cabbage
½ lb. (250 g.) finely minced veal
½ lb. (250 g.) finely minced pork
1 peeled, grated onion
2 tablespoons white breadcrumbs
1 tablespoon flour
Salt, pepper, ground nutmeg
¾ pint (450 ml.) milk (approx.)

COOKING TIME: 1½–2 hours

Make up the stuffing by blending
thoroughly the veal, pork and
onion. Work in the bread-
crumbs and flour, season
to taste with salt, pepper and
nutmeg, and beat to a firm
consistency with the milk.

Remove the outer ragged
leaves of the cabbage, trim the
stalk, slice off the top and set
aside. Scoop out the inner part of
the cabbage with a knife and
spoon, leaving a shell of at least
1 in. (25 mm.) all round.

Press the stuffing into the
cavity, replace the lid and keep
in place with fine string or soft
tape. Wrap in foil and set in a
large pan.

Pour boiling water into the
pan to reach just below the top of
the cabbage, add salt and cover
with a lid. Simmer gently for
about 1½ hours, or until the
cabbage is tender, adding more
water if necessary. Lift out, and
remove the foil and string.
Serving Arrange the cabbage
on a hot dish, surrounded with
small buttered potatoes, and
serve with a white sauce.
Photograph on pages 212–13.

CABBAGE CASSEROLE

1 winter or spring cabbage
*1 lb. (500 g.) leg of lamb or lean
  pork*
2 tablespoons oil
2 large onions
4 tomatoes
Salt and paprika
¾ pint (450 ml.) bouillon

COOKING TIME: 1½–1¾ hours
OVEN TEMPERATURE: 180°C (350°F)
– gas mark 4

Remove the outer leaves from
the cabbage, cut it into quarters,
rinse and drain. Cut out the
centre stalk and chop the
cabbage roughly, or cut each
quarter lengthways in half.

Trim the meat of any fat, and
cut into 1 in. (25 mm.) chunks.
Heat the oil in a pan, and fry the
meat for a few minutes until it is
brown and sealed on all sides.
Pour off any excess fat.

Grease an ovenproof dish
lightly and arrange in it layers of
cabbage, meat, sliced onions and
peeled, sliced tomatoes. Begin
and finish with cabbage, and
season each layer lightly with salt
and paprika.

Pour bouillon into the dish
until it stands just level with the
top layer of cabbage. Cover with
a lid and bake in the oven for 1½
hours, or until the meat is tender.
Serving This casserole is
equally good served with boiled
rice or floury potatoes.

BRAISED RED CABBAGE

*1 large red cabbage 3 lb. (1.5 kg.)
  (approx.)*
2 cooking apples
2 oz. (50 g.) butter
*5 fl. oz. (150 ml.) white wine
  vinegar*
*5 fl. oz. (150 ml.) red or black-
  currant juice, or red wine*
Sugar

COOKING TIME: 1½ hours

Remove the outer coarse leaves,
cut the cabbage into quarters,
remove the large tough cores and
shred the cabbage finely. Peel,
core and grate the apples and
mix with the cabbage.

Melt the butter in a large
heavy-based pan, add the
vinegar and mix in the cabbage;
coat thoroughly, then cover with
a tight-fitting lid and simmer
over a gentle heat for 1 hour. Add
a little more vinegar or water if
there is a danger of the cabbage
sticking.

Stir in the fruit juice or wine,
and season to taste with sugar.
The cabbage should be fairly
sharp in flavour. Cover with a lid
and simmer until tender.
Serving The braised cabbage
goes well with fatty meat and
poultry, such as pork, goose or
duck. It may also be served cold,
and can be cooked in advance
and re-heated.
Variations Flavour with
ground cloves, or add 1 teaspoon
of caraway seeds.

CABBAGE DOLMAS

1 large green or white cabbage
Salt and pepper
4–6 tablespoons oil
1 large onion
½ lb. (250 g.) minced cooked lamb
4 oz. (125 g.) boiled long-grain rice
1 tablespoon finely chopped mint
*1 tablespoon finely chopped parsley or
  dill*
1 egg
3 tablespoons tomato paste
¾ pint (450 ml.) bouillon or white wine

COOKING TIME: 2 hours (approx.)
OVEN TEMPERATURE: 160°C (325°F) –
gas mark 3

Remove any damaged leaves from
the cabbage and trim the stalk. Put
the cabbage in a large pan of
boiling, lightly salted water, bring
back to the boil, cover with a lid
and remove the pan from the heat.

Let the cabbage stand in the hot
water for 10 minutes, then drain it
carefully and peel off the large
outer leaves, leaving them whole.
The cabbage should yield at least
eight, and preferably 12, whole
leaves. Set these aside, remove the
stalk from the rest of the cabbage
and chop the leaves finely.

Heat the oil in a pan and lightly
fry the finely chopped onion until
soft. Add the minced lamb and
fry until it is light brown.

Stir in the rice, mint and
parsley, season to taste with salt
and pepper and remove the pan
from the heat. Blend this stuffing
with the lightly beaten egg and lay
a spoonful or two in the centre of

Cabbages, Chinese

each of the large cabbage leaves.

Fold the sides of the leaves over the stuffing, roll them up and hold in place with fine string.

Butter a large ovenproof dish and line with half the chopped cabbage, lay the cabbage rolls on top and cover with the remaining chopped cabbage. Blend the tomato paste with the bouillon or wine and pour the mixture over the cabbage. Cover with a lid and bake for about 1½ hours.
Serving Serve immediately, accompanied with rye bread.

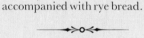

CABBAGE SOUP

½ white or 1 green winter cabbage
2 carrots
2–3 leeks
½ lb. (250 g.) potatoes
3 pints (1.5 l.) bouillon, white stock or water
1 bouquet garni
Salt, pepper, curry powder
Garnish: chopped parsley

COOKING TIME: 30 minutes

Prepare and wash the cabbage; shred it finely. Prepare and roughly chop the carrots, leeks and potatoes. Put all the vegetables in a pan with the bouillon or stock and the bouquet garni; bring to the boil and simmer, covered, over a gentle heat for 30 minutes. Season to taste.
Serving Sprinkle with parsley and serve at once.
Photograph on pages 138–9.

Though grown in the Far East since at least as long ago as the 5th century AD, the Chinese cabbage was unknown in Europe much before 1900. Even now, it is little grown in this country – a pity, since the plant has a particularly delicate flavour.

However, Chinese cabbages are not the easiest of vegetables to grow. They may succumb to frost, and will run to seed if you sow them too early or forget to water them sufficiently. Unlike other cabbages, they must be sown where they are to grow and not transplanted.

In appearance, a Chinese cabbage is more like a large cos lettuce than a conventional cabbage.

Planning the crop

Prepare the ground in late spring, in time for sowing in June or early July. Spread a light dressing of manure or compost, and on dry soils add a bucketful of dampened peat per square yard. Sprinkle lime on the surface if the soil is at all acid.

How many to grow Up to ten cabbages can be grown in a 10 ft (3 m.) row. A single cabbage is sufficient for half-a-dozen people, so a single row of this length should be ample for most families. Bearing in mind that other vegetables are plentiful in late summer, even four or five plants may be sufficient to cover the brief harvesting season – though sometimes they do withstand early frosts.

Varieties Not all the following varieties are widely stocked by seedsmen:

'Chihili': closely resembles a tall, sturdy cos lettuce.

'Pe-tsai': dependable variety; obtainable from most seedsmen.

'Nagaoka' and 'Sampan': F1 hybrids; resistant to bolting.

'Wong-Bok': hardier than some; crisp, tender leaves.

How to grow Chinese cabbages

In mid-June, sow the seeds in the prepared ground ½ in. (12 mm.) deep, spacing the rows 2 ft (610 mm.) apart if you sow more than one. As soon as the seedlings are large enough to handle, thin them out to 12–15 in. (305–380 mm.) apart.

Water the plants well during dry spells and hoe the bed regularly to kill weeds. Scatter slug pellets throughout the bed in late July and August. If the hearts seem loose, raise the outer leaves round them and tie them in place with garden twine.

Pests and diseases During their brief growing season, Chinese cabbages are subject to the same pests that afflict other brassicas. The most likely are APHIDS (p. 282), CABBAGE ROOT FLY (p. 282), CABBAGE WHITEFLY (p. 282), CATERPILLARS (p. 282) and FLEA BEETLE (p. 283).

Disorders include CLUB-ROOT (p. 287), DAMPING OFF (p. 287), LEAF SPOT (p. 288), SPRAY DAMAGE (p. 291) and WIRE STEM (p. 291).

Harvesting and using

Although Chinese cabbages should be left to grow until they are mature and have firm hearts, they will be inedible if they are allowed to run to seed.

The crop generally matures between mid-September and early October.

Cooking Chinese cabbages

Though they cook well and make excellent soup (see cooking instruction and recipes for cabbages, p. 111) they are probably at their best when chopped raw into a salad and served with a vinaigrette or lemon dressing. 🍃🍃

AT-A-GLANCE TIMETABLE FOR CHINESE CABBAGES

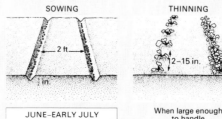
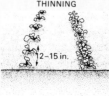

SOWING — JUNE–EARLY JULY

THINNING — When large enough to handle (2–15 in.)

TYING UP — Secure with twine if hearts seem loose

HARVESTING — SEPTEMBER–OCTOBER

Capsicums : see **Peppers and chillis**

Cardoons

This handsome plant, with its great purple flowers and silvery leaves, closely resembles the globe artichoke and may, in fact, be its ancestor. Despite this, cardoons are grown not for their globes but for the midribs and stalks of the young leaves.

Like celery, the stalks are blanched and cooked on their own, or used as flavouring in soups and stews. For centuries an established favourite in French kitchen gardens, the cardoon's distinctive taste deserves greater popularity in Britain.

Planning the crop

Cardoons need a rich, moisture-retentive but well-drained soil, and are best grown in trenches similar to those used for celery. They are large plants and might make a useful screen in summer for the vegetable plot, but be careful to position them so that they do not cut off the light from smaller plants near by.

Varieties 'Improved White' and 'Ivory White' are recommended.

How much to grow Cardoons are still a novelty in Britain, and it would be sensible to grow only a few plants until you decide whether or not you like them.

Even then, about a dozen plants should be quite sufficient for most families.

How to grow cardoons

In early April, dig a trench 12 in. (305 mm.) wide and 12 in. deep, leaving the excavated soil on each side. Fork a generous layer of well-rotted manure into the soil at the bottom.

Sow the seeds in late April or early May in groups of three, 20 in. (510 mm.) apart and ½ in. (12 mm.) deep. Put cloches over the trench during the first month, and in due course remove the two weaker seedlings from each group.

Cardoons need generous water-ing throughout the summer, together with a dose of weak liquid fertiliser every seven days.

They will have finished growing by about mid-September, and this is the time to blanch the stems. On a sunny day, when both the foliage and the earth are dry, tie the leaves firmly together with string and wrap black polythene sheeting around each plant from the bottom to the top.

Tie the polythene in place, and earth up the plants in the same way as for potatoes using the earth left on each side of the trench. In a month, blanching should be complete, and the plants may be dug for use as required.

If preferred, earthing up can be omitted, but the soil does provide extra protection from frost and strong winds.

Pests and diseases Cardoons are normally pest and disease-free.

Harvesting and storing

Dig up the plants as needed, when blanching is complete. This takes about a month.

Alternatively, a number of plants can be dug together and stored, still wrapped in polythene, in a cool, dry place until they are needed. 🪴🪴

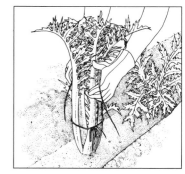

TIE WITH STRING Choose a dry, sunny day, when the leaves are dry, to tie the stems together firmly with raffia or soft string.

WRAP THE LEAVES Wrap brown paper or black polythene round the leaves. Secure with raffia or string before earthing up.

EARTH UP Draw soil round the plants. Though not vital, this gives extra protection.

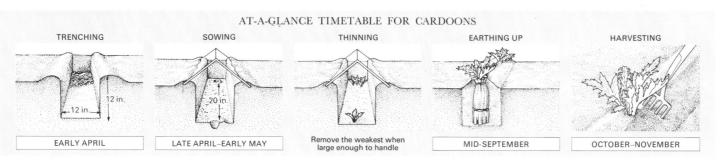

AT-A-GLANCE TIMETABLE FOR CARDOONS

TRENCHING	SOWING	THINNING	EARTHING UP	HARVESTING
EARLY APRIL	LATE APRIL–EARLY MAY	Remove the weakest when large enough to handle	MID-SEPTEMBER	OCTOBER–NOVEMBER

Cooking cardoons

This vegetable is little grown, although it is reminiscent of two other favourite vegetables – celery and globe artichokes.

The edible stems, with their artichoke flavour, can be prepared and cooked like blanched celery, but unlike celery they are not suitable for eating raw.

To prepare cardoons, remove the outer hard stems, which in some varieties are bristly, and trim off the root ends and any pieces of damaged stem.

Separate the individual stems and scrub them clean under cold running water.

Leave the stems in a bowl of water to which the juice of a lemon has been added. This helps to prevent them becoming discoloured before they are cooked.

Cut the stems into pieces 3 in. (75 mm.) long, and at the same time pull any stringy bits from the stems.

Cook the cardoon pieces in boiling, lightly salted water (or white stock) for about 20 minutes, or until tender.

After cooking, drain the pieces of cardoon thoroughly and serve tossed in butter.

Cooked cardoons may also be served coated with cream or sprinkled with chopped parsley, tarragon or chervil.

Alternatively, fold them into a Béchamel or Hollandaise sauce; or the cooked stems may be served in a cheese sauce.

Cooked cardoons may also be served as a salad to accompany cold meat, dressed with oil and vinegar.

Carrots

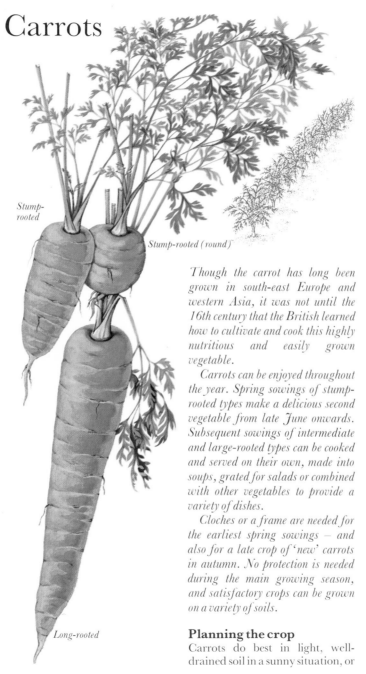

Stump-rooted

Stump-rooted (round)

Long-rooted

Though the carrot has long been grown in south-east Europe and western Asia, it was not until the 16th century that the British learned how to cultivate and cook this highly nutritious and easily grown vegetable.

Carrots can be enjoyed throughout the year. Spring sowings of stump-rooted types make a delicious second vegetable from late June onwards. Subsequent sowings of intermediate and large-rooted types can be cooked and served on their own, made into soups, grated for salads or combined with other vegetables to provide a variety of dishes.

Cloches or a frame are needed for the earliest spring sowings – and also for a late crop of 'new' carrots in autumn. No protection is needed during the main growing season, and satisfactory crops can be grown on a variety of soils.

Planning the crop

Carrots do best in light, well-drained soil in a sunny situation, or one with only minimal shade. Early crops, in particular, do best in full sun. Reasonable crops can be grown on other soils, but clay is unsuitable.

Do not sow carrots in soil that has recently been manured. In a rotation scheme they should follow brassicas, such as cabbages and Brussels sprouts (see pp. 26–27).

How much to grow A 10 ft (3 m.) row will yield up to 13 lb. (6 kg.) of early carrots, or 15 lb. (7 kg.) of maincrop carrots, in really fertile soil.

Varieties Of the three main types of carrots, the cylindrical, non-tapering varieties are best for very early crops under cloches or in frames; the stump-rooted for open sowings on shallow soils; and the tapering, long-rooted kinds for large carrots on deep, rich ground.

The following varieties are recommended:
Cylindrical, non-tapering: 'Amsterdam Forcing'; 'Early Scarlet Horn'; 'Nantes'; 'Paris Forcing' and 'Pioneer' (F1 hybrid).
Stump-rooted: 'Autumn King'; 'Beslicum'; 'Chanteray Red Cored'; 'James's Scarlet Intermediate'; 'Parisian Rondo'.
Long-rooted: 'Scarlet Perfection'; 'St Valery'.

How to grow carrots

The first sowing (which should be of a cylindrical variety) can be made in a frame or under cloches in March. Put cloches in position at least two weeks before sowing to warm up the ground. Just before sowing, break down the soil and apply 4 oz. of general fertiliser per square yard (120 g. per square metre).

Sow the seeds thinly in $\frac{1}{4}$ in. (5 mm.) deep drills, 9 in. (230 mm.) apart. Pelleted seeds are an advantage as they can be placed individually, making subsequent thinning a great deal easier. Replace the cloches or frame lights, and do not remove until the seedlings are growing strongly.

When the seedlings are large enough to handle, thin them first to 1 in. (25 mm.) apart. Later thin them to intervals of about 2 in. (50 mm.).

If you do not use pelleted seeds, thinning can be simplified by

AT-A-GLANCE TIMETABLE FOR CARROTS

SOWING	THINNING	HARVESTING
9–12 in. / 1 in.	3–4 in. / 1 in.	
Short-rooted varieties		
MARCH–APRIL/AUG	When large enough to handle	JUNE–JULY/NOV–DEC
Intermediates/main crop		
MID-APRIL TO JULY	When large enough to handle	JULY–OCTOBER

making a special tool out of an old table knife. Heat the end of the blade, bend the last ½–1 in. (12–25 mm.) at right-angles, and sharpen to give a keen edge.

If space allows, make another sowing of a stump-rooted variety two or three weeks later, either under cloches or in the open.

From about mid-April until July, sow intermediate or long-rooted varieties, with the rows 12 in. (305 mm.) apart, and use the larger thinnings in salads or for cooking. These later sowings do not need cloche protection, but leave at least 3–4 in. (75–100 mm.) between the carrots at the final thinning.

An August sowing of a cylindrical variety, grown under cloches to speed growth, will provide tender carrots in November and December.

Ideally, all thinning should be done on dull days or in the evening. Sun brings out the smell of the carrot foliage, which attracts the carrot fly – the vegetable's worst pest.

Water the plants after thinning, and either scatter bromophos or diazinon granules along the row, or water in a spray-strength solution of diazinon.

Hoe between the rows to keep weeds under control.

Pests and diseases CARROT FLY (p. 282) is the principal pest of this crop.

The diseases and disorders most likely to be encountered are SCLEROTINIA DISEASE (p. 290), SPLITTING (p. 290) and VIOLET ROOT ROT (p. 291).

Harvesting and storing

Pull up early, short-rooted varieties in June and July, easing them with a fork if the ground is hard.

Harvest maincrop carrots in early October, using damaged carrots immediately and storing the rest for use during the winter. Always use a fork to loosen intermediate and long-rooted varieties.

Before storing, remove the soil and cut off the foliage close to the crown. Store the carrots in boxes, between layers of sand, and keep the boxes in an airy, dry, frost-proof shed.

Clamps are not really practicable for small quantities, and are in any case a much less convenient method of storage than boxes.

See also freezing (p. 294); pickling (p. 328); syrups and juices (p. 326) and wine-making (p. 357). 🌢🌢

TRIMMING AND STORING

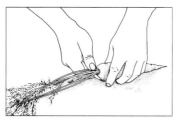

After lifting, cut off the foliage close to the crown. Use damaged roots immediately.

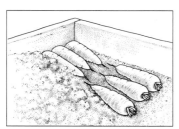

Store the roots in boxes of sand. Pack them closely, with sand between the layers.

Preparing & cooking carrots

Carrots are used as flavouring for stocks, casseroles and stews, and as the base for soups. They may also be served as a cooked vegetable on their own, or eaten raw in salads, with cocktail dips or as a garnish.

To prepare carrots, trim off the tapering root end and the leaves, complete with any woody or discoloured pieces. Scrape young carrots under cold running water, but peel older carrots thinly. Before cooking, cut older carrots into quarters, slices or chunks. Leave young, small carrots whole, or cut them in half. Cook carrots in boiling, lightly salted water, or white stock, for 10–30 minutes – depending on their age and the method of preparation. They can be finished off in melted butter, sprinkled with finely grated cheese, parsley, mint, ginger or coriander. They can also be served in a Béchamel sauce or tossed in cream. Old carrots can be mashed with butter and seasoning, in the same way as potatoes.

As a garnish for soups, chop raw carrots into match-sized strips or pare thin slices along the carrot with a potato peeler. Twist into curls, fasten with cocktail sticks and leave in iced water to settle the shapes. Remove the cocktail sticks before using the garnish.

CARROT MOULD

¾ *lb. (375 g.) carrots*
Salt and pepper
1 teaspoon sugar
1 oz. (25 g.) butter
3 eggs
1 tablespoon chopped parsley

COOKING TIME: 45 minutes
OVEN TEMPERATURE: 180°C (350°F) – gas mark 4

Maincrop carrots may be used for this dish, but young carrots have a more delicate flavour. Trim the roots and tops from the carrots, then scrape or peel them before giving a final wash. Cut the carrots into slices and put in a pan of boiling, lightly salted water.

Simmer, covered, for 12–15 minutes or until quite tender. Drain and mash the carrots to a purée in a liquidiser, vegetable mouli or with a potato masher. Stir the sugar and butter into the purée and season to taste with salt and pepper. If the purée seems too thick, thin it down with a little milk.

Beat the eggs lightly and stir them into the purée, together with the parsley. Spoon the mixture into a buttered mould, set this in a pan of hot water and bake in the oven for about 30 minutes.

Serving Turn the mould out, upside-down, and serve as a dish on its own, accompanied with small buttered potatoes and peas and with a white or cheese sauce.

Variation Make a purée from 1 lb. (500 g.) carrots, add seasoning, butter and cream and serve as a vegetable dish with roast or braised meat.

TURKISH CARROT SALAD

4 large carrots
2 garlic cloves
5 fl. oz. (150 ml.) olive or sunflower oil
½ pint (300 ml.) natural yoghourt
Salt and pepper
Garnish : chopped mint

COOKING TIME: 10 minutes
CHILLING TIME: 1 hour

Peel and wash the carrots and grate them on the coarse side of a grater; peel and crush the garlic.

Heat the oil in a heavy-based pan, add the grated carrots and garlic and cook for about 10 minutes over a gentle heat, stirring frequently. Drain the carrots through a sieve until all the oil has strained off and the carrots have cooled.

Spoon into a bowl and mix with the yoghourt; season to taste with salt and pepper, and chill for at least 1 hour.
Serving Sprinkle with finely chopped fresh mint and serve with cold lamb or chicken.
Variation Mix equal quantities of grated carrot and celeriac with a little finely chopped onion and the juice of a lemon. Dress with soured cream, seasoning to taste.

SUMMER CASSEROLE

1 lb. (500 g.) young carrots
1 lb. (500 g.) new potatoes
1 lb. (500 g.) belly pork
2 oz. (50 g.) butter
¾ pint (450 ml.) white stock
Salt and pepper
2 sprigs of thyme
1 small cauliflower
½ lb. (250 g.) young green peas
Garnish : chopped parsley

COOKING TIME: 1 hour

Trim the carrots, scrape and wash them and chop into rough slices. Scrape the potatoes, leaving small ones whole but cutting larger ones into slices. Remove the rind, bone and gristle from the belly pork and cut into cubes.

Melt the butter in a heavy-based pan and fry the meat until golden-brown ; add the carrots and potatoes and toss well. Stir in the stock, season with salt and pepper and add the fresh thyme. Cover with a lid and simmer over a gentle heat for 35 minutes.

Add the cauliflower, broken into small florets, and the peas. Continue simmering until the ingredients are tender. Correct the seasoning. Remove the thyme and, if necessary, thicken with a little kneaded butter and flour.
Serving Spoon the casserole into a serving dish and sprinkle liberally with finely chopped parsley.
Variation Young green beans and button mushrooms, cooked in a little butter, may also be added for the last 15 minutes of cooking.

CARROTS VINAIGRETTE

1 lb. (500 g.) carrots
1 onion
1 tablespoon finely chopped mint or chives
4 tablespoons olive oil
1 tablespoon white wine vinegar
1 tablespoon lemon juice
Salt and pepper
Garnish : caraway seeds

CHILLING TIME: 30 minutes

Trim and peel the carrots, then wash and dry them. Grate on the coarse side of a grater and mix with the finely chopped or grated onion. Blend in the mint or chives.

Make a dressing from the oil, vinegar and lemon juice, seasoning with salt and freshly ground pepper. Pour the dressing over the carrots, and mix well. Chill in the refrigerator for about 30 minutes.
Serving Sprinkle the salad with caraway seeds and serve with cold roast meat or chicken.
Variation For a slimming salad, mix the grated carrots and onions with one or two grated cooking apples and dress with the juice of a lemon, or half a lemon and half an orange.

HONEY-GLAZED CARROTS

1 lb. (500 g.) young carrots
Salt
1 oz. (25 g.) butter
1 tablespoon honey
½ teaspoon ground cinnamon

COOKING TIME: 20 minutes

Trim off the roots and top ends before scraping and washing the carrots. Leave very small carrots whole ; cut larger ones into halves. Put them in a pan of boiling, lightly salted water, cover with a lid and simmer for about 15 minutes or until just tender. Drain thoroughly.

Melt the butter in a pan, add the honey and stir until melted. Toss the drained carrots in this mixture over a gentle heat until they are evenly coated and light brown. Sprinkle with cinnamon.
Serving Spoon the carrots and glaze into a dish and serve with roast or grilled meat and poultry, or with grilled white fish.

CARROTS À LA VICHY

1 lb. (500 g.) carrots
1 pint (600 ml.) boiling water
1 dessertspoon lemon juice
1 teaspoon salt
1 tablespoon sugar
2 oz. (50 g.) butter
Garnish : chopped mint, chives or parsley

COOKING TIME: 20 minutes

Trim the tops and roots from the carrots, then scrape and wash them. Either leave them whole or cut them into even sizes. If old, maincrop carrots are used, cut them in half lengthways, remove the tough cores and cut the carrots into even chunks.

Put the carrots in a pan, with the boiling water, lemon juice, salt, sugar and butter. Cover the pan with a tight-fitting lid and simmer for about 20 minutes, or until the carrots are tender and the water has reduced to a glaze. Shake the pan occasionally towards the end of the cooking time to glaze the carrots evenly.
Serving Spoon the carrots into a dish and sprinkle with finely chopped mint, chives or parsley.
Variation Replace half the carrots with salad onions and cook as above.
Photograph on pages 141–2.

CARROT SALAD

¾ lb. (375 g.) carrots
1–2 dessert apples
2 oz. (50 g.) raisins
2 tablespoons sugar
Juice and grated rind of 1 lemon
Salt and pepper

Maincrop carrots are ideal for this winter salad. Trim off the roots and tops, peel the carrots and grate them into a bowl, using the coarse blade of a grater.

Peel the apples, cut into quarters and remove the cores. Grate into a bowl with the carrots and mix together with a fork. Blend in the raisins.

Dissolve the sugar in 1 table-spoon of boiling water and mix with the lemon juice and rind. Season this dressing to taste with salt and pepper. Pour the lemon dressing over the carrots.
Serving Serve at once as a side salad, or as a vegetarian dish on its own.
Variations A handful of roughly chopped hazelnuts or peanuts may be added to the carrots before the dressing, and a little soured cream may also be blended in at the last minute.
Photograph on pages 138–9.

Cauliflowers and broccoli

Cauliflowers are the most difficult of the brassica family to grow successfully. They need an open position and rich soil, and must be kept growing quickly.

A setback, such as a spell of drought or a serious check in growth, can result in failure.

Given the right conditions, however, cauliflowers can be harvested all the year round by growing varieties that mature at different times. They also freeze satisfactorily, so surplus heads can be stored before they run to seed.

Broccoli, or winter cauliflowers, which can be harvested from December to May, according to the variety, have large white heads similar to summer cauliflowers. They should not be confused with sprouting broccoli (see p. 104) which have many small, sprig-like heads instead of a single curd.

Planning the crop

Cauliflowers grow best in rich, loamy soils. In an established crop-rotation scheme (see p. 26), grow them on land manured the previous year for pod-bearing crops, applying a general fertiliser at 3 oz. per square yard (90 g. per square metre) at planting time. Unless the soil is alkaline, give a top-dressing of carbonate of lime at 4 oz. per square yard (120 g. per square metre) during the winter or spring before planting.

On a new vegetable plot, dig in manure or compost during the winter before planting cauliflowers, and top-dress with lime after digging.

How much to grow About 14 cauliflowers can be grown in a 20 ft (6 m.) row – about as many as are likely to be eaten while they remain in prime condition. The best plan is to grow different varieties to get a succession of curds, rather than planting a large number of only a single variety that will mature at the same time.

The situation is different, of course, if you plan to freeze surplus cauliflowers.

Varieties Hearting broccoli are now classed as winter cauliflowers. Present-day cauliflowers therefore fall into three main categories – summer-heading; autumn-heading; and winter and spring-heading.
Summer-heading varieties, for sowing:

(a) under glass in late September or early October, and over-wintering in a frame or under cloches before planting out in March.

(b) under glass in January or February.

(c) outdoors in March and April:

'All the Year Round'; 'Classic'; 'Dominant'; 'Early Snowball'.
Autumn-heading varieties, for sowing outdoors from mid-April until mid-May:

'All the Year Round'; 'Autumn Giant'; 'Canberra'; 'Lecerf'; 'Rocket'; 'South Pacific'; and 'White Heart' – which should be sown during the third or fourth week in May.

Winter and spring-heading varieties, for sowing outdoors from March until mid-May:

'April', ready late March/April; 'Royal Oak', ready late May; 'Snow's Winter White', ready January/February; 'St Agnes', ready January; 'St George', ready March/April.

How to raise cauliflowers under glass

For the earliest summer-heading cauliflowers, ready for cutting in May and June, sow in a cold frame in late September or early October or in a heated greenhouse in January or February.

In a frame, prepare the soil in the same way as for an outdoor seed bed (see p. 119). Scatter the seeds lightly and cover with seed compost or sifted soil to a depth of $\frac{1}{4}$ in. (5 mm.).

Keep the frame light closed until germination takes place, then allow a little ventilation during mild weather.

Thin the seedlings to about 2 in. (50 mm.) spacings when they are large enough to handle. During hard night frosts cover the frames with sacking. Keep the plants in

AT-A-GLANCE TIMETABLE FOR CAULIFLOWERS UNDER GLASS

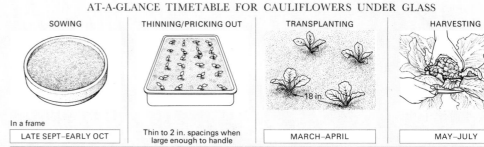

SOWING	THINNING/PRICKING OUT	TRANSPLANTING	HARVESTING
In a frame LATE SEPT–EARLY OCT	Thin to 2 in. spacings when large enough to handle	MARCH–APRIL	MAY–JULY
In a greenhouse LATE JAN–EARLY FEB	Prick out 2 in. apart when large enough to handle	MARCH	MAY–JULY

the frame, ventilating as necessary, until they are planted out in late March or early April.

In a greenhouse, sow in late January or early February in a pan of seed compost at a temperature of 10°C (50°F). When the seedlings are large enough to handle, prick them out 2 in. (50 mm.) apart in each direction into a tray of potting compost.

In early March, put the tray into a cold frame to harden off the plants for several days.

To plant, use a trowel to make holes 18 in. (455 mm.) apart in the prepared bed. Space rows 18 in. apart.

Choose plants with about six leaves and a good ball of soil on the roots. Check that each plant has a growing point – a small half-folded leaf at the tip of the stem. Place the roots in the hole and firm the soil well by pressing with your heel close to the stem.

Water well, and keep watering if necessary. At no stage must the plants be allowed to dry out, or they will produce undersized heads.

How to grow cauliflowers outdoors

For a later crop of summer-heading cauliflowers sow outdoors

in March or April. The same method of sowing, thinning and planting out is suitable also for autumn-heading and winter-heading cauliflowers.

Prepare the seed bed in a sunny, sheltered spot by raking a fine sedge peat, at the rate of not less than a bucketful per square yard, into the soil.

Sow the seed in a drill ¼ in. (5 mm.) deep, spacing drills 12 in. (305 mm.) apart if you sow more than one variety. Mark the names of the varieties on labels as each is sown – they will be indistinguishable otherwise – cover the drills with soil and firm.

Keep the seed bed moist. Thin to 2 in. (50 mm.) spacings when the seedlings are large enough to handle.

Plant out when the plants are 4–6 in. (100–150 mm.) high, following the method advised for the early crop but spacing these larger-growing, later plants 2 ft (610 mm.) apart, with the rows also 2 ft apart.

Keep the plants well watered, and give a dressing of nitrate of soda or Nitro-chalk once or twice during the growing season to improve the quality of the plants and curds.

When the curds begin to form,

break two or three of the large outside leaves over them. This will help to keep the curds pure white, because sunlight turns them yellow and frost turns them brown.

Covering can be left until the curds are nearly mature, or omitted altogether, in the case of some modern varieties which have incurving leaves.

Pests and diseases Like other brassicas, cauliflowers and broccoli are subject to attack by APHIDS (p. 282), CABBAGE ROOT FLY (p. 282), CABBAGE WHITEFLY (p. 282), CATERPILLARS (p. 282) and FLEA BEETLES (p. 283).

The principal diseases and disorders are CLUB ROOT (p. 287), DAMPING OFF (p. 287), DOWNY MILDEW (p. 288), LEAF SPOT (p. 288), SPRAY DAMAGE (p. 291), WHIPTAIL (p. 291) and WIRE STEM (p. 291).

Harvesting and storing

Cut the heads when they are firm. If left too long the curds break up as the plant begins to flower. If a number mature at the same time, pull up the plants and hang them upside-down in a cool shed. They will keep for up to three weeks.

See also freezing (p. 294) and pickling (p. 328).

Preparing & cooking cauliflowers

Although one of our most delicate and versatile vegetables, cauliflowers too often suffer from overcooking. They should be tender, yet remain crisp; and they must be thoroughly drained.

Before cooking, cut off the outer coarse leaves. There is no need to remove the inner, tender leaves and the pale green base leaves. Trim the end of the stalk flush with the base of the cauliflower, and cut a cross in it with a sharp knife to help make the stalk tender.

Depending on the recipe, cook the cauliflower whole, in boiling, lightly salted water, for 12–15 minutes; or for 8–10 minutes if divided into florets. A little lemon juice in the water helps to preserve the white colour.

Cauliflower may be served as an accompanying vegetable, either on its own or with a white, cheese or parsley sauce. It may also be used in soups, soufflés, gratins and salads. Its crisp, nutty texture and taste also make it perfect for cocktail dips and for deep-frying in batter.

CAULIFLOWER WITH BUTTERED CRUMBS

1 cauliflower
Salt and pepper
3 oz. (75 g.) butter
2 oz. (50 g.) dry breadcrumbs
2 tablespoons finely chopped parsley
1 tablespoon lemon juice

COOKING TIME: 15 minutes

Cut the outer leaves and the tough base from the cauliflower, divide it into florets and wash these well. Put the cauliflower into a pan of boiling, lightly salted water, bring it back to the boil and simmer, covered, for 5–7 minutes or until just tender. Drain thoroughly.

Melt the butter in a large frying pan, add the cauliflower florets and sauté over fairly high heat until golden-brown. Lift the cauliflower into a serving dish and keep it warm.

Stir the breadcrumbs and parsley into the remaining butter in the pan. Fry until they are crisp and brown and all the butter has been absorbed. Sprinkle with lemon juice, and season to taste with salt and pepper.

Serving Spoon the buttered crumbs over the cauliflower florets and serve with any kind of meat, poultry or fish, cooked in white sauce.

Continued . . .

AT-A-GLANCE TIMETABLE FOR CAULIFLOWERS OUTDOORS

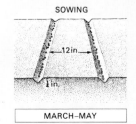

SOWING

—12 in.—

¼ in.

MARCH–MAY

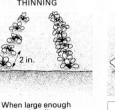

THINNING

2 in.

When large enough to handle

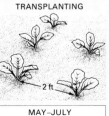

TRANSPLANTING

2 ft

MAY–JULY

HARVESTING

JULY–MAY

Cauliflower recipes (continued)

CAULIFLOWER SOUFFLÉS

Salt and pepper
1 oz. (25 g.) butter
4 oz. (100 g.) mayonnaise
Lemon juice
1 teaspoon dry mustard
2 egg whites
2 dessertspoons fresh white breadcrumbs
Garnish : chopped chives or parsley

COOKING TIME: 20–25 minutes
OVEN TEMPERATURE: 180°C (350°F) –
gas mark 4

Clean the cauliflower and break it into small florets. Put it in a pan of boiling salted water and cook for about 8 minutes, or until barely tender. Drain thoroughly and cool.

Butter four rounded scallop shells thoroughly. Season the mayonnaise to taste with lemon juice, freshly ground pepper and mustard. Beat the egg whites stiff and fold carefully into the mayonnaise, using a metal spoon.

Divide the drained cauliflower over the buttered shells, spoon over the mayonnaise mixture and sprinkle with breadcrumbs. Bake near the top of the oven for about 15 minutes, or until the soufflés are well risen and golden-brown.

Alternatively, arrange the cauliflower florets in a shallow ovenproof dish, well-buttered, and spoon the soufflé mixture over them.
Serving Garnish with chives or parsley and serve the soufflés at once, with cold ham or grilled bacon rolls and with melted butter or a green salad.
Variation Turn the cauliflower florets in a little white sauce instead of mayonnaise and add 4 oz. (100 g.) of chopped prawns.
Photograph on pages 134–5.

CAULIFLOWER AND BACON CHEESE

1 cauliflower
Salt and pepper
6 oz. (175 g.) lean bacon
1 oz. (25 g.) butter
1 oz. (25 g.) flour
½ pint (300 ml.) milk
½ teaspoon dry mustard
3 oz. (75 g.) mature grated Cheddar cheese
Cayenne pepper

COOKING TIME: 25 minutes
OVEN TEMPERATURE: 200°C (400°F) –
gas mark 6

Trim the leaves and stalk from the cauliflower and break it into small, even-sized florets. Cook in boiling, lightly salted water for about 5 minutes. Drain thoroughly in a colander.

Remove the rind and any gristle from the bacon, cut the rashers crossways into narrow strips and fry in a hot pan, without any extra fat, until crisp. Drain the bacon on absorbent kitchen paper.

Make up a white sauce from the butter, flour and milk, stirring until quite smooth. Add the mustard and two-thirds of the cheese, and season to taste with salt, pepper and cayenne. Fold the bacon and drained cauliflower florets carefully into the cheese sauce.

Spoon the mixture into a lightly buttered ovenproof dish, sprinkle the top with the remaining cheese and bake near the top of the oven for about 20 minutes, or until the cheese is brown and bubbly.
Serving This makes a complete dish on its own, suitable for a light lunch.

CAULIFLOWER SOUP

1 cauliflower
1 large carrot
1 leek
2 sticks celery
4 parsley stalks
1 bouquet garni
2 pints (1 l.) white stock
Salt and pepper
1½ oz. (40 g.) butter
1 oz. (25 g.) flour
2 egg yolks
5 fl. oz. (150 ml.) cream
Garnish : bacon

COOKING TIME: 30 minutes

Clean the cauliflower and divide it into florets. Scrape or peel the carrot, clean the leek and celery sticks and chop them all roughly. Put all the vegetables in a pan with the parsley stalks, bouquet garni and stock. Add salt and pepper and bring to the boil. Simmer, covered, for about 15 minutes.

Strain the soup, remove the cauliflower florets, discard the various flavourings, and set the liquid aside. Melt the butter and stir in the flour; gradually add the reserved liquid, stirring all the time to give a smooth soup. Add the cauliflower florets and heat through. Season to taste with salt and pepper.

Beat the egg yolks with the cream, add a little of the hot soup, then blend the egg and cream mixture into the soup. Stir until the soup thickens, but do not let it reach boiling point.
Serving Pour the soup into individual soup bowls and top with diced bacon, fried crisp without any extra fat.
Photograph on page 216.

CAULIFLOWER IN DISGUISE

1 cauliflower – approx. 1½ lb. (750 g.)
1 teaspoon lemon juice
½ lb. (250 g.) lean pork
½ lb. (250 g.) cooked ham or gammon
2–3 tablespoons white breadcrumbs
Salt, pepper, ground nutmeg
2 eggs
5 fl. oz. (150 ml.) milk
½ pint (300 ml.) thick white sauce
Garnish : cucumber slices, tomato quarters, chopped chives or parsley

COOKING TIME: 35 minutes

Trim and wash the cauliflower; put it in a pan of boiling, lightly salted water with the lemon juice. Bring back to the boil and simmer gently for 7 minutes. Drain the cauliflower thoroughly, reserving the water.

Meanwhile, put the pork and ham through the fine blade of a mincer. Blend the breadcrumbs into the mince and season to taste with salt, freshly ground pepper and nutmeg. Bind this mixture with the lightly beaten eggs and the milk to give a soft, pliable texture.

Lightly butter a piece of foil large enough to wrap round the cauliflower. Spread the minced-meat mixture in a circle over the foil, patting it to an even thickness. Place the cauliflower, stalk up, in the centre. Draw the meat and foil up and round the cauliflower, twisting to tighten it.

Put the cauliflower in a large pan of gently boiling water, foil seam up. Cover with a lid and simmer for 25 minutes.

Make the white sauce, using equal parts of single cream and the water reserved from the cooked cauliflower.
Serving Remove the foil and set the cauliflower, stalk end down, on a bed of lettuce leaves on a serving dish. Spoon the white sauce over it and garnish with fresh cucumber slices, wedges of tomatoes and finely chopped chives or parsley. Small buttered potatoes can also be served.

SPICED CAULIFLOWER

1 large cauliflower
2 onions
4–6 tablespoons oil
½ teaspoon mustard seeds
1 teaspoon each of ground ginger and salt
½ tablespoon turmeric
2 large tomatoes
½ teaspoon cumin (optional)
2 tablespoons finely chopped parsley
Sugar

COOKING TIME: 25 minutes

Prepare the cauliflower, divide it into florets and wash. Peel and finely chop the onions; heat the oil in a heavy-based pan and cook the onions for a few minutes until they are soft and transparent. Add the mustard seeds, ginger, salt and turmeric; cook, stirring all the time, for about 5 minutes.

Add the cauliflower florets to the pan, turning them until thoroughly coated with the spice mixture. Skin and finely chop the tomatoes, stir into the cauliflower mixture with the cumin, if used, and the parsley. Add sugar to taste. Cover the pan with a lid and continue cooking over a gentle heat for 10–15 minutes. Stir occasionally to prevent burning.
Serving This is a spicy vegetable dish that goes well with grilled fish, chicken or lamb chops.

CAULIFLOWER AND PRAWN SALAD

1 cauliflower
Salt and pepper
2–3 tomatoes
1 lettuce
5 fl. oz. (150 ml.) mayonnaise
Lemon juice
Garnish: 4 oz. (100 g.) shelled prawns; lemon wedges

COOKING TIME: 10 minutes

Clean and trim the cauliflower, divide it into florets and wash. Cook the cauliflower in boiling salted water for 10 minutes, or until tender yet still crisp. Drain and leave to cool.

Skin the tomatoes, cut them in half, remove the seeds and slice the flesh into wedges. Clean the lettuce; dry and shred it finely. Season the mayonnaise to taste with lemon juice and pepper.

Assemble the salad on individual small plates or shallow dishes: spread a thin base of shredded lettuce and arrange the cauliflower florets and tomato wedges alternately in a circle. Pipe mayonnaise in the centre and over the tomatoes, and set the prawns in the middle.
Serving Garnish with lemon wedges and serve with thin slices of buttered brown bread.
Variation Dress cooked, cooled cauliflower florets with vinaigrette flavoured with finely chopped fennel. Garnish with chopped spring onion.

Celeriac

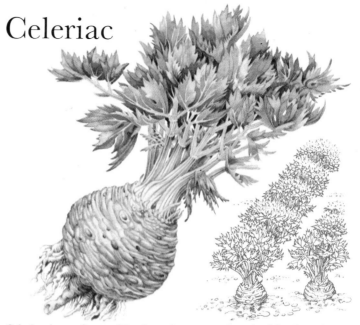

Celeriac has a flavour like that of celery, to which it is very closely related, being only a turnip-rooted form of that plant. Its swollen roots make a good winter substitute for celery in soups, stews and salads.

It is certainly less trouble to grow than trenched celery, which no doubt accounts for its greater popularity on the Continent.

As celeriac needs a long growing season, germinate the seeds in a warm place in March and plant outdoors in late May or June.

It is essential to keep the plants growing steadily throughout the spring and summer, otherwise they will not form roots of adequate size. The first should be ready for lifting by October.

Planning the crop

Grow celeriac in well-drained soil that has been enriched with rotted manure or compost at the rate of a bucketful per square yard in the winter before planting.

Choose a position that gets plenty of sun.

How much to grow A 20 ft (6 m.) row should yield 20 lb. (10 kg.) or more of roots – enough for most families during the autumn and winter.

Varieties Only a few varieties are available. These include:
'Alabaster': white-skinned; turnip-shaped roots.
'Claudia': non-branching roots and few side-shoots.
'Iram': medium-sized, globe-shaped roots.
'Marble Ball': large, globe-shaped roots.

How to grow celeriac

Sow celeriac seeds in mid-March at a temperature of 10–13°C (50–55°F). A greenhouse is the ideal place, but seeds can also be germinated in an airing cupboard and the seedlings grown on a sunny window-sill (see p. 32).

Sow the seeds in a seed pan. Press down the compost to make it level and firm, and sprinkle the seeds thinly over the top. Cover thinly with compost.

AT-A-GLANCE TIMETABLE FOR CELERIAC

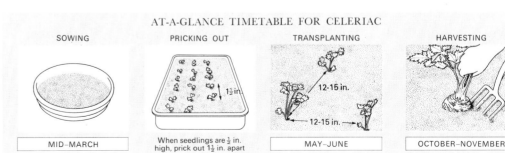

SOWING	PRICKING OUT	TRANSPLANTING	HARVESTING
MID-MARCH	When seedlings are ½ in. high, prick out 1½ in. apart	MAY–JUNE	OCTOBER–NOVEMBER

When the seedlings are ½ in. (12 mm.) high, prick them out about 1½ in. (40 mm.) apart in each direction into a tray of potting compost. Keep them in the greenhouse or indoors for three to five weeks, then put them in a cold frame for a week to harden off.

When setting out the plants in their final bed, set them at 12–15 in. (305–380 mm.) intervals in rows the same distance apart. Plant the seedlings so that the roots are buried and the leaves are just resting on the soil surface. Keep the plants well watered in the early stages, and hoe frequently to kill weed seedlings, otherwise the plants may suffer a serious growth check.

A fortnightly feed of liquid manure will help to keep the plants growing steadily. Apply this just before or just after watering.

During August, September and October, when the roots are swelling, remove any side-growths. If you fail to do so, the roots may not develop fully.

Pests and diseases CARROT FLY (p. 282), CELERY FLY (p. 283) and SLUGS AND SNAILS (p. 285) are the principal pests of celeriac.

LEAF SPOT (p. 288) is the disease most likely to occur.

Harvesting and storing

Use the roots as required during late October and November. Leave them as long as possible, however, so that they attain maximum size. There is no advantage in using them while they are immature.

About the end of November, lift those that remain, remove the foliage and store in damp sand or peat in a cool shed or cellar.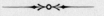

Preparing & cooking celeriac

Although for many years used on the Continent, this root vegetable is only now gaining popularity in Britain. The sweet celery flavour is most pronounced in young roots weighing up to about 1 lb. (500 g.). Older roots tend to become woody and hollow.

To prepare celeriac for cooking, trim off the upper leafy part. Do not discard the leaves, however, as they are excellent for flavouring soups and sauces and on the Continent are considered an essential part of a fresh bouquet garni.

Slice off the root end and scrub the celeriac under cold running water. Peel fairly thickly, and as the celeriac is prepared drop it in a bowl of cold water with 1–2 teaspoons of lemon juice to prevent discoloration.

Cut the celeriac into slices, chunks or narrow strips and cook in boiling salted water for 10–20 minutes, depending on the size of the pieces.

Serve celeriac as an accompanying vegetable – on its own, in a white sauce, or mashed and creamed like potatoes. It makes an excellent soup, and is equally delicious eaten raw as a crisp salad.

CELERIAC SOUP

1 lb. (500 g.) celeriac
2 leeks
2 carrots
1 small onion
2 oz. (50 g.) butter
2 pints (1 l.) white stock or bouillon
4 sprigs parsley
2 sprigs thyme
Salt, pepper and paprika
Milk
Garnish : chopped chives

COOKING TIME: 40 minutes

Pick off a few of the best celeriac leaves, rinse them and set aside. Scrub the celeriac, trim off the foliage and roots, peel and cut into small chunks. Clean the leeks, set a few of the green tops aside and chop the stems finely. Peel and chop the carrots and onion.

Melt the butter in a heavy-based pan and sauté the chopped vegetables for 5 minutes over a gentle heat. Add the stock. Wrap the reserved celeriac leaves, the parsley and the thyme sprigs in the leek tops to make a fresh bouquet garni. Tie with string.

Add the herbs to the pan; season with salt, freshly ground pepper and paprika. Bring to the boil, cover with a lid and simmer until the vegetables are tender. Remove the herbs and let the soup cool slightly.

Blend the soup in a liquidiser and re-heat, adding milk to give the required consistency. Correct the seasoning as necessary.

Serving Pour into soup bowls, garnish with chopped chives and serve with hot, crusty bread.
Variations Garnish with finely grated raw celeriac and sprinkle with paprika. For a richer soup, add ¼–½ pint (150–300 ml.) of double cream. Heat through without boiling.
Photograph on pages 138–9.

CELERIAC SALAD

1 celeriac
Salt
Lemon juice
3 tablespoons mayonnaise
French mustard

CHILLING TIME: 1 hour

Peel the celeriac, cut it into thin slices and then cut it crossways into match-like strips. Put in a pan of boiling, lightly salted water with a little lemon juice to preserve the colour; simmer for 2–3 minutes. Drain thoroughly in a colander and leave to cool.

Season the mayonnaise to taste with mustard, and toss the celeriac in this dressing. Chill in a refrigerator for about 1 hour.
Serving This is a good winter salad with sweet-cured or smoked ham, pork and cheese.
Variations Dress the celeriac with vinaigrette, or oil and lemon juice seasoned with salt and pepper. Alternatively, toss in mayonnaise flavoured with curry and lemon juice.

CELERIAC STEAKS

1 large celeriac
Salt and pepper
Juice of ½ lemon
1 beaten egg
3 tablespoons white breadcrumbs
2 oz. (50 g.) butter
4 eggs
Garnish : finely chopped parsley, tomato wedges

COOKING TIME: 45 minutes

Scrub and trim the celeriac. Peel the root and cook it whole in boiling, lightly salted water with the lemon juice added. Simmer, covered, for about 35 minutes or until just tender.

Drain and cut crossways into four slices, each 1 in. (25 mm.) thick. Trim the slices with a round or fluted pastry cutter. Dip the celeriac slices in beaten egg, and coat with breadcrumbs seasoned with freshly ground pepper. Melt the butter and fry the slices over a gentle heat until they are golden-brown on both sides, turning once only.

Meanwhile, fry the eggs in a separate pan.
Serving Arrange the celeriac steaks on individual plates, top each with a fried egg and decorate with parsley and tomato wedges. Serve as a light luncheon dish or snack.

CELERIAC AU GRATIN

1 large celeriac – 1½ lb. (750 g.)
Salt and pepper
1 tablespoon lemon juice
3 oz. (75 g.) butter
2 eggs
2 oz. (50 g.) breadcrumbs

COOKING TIME: 40 minutes
OVEN TEMPERATURE: 220°C (425°F)
– gas mark 7

Trim the leaves and slice top off the celeriac, together with the root end. Peel it thickly and cut into chunks. Put the celeriac in a pan of boiling, lightly salted water, together with the lemon juice. Cover with a lid and simmer for about 20 minutes, or until the celeriac is quite tender.

Drain the celeriac thoroughly, and mash with a potato masher or in a vegetable mouli. Stir half the butter into the purée and beat in the eggs, one by one. Season to taste with salt and pepper, and spoon the mixture into a buttered ovenproof dish.

Melt the remaining butter in a pan, and fry the breadcrumbs until they are crisp and all the butter is absorbed. Spoon the buttered crumbs over the celeriac purée and bake in the oven for 15–20 minutes or until the topping is crisp.
Serving The dish may be served as a meal on its own, accompanied with boiled or mashed potatoes and a tomato sauce, or as a vegetable dish with roast pork or game.

CELERIAC WITH MUSHROOM STUFFING

1 large celeriac
Salt and pepper
Juice of ½ lemon
½ lb. (250 g.) mushrooms
2 oz. (50 g.) butter
Garnish : paprika

COOKING TIME: 20–25 minutes

Trim the celeriac root, peel it and wash thoroughly. Cut crossways into 1 in. (25 mm.) slices and put in a pan of boiling, lightly salted water with the lemon juice. Cover with a lid and simmer gently for 15 minutes, or until just tender. Drain, and keep the celeriac warm under a dry cloth.

Meanwhile, trim the stalks and any ragged edges off the mushrooms. Leave them whole if small, otherwise slice thickly. Fry the mushrooms in the butter for about 5 minutes or until golden.
Serving Arrange the celeriac slices on individual plates, top with fried mushrooms and sprinkle with paprika. Serve as an appetiser.
Variations Top the slices with cooked ham or tongue and cover with hot, creamed spinach. For a more substantial dish, set a poached egg on the spinach.

Celery

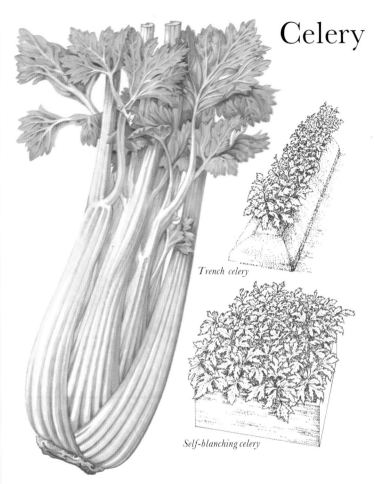

Trench celery

Self-blanching celery

Celery grows wild in damp places in Europe, Asia, North and South Africa and South America. The Greeks cultivated it for the medicinal value of the seeds. Today, however, special forms are grown for their thick, crisp, juicy stalks, which may be eaten raw, mixed in salads, cooked as a vegetable or used to flavour soups and stews.

There is a hard way and an easy way to grow celery. The hard way is to grow it in trenches, and the plants then have to be earthed up or wrapped individually in black polythene to blanch (whiten) the stems. The easy way is to grow self-blanching varieties, which are grown on level ground and need no earthing up.

Blanching is a slight misnomer when applied to celery because the stems may actually be white, pink, red or yellow. But this does not affect its purpose, which is to induce crisper, longer and less-fibrous stems, with a less-bitter flavour.

Self-blanching varieties are planted in a close block instead of in rows, so that they shield each other from the light. Only the outside plants require shading. This is done by banking straw against them, or by planting the celery in an open frame.

The disadvantages of self-blanching varieties are that they are not fully hardy, and their season is limited to late summer and autumn. Trench-grown varieties can be left in the ground for lifting from October until February.

Planning the crop

Celery grows best in an open position in rich soil.

For self-blanching varieties, dig in a bucketful of well-rotted manure or compost per square yard during the winter before planting.

For trench-grown varieties, dig a trench in winter in readiness for planting out in May or June. Make the trench 15 in. (380 mm.) wide to take a single row, or 2 ft (610 mm.) wide for a double row.

Dig out the soil from the trench to a depth of 12 in. (305 mm.) and put the excavated soil on each side. Fork over the bottom of the trench and work well-rotted compost or manure at the rate of a bucketful per square yard into the soil as you do so. Replace some of the soil so that the base of the trench is about 6 in. (150 mm.) below true ground level.

How much to grow A square a little over 5 × 5 ft (1.5 × 1.5 m.) will be sufficient to grow about 50 self-blanching plants. About

26 plants can be grown in a single trench 20 ft (6 m.) long.

Varieties Self-blanching celery can be divided into two types – yellow and green. Yellow varieties include:

'Golden Self Blanching': nutty flavour; non-stringy.

'Latham Self Blanching': vigorous and early maturing with a good flavour.

Green varieties include:

'American Green': creamy-green; crisp and tender.

'Utah': well flavoured, light green, brittle, crisp stems.

Trench-grown celery can be divided into three types – the white, which matures first; the pink, which follows; and the red, which is late and hardier than the others. White varieties include:

'Dwarf White': early maturing; broad sticks; compact growth.

'Giant White': large and solid; for use from October to Christmas.

'Prizetaker White': solid, crisp stems; superb flavour.

Pink varieties include:

'Clayworth's Prize Pink': a large early celery with long, crisp, pink-flushed sticks.

'Giant Pink': solid, very long sticks.

Red varieties include:

'Giant Red': robust growth; solid, dark red stems; will stand well into the New Year.

'Standard Bearer': the latest to mature, with dark red stems that stand well all through the winter.

How to grow self-blanching celery

In March sow the seeds in a pan of seed compost in a greenhouse at a temperature of 10–13°C (50–55°F). Cover the seeds thinly with fine compost.

Alternatively, enclose the pan in a plastic bag and place in an airing cupboard (see p. 32).

For a later crop, sow a second batch of seeds in a cold frame in mid-April.

When the seedlings are large enough to handle, prick them out 2 in. (50 mm.) apart into a tray of potting compost. Grow on in the greenhouse or on a window-sill until early May, then harden them off before planting in late May or early June – late June for the second batch.

Plant the seedlings 9 in. (230

mm.) apart each way to form a block. Use a trowel to loosen and lift the plants from the box, and to plant them. Keep the soil-balls intact while transplanting, and water in well.

Remove side-growths from the base as they appear. If the celery is grown in a frame without a top there is little else to do. If they are grown in an open bed, pack straw round the outside plants in July to blanch the outer rows.

BLANCHING OUTER PLANTS

During July, pack straw round the block to help blanch the outer plants.

How to grow celery in trenches

Raise the seedlings in the same way as for self-blanching varieties, but delay sowing until the second half of March. Make a second sowing in a frame in mid-April.

Plant out the first sowing in late May, the second one a few weeks later, spacing the seedlings for a single row 9 in. (230 mm.) apart along the centre of the prepared trench.

If planting double rows, allow 18 in. (455 mm.) between the rows and set the plants 9 in. (230 mm.) apart.

Water freely, especially during dry spells. Begin earthing up when the plants are 12–15 in. (305–380 mm.) high. This will be about early August for the May-planted celery, and September for those planted in June.

Before drawing soil round the plants, cut off any suckers that grow from the base and tie black polythene or paper round the stems. Water thoroughly, and draw some soil from the ridges on each side into the trenches to form a slight slope reaching about halfway up the stem of each plant.

Three weeks later, draw more earth round the plants to the base of the leaves.

Make the final earthing up three weeks after the second, sloping the soil to form a ridge (see facing page).

Pests and diseases Celery is liable to be attacked by the CARROT FLY (p. 282), CELERY FLY (p. 283) and SLUGS AND SNAILS (p. 285).

Diseases and disorders that may affect celery plants include BOLTING (p. 286), BORON DEFICIENCY (p. 286), LEAF SPOT (p. 288) and SPLITTING (p. 290).

Harvesting and storing

At the end of August start lifting self-blanching celery with a fork, piling up the straw against newly exposed plants.

All must be cleared before severe frosts set in.

Lift celery grown in trenches from late September – that is, about eight weeks after the first earthing up.

Open the ridge from one end, remove the plants with a fork, then earth up again as a protection against frost.

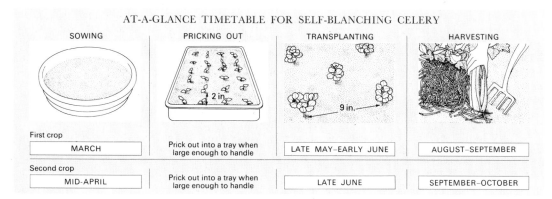

AT-A-GLANCE TIMETABLE FOR SELF-BLANCHING CELERY

SOWING	PRICKING OUT	TRANSPLANTING	HARVESTING
First crop MARCH	Prick out into a tray when large enough to handle	LATE MAY–EARLY JUNE	AUGUST–SEPTEMBER
Second crop MID-APRIL	Prick out into a tray when large enough to handle	LATE JUNE	SEPTEMBER–OCTOBER

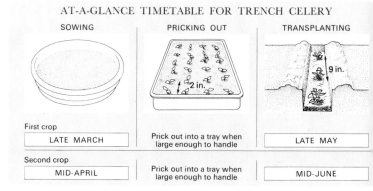

AT-A-GLANCE TIMETABLE FOR TRENCH CELERY

SOWING	PRICKING OUT	TRANSPLANTING
First crop LATE MARCH	Prick out into a tray when large enough to handle	LATE MAY
Second crop MID-APRIL	Prick out into a tray when large enough to handle	MID-JUNE

STAGES IN GROWING TRENCH CELERY

PREPARING THE TRENCH In winter, dig a trench 12 in. (305 mm.) deep and – for a single row – 15 in. (380 mm.) wide and work in well-rotted manure or compost.

PLANTING Depending on when they were sown, set the plants 9 in. (230 mm.) apart in the trench during late May or June. Water thoroughly until the plants are established.

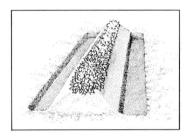

TYING AND EARTHING Start the blanching process by tying black polythene round the plants and drawing soil against them.

FINAL EARTHING The earthing-up process is completed in three stages, the last leaving only the leaves exposed above the ridge.

In extremely severe weather, spread bracken or straw on top of the ridge to prevent damage to the stems.

See also freezing (p. 294); pickles (p. 328); sauces and relishes (p. 339); vinegars (p. 342) and wine-making (p. 357).

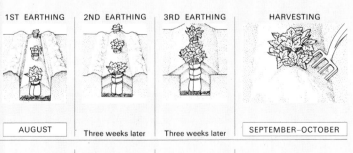

1ST EARTHING	2ND EARTHING	3RD EARTHING	HARVESTING
AUGUST	Three weeks later	Three weeks later	SEPTEMBER–OCTOBER
SEPTEMBER	Three weeks later	Three weeks later	OCTOBER–FEBRUARY

Preparing & cooking celery

Although used principally as a fresh salad ingredient, celery is equally tasty as a cooked vegetable. Prepare celery, either for eating raw and for cooking, by trimming off the lower end and removing entirely the tough outer stems.

For cooking, cut each head in half lengthways, trim off the leaves (which are excellent for flavouring and garnishing) and rinse the stems under cold running water. Alternatively, separate the stems and scrub them in water, peeling off any stringy bits.

Celery to be used fresh should not be left in water longer than absolutely necessary, or the stems will lose their characteristic crispness. Fresh, undamaged leaves may be left on the stems of celery to be served with a cheese-board.

Cook celery, cut into 2–4 in. (50–100 mm.) lengths, in a small amount of boiling, lightly salted water for 15–20 minutes, or steam for 20–30 minutes. Serve boiled or steamed celery in a cheese or parsley sauce, or smother it in melted butter and sprinkle with toasted almonds or grated nutmeg.

Serve celery tassels with cocktail and cheese dips. Cut the cleaned stems into 2 in. (50 mm.) lengths, then cut down at fine intervals almost to the base of each piece. Leave in a bowl of iced water until the strips have curled.

CREAM OF CELERY SOUP

2 heads of celery – approx. 10 oz. (275 g.)
Salt and pepper
1 oz. (25 g.) butter
1 oz. (25 g.) flour
1½ pints (850 ml.) white stock
Sugar ; grated nutmeg
5 fl. oz. (150 ml.) milk
5 fl. oz. (150 ml.) cream
Garnish : bread croûtons

COOKING TIME: 35 minutes

Trim the root ends off the celery, discard the outer stems and scrub the remainder under cold running water. Peel off any tough fibres and cut off the leaves. Chop the celery roughly, blanch in boiling, lightly salted water for 7 minutes, then drain.

Melt the butter in a heavy-based pan. Add the celery and cook over a low heat, stirring all the time, until the celery pieces are thoroughly coated. Stir in the flour and gradually add the hot stock, stirring until it boils.

Season with sugar, pepper and nutmeg, cover with a lid and simmer for about 20 minutes, or until the celery is tender.

Blend the soup in a liquidiser until smooth, or rub through a sieve. Re-heat the soup with the milk and blend in the cream, but do not allow it to boil. Correct the seasoning.

Serving Garnish with crisp bread croûtons, sprinkled with a little nutmeg.

Variation Serve the soup chilled, folding in the cream just before serving, and garnish with a swirl of lightly whipped cream.

CELERY CHEESE SOUFFLÉ

2 heads of celery
½ pint (300 ml.) milk
Salt and pepper
4 oz. (100–125 g.) grated cheese
2 eggs
1 oz. (25 g.) butter
2 tablespoons white breadcrumbs

COOKING TIME: 30 minutes
OVEN TEMPERATURE: 180°C (350°F) – gas mark 4

Trim and clean the celery, separate the stems, scrub thoroughly and either dice finely or grate on the coarse blade of a grater. Put the celery in a pan with enough milk to just cover; bring to the boil and simmer until quite tender and pulpy.

Season the celery purée to taste with salt and freshly ground pepper. Fold in the cheese and whisk in the lightly beaten eggs.

Spoon this mixture into four individual ovenproof dishes and sprinkle lightly with breadcrumbs. Bake for 15 minutes until risen and golden.

Serving Take straight to the table and serve with melted butter, as an appetiser or snack.
Photograph on pages 206–7.

Continued . . .

Celery recipes (continued)

CELERY WITH HAM AND CHEESE

2 heads of celery
Salt and pepper
4 slices of cooked ham
½ pint (300 ml.) white sauce
Grated nutmeg
2 oz. (50 g.) grated cheese

COOKING TIME: 35 minutes
OVEN TEMPERATURE: 190°C (375°F)
– gas mark 5

Trim the roots off the celery, remove any outer damaged stems and cut each head in half lengthways. Clean well in cold water, scrape off any stringy bits, then remove the leafy tops and set aside.

Boil the halved celery in lightly salted water, including the cleaned leaves for extra flavour or retaining them for later use as a garnish. Simmer for 10–15 minutes, then drain carefully in a colander.

Wrap one of the celery halves in a slice of ham and arrange in a buttered ovenproof dish. Make up a fairly thick white sauce, using half celery water and half single cream. Season with salt, pepper and nutmeg to taste.

Fold in two-thirds of the grated cheese and spoon the sauce over the celery and ham rolls. Sprinkle with the remaining cheese and bake near the top of the oven for 15–20 minutes, or until brown and bubbling on top.
Serving Garnish with the reserved celery leaves and serve

with small new potatoes or buttered macaroni.

BRAISED CELERY

2 heads of celery
Salt and pepper
1 small onion
2 small carrots
½ pint (300 ml.) white stock
1 oz. (25 g.) butter
1 oz. (25 g.) flour
Garnish: chopped parsley

COOKING TIME: 1 hour

Trim the roots off the celery and remove damaged stems. Scrub under cold running water, cut in half lengthways and remove the leafy tops.

Put the celery in a pan of boiling, lightly salted water and simmer for 10 minutes. Drain carefully. Arrange the celery in an ovenproof dish, cover with the thinly sliced onion and carrots, pour over the stock and season with salt and pepper. Cover with a tightly fitting lid and simmer over a very low heat for about 45 minutes, or until tender.

Knead the butter and flour together, and add in small pieces to thicken the braising liquid to the desired consistency. Simmer for a further 5 minutes.
Serving Sprinkle with finely chopped parsley and serve straight from the dish with roast or grilled meat or fish.

CELERY AND LETTUCE SALAD

1 head of celery
1 lettuce
1 egg yolk
1 tablespoon olive oil
1 tablespoon white wine vinegar
2½ fl. oz. (75 ml.) cream
Salt, pepper and sugar
Garnish: watercress

Trim the root end off the celery, discard any damaged stems and separate the remainder. Scrub the stems well under cold running water, chop them into 1 in. (25 mm.) pieces and remove any stringy bits.

Strip the outer leaves from the lettuce, separate it into individual leaves and wash and dry them. Shred the lettuce roughly and use it to line the base and sides of a salad bowl. Arrange the celery in the centre.

For the dressing, beat the egg yolk with ½ teaspoon of salt. Add the olive oil slowly, then beat in the vinegar and the cream, little by little. Season to taste with salt, pepper and sugar, and pour the dressing over the celery.
Serving Garnish the salad with sprigs of watercress and serve with cold meats.

Cherries

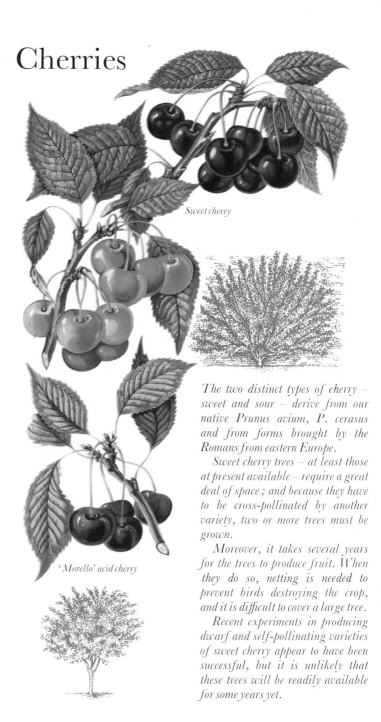

Sweet cherry

'Morello' acid cherry

The two distinct types of cherry – sweet and sour – derive from our native Prunus avium, P. cerasus and from forms brought by the Romans from eastern Europe.

Sweet cherry trees – at least those at present available – require a great deal of space; and because they have to be cross-pollinated by another variety, two or more trees must be grown.

Moreover, it takes several years for the trees to produce fruit. When they do so, netting is needed to prevent birds destroying the crop, and it is difficult to cover a large tree.

Recent experiments in producing dwarf and self-pollinating varieties of sweet cherry appear to have been successful, but it is unlikely that these trees will be readily available for some years yet.

Until then, if you already have a sweet cherry established in your garden, look after it by annual feeding and pruning. If possible, drape plastic netting over the tree in early summer.

If you do not have an established sweet cherry, it is probably not a practical proposition to plant one.

Acid 'Morello' cherries, used mainly for bottling and jam-making, are less vigorous, and may be grown as bush or fan-trained trees. As they are self-fertile, they can be grown singly. Even so, better crops are obtained if a second tree of a different variety is growing near by.

Netting is advisable, although birds are attracted less to acid cherries than to sweet cherries.

Although you may prefer to grow the more popular fruits, such as apples and pears, bear in mind that acid cherries will grow well in cool conditions, such as on a north-facing wall.

Planting an acid cherry tree

A fan-trained tree grown against a wall will attain a span of 15–20 ft (4.5–6 m.). A similar distance is needed between bush trees. A deep, well-drained soil will give the best results, but aspect is unimportant.

Plant between October and late March (see p. 40). When planting a bush tree, drive a supporting stake in the hole and tie the tree to it. Unless secured in this way the tree will tend to rock in high winds, loosening the roots and delaying the tree's development.

How to look after sweet and acid cherry trees

Each January, feed the trees with ½ oz. of sulphate of potash per square yard (15 g. per square metre) over an area roughly equivalent to the spread of the tree. In March, apply 1 oz. of sulphate of ammonia per square yard (30 g. per square metre).

Every third year, apply 3 oz. of superphosphate per square yard (90 g. per square metre).

Water the ground under trees thoroughly during dry spells in summer.

Pruning sweet cherries If the trees are growing as fans against a wall, only light pruning is necessary. In April rub out all new shoots growing towards or away from the wall, but leave unpruned the leaders of shoots that will become part of the main framework. Follow this up during June or July by pinching out the growing tips of all other new shoots after they have produced five or six leaves.

When shoots have reached the top of the wall, shorten them to just above a weak lateral shoot, or bend them over horizontally and fasten to the top wire.

All new shoots must be tied to fit into the fan shape.

In September cut away any dead wood and shorten the shoots that were pinched out in June or July; cut them back to three or four buds.

Limit the pruning of standard sweet cherries to removing dead or diseased branches, and branches that rub against one another. Paint the cut ends with a proprietary sealing compound to keep out silver-leaf infection.

Pruning acid cherries For the first three years, train and prune bush trees in the same way as bush apples (see p. 66) and fan-trained trees as fan peaches (see p. 226). Established acid cherries fruit only on wood that developed during the previous summer. The objective, therefore, is to stimulate plenty of new growth each year by

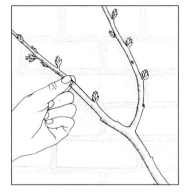

RUBBING OUT A proportion of new shoots will grow towards or away from the wall. Rub these out with your thumb during April, but leave the leaders of main branches.

PINCHING OUT Within a few weeks the remaining shoots will have five or six leaves. At this stage, pinch out the growing tips of new shoots other than branch leaders.

LIMITING THE LENGTH When shoots reach the top of the wall, shorten them to a weak lateral rather than stopping them abruptly.

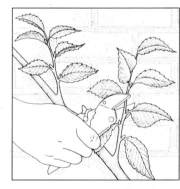

PRUNING NEW GROWTH In September, cut back shoots that were pinched back earlier. Reduce to three or four fruit buds.

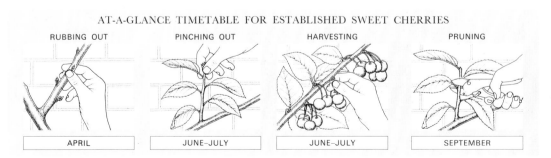

AT-A-GLANCE TIMETABLE FOR ACID CHERRIES		
PLANTING	HARVESTING	PRUNING
OCTOBER–MARCH	JULY–SEPTEMBER	AFTER FRUITING

AT-A-GLANCE TIMETABLE FOR ESTABLISHED SWEET CHERRIES			
RUBBING OUT	PINCHING OUT	HARVESTING	PRUNING
APRIL	JUNE–JULY	JUNE–JULY	SEPTEMBER

heavy feeding and by pruning to produce renewal shoots.

In spring, rub out shoots on fan trees that are growing towards the wall, and either tie back or remove outward-growing shoots. Tie in young shoots that are growing parallel with the wall.

In late summer, after fruiting, cut back a proportion of the older shoots – those up to three years old – to a young replacement shoot. Prune both sides of the fan equally to keep the tree in balance.

Bush trees need similar treatment. After fruiting, cut out some of the less productive branches – but leave those that are more than three years old, otherwise the wound will be too severe.

Seal all cuts with bituminous tree paint to prevent disease spores entering the wounds.

Pests and diseases Apart from birds, the pests most likely to attack cherries are APHIDS (p. 282) and CATERPILLARS (p. 282).

The more troublesome diseases are BACTERIAL CANKER (p. 286), CHLOROSIS (p. 287), HONEY FUNGUS (p. 288), SHOTHOLE (p. 290) and SILVER LEAF (p. 290).

Harvesting and storing

Sweet cherries may be pulled off by hand. They do not keep well, and should be eaten soon after harvesting in June or July.

Pulling off acid cherries, which mature between July and September, can wound the spurs and allow the diseases to which the trees are susceptible to enter. So cut off the cherries with sharp scissors.

See also freezing (p. 294); pickles (p. 328) and wine-making (p. 357).

Preparing & cooking cherries

Sweet white, red and black cherries are often served fresh as a dessert fruit on their own, or they can be added to fresh fruit salads and summer drinks. 'Morello' cherries are the most suitable for cooking. They are used chiefly for preserves, but are also excellent poached and in pies and flans.

Prepare cherries by washing and draining them, after removing the stalks. Ideally, they should be stoned, and a tool known as a 'cherry stoner' can be bought at most good stores. This ejects the stone without breaking the cherry.

Stone the cherries over a plate, so as to catch the juice which will inevitably escape.

COCKTAIL CHERRIES

1 lb. (500 g.) black cherries
2 fl. oz. (50 ml.) water
4 oz. (100 g.) sugar
2 tablespoons Maraschino, Kirsch or brandy

COOKING TIME: 5 minutes

Wash and drain the cherries thoroughly. Discard any that are not perfect, and stone the remainder.

Boil the water and sugar to a syrup, stirring all the time until the sugar has dissolved. Set aside to cool and, meanwhile, pack the cherries into small, clean jars.

Stir the Maraschino, Kirsch or brandy into the syrup and pour this over the cherries. Cover with air-tight seals – preferably screw caps – and store in a cool, dark place for three months before using.

CHERRIES IN RED WINE

1 lb. (500 g.) 'Morello' cherries
5 fl. oz. (150 ml.) red wine
4 oz. (100–125 g.) red-currant jelly
1 teaspoon arrowroot
5 fl. oz. (150 ml.) double cream
Garnish : blanched, split almonds

COOKING TIME: 10 minutes
CHILLING TIME: 1 hour

Wash, drain and stone the cherries; put them in a pan with the wine and red-currant jelly. Bring to the boil over a gentle heat and simmer the cherries for about 5 minutes until they are tender, but still retain their shape.

Lift the cherries out with a slotted spoon and arrange in individual glasses or dishes. Bring the liquid back to the boil, add the arrowroot and stir continuously until thickened. Spoon over the cherries and chill in the refrigerator.
Serving Whisk the cream until firm and pipe over the cherries. Decorate with split almonds.
Photograph on pages 142–3.

CHERRIES WITH DRAMBUIE

1 lb. (500 g.) 'Morello' cherries
7 fl. oz. (200 ml.) water
2 oz. (50 g.) caster sugar
2–3 tablespoons Drambuie

COOKING TIME: 10 minutes
CHILLING TIME: 2 hours

Rinse and drain the cherries and remove the stones. Bring the water and syrup to the boil, stirring until the sugar has dissolved. Add the stoned cherries, cover with a lid and remove the pan from the heat.

Set aside for 15 minutes, then spoon the cherries into serving glasses. Bring the syrup back to the boil, and boil rapidly until it has reduced by half. Leave to cool slightly, then blend in the Drambuie. Spoon this syrup over the cherries, and chill for at least 2 hours to give the flavours time to develop and blend.
Serving Serve with a jug of cream and small macaroons or sponge fingers.
Variations Instead of Drambuie use Kirsch, Maraschino, sweet sherry, white port or cherry brandy.

CHERRY FLAN

¾ lb. (375 g.) 'Morello' cherries
5 fl. oz. (150 ml.) red wine
2 oz. (50 g.) demerara sugar
1½ teaspoons arrowroot
Flan case
Garnish : whipped cream

COOKING TIME: 10 minutes
CHILLING TIME: 30 minutes

Rinse and stone the cherries; put in a pan with the wine and sugar. Bring to the boil over a gentle heat and simmer for about 7 minutes – until the cherries are tender, but not broken up.

Blend the arrowroot with 1 tablespoon of water, stir it into the cherries and simmer for a few minutes, stirring all the time until the mixture thickens. Set aside to cool.

Use an 8 in. (200 mm.) flan case, made from ½ lb. (250 g.) sweet shortcrust pastry and baked blind, or a bought baked flan case. Put the cooled cherry mixture into the flan case and chill for 30 minutes.
Serving Decorate the flan with piped whipped cream and serve cut into wedges.
Variations Fold 1 oz. (25 g.) of blanched, split almonds into the cherry compôte, or flavour the whipped cream with a little Kirsch.
Photograph on pages 136–7.

Chervil

This hardy biennial herb, generally grown as an annual, is a native of south-eastern Europe and western Asia, but has long been naturalised in Britain and elsewhere. It is grown mainly for its bright green, feathery leaves.

The fresh leaves are chopped for adding to salads, garnishing soups and delicately flavoured fish, sprinkling over new potatoes and using in fines herbes. Frozen leaves can be used for the same purposes.

By successional sowing and growing under glass in winter, a year-round supply of fresh chervil leaves can be obtained.

The plant grows to a height of 12–18 in. (305–455 mm.) and bears clusters of white flowers from June to August. In general appearance it is not unlike parsley.

Planning the crop

Early and late-sown plants will thrive in full sun, but those grown in summer benefit from partial shade in hot, dry areas. The herb will do well in any soil, provided the drainage is good.

How much to grow It is usual to grow chervil as a short-term crop, making four to six sowings at intervals during the year and using only tender young leaves. Following this method, ample leaves would be produced by growing up to half-a-dozen plants at any one time.

How to grow chervil

Sow the seeds ¼ in. (5 mm.) deep in an open seed bed at any time between March and August. Allow 12 in. (305 mm.) between rows if more than one is sown, and thin the seedlings to 12 in. spacings.

Water the plants in dry weather and remove flowering stems as soon as they appear. This will not only encourage the growth of young, tender leaves for a longer period, but will also prevent self-sown seedlings from growing like weeds in the surrounding soil.

However, if seeds are wanted for later use you could let one of the heads mature and gather the ripe seeds before they fall.

Chervil can also be grown indoors between October and February.

Plant two or three seeds in a 6 in. (150 mm.) pot filled with seed compost. Remove the weaker plants and grow the remaining one on the kitchen window-sill for a supply of fresh leaves in winter.

Pests and diseases Chervil is normally trouble-free.

Harvesting and storing

Cut or pick the leaves six to eight weeks after sowing. The leaves are too tender for successful drying, but they can be preserved by freezing (see p. 294).

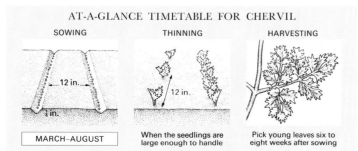

AT-A-GLANCE TIMETABLE FOR CHERVIL

SOWING	THINNING	HARVESTING
12 in. / 1 in.	12 in.	
MARCH–AUGUST	When the seedlings are large enough to handle	Pick young leaves six to eight weeks after sowing

Preparing & cooking chervil

This aromatic herb is similar to parsley, although the lacy leaves are a paler green and have a more delicate flavour. It is one of the traditional herbs for an omelette au fines herbes; it is also used to flavour cream sauces and soups, salads and vinegars, and is attractive as a garnish.

The slight aniseed taste combines well with some vegetables, such as baby carrots, and tiny new potatoes are delicious when tossed in butter and sprinkled with finely chopped chervil. The herb may also be mixed into a mayonnaise sauce with cold asparagus.

Sprinkle chopped chervil over scrambled eggs, poached white fish and grilled tomatoes, and use it to give colour and extra flavour to creamed potatoes.

Add 2 teaspoons of chopped chervil to a white cream sauce, Bernaise or Hollandaise, to accompany roast poultry, poached and baked fish, or boiled cauliflower.

Chervil butter goes well with grilled salmon steaks, roast veal and escalopes. Soften 4 oz. (100 g.) of butter and blend thoroughly with 2 teaspoons of blanched, finely chopped chervil. Season to taste with salt and white pepper, and roll into a sausage shape in damp grease-proof paper.

Chill in the refrigerator until firm, then cut into slices. Stamp out fancy shapes with a small biscuit cutter and use as a garnish.

CHERVIL SOUP

2–3 leeks
3 carrots
½ lb. (250 g.) potatoes
2 sticks of celery
2 pints (1 l.) chicken stock
Salt, pepper, sugar
1 oz. (25 g.) butter
1 oz. (25 g.) flour
Bunch of fresh chervil
Garnish: poached eggs

COOKING TIME: 20 minutes

Trim and clean the leeks; scrape or peel the carrots and potatoes; scrub the celery. Dice all the vegetables and put in a pan with the stock. Bring to the boil and simmer gently for 10–12 minutes, or until the vegetables are tender. Season to taste with salt, pepper and sugar.

Knead the butter with the flour and add to the soup in small pieces, whisking well until it thickens. Remove from the heat.

Cover the chervil with boiling water, drain immediately and chop finely. Stir the chervil into the soup. It must not be allowed to boil, or it will lose both flavour and colour.

Serving Pour into soup bowls, top with poached eggs or halved hard-boiled eggs. Serve.

Variation Sweat the chopped vegetables in the butter before adding the stock; simmer until tender, then blend in a liquidiser. Re-heat the soup and thicken with a cream and egg liaison; add the chopped chervil.

Chicory

Chicory in summer

Chicory chicons

A hardy perennial, native to Europe, chicory is first grown outdoors, then forced and blanched inside to produce a conical head of crisp, white, faintly bitter leaves known as chicons. It is easy to grow, and is a valuable winter vegetable for eating raw in salads or for cooking by boiling, steaming or braising.

The leaves of one variety, 'Sugar Loaf', may also be used, un-blanched, in summer.

The other varieties may be forced, a few roots at a time, to give a continuous supply of chicons between December and March.

Planning the crop

Chicory is deep-rooting and needs a rich soil – either one manured for a previous crop, or one into which well-rotted compost or manure has been incorporated before sowing.

How much to grow A 10 ft (3 m.) row yields up to 6 lb. (3 kg.) of chicons.

Varieties Three varieties are in general cultivation: 'Red Verona', so called because of the pink tinge of its forced leaves; 'Sugar Loaf', whose leaves can be picked in summer and cooked like spinach or used raw in salads; 'Witloof', also called 'Brussels Chicory'.

How to grow chicory

Sow the seeds in the open in May or June. Sow them thinly in drills ¼ in. (5 mm.) deep and 18 in. (455 mm.) apart.

When the seedlings are large enough to handle, thin them to about 9 in. (230 mm.) apart.

Keep weeds under control by hoeing, and water the bed thoroughly during dry spells.

In October or November, when the leaves have died down, cut them off about 1 in. (25 mm.) above the roots and lift carefully with a fork. The roots should by then be 12 in. (305 mm.) or more long, about 2 in. (50 mm.) across the top and parsnip-shaped.

Rub out any side-shoots, leaving only the main crown.

Trim the roots to a length of about 8 in. (200 mm.) and store them in a cool, frost-proof shed or in a shallow trench beneath a layer of soil – marking this so that you can find them later.

Force the roots in batches as they are required for use. To do this, pack them upright, four or five at a time, into a 9 in. (230 mm.) pot filled with soil. The roots should be about 2 in. (50 mm.) apart. Water the pots and cover them with inverted pots of the same size, or with boxes, to keep out the light.

Put the pots in a warm place, such as a greenhouse or kitchen, where the temperature will be 7–16°C (45–61°F). The darkness and warmth will induce chicons to sprout up from the crowns.

Pests and diseases CUTWORMS (p. 283), SLUGS AND SNAILS (p. 285) and caterpillars of the SWIFT MOTH (p. 285) are the principal pests.

STAGES IN BLANCHING CHICORY

LIFTING Cut off the remaining foliage 1 in. (25 mm.) above the roots before or after lifting in October or November. Lift the roots carefully with a fork.

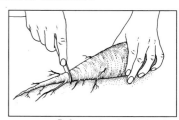

TRIMMING Before storing the roots, reduce the length of each to about 8 in. (200 mm.) by trimming off the lower end. Rub off any side-shoots, leaving the main crown.

FORCING Plant four or five roots in a 9 in. (230 mm.) pot of soil. After watering, cover with another pot to exclude light.

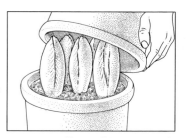

HARVESTING Given sufficient warmth, the chicons will be 6 in. (150 mm.) high a month later. Cut them off at the base.

Chicory is seldom attacked by any disease.

Harvesting and storing

The plants are ready for use when the chicons are about 6 in. (150 mm.) high, which generally takes four weeks.

Cut off the chicons just before using them.

When all the chicons have been picked, throw the roots on to the compost heap. Alternatively, water the pots, and leave the plants to grow a second – but inferior – crop of chicons.

AT-A-GLANCE TIMETABLE FOR CHICORY

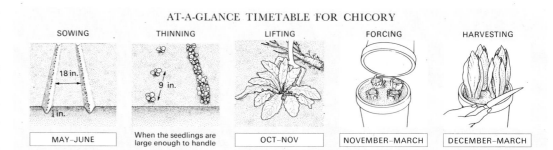

SOWING	THINNING	LIFTING	FORCING	HARVESTING
18 in. / 1 in.	9 in.			
MAY–JUNE	When the seedlings are large enough to handle	OCT–NOV	NOVEMBER–MARCH	DECEMBER–MARCH

Preparing & cooking chicory

Use this delicate vegetable while the blanched chicons are still young and firm, before the leaves begin to turn yellow and the tops show pale green. The central, hard core of chicory is slightly bitter, and this becomes more pronounced with age.

The bitterness can be reduced – and this is advisable for chicory to be used fresh in salads – by blanching the vegetable for 2 minutes in boiling water. A little lemon juice in the water preserves the white colour.

To prepare chicory remove the outer leaves, trim the root end clean, and scoop out any core with a sharp-pointed knife.

Chicory may be used fresh in salads, and it combines particularly well with citrus fruit. As a vegetable dish, it may be boiled for 15–20 minutes, depending on the method of preparation, and served with melted butter, Béchamel, Mornay or Hollandaise sauce.

CHICORY AND EGG SALAD

2–3 heads of chicory
6 tablespoons olive oil
2 tablespoons lemon juice
Salt and pepper
3 hard-boiled eggs
3 tomatoes

CHILLING TIME: 30 minutes

Clean and trim the chicory, cutting out any cores. Blanch for 2 minutes in boiling water, with a little lemon juice added. Drain and refresh in cold water. Dry thoroughly on a cloth or absorbent kitchen paper.

Cut the chicory into thin slices, crossways. Make a dressing from the oil and lemon juice, seasoning to taste with salt and pepper. Pour the dressing over the chicory and toss well. Chill for 30 minutes.
Serving Arrange the chicory on a shallow serving dish and garnish with quartered eggs and tomato wedges. Serve as a lunch salad, on its own or with fingers of toasted cheese.

CHICORY AND GRAPEFRUIT SALAD

2 heads of chicory
2 grapefruits
8 tablespoons olive oil
2 tablespoons white wine vinegar
2 tablespoons grapefruit juice
Salt and pepper
Tabasco sauce

Remove any outer damaged leaves from the chicory. Trim the root ends and scoop out any cores. Wash and dry thoroughly. Cut the chicory, crossways, into thin slices and put in a bowl.

Squeeze the juice from half a grapefruit. Peel off the skin from the remainder and remove all white pith. Divide the grapefruit into segments and cut each in half. Mix with the chicory.

Shake a dressing of oil, vinegar and grapefruit juice, and season with salt, black pepper and a few drops of Tabasco. Pour over the salad and toss well.
Serving This slightly sharp salad goes well with rich meats.

Alternatively, serve it as a salad on its own with cheese.
Photograph on page 216.

BRAISED CHICORY

4 heads of chicory
1 small onion
1 oz. (25 g.) butter
Salt and pepper
5 fl. oz. (150 ml.) stock
Garnish : chopped parsley

COOKING TIME: 45 minutes
OVEN TEMPERATURE: 180°C (350°F) –
gas mark 4

Remove any outer damaged leaves and trim the root bases off the chicory. Cut each head in half lengthways and remove the central bitter cores.

Fry the finely chopped onion in the butter until soft, but not brown. Add the chicory and continue frying until golden on both sides. Sprinkle with salt and pepper, pour over the stock and cover the pan or dish tightly with a lid or foil. Transfer to the oven and cook for 35 minutes.
Serving Sprinkle with the finely chopped parsley and serve straight from the dish, with roast pork or poultry.

CHICORY IN HAM CASES

4 heads of chicory
Salt, pepper and ground ginger
4 slices of ham or gammon
2 teaspoons French mustard (optional)
½ pint (300 ml.) white sauce
3 oz. (75 g.) grated cheese
1 oz. (25 g.) butter

COOKING TIME: 30 minutes
OVEN TEMPERATURE: 190°C (375°F) –
gas mark 5

Remove the outer leaves and trim the root bases. Remove any core, and wash the chicons. Put in a pan of boiling, lightly salted water, bring back to the boil, cover and simmer gently for 12–15 minutes, or until tender. Drain thoroughly in a colander.

Sprinkle the ham slices with a little freshly ground pepper and ginger, and spread lightly with mustard. Lay a head of chicory on each slice, roll up and place, seam down, in a buttered ovenproof dish.

Fold half the cheese into the warm sauce and pour over the ham and chicory. Sprinkle with the remaining cheese and dot with a little butter. Bake near the top of the oven for about 15 minutes, or until the cheese is golden-brown and bubbly.
Serving This is a dish on its own, suitable for lunch or supper. Serve straight from the dish, with small potatoes sprinkled with coarse salt.
Photograph on pages 212–13.

CHICORY WITH LEMON SAUCE

4 heads of chicory
Salt and pepper
Juice of 1 lemon
½ pint (300 ml.) white sauce
2 egg yolks
1 oz. (25 g.) butter
2 tablespoons breadcrumbs

COOKING TIME: 25 minutes
OVEN TEMPERATURE: 220°C (425°F) –
gas mark 7

Trim the outer leaves and root bases off the chicory and scoop out the bitter core. Cut large heads in half lengthways; otherwise leave whole. Put them in a pan of boiling, lightly salted water to which half the lemon juice has been added. Cook, covered, over a gentle heat for about 12 minutes, then drain.

Meanwhile, make up the white sauce, seasoning with salt and freshly ground pepper. Add enough of the remaining lemon juice to give a fairly sharp sauce. Beat the egg yolks with 1 tablespoon of cold water, stir in a little of the hot sauce and return the egg mixture to the pan.

Lay the drained chicory in a buttered ovenproof dish, pour over the sauce, sprinkle the top with breadcrumbs and dot with butter. Bake for about 10 minutes.
Serving This makes an excellent light lunch dish on its own, or it may be served as a vegetable.

Chillis: see **Peppers**

Chinese bean sprouts:
see **Sprouting seeds**

Chives

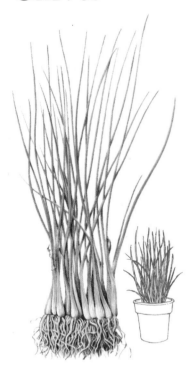

The fine, tubular leaves of this hardy, perennial herb are used to impart a delicate onion flavour to a wide range of dishes.

It is extremely versatile, as omelettes, salads, soups, stews and several sauces can be improved by its addition. Delicious herb bread can be made by mashing chopped chives into butter, inserting the mixture into a French loaf and baking it in the oven.

Chives need little attention and are certainly among the easiest of all garden plants to grow. Fresh clumps can be created every few years by lifting and dividing existing ones.

Chives are in season outdoors from March until autumn, and a winter supply can be obtained by growing them indoors in pots on the kitchen window-sill.

Planning the crop

Chives will grow in any good garden soil in a sunny or semi-shaded position. They may also be grown in pots and window-boxes.

How much to grow Three large clumps should supply sufficient chives for the season. Chives can also be used to make an attractive and useful edging to the vegetable plot, though you will then have more than you need.

How to grow chives

The easiest method is to buy chive plants from a nursery, plant them in the herb bed about 12 in. (305 mm.) apart, and allow them to multiply. Within a few months they will grow into good-sized clumps if the flowers are removed.

Chives can also be grown from seed. Sow these outdoors in March, in groups of three or four at 12 in. (305 mm.) intervals and ¼ in. (5 mm.) deep. Remove the weakest seedlings when they germinate. Any further stock required may be obtained by dividing the plants in September or October.

Even if extra plants are not needed, every three years dig up the clumps in September or October and divide them into groups of half-a-dozen shoots. Re-plant these 12 in. (305 mm.) apart in fresh ground that has been dressed with well-rotted compost.

For a winter supply, take one or two small clumps and set them in 4 in. (100 mm.) pots of potting compost. Place the pots on a window-sill.

Pests and diseases Chives are seldom troubled by pests.

The only disease likely to affect the plants is RUST (p. 290).

Harvesting

Cut the leaves close to the ground as required. Cut each clump in turn; they will soon grow a new crop of leaves.

Cob nuts: see **Nuts**

AT-A-GLANCE TIMETABLE FOR CHIVES

SOWING	THINNING	HARVESTING
12 in. / ¼ in.	Remove the weakest seedlings	
MARCH		MARCH–OCTOBER

Cooking with chives

The finely chopped, dark green leaves are much used as a garnish for salads and sauces, and for flavouring egg and cheese dishes. Chives are a necessary ingredient in tartare sauce to serve with fish, and are used as flavouring in salad dressings.

Try sprinkling tomato and egg sandwiches with chopped chives. The easiest way to chop them is by holding a small bunch in one hand and snipping it with kitchen scissors.

Fold chives into cream and cottage cheese, creamed potatoes and dips, and mix with vegetables and cucumber salads.

Garnish meat, fish and poultry dishes with chive butter. To make this, stir 4 oz. (100 g.) butter until soft, and blend in 4 tablespoons of blanched, finely chopped chives. Alternatively, pound the chopped chives in a mortar and pestle to a paste-like consistency and blend into the soft butter.

Roll into a sausage shape, wrap in damp greaseproof paper and chill in the refrigerator. To use, cut into narrow slices.

CHIVES AU GRATIN

Small bunch of chives
Salt and pepper
8 rashers of streaky bacon
1 oz. (25 g.) butter
4 eggs
7 fl. oz. (200 ml.) milk
2 heaped tablespoons of grated cheese

COOKING TIME: 25–30 minutes
OVEN TEMPERATURE: 180°C (350°F) – gas mark 4

Rinse the chives, blanch for 2 minutes in boiling, lightly salted water, drain and chop roughly. Remove rind and gristle from the bacon and dice the flesh. Fry in half the butter until the bacon begins to crisp, then drain on absorbent kitchen paper.

Grease four individual ovenproof dishes with the remaining butter. Divide the bacon between them and sprinkle with the chives. Beat the eggs lightly with the milk, flavouring with salt and pepper, and pour them over the bacon and chives mixture. Sprinkle with grated cheese.

Set the dishes in a roasting tin and pour in about 1 in. (25 mm.) of hot water. Bake near the top of a pre-heated oven for about 25 minutes, or until the eggs are set.
Serving This is a snack, lunch or supper dish and can be served with bread and green salad.
Variation Skinned, sliced tomatoes may be put on top of the egg mixture before sprinkling with cheese.

SEASONAL COOKING

The following pages present a selection of dishes prepared from spring and summer produce.
Autumn and winter dishes are featured on pages 205 – 16.

Spring dishes

Spring vegetables : page 135   *Spring desserts : page 137*   *Spring soups & salads : page 139*

Summer dishes

Summer vegetables : page 141   *Summer desserts : page 143*   *Summer soups & salads : page 144*

Celeriac and winter kale, cabbages and carrots are the main stand-bys for hot soups on chilly spring evenings. Winter or spring cabbages make a particularly nourishing soup, which becomes a main dish if meat dumplings are added.

The same vegetables can also be used for making crunchy lunch-time salads if cloched or winter-hardy lettuces are in short supply.

New potatoes apart, probably no spring vegetable is greeted with more enthusiasm than the first pickings of small broad beans, and it is a mistake to disguise their flavour by following elaborate recipes. Simply toss the cooked beans in melted butter and sprinkle fresh herbs over them.

But in early spring the housewife has still, for the most part, to rely on what is left of winter crops. To encourage jaded appetites, serve tender broccoli spears, cheese-flavoured salsify, curried cabbage or make individual cauliflower soufflés.

With careful management, spring should find you with a few cooking apples left. Try serving them stuffed with marzipan and baked, or in a pie. For a change, abandon tradition and flavour an apple pie – as the Dutch do – with almonds, with the addition of a few currants or raisins.

Yet however welcome are these changes of flavour, when the time comes to pull the pale stalks of forced rhubarb it would be difficult to improve on the familiar, crisp-topped crumble.

As spring merges into summer, clear the freezer of the last berry fruits to make room for the produce now growing in the garden. Blackberries are ideal for making milk and yoghourt shakes for the children.

Treat the grown-ups to thin, crisp pancakes rolled around a liqueur-flavoured stuffing of raspberries and cream cheese.

Summer, if our hopes are fulfilled, brings sunshine and heat, and lazy meals in the garden. The aim should be to spend as little time as possible over the kitchen stove.

Chilled soups are both delicious and thirst-quenching. Cucumber soup and borsch are unequalled in this respect, and they need a minimum of cooking.

Eat tender, home-grown asparagus – one of the highlights of the gardening year – with your fingers, dipping each piece into hot melted butter or into a cold dressing.

On the occasional chilly day, treat the family to a steamed spinach mould, filled with vegetables or fish in a creamed sauce, or serve braised lettuce as a novel vegetable with the roast Sunday joint.

When you proudly harvest your golden cobs of sweet corn, take care to boil them in water that is unsalted for half the cooking time, otherwise the kernels will go hard. But be liberal when sprinkling salt over tomatoes that you are going to stuff, as this will draw out the excess water while they are draining upside-down.

Summer fruits, like vegetables, are so plentiful that imagination can be given full rein. The berry fruits – strawberries, raspberries and loganberries – are most enjoyable when served fresh with sugar and cream, but fairly large crops are needed to use them like this.

Where only a few plants are grown, it is easy enough to stretch a small amount by using them as a filling for a feather-light choux pastry ring or as a base for a cream mould.

Fruit flans, to serve as a sweet or with Sunday tea on the lawn, can be made with practically any kind of home-grown fresh fruit, including apricots, cherries, gooseberries, loganberries, peaches, raspberries and strawberries.

Spring vegetables

→ 1 ←
SALSIFY WITH CHEESE
recipe on page 254

→ 2 ←
FLORIDA SALAD
recipe on page 185

→ 3 ←
BROCCOLI AU GRATIN
recipe on page 105

→ 4 ←
CAULIFLOWER SOUFFLÉS
recipe on page 120

→ 5 ←
BUTTERED TURNIPS
recipe on page 275

→ 6 ←
BROAD BEANS
WITH BUTTER
recipe on page 90

→ 7 ←
CURRIED CABBAGE
recipe on page 112

→ 8 ←
CRISP BUTTERED
SPINACH
recipe on page 260

Spring desserts

→→◇←

→→ 1 ←←
RHUBARB CRUMBLE
recipe on page 250

→→ 2 ←←
**PANCAKES WITH
RASPBERRY CREAM**
recipe on page 248

→→ 3 ←←
MARZIPAN APPLES
recipe on page 73

→→ 4 ←←
DUTCH APPLE PIE
recipe on page 73

→→ 5 ←←
CHERRY FLAN
recipe on page 128

→→ 6 ←←
**BLACK-CURRANT AND
MINT SHAKE**
recipe on page 153

→→ 7 ←←
GOOSEBERRY MERINGUE
recipe on page 168

→→ 8 ←←
BLACKBERRY MOUSSE
recipe on page 102

→→◇←

Spring
soups & salads

—→✦←—

—→ 1 ←—
CARROT SALAD
recipe on page 117

—→ 2 ←—
COLESLAW WITH
ROQUEFORT DRESSING
recipe on page 111

—→ 3 ←—
HOT POTATO SALAD
recipe on page 241

—→ 4 ←—
CABBAGE SOUP
recipe on page 113

—→ 5 ←—
BROCCOLI VINAIGRETTE
recipe on page 105

—→ 6 ←—
KALE SOUP
recipe on page 176

—→ 7 ←—
CELERIAC SOUP
recipe on page 122

—→ 8 ←—
BEAN SPROUTS
WITH NOODLES
recipe on page 263

—→✦←—

Summer vegetables

→◆◇◆←

→ **1** ←
CARROTS À LA VICHY
recipe on page 117

→ **2** ←
STUFFED TOMATOES
recipe on page 274

→ **3** ←
BRAISED LETTUCE
recipe on page 186

→ **4** ←
SPINACH MOULD
recipe on page 260

→ **5** ←
COLD POTATO SALAD
recipe on page 241

→ **6** ←
BEANS WITH HERBS
recipe on page 93

→ **7** ←
SUMMER VEGETABLE CABARET
recipe on page 233

→ **8** ←
SWEET CORN WITH BUTTER
recipe on page 268

→◆◇◆←

Summer desserts

❧⟐❧

➤ 1 ◄
APRICOT FLAN
recipe on page 77

➤ 2 ◄
STUFFED PEACHES
recipe on page 228

➤ 3 ◄
CHERRIES IN
RED WINE
recipe on page 128

➤ 4 ◄
RASPBERRY FLAN
recipe on page 248

➤ 5 ◄
CHOUX PASTRY
WITH LOGANBERRIES
recipe on page 188

➤ 6 ◄
STRAWBERRY CREAM
recipe on page 266

➤ 7 ◄
GOOSEBERRY FOOL
recipe on page 167

➤ 8 ◄
RED CURRANTS
WITH YOGHOURT
recipe on page 155

❧⟐❧

Summer soups & salads

➤—◦—◦—◦—

➤ **1** ◦
FENNEL À LA
MARTINEZ
recipe on page 162

➤ **2** ◦
ASPARAGUS SALAD
recipe on page 84

➤ **3** ◦
QUICK BORSCH
recipe on page 99

➤ **4** ◦
ARTICHOKES WITH
CURRY MAYONNAISE
recipe on page 79

➤ **5** ◦
GREEK MIXED SALAD
recipe on page 185

➤ **6** ◦
CHILLED
CUCUMBER SOUP
recipe on page 149

➤—◦—◦—◦—

Coriander

This hardy annual herb, a native of south-east Europe that now also occurs in Britain, is grown mainly for its seeds.

Before ripening, these have an unpleasant smell; but, as the small fruits mature, this gives way to a spicy aroma – a sure indication that harvesting is due.

The seeds are ground to a powder which is used in curries and soups, and for flavouring gin, fish, meats, cakes, biscuits and bread.

The plant is easy to grow, and requires little attention.

Planning the crop

Coriander needs a sunny position. It will grow satisfactorily in any well-drained soil, but does best in one enriched with well-rotted manure or compost.

How much to grow

At least 12 plants are needed if the seeds are to be used for occasional curries and for flavouring fish or meat dishes. Grow additional plants if you also wish to use the seeds in biscuits or bread.

Coriander plants grow to about 18 in. (455 mm.) high, with a spread of 6–9 in. (150–230 mm.). There is only one species.

How to grow coriander

Sow the seeds ¼ in. (5 mm.) deep in an outdoor seed bed in April. Thin the plants to 10 in. (255 mm.) spacings as soon as they are large enough to handle.

Pests and diseases Coriander is normally trouble-free.

Harvesting

Your nose is the best harvesting guide. When the seed heads emit a pleasant, spicy odour – following their former disagreeable smell – cut them off and leave them to dry on trays, either in the sunshine or indoors.

When they are dry, shake out the seeds, or rub them off, and place in airtight containers.

Cooking with coriander

This bitter-sweet, aromatic herb is too often neglected in British and European cooking. The dried seeds, picked in late summer, are essential ingredients in the compounds that make up a traditional curry-powder mixture. Whole or ground seeds of coriander are particularly suitable for flavouring chutneys and pickles, curries and other spiced meat dishes.

In eastern European cooking, coriander is a traditional flavouring in cakes, breads and cheeses. As it is mild, it should be used generously.

Strangely, coriander combines well with the stronger-flavoured fennel. The Elizabethans were partial to roast pork that had been rubbed with equal amounts of pounded coriander and fennel seeds, lightly sweetened.

Freshly ground coriander can also be added to milk and rice puddings, and gives a novel flavour to bread-and-butter puddings in place of the usual nutmeg and cinnamon.

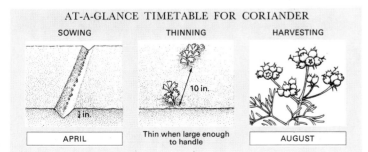

AT-A-GLANCE TIMETABLE FOR CORIANDER

SOWING	THINNING	HARVESTING
APRIL	Thin when large enough to handle	AUGUST

Corn salad

This salad vegetable was introduced to Britain from the Low Countries about 400 years ago. It can be grown throughout the year, but is generally sown as an autumn and winter crop to use when fresh greenstuff for salads is scarce.

Corn salad is a good substitute for lettuce, and can be used in the same ways. Its other name, lamb's lettuce, derives partly from the fact that the leaves are at their greenest and crispest at the end of winter, when lambing starts.

The plant is completely hardy, but will receive less of a check in severe weather if covered with cloches. This will help to ensure a continuous supply of tender young leaves.

Planning the crop

Grow corn salad in sunny, well-drained soil containing a generous amount of well-rotted manure or compost.

How much to grow

A 10 ft (3 m.) row will provide about 20 plants.

Varieties 'Large-leaved Italian' is recommended.

How to grow corn salad

By sowing in March, April, August and September, fresh supplies may be grown all the year round. But for a winter crop sow only in August and September.

Sow the seeds in drills ½ in. (12 mm.) deep, with 9 in. (230 mm.) between rows, and thin the seedlings to 6 in. (150 mm.) spacings. Keep the ground well watered during the first few weeks

---

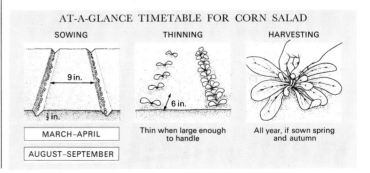

AT-A-GLANCE TIMETABLE FOR CORN SALAD

SOWING	THINNING	HARVESTING
9 in. / ½ in.	Thin when large enough to handle	All year, if sown spring and autumn
MARCH–APRIL AUGUST–SEPTEMBER	6 in.	

after sowing and hoe frequently to keep down weeds.

Cover with cloches to minimise growth check during cold spells.

Pests and diseases Apart from SLUGS AND SNAILS (p. 285), corn salad is generally trouble-free.

Harvesting

The plants are ready for use after they have produced their fourth pair of leaves.

Either use the entire plant after cutting off the roots, or pick a few of the larger leaves from each mature plant. They tend to be rather short-lived, so it is as well to start using the leaves as soon as they are ready.

Cooking with corn salad

This salad plant is ideal for use when ordinary lettuce is scarce and lacking in flavour. Because the leaves grow close to the ground they tend to be dirty when picked, and need careful washing.

Shred the leaves and use in green salads, but avoid mixing them with strong flavours such as onions and garlic. Toss in a slightly sweet dressing of mustard, oil and vinegar or lemon juice, seasoned to taste with salt, pepper and sugar.

Corn salad is particularly good with cold meats, such as tongue and roast chicken.

Courgettes:

see **Marrows and courgettes**

Cress:

see **Mustard and cress**

Cucumbers

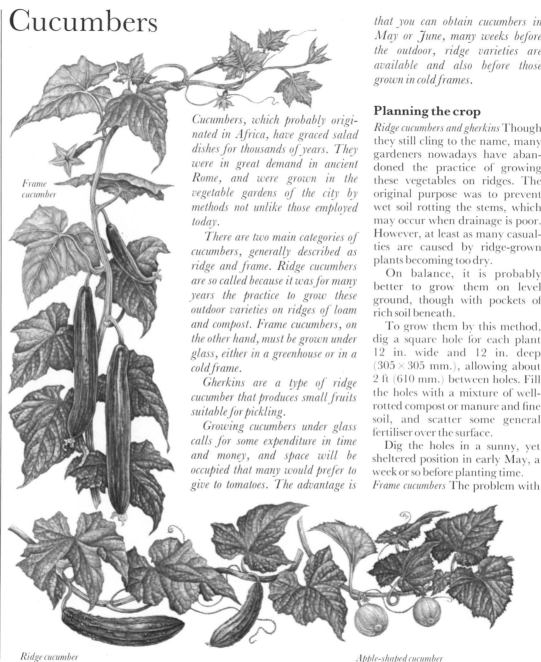

Frame cucumber

Ridge cucumber

Apple-shaped cucumber

Cucumbers, which probably originated in Africa, have graced salad dishes for thousands of years. They were in great demand in ancient Rome, and were grown in the vegetable gardens of the city by methods not unlike those employed today.

There are two main categories of cucumbers, generally described as ridge and frame. Ridge cucumbers are so called because it was for many years the practice to grow these outdoor varieties on ridges of loam and compost. Frame cucumbers, on the other hand, must be grown under glass, either in a greenhouse or in a cold frame.

Gherkins are a type of ridge cucumber that produces small fruits suitable for pickling.

Growing cucumbers under glass calls for some expenditure in time and money, and space will be occupied that many would prefer to give to tomatoes. The advantage is that you can obtain cucumbers in May or June, many weeks before the outdoor, ridge varieties are available and also before those grown in cold frames.

Planning the crop

Ridge cucumbers and gherkins Though they still cling to the name, many gardeners nowadays have abandoned the practice of growing these vegetables on ridges. The original purpose was to prevent wet soil rotting the stems, which may occur when drainage is poor. However, at least as many casualties are caused by ridge-grown plants becoming too dry.

On balance, it is probably better to grow them on level ground, though with pockets of rich soil beneath.

To grow them by this method, dig a square hole for each plant 12 in. wide and 12 in. deep (305 × 305 mm.), allowing about 2 ft (610 mm.) between holes. Fill the holes with a mixture of well-rotted compost or manure and fine soil, and scatter some general fertiliser over the surface.

Dig the holes in a sunny, yet sheltered position in early May, a week or so before planting time.

Frame cucumbers The problem with growing cucumbers in the average greenhouse is that, ideally, they require a night temperature of about 16°C (61°F), together with a high level of humidity. This makes them uneasy company for other greenhouse vegetables that require a lower temperature and less humidity.

Unless you intend filling the entire greenhouse with cucumbers, it is necessary to come to a compromise. Suit the temperature to the tomatoes and plant one or two cucumbers in the warmest position, preferably at the end furthest from the door.

As with outdoor cucumbers, it is necessary to provide a rich mixture of soil and compost. Prepare planting 'pockets' as described for ridge cucumbers – though leaving the surface ridged or mounded over the planting positions – or fill 10 in. (255 mm.) pots with John Innes No. 3 compost.

Alternatively, grow the plants in the compost-filled bags now available from most gardening centres. However they are grown, shade the glass from late March onwards to prevent damage from scorching.

Frame cucumbers, as the name implies, may also be grown in cold frames, though they will crop later than those grown in a warm greenhouse. Dig the growing pockets beneath the higher end of the frame, and obtain some shading material to shield the young cucumbers from scorching on sunny days.

How many to grow A single frame cucumber plant may produce as many as 20 fruits if really well grown, though fewer than ten under average conditions. Two or three outdoor plants, and perhaps a single frame cucumber, should be sufficient, together with one or two of a gherkin variety.

Varieties There are several groups of cucumber varieties, all of which are adapted to particular purposes.

Apart from the major division between ridge and frame cucumbers, there are also gherkins and apple-shaped varieties.

F1 hybrids (see p. 30) in both categories are noted for their heavy cropping and uniformity.

Ridge cucumbers:

'Bedfordshire Prize', 'Long Green Ridge', 'Nadir' and 'Perfection' are sturdy, dependable varieties.

'Baton Vert' and 'Burpee Hybrid': F1 hybrids, grown for early development and vigour.

'Chinese Long Green' and 'Kyoto Three Feet': Japanese varieties noted for the length of their fruits.

'Apple-shaped': a round, yellow cucumber with an excellent flavour; very prolific.

'Venlo Pickling': a good gherkin variety.

Frame cucumbers:

'Butcher's Disease Resisting', 'Conqueror' and 'Telegraph' are among the best varieties for a cool greenhouse.

'Sigmadew': a pale green variety with a thin skin and excellent flavour.

'Femdam', 'Femspot', 'Fernstar', 'Pepinex', 'Rocket' and 'Topsy': all are F1 hybrids that produce only female flowers. Though prolific and disease-resistant, the fruits are smaller than those of conventional varieties. They also require a higher temperature for successful growth.

How to grow ridge cucumbers and gherkins

In late April, sow two or three seeds ½ in. (12 mm.) deep in 3 in. (75 mm.) peat pots filled with seed compost. A temperature of 21°C (70°F) is needed, so place the pots in an airing cupboard, or in a greenhouse near the heater. Remove the weakest seedlings to leave only one in each pot.

Harden off the seedlings during May and plant them out in the prepared beds at the end of the month or in early June, when there is no danger of frost at night.

Alternatively, in the last week or so in May, sow three or four seeds 1 in. (25 mm.) deep and 3 in. (75 mm.) apart from each other in the centre of each planting pocket – which are themselves at 2 ft (610 mm.) spacings. Once germination has taken place, remove the weaker seedlings and leave the strongest to stand alone.

Whichever method is followed, pinch out the growing tip of each plant after six or seven leaves have appeared. This will permit the fruit-bearing shoots to develop.

Unlike frame cucumbers, the female flowers of some ridge varieties require fertilising by the male; therefore, the male flowers must not be removed. The seedsman will advise on this. Pollination will probably be carried out by insects; but if few are about, wait until the male flowers are fully developed, then transfer male pollen to the female flowers with a camel-hair paintbrush.

If a lateral fails to show any sign of fruit production by the time the sixth or seventh leaf appears, nip off the tip.

Keep the soil moist by watering round the plants. Feed them regularly with a liquid fertiliser, and protect them with slug pellets.

As the fruits swell and ripen, keep them off the soil with pieces of board or glass.

How to grow frame cucumbers in a greenhouse

The main snag about growing cucumbers in this way is the high temperature required if they are grown early in the season to fruit before those grown in frames or outdoors. All varieties need at least 21°C (70°F) to germinate, and though in most cases this can be lowered as the seedlings progress, they must be grown in a greenhouse where the night temperature does not drop below 16°C (61°F) throughout the growing period.

Begin sowing at any time between late February and March, placing the seeds in compost-filled 3 in. (75 mm.) peat pots.

Insert a single seed edgeways ½ in. (12 mm.) deep into each pot and place the pots in a propagator, above the greenhouse heater or in an airing cupboard (see p. 32).

While the seeds are germinating, rig horizontal wires across the end of the greenhouse from one glazing strut to another. These will be used to train the laterals. Rig the wires about 12 in. (305 mm.) away from the glass.

When the seedlings have developed two rough leaves – that is, the leaves that follow the initial seed leaves – transplant them to the prepared greenhouse bed, or into the large pots in which they will complete their growth. Fix a vertical stake beside each plant.

When the plants have grown up

GROWING RIDGE CUCUMBERS

PREPARING THE SOIL Make planting stations, 2 ft (610 mm.) apart, by filling spade-depth holes with a mixture of well-rotted compost or manure and soil.

PINCHING OUT LEADERS Shortly after planting, when six or seven leaves have developed, pinch out each plant's growing tip to encourage growth of fruit-bearing laterals.

PINCHING OUT LATERALS If any laterals show no signs of fruiting, pinch out the tip beyond the sixth or seventh leaf.

AT-A-GLANCE TIMETABLE FOR RIDGE CUCUMBERS

	SOWING	TRANSPLANTING/THINNING	PINCHING OUT	HARVESTING
In pots	LATE APRIL	LATE MAY–EARLY JUNE	Remove growing tip when plant has six or seven leaves	JULY–SEPTEMBER
Outdoors	LATE MAY	Remove weakest seedling	Remove growing tip when plant has six or seven leaves	JULY–SEPTEMBER

TRAINING GREENHOUSE CUCUMBERS

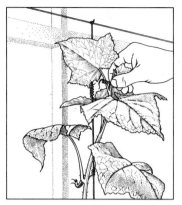

PINCHING OUT LEADERS Remove the tip of each leader, or main shoot, when it reaches roof height. Lateral shoots will develop.

PINCHING OUT LATERALS Pinch out laterals just beyond the second leaf after the fruit. Restrict to 2 ft (610 mm.) if no fruits form.

to the height of the roof, pinch out the tips of the leading shoots. This will encourage the growth of the lateral shoots, which should then be attached to the horizontal wires with twine.

It is often recommended that male flowers should be removed to prevent the fruits from becoming bitter due to pollination, but this is generally unnecessary. Natural pollination of frame types is fairly uncommon, and fruits picked when young, as they should be, will not be seedy or bitter.

If no cucumbers have appeared on the laterals by the time they are 2 ft (610 mm.) long, pinch out the growing tips. If laterals do produce fruit, pinch them out in any event just beyond the second leaf after the first cucumber.

Laterals frequently put out fruit-bearing side-shoots. When this occurs, treat them in the same way as the laterals themselves by pinching out the growing tips two leaves beyond the first cucumber.

Shade the plants from strong sunlight, and water them well. Keep the air as moist and well-ventilated as the other plants in the greenhouse will bear. To provide these conditions, spray the greenhouse floor twice a day.

Once the fruits begin to swell, give the plants a fortnightly feed of liquid fertiliser.

How to grow frame cucumbers in a cold frame

Prepare the planting stations by early May, so that the plants can be set out at the end of the month. Sow seeds in peat pots in the same way as for greenhouse cultivation, but leave them to germinate within the cold frame.

When the seedlings are growing well, transplant them to their final growing situation – that is, a single plant beneath each frame light at the highest point of the frame.

Replace the lid of the frame and cover the glass with greenhouse shading or a coat of limewash. Open the lid 2 in. (50 mm.) on the sheltered side during warm days, but close it to the merest crack at night.

The required openings can be obtained by means of a wedge.

Water the plants frequently, and spray the inside of the frame twice a day during hot weather. This will help maintain the necessary degree of humidity.

When the plants have developed about six leaves, pinch out the growing tips to promote development of laterals.

Spread the laterals evenly over the floor of the frame. Remove the male flowers (readily identifiable by their thin stalks) before they open, and pinch out all fruiting shoots two leaves beyond the first cucumber.

It is important, too, to pinch out any shoot that climbs over the front edge of the frame.

Pests and diseases APHIDS (p. 282), GLASSHOUSE RED SPIDER MITES (p. 283) and GLASSHOUSE WHITEFLY (p. 283) are the pests most likely to occur.

Diseases to which cucumbers are susceptible include CUCUMBER MOSAIC VIRUS (p. 287), GREY MOULD (p. 288), POWDERY MILDEW (p. 289) and SOIL-BORNE DISEASES (p. 290).

Harvesting and storing

Despite the temptation to discover how big your cucumbers will grow, they will taste much better if you harvest them before they reach maximum size.

It is equally important, however, not to cut the fruits too early. As a rough guide, a mature cucumber should have parallel sides. One whose sides dwindle to a point is not developing properly and may have a bitter flavour. This occurs usually towards the end of the cropping season.

Depending on the variety, outdoor cucumbers can be harvested from the end of July to at least the middle of September. Frame plants have a rather longer season, from early July to the end of September. But however they are grown, they are at their best if eaten immediately after cutting.

See also pickles (p. 328); salting (p. 346); sauces, ketchups and relishes (p. 339) and vinegars (p. 342).

GROWING IN FRAMES

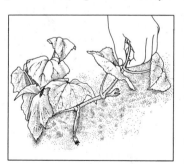

PINCHING OUT LEADERS Remove the growing tip of each plant when six leaves have formed. Fruit-bearing laterals will develop.

PINCHING OUT LATERALS Spread the shoots evenly over the frame. Pinch out each tip just beyond the second leaf after the fruit.

AT-A-GLANCE TIMETABLE FOR GREENHOUSE AND FRAME CUCUMBERS

	SOWING	TRANSPLANTING	PINCH OUT LEADER	PINCH OUT LATERALS	HARVESTING
			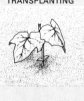		
Greenhouse	LATE FEB–MARCH	Transplant when two leaves have developed	Pinch out when plant reaches roof	Pinch out shoots two leaves beyond fruit	JUNE–SEPTEMBER
Frame	APRIL–MAY	Transplant when two leaves have developed	Pinch out when six leaves have developed	Pinch out shoots two leaves beyond fruit	JULY–SEPTEMBER

Preparing & cooking cucumbers

This vegetable is mainly used fresh in mixed or green salads, or on its own in various dressings. It can, however, also be cooked as a separate vegetable dish. Cucumber is excellent as a base for chilled summer soups, and firm cucumbers may also be cooked as courgettes. The bitterness of the skin, which is most obvious in cooked cucumber, can be reduced by blanching in boiling water for 2 minutes.

For use in fresh salads, wash and dry the cucumber and trim off both flower and stalk end. Peeling is unnecessary, unless the skin is very rough and bruised. Cut crossways into narrow slices or, especially if there are a number of seeds, cut in half lengthways, scoop out the seeds, and then chop into 1 in. (25 mm.) chunks.

Cook sliced or diced cucumber in boiling, lightly salted water for 10 minutes, or steam in butter for about 15 minutes. Serve with a cream sauce flavoured with dill or tarragon. Alternatively, bake peeled, thickly sliced cucumber, liberally dotted with butter and sprinkled with fresh herbs, in the oven for 30 minutes at 190°C (375°F) – gas mark 5.

Small cucumbers, which are known as gherkins, are usually pickled whole.

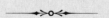

CUCUMBER IN DILL DRESSING

1 cucumber
Salt and pepper
2½ fl. oz. (75 ml.) soured cream
2½ fl. oz. (75 ml.) natural yoghurt
1 heaped tablespoon finely chopped dill.

CHILLING TIME: 30 minutes

Wash the cucumber, but do not peel it unless the skin is bruised or rough. Cut it crossways into paper-thin slices, arrange these on a flat dish and sprinkle with 1 tablespoon salt. Chill in the refrigerator for 30 minutes to let the water drain out of the cucumber.

Rinse the cucumber slices in a colander under cold running water, then dry them on a clean cloth or kitchen paper. Blend the soured cream and the yoghurt, stir in the finely chopped dill and fold in the cucumber slices. Season to taste with salt and pepper.
Serving Serve this salad at once, as an accompaniment to roast chicken or veal; or serve with baked or grilled oily fish, such as salmon or trout.

CUCUMBER AND PEPPER SALAD

1 cucumber
1 tablespoon tarragon vinegar
1 teaspoon salt
1 green pepper
1 small onion
5 fl. oz. (150 ml.) natural yoghourt
Pepper and dry mustard
Garnish: 1 tablespoon coriander seeds

Peel the cucumber and grate on the coarse side of a grater. Sprinkle with vinegar and salt, leave for 30 minutes to draw out the water, then drain.

Trim the base off the pepper, remove the stalk end and all seeds and chop the flesh roughly. Peel and finely chop the onion. Mix these ingredients with the drained cucumber. Season the yoghourt to taste with freshly ground pepper and mustard, spoon over the cucumber, pepper and onion mixture and blend thoroughly.
Serving Sprinkle the salad with coriander seeds, and serve as a side dish with roast lamb or baked white fish.
Variations Garnish with chopped parsley instead of coriander, or with finely chopped fennel leaves to accompany grilled chicken.

CHILLED CUCUMBER SOUP

1 large cucumber
Salt and pepper
½ pint (300 ml.) natural yoghourt
5 fl. oz. (150 ml.) single cream
1 garlic clove
2 tablepoons olive oil
2 tablespoons white wine vinegar
2 oz. (50 g.) chopped walnuts

CHILLING TIME: 1–2 hours

Peel the cucumber and dice into tiny cubes. Put these on a flat dish, sprinkle lightly with salt and leave for 30 minutes. Rinse the cubes in a colander under cold running water and drain thoroughly.

In a bowl, blend the yoghourt with the cream, the crushed garlic, the oil and the vinegar, and season to taste with salt and pepper. Fold in the cucumber and just over half the chopped walnuts; blend thoroughly, then chill in the refrigerator for about 2 hours.
Serving Spoon the chilled soup into individual bowls, sprinkle the remaining chopped walnuts on top, and serve.
Photograph on page 144.

BRAISED CUCUMBER

2 cucumbers
Salt and pepper
1 medium-sized onion
2 oz. (50 g.) butter
2 tablespoons of freshly chopped tarragon
1 tablespoon lemon juice

COOKING TIME: 20 minutes

Peel the cucumbers and cut them into 2 in. (50 mm.) chunks. Slice the chunks into ½ in. (12 mm.) sticks and put them in a pan of boiling, lightly salted water. Cook for 3 minutes, then drain the cucumber through a colander.

Peel the onion and chop it finely. Melt the butter in a heavy-based pan, without letting it become brown. Add the onion and cook over gentle heat for about 5 minutes, or until it is soft and transparent. Stir in the finely chopped tarragon and add the drained cucumber.

Cover with a lid and cook over gentle heat for about 7 minutes, then season to taste with lemon juice, salt and freshly ground pepper.
Serving Spoon the cucumber and onion into a dish and pour the braising juices over them – if necessary first reducing these by rapid boiling. This makes an unusual vegetable dish with white meat, such as veal and chicken, and white fish.

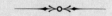

Continued...

Cucumber recipes (continued)

CUCUMBER SALAD

1 cucumber
½ tablespoon salt
Pepper
3 tablespoons caster sugar
2 tablespoons boiling water
Juice of ½ lemon
Garnish : finely chopped parsley

CHILLING TIME: 30 minutes

Wash and dry the cucumber and cut crossways into paper-thin slices. Arrange in a shallow dish and sprinkle with the salt and a little pepper. Set aside for 30 minutes, after which the cucumber will have produced a fair amount of liquid. Do not drain this off, but let it form part of the dressing.

Dissolve the sugar in the water and mix with lemon juice. Spoon the cucumber, with the liquid, into a serving bowl, pour the sweetened lemon juice over it and leave to chill for 30 minutes.
Serving Sprinkle with finely chopped parsley and serve as a side salad with roast chicken and pork. Alternatively, drain the cucumber from the dressing and stuff into hollowed-out tomatoes.
Variation Turn the slices in a dressing made from equal amounts of soured cream and yoghourt, flavoured with fresh dill.

COLD STUFFED CUCUMBERS

2 cucumbers
7 oz. (200 g.) tin of tuna fish
4–5 sticks of celery
4 tablespoons mayonnaise
1 tablespoon lemon juice
1 tablespoon chopped parsley
Salt and pepper
Garnish : watercress

Chill the cucumbers in the refrigerator and, meanwhile, prepare the stuffing. Drain the oil from the tuna fish and mash this with a fork; scrub the celery sticks thoroughly, chop them finely and blend with the tuna fish. Fold in the mayonnaise and parsley, sharpen the flavour with lemon juice and season to taste with salt and pepper.

Cut each cucumber into two, then slice them lengthways into halves. Scoop out the seeds with a pointed teaspoon, leaving a shell all round. Spoon the tuna-fish stuffing into the hollows.
Serving Arrange the cucumber halves on a bed of watercress on individual plates and serve as a first course, accompanied with thin triangles of buttered brown bread.
Variations Fill the cucumbers with cold diced chicken in a cream sauce, asparagus tips in oil-vinaigrette, or peeled prawns in lemon mayonnaise.

INDIAN CUCUMBER SALAD

1 cucumber
1 tablespoon salt
1 garlic clove
5 fl. oz. (150 ml.) natural yoghourt
2 tablespoons chopped parsley
2 tablespoons lemon juice
Cayenne

CHILLING TIME: 30 minutes

Peel the cucumber, cut it crossways into thin slices and arrange on a flat dish. Sprinkle with the salt, and leave for 1 hour to extract the water in the cucumber. Drain thoroughly.

Peel and crush or finely chop the garlic; blend it into the yoghourt, together with the finely chopped parsley, lemon juice and cayenne to taste. Pour this dressing over the cucumber, mix well and chill in the refrigerator for 30 minutes.
Serving This cool, refreshing salad is ideal as a side dish with curry dishes and with grilled, devilled chicken.
Variation Soured cream may be used instead of yoghourt.

CUCUMBER CASSEROLE

2 cucumbers
6 tablespoons oil
1 large onion
1 lb. (500 g.) minced veal, lamb or beef
1 dessertspoon tomato paste
5 fl. oz. (150 ml.) bouillon or water
Salt and pepper
½ pint (300 ml.) white sauce
Paprika

COOKING TIME: 1 hour
OVEN TEMPERATURE: 180°C (350°F) – gas mark 4

Peel the cucumbers and cut them crossways into thin slices. Heat the oil in a pan and fry the cucumber slices quickly for a few minutes. Lift them out and drain on absorbent kitchen paper.

Add the peeled and finely chopped onion to the oil in the pan and fry over gentle heat for about 5 minutes, or until it is soft but not coloured. Stir in the minced meat and continue frying until this is brown and sealed. Add the tomato paste and bouillon, and season to taste with salt and pepper.

Cover with a lid and simmer for about 20 minutes, or until most of the liquid has been absorbed. Butter an ovenproof dish, and line the base with cucumber slices. Cover with a layer of meat and continue with these layers, finishing with cucumber.

Make up a fairly thick white sauce and season it with paprika. Spoon this into the dish and bake in the oven for about 35 minutes,

or until it is bubbling and brown.
Serving This makes a complete dish, reminiscent of moussaka, and can be served with a green salad and a chilled soured-cream sauce.

CUCUMBER SAUCE

1 cucumber
Salt and pepper
1 tablespoon tarragon vinegar
5 fl. oz. (150 ml.) double cream
Sugar (optional)
Garnish : chopped tarragon

CHILLING TIME: 30 minutes

Peel the cucumber and grate on the coarse side of a grater. Arrange in a bowl, sprinkling with salt, pepper and vinegar. Set aside for 30 minutes to let the juices drain out.

Beat the cream lightly, fold in the cucumber and the liquid and correct the seasoning. A little sugar may be added if necessary. Chill in the refrigerator for 30 minutes.
Serving Sprinkle with freshly chopped tarragon and serve the sauce with cold roast chicken, cold trout or salmon.
Variation Add a little freshly grated horseradish to the sauce and sweeten to taste with sugar.

Currants, Black

These hardy shrubs do well in any part of the country. They are easy to grow and long-lived.

The dark, acid berries are richer in vitamin C than any other garden fruit, and for this reason are used for medicinal drinks. For the house-wife, they are a versatile fruit that can be used to make jam, jelly, fruit syrup, pies, puddings and other desserts, as well as ice creams and water ices. They also freeze well.

Planning the crop

Black currants thrive in full sunshine, but will also do well in slightly shaded positions. Avoid pockets and hollows subject to late spring frosts.

Black currants will grow in any soil that is well-drained, but they do best in well-manured ground.

How many bushes to grow A mature bush will yield about 10–15 lb. (5–7 kg.) of fruit and will occupy a space of 30 sq. ft (2.75 sq. m.).

Varieties The following are given in the order in which they fruit:

'Boskoop Giant': early; large fruits; vigorous.

'Seabrook's Black': second early; compact growth; partly resistant to gall mite.

'Blackdown': second early; resistant to mildew.

'Wellington XXX': mid-season; heavy cropper; sweet fruits; do not spray with lime-sulphur.

'Baldwin': late; medium-size currants; compact bush.

'Malling Jet': very late; also flowers late, and so escapes frost.

How to grow black currants

Buy certificated disease-free plants from a reputable nursery. Enrich the soil with garden compost or farmyard manure.

Planting is best done in autumn, but can be carried out at any time until March provided the soil is not frozen. Plant the bushes 5–6 ft (1.5–1.8 m.) apart in each direction. Put them in a little deeper than they were in the nursery, using the soil mark on the stem as a guide.

After planting, prune all the shoots to about 1 in. (25 mm.) above ground level, cutting just above a bud. This means that the bushes will yield no fruit the first summer; instead, their energy will be used to produce vigorous new growth that will provide a crop during the second summer after planting.

After this pruning, mulch the plants with a layer of compost, peat or manure. Repeat this mulch every spring, at the rate of two buckets per square yard, to feed the plants and to conserve moisture in the soil.

Dress the soil in January with 1 oz. of sulphate of potash per square yard (30 g. per square metre), and in March with 1 oz. of sulphate of ammonia. Every third year, apply a dressing of 2 oz. of superphosphate per square yard (60 g. per square metre).

PLANTING Dig a hole broad enough to spread the roots. Set the bushes slightly deeper than they were in the nursery.

PRUNING Cut each shoot of the newly planted bushes to within 1 in. (25 mm.) of ground level, cutting above an outward-facing bud.

After spells of hard frost, ensure that the bushes – which are shallow-rooted – have not been lifted. If they have, firm them in with your feet. Do not disturb the roots by weeding with a fork or hoe; regular mulching should keep down weeds.

Water the plants regularly during dry periods. In the first autumn after planting, cut down the weakest of the current season's shoots to just above the soil. During the following autumn, cut out a few of the weaker shoots to stimulate new growth.

In succeeding autumns remove a proportion of the older wood to make way for replacement shoots.

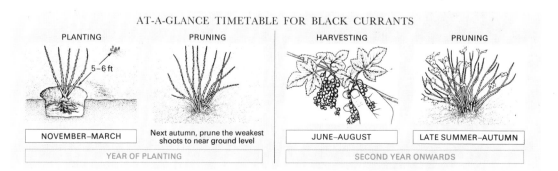

PLANTING — NOVEMBER–MARCH

PRUNING — Next autumn, prune the weakest shoots to near ground level

YEAR OF PLANTING

HARVESTING — JUNE–AUGUST

PRUNING — LATE SUMMER–AUTUMN

SECOND YEAR ONWARDS

Cut low down to promote new growth from near ground level. Aim to cut out between a quarter and one-third of the old wood.

If you have inherited untended black-currant bushes, cut out the old wood from the centre to let in light and air, then the oldest-looking (darkest) remaining shoots. Really hard pruning is needed to stimulate new growth.

How to raise new bushes Black currants are easily increased from hardwood cuttings. In early October, take these from current season's shoots that are well-ripened and healthy looking. Cut off the unripened tip just above a bud, and the bottom just below a bud, to make a cutting about 8 in. (200 mm.) long.

Dig a 6 in. (150 mm.) deep, V-shaped trench, with one side vertical. If the soil is heavy, add sand to the trench to improve drainage.

Place the cuttings in the trench, against the vertical side, 6 in. (150 mm.) apart, with two buds showing above ground. Fill in the trench and firm the soil.

By the following autumn they should have rooted and be ready for their permanent positions. Remove them carefully with a fork and re-plant them, cutting them back as already described for planting young plants bought from a nursery.

Pests and diseases The principal pests of black currants are APHIDS (p. 282), BLACK-CURRANT GALL MITE (p. 282), BLACK-CURRANT LEAF MIDGE (p. 282) and CAPSID BUGS (p. 282).

Diseases most likely to occur are AMERICAN GOOSEBERRY MILDEW (p. 286), GREY MOULD (p. 288), HONEY FUNGUS (p. 288), LEAF SPOT (p. 288) and REVERSION (p. 290).

Harvesting and storing

Pick black currants only when they are properly ripe – that is, a week or so after they have turned black. The fruits at the top of each cluster generally ripen first.

See also bottling (p. 309); drying (p. 343); freezing (p. 294); fruit cheeses and butters (p. 323); jams (p. 314); pickles (p. 328); syrups and juices (p. 326) and wine-making (p. 357).

PRUNING BLACK CURRANTS

ANNUAL PRUNING From the second autumn onwards, remove some older wood each year to make way for younger shoots that will produce fruit the following year.

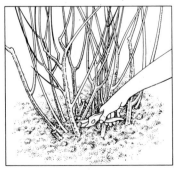

NEGLECTED BUSHES To restore untended bushes, remove crowded shoots from the centre and cut out the older shoots from the outside.

RAISING NEW BUSHES

TAKING A CUTTING In early October, take well-ripened cuttings, about 10 in. (255 mm.) long, of current season's growth. Check that the shoots look healthy.

PREPARING A CUTTING Cut off the soft, pale-coloured tip just above a bud, and trim the base of the cutting just below a bud. Final length should be about 8 in. (200 mm.).

ROOTING THE CUTTINGS Set the cuttings in a V-shaped trench about 6 in. (150 mm.) deep, replace the soil and firm it.

Cooking black currants

Black currants are cooked and used as pie and pudding fillings, for flavouring ice creams and sorbets, and for making jam and fruit syrups. In some recipes they are mixed with red currants and other soft fruits (see pp. 155–6). Always use the berries as soon as possible after harvesting as they tend to deteriorate fairly rapidly.

Like all soft fruits they should be handled carefully to avoid bruising. The blossom and stalk ends are usually snipped off with scissors, but this is unnecessary if the fruit is to be sieved for a purée.

The berries are easily stripped from the stalks with a table fork.

Wash currants by placing them in a colander, and dipping this in several lots of cold water. Let all the water drain off before using the fruit.

AMERICAN BLACK-CURRANT TART

1–1½ lb. (500–750 g.) black currants
1½ tablespoons cornflour
6 oz. (175 g.) sugar
Shortcrust pastry made with ½ lb. (250 g.) flour
2 tablespoons lemon juice
1 oz. (25 g.) butter
1 egg

COOKING TIME: 45 minutes
OVEN TEMPERATURE: 190°C (375°F) – gas mark 5

Strip the black currants from the stalks, rinse and drain them thoroughly and place in a bowl. Blend the cornflour and the sugar with 2½ fl. oz. (75 ml.) water until smooth, and stir this thickening into the currants. Leave to stand for 15 minutes.

Line an 8 in. (200 mm.) pie plate with the prepared pastry, spoon the black-currant mixture over it, sprinkle with lemon juice and dot with butter. Use the pastry trimmings to make a lattice pattern over the top, brush with the lightly beaten egg, and dust with a little sugar.

Bake the tart in the centre of the oven for about 45 minutes, or until the pastry is golden-brown.
Serving Serve the tart lukewarm or cold, with either a bowl of whipped cream or a jug of fresh cream.

Currants, Red and white

BLACK-CURRANT PUDDING

1 lb. (500 g.) black currants
½ lb. (250 g.) self-raising flour
6 oz. (175 g.) caster sugar
4 oz. (100–125 g.) shredded suet
5 fl. oz. (150 ml.) milk
Butter

COOKING TIME: 2 hours

Sift the flour into a bowl, blend in half the sugar and all the suet, and mix to a stiff dough with the milk. Knead the dough on a floured surface until smooth and elastic. Leave to rest for 15 minutes under an inverted bowl.

Meanwhile, trim the currants, rinse in a colander and drain thoroughly.

Grease a 2 pint (1 l.) pudding basin. Roll out three-quarters of the suet pastry, ¼ in. (5 mm.) thick, and line the basin with this. Arrange half the currants over the pastry, add the remaining sugar and top with the rest of the currants.

Roll out the reserved suet pastry to form a lid to fit the basin, and seal the edges. Cover the basin with buttered, greaseproof paper, or foil or a cloth, and tie securely in place with string, leaving room for expansion.

Place the basin in a pan of boiling water and steam for 2 hours, topping up with hot water as necessary.
Serving Turn out the pudding and serve warm with custard.
Photograph on pages 214–15.

BLACK-CURRANT AND MINT SHAKE

½ lb. (250 g.) black currants
1 dozen mint leaves
Sugar
1 pint (600 ml.) milk
¼ pint (150 ml.) vanilla ice cream
Garnish: mint leaves

Strip the black currants from the stalks and, if necessary, rinse and drain. Put them in a pan with the rinsed mint leaves and 6 tablespoons of water. Bring to the boil over gentle heat and continue simmering until the berries burst and release their juices. Rub the currants through a sieve, sweeten to taste with sugar and set the purée aside to cool. Chill in the refrigerator. Combine in the blender the black-currant purée with the cold milk and the ice cream. Blend until perfectly smooth.
Serving Pour the milk shake into tall glasses, each containing a couple of ice cubes. Garnish with a small sprig of mint and serve with drinking straws.
Variations About ½ pint (300 ml.) of fruit syrup may be used instead of the purée. Cream may take the place of the ice cream, and yoghourt used instead of milk.
Photograph on pages 136–7.

Red currants

White currants   *Bush*   *Cordon*

These delicious fruits are related to black currants but do not have the same growing habit. They are therefore cultivated in a different way.

They can be grown as bushes or as cordons, the latter being ideal for the small garden as they occupy much less space and can be grown as an ornamental edging or divider.

For the space they occupy, red and white currants produce a large amount of fruit from mid-June to late July. Like black currants, they are long-lived plants.

Planning the crop

An open site in full sun or semi-shade is best for currants, but cordons can also be grown successfully against walls of any aspect.

Whatever the position it should not be subject to late frosts, because the plants flower early.

Red and white currants grow well in any moisture-retaining soil, as long as it is not liable to become waterlogged.

How many bushes to grow Red and white currant bushes yield about 8–10 lb. (4–5 kg.) of fruit, and cordons about 2–3 lb. (1–1.5 kg.). Each mature bush occupies about 25 sq. ft (2.3 sq. m.). Eight single cordons can be planted against a wall or fence 10 ft (3 m.) long.

Varieties Some recommended varieties in order of fruiting are:
Red currants 'Jonkheer van Tets': very early; 'Laxton No. 1': early; 'Red Lake': mid-season; 'Rivers Late Red': late; 'Wilson's Long Bunch': late.
White currants 'White Grape'; 'White Versailles'.

How to grow red and white currants

Red and white currants, like gooseberries, are susceptible to a deficiency of potash. Before planting, apply a general fertiliser at 4 oz. per square yard (120 g. per square metre), together with a dressing of well-rotted manure or compost if the soil is low in humus.

The best month for planting is October, but any time until March is suitable provided the soil is not frozen.

Space bushes 5 ft (1.5 m.) apart each way, and cordons 15 in. (380 mm.) apart.

After planting a bush, cut back

153

all the branches to four buds above the base of the stems. The top bud should point outwards.

Before planting cordons, stretch support wires between end posts or along a fence. Set the bottom wire 18 in. (455 mm.) from the ground and two more spaced 2 ft (610 mm.) apart above the bottom wire.

Canes tied to these will support the cordons.

After planting a cordon, choose the strongest shoot to become the leader and eventually constitute the main stem. Cut off all others to within 1 in. (25 mm.) of the base. Prune lateral shoots that grow from the main stem to two buds.

Secure the cordon to the cane with soft string, and fasten the cane to the wires.

Mulch the bushes and cordons in winter with a 2 in. (50 mm.) layer of well-rotted compost or manure and feed them with 1 oz. of sulphate of potash per square yard (30 g. per square metre).

In spring, a further feed of 1 oz. of sulphate of ammonia per square yard (30 g. per square metre) will promote growth. Every third year apply 2 oz. of superphosphate per square yard (60 g. per square metre).

PRUNING AFTER PLANTING

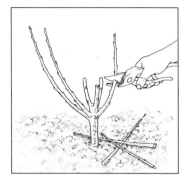

BUSHES Immediately after planting, cut back each shoot to an outward-pointing bud – about the fourth above the base of the shoot. Fruiting stems will grow from these.

CORDONS Choose the strongest shoot – two shoots for a double cordon – and cut the remainder back to the base. Fasten the stem to the stake with soft string.

Pruning

Bushes and cordons both need to be pruned in winter and summer. Leave winter pruning, in which growth is always cut back to an undamaged bud, until February.

Bushes During the second winter shorten each branch by half, cutting back to an outward-facing bud. In succeeding winters cut back leading shoots halfway, and laterals to two buds. The aim is to achieve a goblet-shaped bush, with an open centre.

From about the fifth winter onwards, cut back all current season's shoots by about 1 in. (25 mm.). Remove congested old wood from the centre of the bush, aiming to replace it with new growth.

In late June, cut back laterals to three or five leaves.

Cordons Winter pruning of cordons consists of shortening the leading shoots by one-third and laterals to one bud. Do not allow the leader to exceed a height of 6 ft (1.8 m.).

In late June cut back laterals to three or five leaves on both bushes and cordons.

Raising new plants

Red and white currants can be

WINTER AND SUMMER PRUNING

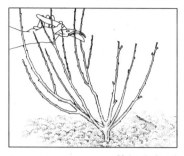

BUSHES: SECOND WINTER Halve the length of each shoot, cutting back to just above an outward-facing bud in each case to ensure an open structure.

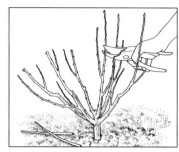

BUSHES: SUCCEEDING WINTERS Cut back leading shoots to half their length, and laterals to two buds. The aim is to achieve an open-centred, goblet-shaped bush.

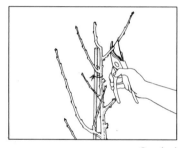

CORDONS: WINTER PRUNING Cut back each leading shoot by one-third, and reduce each of the lateral shoots to a single bud.

BUSHES/CORDONS: SUMMER Towards the end of June, prune lateral shoots on red and white currants to three or five leaves.

raised from cuttings of the current year's growth.

In October, cut off some well-ripened shoots. Trim the soft wood off the top, just above a bud, and some wood off the bottom, just below a bud, to produce cuttings 10–15 in. (255–380 mm.) long. Rub off all except the top four buds.

Dig a 7–8 in. (180–200 mm.) deep, V-shaped trench, with one side vertical, and put the cuttings in this against the vertical face, 6 in. (150 mm.) apart. Then carry out the procedure described for black currants (see p. 152).

When putting the young currant plants into their permanent positions, plant them at the same depth as they were while rooting, and remove any low, unwanted side-shoots so that the bush has a clean stem about 4–6 in. (100–150 mm.) long.

Cut back all upper branches halfway to an outward-facing bud. After that, prune them as already described.

Pests and diseases APHIDS (p. 282), BLACK-CURRANT GALL MITE (p. 282), BLACK-CURRANT LEAF MIDGE (p. 282) and CAPSID BUGS

AT-A-GLANCE TIMETABLE FOR RED AND WHITE CURRANTS

PLANTING	SUMMER PRUNING	HARVESTING	WINTER PRUNING
OCTOBER–MARCH	JUNE	LATE JUNE–JULY	FEBRUARY
FIRST YEAR	SUCCEEDING YEARS		

(p. 282) are the pests most likely to harm currant crops.

Diseases that may occur are CORAL SPOT (p. 287); GREY MOULD (p. 288), HONEY FUNGUS (p. 288) and LEAF SPOT (p. 288).

Harvesting and storing

Pick the fruits as soon as they are ripe and use them immediately, since they do not keep for long.

See also bottling (p. 309); freezing (p. 294); jams (p. 314) and jellies (p. 320). ✒✒

RAISING NEW PLANTS

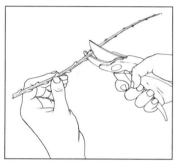

TRIMMING A CUTTING After cutting off the soft tip, remove some wood at the base to give a cutting 10–15 in. (255–380 mm.) long. Remove all but the top four buds.

INSERTING A CUTTING Placed in a trench, with two buds above ground level, the cuttings will root by the following autumn.

Preparing & cooking red and white currants

Red and white currants may be served as fresh dessert fruits, left on the stalks after rinsing and draining. Red currants are also used in fresh fruit salads and cooked in compôtes, pastries, jams and jellies. Before cooking, red and white currants are stripped from the stalks, which is most easily done by running the prongs of a fork down the length of the stalk.

Frosted red currants are attractive as a garnish to sweet fruit mousses, trifles, cakes and ice creams, or they can be served on their own as a dessert fruit. Rinse and drain clusters of the currants, thoroughly brush with lightly beaten egg white and dredge heavily with sugar. Leave on a wire rack to dry before use.

———◦———

RED-CURRANT COMPÔTE

1 lb. (500 g.) red currants
7 oz. (200 g.) caster sugar
1–2 tablespoons brandy
5 fl. oz. (150 ml.) single cream

CHILLING TIME: 1 hour

Strip the currants from the stems, rinse in a colander and drain thoroughly. Put alternate layers of currants and sugar in a bowl. Leave in a warm room for several hours until the sugar has dissolved, then stir in the brandy.

Spoon the red currants, with their juice, into serving glasses, and chill the compôte in the

refrigerator for about 1 hour.
Serving Offer a separate jug of cream with the currants.
Variation Make a syrup from the sugar and 2 tablespoons of water, and pour this hot over the red currants. Leave them to cool in the syrup, then chill them for a couple of hours.

———◦———

RED CURRANTS WITH YOGHOURT

¾ lb. (375 g.) red currants
2 tablespoons of sherry
3 oz. (75 g.) sugar
2 oz. (50 g.) ratafia biscuits
½ pint (300 ml.) natural yoghourt

CHILLING TIME: 30 minutes

Strip the currants from the stems, rinse in a colander and drain thoroughly. Put two-thirds of the currants in a bowl with the sherry and sugar, and stir until the sugar has dissolved. Crush the ratafia biscuits to coarse crumbs with a rolling pin and fold these and the red currants and juice into the yoghourt.

Spoon the mixture into four serving glasses and chill for 30 minutes in the refrigerator.
Serving Just before serving, garnish each glass with the reserved red currants and sprinkle with a little extra sugar.
Variations Black or white currants may be used instead of red currants.
Photograph on pages 142–3.

SUMMER PUDDING

6–8 slices of stale, crustless white bread, ½ in. (12 mm.) thick
1½ lb. (750 g.) mixed red and black currants
4 oz. (100 g.) sugar

COOKING TIME: 10 minutes
CHILLING TIME: 8 hours

Line the base and sides of a 2 pint (1 l.) pudding basin with the bread slices cut to shape so as to fit together closely. Set some of the bread aside for the top.

Top and tail the black currants and strip the red currants from the stems. Rinse and drain thoroughly. Put the fruit in a pan with the sugar and bring to the boil over a very gentle heat. Simmer for a few minutes only, until the sugar has dissolved and the juices begin to run.

Remove the pan from the heat, reserve 2 tablespoons of the juices and spoon the remainder, with the fruit, into the prepared basin. Cover the top closely with bread.

Fix a saucer or plate over the pudding, inside the basin, and place a heavy weight on top. Chill in the refrigerator for 8 hours.
Serving Turn the pudding out, upside-down, on to a serving dish and pour the reserved fruit juice over any parts of the bread not soaked through and coloured. Serve with a bowl of lightly whipped cream.

CURRANT SOUP

½ lb. (250 g.) red currants
½ lb. (250 g.) black currants
5 fl. oz. (150 ml.) water
1½–2 tablespoons of cornflour
Sugar
Cream (optional)
Garnish : small macaroons

COOKING TIME: 20–30 minutes

Rinse and drain the currants, but do not strip from the stalks. Put in a pan with the water and bring to the boil over a low heat; simmer gently until the berries burst and the juices flow freely.

Strain through butter muslin or a jelly bag until all the juice has dripped through. Do not squeeze the bag, or the juice will be cloudy.

Make up the juice with cold water to 2 pints (1 l.); bring back to the boil and thicken with the cornflour mixed with a little cold water. Boil gently for a few minutes to cook the flour through and to let the soup thicken to the required consistency. Add sugar to taste.
Serving Pour into soup plates, trail a little cream over the surface, and top with a few macaroons. Serve as a first course.
Variation Chill the soup for a couple of hours in the refrigerator and serve as above, as either a first or a last course.

———◦———

Continued . . .

Red and white currant recipes (continued)

CURRANT MOUSSE

1 lb. (500 g.) mixed red and black currants
1¼ pints (725 ml.) water
4 tablespoons of cornflour
½ lb. (250 g.) sugar (approx.)
Vanilla sugar
Single cream

COOKING TIME: 20–25 minutes
CHILLING TIME: 1 hour

Rinse and drain the currants, put them in a pan with the water and bring to the boil over gentle heat. Simmer gently for about 10 minutes, or until the currants burst and the juices flow freely. Strain through a sieve lined with muslin and leave the juices to drip through for 30 minutes.

Measure the juice and, if necessary, make up to 2 pints (1 l.) with cold water. Blend the cornflour with a little of the juice and put the remainder in a pan. Stir in the blended cornflour and bring the mixture to the boil, stirring continuously until it thickens.

Remove from the heat; add the sugar, and also about 1 teaspoon of vanilla sugar to taste. Pour into a serving dish and sprinkle the top with a little sugar to prevent a skin forming.
Serving This is the classic and traditional Danish summer sweet known as Rödgröd. It is served lukewarm or chilled, with a jug of cream, and eaten from soup plates. Blanched, flaked almonds are sometimes sprinkled on top.

RED-CURRANT BOATS

¾ lb. (375 g.) red currants
4–5 oz. (100–150 g.) sugar
2 teaspoons arrowroot
4 oz. (100–125 g.) flour
Salt
2 oz. (50 g.) caster sugar
2 oz. (50 g.) butter
2 egg yolks
Garnish : custard, whipped cream

COOKING TIME: 12 minutes
OVEN TEMPERATURE: 190°C (375°F) – gas mark 5

Strip the currants from the stems, rinse and drain them and put in a pan with the sugar and 2 tablespoons of water. Bring to the boil over gentle heat. Stir the arrowroot with a little water and blend into the red currants, stirring carefully until thickened. Remove the pan from the heat and leave the currants to cool.

Sift the flour with a pinch of salt and add the caster sugar, softened butter and egg yolks. Knead the dough lightly and set it aside to rest in a cool place.

Roll out the pastry and use it to line 12–14 boat-shaped moulds. Prick them with a fork and bake blind in the oven for 5–7 minutes, or until they are light golden-brown.

Ease the pastries from the moulds and leave to cool.
Serving Spread a little rich custard sauce over the base of the pastries, fill them with the cooled red currants and decorate with a little whipped cream on top.

Damsons

The fruit of the damson is the smallest in the plum family, but a tree will succeed in exposed, wet districts where plums are difficult to grow and gages may not survive.

Damsons are self-fertile, so that only one tree needs to be planted to produce a crop.

Planning the crop

Damsons do best in deep, well-drained heavy loams, but they can be grown in most soils.

How many to grow One tree is sufficient to supply the average family.

Varieties Two self-fertile varieties are generally easy to obtain:
'Merryweather': large, black, fine-flavoured fruits in late August and early September.
'Prune': small, tapering, blue-black fruits of good flavour in September and October.

How to grow damsons

Damsons can be grown as a bush or may be fan-trained on a wall. If more than one tree is to be grown, set them 12 ft (3.6 m.) apart. Plant two-year-old trees in October or November (see p. 42).

To establish the framework of the tree, prune and train basically as for apples (see pp. 64–68), but prune in early spring as growth begins – not in winter. Another difference is that a damson should have a more crowded and compact head than an apple.

When the tree is established little pruning is needed, as damsons fruit on both old and new wood.

The general cultivation of damsons is the same as that of plums (see p. 236).

Pests and diseases Among pests attacking damsons are APHIDS (p. 282), CATERPILLARS (p. 282), FRUIT TREE RED SPIDER MITES (p. 283) and PLUM SAWFLY (p. 284).

Diseases that may occur are BACTERIAL CANKER (p. 286), BROWN ROT (p. 286), HONEY FUNGUS (p. 288), RUST (p. 290), SHOTHOLE (p. 290) and SILVER LEAF (p. 290).

Harvesting and storing

Pick the fruit by the stalk to avoid bruising.

See also bottling (p. 309); freezing (p. 294); fruit cheeses and butters (p. 323); jams (p. 314); jellies (p. 320); pickles (p. 328); syrups and juices (p. 326) and wine-making (p. 357).

AT-A-GLANCE TIMETABLE FOR DAMSONS

PLANTING	PRUNING	HARVESTING
OCTOBER–NOVEMBER	MARCH–APRIL	SEPTEMBER–OCTOBER

Preparing & cooking damsons

These small plums are rarely used as fresh dessert fruits, being more often used for pie and pudding fillings and for that classic preserve, damson cheese.

To prepare damsons for cooking, wash and dry them and remove any stalks. Cut with the point of a knife along the indentations on the skin and twist the damson into two halves. Prise out the stone with the point of a knife, doing this over a plate.

For purées, cook damsons in just enough water to prevent sticking. Cook for 15–20 minutes, depending on the ripeness of the fruit.

STEWED DAMSONS

1 lb. (500 g.) damsons
1 pint (600 ml.) water
3 tablespoons cornflour
Sugar
Garnish : blanched, split almonds

COOKING TIME: 20 minutes
CHILLING TIME: 1 hour

Wash the damsons, cut them in half and remove the stones. Put in a pan with the water and bring to the boil; simmer gently for about 10 minutes, or until just tender but not mushy. Blend the cornflour with cold water and stir into the damsons; continue stirring until the damsons have reached boiling point and are beginning to thicken.

Remove the pan from the heat, sweeten to taste with sugar and pour into a serving bowl. Sprinkle the top with a little sugar to help prevent a skin forming. Decorate with split almonds in a circular or star-like pattern. Chill for about 1 hour in the refrigerator.
Serving Serve chilled or lukewarm, with a separate jug of cream.

DAMSON AND APPLE PIE

¾ lb. (375 g.) damsons
¾ lb. (375 g.) cooking apples
3 oz. (75 g.) sugar
½ lb. (250 g.) shortcrust pastry

COOKING TIME: 35–40 minutes
OVEN TEMPERATURE: 200°C (400°F) – gas mark 6

Wash and dry the damsons, cut them in half and remove the stones. Peel and core the apples and cut them into chunks. Put a pie funnel in the centre of a pie dish and arrange the mixed damsons and apple round it. Sprinkle the fruit with the sugar and add 3 tablespoons of water.

Roll out the pastry and cover the pie. Use the trimmings for decorations, and brush the pastry with a little milk. Sprinkle with caster sugar, make a slit in the centre, and bake in the oven for 35–40 minutes, or until golden-brown.
Serving Serve warm or cold, with a jug of cream or custard sauce.

DAMSON PUFFS

½ lb. (250 g.) damsons (prepared weight)
3 oz. (75 g.) sugar
¾ lb. (375 g.) puff pastry
1 egg
Cream

COOKING TIME: 20 minutes
OVEN TEMPERATURE: 220°C (425°F) – gas mark 7

Wash and dry the damsons, cut in half and remove the stones. Chop the flesh roughly and mix with the sugar. Roll out the pastry, ¼ in. (5 mm.) thick, and cut into eight squares. Place some chopped damsons in the centre of each, bring up the long edges and seal over the top.

Set the pastries on a moist baking tray, seams down, brush with the lightly beaten egg and sprinkle with a little sugar. Make a small slit in each pastry for the steam to escape, then bake in the oven for about 20 minutes, or until the pastries are well risen and golden.
Serving Serve lukewarm as a dessert course, with a jug of cream, or as pastries with tea or coffee.
Variation Arrange the sugared damsons in a pie dish and cover with the rolled-out puff pastry. Bake until risen and golden.

DAMSONS WITH BAKED CUSTARD

1 lb. (500 g.) damsons
Whole blanched almonds
3 eggs
4 oz. (100–125 g.) sugar
Vanilla essence
5 fl. oz. (150 ml.) single cream
Pinch of baking powder

COOKING TIME: 40 minutes
OVEN TEMPERATURE: 180°C (350°F) – gas mark 4

Wash and dry the damsons, cut them in half and remove the stones. Put a whole blanched almond in each damson half, and arrange these over the base of an ovenproof dish. Sprinkle with half the sugar.

Separate the eggs and beat the yolks with the remaining sugar and a few drops of vanilla essence until creamy and fluffy. Bring the cream to the boil over gentle heat and beat it gradually into the egg yolks. Pour this custard mixture back into the pan and heat through until it thickens, without boiling. Strain into a bowl.

Whisk the egg whites with a tiny pinch of baking powder until stiff, and mix carefully into the custard. Spoon it over the damsons and set the dish in a roasting tin with about 1 in. (25 mm.) of cold water. Bake for about 30 minutes, or until the custard is set and golden-brown.
Serving Serve straight from the oven. A jug of cream may be offered, but this is not necessary.

DAMSON CHARLOTTE

1½ lb. (750 g.) damsons
4 oz. (100–125 g.) sugar
4 oz. (100–125 g.) sponge fingers
2½ fl. oz. (75 ml.) cream
2 teaspoons powdered gelatine
2½ fl. oz. (75 ml.) milk

COOKING TIME: 20 minutes
CHILLING TIME: 2–3 hours

Wash the damsons, cut them in half and remove the stones. Put the damsons in a pan with the sugar and just enough water to prevent sticking. Simmer gently for about 15 minutes, until soft and tender. Rub through a sieve, and set the purée aside to cool.

Line a charlotte mould or round cake tin with the sponge fingers, brushing them with a little of the purée to hold them together. Beat the cream lightly and fold it into the damson purée.

Dissolve the gelatine in the hot milk and strain into the mixture. Beat steadily until it is stiff and beginning to set, then pour the damson purée into the prepared mould. Chill the charlotte in the refrigerator for several hours until set.
Serving Dip the base of the mould into hot water to loosen it, invert on to a plate, and serve with a jug of fresh cream.
Photograph on pages 214–15.

Dill

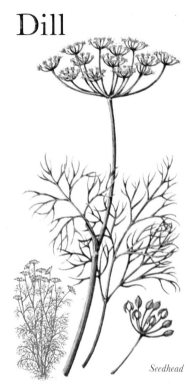

Seedhead

Fresh or dried leaves of dill, a hardy annual herb, add an aniseed flavour to fish, poultry, soups and stews.

How to grow dill

Dill can be grown in any well-drained soil in an open, sunny position. The plants grow to a height of 3 ft (1 m.).

Sow the seeds at monthly intervals from March to July to get a constant supply throughout the summer and autumn.

Sow about ¼ in. (5 mm.) deep, and leave 9 in. (230 mm.) between drills if you sow more than one.

Thin the first sowing – to provide seeds – leaving 9 in. between plants. Use the thinnings to provide tender young leaves. Subsequent sowings, for leaves only, need be thinned to only 3–4 in. (75–100 mm.).

Pests and diseases Dill is usually trouble-free.

Harvesting and storing

The leaves will be ready for picking about eight weeks after sowing.

Pick leaves for using fresh when needed, and those for drying (see p. 343) or freezing (see p. 294) before the plants start flowering.

Leave plants from the earliest sowing to provide seeds for the winter. Pick the seeding heads when they have turned brown, and complete the drying out by spreading the seeds on a tray in a warm, dry place. Store the seeds in air-tight jars. 🌿🌿

AT-A-GLANCE TIMETABLE FOR DILL

SOWING	THINNING	HARVESTING
MARCH–JULY	When large enough to handle	MAY–SEPTEMBER

¼ in. / 9 in.

Preparing & cooking dill

This pungently aromatic herb, with its aniseed flavour, combines particularly well with both hot and cold fish dishes, and is also useful for salads, cold sauces and dressings. Both the leaves, fresh and dried, and the dried seeds are used in cooking. They are also used to flavour vinegar and as a pickling ingredient with gherkins and cucumbers.

Use the leaves chopped in salad dressings or sprinkle them on buttered new potatoes; on egg, tomato and cucumber sandwiches; on fish and tomato soups; and on grilled and baked fish. The seeds, too, can be added to salad dressings, creamed cabbage and white chicken stews.

The feathery, pale green leaves are attractive as a garnish, and feature particularly in Scandinavian cooking. Raw, smoked and pickled salmon are traditionally served with a strong mustard and dill dressing, which can also be served with smoked mackerel and trout.

DILL SAUCE

2 tablespoons finely chopped dill leaves
5 fl. oz. (150 ml.) double cream
Salt and pepper

CHILLING TIME: 1 hour

Blanch the dill leaves for 1 minute, drain, dry thoroughly and chop finely.

Whip the cream lightly and fold in the chopped dill. Season to taste with salt and ground white pepper. Chill in the refrigerator for 1 hour.

Serving The sauce is excellent with cold meat, such as lamb or chicken, and with fish dishes such as trout and salmon.

Variation For a hot sauce, flavour a white sauce with white wine vinegar and sugar, fold in the chopped dill and enrich the sauce with cream mixed with one or two egg yolks. Serve with baked ham or poached white fish.

MUSTARD AND DILL DRESSING

2 tablespoons prepared French mustard
1 tablespoon sugar
1 egg yolk
6 tablespoons olive oil
2 tablespoons white wine or dill vinegar
1 heaped teaspoon fresh, chopped dill
Salt and pepper

Beat the mustard with the sugar and egg yolk until smooth. Add the oil and vinegar, little by little, beating thoroughly after each addition. Fold in the dill and season to taste with salt and pepper.

MATJES HERRINGS IN DILL DRESSING

4 matjes-herring fillets
5 fl. oz. (150 ml.) whipping cream
Salt and pepper
½ teaspoon paprika
1 tablespoon caster sugar
1 teaspoon mustard powder
1 teaspoon lemon juice
2 tablespoons finely chopped dill

CHILLING TIME: 1 hour

Marinated herring fillets – matjes herrings – can be bought from most delicatessen shops, either by weight or tinned. Drain the fillets from the marinade and remove any bones. Cut the fish into bite-sized pieces and arrange in a bowl. Chill in the refrigerator for about 1 hour.

Whip the cream lightly and season it sweet and sour with salt, pepper and paprika, sugar, mustard and lemon juice. Fold in half of the freshly chopped dill, and spoon the dressing over the herring fillets.

Serving Sprinkle the remaining dill on top of the matjes herrings and serve at once as a first course, accompanied with pumpernickel and ice-cold butter.

Dwarf beans:

see **Beans, French**

Egg plants:

see **Aubergines**

Endive

Batavian endive

Curled endive

Endives have been grown as a winter salad vegetable in English gardens since the 16th century, but have never achieved the popularity they deserve. Perhaps this is due to the bitter taste of the leaves in their green state – a condition that is easily corrected by blanching to provide interesting salads in the season when lettuces are in short supply.

Two kinds of endives are grown. The curly variety is sown in June and July to provide salads from September to November, while the hardier, wavy-leaved Batavian type is not sown until August. This will provide endives for the table until well into winter.

Endives may be served raw in salads, or braised with white or cream sauce. They are an ideal accompaniment to grilled steak.

Planning the crop

Endives do best in a light, well-drained soil containing plenty of rotted manure or compost. Plants sown in July or later may be grown in beds from which early potatoes or peas have been harvested. Endives grown for mid-winter eating should be sown in a sheltered position.

How much to grow Nine or ten plants can be grown in a 10 ft (3 m.) row. Two such rows, one containing early and the other late endives, should be sufficient for most families.

Varieties 'Batavian Broad Leaved': large leaves; crisp and tender.

'Exquisite Curled': delicately curled leaves; excellent for autumn salads.

How to grow endives

Sow the seeds thinly in drills ½ in. (12 mm.) deep and drawn 15 in. (380 mm.) apart in the position where the plants are to grow. Water them thoroughly, keep them well-weeded and thin the seedlings to 12–15 in. (305–380 mm.) apart.

To save seeds, three or four may be sown at 12–15 in. intervals and the weakest removed after germination.

It is inadvisable to sow endives before mid-June, partly because they should be grown as a successor to lettuce, and partly because early plants have a tendency to run quickly to seed.

Pests and diseases SLUGS AND SNAILS (p. 285) may attack the plants. Endives are generally disease-free.

Harvesting

Endives must be blanched to make them suitable for eating. When the leaves are completely dry, bind them in the same way as for hearting cos lettuces (see p. 184).

Cover each endive with an upturned flower pot, blocking the drainage hole.

After seven to ten days in early autumn, or three weeks in winter, the centres of the plants turn to a creamy-white shade and are then ready for eating. Use the endives as soon as possible after lifting, as even a short period of storage will cause the leaves to toughen.

BLANCHING ENDIVES

SECURE WITH STRING Choose a sunny or windy day, when the leaves of mature plants are dry, to tie them loosely with soft string.

COVER WITH A POT Place an upturned flower pot, or similar lightproof cover, over each plant. Place a stone over the drainage hole.

AT-A-GLANCE TIMETABLE FOR ENDIVES

SOWING	THINNING	BLANCHING	HARVESTING
Curly-leaved types			
JUNE–JULY	When large enough to handle	SEPTEMBER–OCTOBER	ONE WEEK LATER
Batavian types			
AUGUST	When large enough to handle	NOVEMBER	THREE WEEKS LATER

Preparing & cooking endive

The curly, pale green leaves of this salad vegetable are excellent for winter salads. They are best tossed in a piquant or sweet dressing on their own.

To prepare endives for use in salads, cut off any outer damaged leaves, trim off the root base, separate the spears and divide into small sprigs complete with sections of white stalk. Wash thoroughly and dry on a cloth.

For cooking, trim the root bases, leave the endives whole cut large ones in half lengthways. Wash and drain.

ENDIVE AND OLIVE SALAD

1 endive
4 oz. (100–125 g.) green olives
1 egg yolk
Salt
1 tablespoon olive oil
1 tablespoon lemon juice
2 fl. oz. (50 ml.) single cream
Dry mustard or paprika, sugar

Prepare the endive and arrange the leaves and olives in a salad bowl. Make up the dressing: beat the egg yolk with salt until smooth and add the oil, drop by drop. Stir in the lemon juice and the cream, and season with mustard and a little sugar.
Serving Just before serving, pour the dressing over the endive and toss well. Serve as a side salad with roast meat or poultry.

BRAISED ENDIVE

2–3 endives
2 oz. (50 g.) streaky bacon
1 oz. (25 g.) butter
1 carrot
1 onion
½ pint (300 ml.) white stock
Salt and pepper
Garnish: chopped parsley

COOKING TIME: 50 minutes
OVEN TEMPERATURE: 180°C (350°F) – gas mark 4

Trim the bases of the endives, wash thoroughly and divide each head into two. Put in a pan of boiling, lightly salted water and blanch for about 3 minutes. Refresh at once under cold running water and drain thoroughly.

Remove rind and gristle from the bacon and chop the flesh. Melt the butter in a fireproof casserole dish and fry the bacon for 2 minutes.

Add the peeled and sliced carrot and the peeled, finely chopped onion.

Lay the endives on top of the vegetables, pour over the stock and season with salt and pepper. Cover with a lid and cook in the oven for 45 minutes.
Serving Serve the endives straight from the dish, with the cooking liquid, and sprinkled with finely chopped parsley. They are excellent with roast or grilled lamb or veal. The liquid may be thickened with a little kneaded butter and flour.

Fennel

There are two distinct varieties of fennel: the tall, perennial herb that grows wild on waste ground and is cultivated for the fine flavour of its leaves, seeds and stems; and the usually smaller Florence fennel (see facing page), a biennial that is grown mainly for its swollen stem base and is used as a vegetable.

The leaves of both plants, dried or fresh, impart a delicate aniseed flavour to fish, cheese dishes, sauces, pickles and chutneys.

The young stems or leaf stalks of common fennel may be braised like celery or chopped into salads. The seeds, whose aniseed taste is particularly pronounced, may be used in soups, bread and cakes.

Planning the crop

Fennel grows well in a warm, sunny position in any reasonably well-drained garden soil.

How much to grow Unless a regular supply of seeds is needed, or stems and stalks for cooking, three plants of common fennel – which grow to a height of 5–8 ft (1.5–2.5 m.) – would be adequate for the needs of all but the most fervent fennel lovers.

How to grow fennel

When growing the plants for seeds, sow thinly in ½ in. (12 mm.) drills in March to allow time for the seeds to ripen in September or October. If grown for the leaves and stalks, sow in April or May.

In both cases, thin the seedlings to 12 in. (305 mm.) spacings.

Pests and diseases Fennel is generally trouble-free.

Harvesting and storing

Pick the leaves as required from June onwards, pinching off the flower heads as they form unless you wish to harvest the seeds.

Gather the seed heads on a dry day in early autumn, when they have turned pale brown, and hang them in a warm place for a week or two, with a tray underneath to catch any seeds that fall.

Make sure that the seeds are dry before storing them in air-tight containers.

See also drying (p. 343) and freezing (p. 294).

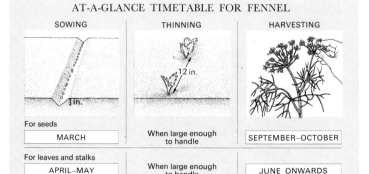

AT-A-GLANCE TIMETABLE FOR FENNEL

SOWING	THINNING	HARVESTING
	12 in.	
½ in.		
For seeds	When large enough to handle	
MARCH		SEPTEMBER–OCTOBER
For leaves and stalks	When large enough to handle	
APRIL–MAY		JUNE ONWARDS

Cooking with fennel

The blue-green leaves of fennel are most attractive as a garnish. They are sweetly aromatic, with an aniseed flavour that is reminiscent of dill, but less pungent.

Both the leaves and the seeds are used for the same cooking purposes as dill. But while dill is traditionally used in northern European cooking, the flavour of fennel is more usually found in Mediterranean dishes. Bass and other oily fish are often grilled on a bed of fennel leaves.

The dried seeds are used chiefly in pickles, seed cakes and herbal teas. The fresh leaves, finely chopped, are added to dressings for cucumbers and green salads, to fish soups and stews, and to young buttered vegetables.

Fennel, Florence

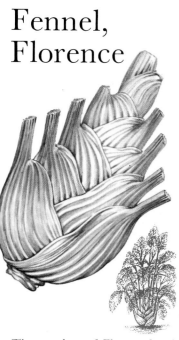

The stem base of Florence fennel, also called finocchio, may be chopped raw into salads; but it is more usually simmered in a stock.

The ferny leaves of Florence fennel make an attractive backdrop to the herb or vegetable bed.

Planning the crop

Florence fennel requires more attention than the common species. Dig well-rotted manure or compost into the ground during the previous winter, and rake in a dressing of general fertiliser at 2 oz. per square yard (60 g. per square metre) shortly before sowing the seeds in April.

Plant it in a sunny position in well-drained soil.

How much to grow Florence fennel is a dish for special occasions, for which half a stem base per person should be sufficient. A 10 ft (3 m.) row, yielding 10–12 plants, would be enough for most families.

How to grow Florence fennel

Sow the seeds thinly in a ½ in. (12 mm.) drill in April, thinning the seedlings to 12 in. (305 mm.).

Keep the plants well-watered and, when the stem bases begin to swell, draw earth around them in the same way as for potatoes.

Pests and diseases Florence fennel is generally trouble-free.

Harvesting

Gather the swollen stem bases for cooking in late summer or early autumn. Use the leaves for flavouring or as a garnish. See also freezing (p. 294).

AT-A-GLANCE TIMETABLE FOR FLORENCE FENNEL

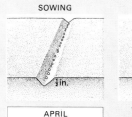

SOWING

½ in.

APRIL

THINNING

12 in.

When large enough to handle

HARVESTING

AUGUST–SEPTEMBER

Preparing & cooking Florence fennel

This delicate vegetable has the same sweet aniseed flavour as common fennel. It is made up of tightly compressed fleshy leaves, like an onion, and is used as a vegetable or salad ingredient.

To prepare Florence fennel, trim away the leafy top stems close to the root. Do not discard the leaves, which can be added to the cooking liquid for extra flavour or used, finely chopped, as a garnish. As they are more pungent than the leaves of common fennel, use them with discretion.

Trim the root base and wash the fennel roots in cold water.

For salads, cut the fennel roots in half lengthways and then across into thin slices. For cooking, leave fennel roots in halves and cook in a small amount of boiling, lightly salted water for 15–20 minutes, depending on size.

Drain thoroughly, sprinkle with ground coriander or nutmeg and serve with melted butter. Cooked fennel may also be covered with finely grated cheese, and melted butter poured over it.

---※---

FLAMBÉ MACKEREL AND FENNEL

Large bunch of fennel leaves
4 mackerel
Salt and pepper
2 oz. (50 g.) melted butter
2 tablespoons brandy

COOKING TIME: 20 minutes

Wash and dry the fennel leaves on a cloth or absorbent paper and place over the base of a grill pan, beneath the grid.

Split the mackerel along the belly and remove the entrails and all traces of blood. Heads and tails may be left on or removed.

Make three slashes through the skin on each side of the fish, sprinkle inside and out with salt and pepper. Place the mackerel on the buttered grid, brush the fish liberally with butter, and grill under moderate heat for about 15 minutes.

Turn the fish once only, halfway through cooking, and brush with more butter.

Remove the grill pan, warm the brandy in a ladle, set it alight and pour over the mackerel and fennel, making sure that the fennel catches fire.

Serving Serve the mackerel, with any pan juices poured over them, as soon as the flames die down. Small new potatoes are a good accompaniment.

Variation Lay mackerel or trout fillets for barbecuing on sprigs of fresh fennel leaves, and wrap in foil.

BUTTERED FENNEL

4 roots of Florence fennel
Salt and pepper
3 oz. (75 g.) melted butter

COOKING TIME: 20 minutes

Trim away the upper stems, leaving just the bulbous roots. Set the fine, feathery leaves aside. Trim the root base, cut each fennel in half lengthways and rinse in cold water.

Put the fennel in a pan with the minimum amount of boiling, lightly salted water and simmer, covered, for 15–20 minutes or until just tender. Overcooking reduces the sweet aniseed flavour. Drain thoroughly in a colander and keep warm on a serving dish.

Melt the butter.

Serving Chop the reserved fennel leaves finely, and sprinkle them over the roots with freshly ground pepper. Pour the melted butter over the leaves and serve with roast chicken or grilled fish.

Variation Sprinkle the fennel with finely grated cheese, pour the butter over it and set under a hot grill for a few minutes to melt the cheese.

---※---

Continued . . .

Florence fennel recipes (continued)

FENNEL À LA MARTINEZ

4 roots of Florence fennel
¾ pint (450 ml.) white stock or bouillon
3 tablespoons mayonnaise
1 dessertspoon tomato ketchup
1 tablespoon Pernod
Worcester sauce
Juice of ½ small orange
2 tablespoons lemon juice
Tabasco

COOKING TIME: 20 minutes

Trim the roots off the fennel and slice the stems at the top, level with the bulbs. Set the leaves aside. Cut the fennel in half and rinse in cold water.

Put the fennel in a pan with the stock or bouillon. Bring to the boil, cover with a lid and simmer gently for 20 minutes, or until tender. Drain in a colander and leave to cool completely.

Blend the mayonnaise with the ketchup and Pernod; add a few drops of Worcester sauce, mixing well. Stir in the strained orange and lemon juice and flavour to taste with two or three drops of tabasco.

Serving Arrange two fennel halves, rounded sides up, on individual serving plates, spoon the mayonnaise sauce over them and decorate with the reserved leaves. Serve as a first course.

Photograph on page 144.

ITALIAN FENNEL SALAD

3 roots of Florence fennel
4 oz. (100 g.) smoked ham
2 cooking apples
1 orange
4 fl. oz. (100 ml.) olive oil
3 tablespoons white wine vinegar
1 garlic clove
Salt and pepper

Trim the stems from the fennel roots and set the leaves aside. Cut each root in half lengthways, and cut across into very thin slices.

Dice the ham; peel, core and dice the apples; peel the orange and divide into segments. Mix all these ingredients together in a salad bowl.

Make a dressing from the oil, vinegar, crushed garlic and salt and pepper. Pour this over the salad ingredients and toss well.

Serving Sprinkle the salad with the finely chopped fennel leaves and serve the salad on its own, or with cold roast poultry or veal.

Variation Mix sliced fennel roots with roughly chopped walnuts and turn them in a dressing of 3 tablespoons of mayonnaise blended with 2 teaspoons of oil, 1 teaspoon of white wine vinegar, a little lemon juice, and salt and pepper.

Fenugreek:
see **Sprouting seeds**

Figs

Gardeners have tried to grow figs in Britain since the time of Henry VIII. Some have been successful, but many have been discouraged after severe winters or dismal summers have ruined their crops.

Figs are natives of Mediterranean countries, and they can be grown successfully in this country, particularly in the south and west, but they require more attention and understanding than most fruits.

North of the Trent they must be grown under glass for the fruit to ripen, but the gardener must then consider whether to use greenhouse space for more reliable and productive crops, such as tomatoes.

Even in the south and west, figs do best when grown on a south-facing wall, which will capture the sun and warmth. Once again, though, the gardener must decide whether to use the wall space for growing a more consistent crop, such as peaches.

A basic point to understand is that figs harvested during summer were formed during the previous year, and are present during the winter as embryo fruits next to the terminal growth buds on young shoots. It is these shoots and tiny fruits that require protection during cold weather.

Planning the crop

In a suitably mild district, choose a position against a south-facing wall or in a sunny corner between two walls.

The root system must always be restricted to stop the tree from making rank, unfruitful wood, so dig a hole about 3 ft (1 m.) square and 3 ft deep against the wall and

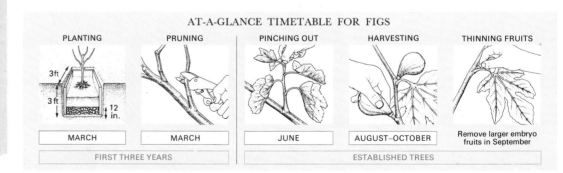

AT-A-GLANCE TIMETABLE FOR FIGS

PLANTING	PRUNING	PINCHING OUT	HARVESTING	THINNING FRUITS
3ft / 3ft / 12 in.				Remove larger embryo fruits in September
MARCH	MARCH	JUNE	AUGUST–OCTOBER	
FIRST THREE YEARS		ESTABLISHED TREES		

line the sides with bricks, concrete or stone slabs. Put brick rubble to a depth of 12 in. (305 mm.) in the bottom and ram it down hard.

Fill the hole with 2 parts of good, but not rich, garden soil mixed with 1 part of mortar rubble to which 2 lb. (1 kg.) of bonemeal has been added.

Figs may also be grown in 15 in. (380 mm.) pots of potting compost. Sink the pot into the ground, with the rim just above ground level, to reduce loss of moisture. Each winter, dig around the pot and remove any roots that have grown through the drainage hole.

Varieties There are two varieties generally grown in this country:

'Brown Turkey': brown-green fruits; usually grown against a wall.

'White Marseilles': pale green fruits; can be grown as a bush tree in a warm, sheltered spot.

How to grow figs

Plant the tree in March. Make a hole in the prepared bed just big enough to take the roots.

Spread these out and cover with soil, firm the ground with your feet and give a light mulch of well-rotted manure or compost.

For the first three winters, train the trees in the same way as bush apples (p. 66) or fan peaches (p. 226).

In subsequent summers, before the end of June, pinch out side-shoots to five leaves from their base.

If grown as a fan, train in further branches where there is room. Early in the season, rub out shoots growing towards or away from the wall.

Feeding is unnecessary during the three years the framework is being built up. In subsequent years, mulch with rotted manure or compost at the rate of a bucketful per square yard in April or May. At the end of September remove all immature figs larger than peas that have grown during the summer, as they will not survive the winter.

The smaller fruitlets that are left towards the end of the shoots will mature the following year.

Protect these in winter by tying spruce branches or ferns over the shoots, or by loosening the branches from their supports, collecting them in bundles and covering with straw or canvas. Gradually remove the protection in April and May as the danger of hard frost diminishes.

Raising new trees

Take 4–6 in. (100–150 mm.) heel cuttings of semi-ripe wood in August or September. Insert them in 3 in. (75 mm.) pots of equal parts (by volume) of peat and sand, and place them in a cold frame. Plant out 18 months later, when they should have strong roots.

Pests and diseases Figs are generally free of pests.

Diseases liable to attack fig trees are CORAL SPOT (p. 287), FIG CANKER (p. 288) and GREY MOULD (p. 288).

Harvesting figs

Leave the fruits to ripen on the tree, which will usually be between mid-August and October. The fruit is ripe when it hangs down, the stalk softens and the skin splits.

See also bottling (p. 309) and drying (p. 343). 🍂🍂

STAGES IN GROWING FIGS

PLANTING To restrict the roots, dig a hole 3 ft (1 m.) square and deep. Line with bricks or stone slabs. Place rubble on the bottom.

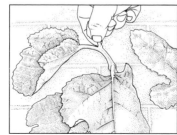

PINCHING OUT SHOOTS Stopping young growths after the fifth leaf, during June, will encourage new fruit-bearing shoots to form.

REMOVING FRUITS Only the smallest embryo fruits will survive the winter. In late September, remove those larger than peas.

Preparing & cooking figs

The few home-grown figs that ripen in Britain are such a rare delicacy that it is wasteful to serve them in any other way than as fresh dessert fruit.

Wipe the figs carefully. Cut them open and scoop out the sweet seeds and the juice, leaving the purple-green skins. Fresh cream or vanilla ice cream may be offered with them, but this is not really necessary. Provide a knife and small spoon.

For more sophisticated occasions, fresh figs can be dressed with delicate sweet sauces, flavoured creams or yoghourt.

FIGS IN BRANDY

8 figs
4 tablespoons brandy
Honey
5 fl. oz. (150 ml.) double cream

CHILLING TIME: 1 hour

Remove the stalks, put the figs in a bowl and cover with boiling water. Leave for 1 minute, then peel the figs and cut into quarters. Put the figs in a bowl and pour over them the brandy sweetened with a little honey. Leave to chill in the refrigerator for 1 hour.

Drain the brandy from the figs. Whisk the cream lightly, fold in the drained liquid and continue whisking until the cream is stiff enough to pipe. Spread a layer of cream over the base of four serving glasses, arrange six fig quarters on top, and pipe the remaining cream over them. Top with two fig quarters.

Serving Serve with sponge fingers.

FIGS WITH ORANGE JUICE

8 figs
Juice and grated rind of 1 orange
½ teaspoon ground cinnamon
1 tablespoon icing sugar

CHILLING TIME: 2 hours

Remove the stalks from the figs, put the figs in a bowl and pour boiling water over them. Leave for 1 minute, then drain and peel the figs.

Cut each fig into quarters and arrange them in four individual serving dishes. Grate the rind from the orange and squeeze out the juice; mix the rind with the cinnamon and set aside.

Dissolve the icing sugar in the orange juice and spoon this equally over the figs. Chill in the refrigerator for 2 hours.

Serving Just before serving, sprinkle each dish with the grated orange rind and cinnamon.

Variation Mix the orange juice with 2 tablespoons of curaçao and pour over the figs. Decorate with whipped cream.

Photograph on pages 208–9.

Filberts:
see **Nuts**

Florence fennel:
see **Fennel, Florence**

French beans:
see **Beans, French**

Garlic

Originating probably from the Kirghiz Desert in Central Asia, garlic has been cultivated in Mediterranean countries since the earliest times and in Britain since at least the beginning of the 16th century.

Its chief use is as a culinary herb whose spirited flavour has gained in popularity with the British in the past few decades, probably as a side-effect of the continental holiday boom. The juice of the garlic is also a powerful antiseptic, and was used as such by the French Army during the First World War.

Its unique flavour is powerful, and in cooking should be used with caution. Nevertheless, it is indispensable in the modern kitchen and is little trouble to grow.

Planning the crop

Garlic does best in a sunny position and in soil that is light and well-manured.

How much to grow A single clove – the name given to the small divisions of the garlic bulb – goes a long way when used to flavour dishes, and there are a dozen or more cloves in each bulb. About 12–15 plants should therefore be ample.

How to grow garlic

Plant garlic in late February or March in ground that has been raked to a fine tilth. Strip the papery outer skin from a garlic bulb, carefully separate the cloves and plant them 6 in. (150 mm.) apart, pointed end upwards and only just covered by soil. Allow 12 in. (305 mm.) between rows.

If you have difficulty in obtaining bulbs from a seedsman, buy them instead from a greengrocer or delicatessen.

Pests and diseases ONION EELWORM (p. 284) sometimes attacks garlic. The disease most likely to occur is WHITE ROT (p. 291).

Harvesting and storing

Lift garlic when the foliage dies down in late summer, easing the plants out of the ground with a fork to avoid damaging them.

Dry the bulbs thoroughly in the sun and store them in a cool, dry place – never in the kitchen. Put aside a few bulbs for planting in the following year.

See also drying (p. 343); freezing (p. 294); pickles (p. 328) and vinegars (p. 342).

AT-A-GLANCE TIMETABLE FOR GARLIC

PLANTING

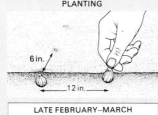

LATE FEBRUARY–MARCH

HARVESTING

AUGUST

Cooking with garlic

The pungent aroma and flavour of garlic is unique, and while shallots are often recommended as a substitute the two flavours cannot be compared.

Used with discretion, garlic gives heightened flavour to almost any savoury dish. A sliced clove rubbed over the inside of the salad bowl, over chops, steaks and fish fillets leaves a faint but distinct flavour. Raw, chopped garlic in butters, salad dressings and marinades, in vinegars and crushed with salt has a similar effect.

For stronger flavours in stews and casseroles, and as larding strips in joints of lamb and pork, whole or halved cloves are used and cooked with the ingredients.

Garlic may be crushed in a special garlic press, or finely chopped and fried with other vegetables for a braising base. Many cookery experts maintain that a garlic press results in loss of flavour, due to the juices escaping.

For cooked dishes to be frozen and stored for any length of time, omit garlic at the initial stage and add it to the dish when reheating it.

GARLIC DRESSING

6 tablespoons olive oil
3 tablespoons lemon juice
Salt and pepper
2–3 garlic cloves

Blend the oil and lemon juice and season to taste with salt, freshly ground black pepper and the crushed or finely chopped garlic. Shake vigorously and use to dress green salads, tomatoes, mixed vegetables and rice salads.

GARLIC BREAD

6 garlic cloves
6 oz. (175 g.) unsalted butter
1 French loaf (or sandwich loaf)

COOKING TIME: 15 minutes
OVEN TEMPERATURE: 180°C (350°F)
– gas mark 4

Peel the garlic cloves and crush them, or chop very finely. Stir into the softened butter until thoroughly blended.

Cut the loaf into slices about 1½ in. (40 mm.) thick, stopping each cut just short of the bottom crust. Spread each slice liberally with butter, then press together to regain the loaf shape. Wrap the loaf in foil and heat through in the oven for about 15 minutes, until crisp.
Serving Serve with spicy meat dishes, with tomato and onion soups and cheese salads.
Variations Spread toast to accompany patés with garlic butter, or fry bread croûtons for soups in garlic butter.
Photograph on page 216.

SPAGHETTI ITALIAN STYLE

1 lb. (500 g.) spaghetti
Salt and pepper
4 garlic cloves
4 tablespoons olive oil
4 tablespoons dry white wine
3 oz. (75 g.) grated Parmesan cheese

COOKING TIME: 20 minutes

Bring a large pan of lightly salted water to the boil, add the spaghetti and continue cooking for 12–15 minutes, or until just soft. Drain the spaghetti through a colander and keep it warm.

While the spaghetti is cooking, peel the garlic and chop it. Heat the oil in a pan and fry the garlic over a gentle heat for about 4 minutes, without letting the garlic become brown. Stir in the white wine, increase the heat and let the mixture boil for a few minutes to reduce it slightly. Add the drained spaghetti to the pan and toss quickly and thoroughly to coat every strand with oil and garlic.
Serving Spoon the spaghetti into a serving dish, season with freshly ground pepper, and sprinkle the top thickly with Parmesan cheese. Serve as a first course, accompanied with crusty bread and butter.

TOURNEDOS WITH GARLIC BUTTER

4 tournedo steaks, 1 in. (25 mm.) thick
Salt and pepper
½ lb. (250 g.) butter
1½ lb. (750 g.) potatoes
3–4 garlic cloves
Garnish: chopped parsley

COOKING TIME: 20–30 minutes

Trim the steaks and sprinkle with freshly ground pepper, but no salt. Brush with a little melted butter and put under a hot grill for 7–15 minutes, depending on whether rare or well-done steaks are preferred. Turn once only.

Meanwhile, boil the potatoes in their skins until almost cooked. Drain and peel them, then cut into even slices about ¼ in. (5 mm.) thick. Melt 2 oz. (50 g.) of the butter in a heavy-based pan and sauté the potatoes until crisp and golden-brown on both sides, turning frequently. Sprinkle with salt.

Stir the remaining butter until soft, then mix in the crushed garlic cloves. Shape into a sausage and cut into thick slices.

Arrange the steaks on a fireproof dish and surround with the sauté potatoes. Lay the garlic butter over the steaks and potatoes and set under a hot grill for about 2 minutes, or until the butter begins to melt.
Serving Sprinkle with finely chopped parsley and serve at once, with a green salad.

FRENCH SAGE AND GARLIC SOUP

7–8 garlic cloves
2 pints (1 l.) water
Salt and pepper
4 slices of white or brown bread
Olive oil
1 sprig each of sage and thyme
1 bay leaf
2 egg yolks

COOKING TIME: 15 minutes

Peel the garlic cloves and crush six of them with a broad-bladed knife. Put the water in a pan and bring to the boil with a pinch of salt and pepper. Add the crushed garlic cloves and simmer, covered, for 5 minutes.

Rub the remaining garlic cloves lightly over the bread slices, place them in soup bowls and sprinkle the bread with a few drops of olive oil.

Remove the pan from the heat, then add the sage, thyme and bay leaf. Cover the pan and leave to infuse for 3 minutes, then strain the liquid into another pan.

Beat the egg yolks lightly and stir in a little of the hot liquid. Return this egg mixture to the pan, stirring all the time until it thickens, but do not allow it to boil. Correct the seasoning with salt and pepper.
Serving Pour the soup over the bread and serve at once.
Variation Use mayonnaise instead of egg yolks to thicken the soup.

Globe artichokes:
see **Artichokes, Globe**

Gooseberries

Dessert gooseberries

Dessert gooseberries

Culinary gooseberries

Though gooseberries are native to northern Europe, only in Britain are they truly popular. Ever since Tudor times, gooseberry fools, tarts, crumbles, jellies and pies have featured on English tables.

To this day, a Great Gooseberry contest is held yearly at Egton Bridge, in North Yorkshire. There, fabulous fruits the size of a hen's egg and weighing nearly 2 oz. (50 g.) are displayed to the envy of visiting gardeners.

Even if such results are beyond the skills of most gardeners, more modest gooseberries are easy to grow. They do well in any part of Britain, and may be grown either as bushes or cordons.

If different varieties are planted, a succession of berries may be obtained from May to August. The different varieties may be sweet or acid, white, yellow, green or pink. The sweet fruits can be eaten raw for dessert, while the acid ones are more suitable for cooking, as well as for making jam and wine.

Planning the crop

Gooseberries do equally well in semi-shade or full sun. They need a site protected from cold winds and not subject to late frosts. Any moist, well-drained soil is suitable, but the best results are obtained from a deep, well-manured loam. Make sure that it is free from perennial weeds such as bindweed.

If possible, grow gooseberries in a fruit cage as birds may otherwise destroy the buds in late winter.

How many bushes to grow A mature, well-tended gooseberry bush will yield up to 8–10 lb. (4–5 kg.), and cordons about 5 lb. (2.5 kg.).

Varieties *Early* 'Keepsake': green; dessert or cooking.

'May Duke': red; dessert or cooking when green.

Mid-season 'Careless': white; cooking.

'Golden Drop': yellow; dessert.

'Lancer': green; dessert or cooking.

'Langley Gage': green-white; dessert only.

'Leveller': yellow; dessert or cooking.

'Whinham's Industry': red; dessert or cooking.

Late 'Warrington': red; dessert or cooking.

'White Lion': white; dessert or cooking.

'Whitesmith': white; dessert or cooking.

How to grow gooseberries

Before planting, work liberal supplies of manure or compost into the soil, at least a bucketful to the square yard. This is essential if the soil is light and shallow, otherwise crops will be poor. It also makes heavy soil easier to work and improves the drainage.

At the same time, apply 1 oz. of sulphate of potash per square yard (30 g. per square metre).

Buy two or three-year-old plants and put them into the ground between October and March. Plant bushes 5 ft (1.5 m.) apart, single cordons 15 in. (380 mm.), double cordons 2 ft (610 mm.), triple cordons 3 ft (1 m.). Leave 5 ft (1.5 m.) between rows. Plant firmly.

(For method of training cordons see Raising new bushes, column 5.)

Cordons are best grown against a fence. Staple three horizontal support wires at 12 in. (305 mm.) intervals. Tie each cordon to a cane with soft string and secure the cane to the wires.

In winter, firm any plants loosened by frost.

Every spring feed the plants with ¾ oz. of sulphate of potash per square yard (22 g. per square metre) and give them a mulch of well-rotted compost or manure. This will help keep down weeds.

Any weeds that do come up between plants should be killed with paraquat. Never hoe, as this can damage the roots.

If you do not grow the bushes in a cage, protect the buds from birds by stringing black cotton between the shoots in November.

Netting draped over the plants on spring nights will provide blossom with some protection against frost. Take it off during the day so as not to discourage pollinating insects. Remove any suckers that appear, and make sure the plants never dry out during hot weather.

Pruning

Prune the bushes in winter. If bird damage to buds is probable, leave pruning until the buds start to swell so that you can make sure of cutting back to an undamaged bud.

It is best to prune spreading, drooping bushes to an inward-pointing bud; upright varieties to an outward-pointing one.

One-year-old bushes Shorten the strongest three or four shoots on a one-year-old bush by about three-quarters and remove the others at their base.

Cut out any low shoots to create a clean stem 4–6 in. (100–150 mm.) long.

Two-year-old bushes Cut off half the new wood growing from the eight to ten best shoots (two-thirds if the new growth is spindly or drooping). Remove all other shoots, cutting just above the bottom bud.

Mature bushes Prune mature bushes and cordons in the same way as red currants (see p. 154).

Raising new bushes

Gooseberries can be raised from cuttings in exactly the same way as described for red and white currants (see p. 154).

To create a single cordon after planting out the rooted cutting in its permanent position, select the strongest shoot and remove the

PRUNING GOOSEBERRIES

ONE-YEAR-OLD Shorten three or four strong shoots by three-quarters. Remove others completely, and any low-growing shoots.

TWO-YEAR-OLD Cut out all but eight to ten strong shoots, aiming to produce a goblet-shaped bush with an open centre.

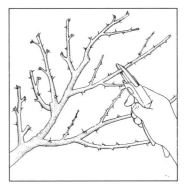

ESTABLISHED BUSH Prune current season's shoots to about 1 in. (25 mm.). Cut out crossing and inward-growing branches.

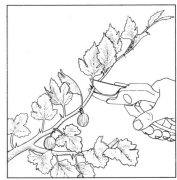

SUMMER PRUNING Shorten lateral shoots to about five leaves. Cut leaders on cordons when the required height is reached.

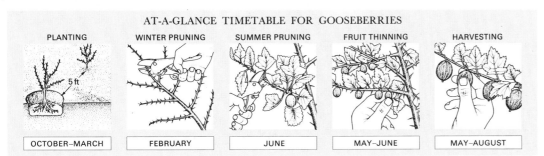

AT-A-GLANCE TIMETABLE FOR GOOSEBERRIES

PLANTING	WINTER PRUNING	SUMMER PRUNING	FRUIT THINNING	HARVESTING
OCTOBER–MARCH	FEBRUARY	JUNE	MAY–JUNE	MAY–AUGUST

others flush with the main stem. Support the young cordon by tying it to a cane with soft string.

To make a double cordon, choose the two strongest shoots that emerge from the main stem about 9 in. (230 mm.) from its base. Until they are 6 in. (150 mm.) long, train them horizontally in the same way as for an espalier (see p. 41). After that, train them against vertical canes.

For a triple cordon, select the best three shoots 9 in. (230 mm.) above ground level. Train the two outside shoots as for a double cordon, and the middle one as for a single cordon.

Pests and diseases The worst pests are APHIDS (p. 282), CAPSID BUGS (p. 282) and GOOSEBERRY SAWFLIES (p. 283).

The most serious diseases are AMERICAN GOOSEBERRY MILDEW (p. 286), GREY MOULD (p. 288), HONEY FUNGUS (p. 288), LEAF SPOT (p. 288), RUST (p. 290) and SCALD (p. 290).

Harvesting and storing

Thin heavy-cropping plants from late May onwards, removing some berries from each branch so that, ideally, there are 3 in. (75 mm.) intervals between those remaining, which will then grow larger. The unripe picked fruit can be used for cooking or preserving.

This thinning can be carried out several times, especially on dessert varieties.

See also bottling (p. 309); chutneys (p. 335); freezing (p. 294); fruit cheeses and butters (p. 323); jams (p. 314); jellies (p. 320); pickles (p. 328); syrups and juices (p. 326) and wine-making (p. 357).

Preparing & cooking gooseberries

Sweet red or yellow gooseberries are usually served fresh as a dessert fruit. The smaller and harder acid gooseberries are suitable only for cooking. They are used as fillings for pies and puddings, for creamed desserts such as fools, and for sauces – both sweet and savoury.

To prepare gooseberries, both for dessert fruits and for cooking, snip off flower and stalk ends with scissors (called topping and tailing). Wash them carefully, placing the berries in a colander and dipping this into several lots of cold water. Allow the fruit to drain; dry dessert berries on absorbent kitchen paper.

STEWED GOOSEBERRIES

1 lb. (500 g.) gooseberries
1 pint (600 ml.) water
4 tablespoons cornflour
2 tablespoons ginger wine
6 oz. (175 g.) sugar (approx.)

COOKING TIME: 25 minutes

Top, tail and wash the gooseberries. Put them in a pan with the water and bring to the boil. Simmer gently until the berries are soft.

Blend the cornflour with a little cold water, stir it into the gooseberries and continue stirring until the mixture thickens. Remove the pan.

Blend the ginger wine into the stewed gooseberries and sweeten to taste with sugar. Pour into a serving bowl.
Serving The gooseberries may be served lukewarm or chilled, with a jug of fresh cream.
Variation If available, tie a few heads of elderflowers in muslin and cook them with the gooseberries. Remove the elderflowers before thickening and omit the ginger wine.

SAVOURY GOOSEBERRY SAUCE

½ lb. (250 g.) green, slightly immature, gooseberries
2 oz. (50 g.) sugar
1 tablespoon finely chopped chives
1 oz. (25 g.) butter

COOKING TIME: 25 minutes

Top, tail and wash the gooseberries. Put the sugar in a pan with 3 tablespoons of water. As soon as the sugar has dissolved, add the chives and the gooseberries. Simmer over gentle heat until the berries are tender and the skins burst.

Rub the gooseberries through a coarse sieve. Return the purée to the pan and heat through. Stir in the butter and correct the seasoning.
Serving Traditionally, gooseberry sauce is served with fried and grilled mackerel. It also goes well with roast goose or cold roast pork.

GOOSEBERRY FOOL

1 lb. (500 g.) gooseberries
5 tablespoons water
3–4 oz. (75–100 g.) sugar
2 tablespoons ginger wine (optional)
½ pint (300 ml.) milk
½ vanilla pod
1 tablespoon caster sugar
2 egg yolks
5 fl. oz. (150 ml.) double cream
Garnish: sponge fingers, whipped cream

COOKING TIME: 45 minutes
CHILLING TIME: 30 minutes

Top and tail the gooseberries, then wash them and drain. Put the berries in a pan with the water, cover with a lid and simmer for about 20 minutes until soft and pulpy. Rub the gooseberries through a sieve and sweeten the purée with sugar. Flavour with ginger wine if you wish. Set aside to cool.

Meanwhile, put the milk and vanilla pod in a pan and heat through gently without boiling. Remove from the heat, cover with a lid and leave to infuse for 10 minutes. Discard the vanilla pod and stir in the caster sugar.

Whisk the egg yolks until creamy, and gradually beat in the milk. Strain this custard back into the pan, or preferably into a double saucepan. Heat the custard, stirring continuously until it thickens. Pour into a bowl and leave to get cold. Sprinkle with a little sugar.

Whip the cream lightly and fold it carefully into the cooled custard; then fold this into the gooseberry purée, blending the mixture evenly.

Spoon the mixture into serving glasses and chill for 30 minutes.
Serving Serve with sponge fingers, and decorate the top of each glass with a little whipped cream.
Photograph on pages 142–3.

SWEET GOOSEBERRY SAUCE

½ lb. (250 g.) gooseberries
2 oz. (50 g.) sugar
1 oz. (25 g.) butter
Ground cloves

COOKING TIME: 15 minutes

Top, tail and wash the gooseberries. Put them in a pan with very little water, and simmer over a low heat until the berries pop open and the juice runs. Rub the gooseberries through a sieve.

Return the purée to a clean pan and reduce by fast boiling if it is too liquid. Stir in the sugar, butter and pinch of cloves and heat through, stirring continuously until the sauce is smooth and shiny.
Serving The sauce may be served hot or cold with steamed or boiled puddings, ice creams and fruit flans.

Continued ...

Gooseberry recipes (continued)

GOOSEBERRY TRIFLE

1 lb. (500 g.) green gooseberries
3 oz. (75 g.) sugar
3–4 sponge trifle cakes
3 tablespoons ginger wine
½ pint (300 ml.) custard sauce
5 fl. oz. (150 ml.) whipping cream
Garnish : gooseberry jelly

COOKING TIME: 15 minutes
CHILLING TIME: 1 hour

There is no need to top and tail the gooseberries. Simply rinse them and place in a pan with 3 tablespoons of water, and bring to the boil over a gentle heat. Add the sugar and simmer the berries until they are soft and pulpy, which will take 12–15 minutes. Rub the gooseberries through a sieve and set the purée aside to cool.

Meanwhile, cut the sponge trifle cakes in half lengthways and arrange them over the base of a serving dish. Sprinkle the ginger wine over them and leave until this has been soaked up.

Prepare a fairly thick custard sauce and keep it warm. Spoon the gooseberry purée over the sponge cakes, pour the custard over the top and leave the trifle to chill in the refrigerator.
Serving Just before serving, spread or pipe the whipped cream over the trifle and decorate with gooseberry jelly.

GOOSEBERRY MERINGUE

1 lb. (500 g.) gooseberries
5 tablespoons water
6 oz. (175 g.) sugar
2 eggs
3 tablespoons crushed macaroons
2 tablespoons milk
Grated rind and juice of 1 lemon
½ tablespoon white wine vinegar

COOKING TIME: 1¼–1½ hours
OVEN TEMPERATURE: 180°C (350°F)
– gas mark 4

Wash and drain the gooseberries, put them in a pan with the water, cover with a lid and simmer for about 20 minutes until they are soft and pulpy. Rub through a sieve and sweeten with 2 oz. (50 g.) sugar. Leave to cool.

Separate the eggs and beat the yolks with 1 oz. (25 g.) of sugar until they are creamy and fluffy. Fold in the macaroons, milk, lemon juice and rind.

Spoon this custard mixture into a lightly buttered, ovenproof dish and bake for 30 minutes.

Remove the custard from the oven and spread the gooseberry purée on top. Whisk the egg whites with the remaining sugar and vinegar until stiff, and spread over the purée.

Return the dish to the oven, reduce the temperature to 150°C (300°F) – gas mark 2 – and bake for about 20 minutes.
Serving Take the dish straight from the oven and serve at once.
Photograph on pages 136–7.

Grapes

Vines have been grown successfully in this country since the time of the Romans. The first are believed to have been planted only 70 years after Julius Caesar's invasion in 55 BC.

Later, the fortunes of Britain's vines followed those of the monasteries, where they were extensively grown.

With the Dissolution of the Monasteries by Henry VIII in the 16th century, the number of vineyards rapidly declined.

A revival of grape growing came

in the late 18th century. This time, however, the vines were not grown in the open but under glass, mostly on the large estates of landed gentry.

Today the growing of grapes depends on two factors – locality and cost. South of a line roughly from Pembroke to the Wash, grapes can be grown in the open on wire supports, or against a sunny, south-facing wall, or in a greenhouse – which should be reserved for the best varieties of dessert grapes.

In sheltered places north of the line, grapes can be grown against a south-facing wall if given some protection with glass or plastic to aid ripening. Alternatively, they can be grown in a greenhouse, preferably with some heat in late spring and early autumn.

A greenhouse provides ideal conditions for vines, but gardeners interested in the money-saving possibilities of fruit growing must decide if the space could be better used for a more cost-effective crop, such as tomatoes.

Only an enthusiast, undismayed by cost, should consider buying a new greenhouse solely for growing grapes.

The minimum size of a greenhouse for growing grapes is 8 ft (2.5 m.) long, 7 ft (2.1 m.) to the ridge and 5 ft (1.5 m.) to the eaves.

Planning an outdoor crop

Choose a sheltered position in full sun for growing grapes in the open in the south. Avoid frost pockets and sites in even partial shade. A slope facing south or south-west is ideal.

For growing vines on a wall or

fence, choose a site facing south, south-west or south-east. Vines grown this way succeed in areas too cold for growing completely in the open. In more favourable areas the extra warmth radiating from the wall makes the grapes sweeter and better flavoured.

Vines grow best in a sandy, gravelly soil that warms up quickly in the sun, but they will succeed in any type of soil if the drainage is good. Drainage is vitally important.

On heavy soils dig a trench at least 2 ft (610 mm.) deep, leading away from where the vine is to be planted. Place a layer of rubble, broken bricks or clinker at the bottom of the trench. The deeper the trench and the greater the amount of rubble the better, because the roots of an established vine go deep and must never be allowed to become waterlogged.

Two or three months before planting, prepare the ground by forking in well-rotted manure or compost at the rate of a bucketful per square yard, plus John Innes base fertiliser at the rate of 3 oz. per square yard (90 g. per square metre).

To grow vines in a row, set support posts 5 ft (1.5 m.) high at

PREPARING SUPPORT WIRES FOR OUTDOOR GRAPES

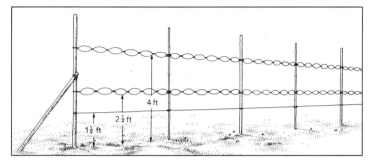

4 ft
2½ ft
1½ ft

Drive in support posts, and staple three lengths of wire to them at the distances shown. Use a single strand at the bottom and two loosely twisted strands in the centre and on top.

intervals of 8–10 ft (2.5–3 m.). The end posts should be at least 2½ in. (65 mm.) in diameter, and intermediate posts about 2 in. (50 mm.) in diameter. Allow 5 ft between rows.

Staple a single strand of 12-gauge galvanised wire to the posts 18 in. (455 mm.) from the ground.

Loosely twist two strands together and staple them 2½ ft (760 mm.) from the ground, with another length of twisted wire 18 in. (455 mm.) above this.

If fruiting shoots are trained through the double wire, the twisting will save the trouble of tying them.

To grow vines on a wall, fix support wires 12 in. (305 mm.) apart and held 5 in. (130 mm.) away from the wall with vine eyes, obtainable from garden shops.

How many to grow An established vine in the open will produce at least ten bunches of grapes – about 5 lb. (2.5 kg.) in a good year. A cordon on a wall may produce 15–20 lb. (7–10 kg.) or more, depending on the amount of wall covered.

Generally, it is best for a beginner to start with only a few vines, adding more later if sufficient space is available.

Outdoor varieties Choose early ripening grapes for cooler areas. In more favourable districts grow early varieties in the open or on walls, and mid-season varieties on walls only, where the extra protection will hasten ripening.

Generally, white grapes can be grown more successfully than red, except in the hottest summers.

'Cascade' ('Seibel 13/053'): mid-season; small bunches of deep purple grapes; heavy cropper for wine-making.

'Madeleine Sylvaner 28/51': early white; consistent cropper; fair wine grape.

'Noir Hatif de Marseilles': early black; small fruits with good muscat flavour; for dessert and wine.

'Precoce de Malingre': early white; good-flavoured, non-muscat dessert and wine grape.

'Riesling Sylvaner': mid-season white; excellent for hock; acceptable as dessert.

'Seyve Villard 5/276': mid-season white; heavy cropper; makes excellent wine; pleasant dessert grape.

'Siegerrebe': early, deep golden grape with fine muscat flavour; recommended for both dessert and for making wine.

PREPARATION FOR PLANTING

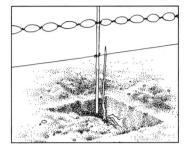

Before planting drive a stout cane into the hole, leaving 6 ft (1.8 m.) above ground. Tie the cane to the wires.

How to grow grapes in the open

Vines can be planted at any time while they are dormant, generally between October and March. For the beginner March is probably best, as the risk of long periods of severe frost is then over. Nurseries generally supply vines that are one-year-old.

If planting must be done in autumn, pile a layer of peat or well-rotted compost over the lower buds to protect them from frost, and draw it back from the plant when growth begins in spring.

When planting, dig a hole wide enough for the roots to be spread out evenly and deep enough for the vine to be at the same level as it was in the nursery.

The soil mark on the stock will indicate this.

Before planting, drive a stout cane into the soil so that 6 ft (1.8 m.) is left above ground level. This will provide a support for tying replacement shoots. Alternatively, plant against a fence post.

Plant the vines 4 ft (1.2 m.) apart – or 5 ft (1.5 m.) if the soil is fairly rich.

PREPARING SUPPORT WIRES FOR GROWING OUTDOOR GRAPES

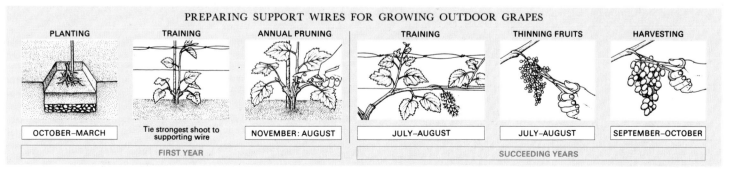

PLANTING — OCTOBER–MARCH
TRAINING — Tie strongest shoot to supporting wire
ANNUAL PRUNING — NOVEMBER: AUGUST
FIRST YEAR

TRAINING — JULY–AUGUST
THINNING FRUITS — JULY–AUGUST
HARVESTING — SEPTEMBER–OCTOBER
SUCCEEDING YEARS

Allow only the strongest shoot to grow in the first year. Tie this to the support, and pinch out all other shoots at one or two leaves.

In the following November the vine will be ready for training by the double Guyot system, one of the simplest ways of growing vines in the open.

By this method, grapes are grown on laterals from stems produced in the previous year while, at the same time, replacement stems are trained for fruiting in the following year.

Guyot system of training After leaf-fall in November, but no later than the end of December, cut the vine down to three or four buds.

The following summer, allow the three strongest shoots to grow, and pinch out any others.

In November, tie two of the shoots along the bottom wire. Cut the third shoot back to three buds.

In the following summer, train the fruiting laterals from the two horizontal stems through the double wires. In August, cut the tops of the laterals to two or three leaves above the top wire and remove all sub-laterals. Tie the three replacement shoots to the cane, and pinch back the laterals growing from them to one leaf.

In November, remove completely the two shoots carrying the laterals that have fruited. Tie two replacement shoots to the bottom wire and cut back the third to three buds.

Repeat this system of training each year.

Restrict the crop to four bunches of grapes in the first fruiting year, six in the second, and allow full cropping thereafter.

Keep the ground well-watered, especially in the year after planting. As a mulch only, dress the rows as generously as possible with peat, well-rotted garden compost or spent mushroom compost every spring.

In February, apply along each side of the row a general fertiliser at the rate of 2 oz. per square yard (60 g. per square metre).

In April, apply magnesium sulphate (Epsom salts) as a top-dressing at 2 oz. to the square yard.

How to grow grapes on a wall

The simplest method of growing grapes on a wall or fence is to train them on a single cordon, or rod.

Plant as in the open (see p. 169), setting the vines 4 ft (1.2 m.) apart, and 9 in. (230 mm.) from the wall.

After planting, choose the strongest leader to grow on as the rod and cut out the others to one bud. Tie the leader to a cane and secure the cane to the wires.

During the following growing season pinch out flowers as they appear and, about the middle of August, cut back laterals to five leaves.

In November, remove immature wood on the stem by cutting back to ripe, nut-brown wood of not less than pencil thickness.

Repeat this sequence during the second year after planting, but during summer pruning also cut back sub-laterals to one leaf.

TRAINING VINES ON SUPPORT WIRES IN THE OPEN

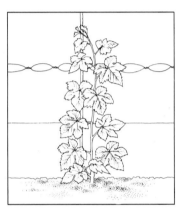

FIRST SUMMER AFTER PLANTING Tie the strongest shoot to the support. Pinch out other shoots to one or two leaves.

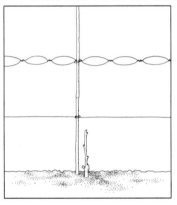

NOVEMBER AFTER PLANTING Cut the vine down to three or four buds. Cover with peat or straw as a protection against frosts.

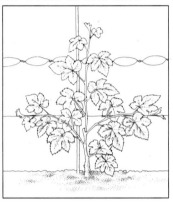

NEXT SUMMER Allow the three strongest shoots to grow. Train them to the support wires and pinch out any other shoots.

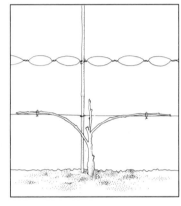

FOLLOWING NOVEMBER Tie two of the shoots along each side of the bottom wire and cut the third shoot back to three buds.

SUBSEQUENT SUMMERS Train the laterals from the horizontal stems through the twisted wires. Remove sub-laterals and, in August, cut the lateral tips to two or three leaves above the top wire. Tie replacement stems to the cane and pinch back laterals to one leaf.

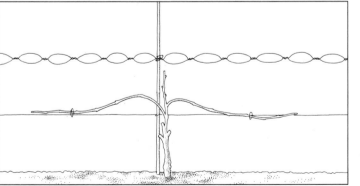

EACH NOVEMBER Cut back to the base the two stems that have carried fruit. Tie two of the replacement shoots to the bottom wire and prune the remaining shoot to three buds. These buds will provide the following season's shoots. Repeat this training every year.

This training should produce a well-spurred cordon for providing a limited harvest in the following season.

In the first cropping year allow only three bunches to a cordon. In the following year allow four or five.

Thereafter, allow only one bunch per foot run, which usually means that you will harvest a bunch from each spur.

TRAINING A SINGLE CORDON

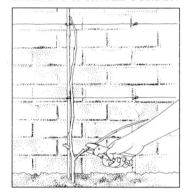

AFTER PLANTING Choose the strongest leader as the rod, and cut the others to one bud. Tie the leader to a cane and to the wires.

THE FOLLOWING SUMMER Pinch out all flowers. In August, cut back laterals as part of the training to produce fruiting spurs.

How to grow grapes in a greenhouse

Greenhouse vines are usually grown, like those trained against walls, as single-stem cordons. However, a gardener who moves into a home with a greenhouse vine may find that it has a number of spaced-out rods. Each of these should be treated in the same way as a single cordon.

Planning the crop Before planting a vine, decide whether to plant inside the greenhouse or whether to set it in an outside border and train it indoors through an aperture.

Although the gardener has less control over the management of a vine in an outside border, watering is easier.

Prepare the soil by mixing 10 parts of good loam with 1 part crushed bricks and old mortar. Two weeks before use, for each cubic yard, add 10 lb. (5 kg.) John Innes base fertiliser, 5 lb. (2.5 kg.) bone-meal and 5 lb. dried blood.

In the house, set up support wires 12 in. (305 mm.) apart and held 18 in. (455 mm.) from the roof by vine eyes screwed into the glazing bars or by securing them to the gable ends of the greenhouse.

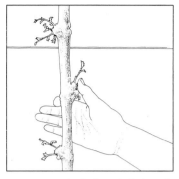

RUBBING OUT In April, as the buds swell, select the strongest shoot from each spur and rub out the others with your thumb.

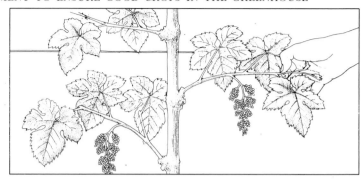

PINCHING OUT About a fortnight after rubbing out the unwanted buds, stop the shoots with the longest flowering trusses at two leaves beyond the bunch. Pinch out the others at the fourth or fifth leaf, and sub-laterals at the first. Tie laterals to supporting wires.

How many to grow Single-stem cordons are set 4 ft (1.2 m.) apart, so the number planted depends on the length of the house.

Greenhouse varieties The amount of artificial heat required in a particular locality generally dictates the varieties that can be grown. The two most successful varieties for a cold greenhouse are:

'Black Hamburgh': large black berries with good flavour when fully ripe; reliable and hardy; mid-season.

'Buckland Sweetwater': the best general-purpose white grape;

large, sweet berries; early crop.

Other varieties include:

'Alicante' ('Black Tokay'): large berries; requires a warm house in the north but ripens without heat in the south.

'Foster's Seedling': white, good-flavoured, large berries; suitable for cold greenhouse; mid-season.

'Muscat Hamburgh': black, medium-sized berries with an excellent muscat flavour; needs heat in the north; mid-season to late.

'Muscat of Alexandria': large white berries with superb muscat flavour; requires artificial heat

and cross-pollination to set well; mid-season to late.

How to grow greenhouse grapes For the first two or three years after planting, train the cordon in the same way as when growing a vine on a wall (see facing page). For an established tree follow this annual routine:

November–December Prune the previous summer's growth back to one bud. After pruning, scrub the rods gently with tar-oil winter wash, diluted according to the manufacturer's instructions.

After pruning, wash the glass

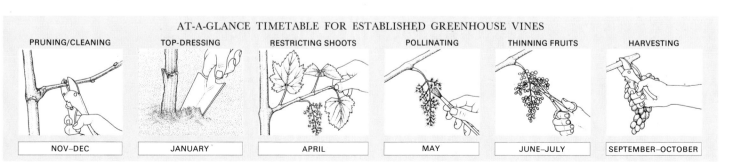

AT-A-GLANCE TIMETABLE FOR ESTABLISHED GREENHOUSE VINES

PRUNING/CLEANING	TOP-DRESSING	RESTRICTING SHOOTS	POLLINATING	THINNING FRUITS	HARVESTING
NOV–DEC	JANUARY	APRIL	MAY	JUNE–JULY	SEPTEMBER–OCTOBER

and superstructure with a suitable disinfectant, obtainable from a horticultural supplier.

January–March Keep the ventilators open. The vines, which are hardy and untroubled by frost, are dormant at this time.

Top-dress the rooting area in January with a mixture of 4 oz. per square yard (120 g. per square metre) of John Innes base fertiliser, plus an equal amount of dried blood.

Follow this with a light dressing of well-rotted manure or compost.

April Close the ventilators to increase the temperature and induce the buds to break. Spray the rods, soil and path with water twice daily.

The buds will swell quickly. Select the strongest shoot from each spur, and rub out the others with your thumb.

Two weeks later, keep the best with the longest flowering trusses, stopping these at two leaves beyond the bunch. Pinch out the others at the fourth or fifth leaf, and sub-laterals at the first.

May As the laterals reach 9 in. (230 mm.), tie them to the supporting wires. When the flowers open, use a camel-hair brush to distribute pollen between them. Once the vine is in full growth, and the flowers have set, give a weekly liquid feed, according to the manufacturer's instructions.

Keep the temperature high and the humidity fairly low until the flowers have set, then increase ventilation to lower the temperature. Keep damping down the border and path.

June–August Ventilate freely. As the berries swell, thin them gradually over seven to ten days. With a free-setting variety remove half the berries from the inside of the bunch, leaving more on the shoulders.

When the grapes begin to show colour, reduce watering to a mere dampening of the border.

Stop applications of liquid feed.

September–October Cut the bunches of grapes as they ripen. Increase the temperature by closing the greenhouse ventilators until the last bunches are cut.

Pests and diseases The most common pests attacking grapes are GLASSHOUSE RED SPIDER MITES (p. 283), MEALY BUGS (p. 284) and SCALE INSECTS (p. 285).

Diseases and disorders that may occur include GREY MOULD (p. 288), HONEY FUNGUS (p. 288), MAGNESIUM DEFICIENCY (p. 288), POWDERY MILDEW (p. 289), SCALD (p. 290), SHANKING (p. 290) and SPLITTING (p. 290).

Harvesting and storing

Grapes are ready for harvesting when they change colour.

Cut the bunch with scissors. If not bruised, grapes will keep in a cold place for up to two months.

See also drying (p. 343); pickles (p. 328); sauces, ketchups and relishes (p. 339) and wine-making (p. 357).🙠🙠

HOW TO PRODUCE LARGE, EVEN BUNCHES OF GRAPES

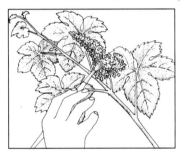

POLLINATING When the flowers open in May, assist pollination by stroking along the trusses with a soft camel-hair brush.

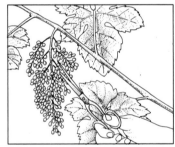

FIRST THINNING As the berries swell, usually in June, begin thinning by removing some of the berries from inside the bunches.

FINAL THINNING Spread thinning gradually over seven to ten days. Leave more on the shoulders to give the bunch a good shape.

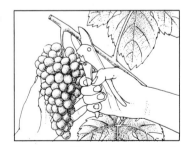

HARVESTING When grapes are ready for picking they change colour and often develop a bloom. Cut the stem with secateurs.

Preparing & serving grapes

Most luscious of all dessert fruits, the juice and sweetness of grapes are best enjoyed in the fresh berries. They can be eaten on their own, in fresh fruit salads, as edible garnishes to savoury and sweet dishes or as accompaniments to cheese-boards.

For special occasions, grapes can be sugar-frosted. Brush the berries with lightly beaten egg white, dredge with sugar and leave on a wire rack for about 15 minutes before serving.

Grapes are seldom cooked, but they are sometimes peeled for garnishes and fruit salads, and often have the pips removed. Most grapes can be peeled by pulling the skin away with the fingertips, beginning at the stalk.

If the skins are tough, dip a few grapes at a time in boiling water for 30 seconds, then plunge them into cold water.

The simplest way to remove the pips is to cut the grapes in half and ease the pips out with the tip of a knife. But if grapes must be left whole, dig the rounded end of a clean hair-grip into the grapes at the stalk end and scoop out the pips.

BANANAS AND GRAPES

½ lb. (250 g.) grapes
Juice of ½ lemon
1 oz. (25 g.) clear honey
5 fl. oz. (150 ml.) double cream

Separate the grapes into single berries, wash and dry them and remove the pips. Peel the bananas, cut them in half lengthways and sprinkle with lemon juice to prevent them going brown. Set two banana halves on each serving plate and smear with honey. Whip the cream, and pipe it along the edges and between the bananas.

Serving Decorate the bananas with the grapes, which for special occasions may be sugar-frosted.

Variation Flavour the whipped cream with 1–2 tablespoons of Drambuie.

CRISP CAMEMBERT AND GRAPES

8 small Camembert cheeses
1 egg
2 tablespoons fine breadcrumbs
Oil for frying
Large bunch of grapes

COOKING TIME: 2–3 minutes
CHILLING TIME: 30 minutes

This is a novel way of serving small triangular Camembert cheeses, which should preferably be on the firm side. Remove from the wrapping paper, and turn the triangles in the lightly beaten egg. Coat the cheeses with breadcrumbs and let them rest in the refrigerator for about 30 minutes to settle the coating.

Heat the oil in the deep-fryer until smoking hot, then drop in the Camembert triangles a few at a time. Fry for about 1 minute, or until they are golden-brown.

Drain on absorbent paper. **Serving** Serve the deep-fried Camembert – crisp on the outside but melting soft inside – at once, accompanied with dark rye bread, ice-cold butter and juicy, fresh grapes.

GRAPES IN ASPIC

½ lb. (250 g.) grapes
½ pint (300 ml.) aspic jelly
3 tablespoons mayonnaise
Paprika

CHILLING TIME: 1 hour

Seedless grapes are the most suitable for setting in aspic, but other grapes can also be used after peeling and removing the pips. Separate the grapes into individual berries, rinse and dry.

Make up the aspic jelly as directed on the packet and let it cool a little. Before it starts to set, rinse four small individual moulds in cold water and pour a little aspic over the base of each, to a depth of about ½ in. (12 mm.) Leave in the refrigerator until the aspic has set.

Divide the grapes equally over the four moulds, pour most of the remaining aspic over them and return the moulds to the refrigerator until the aspic has set. Spoon the remaining aspic into the moulds to provide a firm base for turning out, and leave once more to set.

Serving Dip the moulds quickly into hot water, then turn out, upside-down, on to individual plates. Decorate with rosettes of mayonnaise, flavoured and coloured with a pinch of paprika. Serve as an accompaniment to grilled sole or plaice, or with cold meat and chicken.

GRAPES IN FRENCH DRESSING

½ lb. (250 g.) seedless grapes
2 teaspoons French mustard
1 teaspoon caster sugar
6 tablespoons olive oil
3 tablespoons white wine vinegar
Salt and pepper

CHILLING TIME: 30 minutes

Strip the grapes from the stalks. Rinse and drain them thoroughly, discarding any that are bruised or mouldy.

Make up the dressing by stirring the mustard with the sugar and gradually adding first the oil, then the vinegar. Season to taste with salt and freshly ground pepper. Put the grapes in a bowl, pour the dressing over them and toss well. Chill in the refrigerator for about 30 minutes.

Serving Drain the grapes from the dressing and arrange in a bowl lined with shredded lettuce. Serve as an unusual salad with cold ham or baked fish, or as part of a selection of buffet salads.

Variation Toss the grapes in oil-vinaigrette instead of a French dressing.

GRAPE SALAD

¾ lb. (375 g.) black or green grapes
Juice and rind of 1 lemon
4 oz. (100 g.) sugar
1 egg yolk
7 fl. oz. (200 ml.) olive oil
5 fl. oz. (150 ml.) double cream

CHILLING TIME: 1 hour

Peel the grapes if the skins are tough, otherwise leave them on. Remove the pips, either cutting the grapes into halves or leaving them whole. Dissolve the sugar in 4 tablespoons of hot water and stir in the juice and grated rind of the lemon. Pour this syrup over the grapes and leave to chill for 1 hour.

Meanwhile, make a mayonnaise from the egg yolk and olive oil, whisk the cream lightly and fold it carefully into the mayonnaise. Flavour to taste with a little of the syrup in which the grapes were marinating. Drain the grapes and fold them into the mayonnaise and cream mixture, setting a few aside.

Serving Decorate with the reserved grapes and serve the salad as a novel addition to the cheese-board.

Photograph on pages 208–9.

Greengages: see **Plums and gages**

Haricot beans: see **Beans, French**

Hazelnuts: see **Nuts**

Horseradish

Originally a native of south-east Europe, this hardy herb is now established along roadsides, field boundaries and railway embankments in many parts of Britain.

Whether or not it occurs naturally in your area, it is a good idea to grow a few plants in a corner of the garden. As an accompaniment to roast beef and to some fish dishes, a sauce made from freshly grated horseradish root has no equal.

The fact that horseradish is easy to grow has its drawbacks, since if it begins to spread it is difficult to get rid of. The roots are deep and tough; if even a small piece is left in the ground a new plant will grow.

Planning the crop

Grow horseradish in any odd corner of the garden, but preferably one that is sunny or in only partial shade. The plants do best in rich, well-drained soil.

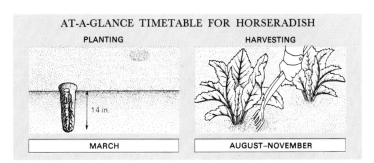

AT-A-GLANCE TIMETABLE FOR HORSERADISH

PLANTING — 14 in. — MARCH

HARVESTING — AUGUST–NOVEMBER

How much to grow Horseradish roots grow to a length of 12 in. (305 mm.) or more, and to a thickness of ¾ in. (20 mm.). Three or four plants should be ample, spaced about 2 ft (610 mm.) apart.

How to grow horseradish

Roots for planting can be obtained either by digging them up from waste ground in late summer and storing them until the following spring, or by buying them from a good nursery or herb-grower.

Dig the patch deeply in winter, working in plenty of compost.

In March, drive holes in the ground with a crowbar to a depth of 14 in. (355 mm.), spacing the holes 2 ft (610 mm.) apart. Drop a piece of root into each hole.

Ideally, the pieces should be about 12 in. (305 mm.) long with crowns (tufts of new foliage) at one end. However, roots 3–4 in. (75–100 mm.) long will do, though in a smaller hole.

Raising new plants Fresh stock can be obtained by keeping some of the autumn-harvested roots for planting in the following year.

Pests and diseases Although seldom troubled by pests, horseradish may be affected by LEAF SPOT (p. 288), SHOTHOLE (p. 290) and WHITE BLISTER (p. 291).

Harvesting and storing

Horseradish plants grown from small pieces of root should be left in the ground for at least two years. If grown from large pieces, dig up the plants from late summer onwards. Store in boxes of sand.

See also sauces, ketchups and relishes (p. 339) and vinegars (p. 342).

Cooking with horseradish

Horseradish sauce is as traditional with roast beef as is Yorkshire pudding, but a major drawback lies in the preparation. The skin emits fumes more powerful than those of the strongest onion. Some people counter this by wearing glasses, while others resort to the old folklore remedy of holding a piece of bread in the mouth.

Perhaps the easiest way is to put it through the mincer or shredder attachment of an electric food mixer.

However, once grated, horseradish should be used immediately as it quickly loses its pungent flavour. This also happens if it is cooked.

Grated horseradish is used in creams, sauces and mayonnaises to flavour roast beef, fish (especially smoked), boiled poultry, and with tomato salads or as a stuffing for hard-boiled eggs. Grated horseradish is also used as a garnish with roast meat and with steak tartare.

HORSERADISH SAUCE

3 rounded tablespoons grated
  horseradish
5 fl. oz. (150 ml.) soured cream
Salt and pepper
Pinch of dry mustard

Fold the freshly grated horseradish into the soured cream and season to taste with salt, freshly ground black pepper and mustard.

Serve with hot or cold roast beef, cold ham, smoked trout or salmon.

HORSERADISH CREAM

2 rounded tablespoons grated
  horseradish
5 fl. oz. (150 ml.) whipping cream
2 oz. (50 g.) cooked macaroni
1 tablespoon white wine vinegar
Salt and sugar
Garnish: paprika, watercress sprigs

Whip the cream until it holds its shape, and fold in the freshly grated horseradish. Dice the cooked, cooled macaroni and fold it into the cream. Season to taste with vinegar, salt and sugar. Turn the cream into a small bowl, sprinkle lightly with paprika, and garnish with a few sprigs of watercress.

Serving This is a classic accompaniment to cold roast beef. It also goes well with smoked buckling, mackerel and trout, or with cold ham.

Variation Add a little diced ham or beef to the horseradish cream, pile the mixture on lettuce leaves, garnish with sliced tomatoes and serve as a salad on its own.

Hyssop

Hyssop, a hardy evergreen herb, was once widely grown for its minty leaves which were used to flavour stews, soups, meat stuffings and salads. Nowadays it is rarely grown, possibly because many people find it too bitter. But it is still used in making the liqueur, Chartreuse.

From July to September hyssop bears spikes of blue, pink or white flowers, according to variety, so it can make an attractive, low ornamental hedge round a herb garden. It grows to 18 in. (455 mm.) or more in height.

Planning the crop

Hyssop grows best in a sunny position and on well-drained soil.

How much to grow Unless you are growing hyssop for decorative purposes a single plant is sufficient, since only a few of the pungent leaves are needed for each dish.

Varieties Seed sold as hyssop is generally the common blue-flowered species, but specialist seedsmen may stock 'Albus', the white form, and 'Roseus', which has pale pink flowers.

How to grow hyssop

Sow the seeds outdoors in late April or May in drills ¼ in. (5 mm.) deep. When the seedlings are large enough to handle, thin them to 3 in. (75 mm.) apart.

Set them in their permanent positions at any time between September and March. If more than one plant is to be grown, space them at 12 in. (305 mm.) intervals.

To encourage the plants to bush

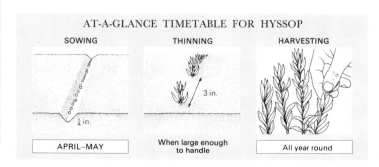

AT-A-GLANCE TIMETABLE FOR HYSSOP		
SOWING	THINNING	HARVESTING
APRIL–MAY	When large enough to handle	All year round

out, remove the tips of the main shoots. Once plants are established, trim them with shears each April.

Raising new plants An existing stock of plants can be increased by taking 2 in. (50 mm.) cuttings of side-shoots in April or May. Remove the lower leaves and insert the cuttings in equal parts of peat and sand in a cold frame, shading the glass in hot weather.

Plant the rooted cuttings directly into their permanent site, or grow them on in 3 in. (75 mm.) pots of potting compost and plant out in September.

Large and bushy plants can be divided in spring.

Pests and diseases Hyssop is usually trouble-free.

Harvesting and storing

Pick the leaves at any time of year, as needed. For salads they are at their best in early summer.

See also drying (p. 343) and freezing (p. 294).

See also drying (p. 343) and freezing (p. 294).

Cooking with hyssop

The finely chopped leaves may be used instead of mint and can be sprinkled over vegetables, salads, meat stews and vegetable soups.

Hyssop is also added to fruit salads and cups, sprinkled over grapefruit and added to apple and apricot pies and flans.

To make a herbal tea with hyssop leaves, steep 1 oz. (25 g.) of fresh leaves in 1 pint (600 ml.) of boiling water for 5–10 minutes and strain the infusion.

Jerusalem artichokes:
see **Artichokes, Jerusalem**

Kale and rape kale

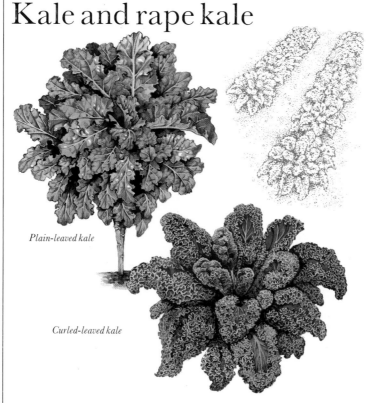

Plain-leaved kale

Curled-leaved kale

Both kale and rape kale, two related brassicas which are descended from the wild cabbage, are valuable winter vegetables. They provide greens from December to April when other greenstuff may be scarce.

The kales are extremely hardy, surviving conditions that will harm broccoli and Brussels sprouts. Indeed, it is considered that frosts improve their flavour.

The leaves of kale, which is also known as borecole, may be either curled or plain.

Rape kale, too, has plain or curled leaves. It is sown later than true kale and produces a later crop.

Planning the crop

Kales are best grown on well-drained, medium or heavy loam which has been well manured for a previous crop. Two weeks before planting kale – or sowing rape kale – dress the surface with 2 oz. per square yard (60 g. per square metre) of general fertiliser.

Like all brassicas, kale thrives in an alkaline soil, so apply lime after digging the plot during the previous winter.

How much to grow A 30 ft (9 m.) row will yield an average of 18 lb. (about 8.5 kg.) of kale or rape kale. The amount needed may to some extent depend on the quantity of summer vegetables you have stored in the freezer.

Varieties Curled-leaved kale:
'Dwarf Green Curled': hardy; fine quality; tightly curled.
'Pentland Brigg': very hardy; young shoots and flower stalks may be eaten.
Plain-leaved kale varieties:
'Cottager's': purple-tinged leaves; abundant side-shoots in spring.
'Frosty': dwarf habit; prolific; hardy, and ideal for exposed gardens.
'Thousand headed': the hardiest plain-leaved variety; pick shoots in late winter and spring.

Rape kale varieties are sold under different names, but there is not much to choose between them in terms of cropping and flavour. They include: 'Asparagus Kale', 'Favourite', 'Hungry Gap' and 'Ragged Jack'.

How to grow kale

Sow the seeds in a ½ in. (12 mm.) deep drill in April. Thin the seedlings to about 2 in. (50 mm.) apart so that they have space to form sturdy plants.

Transplant them to the prepared permanent bed in July, spacing them 2 ft (610 mm.) apart in each direction. Firm the plants in with your feet or with the dibber, and keep them watered until they are well established.

An application of bromophos or diazinon granules to the soil at planting time will prevent the risk of attack by cabbage root fly.

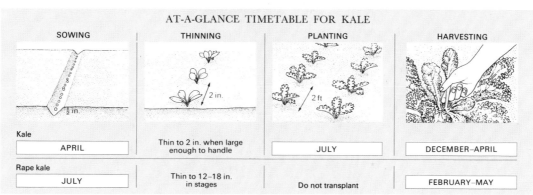

AT-A-GLANCE TIMETABLE FOR KALE

SOWING	THINNING	PLANTING	HARVESTING
Kale	Thin to 2 in. when large enough to handle		
APRIL		JULY	DECEMBER–APRIL
Rape kale	Thin to 12–18 in. in stages		
JULY		Do not transplant	FEBRUARY–MAY

How to grow rape kale

Delay sowing rape kale until early July. If sown earlier it will put on too much foliage and the large, succulent leaves may fail to survive the winter.

Sow directly into the permanent bed in drills ½ in. (12 mm.) deep and 18 in. (455 mm.) apart. Thin the seedlings in stages until they are 12–18 in. (305–455 mm.) apart.

Alternatively, to save seed, sow in groups of three or four at 12–18 in. spacings, removing all but the strongest seedling in each group when large enough to handle.

Hoe frequently to destroy weeds, and tread the ground around the plants occasionally to prevent winds rocking them. If they become excessively large and floppy, push a bamboo cane into the soil alongside each plant and tie the plant to it.

Pests and diseases Pests that may attack kales include CABBAGE ROOT FLY (p. 282), CABBAGE WHITEFLY (p. 282), CATERPILLARS (p. 282) and FLEA BEETLE (p. 283).

The disease most likely to give trouble is CLUB ROOT (p. 287).

Harvesting kales

The leaves of kale are ready for cutting from Christmas onwards. Cut the centre of each plant first to encourage the production of fresh side-shoots.

Start cutting rape kale either in February or when the true kale has finished.

When either type starts to flower, pull up the plants. Chop the tough stems into small pieces, to speed rotting, before putting them on the compost heap.

Preparing & cooking kale

This much-neglected winter vegetable is useful for its crisp, curly leaves which are rich in both iron and vitamin C. It is more popular in the north of England and in Scotland than in the south, being used as a vegetable, for soups and in purées.

Raw kale is also suitable for a winter salad. Toss the freshly chopped leaves in a well-peppered lemon dressing and garnish with quartered hard-boiled eggs.

To prepare kale for cooking, strip the long leaves from the tough stems and then shred them away from the white midribs. Wash thoroughly in cold, running water.

For cooking, boil kale in the minimum amount of boiling, lightly salted water for 10–15 minutes. Drain in a colander and chop the leaves roughly, then heat through with a little butter and season with pepper and ground cloves.

Its rather strong taste makes kale an excellent vegetable to accompany fatty and smoked meats, such as pork and bacon joints.

KALE SOUP

½ lb. (250 g.) kale
1 onion
3 carrots
3 potatoes
3 leeks
2 oz. (50 g.) butter
2 pints (1 l.) white stock or bouillon
Salt, pepper, sugar
Milk
Garnish : hard-boiled eggs

COOKING TIME : 40 minutes

Strip the kale away from the midribs. Wash the leaves and cook in boiling, lightly salted water for 10 minutes. Drain thoroughly and chop finely. Set aside.

Peel the onion, carrots and potatoes and chop finely. Clean the leeks and cut crossways into narrow slices. Melt the butter in a pan and add the vegetables, tossing them well in the butter for about 3 minutes.

Pour the stock over the vegetables, and season with salt and pepper. Bring to the boil and simmer for 20–25 minutes.

Blend the soup in a liquidiser, return the purée to the pan and heat through, adding milk to give the required consistency. Fold in the chopped kale and season to taste with salt, pepper and sugar.
Serving Pour into soup bowls and garnish with chopped hard-boiled eggs.
Photograph on pages 138–9.

KALE AND POTATO CAKES

½ lb. (250 g.) kale
1 lb. (500 g.) mashed potatoes
2 eggs
2 oz. (50 g.) breadcrumbs
Salt and pepper
2 oz. (50 g.) butter

COOKING TIME : 10 minutes

Shred the kale from the midribs, wash it thoroughly in cold water and put in a pan of boiling, lightly salted water for 2 minutes to blanch. Drain thoroughly in a colander and leave to cool slightly.

Chop the kale finely and stir it into the mashed potatoes. Blend in the eggs and add as many breadcrumbs as the mixture will absorb to achieve a fairly stiff consistency. Season to taste with salt and pepper. Shape the mixture into oblong balls, the size of eggs.

Melt the butter and fry the kale and potato cakes for about 8 minutes, turning them once or twice until they are brown and crisp.
Serving Serve with hot or cold gammon, or with bacon or grilled sausages, using the pan juices as a gravy.

CREAMED KALE

2 lb. (1 kg.) kale
Salt and pepper
1½ oz. (40 g.) butter
1½ oz. (40 g.) flour
½ pint (300 ml.) milk
Sugar
2½ fl. oz. (75 ml.) cream

COOKING TIME : 25–30 minutes

Strip the kale from the tough midribs and wash it thoroughly in cold, running water. Put it in a large pan with a small amount of boiling, lightly salted water and cook for about 15 minutes. Drain thoroughly, then chop the kale finely with a sharp knife or put it through a mincer or vegetable mouli.

Melt the butter in a pan, stir in the flour and cook through for a few minutes. Gradually stir in the milk to make a white sauce, adding a little of the cooking liquid from the kale if necessary.

Fold in the chopped kale, heat through and season to taste with salt, pepper and a little sugar. Add the cream, and heat through without boiling.
Serving Kale cooked in this fashion is good with fried or grilled sausages, gammon steaks, braised pork or cold ham.
Variation Spinach may be treated in the same way, and seasoned with ground nutmeg.

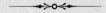

TIMBALE OF KALE

½ lb. (250 g.) kale
4 eggs
Salt and pepper
Pinch of ground cloves
5 fl. oz. (150 ml.) milk
5 fl. oz. (150 ml.) single cream
1 oz. (25 g.) butter

COOKING TIME: 50 minutes
OVEN TEMPERATURE: 180°C (350°F)
– gas mark 4

Strip the kale from the coarse midribs, wash thoroughly and cook without any extra water for 15 minutes over gentle heat. Drain well, then chop the leaves finely or put them through a mouli or a liquidiser.

Beat the eggs lightly with salt, pepper and cloves, and gradually beat in the milk and cream. Strain into a basin and blend in the chopped kale.

Butter a ring mould thoroughly and spoon in the kale mixture. Set the mould in a roasting tin and half fill it with water. Bake in the oven for 35 minutes, or until set.

Serving Remove the mould from the oven, turn out upside-down and fill the centre with buttered baby carrots, or Jerusalem artichokes, coated with a white sauce. Grilled bacon or boiled gammon would go well with this dish.

Photograph on pages 212–13.

COLCANNON

¾ lb. (375 g.) kale
1 onion
5 fl. oz. (150 ml.) milk
¾ lb. (375 g.) mashed potatoes
Salt and pepper
2 oz. (50 g.) melted butter

COOKING TIME: 25 minutes

Shred the kale from the midribs and wash it in cold, running water. Put in a pan of boiling, lightly salted water and cook for 15 minutes. Drain thoroughly in a colander and chop the kale finely.

Meanwhile, peel the onion, chop it finely and put in a pan with the milk. Bring to the boil, then remove from the heat, cover with a lid and leave to infuse while the kale is cooking.

Blend the mashed potatoes with the chopped kale. Heat through over gentle heat, adding as much of the milk and onion mixture as it will absorb to give the consistency of creamed potatoes.

Serving Spoon the colcannon into a serving dish, make a depression in the centre and pour in the melted butter. Serve with roast, grilled or fried meat dishes.

Variation Cabbage may be used instead of kale. However, in Scotland and Ireland, where this dish originates, kale is always used. In some areas the dish is known as kailkenny.

Kohl-rabi

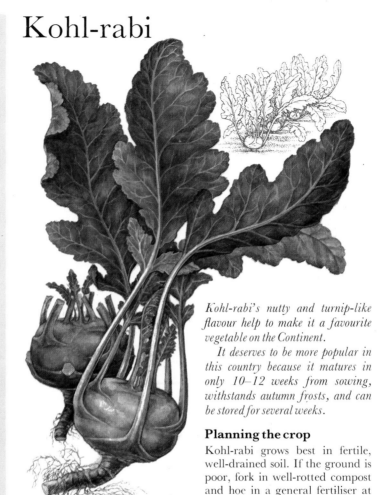

Kohl-rabi's nutty and turnip-like flavour help to make it a favourite vegetable on the Continent.

It deserves to be more popular in this country because it matures in only 10–12 weeks from sowing, withstands autumn frosts, and can be stored for several weeks.

Planning the crop

Kohl-rabi grows best in fertile, well-drained soil. If the ground is poor, fork in well-rotted compost and hoe in a general fertiliser at the rate of 2 oz. per square yard (60 g. per square metre).

How much to grow If your family enjoys root vegetables, sow rows about 10 ft (3 m.) long at four-week intervals from March to August for a constant supply.

Varieties Although the flesh is white in all varieties, some may have green or purple skins:

'Primavera White': very early; green-skinned; bolt-resistant.

'Purple Vienna': purple skin; hard white flesh.

'White Vienna': pale green skin; especially delicate flavour.

How to grow kohl-rabi

Sow the seeds in a drill about ½ in. (12 mm.) deep where the plants are to grow, spacing the rows 15 in. (380 mm.) apart. Thin to 9 in. (230 mm.). Keep them watered.

Pests and diseases The pests most likely to affect this crop are APHIDS (p. 282), CABBAGE ROOT FLY (p. 282), CABBAGE WHITEFLY (p. 282), CATERPILLARS (p. 282) and FLEA BEETLE (p. 283).

The principal diseases and disorders are CLUB ROOT (p. 287), DAMPING OFF (p. 287), DOWNY MILDEW (p. 288), LEAF SPOT (p. 288), SPRAY DAMAGE (p. 291), WHIPTAIL (p. 291) and WIRE STEM (p. 291).

Harvesting and storing

Pull the plants out of the soil when the bulbous stems are about the size of a tennis ball.

Although the final autumn crop can be left in the ground until needed, it is better lifted when mature. Trim the leaves and roots, and store in a dry, cool place.

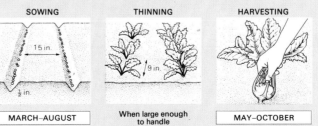

AT-A-GLANCE TIMETABLE FOR KOHL-RABI

SOWING	THINNING	HARVESTING
15 in. — ½ in.	9 in.	
MARCH–AUGUST	When large enough to handle	MAY–OCTOBER

Preparing & cooking kohl-rabi

This root vegetable resembles a turnip in appearance, and is also somewhat similar in taste. The roots are white or purple and should be used while young, before they become coarse. They are suitable for cooking as an accompanying vegetable, and may also be used raw in salads.

To prepare kohl-rabi, cut off the leafy tops and trim away the root base and any fibrous roots. Scrub thoroughly in cold running water, and peel rather thickly. Cut the roots crossways into $\frac{1}{2}$ in. (12 mm.) slices, or finger-wide strips.

Blanch the prepared vegetable for 5 minutes in boiling water with a little added lemon juice. Refresh it in cold water before cooking.

Cook kohl-rabi, either in slices or strips, for 10–15 minutes in a very small amount of boiling, lightly salted water, adding butter at the rate of about 3 oz. (75 g.) to every pound of vegetable. Serve the kohl-rabi with part of the cooking liquid poured over it, or in a white sauce. Alternatively, it may be mashed with butter, and either milk or cream.

For a fresh salad, cut the peeled kohl-rabi into narrow strips, or grate the roots on the coarse side of a grater and toss in French dressing.

SUGAR-BROWNED KOHL-RABI

1 lb. (500 g.) kohl-rabi
1 oz. (25 g.) sugar
1 oz. (25 g.) butter

COOKING TIME: 25 minutes

Peel the kohl-rabi and cut into finger-wide strips. Blanch for 5 minutes and refresh in cold water. Return the kohl-rabi to the pan with a small amount of boiling, lightly salted water. Bring to the boil and simmer gently for about 10 minutes, or until tender but still firm. Drain thoroughly in a colander and allow to cool slightly.

Melt the sugar in a heavy-based frying pan, without stirring, until it bubbles and is pale brown. Add the butter and stir until blended. Stir in the kohl-rabi strips and shake the pan frequently to coat them evenly with the caramel. Avoid stirring as much as possible.
Serving Spoon the sugar-browned kohl-rabi into a dish and serve with roast meat. It is particularly good with pork.

KOHL-RABI IN MORNAY SAUCE

1 lb. (500 g.) kohl-rabi
4 oz. (100 g.) butter
1 oz. (25 g.) flour
$\frac{1}{2}$ pint (300 ml.) milk
4 oz. (100 g.) grated Cheddar cheese
Salt and pepper
2 tablespoons of double cream

COOKING TIME: 30 minutes

Peel the kohl-rabi and cut into slices or strips. Blanch for 5 minutes, refresh in cold water and steam in 3 oz. (75 g.) of butter and 3–4 tablespoons of water for about 10 minutes.

Meanwhile, prepare the sauce. Melt the remaining butter in a pan, stir in the flour and cook for a few minutes. Gradually stir in the milk until the sauce is smooth and thick.

Add 2 tablespoons of the cooking liquid, fold in the cheese and season to taste with salt and freshly ground pepper. Stir in the cream, and heat through without boiling. Drain the kohl-rabi.
Serving Arrange the kohl-rabi in a dish and spoon the Mornay sauce over it. Serve with grilled or roast meat.
Variation Use only half the cheese in the sauce, sprinkling the remainder over the completed dish. Dot with a little extra butter and set under a hot grill for a few minutes until the cheese has melted.

KOHL-RABI CASSEROLE

1 lb. (500 g.) kohl-rabi
1 lb. (500 g.) potatoes
$\frac{1}{2}$ lb. (250 g.) streaky bacon
1 onion
1 oz. (25 g.) butter
Salt and pepper
5 fl. oz. (150 ml.) white stock
Garnish : chopped chervil

COOKING TIME: $1\frac{1}{4}$ hours
OVEN TEMPERATURE: 180°C (350°F) – gas mark 4

Peel the kohl-rabi and cut into finger-wide strips, then cut these in half. Peel and dice the potatoes.

Remove rind and gristle from the bacon and chop the flesh roughly. Peel the onion and chop finely. Melt the butter in a pan and fry the onion until soft and golden, but not brown. Lift out with a slotted spoon. Fry the diced bacon in the butter until crisp, then remove and drain.

Put a layer of potatoes over the base of an ovenproof dish, add a layer of kohl-rabi and a layer of onion and bacon. Sprinkle the layers lightly with salt and pepper and continue with these layers until all the ingredients are used up, finishing with potatoes. Pour the stock into the casserole, cover with a lid and cook for 1 hour.
Serving Serve as a dish on its own, straight from the oven, sprinkled with finely chopped chervil.

KOHL-RABI WITH CHIVES AND PARSLEY

1 lb. (500 g.) kohl-rabi
3 oz. (75 g.) butter
Sea salt
1 tablespoon finely chopped chives
1 tablespoon finely chopped parsley

COOKING TIME: 15 minutes

Trim and peel the kohl-rabi and cut into $\frac{1}{2}$ in. (12 mm.) slices. Blanch for 5 minutes in boiling water, with a little lemon juice added. Drain, and refresh in cold water.

Melt the butter in a pan, add 2 tablespoons of water and the kohl-rabi slices. Cover with a lid and simmer gently for 10 minutes. Sprinkle the kohl-rabi liberally with sea salt, lift the slices out and arrange in a shallow serving dish.

Stir the chives and parsley into the cooking liquid and spoon this over the vegetable.
Serving Serve with roast meat, or with oily fish that has been grilled or baked.

Land cress

Land cress, an annual also known as American cress or winter cress, is one of the few vegetables that will thrive in a damp, shady part of the garden. It is also hardy, so it is worth growing to provide water-cress-flavoured leaves for winter salads and garnishes.

Planning the crop

Choose a site that is moist and, preferably, shaded. When digging, add well-rotted manure or compost to the soil at the rate of a bucketful per square yard.

How much to grow Sow in March for use in summer, and in September for winter use. About six to eight plants in summer, and eight to ten in winter, will give a constant supply of leaves.

Varieties Seed merchants sell the seed simply as land cress or American cress.

How to grow land cress

Sow the seed in a drill about $\frac{1}{4}$ in. (5 mm.) deep. If the ground is even slightly dry, water the site thoroughly before sowing.

When the seedlings are large enough to handle, thin them to 8 in. (200 mm.) apart.

Keep the ground well watered, particularly during dry spells, and mulch with well-rotted manure or compost, or with dampened peat.

Land cress can also be grown in 7 in. (180 mm.) pots of garden soil mixed with an equal amount of dampened peat. Sow three or four seeds to a pot and remove all but the strongest when the seedlings are large enough to handle. Put the pots in a partially shaded place and water regularly.

Pests and diseases SLUGS AND SNAILS (p. 285) are the pests most likely to occur. Land cress is generally disease-free.

Harvesting land cress

The cress grows quickly, and the first pickings may be expected about eight weeks after sowing. Pick the outer leaves first, leaving the centre to produce more.

As the plant gets older, discard the tougher, outer leaves and pick only from the centre. ✿✿

Serving land cress

Land cress resembles watercress, although the green leaves are smaller and have a less delicate flavour. For this reason, pick them while they are young.

Land cress may be used as a substitute for watercress garnishes, particularly with roast chicken and game. It may also be used as a basis for soups (see Watercress soup, p. 276).

Pick the leaves just before they are needed and prepare in the same way as watercress.

Use land cress as an ingredient in mixed or green salads, or combine the sprigs with segments of grapefruit or orange and toss in oil-vinaigrette, French dressing or Roquefort dressing.

AT-A-GLANCE TIMETABLE FOR LAND CRESS

SOWING	THINNING	HARVESTING
	8 in.	
Winter crop	When large enough to handle	NOVEMBER ONWARDS
SEPTEMBER		
Summer crop	When large enough to handle	MAY ONWARDS
MARCH		

Leeks

The leek has been the national emblem of Wales ever since AD 640, when the Welsh forces under King Cadwallader, wearing the vegetable as a badge of recognition, defeated an invading Saxon army.

In England it was used to make soups and stews during Lent, at a time of year when other vegetables were scarce. This points to one of the qualities for which the leek is still valued – its ability to survive the hardest of winters.

It is also an easy vegetable to grow, provided it is sown sufficiently early to give a long growing season.

For many years, in the Newcastle area, the growing of exhibition leeks has been a passion. With the aid of closely guarded techniques and fertilisers, experts raise 9 lb. (4.5 kg.) giants, whose blanched bases measure 20 in. (510 mm.) or more.

These are massive compared with the specimens that most of us manage to grow, but leeks of more modest size remain one of the most worthwhile vegetable crops.

Planning the crop

Leeks will thrive in any well-drained soil, even in the coldest areas, provided it is well manured during the winter before planting.

How much to grow A 10 ft (3 m.) row will yield an average of 10 lb. (5 kg.) of leeks. Two rows should be sufficient for most families.

Varieties 'Catalina': long, thick stems; mild flavour.

'Lyon': long, thick stems; equally suitable for exhibition or table use.

'Malabar': very rapid growth; ready in autumn; medium length.

'Musselburgh': very hardy; a long-stemmed Scottish variety.

'Yates Empire': maincrop variety; long, thick stems; blanches pure white.

How to grow leeks

Sow leeks ½ in. (12 mm.) deep in an outdoor seed bed during March. In late June or July, when the seedlings will be about 8 in. (200 mm.) high, transplant them to their final bed, first trimming the tops to reduce transpiration.

With a dibber, make holes 6 in. (150 mm.) deep and 9 in. (230 mm.) apart, leaving 15 in. (380 mm.) between rows.

Drop the young leeks into the holes. Do not replace the soil; instead, water the seedlings thoroughly.

The amount of soil carried into the holes by the water will be sufficient to set the leeks in place without settling between the leaves. The holes will soon fill up as a result of watering and hoeing.

During the rest of the summer, hoe the bed regularly to keep down weeds, and water thoroughly during dry spells.

During the autumn, draw soil round the developing stems to increase the length of the blanched part.

Pests and diseases ONION FLY (p. 284) is the most likely pest.

RUST (p. 290) and WHITE ROT (p. 291) are the principal diseases.

Harvesting and storing

To extend the harvesting period, start lifting the leeks when they are about ¾ in. (20 mm.) thick.

Ease them out of the soil with a fork, otherwise they may break. Continue lifting the leeks during the winter as they are needed. They will keep growing during the winter, though only slowly during the coldest months.

See also freezing (p. 294).

CULTIVATING LEEKS

TRANSPLANTING Unlike most crops, which need firm planting, it is sufficient to drop leeks into a dibber hole and water them in.

EARTHING UP During the autumn, draw soil round the base of the plants to increase the length of the blanched stems.

Preparing & cooking leeks

Together with potatoes and onions, leeks are certainly one of the most versatile and popular of vegetables. They are used to flavour soups and stews, and a few leaves wrapped round sprigs of parsley and thyme make a quick and fresh-tasting bouquet garni.

Leeks are also used as an accompanying vegetable, and may be boiled, steamed, braised or fried. Young leeks, finely chopped, can be used as a salad vegetable and dressed with oil-vinaigrette; or, cooked whole, they may be served hot, luke-warm or cold as an appetiser.

To clean leeks for cooking, slice off the root base, cut off the upper green leaves and remove any tough or damaged outer leaves. If the leeks are to be cooked whole, as for braising, make a downward slit into the white part, long enough to prise the leaves apart but not so deep that the stem splits in two.

Rinse the leeks thoroughly under cold, running water, washing away all traces of soil and grit.

Alternatively, cut the leeks in half lengthways and rinse them well; or wash them first, then cut crossways into 1–2 in. (25–50 mm.) pieces, or into even thinner slices.

Boil leeks in a minimum of boiling, lightly salted water.

PREPARING LEEKS FOR COOKING

TRIM THE ENDS With a sharp knife, remove the root base and cut off the green leaves from the top of the stem.

CUTTING LENGTHWAYS Before cooking leeks whole, slit the top of the stem for a few inches and prise the leaves apart.

CUTTING CROSSWAYS Instead of cooking them whole, leeks may be cut crossways into 1–2 in. (25–50 mm.) pieces.

CUTTING IN HALF If the whole leeks are not required, the stems may be cut lengthways instead of slicing into pieces.

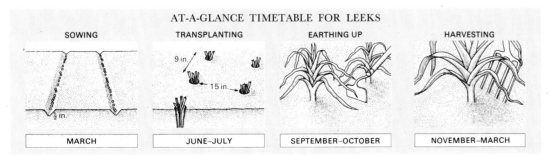

AT-A-GLANCE TIMETABLE FOR LEEKS

SOWING	TRANSPLANTING	EARTHING UP	HARVESTING
MARCH	JUNE–JULY	SEPTEMBER–OCTOBER	NOVEMBER–MARCH

Whole and halved leeks require about 15–20 minutes; rings and slices about 10 minutes.

Drain thoroughly, return the leeks to the pan and heat for a few minutes to steam off any remaining water.

Serve leeks on their own, with a knob of butter, or coated with a white sauce or cheese sauce.

LEEK SOUP

6–8 leeks
2 oz. (50 g.) butter
1 pint (600 ml.) chicken stock
1¼ pint (725 ml.) milk
Salt and pepper
4 oz. (100–125 g.) grated cheese

COOKING TIME: 40 minutes

Trim the root bases and upper green leaves off the leeks, and set a few of the better pieces of the leaves aside. Rinse the leeks thoroughly in cold water and cut crossways into narrow slices. Melt the butter in a pan, add the leeks, and cover.

Cook over gentle heat for 8 minutes, then add the stock and milk. Season with salt and pepper. Bring to the boil and simmer for 20 minutes, or until tender.

Cool the soup slightly, then blend in a liquidiser or rub it through a sieve. Return the soup to the pan and re-heat; add the cheese, stirring all the time until the cheese has melted.
Serving Pour into bowls and garnish with chopped leek leaves.

BRAISED LEEKS

1½ lb. (750 g.) leeks
Salt
1 pint (600 ml.) white stock
3 oz. (75 g.) butter
1 bouquet garni
Garnish : chopped parsley

COOKING TIME: 50 minutes

Trim the roots and upper parts of the leaves from the leeks. Split the green parts lengthways so that they can be opened out, and wash under cold, running water.

Put the leeks in a heavy-based pan and pour over just enough stock to cover them. Add salt (depending on the saltiness of the stock), the butter and the bouquet garni. Bring to the boil over high heat, then cover the leeks with greaseproof paper and a lid.

Lower the heat and simmer gently for about 45 minutes, or until the white parts of the leeks are tender and most of the liquid has evaporated.

Lift the leeks on to a serving dish. Remove the bouquet garni. Reduce the braising liquid, if necessary, by rapid boiling and pour this glaze over the leeks.
Serving Garnish with parsley. Serve with roast poultry and beef, or with grilled steaks.

CHEESY LEEKS

6–8 leeks
Salt and pepper
2 oz. (50 g.) butter
2 oz. (50 g.) flour
4 fl. oz. (125 ml.) cream (approx.)
3 oz. (75 g.) grated cheese
Paprika
2 tablespoons white breadcrumbs

COOKING TIME: 40 minutes
OVEN TEMPERATURE: 190°C (375°F) – gas mark 5

Trim the roots and upper green parts off the leeks, wash thoroughly and cut in half lengthways. Put in a pan with a small amount of boiling, lightly salted water and simmer for about 6 minutes. Drain, and set the cooking water aside.

Melt the butter in a pan and stir in the flour, cook for a few minutes, then gradually add about 5 fl. oz. (150 ml.) of the reserved cooking liquid. Continue stirring until the sauce is smooth and thick, then add cream to give the required consistency. Season to taste, and stir in two-thirds of the cheese.

Arrange the leeks in a buttered ovenproof dish, spoon the sauce over them and sprinkle with a little paprika. Mix the remaining cheese with the breadcrumbs and sprinkle over the sauce. Dot with a little butter and cook in the oven for about 20 minutes, or until the topping has crisped.
Serving This makes a good dish on its own, or with grilled or fried bacon, or chops.

CRISP-FRIED LEEKS

8 leeks
Salt
1 egg
3–4 tablespoons breadcrumbs
2 oz. (50 g.) butter

COOKING TIME: 25 minutes
CHILLING TIME: 1 hour

Trim the roots and tough upper parts from the leeks, leaving them whole. Wash thoroughly under cold running water to remove all traces of grit.

Put the leeks in a large pan containing a small amount of boiling, lightly salted water. Cover with a lid and simmer for about 15 minutes, or until the leeks are just tender but not disintegrating.

Drain the leeks well, patting them dry in absorbent kitchen paper.

Beat the egg lightly, turn the leeks in it, then coat thickly on all sides with fine breadcrumbs. Chill the coated leeks in the refrigerator for about 1 hour to allow the breadcrumb coating to set.

Melt the butter in a wide pan, and fry the leeks until they are golden-brown and crisp on both sides.
Serving These crisp leeks go well with grilled meat and fish; also with fricassées and other cream-based dishes.
Variation Deep-fry the coated leeks in oil instead of shallow-frying them. This is easier if the whole leeks are cut in half, crossways, before coating them.

CRÈME VICHYSSOISE

2 lb. (1 kg.) leeks
1 lb. (500 g.) potatoes
2 oz. (50 g.) butter
1 stick celery
1 pint (600 ml.) chicken stock
1 pint (600 ml.) milk
Salt, pepper and nutmeg
½ pint (300 ml.) cream
Garnish : chopped chives

COOKING TIME: 40 minutes
CHILLING TIME: 3 hours

Trim off the roots and coarse upper leaves; wash the leeks thoroughly and cut into narrow slices. Peel and dice the potatoes. Melt the butter in a pan, and add the leeks and potatoes; cook over gentle heat for about 7 minutes, stirring continuously to prevent sticking.

Add the chopped celery, the stock and the milk and bring to the boil. Season to taste with salt, pepper and ground nutmeg. Simmer for about 25 minutes, or until the vegetables are tender.

Rub the soup through a sieve or blend it in a liquidiser. Correct the seasoning and stir in the cream. Chill in the refrigerator for about 3 hours.
Serving This classic soup is always served chilled, in individual soup bowls, and garnished with freshly chopped chives.
Variations Grated fresh carrots, or the finely chopped white flesh of leeks, are other alternatives for an edible garnish.

Continued . . .

Leek recipes (continued)

LEEKS IN PAPILLOTES

4 leeks
Salt and pepper
6 oz. (175 g.) fresh white breadcrumbs
2 oz. (50 g.) melted butter
1 small onion
2 oz. (50 g.) cooked ham
Grated rind of ½ lemon
2 tablespoons finely chopped parsley
2 eggs
Flour

COOKING TIME: 30 minutes

Trim and wash the leeks, leave them whole and put in a large pan with a little boiling, lightly salted water. Bring to the boil and simmer for 8 minutes. Drain carefully.

Put the breadcrumbs in a bowl, stir in the melted butter and the peeled onion – finely chopped or grated. Dice the ham and add to the breadcrumbs, together with the lemon rind and parsley.

Beat the eggs lightly and use them to bind the forcemeat mixture, adding a little water if necessary. Season to taste with salt and pepper.

Cut eight pieces of greaseproof paper to fit the leeks; sprinkle lightly with flour. Spread half the forcemeat equally over the paper pieces, lay a leek on top and cover with more forcemeat. Sprinkle with a little more flour and wrap the paper loosely round each leek, twisting the ends securely.

Put the parcels in boiling water and simmer for 20 minutes.

Serving Remove the paper cases and arrange the leeks in a serving dish.

They make a satisfying dish when served with potatoes, and either a cheese sauce or horseradish cream.

Variation Use sausage meat instead of herb forcemeat, and serve with a tomato sauce.

LEEK AND HAM SOUFFLÉ

1 lb. (500 g.) leeks
Salt and pepper
1 oz. (25 g.) butter
3 oz. (75 g.) chopped cooked ham
½ pint (300 ml.) thick white sauce
3 eggs, separated

COOKING TIME: 1¼ hours
OVEN TEMPERATURE: 180°C (350°F) – gas mark 4

Trim off the roots and all green leaves. Wash the leeks thoroughly under cold, running water and cut crossways into ½ in. (12 mm.) pieces.

Put the leeks in a pan with a good pinch of salt, ½ pint (300 ml.) of boiling water and the butter. Cook over high heat until most of the liquid has evaporated, then lower the heat and simmer, covered, for about 20 minutes or until the leeks are quite tender. Drain if necessary.

Fold the leeks and chopped ham into the prepared white sauce and beat in the egg yolks, one at a time. Whisk the egg whites until stiff,

then fold them carefully into the soufflé mixture with a metal spatula.

Spoon the mixture into a buttered, straight-sided soufflé dish and set this in a roasting pan of hot water.

Bake in the oven for about 45 minutes or until it has risen and is golden-brown.

Serving A soufflé must be served as soon as it is taken from the oven, before it collapses. Serve this leek and ham soufflé with a small bowl of melted butter mixed with finely chopped chives.

LEEK CHIFFONADE SALAD

2 lb. (1 kg.) young leeks
1 bay leaf
Salt and pepper
½ teaspoon mustard
1 teaspoon sugar
4 tablespoons olive oil
2 tablespoons white wine vinegar
2 hard-boiled eggs
1 tablespoon chopped parsley
1 tablespoon chopped chives
1 small onion

COOKING TIME: 30 minutes
CHILLING TIME: 30 minutes

Trim the roots from the leeks and cut off most of the upper green parts, leaving about ½ in. (12 mm.). Wash the leeks thoroughly under cold, running water, then tie them in small bundles with soft string to prevent them

breaking up during cooking.

Put the leeks in a pan with a small amount of boiling, lightly salted water; add the bay leaf and cover the pan with a lid. Simmer for about 30 minutes, or until just tender.

Lift out the leeks, remove the strings and leave to drain and cool completely.

For the dressing, stir the mustard with the sugar and gradually add first the oil, then the vinegar. Season to taste with salt and pepper. Chop the hard-boiled eggs and fold into the dressing, together with the parsley, chives and finely chopped onion.

Spoon this dressing over the leeks and chill in the refrigerator for about 30 minutes.

Serving Serve the leeks as a side salad with any type of cold meat, or as part of an hors-d'oeuvre spread.

FRENCH LEEK FLAN

1½ lb. (750 g.) leeks
6 oz. (175 g.) shortcrust pastry
4 oz. (100–125 g.) butter
2 oz. (50 g.) flour
5 fl. oz. (150 ml.) milk
Salt, pepper and nutmeg
3 oz. (75 g.) grated mature Cheddar cheese

COOKING TIME: 1 hour
OVEN TEMPERATURE: 190°C (375°F) – gas mark 5

Roll out the pastry, made from 6 oz. (175 g.) flour, and use it to

line an 8 in. (200 mm.) flan ring set on a baking sheet. Put aside to chill.

Trim the root bases and all the leafy tops from the leeks, wash thoroughly and cut them crossways into thin slices. Melt the butter in a pan, add the leeks and simmer, covered with a lid, for about 20 minutes or until soft and tender.

Stir occasionally to prevent the leeks browning. Stir the flour into the leeks and gradually add the milk, stirring until the mixture is smooth and has a purée-like texture.

Season to taste with salt, pepper and grated nutmeg. Remove from the heat and stir in the grated cheese.

Spoon the leek mixture into the pastry shell and bake in the centre of a pre-heated oven for about 30 minutes, or until the filling is golden-brown.

Serving This pie or quiche may be served hot or cold as a main course, accompanied with a green salad. It is also excellent for a picnic meal.

Photograph on pages 212–13.

Lettuces

Winter butterhead: 'Valdor'

Cos: 'Little Gem'

Bronze-tinted
butterhead:
'Continuity'

Summer butterhead:
'All the Year Round'

Loosehead: 'Salad Bowl'

Miniature butterhead: 'Tom Thumb'

Crisp-heart: 'Webb's Wonderful'

Although lettuces were popular with the Romans and Greeks – the philosopher Theophrastus identified three sorts in the 4th century BC – they are believed to have a much longer history, and may have been grown thousands of years earlier in the Far East. In Britain, the lettuce was already popular by the 16th century, and today it is the most widely grown salad vegetable.

There are two main types: cos, which are generally oblong with crisp leaves; and cabbage lettuces, which are further divided into smooth-leaved, globular butterheads and crinkly leaved crisp-heart or iceberg types.

In addition, there is the variety 'Salad Bowl', which produces a profusion of leaves but no heart. Some seedsmen also sell packets of mixed seeds, giving lettuces which mature over an extended period.

Although lettuces are among the easiest vegetables to grow in summer and early autumn, they need the protection of glass or polythene cold frames or cloches if their season is to be extended from mid-March to early December. A heated green-house or frame is necessary for harvesting lettuces from mid-December to March.

If lettuces are to be grown for early or late crops, choose only varieties recommended for this purpose by seed merchants.

In a small garden, lettuces need not occupy a special bed. They can be planted as a catch-crop between slower-maturing vegetables, such as parsnips. The lettuces will be out of the ground before the other crop needs the space.

Planning the crop

Lettuces grow best on a fertile, well-drained soil. Before sowing or planting apply a general fertiliser at the rate of 2 oz. per square yard (60 g. per square metre). Prepare the soil in the same way for growing in frames or under cloches.

How many to grow Avoid the risk of summer gluts alternating with shortages by sowing a row 10–12 ft (3–3.6 m.) long every three weeks in the open from early April to late July.

A single row apiece of earlier and later crops should be sufficient.

Varieties These are listed in groups in the order of sowing to produce lettuces from March to early December.

Butterheads for September sowing in ' the open (in the south) to mature in April.

'Arctic King': extremely hardy; smaller and more compact than 'Imperial Winter'.

'Imperial Winter': large and hardy.

'Valdor': large, solid heads; very hardy.

Butterheads for sowing in cold frames or cloches in October for cutting in March/April.

'Emerald': large heads.

'Knap': large, firm heads.

'May Queen': may also be sown in the open in March to mature in June.

Butterheads for sowing in cold frames or cloches in January. Transplant outdoors in late March to mature in May.

'Fortune': large, medium-green heads.

'Tom Thumb': quick-growing heads no larger than a tennis ball; may be grown to maturity under glass, or transplanted outside, or sown outside in March.

'Unrivalled': may also be sown in the open from March to July.

Butterheads for successional sowings from March to July, to mature in 10–12 weeks.

'All the Year Round': solid, pale green hearts; reliable even in dry summers with minimal watering.

'Continuity': compact and long-standing; one of the best varieties for light soils.

'Suzan': pale leaves; large hearts; may also be sown under glass in January.

Crisp-heart or iceberg varieties.

'Cornell 456': light green; large hearts.

'Great Lakes': large, crisp hearts; slow to bolt.

'Minetto': very early; slow to run to seed.

'Webb's Wonderful': large hearts; slow to run to seed.

'Windermere': smaller but quicker maturing than 'Webb's Wonderful'.

Cos varieties.

'Little Gem': dwarf and compact; one of the earliest maturing cos.

'Lobjoits Green': dark green hearts about 9 in. (230 mm.) tall.

'Winter Density': dark green hearts; may be sown outdoors in September for cutting the following May.

Forcing varieties to sow in cold frames or cloches, or a cold greenhouse, in the first week of August to crop in November and December.

'Emerald': large, solid hearts; hardy.

'Kwiek': large hearts.

Loosehead lettuce.

'Salad Bowl': produces numerous tender, curled leaves; practically non-bolting; an excellent choice for trouble-free cropping over a long period.

How to grow lettuces

From March to late July sow seeds in drills about ¼ in. (5 mm.) deep and 12 in. (305 mm.) apart. Thin the seedlings to 3 in. (75 mm.) apart as soon as they are large enough to handle.

Thin finally according to variety. For instance, space the dwarf 'Tom Thumb' 6 in. (150 mm.) apart, most butterheads 9 in. (230 mm.), and large iceberg varieties, such as 'Webb's Wonderful', 12 in. (305 mm.) apart.

The second thinnings can be used in salads, or transplanted to another bed. In this case, space them as advised for thinning, and plant with a dibber or trowel. After firming the soil, water the roots well.

Do not transplant outdoor lettuces after the end of April as, during long dry spells, the plants are likely to bolt (run to seed prematurely).

Keep the plants well watered and hoe regularly to keep down the weeds.

Most cos varieties will form a compact heart without any assistance. If any do not, slip a rubber band over the leaves, or tie them with soft string.

How to grow forcing varieties Sow varieties such as 'Kwiek' or 'Emerald' not later than the first week in August to produce a crop in November or December.

Sow the seeds in a bed prepared as for the summer sowings. In September, transplant the seedlings to a cold frame, under cloches or to a bed in a cold greenhouse, setting the plants 9 in. (230 mm.) apart. Ventilate on all mild days.

For a crop in March or April,

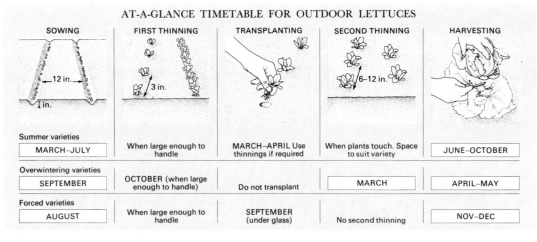

AT-A-GLANCE TIMETABLE FOR OUTDOOR LETTUCES

	SOWING	FIRST THINNING	TRANSPLANTING	SECOND THINNING	HARVESTING
Summer varieties	MARCH–JULY	When large enough to handle	MARCH–APRIL Use thinnings if required	When plants touch. Space to suit variety	JUNE–OCTOBER
Overwintering varieties	SEPTEMBER	OCTOBER (when large enough to handle)	Do not transplant	MARCH	APRIL–MAY
Forced varieties	AUGUST	When large enough to handle	SEPTEMBER (under glass)	No second thinning	NOV–DEC

AT-A-GLANCE TIMETABLE FOR LETTUCES UNDER GLASS

SOWING	FIRST THINNING	SECOND THINNING	HARVESTING
OCTOBER–JANUARY	When ½ in. high remove the weakest seedlings	LATE FEBRUARY	MARCH–MAY

sow a forcing variety, such as 'May Queen', in October directly in the frame or under cloches. Sow three or four seeds ½ in. (12 mm.) deep in groups about 3 in. (75 mm.) apart in each direction. When the seedlings are about ½ in. (12 mm.) high, remove all but the strongest plant from each station.

Water sparingly or not at all during the winter, and make a final thinning to 6 in. (150 mm.) spacings in late February when the plants start to grow again.

How to grow overwintering varieties Sow fully hardy varieties such as 'Imperial Winter' in their permanent bed in September. Thin to only 3 in. (75 mm.) in October; then, if severe weather kills some plants, enough will survive to yield a good crop.

In March, thin to 6–8 in. (150–200 mm.) apart and give a top-dressing of general fertiliser at the rate of 2 oz. to the yard run (60 g. to the metre).

Pests and diseases The main pests are APHIDS (p. 282), CUTWORMS (p. 283), SLUGS AND SNAILS (p. 285) and WIREWORM (p. 285).

The principal diseases of lettuces are DAMPING OFF (p. 287), DOWNY MILDEW (p. 288) and GREY MOULD (p. 288).

Harvesting

Start using a crop of lettuces as soon as the first hearts form. Morning is the best time to gather them.

Either cut the lettuces with a sharp knife just above ground level, or pull the whole plant and cut the root off afterwards.

Pick leaves from 'Salad Bowl' as required.

Preparing & serving lettuces

Use lettuces of all types while they are as fresh as possible, before the leaves lose their crispness and fresh green colour. Although lettuces can be cooked as a vegetable or as a soup, they are used chiefly in salads.

It is the dressing or marinade that gives a salad its distinctive taste. Oil-vinaigrette or French dressings are the most usual marinades, often with added fresh herbs such as chives, parsley, dill, fennel or marjoram.

It is essential that any salad be made up at the last possible moment and, ideally, it should not be tossed in its dressing until served. It is important to use only enough dressing to coat the ingredients, not to drench them.

Prepare lettuces, whether for cooking or for use in a salad, by cutting off the root and removing the outer rough or damaged leaves. For cooking, lettuces are usually left whole, but for salads separate the leaves and cut off any bruised parts. Wash lightly in cold water and dry thoroughly in a salad basket or on a soft towel.

Avoid, if possible, washing the tender inner hearts. Small leaves may be left whole, but larger ones should be shredded, preferably by tearing them rather than cutting with a knife.

Shredded lettuce is used as a base for shellfish cocktails, such as those made with shrimps or lobsters in mayonnaise sauces, as a garnish for chilled soups and as a constituent of sandwich fillings.

GREEK MIXED SALAD

1 lettuce
2 sticks of celery
1 small cucumber
3 tomatoes
½ green pepper
2 oz. (50 g.) anchovy fillets
3 oz. (75 g.) cheese
8–12 black olives
6 tablespoons olive oil
2 tablespoons white wine vinegar or lemon juice
1 teaspoon chopped marjoram
Salt and pepper

Trim the root and outer leaves from the lettuce. Separate the leaves, wash and dry them, then shred them. Scrub the celery and chop into pieces.

Wash, wipe and dice the cucumber, without peeling. Cut the tomatoes into quarters and then in half again. Remove the stalk end, seeds and membranes from the pepper, and dice the flesh.

Mix all these salad ingredients together and arrange on a flat dish. Cut the drained anchovy fillets and cheese into bite-sized pieces and lay them over the salad, together with the olives.

Make a dressing from the oil, vinegar, finely chopped marjoram, and season with salt and pepper.
Serving Pour the dressing over the salad and serve at once as a first course, accompanied with coarse wholemeal bread and butter.
Photograph on page 144.

LETTUCE WITH SOURED-CREAM DRESSING

1–2 lettuces
1 green pepper
1 red pepper
2 hard-boiled eggs
1 garlic clove
4 tablespoons olive oil
1 tablespoon white wine vinegar
2 tablespoons soured cream
Salt and pepper

Cut the stalk base from the green and red pepper; slice each in half lengthways and remove all the seeds and membranes. Wash and dry, then cut crossways into thin slices.

Remove the root and outer leaves from the lettuces, separate the leaves and wash and dry thoroughly. Use a few of the leaves to line a bowl, and shred the remainder. Mix the shredded lettuce with the peppers and place in the bowl.

Separate the yolks from the hard-boiled egg whites and mash with a fork. Blend in the crushed garlic and gradually stir in the oil, vinegar and soured cream. Stir until quite smooth, and season to taste with salt and pepper.
Serving Pour the soured-cream dressing over the salad and sprinkle with the chopped egg whites. Serve as a light salad dish on its own.
Variation A handful of black olives may be added to the salad.

FLORIDA SALAD

1 lettuce
2 sweet oranges
1 grapefruit
2 tomatoes
4 tablespoons olive oil
1 tablespoon sugar
1 tablespoon hot water
Salt and pepper
Garnish : chopped chives

Remove the root and outer leaves from the lettuce; separate into single leaves, then wash and dry thoroughly. Break the lettuce into shreds and arrange in a bowl.

Peel the oranges and the grapefruit, removing all the white pith, and divide the fruit into segments. Cut the tomatoes into quarters, and add the orange and grapefruit segments and tomato quarters to the lettuce.

Put the oil in a small bowl. Melt the sugar in the water and blend this into the oil, seasoning to taste with salt and pepper.
Serving Pour the dressing over the salad, toss well and sprinkle with finely chopped chives.
Photograph on pages 134–5.

Continued . . .

Lettuce recipes (continued)

LETTUCE WITH LEMON DRESSING

1–2 lettuces
Juice of 1 lemon
2 tablespoons sugar
Pinch of salt
1 tablespoon boiling water

Trim the lettuces, remove any damaged leaves and wash and dry the remainder thoroughly. Line a salad bowl with whole lettuce leaves and arrange the hearts, divided into quarters, in the centre.

Squeeze out the lemon juice and strain it. Dissolve the sugar and salt in the boiling water and mix with the lemon juice. Leave to cool.
Serving Pour the lemon dressing over the lettuce and serve at once.

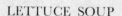

LETTUCE SOUP

1 large lettuce – approx. 1 lb. (500 g.)
Salt and pepper
1 pint (600 ml.) white stock
Nutmeg and sugar
2 oz. (50 g.) butter
1 small onion
1 pint (600 ml.) milk
1 oz. (25 g.) flour
Garnish : grated cheese

COOKING TIME: 25 minutes

Separate the lettuce leaves and wash them thoroughly. Blanch for 5 minutes in boiling, lightly salted water, then drain and refresh in cold water.

Shred the leaves and put them in a pan, together with the stock. Bring to the boil and simmer for 5 minutes. Season to taste with salt and pepper, grated nutmeg and sugar.

Blend the soup in a liquidiser or rub it through a sieve. Melt the butter in a pan and cook the finely chopped onion for about 5 minutes, or until soft but not browned.

Stir in the flour and let it cook for a few minutes before gradually adding the milk. Blend in the lettuce purée and heat the soup through ; correct the seasoning.
Serving Pour the soup into bowls and offer a separate bowl of grated cheese.
Variations For a more substantial soup, boiled rice can be added after the lettuce purée. Alternatively, enrich the soup by adding a few tablespoons of cream to the hot, but not boiling, soup.
Photograph on pages 210–11.

WALDORF SALAD

1 lettuce
1 lb. (500 g.) red dessert apples
2 tablespoons lemon juice
1 teaspoon caster sugar
5 fl. oz. (150 ml.) mayonnaise
½ head of celery
2 oz. (50 g.) shelled walnuts

Wash and dry the apples. Remove the cores, cut one apple into thin slices and dice the remainder. Mix the lemon juice with the sugar and 1 tablespoon of the mayonnaise, and brush over the apple slices to prevent them going brown. Blend the diced apples into the remainder of this dressing.

Clean the celery and chop it roughly. Chop the walnuts. Mix these two ingredients thoroughly with the diced apples, adding the rest of the mayonnaise.

Trim the root and outer leaves from the lettuce, separate into single leaves and rinse and dry well. Line a bowl with the lettuce leaves and pile the diced apple mixture in the centre.
Serving Arrange the apple slices in an overlapping pattern between the lettuce leaves and the centre filling. Serve as a side salad with rich roast meats or poultry.
Variation Sliced bananas are sometimes added to the diced-apple mixture.

BRAISED LETTUCE

2 large cabbage lettuces
1 oz. (25 g.) butter
2 oz. (50 g.) streaky-bacon rashers
1 small onion
1–2 carrots
5 fl. oz. (150 ml.) chicken stock
Salt and pepper
Garnish : chopped parsley

COOKING TIME: 50 minutes
OVEN TEMPERATURE: 180°C (350°F) – gas mark 4

Remove the root bases and outer leaves of the lettuces. Cut both into quarters, wash thoroughly and blanch for 5 minutes in boiling salted water. Refresh under cold running water and dry well.

Melt the butter in a fireproof dish and fry the chopped bacon for 2–3 minutes. Add the chopped onion and the sliced carrots.

Fry for 5 minutes, then add the lettuce quarters. Pour the stock over the fried mixture and season with salt and pepper. Cover with a lid and bake in the oven for about 35 minutes.
Serving Braised lettuce is excellent with grilled or roast meat. Serve it straight from the dish, sprinkled with finely chopped parsley.
Photograph on pages 140–1.

LOW-CALORIE LETTUCE SALAD

8 large lettuce leaves
½ lb. (250 g.) cottage cheese
Salt and pepper
2 oz. (50 g.) cooked ham
2 sticks of celery
1 dessert apple
1 small green pepper
1 tablespoon chopped chives
Lemon juice

CHILLING TIME: 1 hour

Beat the cottage cheese smooth, or blend it in the liquidiser. Season lightly to taste with salt and pepper. Dice the ham. Scrub the celery and cut into small pieces.

Cut the apple into quarters, remove the cores and slice the flesh. Peel only if the skin is tough or bruised. Remove the stalk base, seeds and membranes from the pepper, and cut into small pieces.

Fold all these ingredients, together with the finely chopped chives, into the cottage cheese. Sharpen to taste with lemon juice.

Rinse the lettuce leaves and pat them dry on absorbent kitchen paper. Spread the cottage-cheese filling equally over the lettuce leaves, roll them up and hold in place with wooden cocktail sticks. Chill in the refrigerator for 1 hour.
Serving For a low-calorie main course serve these lettuce rolls sprinkled with lemon juice and accompanied by sliced tomatoes. Alternatively, serve with French dressing or salad cream and crusty bread and butter.

Loganberries

This fine hybrid berry is said to have resulted from an accidental cross between a blackberry and a raspberry that took place in 1881 in the garden of Judge Logan, of Santa Cruz, California. The Judge was swift to appreciate the possibilities of the new fruit, and within a short time it was being grown commercially in many parts of the United States.

There are several reasons for its popularity – in Great Britain as well as in the States. In particular, it is a plant of only moderate vigour, so it is suitable for small gardens. The stems are not so aggressively thorny as those of the blackberry.

Loganberries are larger than the fruits of either ancestor; in taste, they are sharper than both.

Delicious though they are, if eaten raw, the fruits need a good deal of sugar, or mixing with other fruits in a salad. However, for cooking in pies, or making into jam, they have few equals, and will retain their shape and flavour even after lengthy periods of freezing.

Quite a number of other hybrid berries have been brought into cultivation. These include the boysenberry, the veitchberry and the youngberry. Their flavour varies according to their origin, but none has so far achieved the distinctive taste of the loganberry.

Planning the crop

Loganberries will give high yields in most moisture-retentive, fertile soils, other than chalk. Choose a sunny site – ideally a wall or fence with a southerly aspect.

How many to grow Since loganberries require a good deal of space – about 12 ft (3.6 m.) between plants – one or two are sufficient for most gardens.

Varieties The virus-free 'LY. 59' is the one generally recommended. There is also a thornless variety, 'L. 654', which, though it does not crop quite so heavily as 'LY. 59', is easier to pick from and to prune.

How to grow loganberries

In late summer, cultivate the ground thoroughly and remove all perennial weeds.

Plant at any time during the dormant season, though preferably in November or December, and at once cut the canes back to a bud 9 in. (230 mm.) above ground level.

Mulch with well-rotted manure or compost after planting.

Training and pruning Train your loganberries along horizontal wires secured 12 in. (305 mm.) apart, with the top wire about 6 ft (1.8 m.) above the ground. A 12 ft (3.6 m.) span is needed for each plant.

Secure the wires to stout posts at each end, or by means of vine eyes to a wall.

Loganberries fruit best on canes that developed during the previous summer. After fruiting, cut back to ground level the canes from which the berries were gathered.

Tie the young growths to the wires with soft string, ready for the following season's crop.

Because fungal diseases may be transmitted from the older canes to the new growth, it is an advantage to keep them separate. This is most easily done by training each year's shoots to one side of the central root, as described for blackberries (see p.100).

Watering and feeding Loganberries require watering only in the driest weather.

Feed them in January with 1 oz. of sulphate of potash per square yard (30 g. per square metre), and again in April with a similar amount of sulphate of ammonia. Every third year, in January, apply superphosphate at 3 oz. per square yard (90 g. per square metre).

Raising new plants The best way to obtain new plants is by layering the tips of canes that grow closely to the ground. In July, as the new shoots are growing, dig a 6 in. (150 mm.) deep hole close to a convenient cane, insert the tip, and firm it into the soil.

After a few weeks, new growth will be seen above the layered tip, which means that it has taken root. In October, sever the new plant from the parent plant but leave it where it is growing for a week or two longer. Transplant to its final position in November.

Pests and diseases APHIDS (p.282), LEAFHOPPERS (p. 283) and RASPBERRY BEETLE (p. 285) are the pests most likely to occur.

Diseases of loganberries include CANE SPOT (p. 287), GREY MOULD (p. 288) and SPUR BLIGHT (p. 291).

Harvesting and storing

Loganberries ripen in August, midway between raspberries and blackberries. Pick the fruits when they are claret-red, acid and juicy, yet perfectly dry on the outside. Use them at once, whether they are to be eaten fresh or preserved for use in winter.

See also bottling (p. 309); freezing (p. 294); jellies (p. 320) and syrups and juices (p. 326).

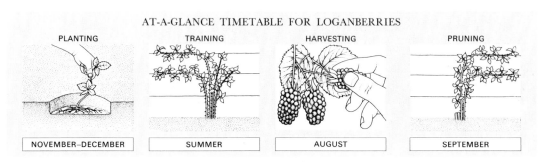

AT-A-GLANCE TIMETABLE FOR LOGANBERRIES

PLANTING	TRAINING	HARVESTING	PRUNING
NOVEMBER–DECEMBER	SUMMER	AUGUST	SEPTEMBER

Preparing & cooking loganberries

These elongated, deep claret-red berries resemble large raspberries, but are juicier and with a fresh, sharp flavour reminiscent of cultivated blackberries.

Loganberries are excellent dessert fruits, served with sugar and cream, and they may also be used in cooking in the same way as blackberries for pie and pudding fillings, and for jams and jellies. They freeze well, with or without sugar.

Prepare loganberries by hulling – that is, by removing the long flower stalk round which the berry is shaped. Rinse carefully in cold water by placing the berries in a colander and dipping this in the water several times. Drain thoroughly, and use the berries fresh, or in creamed or cooked desserts.

CHOUX PASTRY WITH LOGANBERRIES

¾–1 lb. (375–500 g.) loganberries
3 tablespoons icing sugar
1 oz. (25 g.) butter
1 tablespoon caster sugar
5 fl. oz. (150 ml.) milk
4 oz. (100–125 g.) flour
3 eggs
½ pint (300 ml.) double cream (or half single and half double)

COOKING TIME: 1 hour
OVEN TEMPERATURE: 220°C (425°F) – gas mark 7

Hull and rinse the loganberries, put them in a bowl and sprinkle with half the icing sugar. Set aside.

Put the butter, caster sugar and milk in a pan and bring to the boil over moderate heat. Sift the flour and stir it into the milk; remove the pan from the heat and beat the mixture quickly until it leaves the sides of the pan clean.

Beat two eggs, one after the other, into the choux dough and add the yolk from the third egg. The dough should now be smooth and shiny, but if necessary beat in the remaining egg white.

Spoon the choux dough into a forcing bag fitted with a large plain nozzle and pipe a ring, about 1½ in. (40 mm.) wide and 8 in. (200 mm.) in diameter, on to a greased baking sheet. Bake in the centre of a hot oven for 30 minutes, or until brown.

Cool the pastry ring on a wire rack, then split in half horizontally with a sharp knife.

Whip the cream with the remaining icing sugar until it is fluffy but not stiff, spoon it into the bottom half of the choux ring and place the drained loganberries on top. Cover with the upper half of the pastry.

Serving Dust the pastry lightly with sifted icing sugar before serving.

Variation Pipe the pastry on to the baking sheet in four round buns, and bake as already described. Split halfway through, and fill the choux buns with cream and loganberries.

Photograph on pages 142–3.

LOGANBERRY ICE CREAM

1 lb. (500 g.) loganberries
Juice of ½ lime
3 oz. (75 g.) caster sugar (approx.)
½ pint (300 ml.) double cream

FREEZING TIME: 12 hours

Set the freezing compartment of the refrigerator to its coldest setting 1 hour in advance. Hull the loganberries, wash and drain them thoroughly and put them in the liquidiser to make a purée.

Rub the purée through a sieve in order to remove the pips. Add the strained lime juice to the purée and sweeten to taste with sugar.

Whip the cream well, but not stiff, and blend it thoroughly and evenly into the loganberry purée. Spoon the mixture into a plastic container, cover with a lid and freeze for about 12 hours, or until firm.

Serving Remove the ice cream from the freezing compartment 1 or 2 hours before use, and leave in the body of the refrigerator to thaw slightly. Serve this beautiful claret-coloured ice cream in individual glasses, decorating it if you wish with sugar-frosted wedges of lime.

LOGANBERRY MOUSSE

1 lb. (500 g.) loganberries
4–5 oz. (125–150 g.) sugar
3 teaspoons powdered gelatine
½ pint (300 ml.) double cream

CHILLING TIME: 2 hours

Hull and rinse the loganberries. Set about a dozen of the finest berries aside and put the remainder in a bowl. Sprinkle with the sugar.

Leave the bowl in a cool place for several hours, until the sugar has melted and the juices are flowing from the loganberries. Correct the sweetening if necessary.

Dissolve the gelatine in 3 tablespoons of water and stir into the loganberries. Whip the cream lightly and fold it into the fruit mixture when this is beginning to set. Spoon the mousse into a serving dish and leave to chill in the refrigerator until set firm.

Serving Decorate with the reserved loganberries just before serving.

Variation Spoon the mousse into a wetted, decorative mould and turn out before serving.

Photograph on pages 214–15.

LOGANBERRY CREAM

¾ lb. (375 g.) loganberries
3 egg yolks
3 tablespoons caster sugar
4 fl. oz. (125 ml.) milk
½ oz. (15 g.) powdered gelatine
8 fl. oz. (250 ml.) cream (half single, half double)

COOKING TIME: 5 minutes
CHILLING TIME: 3 hours

Hull the loganberries, rinse in a colander and leave to drain thoroughly.

Beat the egg yolks with the sugar until light and fluffy. Heat the milk to just below boiling point and beat into the eggs. Strain this custard into a bowl. Stir in the gelatine dissolved in a little warm water, blending thoroughly.

As the custard cools and is just beginning to set, fold in ½ lb. (250 g.) of the loganberries, gently but thoroughly. Whisk the cream lightly, not to a stiff consistency, and fold it into the loganberry custard using a metal spoon.

Spoon the mixture into a glass dish or individual glasses and leave in the refrigerator until set and chilled.

Serving Decorate with the reserved loganberries.

Lovage

Lovage, a many-purpose perennial herb, is believed to have been brought to this country by the Romans. From the Middle Ages its leaves have been used in medicines and for giving a musky, lemon-like flavour to soups, stews, sauces and salads.

A cordial, made from this herb and called by the same name, was served in inns up to the last century.

Planning the crop

Lovage grows best in a well-drained soil in a sunny position or in partial shade. It reaches a height of 4 ft (1.2 m.).

How many plants to grow Two or three plants will provide sufficient fresh and dried leaves for occasional flavouring of dishes, but additional plants will be needed if they are to be used as a vegetable or for candying.

How to grow lovage

Sow the seeds in September or March in a drill about ½ in. (12 mm.) deep, either in a seed bed or where the plants are to grow. When the seedlings are large enough to handle, thin them to 12 in. (305 mm.) apart; or transplant them in their permanent positions at 12 in. spacings.

During the summer, remove any flowering stems to promote the growth of young leaves.

Raising new plants An existing stock of plants may be increased by dividing the roots in March and replanting the divisions at 12 in. (305 mm.) spacings.

Pests and diseases Lovage is generally trouble-free.

Harvesting and storing

Pick the leaves as required during summer and autumn – from about June until October.

See also freezing (p. 294).

Cooking with lovage

This perennial herb has almost disappeared from general use, although it was extremely popular in medieval herb gardens. It resembles a giant celery in shape and provides a distinctive feature in any herb garden or vegetable garden.

The taste is also similar to that of celery, though it is much stronger and has an additional lemon and yeast flavour.

In southern Europe, the stems are candied and used for decoration in the same way as angelica, and the dried seeds are used like caraway seeds in breads and biscuits.

The roots, too, are edible, but few gardeners would wish to grow sufficient plants to use them for this purpose.

In general, it is the glossy, dark green leaves that are used for flavouring – especially in vegetable soups and in stews, where they give an impression of substance and body due to their distinctive yeasty taste.

Use the washed and finely chopped leaves to flavour stocks and any kind of vegetable soup, fish chowders and cooked vegetables.

The leaves may also be used in omelettes, salad dressings and cream sauces, or they may be mixed sparingly in salads.

Marjoram

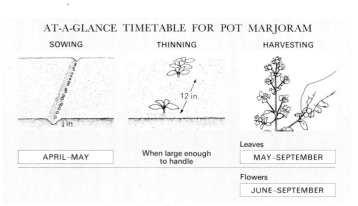

Sweet marjoram

Pot marjoram

Two types of the herb marjoram are grown for their aromatic leaves and flowers, which are used to flavour a wide variety of dishes.

One, called sweet or knotted marjoram, is usually grown as a half-hardy annual. It is generally considered to have a finer flavour than the other type, pot marjoram, which is a hardy perennial.

Planning the crop

Like most herbs, marjoram grows best in full sun and in a well-drained, fertile soil.

How much to grow Two or three plants of each type of marjoram will provide a plentiful supply of leaves all the year, including those which are to be frozen for use during winter. Sweet marjoram can be grown as a pot plant.

Varieties Seed is sold as sweet marjoram or pot marjoram.

How to grow marjoram

Sow seeds of sweet marjoram in a pan of seed compost under glass in early March at a temperature of 10–13°C (50–55°F).

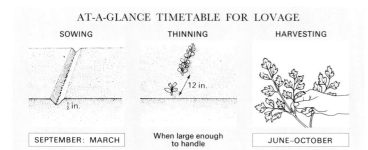

AT-A-GLANCE TIMETABLE FOR LOVAGE

SOWING	THINNING	HARVESTING
½ in.	12 in. When large enough to handle	
SEPTEMBER: MARCH		JUNE–OCTOBER

AT-A-GLANCE TIMETABLE FOR POT MARJORAM

SOWING	THINNING	HARVESTING
½ in.	12 in. When large enough to handle	Leaves MAY–SEPTEMBER
APRIL–MAY		Flowers JUNE–SEPTEMBER

Prick out the seedlings when they are large enough to handle into 2½ in. (65 mm.) pots of potting compost. Put a single seedling in each pot.

Harden off (see p. 34) before planting out 12 in. (305 mm.) apart in their permanent positions in May.

Clusters of flowers appear from June to September from knot-like bracts. It is from these that the plant gets one of its common names.

For winter pot plants, take cuttings of basal shoots in August (see p. 29).

Sow pot marjoram in April or May in ¼ in. (5 mm.) deep drills in the open. Thin to 12 in. (305 mm.) apart.

The plants grow to a height of about 12 in.

Raising new plants Propagate established plants of pot marjoram by taking 2 in. (50 mm.) cuttings of basal shoots in April or May. After removing the lower leaves, insert them in equal parts (by volume) of peat and sand in a shaded cold frame – either directly into the bed of the frame or into pots containing this mixture.

Plant out in their permanent positions when rooted.

Pests and diseases Marjoram is generally trouble-free.

Harvesting and storing

Pick the leaves and flowers of sweet marjoram when needed during the summer. For freezing (see p. 294), pick before the flowers open – generally in July.

The leaves of pot marjoram can be picked from spring to autumn, as required.

190

Cooking with marjoram

The hairy leaves of sweet marjoram have a flavour reminiscent of thyme, although they are sweeter, and are often used as a substitute for this herb. They are excellent for flavouring roast or grilled meat, in stuffings for meat, poultry and oily fish, and in omelettes, soups and stews.

Pot marjoram has the same culinary uses as sweet marjoram, but the leaves lack the sweetness and often have a bitter taste.

Use marjoram in a bouquet garni for soups and stews, and to flavour minestrone, tomato and chicken soups. Oily fish, such as mackerel and trout, can be stuffed with marjoram leaves prior to grilling or baking. Wrap a few leaves in muslin and add them to beef and pork stews, veal fricassées, casseroles, and to braised chicken, duck and game birds.

Sprinkle tomato salads with finely chopped marjoram, or mix with sugar to flavour bread-and-butter and rice puddings. The leaves can also be used to flavour home-made vinegars.

PIZZAIOLA SAUCE

1 tablespoon freshly chopped marjoram
2 onions
2 garlic cloves
1 green pepper
1 dessertspoon oil
2 oz. (50 g.) mushrooms
1 lb. (500 g.) tomatoes
5 fl. oz. (150 ml.) stock
Tomato paste
Chilli sauce
Salt and pepper

COOKING TIME: 30 minutes

Mince the peeled onions and garlic cloves. Remove the stalk base, seeds and membranes from the green pepper, and dice the flesh. Heat the oil in a pan and fry the onions and garlic over gentle heat for 3–5 minutes.

Add the diced pepper and cook for a further 15 minutes before adding the trimmed and roughly chopped mushrooms and the skinned and chopped tomatoes.

Stir in the marjoram and add the stock; blend thoroughly, cover with a lid and simmer for 10 minutes. Season to taste with tomato paste, chilli sauce, salt and pepper.

Serving Serve the sauce hot with grilled or fried sausages, beefburgers, or baked meat loaves. It is ideal with spaghetti and noodles, accompanied by a bowl of grated cheese.

Marrows and courgettes

Marrow 'All Green Bush'

Trailing habit

Courgette 'Zucchini'

Bush habit

Although not especially nutritious, marrows provide a considerable yield from a modest area. They may even be planted on a compost heap, if this will remain undisturbed until autumn.

In addition to being served as a second vegetable, or as a dish on their own, marrows are used in making chutney, jams and pickles.

Small marrows, called courgettes, are nowadays more popular than the fully grown vegetables and can be used as an accompaniment to a wider range of dishes. This, and the fact that so many courgettes come to maturity at the same time, makes them an excellent crop for the freezer.

Although any immature marrow may be called a courgette, some varieties are particularly suitable for producing baby marrows.

Planning the crop

Marrows and courgettes both require a sunny position and a deep, rich soil. They can be sown or planted directly in the soil, or on an old heap of thoroughly rotted manure or compost if this will not be needed for a time.

When planting in soil, in early May, take out a good spadeful where each plant is to be grown and work in a bucketful of manure or compost at the bottom of the hole. Return the topsoil, and form a ridge about 2 in. (50 mm.) high surrounding each planting site to help retain moisture when watering the plants.

On a compost heap, mix a little soil into the planting position and make sure that the heap does not dry out during spells of sunny weather.

Trailing marrows are more suitable than bush marrows for growing in this way.

How many to grow One or two marrow plants should be sufficient. Bush marrows, grown 2 ft (610 mm.) apart, occupy less space than trailing varieties, which require 3–4 ft (1–1.2 m.) between plants.

Courgettes occupy the same amount of space as bush marrows. Even so, four to six plants should provide an adequate crop, for both immediate use and for freezing.

Varieties (trailing) 'Long Green Trailing': very large fruits; dark green with paler stripes.
'Long White Trailing': very large; heavy cropper; stores well.

Varieties (bush) 'All Green Bush': medium size; dark green; good flavour.
'Golden Zucchini' (courgette type) F1 hybrid: slender, golden-yellow fruits of fine flavour.
'Prokor' (F1 hybrid): very early and heavy cropper; medium-size fruits.
'White Bush': medium size; creamy-white; very prolific.
'Zucchini' (courgette type) F1 hybrid: extremely early and prolific; tender and tasty flesh.

How to grow marrows

Marrows and courgettes are both raised in the same way. Prepare the beds, as already described, in early May and sow the seeds indoors or under cover at about the same time.

The best method is to sow two seeds 1 in. (25 mm.) deep in each of a number of peat pots (see p. 33) containing seed compost. Place the pots in a cold frame or on a shaded window-sill indoors. When the seed leaves have developed, remove the weaker of the two plants from each pot.

At the end of May, plant out the seedlings in their peat pots.

Plant bush marrows and courgettes 2 ft (610 mm.) apart; allow 3–4 ft (1–1.2 m.) between trailing marrows. Water the plants thoroughly after planting, and throughout the growing season during dry spells.

If preferred, marrow seeds may be sown in pairs direct into prepared planting sites in mid-May; or, with cloche protection, at the beginning of the month. Remove the weaker seedling of each pair.

Marrows and courgettes produce both male and female flowers. The latter is distinguished by an embryo fruit behind the bloom, while the former has no swelling behind it.

Fertilisation is generally carried out by insects, which carry the pollen from the male to the female flowers. However, in dull, cold or wet weather, when there are few insects about, it is as well to pollinate the flowers by hand to make sure that the fruits form.

POLLINATING MARROW PLANTS

In dull or cold weather, when insects may be scarce, pollinating by hand helps fruits to form. Transfer pollen from male to female flowers with a soft brush; or, as here, rub the male flower directly on to the open blooms of the female flowers.

Pests and diseases APHIDS (p. 282), GLASSHOUSE RED SPIDER MITES (p. 283) and GLASSHOUSE WHITEFLY (p. 283) are the pests most likely to give trouble.

Diseases that may occur are CUCUMBER MOSAIC VIRUS (p. 287), GREY MOULD (p. 288) and POWDERY MILDEW (p. 289).

Harvesting and storing

Marrows are best if eaten in summer when the fruits are 9–12 in. (230–305 mm.) long and when the skins yield to gentle pressure of the fingers.

A few late marrows, however, may be left on the stalk to ripen until early October.

Harvest them just before the first frosts are expected and hang them in nets in an airy, frost-free place.

Stored in this way, they will last for several weeks.

Ideally, you should begin cutting courgettes when the fruits are 4 in. (100 mm.) long.

See also chutneys (p. 335); freezing (p. 294); fruit cheeses and butters (p. 323); jams (p. 314) and pickles (p. 328).

Recipes on next page

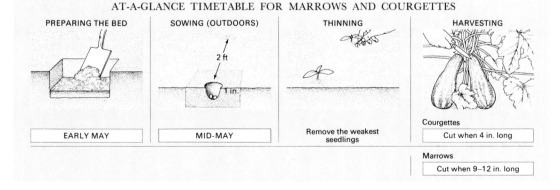

AT-A-GLANCE TIMETABLE FOR MARROWS AND COURGETTES

PREPARING THE BED	SOWING (OUTDOORS)	THINNING	HARVESTING
EARLY MAY	MID-MAY	Remove the weakest seedlings	Courgettes — Cut when 4 in. long / Marrows — Cut when 9–12 in. long

Preparing & cooking marrows and courgettes

Although very large vegetable marrows are often grown for exhibition, for cooking purposes the fruits should be picked when 9–12 in. (230–305 mm.) long – before the seeds have fully developed and the fibres become coarse and stringy.

Marrows have a high water content and tend to be insipid when subjected to prolonged boiling in a large amount of water. Cooked in the minimum of water, or steamed, the fresh taste is retained and excess water evaporated.

Very young and tender marrows, to be cut into rings and stuffed, need only washing. Prepare mature marrows for cooking by peeling lengthways. Cut the peeled marrow in half, scoop out the seeds and any fibrous parts with a spoon, and cut into chunks for boiling, steaming or frying.

For rings, cut a whole marrow crossways into 2 in. (50 mm.) slices, then scoop out the seeds. For whole, stuffed marrow, cut the peeled marrow in half lengthways and remove the seeds.

Boil marrow in a small amount of lightly salted water for about 10 minutes, or steam for 20 minutes. Cooked marrow should be firm, not squashy. Serve boiled or steamed marrow either tossed in butter or with a white or cheese sauce. Marrow is also excellent stuffed and baked, either whole or in slices.

Courgettes are ready for eating when 4–6 in. (100–150 mm.) long. Although they contain seeds, these are so immature and soft that there is no need to remove them. Neither do courgettes have to be peeled for cooking.

Courgettes may also be used fresh in salads, when it is advisable to blanch them for 2–3 minutes in boiling, lightly salted water to remove any excess bitterness from the skin.

Prepare courgettes, both for cooking and for salads, by washing them and trimming both ends. Cut off any discoloured or bruised pieces on the skin. Courgettes may be cooked whole or in slices; or they may be cut in half lengthways, filled with stuffing and baked.

Boil courgettes in lightly salted water for 10–15 minutes. Sliced courgettes may be steamed in butter for about 10 minutes; halved courgettes may be parboiled for 5 minutes then finished off in the oven, in a well-buttered dish, for about 25 minutes at a temperature of 190°C (375°F) – gas mark 5.

MARROW SOUP

1 lb. (500 g.) marrow
1½ oz. (40 g.) butter
1 small onion
1 turnip
2 carrots
2 pints (1 l.) chicken stock
Salt, pepper, ground ginger
5 fl. oz. (150 ml.) cream
Garnish : bread croûtons

COOKING TIME: 45 minutes

Peel the marrow, cut it in half lengthways and scoop out the seeds. Chop the flesh roughly. Melt the butter in a pan and add the marrow, the finely chopped onion and the peeled and diced turnip and carrots. Fry over gentle heat for about 5 minutes until the vegetables are soft, but not brown.

Add the stock to the pan, with salt and pepper to taste, bring to the boil, cover with a lid and simmer for about 30 minutes or until all the vegetables are tender.

Blend the soup in a liquidiser or rub it through a sieve. Return the purée to a clean pan, heat it through and correct the seasoning, adding ground ginger to taste. Gradually blend in the cream, and heat without letting the soup reach boiling point.
Serving Pour into individual soup bowls and top with crisp bread croûtons.
Variation For a richer soup, beat 1–2 egg yokes with the cream. Add the mixture just before serving.

BAKED MARROW

1 medium-size marrow
4 oz. (100–125 g.) lean pork
4 oz. (100–125 g.) veal
1 small onion
1 oz. (25 g.) butter
2 tablespoons chopped parsley
2 oz. (50 g.) white breadcrumbs
Salt and pepper
1 egg

COOKING TIME: 1 hour
OVEN TEMPERATURE: 180°C (350°F) –
gas mark 4

Peel the marrow, cut it in half lengthways and scoop out the seeds; or cut a slice off at one end and leave the marrow whole, scooping out the seeds with a long-handled spoon.

Put the pork and veal through the fine blade of a mincer. Peel the onion and chop it finely. Melt the butter and fry the onion for 5 minutes until it is soft, but not coloured; then add the minced meat and seal over a high heat for a few minutes.

Remove the pan from the heat, blend in the chopped parsley and breadcrumbs and season the stuffing with salt and pepper. Beat the egg lightly and use it to bind the stuffing.

Spoon the stuffing into the two marrow halves and put them together. Tie in place with two or three pieces of fine string and wrap the stuffed marrow in buttered foil. Place in a roasting tin and bake in the oven.
Serving Cut the stuffed marrow into thick slices and serve with buttered rice and a tomato sauce.
Variations Baked marrow can be stuffed with any type of forcemeat, herb-flavoured sausage meat, cheese, rice and tomato, or minced beef.
Photograph on pages 206–7.

BUTTERED MARROW

1 medium-size marrow
2–3 oz. (50–75 g.) butter
Salt and pepper
2 tablespoons freshly chopped herbs –
parsley, tarragon, marjoram or basil

COOKING TIME: 10 minutes

Peel the marrow, cut it in half lengthways and scoop out the seeds. Cut into 2 in. (50 mm.) pieces.

Melt the butter in a heavy-based pan, add the marrow pieces, flavour with salt and pepper, and cover the pan with a lid. Cook over a gentle heat for 7–10 minutes, shaking the pan occasionally to prevent sticking.
Serving Spoon the buttered marrow into a dish and sprinkle with the freshly chopped herbs. Serve with roast or grilled meat.
Variations Par-boil the marrow pieces for 5 minutes, drain and coat with egg and breadcrumbs, and shallow-fry in hot fat until brown.

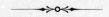

COURGETTES AU GRATIN

6–8 courgettes
Salt and pepper
2 oz. (50 g.) butter
4 lean bacon rashers
1 onion
4 tomatoes
1 teaspoon chopped tarragon
4 tablespoons breadcrumbs

COOKING TIME: 35 minutes
OVEN TEMPERATURE: 190°C (375°F) –
gas mark 5

Wipe the courgettes and trim off the stalk and blossom ends. Put in a pan of boiling, lightly salted water and cook for 5 minutes. Drain, and leave to cool slightly.

Cut the courgettes in half and scoop out most of the flesh with a pointed teaspoon. Chop the flesh finely and set the courgette shells in a buttered ovenproof dish.

Melt half the butter in a pan and fry the diced bacon until it starts to become crisp, then add the finely chopped onion and continue cooking until soft.

Skin the tomatoes, cut them into quarters and remove the seeds. Chop the pulp finely and add to the pan, together with the courgette flesh and the chopped tarragon.

Continue cooking until the ingredients are well blended. Season to taste with salt and pepper, and spoon the stuffing into the courgette hollows.

Melt the remaining butter, and fry the breadcrumbs until they are brown and crisp. Spread them over the courgettes, dot with a few flakes of butter and bake in the oven for about 20 minutes, or until the topping is crisp.

Serving This makes a light lunch or supper dish on its own, served with a cheese sauce. Alternatively, serve it as an accompaniment to boiled gammon or bacon, or baked fish.

COURGETTE SALAD

4 courgettes
Bunch of watercress
1 small head of celery
1 green pepper
1 shallot
½ teaspoon each of salt and pepper
4 tablespoons olive oil
2 tablespoons tarragon vinegar
2 tablespoons dry white wine
1 tablespoon chopped parsley or
*   1 dessertspoon chopped tarragon*
Garnish : black olives

CHILLING TIME: 1 hour

Wipe the courgettes clean, trim off the stalk and blossom ends, and blanch in boiling, lightly salted water for 3 minutes. Drain and refresh in cold water, then leave the courgettes to cool.

Meanwhile, remove the stalks and yellowed leaves from the watercress, rinse and shake dry and divide into small sprigs. Separate the celery sticks, scrub clean and cut into bite-size pieces.

Remove the stalk base, seeds and membranes from the pepper and chop the flesh roughly. Peel the shallot and chop it finely.

Cut the cooled courgettes crossways into thin slices. Put them in a salad bowl with the watercress, celery, green pepper and shallot, and blend well.

Stir the salt and pepper with the oil, then add the vinegar, white wine and parsley. Blend this dressing well, pour it over the salad ingredients and toss to give them an even gloss. Chill in the refrigerator for 1 hour.

Serving Garnish the salad with whole black olives. Serve as a first course with chunks of wholemeal bread and butter.

SICILIAN CAPONATA

1 lb. (500 g.) courgettes
2 onions
1 green pepper
6 large tomatoes
1 aubergine
4 fl. oz. (100 ml.) olive oil
4 oz. (100 g.) black olives
5 fl. oz. (150 ml.) dry white wine
Sugar
Salt and pepper

COOKING TIME: 15 minutes

Wash the courgettes, dry them thoroughly, trim off the stalk and blossom ends, and cut into thin slices. Peel the onions and chop them finely. Remove the stalk end, seeds and membranes from the pepper, and dice the flesh. Skin the tomatoes and chop them roughly. Wash and dry the aubergine and cut it crossways into narrow slices.

Heat the oil in a heavy-based pan and fry the onions for 3–5 minutes, until soft and golden. Add the courgettes, green pepper and aubergine slices. Stir continuously for about 3 minutes until the vegetables are softening, then add the tomatoes, olives and half the wine.

Cook the vegetable mixture over very gentle heat until thoroughly combined, stirring frequently to prevent burning and gradually adding the rest of the wine. Season to taste with sugar, salt and pepper.

Serving This Sicilian dish is served as a first course, hot or cold, with crusty bread.

PORK WITH COURGETTES SPANISH STYLE

4 lean pork steaks
Salt, pepper and paprika
1 onion
2 tablespoons oil
¾ lb. (375 g.) tomatoes
¾ lb. (375 g.) courgettes
1 tablespoon tomato paste
1 teaspoon sugar
5 fl. oz. (150 ml.) chicken stock
1 oz. (25 g.) butter
Garnish : chopped chives

COOKING TIME: 65 minutes
OVEN TEMPERATURE: 160°C (325°F) –
gas mark 3

Trim excess fat from the pork steaks and season them with salt, pepper and paprika. Peel the onion and chop finely.

Heat the oil in a pan and seal the pork steaks until they are brown on both sides – about 2 minutes on each side. Lift into a lightly buttered ovenproof dish. Fry the onion in the oil until golden, then spoon it over the steaks.

Skin and roughly chop the tomatoes and lay them over the onion. Slice the washed and dried courgettes thinly and arrange over the tomatoes. Blend the tomato paste and sugar with the chicken stock; pour over the contents of the casserole until it comes just below the courgettes.

Cover the dish with a lid and bake in the oven for 50 minutes. Remove the lid from the dish, brush the courgettes with melted butter and return to the oven for a further 15 minutes, or until the courgettes have browned.

Serving Garnish with finely chopped chives and serve straight from the oven with buttered noodles or rice.

Variation Sprinkle the courgettes with finely grated cheese instead of brushing with butter, and continue baking until the cheese has melted.

Continued . . .

Marrow recipes (continued)

STUFFED MARROW RINGS

1 marrow
Salt and pepper
3 oz. (75 g.) butter
1 large onion
½ lb. (250 g.) minced beef
4 large tomatoes
1 dessertspoon chopped marjoram
2 oz. (50 g.) boiled rice

COOKING TIME: 1 hour
OVEN TEMPERATURE: 190°C (375°F)
– gas mark 5

Cut the marrow, crossways, into 2 in. (50 mm.) slices. Remove the peel and scoop out the seeds with a teaspoon. Arrange the marrow rings in a single layer in a buttered ovenproof dish, and sprinkle them with salt and pepper.

Melt two-thirds of the butter in a pan and fry the finely chopped onion over moderate heat until soft. Crumble in the mince and continue frying until the mixture is brown and separated into grains.

Meanwhile, skin the tomatoes and chop the flesh roughly. Add to the pan, together with the finely chopped marjoram. Continue cooking until all the ingredients are well blended.

Bind this stuffing with as much of the boiled rice as it will absorb without becoming too solid. Season to taste with salt and pepper.

Spoon the stuffing into the marrow rings and dot with flakes of the remaining butter. Cover the dish tightly with a lid or foil and bake for 45 minutes.
Serving The rings make a complete meal with a hot tomato sauce.

————◇————

MARROW PURÉE

1 marrow – approx. 2 lb. (1 kg.)
Salt and pepper
2 oz. (50 g.) butter
4 tablespoons breadcrumbs
Nutmeg
3 tablespoons cream

COOKING TIME: 15–20 minutes

Cut the marrow into slices, remove the peel and seeds, and cut the flesh into chunks. Put the marrow into a pan of boiling, lightly salted water and cook for 10 minutes, or until tender. Drain the marrow thoroughly and mash with a potato masher, or put it through a vegetable mouli, to make a finer purée.

Melt half the butter in a pan and fry the breadcrumbs until golden-brown and crisp, and all the butter has been absorbed. Return the marrow purée to the pan and cook over low heat to evaporate any excess water.

Add the remaining butter and continue cooking, stirring all the time, until the purée has thickened. Blend in the buttered breadcrumbs and season to taste with salt, pepper and grated nutmeg. Stir in the cream.
Serving Serve with grilled or roast meat, or with baked fish.

Medlars

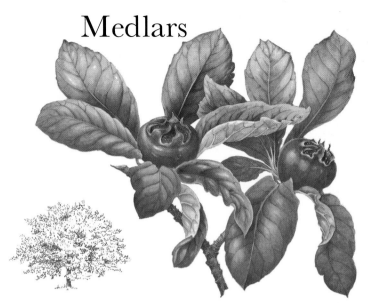

Medlars are somewhat out of fashion nowadays, and the trees are certainly too large for planting in most modern gardens. They attain a height and spread of about 15-20 ft (4.5–6 m.).

However, if you inherit one in a garden that you take over, or if you have a garden large enough to plant one, you will find the medlar a most attractive tree.

The branches are gnarled and twisted, and large pink or white flowers are borne in early summer. In autumn, the dull green leaves flare into brilliant colour.

Planning to grow a medlar

A well-drained loam suits medlars best. They need an open, sunny position, preferably with shelter from northerly and easterly winds.

Varieties Two varieties are generally available:

'Dutch': widely spreading branches; large fruits.

'Nottingham': branches are more erect; smaller, more richly flavoured fruits.

How to grow medlars

Buy a three or four-year-old standard or half-standard from a nursery. Plant it (see p. 42) in well-manured soil at any time between October and March, though the earlier the better. Support the tree with a stake.

Prune back the leaders of the main framework branches by half each winter for two years, then by a quarter for the next two years. Cut strong side-shoots to about 6 in. (150 mm.).

Mature trees require little or no pruning.

Pests and diseases Medlars are generally trouble-free.

Harvesting and storing

The fruits part easily from the tree in October or early November, and this is the time to pick them.

Gather the fruits on a dry day and store them, eye downwards, in a single layer in a cool place.

After three or four weeks, the colour of the fruits will deepen to dark brown, and they will become soft to the touch. They may then be eaten raw, or cooked.🌰🌰

AT-A-GLANCE TIMETABLE FOR MEDLARS

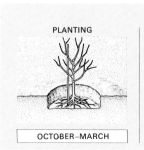

PLANTING

OCTOBER–MARCH

PRUNING TREES

OCTOBER–MARCH

HARVESTING

OCTOBER–NOVEMBER

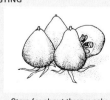

Store for about three weeks before eating

Preparing & cooking medlars

Medlars were popular after-dinner dessert fruits in Victorian days, their flavour often being complemented by a glass of port. But there are other ways of enjoying their distinctive taste.

Ripe medlars can be cut across and their soft flesh scraped out with a teaspoon, sweetened to taste with soft brown sugar and mixed with thick cream. Or try beating the fresh, sweetened pulp to a fine purée, and blending it with cream and cider, to make a delicious fool.

Medlars can also be roasted in the oven, like apples. Stick a whole clove in each cleaned fruit and set in a shallow, buttered, ovenproof dish. Bake in the oven at a temperature of 180°C (350°F) – gas mark 4 – for about 10 minutes, or until soft but not mushy. Serve lukewarm with a bowl of sugar and cream, or with a caramel or cider sauce.

Try using medlar sauce as a change from apple sauce with fatty meats, such as pork and goose. To make it, spoon the flesh from ripe medlars and cook to a pulp with very little water and 1–2 tablespoons of lemon juice. Simmer over low heat, stirring frequently until quite soft, then sweeten to taste with brown sugar and add a little ground cloves or cinnamon.

Medlar jelly provides a rose-coloured and distinctive accompaniment to game dishes. Make the jelly as for crab-apple jelly (see p. 322), letting the fruit cook for a fairly long time over low heat to extract all the juices.

Medlars need the addition of lemon juice to obtain a good set. Allow the juice and pared rind of 1 medium-size lemon to 1 lb. (500 g.) of medlars.

——◆◇◆——

MEDLAR FOOL

1½ lb. (750 g.) ripe medlars
4 oz. (100–125 g.) sugar
4 tablespoons sweet cider
5 fl. oz. (150 ml.) double cream

CHILLING TIME: 2 hours

Scrape the pulp from the medlars and beat into a smooth purée with a fork. Stir in the cider and sweeten to taste with the sugar.

Whip the cream lightly – but not too thick – fold it into the purée and spoon into glasses. Chill in the refrigerator for about 2 hours.

Serving Decorate with candied violets, or top with toasted hazelnuts.

Variation Instead of the cream, blend the purée with ½ pint (300 ml.) of rich custard sauce and chill in the refrigerator until set. A little cream can be piped over the top.

——◆◇◆——

Melons

Casaba melon

Cantaloupe melon

Melons are fairly easy to grow under cloches, in cold frames or in an unheated greenhouse, though results vary from year to year with the amount of sunshine. Most gardeners begrudge the amount of greenhouse space needed, so cloches and frames are the usual choice.

It is essential to choose a variety suited to cool conditions – not a hot-house melon.

Planning the crop

Melons require a warm situation and a moist, well-manured soil.

Whether you are growing them in a greenhouse border, in a frame or under cloches, prepare the ground well in advance by making up the soil from good-quality turves which have been stacked for at least four months. Do not use manure, as this tends to produce over-luxuriant growth.

How many to grow Three or four plants will yield about a dozen melons. It is a good idea to raise the plants in two batches so that they do not all ripen at the same time.

Varieties Two types of melon are grown in this country – cantaloupes, which are comparatively hardy and can be grown in frames; and casabas, which have larger fruits and are grown in greenhouses. Cantaloupes have more flavour than casabas.

Recommended varieties of cantaloupes include the orange-fleshed 'Charentais'; the green 'Ogen'; the F1 hybrid 'Sweetheart', with scarlet flesh; and the early-maturing 'Tiger', with orange flesh.

Fine, orange-fleshed varieties of casabas include 'Blenheim Orange', 'King George' and 'Superlative'; the green 'Emerald Gem', 'Honeydew' and 'Ringleader'; and the white-fleshed 'Hero of Lockinge'.

Growing melons under frames and cloches

While it is possible to sow seeds beneath cloches or a frame in late April or early May, results will be more reliable from an indoor sowing, with artificial heat, in mid-April.

Sow the seeds in 3 in. (75 mm.)

GROWING MELONS UNDER CLOCHES

PLANTING Water before removing the plant from its pot, to keep the soil intact. Plant with the soil-ball just above the surface.

PINCHING OUT Encourage fruit-bearing side-shoots to form by pinching out the tip when the plant has four or five leaves.

peat pots containing John Innes seed compost or a peat-based compost. Press a single seed edgeways into each pot $\frac{1}{2}$ in. (12 mm.) deep, water the pots well and enclose in a plastic bag. Leave in the airing cupboard, or near the heater in a greenhouse, until the seeds germinate.

To provide a succession, sow a second batch of seeds two or three weeks later.

When the seedlings appear, place them on a warm window-sill or near the glass in a greenhouse. Do not allow the roots to become cramped. Pot on, if necessary, into 8 in. (200 mm.) pots. Plant them out in frames or under cloches from the middle of May onwards. Place frames or cloches in position a fortnight before planting to warm the soil.

Set the plants 3 ft (1 m.) apart under cloches. Set one plant in the centre of an average-size garden frame or under a Dutch light.

Disturb the roots as little as possible when planting, and water the plants to ensure that they do not suffer a growth check. Plant so

that the top of the soil-ball is just above the surface. This will lessen the chances of collar rot.

As each plant develops four or five rough leaves – that is, excluding the original seed leaves – pinch out the growing point to encourage side-shoots to form.

In due course, select the four strongest shoots and pinch out any others that form. In a frame, direct these towards the corners; under cloches, train two in each direction.

Allow only one melon to form

on each shoot. Remove any other fruits that develop, leaving similar-size fruits on each shoot. Pinch out the tip of the shoot two leaves beyond the fruit.

Growing melons in a greenhouse

Different methods are needed for growing melons indoors, mainly because they require supporting. They are usually grown as double-stemmed cordons.

Sow in March if you are able to maintain a minimum temperature of 16°C (61°F) while the seedlings are growing. Otherwise wait until April, and sow as for frame or cloche crops. When the young plants have developed four or five leaves, transplant them to their final growing positions – either in the greenhouse border (in prepared stations, as already described) or in 9 in. (230 mm.) pots filled with John Innes No. 3 potting compost. Set the plants, or pots, 2$\frac{1}{2}$ ft (760 mm.) apart.

Insert two, eave-height canes, 10 in. (255 mm.) apart, alongside each plant. Fasten horizontal wires, using vine eyes, to the glazing bars on the side wall of the

TRAINING GREENHOUSE MELONS

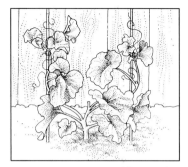

SECURING TWO LATERALS After removing the growing tip when 6 in. (150 mm.) high, train the two strongest side-growths to canes.

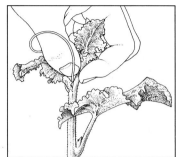

PINCHING OUT THE TIPS After training each pair of shoots up the canes and wires, pinch out when 5–6 ft (1.5–1.8 m.) long.

greenhouse and to the underside of the roof, at 12 in. (305 mm.) intervals. The eyes keep leaves from touching the glass.

Pinch out each plant's growing point when it is 6 in. (150 mm.) high. Pinch out all but the two strongest of the side-shoots that will then form; tie to the canes.

Continue tying-in the two shoots, first to the canes and then to the wires, until they are 5–6 ft (1.5–1.8 m.) long. At this stage, pinch out their growing points.

Laterals will develop from the

two stems as soon as the tops are pinched out. Tie these to the wires, and pinch out their tips when they have developed four or five leaves. Pollinate the flowers that grow on sub-laterals; remove flowers that grow on the main stems.

The aim is to produce four female flowers on each stem for simultaneous pollination.

Pollination Melons produce both male and female flowers, the latter being distinguished by the swelling of the embryo fruits

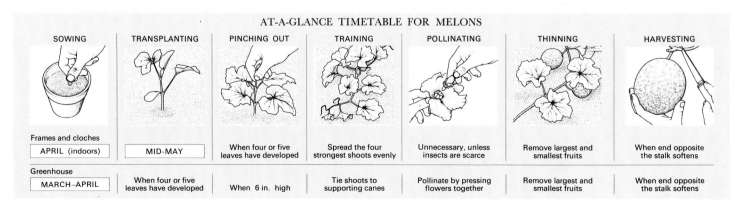

AT-A-GLANCE TIMETABLE FOR MELONS

	SOWING	TRANSPLANTING	PINCHING OUT	TRAINING	POLLINATING	THINNING	HARVESTING
Frames and cloches	APRIL (indoors)	MID-MAY	When four or five leaves have developed	Spread the four strongest shoots evenly	Unnecessary, unless insects are scarce	Remove largest and smallest fruits	When end opposite the stalk softens
Greenhouse	MARCH–APRIL	When four or five leaves have developed	When 6 in. high	Tie shoots to supporting canes	Pollinate by pressing flowers together	Remove largest and smallest fruits	When end opposite the stalk softens

ASSISTING POLLINATION

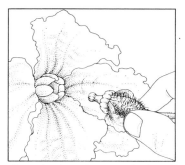

Because insects may be scarce under glass, aid pollination by pressing male flowers, after removing petals, to female flowers.

behind the blooms. In half-open frames or open-ended cloches, the chances are that bees or other insects will pollinate the plants. In enclosed greenhouses, however, or in cold weather, hand pollination is necessary.

When the young fruits begin to swell, remove the largest and the smallest, leaving only those of the same size on each plant. Any large fruit remaining will develop at the expense of the others.

Pests and diseases APHIDS (p. 282), GLASSHOUSE RED SPIDER MITES (p. 283) and GLASSHOUSE WHITE-FLY (p. 283) are the pests most likely to affect melons.

The chief diseases are CUCUMBER MOSAIC VIRUS (p. 287) and SOIL-BORNE DISEASES (p. 290).

Harvesting and storing

Cut melons from the stalks only when they are completely ripe. The best means of testing this is to press the end of the fruit furthest from the stalk. If the skin yields to the touch, the melon is ripe.

See also freezing (p. 294).

Preparing & serving melons

Cool, refreshing, ripe melons are equally suitable for a first course or a dessert course.

Casaba melons – most suitable for growing in greenhouses – are larger, firmer and have paler flesh than the cantaloupe melons grown in frames and under cloches. The latter are sweeter and for the most part have orange-yellow flesh.

Melon is usually served lightly chilled, but bear in mind that prolonged refrigeration destroys the delicate flavour. An hour's chilling before serving is sufficient.

Melons may be stored wrapped in plastic film in the refrigerator overnight, but some loss of flavour is inevitable.

Prepare a large melon for serving in sections by cutting it in half lengthways, and then cutting each half lengthways into segments. Scoop out the pips and loose fibres with a spoon. The skin may be left on, or the melon detached from it by running a sharp knife blade between flesh and skin, leaving the skin in position.

Small cantaloupe melons usually yield only two portions. Trim a narrow slice from both ends and cut the melon in half crossways. Scoop out the pips and fibres.

As either a first or last course, serve melon segments with sugar and a squeeze of lime or lemon juice. For a first course, melon also combines well with smoked meat. Or the flesh may be diced, and either tossed with cubes of mild cheese in a French dressing, or served on its own in mayonnaise sharpened with lemon juice.

For a dessert course, garnish melon segments with Maraschino cherries or finely chopped stem ginger. Fill half melons with soft fruits, sprinkled with liqueur or white wine.

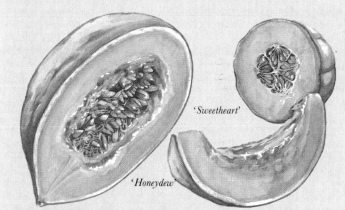

'Sweetheart'

'Honeydew'

Sliced melons, showing their distinctive flesh colour and characteristic shapes.

SAVOURY MELON BASKET

1 medium-size melon
4 sticks of celery
1 green pepper
3 oz. (75 g.) Emmenthal cheese
6 tablespoons olive oil
3 tablespoons vinegar
1½ teaspoons French mustard
Salt and pepper
Paprika

CHILLING TIME: 1 hour

Wash the melon and wipe it dry. Cut a narrow slice from the stalk end so that the melon will stand upright.

Mark the centre of the top of the melon, and make a vertical cut ½ in. (12 mm.) to the left of the centre and halfway down the melon. Make a similar cut ½ in. to the right of the centre, then cut each side horizontally, stopping at the vertical cuts.

Lift the two sections away, leaving the lower half of the melon with a handle 1 in. (25 mm.) wide. Scoop out the pips and fibres and remove the melon flesh with a small ball scoop, both from the basket and from the removed sections.

Scrub and dice the celery sticks. Remove the stalk end, seeds and membranes from the pepper and chop the flesh roughly. Dice the cheese; mix ingredients with the melon balls.

Make a French dressing from the oil, vinegar and mustard, and season to taste with salt and

pepper. Pour the dressing over the melon, celery, pepper and cheese and marinate in the refrigerator for about 1 hour.
Serving Drain the melon salad from the dressing and spoon it into the basket. Sprinkle with paprika and serve with brown bread and butter as a first course.

SWEET MELON BASKET

1 medium-size melon
1 lb. (500 g.) red currants
1 egg white
Caster sugar

CHILLING TIME: 1 hour

Wash and wipe the melon dry. Prepare a basket as described under Savoury Melon Basket, but without scooping out the melon flesh. Simply loosen it into large flakes with a spoon and add the sliced flesh from the removed sections. Chill for 1 hour.

Meanwhile, rinse the red currants in cold water and let them drain and dry thoroughly. Do not strip them from the stalks. Beat the egg white lightly and dip the currants in this; dredge them well with sugar and leave on a wire rack until dry.
Serving Fill the top of the melon basket with the frosted red currants, letting a few hang decoratively over the edge.
Photograph on pages 208–9.

Continued . . .

Melon recipes (continued)

MELON WITH COINTREAU

2 cantaloupes or 1 medium-size
  casaba melon
Caster sugar
1 miniature bottle of Cointreau

CHILLING TIME: 1 hour

Cut the melons in half, scoop out the pips and fibres and cut the flesh from the skin. Dice the melons and arrange in four serving bowls or glasses. Sprinkle with a little sugar – cantaloupe melons will need hardly any – and chill for 1 hour.
Serving Just before serving, spoon the Cointreau over the melon cubes.

MELON ITALIAN STYLE

1 small casaba melon
16 paper-thin slices of Italian salami
Small bunch of watercress
4 tablespoons olive oil
1½ tablespoons lemon juice
Salt and pepper

CHILLING TIME: 1 hour

Chill the ripe melon in the refrigerator for 1 hour before preparing it. Cut it in half lengthways, and cut each half into four long slices; scoop out the seeds and remove the skin. Arrange four slices of salami on each plate and set two melon slices on top.

Wash the watercress, remove any tough stalks and yellow leaves and set a few sprigs aside for garnishing. Shake the watercress dry in a salad shaker, or dry in absorbent paper.

Make a dressing from the oil and lemon juice, and season with salt and pepper. Pour this over the watercress in a sauce boat.
Serving Dressed watercress must be served as soon as it is made. Garnish the melon with the reserved watercress, and serve the dressing separately.
Photograph on pages 210–11.

MELON WITH RASPBERRIES

2 small casaba melons
½ lb. (250 g.) raspberries
4 tablespoons Cherry Heering
Icing sugar

CHILLING TIME: 1 hour

Put the melons in the refrigerator for about 1 hour before preparing and serving them.

Remove the melons from the refrigerator, cut them in half crossways and scoop out the seeds. Cut a slice from the base of each half melon so that it will stand upright, and arrange on individual plates. Fill the hollows with the cleaned, rinsed and drained raspberries, and spoon Cherry Heering over them.
Serving Just before serving, dust the raspberries lightly with sifted icing sugar.

Mint

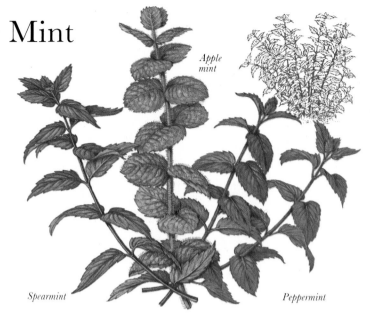

Apple mint

Spearmint

Peppermint

One of the features of this indispensable herb is the extraordinary range of flavours and scents provided by its many varieties. Ginger mint, spearmint, peppermint, Eau-de-Cologne mint, pineapple mint, bergamot mint and penny royal – the latter with an odour so pungent that it was said to drive fleas away – all of these were grown in the old-fashioned herb garden and several are still available today.

But the most important varieties to the modern housewife are those which, when freshly picked, are famed as accompaniments to a wide range of dishes, from roast lamb, new potatoes or young peas, to cream cheese sandwiches, jellies and chutneys.

The mint most often used in this context is the common green spearmint. However, the round-leaved apple mint, with its more subtle flavour, is also rapidly gaining popularity.

Both types – and, indeed, all mints – are grown in the same way and need the same conditions. The only difficulty lies not in obtaining a crop, but in preventing it from spreading to surrounding areas.

Planning the crop

A deep, moist soil in a semi-shaded position is generally advised; but, in fact, mint will grow almost anywhere, including damp, dark corners where few other plants would survive.

Mint may also be grown in a window-box.

If you grow mint in a herb or vegetable bed, sink an old, bottomless bucket or box into the soil and plant the roots inside. This will help to prevent them spreading.

How much to grow Mint grows rapidly, so three or four roots of your chosen variety should provide an ample supply for both cooking and storing.

Varieties Some of the more unusual varieties have already been mentioned, but it may be necessary to enquire at several nurseries or specialist herb farms to obtain a particular sort.

However, the two most commonly used in the kitchen – apple mint and spearmint – are readily available.

How to grow mint

Prepare the ground in February and dig a spadeful or two of well-rotted compost or manure into the planting site.

If possible, obtain a few roots in

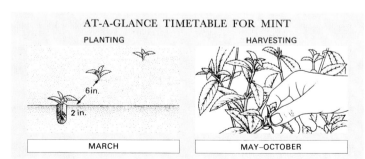

AT-A-GLANCE TIMETABLE FOR MINT

PLANTING | HARVESTING

6 in.
2 in.

MARCH | MAY–OCTOBER

March from a neighbour, and plant them 2 in. (50 mm.) deep and 6 in. (150 mm.) apart.

Alternatively, buy three or four potted plants from a nursery. Invert the pots and tap their edges on a table to remove the plants, then set them in the soil 6 in. (150 mm.) apart.

Whether growing from roots or plants, water the soil well to help get the mint established. Thereafter, it requires little attention other than ensuring that it does not spread beyond its allotted space in the herb bed.

Raising new plants Mint can be propagated from early spring to late autumn by digging up pieces of root or by taking cuttings of young shoots and re-planting them.

For a fresh supply of mint during the winter, place young plants or pieces of root in pots of potting compost in early October and stand them on the kitchen window-sill.

Pests and diseases Mint is seldom troubled by pests.

RUST (p. 290) is the most likely disease.

Harvesting and storing

Pick the fresh, green leaves at any time from May until early autumn.

A way to maintain a supply of mint sauce throughout the winter is to chop a bunch of leaves, place them in a jar and cover them with golden syrup. Take out a few teaspoonfuls as required and mix them with white vinegar.

See also drying (p. 343); freezing (p. 294) and vinegars (p. 342).

Cooking with mint

This most traditional of herbs in British cooking is associated with fresh summer vegetables, lamb and mutton, and salads. It has been of culinary importance for hundreds of years.

Gather the leaves while they are young and use them finely chopped for garnishing. Add whole sprigs when cooking new potatoes, young peas and carrots, beans and spinach; add sprigs to fruit and wine cups.

Iced mint tea, made by pouring boiling water over freshly gathered leaves, makes a refreshing summer drink.

A classic mint julep consists of a few mint leaves placed in a glass with crushed ice, a little sugar syrup and 2 tablespoons of whisky. Fill the glass with crushed ice, pour more whisky over the ice and decorate the glass with a sprig of mint.

Finely chopped mint gives additional flavour to salads and dressings, vegetable soups, cream and cottage cheeses, stewed fruit and apple sauces.

Use sugar-frosted mint leaves as an edible garnish with fresh summer fruits such as melon, peaches and apples. Brush small sprigs or individual mint leaves lightly with beaten egg white, dredge with caster sugar and leave to dry. Use the frosted leaves the same day.

MINT SAUCE

3 tablespoons chopped mint
1½ tablespoons caster sugar
5 fl. oz. (150 ml.) white wine vinegar

Sprinkle the mint with half the sugar and chop the leaves finely on a board. Put the mint in a bowl and add 2 tablespoons of boiling water, stirring until the sugar has dissolved. Add the vinegar gradually, with the remaining sugar.

Leave the sauce to rest for about 30 minutes before using. **Serving** This is the traditional sauce to accompany roast lamb.

MINT AND CUCUMBER SALAD

1 tablespoon finely chopped mint
1 cucumber
1 garlic clove
½ pint (300 ml.) natural yoghourt
½ teaspoon sea salt

CHILLING TIME: 30 minutes

Chop the freshly gathered mint finely. Wash and dry the cucumber; do not peel it, but grate coarsely and mix with the mint. Add the crushed garlic.

Stir the yoghourt with the sea salt and fold it into the mint and cucumber mixture. Chill in the refrigerator for 30 minutes. **Serving** This is a refreshing salad to serve with cold meat.

Mulberries

Mulberry trees were first planted in Britain at Syon House, Brentford, in 1548, and during the next two centuries were widely grown throughout the London area. Like their Far Eastern ancestors, they were grown not so much for their fruits as for their leaves, which are the sole food of silkworms.

The London silk-weaving industry was relatively short-lived, but many of the original trees survive to this day, including a number planted by James I in 1610 in the grounds of Buckingham Palace.

From this it will be gathered that the trees have a long life span and are consequently slow to mature. So unless you are growing them for posterity, or as a novelty, they do not warrant space in a small garden.

However, if you have room to spare, the mulberry is worth considering both for its fine appearance and for the abundance of its delicious fruits from which excellent jams and wines can be made.

Unless netting is used, birds may strip much of the crop.

Planning the crop

Mulberries will grow almost anywhere in Britain where there is a

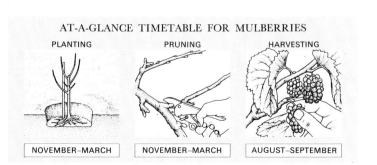

AT-A-GLANCE TIMETABLE FOR MULBERRIES

PLANTING — NOVEMBER–MARCH

PRUNING — NOVEMBER–MARCH

HARVESTING — AUGUST–SEPTEMBER

deep, moist soil, though in the north of England and in Scotland they will do better if protected by a south-facing wall.

They can be grown either as bushes or standard trees, the latter eventually achieving a height of 30 ft or more, which is a great deal too big for the average modern garden.

How many to grow Mulberries are self-fertile, and a single tree would be ample for most families.

Varieties There are two species, the black mulberry that produces fine, dark fruits, and the white type with pale fruits that are relatively tasteless.

When fed to silkworms, leaves of the white mulberry produce better silk than those of the black: but this is unlikely to concern gardeners today.

How to grow mulberries

The usual way to acquire a mulberry is by purchasing a young tree from a nursery in autumn or spring.

Plant it in an open, sunny position in well-manured ground, taking particular care not to damage the roots.

However, supplies are by no means plentiful and you may experience difficulty in finding a nursery which has young trees in stock.

The alternative is to take a cutting from a friend's tree in either autumn or early spring, preferably a 12 in. (305 mm.) cutting that has some older, two-year-old wood at the base. Plant the cutting deeply so that all but two or three buds are buried below ground.

Even longer branches can be rooted with a good chance of success, though any lateral branches should be trimmed off and about half the main branch buried.

Large branches can be planted in the position where the tree is to grow, but shorter cuttings are better grown in a nursery bed for a year or two until they are well rooted.

Avoid using any shoots which are growing from near the base of the tree. The more desirable black mulberry was sometimes grafted on to a white species, and the basal shoots may therefore be of the white sort.

Pruning Mulberries tend to bleed when cut, so avoid heavy pruning. It is necessary only to remove dead wood, or inward-growing branches that rub against their neighbours.

Pests and diseases Birds are fond of the ripe fruits, and may strip much of the crop unless the tree can be netted.

The principal disease of this tree is MULBERRY CANKER (p. 289).

Harvesting and storing

The best way to gather mulberries is to wait until the fruit ripens in late summer, then spread a cloth or large sheet of plastic beneath the branches and shake the tree gently.

Any unripe fruits can remain on the tree to be gathered later.

Mulberries may be eaten fresh, or used in cooked dishes.

See also bottling (p. 309); freezing (p. 294); fruit cheeses and butters (p. 323) and wine-making (p. 357).

Preparing & cooking mulberries

When the blood-red mulberries become ripe during August and September the fruits should be gathered and used as soon as possible. They may be used for jams but, as their pectin content is low, additional pectin stock is necessary.

The slightly acid, juicy berries may also be served as fresh dessert fruits with sugar and cream. Handle the berries as little as possible. Wash them if necessary, and remove calyces and damaged parts. Both berries and juice stain cloth badly, and the stains are almost impossible to remove.

Mulberry with junket was a popular dish in the 17th century. Today, a similar sweet is made by arranging layers of sweetened mulberries with layers of natural yoghourt in serving glasses, sprinkling the top with soft brown sugar and leaving them to chill until the sugar has melted.

All recipes for raspberries and loganberries are also suitable for mulberries, and they are excellent for fruit pies.

BAKED MULBERRIES

1 lb. (500 g.) mulberries
4 oz. (100–125 g.) sugar
1 pint (600 ml.) milk
½ vanilla pod
2 tablespoons caster sugar
4 egg yolks

COOKING TIME: 20 minutes
OVEN TEMPERATURE: 180°C (350°F) – gas mark 4

Pick over the mulberries, remove any damaged berries and place the remainder in a deep pie dish. Dredge with the sugar and bake in the oven for about 15–20 minutes, or until the juices are flowing.

Meanwhile, prepare a custard sauce. Heat the milk with the vanilla pod over gentle heat, but do not let it reach boiling point. Remove the pan from the heat, cover with a lid and leave to infuse for 10 minutes.

Remove the vanilla pod and stir in the caster sugar. Beat the egg yolks in a bowl and gradually whisk in the hot milk. Strain the mixture back into a pan or double saucepan and stir constantly over low heat until the custard thickens.

Serving Serve the baked mulberries lukewarm, straight from the dish, with a jug of the warm custard.

Variation Cream may replace the custard sauce.

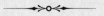

MULBERRY TANSY

1 lb. (500 g.) mulberries
2 oz. (50 g.) butter
4 oz. (100–125 g.) sugar
2 egg yolks
3 tablespoons fresh white breadcrumbs
5 fl. oz. (150 ml.) double cream

COOKING TIME: 20 minutes
CHILLING TIME: 1 hour

Melt the butter in a pan with 4 tablespoons of cold water. Add the mulberries, and cover the pan with a lid. Simmer over gentle heat for about 10 minutes, stirring occasionally, until the berries have burst and released their juice.

Rub the mulberries through a sieve and return the purée to the pan. Add sugar to taste and, if necessary, reduce the purée to a thicker consistency by rapid boiling.

Remove the pan from the heat and blend in the beaten egg yolks and the breadcrumbs. Return to a low heat, stirring constantly until the mulberry purée has thickened. Set aside to cool.

Whisk the cream lightly and fold it into the purée. Spoon the mixture into a serving dish and chill in the refrigerator for 1 hour.

Serving Whipped cream may be piped over the tansy before serving, and a few fresh mulberries used for decoration.

Mushrooms

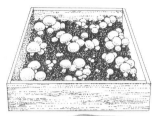

'*Mushroom*' *is a term used in the countryside to describe several wild, edible fungi, some of which are closely related to the familiar companion of liver and bacon. Most are obtainable only from meadows and woodlands; in fact, just a* single species, related to the common or field mushroom, is cultivated.

Not only is it a valuable commercial crop; it is also well worth growing by householders, for mushrooms are at their finest when eaten within a short time of picking. They can be grown indoors or out, so limited garden space need not be a problem.

In the wild, the common mushroom grows best in fields in which horses or cows have been kept, where it is greatly enriched by manure. A similar soil is required when growing it under less natural conditions, whether in a corner of the lawn, in frames, or in boxes tucked away at the back of a shed.

Soil preparation is the most critical part of mushroom growing, but even this labour can be avoided by buying one of the complete kits that include mushroom spores, the correct compost and a tub.

Planning the crop

Mushrooms grown outdoors require a shady corner of the lawn that has been enriched with very well-decayed manure or compost, yet contains no fungicides or weedkillers. The chief disadvantage of such a site is that cropping is rather uncertain and of limited duration, and it will not be possible to cut the grass once the mushrooms start to appear.

Indoors, mushrooms may be grown in any dimly lit corner of a shed, cellar or room where a fairly steady temperature of 10–13°C (50–55°F) is assured. It is necessary first to prepare the compost.

Use fresh, damp, strawy manure if possible, mix it thoroughly and pile it in a heap to generate heat.

After a week, turn the heap over and repeat the process every two or three days until the manure becomes crumbly and has lost its smell. It is then ready for use. Pack it firmly into open boxes or tubs to a depth of 10–12 in. (255–305 mm.).

If no manure is available, buy ready-mixed mushroom compost from a nursery or a commercial grower.

How much to grow Mushrooms tend to crop in flushes. Large quantities may spring up within a few days, while at other times only a few may appear.

Even so, a single box – say, 3 × 2 ft (1 m. × 610 mm.) – or one of the mushroom-growing kits, should be sufficient.

Varieties Only a single form of mushroom is grown – *Agaricus bisporus albida*. This may be creamy, off-white or flushed with brown. There is no difference in flavour, but the brown sort is less prone to disease.

How to grow mushrooms

To grow mushrooms outdoors, choose a warm, damp day

STAGES IN GROWING MUSHROOMS

PLANTING THE SPAWN Insert the pieces of spawn 2 in. (50 mm.) deep when the compost temperature falls to 24°C (75°F).

COVERING WITH SOIL Use subsoil, dug from 12 in. (305 mm.) below ground, to cover the compost ten days after planting the spawn.

between late spring and early autumn and lift small squares of turf about 2 in. (50 mm.) thick and 12 in. (305 mm.) apart.

Insert a walnut-size piece of spawn into each hole and replace the turf afterwards.

The best means of raising mushrooms in boxes is to wait until the natural heat of the decaying manure drops to a temperature of 24°C (75°F). When this occurs, insert the small pieces of spawn about 2 in. (50 mm.) deep into the compost, allowing 10 in. (255 mm.) between each piece.

Water the compost lightly, and within a few days the spawn will start to spread fine threads – the mycelium, or mushroom plant – throughout the box.

Ten days after planting, cover the compost with a layer of sterile subsoil to help maintain the temperature and to prevent loss of moisture. Mushrooms will generally appear about eight to ten weeks after planting, and will

continue to do so for some three months afterwards.

These methods do not apply to the kits sold by nurserymen. Each pack contains instructions.

Pests and diseases The larvae of various species of MUSHROOM FLY (p. 284) may tunnel into the stalks and caps, rendering the plants inedible.

A variety of MUSHROOM DISEASES (p. 289) may occur.

Harvesting and storing

Mushrooms taste best if cooked and eaten immediately after picking. If you want button mushrooms – which can be eaten raw – pick them just before the membrane between the cap and stalk separates to reveal the gills.

See also drying (p. 343); freezing (p. 294); pickling (p. 328) and sauces, ketchups and relishes (p. 339).

Recipes on next page

AT-A-GLANCE TIMETABLE FOR MUSHROOMS (INDOORS)

PLANTING SPAWN	COVERING COMPOST	HARVESTING

All year, subject to suitable temperature	Ten days after planting	From eight weeks after planting

Preparing & cooking mushrooms

A few hours after picking, mushrooms become limp and begin to sweat, with a subsequent loss of flavour. So use them fresh, and never store in the refrigerator.

Just a few mushrooms can add a special touch to the most ordinary dish. Serve them grilled or fried with breakfast bacon, sausages or kidneys; fold them into an omelette; or use as a savoury topping to scrambled eggs.

Add chopped, lightly fried mushrooms to a white sauce and serve with grilled fish or left-over chicken, or fold them into a brown sauce to go with roast lamb or beef, chops or steaks. Alternatively, blend chopped, sautéed mushrooms into forcemeat stuffing for a roasting or boiling chicken, for thick veal chops or crown of lamb.

Finely chopped mushrooms blended into softened butter make an attractive garnish to steaks and chops – as an alternative to grilled mushrooms – and to plain omelettes. They may also be used to enrich and flavour white sauces.

Prepare mushrooms for cooking, salads or garnishing by trimming away the dirty base of the stalks. Do not peel unless the edges are ragged or discoloured. Although mushrooms may be cleaned in cold water, less loss of flavour occurs if they are wiped with a clean cloth dipped in milk.

For grilling, mushrooms may be left whole and brushed with melted butter or oil. Grill under moderate heat for 6–8 minutes, turning them once.

Fry small whole or sliced mushrooms in butter over gentle heat for 3–5 minutes, and use them as a garnish. If large mushrooms are to be fried, either quarter them or cut them into narrow slices.

MUSHROOM AND BACON OMELETTE

½ lb. (250 g.) mushrooms
1 onion
2 oz. (50 g.) butter
6 thick bacon rashers
4 eggs
6 tablespoons milk
1 teaspoon cornflour
Salt and pepper
Garnish : chopped chives

COOKING TIME: 20 minutes

Trim the mushroom stalks, but do not remove them entirely. Wipe the caps and chop the mushrooms roughly. Peel the onion and chop it finely. Melt most of the butter in a pan and fry the mushrooms and onions lightly until soft, which will take about 5 minutes. Remove from the heat.

Cut the rind and gristle from the bacon rashers, cut them in half crossways, and fry in the remaining butter until crisp. Add the bacon and most of the fat to the mushroom and onion mixture.

Beat the eggs lightly with the milk, cornflour, salt and pepper. Pour this mixture over the mushrooms and bacon, return the pan to the heat and cook slowly until the eggs have set. While cooking, lift the edges occasionally with a knife to allow the liquid egg to run underneath.

Serving Sprinkle the top of the omelette with finely chopped chives and serve with crusty bread and butter.
Photograph on pages 206–7.

MUSHROOMS IN SOURED CREAM

1 lb. (500 g.) mushrooms
1 onion
1 garlic clove
2 oz. (50 g.) butter
1 tablespoon chopped parsley
1–2 tablespoons flour
4 fl. oz. (100–125 ml.) bouillon
Salt and pepper
2½ fl. oz. (75 ml.) soured cream

COOKING TIME: 20 minutes

Trim the mushrooms and wipe them clean. Cut them into quarters or thick slices. Peel the onion, chop it finely and peel and crush the garlic. Melt the butter in a pan and fry the onion and garlic for about 5 minutes, or until soft and transparent. Stir in the parsley and add the mushrooms.

Continue frying for 5 minutes over gentle heat, then stir in the flour and cook through.

Gradually add the bouillon, made from a stock cube, stirring all the time until the mixture thickens. Season to taste with salt and pepper, and cook for another 5 minutes. Stir in the soured cream and heat through, but do not boil.
Serving Pile on to hot buttered toast, or spoon into warm vol-au-vent cases, and serve as a first course or as a light snack.
Photograph on pages 212–13.

MUSHROOM SOUFFLÉ

1 lb. (500 g.) small mushrooms
2 shallots
2 oz. (50 g.) butter
Salt and paprika
1 tablespoon lemon juice
½ pint (300 ml.) thick white sauce
5 eggs

COOKING TIME: 1 hour
OVEN TEMPERATURE: 180°C (350°F) – gas mark 4

Trim and wipe the mushrooms, and chop them roughly. Peel the shallots and chop them finely. Melt the butter in a pan and fry the mushrooms and shallots lightly for 2 minutes. Season with salt, paprika and lemon juice.

Blend the mushrooms and shallots into the slightly cooled white sauce. Beat the eggs and fold them in thoroughly. Spoon the mixture into a buttered soufflé dish ; set this in a roasting pan of hot water and bake just above the centre of the oven for about 50 minutes, or until well risen and golden.
Serving Grilled bacon goes well with this light mushroom soufflé.

CREAM OF MUSHROOM SOUP

½ lb. (250 g.) mushrooms
1 small onion
1½ oz. (40 g.) butter
1 oz. (25 g.) flour
¾ pint (450 ml.) white stock
¾ pint (450 ml.) milk
Salt and pepper
1 egg yolk
2½ fl. oz. (75 ml.) double cream

COOKING TIME: 40 minutes

Trim the mushrooms and wipe them clean. Chop them roughly, including the stalks. Peel the onion and chop it finely. Melt the butter in a pan and cook the mushrooms and onions, covered, for 5 minutes. Lift out one-third of the mushrooms, set aside and keep them warm.

Stir the flour into the pan and gradually stir in the stock. Bring to the boil and simmer, covered, for about 25 minutes. Rub the soup through a sieve or blend it in the liquidiser.

Return the purée to the pan, stir in the milk and bring to the boil. Season to taste with salt and pepper and simmer for a further 5 minutes.

Beat the egg yolk with the cream, stir in a little of the hot soup and add the mixture to the pan. Heat through, but do not let the soup reach boiling point again.
Serving Pour the soup into individual bowls, and garnish with the reserved hot mushrooms.

Mustard and cress

Mustard   *Cress*

Pungent, spicy mustard and cress are quick-growing plants that are cut as seedlings for sandwiches and salads.

The cress seedlings add the peppery tang to the mixture – which is not to everybody's taste. If cress is to be sown, therefore, a much smaller quantity is needed than of the mustard – say, not more than a quarter of the total.

Plants grown in the garden become gritty, so normally they are sown indoors on dampened material such as peat, cottonwool or flannel.

However, the seeds may be sown on soil or seed compost if preferred.

How much to grow

A 1 oz. (25 g.) packet of mustard and a quarter of a 1 oz. packet of cress will be enough to sow four seed pans or plastic containers, each measuring about 6×4 in. (150×100 mm.). A pan of this size will produce enough for two salads or a substantial number of sandwiches. Stagger the sowings so that there is a constant supply.

Varieties Most seedsmen stock only one variety of mustard, White, and one of cress, Curled. Commercially, much of the crop sold as mustard is, in fact, rape.

How to grow mustard and cress

Place a layer of cottonwool, flannel or sacking in a seed tray or plastic container. Sow the cress first and the mustard three or four days later – either with the cress or in a separate tray – so that the crops mature at the same time.

Spread the seeds thickly and evenly on top of the material and press them down lightly. Sprinkle thoroughly with lukewarm water and cover the tray with brown paper or black polythene.

In winter, place the tray in a warm position in the house or in a heated greenhouse. A temperature of 10–16°C (50–61°F) is ideal. From spring to autumn, the tray can be placed under a cloche or in a cold frame.

Remove the cover when the seedlings are about 1½ in. (40 mm.) high, and allow a few days for them to green up and expand fully before cutting. Keep moist.

Pests and diseases Both mustard and cress are generally free from pests. DAMPING OFF (p. 287) is the principal disease risk.

Harvesting

Use scissors to cut the crop when the white stems are about 2 in. (50 mm.) long – about 11–14 days after sowing the cress. 🥬🥬

Serving mustard and cress

If the mustard and cress have been grown on a soil-less medium there is no need to wash or rinse them. If grown in soil, place the crop in a colander, rinse it under a fine spray of water and drain thoroughly.

Use mustard and cress as an ingredient in green and mixed salads, as a garnish sprinkled over grilled steaks, and over vegetables in cream sauces. Mustard and cress are also used with creamed soups and egg dishes, and with any pale savoury dish to which they would add welcome colour.

Mustard and cress are excellent sandwich fillings, either on their own or sprinkled on top of meat and fish-paste fillings.

AT-A-GLANCE TIMETABLE FOR MUSTARD AND CRESS

SOWING — Sow seeds on damp surface, then cover

UNCOVERING — Remove when seedlings are 1½ in. high

HARVESTING — About 11–14 days after sowing

New Zealand spinach : see **Spinach**

Nuts

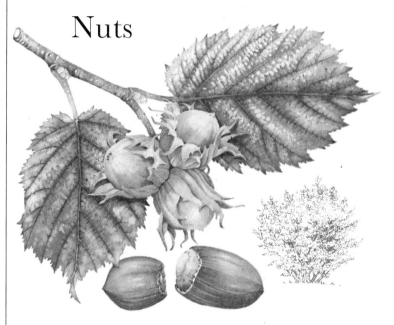

Hazel is the general name given in this country to trees of the genus Corylus, which includes cobnuts and filberts.

Somewhat confusingly, it is cobnuts that are most generally known as hazels, while one variety of filbert is called a Kentish Cob. However, this helps to emphasise the fact that the only differences between them are small variations in the shape and size of the nuts, and slight subtleties of flavour.

Even when grown as a bush, a hazel occupies a good deal of space; but if you have a large garden, it is well worth planting one both for its decorative value in spring, when the branches are covered with long, pale yellow catkins, and for the protein-rich nuts that ripen in September and October.

Unfortunately, squirrels are just as aware as humans that the nuts are excellent for winter storage. There is no simple defence against them.

Nut-lovers sometimes wonder whether they can hope to harvest almonds from their ornamental Prunus trees. However, in most years either frost damages the blossom or cool weather in summer prevents the formation of sweet, edible nuts.

When, in a good year, some edible nuts can be harvested, this should be regarded as a bonus. Almonds are not worth planting as part of a food-growing programme.

The same is true of walnuts, the

203

reason being the length of time before you can hope to harvest your first crop – fully 15 years – and the massive size of the mature tree.

However, if you take over a property with an established walnut tree you will have little to do beyond picking any nuts that escape the attention of squirrels.

How many trees to grow

Even if pruned into bush form, a mature hazel stands 6 ft (1.8 m.) high and has a spread of 12 ft (3.6 m.). Unless your garden is considerably larger than average, a single bush should be sufficient.

Where space is scarce, a well-pruned hazel makes an attractive specimen tree in a lawn.

Position and soil Hazels do equally well in open sun or partial shade; but grow them, if possible, in a position that is sheltered from the north and east winds.

Any well-drained soil is suitable, including chalky soils.

Varieties 'Cosford' (cobnut): large, smooth oval nuts in small husks; produces catkins freely; good pollinator.

'Pearson's Prolific' (cobnut):

early maturing and prolific; small, sweet, round nuts in hairy husks; a good pollinator for the filberts.

'Kentish Cob' (filbert): good flavour; large, long nuts; crops heavily when interplanted with a suitable pollinator, such as 'Pearson's Prolific'.

'Red Filbert' (filbert): one of the best-flavoured varieties; small, narrow nuts covered by reddish husks; poor catkin producer and needs a pollinator to crop heavily.

'White Filbert' (filbert): similar to 'Red Filbert', but lacking the red skin and with distinctive, pale green foliage.

How to grow hazels

A bush is the best form in which to grow a nut tree in the average-sized garden. Its main stem will have been pruned to 18 in. (455 mm.) at the nursery.

Plant the young bush in October or November. After planting, and for three or four subsequent autumns, reduce the previous season's wood by half, cutting back to an outward-pointing bud. This will build up the bush.

Cobnuts and filberts are self-fertile. Pollen from the male catkins, which are borne on twigs grown in the previous season, is

blown on to the tiny female flowers, which grow on shoots formed the previous year. To ensure that this fertilisation takes place, pruning on bushes that have begun flowering – generally when they are four or five years old – should be left until March.

Cut back shoots that have borne fruit the previous season to two or three buds to encourage renewed growth.

In August, cut out entirely all strong growth at the centre of the bush.

Remove all suckers at their point of origin.

Mulch the bush with decayed compost in autumn or spring.

Pests and diseases Hazelnuts are subject to attack by NUT WEEVIL (p. 284), and to damage caused by a number of caterpillars, including those of the WINTER MOTH (p. 285).

HONEY FUNGUS (p. 288) is the principal disease.

Harvesting and storing

Pick the nuts when they have turned brown. Put them in a warm place for a few days to dry out, then store them in containers in a cool place.

See also salting (p. 346).

AT-A-GLANCE TIMETABLE FOR HAZELNUTS

PLANTING	PRUNING	PRUNING	HARVESTING
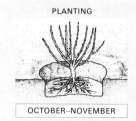			
OCTOBER–NOVEMBER	NOVEMBER	MARCH: AUGUST	SEPTEMBER–OCTOBER
	FIRST FOUR OR FIVE YEARS	SUBSEQUENT YEARS	

Preparing & cooking nuts

These small, sweet-tasting nuts are a traditional feature of the Christmas fruit basket. They are apt to dry out in their shells, but this can be prevented by storing them in layers of salt in air-tight jars (see Salting, p. 346).

Hazelnuts are used as a garnish, and also in making confectionery. The shelled nuts can be used with their brown skins intact, but for confectionery purposes the brown skins are removed.

This is done by spreading the nuts over a grill pan and setting them for a few minutes under a moderate heat. When the skins begin to split, rub them off between the fingers.

HAZELNUT TRUFFLES

2 oz. (50 g.) hazelnuts
2 oz. (50 g.) unsalted butter
4 oz. (100 g.) breakfast oats
4 oz. (100 g.) caster sugar
2–3 tablespoons chocolate or cocoa powder
Rum essence
3–4 tablespoons black coffee

Rub the skins off the nuts. Beat the butter until it is soft, and work in the oats, sugar and chocolate powder until well blended. Add a few drops of rum essence and enough coffee to bind the mixture without making it sticky.

Leave the mixture to firm slightly, then divide it into

small pieces and shape into round balls between the palms of the hands. Set a hazelnut on top of each ball and press down lightly, or chop the nuts finely and use them to coat the balls.

Use the truffles on the day they are made, or store them in a plastic box in the refrigerator for a few days.

SUGAR-COATED HAZELNUTS

4 oz. (100 g.) hazelnuts
4 oz. (100 g.) icing sugar
4 tablespoons water

COOKING TIME: 15 minutes

Rub the skins off the nuts. Put the nuts, sifted sugar and water in a heavy-based pan and boil rapidly, without stirring, for about 10 minutes until the water has evaporated. Reduce the heat and continue cooking until the sugar has caramelised to a golden-brown colour.

Pour the nuts on to an oiled baking sheet and separate them from each other with a fork. Leave to cool, then break the nuts apart with the caramel. Store in an air-tight tin.

SEASONAL COOKING

The following pages present a selection of dishes prepared from autumn and winter produce.
Spring and summer dishes are featured on pages 133–44.

Autumn dishes

Autumn vegetables : page 207

Autumn desserts : page 209

Autumn soups & salads : page 211

Warming soups are sure of a welcome on chilly autumn evenings. For economy, make them from lettuces that show signs of running to seed or from surplus, very ripe tomatoes.

More unusual is the green-gold soup made from sweet corn. If you would prefer it to have an extra 'bite', leave the corn kernels and leeks floating in it and thicken with egg yolks and cream.

The run-of-the-mill green side-salad can now give way to more substantial dishes. Try aubergines in a sweet and spicy sauce, or chilled melon with either salami or paper-thin slices of smoked pork fillet.

You can cut down on the meat bill by treating vegetables as the main ingredient rather than as an accompaniment. Both stuffed marrows and stuffed peppers need only small amounts of meat, yet they make good main dishes.

For quick meals, eggs and bacon combine well with a variety of vegetables, as in a mushroom omelette. For an autumn picnic, try golden onion flan.

Produce sold in the shops cannot compare with the flavour of freshly picked autumn fruits, whether you stick to old-time favourites – such as blackberry and apple pie, and Victoria plums in wine – or try more elaborate concoctions.

For a special occasion, fill melons with late-ripening red currants or autumn raspberries, or top a cheese-cake with poached blueberries.

Grapes, like apples and pears, are usual additions to the cheese-board, but as an original accompaniment to ham or baked fish try serving them with a sweet mayonnaise dressing.

For a change, too, emulate the American Thanksgiving Day offering with a traditional pumpkin pie – served on the fourth Thursday of November in that country.

Winter dishes

Winter vegetables : page 213

Winter desserts : page 215

Winter soups & salads : page 216

Vegetable soups will provide nourishing and economical fare throughout the winter. Ring the changes with Brussels sprouts, cauliflowers and spinach, using stock made from bones or a chicken carcase.

Served with crisp-fried bread cubes, diced bacon, or hot, crusty garlic bread, the soup will keep the family satisfied for hours.

Iron and vitamins, so essential in the winter diet, are readily available in kale, spinach and apples. So make plenty of crisp winter salads with mixed vegetables and fruit.

Brussels sprouts, the traditional vegetable with the Christmas turkey, are transformed by flavouring with chestnuts. When everyone is tired of cold turkey, the left-overs can be added to creamed sweet corn (taken from the freezer) and either piled on to slices of toast or folded into mushroom and soured cream and served in a vol-au-vent case.

January's depressing crop of household bills provides an extra incentive for making the most of garden produce. Satisfy winter appetites by serving large baked potatoes, topped with a knob of butter; or mix in some diced, left-over meat or fish.

There can be few more economical dishes than a leek flan, made without eggs or cream, or a mould of kale.

When it comes to sweets, the freezer and store cupboard afford plenty of scope. On a cold day, make up for a scant main course with a steaming black-currant pudding, an apple cake (still warm), or pears in cinnamon-flavoured syrup.

As a change from pies and crumbles, serve sliced apples wrapped in golden puff pastry. Use damsons to make an elegant charlotte set within sponge fingers, or make a mousse with loganberries.

1

2

3

Autumn vegetables

—◦—

→ 1 ←
**BAKED BEANS
AND MUSHROOMS**
recipe on page 96

→ 2 ←
BAKED MARROW
recipe on page 192

→ 3 ←
ONION QUICHE
recipe on page 220

→ 4 ←
**MUSHROOM AND
BACON OMELETTE**
recipe on page 202

→ 5 ←
STUFFED TOMATOES
recipe on page 274

→ 6 ←
COLD STUFFED PEPPERS
recipe on page 235

→ 7 ←
**CELERY CHEESE
SOUFFLÉ**
recipe on page 125

→ 8 ←
POTATO NESTS
recipe on page 242

—◦—

Autumn
desserts

—→●◆—

—→ 1 ←—
SWEET MELON BASKET
recipe on page 197

—→ 2 ←—
CROÛTES AUX POIRES
recipe on page 231

—→ 3 ←—
GRAPE SALAD
recipe on page 173

—→ 4 ←—
PLUMS IN RED WINE
recipe on page 238

—→ 5 ←—
BLACKBERRY AND
APPLE PIE
recipe on page 101

—→ 6 ←—
BLUEBERRY CHEESECAKE
recipe on page 103

—→ 7 ←—
FIGS WITH
ORANGE JUICE
recipe on page 163

—→ 8 ←—
PUMPKIN PIE
recipe on page 243

—→●◆—

1

2

3

4

5

Autumn soups & salad.

→ 1 ←
PEARS AND PEPPERS
WITH YOGHOURT
recipe on page 231

→ 2 ←
AUBERGINES
À LA GRECQUE
recipe on page 86

→ 3 ←
MELON ITALIAN STYLE
recipe on page 198

→ 4 ←
SPINACH SALAD
recipe on page 261

→ 5 ←
LETTUCE SOUP
recipe on page 186

→ 6 ←
PEPPERS AND
TUNA-FISH SALAD
recipe on page 235

→ 7 ←
CREAMED TOMATO SOUP
recipe on page 274

→ 8 ←
SWEET CORN AND
LEEK SOUP
recipe on page 269

Winter
vegetables

➤❯◦❮◄

➤ 1 ◄
BAKED POTATOES
recipe on page 241

➤ 2 ◄
FRENCH LEEK FLAN
recipe on page 182

➤ 3 ◄
STUFFED CABBAGE
recipe on page 112

➤ 4 ◄
BRUSSELS SPROUTS
WITH CHESTNUTS
recipe on page 108

➤ 5 ◄
SWEET-CORN TOASTS
recipe on page 269

➤ 6 ◄
MUSHROOMS IN
SOURED CREAM
recipe on page 202

➤ 7 ◄
CHICORY IN HAM CASES
recipe on page 131

➤ 8 ◄
TIMBALE OF KALE
recipe on page 177

➤❯◦❮◄

Winter desserts

➤◦◄

➤ **1** ◄
APPLE PUFFS
recipe on page 73

➤ **2** ◄
DANISH APPLE CAKE
recipe on page 72

➤ **3** ◄
APRICOT COMPÔTE
recipe on page 77

➤ **4** ◄
BLACK-CURRANT PUDDING
recipe on page 153

➤ **5** ◄
DAMSON CHARLOTTE
recipe on page 157

➤ **6** ◄
RHUBARB AND BANANA FOOL
recipe on page 250

➤ **7** ◄
LOGANBERRY MOUSSE
recipe on page 188

➤ **8** ◄
CINNAMON PEARS
recipe on page 231

➤◦◄

Winter soups & salads

—◦—

→ 1 ←
APPLE SALAD
recipe on page 73

→ 2 ←
CHICORY AND
GRAPEFRUIT SALAD
recipe on page 131

→ 3 ←
HARICOT-BEAN SALAD
recipe on page 93

→ 4 ←
BRUSSELS-SPROUTS
SOUP
recipe on page 107

→ 5 ←
CREAM OF
SPINACH SOUP
recipe on page 261

→ 6 ←
CAULIFLOWER SOUP
recipe on page 120

→ 7 ←
GARLIC BREAD
recipe on page 164

—◦—

Onions

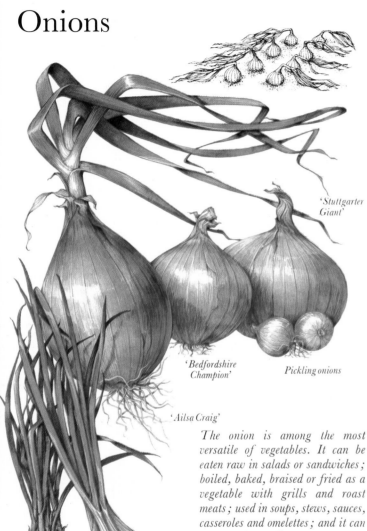

'Stuttgarter Giant'

'Bedfordshire Champion'

Pickling onions

'Ailsa Craig'

The onion is among the most versatile of vegetables. It can be eaten raw in salads or sandwiches; boiled, baked, braised or fried as a vegetable with grills and roast meats; used in soups, stews, sauces, casseroles and omelettes; and it can be pickled or used in chutneys.

Onions are essential to so many recipes that the gardener faces a challenge in trying to keep up with all the demands from the kitchen. However, most of these may be met by careful planning, and by planting the right varieties of onions at the right time.

Welsh onions   Spring onions

Apart from onions grown specially for salads and pickling, there are four groups grown from seed:

Japanese varieties Sow these in August in their permanent bed for harvesting the following June.

August-sown varieties The bulbs are larger than those of the Japanese varieties. Sow the seeds in August, transplant the seedlings to their permanent bed in spring, and pull and store the bulbs in August.

January-sown varieties Germinate under glass and transplant to the permanent bed for an autumn crop.

Spring-sown varieties Sow directly in the permanent bed for harvesting in September. They will keep well into the following spring.

In addition to onions grown from seed, onion sets – immature bulbs ripened during the previous summer – may be planted in April to produce an autumn crop to ripen at the same time as the January-sown varieties. Onion sets are sold by seed merchants and garden centres.

Planning the crop

Onions need a site in full sun, and do best on light, deep loam which – for maincrop varieties – has been well manured. Dig the plot deeply in the autumn, even as early as mid-September, and work in two buckets of well-rotted manure or compost per square yard.

Spring onions, pickling onions and Welsh onions will grow satisfactorily on any fertile, well-drained soil.

Onions of all types grow best in firm ground, so prepare the bed well in advance to give it a chance to settle.

In February give a dressing of 4 oz. of bonemeal and 2 oz. of sulphate of potash per square yard (120 g. and 60 g. per square metre).

Alternatively, rake in 3 oz. (90 g.) of general fertiliser before sowing or planting.

How many to grow A bed 30 × 3 ft (9 × 1 m.) should produce about 100 onions weighing at least 25 lb. (12 kg.); but with good feeding and care the yield may be twice as great.

This applies to both onions grown from seeds and to those grown from sets.

If sown in succession, rows of spring onions only a few feet long should keep the family supplied.

The number of pickling onions to grow is very much a matter of taste. A 10 ft (3 m.) row will yield 100–150 small onions.

Varieties These first four groups, comprising maincrop onions, are described in the order that the bulbs will ripen:
Japanese varieties:

'Express Yellow': dark yellow skin; quicker maturing than 'Kaizuka'.

'Kaizuka Extra Early': flat, pale yellow bulbs.
For August sowing:

'Hygro': high yielding; globe shaped; good keeper.

'Reliance': large and mild flavoured; good keeper.

'Ailsa Craig': large, globe-shaped bulbs; mild flavour.
For January sowing under glass:

'Superba' (F1 hybrid): one of the largest varieties; golden and globe shaped; good for storing.
For spring sowing:

'Bedfordshire Champion': large, globe shaped; heavy cropper; good keeper.

'Dura': medium sized; keeps for an exceptionally long time.

'Hyduro': golden skin; heavy cropper; good keeper.
Onion sets:

'Dobies' All-Rounder': round and thin necked; long keeping.

'Sturon': heavy cropper; large, round bulbs; good keeper.

'Stuttgarter Giant': resistant to bolting; long keeping.

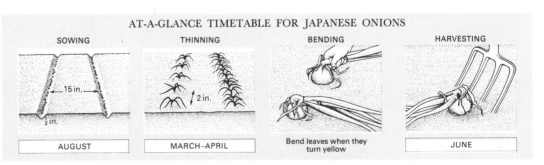

AT-A-GLANCE TIMETABLE FOR JAPANESE ONIONS

SOWING	THINNING	BENDING	HARVESTING
15 in. / 1 in.	2 in.	Bend leaves when they turn yellow	
AUGUST	MARCH–APRIL		JUNE

Spring onions:
  'White Lisbon': quick growing; mild flavour.
Pickling onions:
  'Paris Silver Skin': very quick growing; early ripening.

How to grow onions

It is important to choose a sowing date and method of cultivation suited to the type of onion you are growing.

Japanese varieties Sow from the middle to the end of August in drills ½ in. (12 mm.) deep, with the rows 15 in. (380 mm.) apart, in the prepared permanent bed.

Do not transplant, but in the spring thin to 2 in. (50 mm.) apart. Water in dry spells, and hoe frequently to keep down the weeds until the bulbs are ready for pulling in June. Use them to fill the period before maincrop varieties ripen.

August sowing (maincrop) In the middle of the month prepare a seed bed on well-drained soil which has been raked to a fine tilth. Sow the seeds fairly thickly in

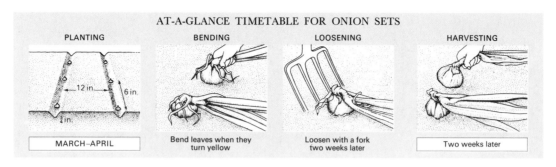

AT-A-GLANCE TIMETABLE FOR ONION SETS

PLANTING — 12 in. — 6 in. — ½ in. — MARCH–APRIL
BENDING — Bend leaves when they turn yellow
LOOSENING — Loosen with a fork two weeks later
HARVESTING — Two weeks later

drills ½ in. (12 mm.) deep and 9 in. (230 mm.) apart.

In the following March, as soon as the soil can be worked easily, transplant the seedlings to the prepared permanent bed. The bed must be firm, and on light soils it is helpful to tread it before raking, or to firm it with a roller.

Use a trowel to plant the seedlings, leaving about ½ in. (12 mm.) of white stem covered with soil. Space the seedlings 6 in. (150 mm.) apart in rows 12 in. (305 mm.) apart.

Keep the plants watered, and hoe regularly between the rows.

Hand-weed between the onions in the rows.

January sowing (maincrop) Sow in pans or pots of seed compost. Firm the compost level ½ in. (12 mm.) from the top of the container. Dust the surface with lime to make the seeds easier to see, and sow them at 1 in. (25 mm.) spacings.

Press each seed just under the surface with the point of a pencil, or tap the side of the pan so that the seeds settle into the compost. Sift a little compost over them and water through the fine rose of a can, or with a sprayer.

Cover with glass, then a folded sheet of newspaper, and place in a cold greenhouse, a cold frame or under cloches. Remove the newspaper as soon as the seeds germinate, and take off the glass before the seedlings reach it.

Harden off the seedlings (see p. 34) in mid-March and plant out in April. Treat them in the same way as August-sown seedlings.

Spring sowing (maincrop) Sow the seeds directly into the prepared permanent bed in March, or as soon as the soil can be raked to a fine tilth. Sow ½ in. (12 mm.) deep in drills 12 in. (305 mm.) apart.

When the seedlings are 2 in. (50 mm.) high, thin them to 1 in. (25 mm.) apart. When they are 4–6 in. (100–150 mm.) high, thin them again to 4 in. apart. Use the thinnings in salads.

Lift the bulbs in late September for storing.

Onion sets Plant the sets in the prepared permanent bed in March or April. Make drills about ¾ in. (20 mm.) deep and 12 in. (305 mm.) apart. Space the bulbs 6 in. (150 mm.) apart in the drills, and cover with soil so that only the tips are showing.

Firm the soil and cover the bed with netting to prevent birds from lifting them out. Check frequently and replace any bulbs which have been forced out of the soil as the roots grow.

Cultivate as for August-sown onions.

Spring or salad onions Thinnings of maincrop onions can be used when they are about 4–6 in. (100–150 mm.) high for salads, but for a regular supply it is better to grow the mild, quick-growing variety called 'White Lisbon'.

Sow the seeds thinly in a ½ in. (12 mm.) drill in September for the first crop to be pulled during the spring. In February, a second sowing can be made in a cold frame or under cloches for pulling in June. There is no need to thin the crop.

Further sowings can be made at four-weekly intervals from March to early July to provide a constant supply through the summer and autumn.

Pull the onions when they are about 6 in. (150 mm.) high. Any left-overs that start to form bulbs can be left for pickling.

Onions for pickling Pickling

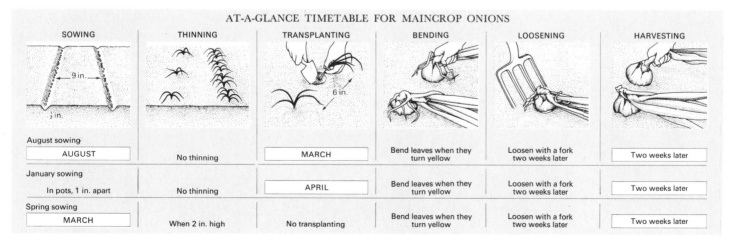

AT-A-GLANCE TIMETABLE FOR MAINCROP ONIONS

	SOWING	THINNING	TRANSPLANTING	BENDING	LOOSENING	HARVESTING
August sowing	AUGUST	No thinning	MARCH	Bend leaves when they turn yellow	Loosen with a fork two weeks later	Two weeks later
January sowing	In pots, 1 in. apart	No thinning	APRIL	Bend leaves when they turn yellow	Loosen with a fork two weeks later	Two weeks later
Spring sowing	MARCH	When 2 in. high	No transplanting	Bend leaves when they turn yellow	Loosen with a fork two weeks later	Two weeks later

onions do best on light soil that has not recently been manured, as it is necessary to keep them small. If the soil is very fertile, sow the seeds more thickly than usual. Sow the seeds in March or April in a bed raked to a fine tilth. Either scatter the seeds, or sow them ½ in. (12 mm.) deep in drills 6–8 in. (150–200 mm.) apart.

Little thinning is necessary, provided the plants have space to form small bulbs, and the crop will be ready for pulling in July.

Welsh onions These hardy, non-bulbous perennials, also known as ciboules or green onions, grow to a height of 12 in. (305 mm.) and resemble multi-stemmed salad onions.

The pencil-thick shoots grow together in close tufts. The shoots are used as salad onions, and the leaves in the same way as chives (see p. 132).

Prepare the ground as for maincrop onions and sow from February to May where the plants are to mature, thinning to give 10 in. (255 mm.) spacings between the plants. Lift and divide the clumps every three years.

Pests and diseases Pests which may attack plants of the onion family include ONION EELWORM (p. 284) and ONION FLY (p. 284).

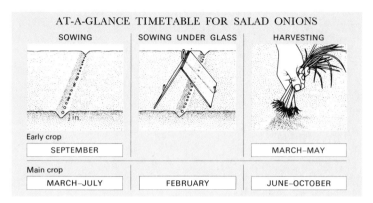

AT-A-GLANCE TIMETABLE FOR SALAD ONIONS

SOWING	SOWING UNDER GLASS	HARVESTING
Early crop SEPTEMBER		MARCH–MAY
Main crop MARCH–JULY	FEBRUARY	JUNE–OCTOBER

Diseases include DOWNY MILDEW (p. 288), NECK ROT (p. 289) and WHITE ROT (p. 291).

Harvesting and storing maincrop onions

When the outer leaves begin to turn yellow, bend over the tops to encourage early ripening. Two weeks later, push a fork underneath the bulbs to loosen the roots.

After another fortnight – or sooner if the weather is particularly wet and the onions show any sign of splitting – lift the bulbs and spread them out in a greenhouse or shed to ripen fully. This will take some days – or even weeks with large bulbs. Complete the ripening in a cool, dry place.

At all stages handle bulbs carefully to avoid the risk of bruising. Do not trim off the withered tops at this stage, as they will be needed if you string the onions.

To store, secure the onions one above the other to a length of rope and hang them in a cool, dry place. Alternatively, hang them in bags of nylon or string netting.

STORING ONIONS

When they are completely dry, bind the onions to a length of rope. Start at the base; trim off surplus leaves afterwards.

AT-A-GLANCE TIMETABLE FOR PICKLING ONIONS

SOWING	THINNING	HARVESTING
MARCH–APRIL	Only if plants need space to develop	JULY

Preparing & cooking onions

Onions have been used as a flavouring in cooking since earliest times, being gathered in the wild long before the development of the first kitchen gardens. Today's ploughman's lunch is simply a version of the farmworker's traditional midday meal, which for long consisted of a hunk of coarse bread, a couple of onions and a mug of weak ale – plus a lump of cheese when times were favourable.

As a flavouring, onion is invaluable in stocks and soups, casseroles and sauces. Shallow or deep-fried, it does duty as an edible garnish; raw and finely chopped, it adds a crunchy texture and flavour to tomato and green salads and to sandwich fillings.

Onions are also excellent as an accompanying vegetable, either boiled and served in a white or cheese sauce, or glazed and sprinkled with parsley. They may be served as a first course – stuffed or baked – or used in flans and pies they make excellent main courses.

To prepare onions for cooking, cut off the upper part with the stalk attached. Trim off the roots, but do not remove the root base entirely as this holds the onion together, making slicing and chopping easier. Peel off the dry, outer layers of skin.

To slice an onion, lay it on its side and make a series of close cuts, starting at the neck end. Discard the root end when the onion has been sliced.

For chopping, first cut the onion into halves, from neck to root base, and then cut each half into thin vertical slices. Finish each cut just short of the root base, so that the onion does not disintegrate.

Place the sliced halves, cut sides down, on a chopping board and cut down across the previous cuts. To dice an onion or chop it finely, cut a third time across the

Continued ...

PREPARING ONIONS

TOPPING AND TAILING Cut off the stem and also the root end.   *SLICING Cut the onion crossways into slices with a sharp knife.*   *CHOPPING Cut the onion lengthways first, then cut again crossways.*

Onion recipes (continued)

two sets of cuts made previously.

If the fumes worry you excessively, work with your hands and the onions immersed in water.

Clean salad onions by trimming the green stalks to just above the white part, trimming off the roots and peeling off the thin, outer layer.

It is advisable to keep a special chopping board for onions, as the flavour may otherwise be passed on to other foods.

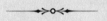

ONION SAUCE

1 large onion
1½ tablespoons butter
2 tablespoons flour
½ pint (300 ml.) milk
Salt and pepper

COOKING TIME: 15 minutes

Peel the onion and chop it finely. Melt the butter in a heavy-based pan and fry the onion over gentle heat for about 5 minutes, or until soft but not coloured. Blend in the flour; cook for a few minutes, then gradually blend in the milk.

Stir continuously until the sauce thickens and is free of lumps. Season to taste with salt and pepper, and simmer gently for 5 minutes.
Serving This is the traditional sauce to serve with tripe, and it is also excellent with mutton and fried herrings.

CREAM OF ONION SOUP

1 lb. (500 g.) onions
2 oz. (50 g.) butter
2 tablespoons flour
2 pints (1 l.) white stock
Salt and pepper
2½ fl. oz. (75 ml.) dry white wine
2½ fl. oz. (75 ml.) double cream
Garnish : 1 tablespoon chopped chives ;
   1 tablespoon chopped dill

COOKING TIME: 50 minutes

Peel the onions and chop roughly. Melt the butter in a pan and cook the onions for 5–10 minutes, or until soft and transparent. Stir in the flour and cook through for 2 minutes. Gradually stir in the stock, bring to boiling point, then simmer for about 25 minutes or until the onions are tender.

Blend the soup in a liquidiser or rub through a sieve. Re-heat the soup and season to taste with salt and pepper. Stir in the wine and simmer the soup for a further 10 minutes, then add the cream and heat through without boiling.
Serving Pour into soup bowls and garnish with the mixed, finely chopped herbs.
Variations Creamed onions, to serve as an accompanying vegetable, are made by boiling button-size onions until tender, then folding them into a white sauce flavoured with mustard. They may also be spooned into an ovenproof dish, topped with grated cheese or breadcrumbs and baked until bubbling and brown.

ONION DOLMAS

6 large onions
Salt and pepper
1 tablespoon breadcrumbs
5 fl. oz. (150 ml.) milk or cream
½ lb. (250 g.) minced veal
½ lb. (250 g.) lean minced pork
1 tablespoon tomato purée
1 teaspoon basil
1 oz. (25 g.) butter

COOKING TIME: 40 minutes
OVEN TEMPERATURE: 220°C (425°F) –
gas mark 7

Peel the onions and leave the root bases intact. Put them in a pan of boiling, lightly salted water and simmer for 10 minutes. Leave the onions in a colander to drain and cool, then carefully peel off the outer layers, keeping them intact.

Meanwhile, steep the breadcrumbs in the milk or cream and mix them gradually into the minced veal and pork, blending in the tomato purée and basil. Beat this stuffing until well combined, so that it remains elastic and not too firm. Season to taste.

Spoon some stuffing over each onion layer, fold the edges over, and place in a well-buttered ovenproof dish, seam downwards. Bake the onion parcels in the oven for 30 minutes, basting occasionally with a little of the reserved onion water.
Serving These dolmas may be served hot or cold as a substantial first course, or hot as a main course with buttered rice and a salad.

ONIONS WITH FORCEMEAT

4–6 large onions
2 oz. (50 g.) butter
6 oz. (175 g.) minced veal
3 slices white bread
Milk
1 tablespoon finely chopped parsley
2 egg yolks
Salt and pepper
Breadcrumbs

COOKING TIME: 1 hour
OVEN TEMPERATURE: 190°C (375°F)
– gas mark 5

Peel the onions and cut a slice off the top of each. Use a teaspoon to scoop out most of the inside, leaving an unbroken shell about ¼ in. (5 mm.) thick. Chop the removed onion finely, and fry lightly in half the butter until it is soft but not brown. Mix the fried onions into the minced veal and add the crustless bread, soaked in a little milk and squeezed dry.

Combine these stuffing ingredients thoroughly, blend in the parsley and bind the stuffing with the lightly beaten egg yolks. Season to taste with salt and pepper.

Spoon the stuffing into the onions and set them in a well-buttered ovenproof dish. Sprinkle the top of each with breadcrumbs, top with a knob of butter and bake in the oven for about 1 hour, or until the onions are tender.

Baste frequently with melted butter.

Serving Onions stuffed in this fashion can be served as a complete meal, with crusty bread and hunks of cheese.
Variations Use minced beef instead of veal, or substitute finely chopped mushrooms for half of the veal.

ONION QUICHE

1 lb. (500 g.) onions
2 oz. (50 g.) butter
6 oz. (175 g.) shortcrust pastry
3 eggs
½ pint (300 ml.) soured cream
3 tablespoons dry white wine
Salt and pepper
1 tablespoon chopped basil
4 bacon rashers

COOKING TIME: 1¼ hours
OVEN TEMPERATURE: 200°C (400°F) –
gas mark 6

Trim the roots and tops from the onions, then peel them and cut into slices. Melt the butter in a pan, add the onions and sprinkle lightly with salt and pepper. Cover the pan with a tight-fitting lid and cook the onions over low heat for about 30 minutes, until they are soft and golden but not brown. Drain the onions through a colander and set them aside to cool.

Meanwhile, prepare the shortcrust pastry made from 6 oz. (175 g.) flour. Roll it out and use to line an 8 in. (200 mm.) flan ring set on a baking sheet. Chill the pastry in the refrigerator while making the filling.

Beat the eggs lightly and season with salt and pepper. Beat in the wine, soured cream and finely chopped basil, and finally fold in the drained onions.

Spoon this filling into the chilled flan case; lay the bacon rashers in a criss-cross pattern over the top. Bake in the oven for about 40 minutes, or until the top of the filling is set and firm.
Serving This quiche can be served hot or cold as a main course, accompanied with a green or tomato salad.
Photograph on pages 206–7.

———◆○◆———

GLAZED ONIONS

1 lb. (500 g.) button onions
1 oz. (25 g.) sugar
2 oz. (50 g.) butter

COOKING TIME: 10–15 minutes

Bring a pan of water to the boil, drop in the unpeeled onions and bring back to the boil. Simmer for 5–7 minutes, then drain and peel the onions. Rinse under cold water and leave to drain.

Heat a heavy-based pan, add the sugar and let it melt and bubble without stirring until light brown, then stir in the butter. Add the onions and toss them gently in the caramel for 5–6 minutes, or until evenly coated and glazed.
Serving Glazed onions make an attractive, edible garnish to roast meats and game.

STUFFED ONIONS

4 large onions
4 oz. (100 g.) butter
4 oz. (100 g.) lean, cooked ham
2 tablespoons tomato purée
2 oz. (50 g.) grated Cheddar cheese
Salt, pepper, cayenne
Water or bouillon
5 fl. oz. (150 ml.) soured cream

COOKING TIME: 1 hour 10 minutes
OVEN TEMPERATURE: 190°C (375°F) – gas mark 5

Peel the onions, cut a slice off the top of each and set these aside. Scoop out most of the centres of the onions and chop finely. Melt a quarter of the butter in a pan and fry the onions over gentle heat until soft and golden, which will take 8–10 minutes. Remove from the pan.

Mince the ham or chop it finely. Blend it with the onions, the tomato purée and the grated cheese. Season this stuffing with salt, pepper and cayenne to taste, and bind with 1–2 tablespoons of bouillon or water. Spoon the stuffing into the onions, replace the lids and tie the onions with soft string. Set in a well-buttered fireproof dish and pour the remaining butter over the onions. Bake in the oven for 1 hour. After 30 minutes, spoon the soured cream over the onions.
Serving Remove the string from the onions and serve as a main course, with sauté potatoes and the reduced pan juices.

Parsley

Parsley had widely different reputations among the ancient Greeks and the Romans.

At banquets, the Greeks wore sprigs of parsley on their heads in the belief that it created both gaiety and a good appetite. The Romans, however, planted it on graves. This association with death persisted until the Middle Ages, and people believed that to transplant parsley invited death and crop failure.

Today, parsley is widely used for garnishing hot and cold dishes and for flavouring sauces and stuffings. It is also an essential ingredient in fines herbes and a bouquet garni.

Although a biennial, parsley is best grown as an annual, since fewer and smaller leaves will be produced on the flowering stems during the second year. To ensure a constant supply, make two sowings – one in March for summer and autumn use, and another in July for winter and spring.

Parsley can also be grown in a pot indoors for winter use (see p. 29).

In the garden, parsley need not take up space in the vegetable plot.

Instead, it can form an edging to a path or add an attractive splash of greenery to a flower border.

Planning the crop

Parsley needs a well-drained, fertile soil in a sunny or partly shaded position. Prepare the soil by working in a moderate dressing of well-rotted compost or manure during the previous winter.

Grow the winter crop in a sheltered, south-facing position.

How much to grow Since parsley is a cut-and-come-again herb, about six plants will give an adequate and constant supply.

Varieties Well-flavoured varieties with tightly curled, bright green sprigs, include the following: 'Champion Moss Curled'; 'Dobies Perfection'; 'Imperial' and 'Suttons Curly Top'.

How to grow parsley

Sow in drills $\frac{1}{4}$ in. (5 mm.) deep where the plants are to grow. The seed is slow to germinate – sometimes taking up to five weeks – so help germination by watering through a fine rose to keep the soil

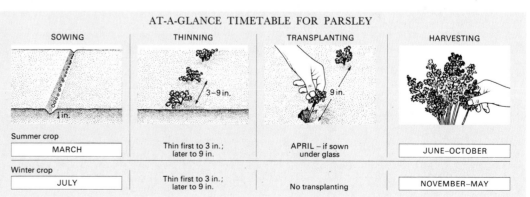

AT-A-GLANCE TIMETABLE FOR PARSLEY

SOWING	THINNING	TRANSPLANTING	HARVESTING
1 in.	3–9 in.	9 in.	
Summer crop	Thin first to 3 in.; later to 9 in.	APRIL – if sown under glass	
MARCH			**JUNE–OCTOBER**
Winter crop	Thin first to 3 in.; later to 9 in.	No transplanting	
JULY			**NOVEMBER–MAY**

moist until the seedlings appear.

To mark the rows, so that weed seedlings growing on either side can be identified and removed even before the parsley germinates, mix a few lettuce or radish seeds with those of the parsley. The seedlings of these crops will generally appear within a week.

When the seedlings are large enough to handle, first thin to 3 in. (75 mm.) apart; then, when they are well established, thin them again to 9 in. (230 mm.).

If the weather in early spring is severe, sow the seeds in a box of seed compost and place in a cold greenhouse, frame or cloche. Plant the seedlings outside, 9 in. (230 mm.) apart, in April.

Provide partial shade for July-sown seeds and seedlings, keeping the ground moist to encourage germination and growth. In cold districts, cover the summer-sown parsley with cloches to encourage continued growth during the winter, or transfer one or two plants to pots for growing indoors.

Pests and diseases Parsley is occasionally attacked by APHIDS (p. 282) and the CARROT FLY (p. 282).

It is also susceptible to LEAF SPOT (p. 288) and to certain VIRUS DISEASES (p. 291).

Harvesting and storing

Cut only one or two sprigs at a time from each plant until the parsley is well established. Cut out all stems that are going to seed, otherwise the plants will not produce new growth.

From June onwards, sprigs of parsley can be cut for drying (p. 343) and freezing (p. 294).

Cooking with parsley

Parsley is the most commonly used of our herbs, indispensable in cooking and as a colourful garnish. Parsley is essential in a bouquet garni and as a flavouring for many soups and stocks. Chopped parsley is added to white sauces, used in omelettes aux fines herbes, and is often blended into salad dressings, mayonnaises, stuffings and forcemeats.

Sprinkle fresh, finely chopped parsley over cooked vegetables, cream soups, tomato salads, fricassées of veal and chicken, grilled kidneys, grilled and fried fish – in fact, over almost any type of savoury dish. Small sprigs of fresh parsley are also used for garnishing.

Sprinkle some finely chopped parsley over the lemon wedges served with fish.

Alternatively, cut the lemon in half and remove a thin slice so that it will stand upright. Make a series of V-shaped indentations round the edge with a pair of scissors, and push small sprigs of parsley into the lemon flesh.

Small new potatoes are often tossed in butter and finely chopped parsley before serving. For a change, heat boiled potatoes in butter, add a few tablespoons of white stock and the juice of half a lemon, and serve them in this sauce, liberally sprinkled with chopped parsley.

Whether for use in cooking or as a garnish, parsley should be used absolutely fresh. Wash it carefully under cold running water and shake well to dry. Shorten the stems and, if it is to be kept for even a few hours, stand the parsley in a jar of water.

For garnishing, divide parsley into small sprigs and use fresh, or deep-fry the sprigs in hot oil or lard for 1 minute and use to garnish fried or grilled fish.

Small wooden chopping bowls with a curved-bladed, two-handled knife are excellent for chopping all types of fresh herbs, as are miniature moulis. Large quantities of parsley are best chopped on a board, using a sharp knife, but small amounts are easier snipped with scissors.

MAITRE D'HÔTEL BUTTER

4 oz. (100–125 g.) butter
1 tablespoon finely chopped parsley
Salt and pepper
Lemon juice

CHILLING TIME: 1 hour

Soften the butter in a bowl with a wooden spoon. Blend in the parsley, incorporating it evenly and thoroughly. Season to taste with salt and pepper and a few drops of lemon juice.

Roll the butter flat between two sheets of damp greaseproof paper, and chill in the refrigerator until firm.

Serving Cut the butter into small shapes with fancy biscuit cutters and use to garnish grilled or fried meat and fish, and boiled vegetables.

PARSLEY BUTTER SAUCE

4 oz. (100–125 g.) butter
1 tablespoon flour
½ pint (300 ml.) water
2 tablespoons finely chopped parsley
Salt and pepper
1 dessertspoon lemon juice

COOKING TIME: 10 minutes

Knead 1 tablespoon of the butter with the flour; bring the water to the boil in a pan and gradually whisk in small knobs of the kneaded butter and flour. Whisk steadily until thoroughly blended, then gradually heat in the remaining butter and the parsley. Season to taste with salt and pepper, and blend in the lemon juice.

Serving This is a traditional sauce with boiled bacon and salt beef, grilled and steamed fish, and with vegetables.

Variation Stir the parsley and lemon juice into a well-flavoured white sauce.

PARSLEY DIP

4 oz. (100–125 g.) cream cheese
1–2 tablespoons finely chopped parsley
Worcester sauce
Tabasco
Lemon juice
Salt and pepper

CHILLING TIME: 1 hour

Put the cream cheese in a bowl and stir it with a few tablespoons of lukewarm water until smooth and soft. Blend in the parsley and season dip to taste with Worcester sauce and tabasco, lemon juice, salt and pepper. Spoon into a bowl and chill in the refrigerator.

Serving This dip can be served as part of an hors-d'oeuvre, or with pre-dinner drinks, with fresh cauliflower sprigs, radishes, celery and carrot sticks, salty and savoury biscuits or potato crisps.

Variation Finely chopped chives, or a mixture of chives and parsley, can also be used for a dip.

Parsley, Hamburg

Hamburg, or turnip-rooted, parsley is grown for its roots, which are cooked like parsnips. The tops can be eaten, but they are coarser and of poorer flavour than those of parsley.

The vegetable provides a welcome change of flavour in winter, either on its own or as an addition to stews and soups.

Planning the crop

Hamburg parsley grows best in well-drained, fertile soil, preferably enriched with well-rotted manure or compost during the winter before sowing.

How much to grow About 40 roots can be grown in a 30 ft (9 m.) row to provide a family of four with vegetables for perhaps 20 meals.

How to grow Hamburg parsley

Sow the seeds in March or early April in a ¼ in. (5 mm.) deep drill, leaving 12 in. (305 mm.) between drills if you sow more than one row. Thin the seedlings when they are large enough to handle, leaving them 9 in. (230 mm.) apart. Hoe regularly.

Pests and diseases Hamburg parsley is generally free from pests, but crops are occasionally attacked by the disease PARSNIP CANKER (see p. 289).

Harvesting and storing

The roots, about 6–7 in. (150–180 mm.) long, will be ready to lift and use from September. They are hardy and may be left in the ground until needed, or they can be lifted and stored in boxes of moist sand for use as required during the winter. 🪶🪶

Cooking Hamburg parsley

The flavour of Hamburg parsley is reminiscent of both kohl rabi and celeriac. On the Continent it is used to give extra flavouring to thick meat and vegetable soups, rather as the English use turnips for flavouring.

Unlike both kohl rabi and turnips, which taste best when pulled young, the roots of Hamburg parsley should be left to mature before being harvested.

Prepare them like other root vegetables, peeling off the skin and trimming the roots and tops. Cut into even chunks and cook in boiling, lightly salted water for about 25 minutes, or until tender. Serve tossed in butter and finely chopped parsley, or coat them with a Béchamel or cheese sauce.

Hamburg parsley can also be creamed and made into a purée with butter, cream and eggs and flavoured with paprika.

Alternatively, use Hamburg parsley instead of celeriac or parsnips in the recipes given for these crops. (See p. 122 for celeriac and p. 224 for parsnips.)

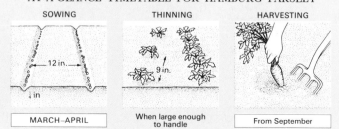

AT-A-GLANCE TIMETABLE FOR HAMBURG PARSLEY

SOWING	THINNING	HARVESTING
12 in. / ¼ in. / MARCH–APRIL	9 in. / When large enough to handle	From September

Parsnips

Long variety

Short-rooting variety

Parsnips are the earliest vegetable seeds to be sown in the open – in early March in the south, if the weather is favourable. As they are not harvested until the following winter, this means that the crop occupies ground for almost a year.

On the credit side, parsnips require little attention once the seedlings have been thinned. They are harvested when fresh vegetables are scarce, and they are very hardy.

One way to get a little extra out of the parsnip bed is to sow a catch-crop of 'Tom Thumb' lettuces between the rows when sowing the parsnips. The lettuces mature and are cut before the parsnips need all the space.

Another way is to sow radish seeds in the drills with the parsnips. They will grow quickly to show the line of the drill for early hoeing before the parsnips germinate. The radishes will be ready for use when the parsnips are thinned.

Planning the crop

Parsnips will grow in almost any soil, but they do best in deep, rich, fairly light ground. Choose an open, sunny position and use a bed that has been well manured for a previous crop. Do not use fresh manure, or the parsnips will 'fork', or split up into several roots, rather than making one long, clean root.

How many to grow As the germination of parsnips can be unreliable, the seeds must be sown fairly thickly.

About 50 parsnips can be grown in a 30 ft (9 m.) row to provide vegetables for perhaps 25 meals for a family of four.

Varieties Long varieties for good, deep soil: 'Exhibition Long-rooted'; 'Improved Hollow Crown'; 'Tender and True'.

Medium varieties: 'Dobies Intermediate'; 'Suttons White Gem'.

Short-rooting varieties for shallow soil: 'Avonresister'; 'Offenham'.

How to grow parsnips

Sow the seeds in March as soon as the soil is dry enough and the weather not too severe. First rake into the surface a general fertiliser at the rate of 2–3 oz. per square yard (60–90 g. per square metre).

Make drills ½ in. (12 mm.) deep and 15 in. (380 mm.) apart.

Give the seedlings a preliminary thinning when they are about 1 in. (25 mm.) high, then continue thinning until they are 6–9 in. (150–230 mm.) apart.

Alternatively, sow three or four seeds in groups 15 in. apart, and remove the weakest seedlings.

Hoe regularly between the plants to keep down the weeds.

Pests and diseases The pest most likely to attack parsnips is the CELERY FLY (p. 283).

The most common diseases and disorders are PARSNIP CANKER (p. 289) and SPLITTING (p. 290).

Harvesting and storing

Parsnips can be used as soon as the leaves die back in autumn, but it is better to wait until sharp frosts improve their flavour. When lifting the roots take care not to damage them with the fork.

Parsnips may be left in the soil until they are needed, but the last of the crop should be dug up during February, or before the roots start to produce new leaves, put in a cool place and covered with soil.

AT-A-GLANCE TIMETABLE FOR PARSNIPS

SOWING	THINNING	HARVESTING
15 in. / ½ in.	6–9 in.	
MARCH	Thin gradually until 6–9 in. apart	SEPT–FEB

Preparing & cooking parsnips

This sweet root vegetable was eaten by our ancestors in the same way as potatoes are today, and did not lose favour until long after the introduction of potatoes. Parsnip was the traditional vegetable with roast beef and boiled cod.

Prepare the roots for cooking by cutting off the tops and the tapering roots. Peel the parsnips thinly and cut lengthways into thick slices. Cut large roots into quarters and take out the woody cores.

Parsnips may be boiled in lightly salted water for about 20–25 minutes, depending on the size and method of preparation, or they may be steamed in butter and a little white stock or white wine. Boiled parsnips can be served tossed in butter and parsley, or Mornay sauce.

Butter-steamed parsnips are excellent served in the cooking liquid and garnished with parsley, or folded into soured cream.

Parsnips can also be roasted, in the same way as potatoes, and either shallow-fried or deep-fried, after par-boiling for 5 minutes. They are often boiled and mashed and made into a purée with butter and nutmeg, either on their own or mixed with equal amounts of mashed carrots or potatoes.

FRIED PARSNIPS

1 lb. (500 g.) parsnips
Salt and pepper
1 egg
4 tablespoons breadcrumbs
2 oz. (50 g.) butter
Garnish : lemon slices

COOKING TIME: 25–30 minutes

Trim the tops and roots off the parsnips, then peel and cut in half lengthways. Put the parsnips in a pan of boiling, lightly salted water and cook for 15 minutes. They should still be firm and not quite tender. Drain thoroughly.

Dip the parsnips in the lightly beaten egg, and coat with breadcrumbs seasoned with salt and pepper. Melt the butter in a pan and shallow-fry the coated parsnips until they are golden and crisp on both sides, turning once.

Serving Garnish the fried parsnips with thin slices of lemon, and serve with roast or grilled beef or pork.

Variation Par-boil halved or quartered parsnips in boiling salted water for 5 minutes. Drain and roast in the oven round a joint of meat for the last 30–40 minutes.

PARSNIP PURÉE

1¾ lb. (875 g.) parsnips
Salt and pepper
2 oz. (50 g.) butter
1 egg yolk
1 tablespoon honey
Ground cinnamon
Garnish : chopped parsley

COOKING TIME: 30 minutes

Trim the tops and roots from the parsnips, peel them and cut into thick slices. Mature parsnips are suitable, but the hard central cores must be removed. Put the parsnips in a pan of boiling, lightly salted water, cover, and simmer for about 20 minutes or until quite tender.

Drain the parsnips, mash them to a purée or put them through a vegetable mouli. Return the purée to the pan, add the butter and beat until heated through and fluffy. Beat in the egg yolk and honey, and season to taste with salt, pepper and cinnamon.

Serving Spoon the purée into a dish and sprinkle with finely chopped parsley. The addition of honey and cinnamon brings out the naturally sweet flavour of the parsnip, and makes the purée an ideal accompaniment for roast meat and baked ham.

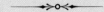

Peaches and nectarines

'Peregrine' (peach)

Peaches have been grown in England since long before the Norman Conquest. The Anglo-Saxons called the peach tree Perseoctreou – the Tree of Persia – a name that is still reflected in its botanic title Prunus persica.

Despite this, the tree almost certainly originated in China, where all the main types of peaches and nectarines (smooth-skinned peaches)

'Lord Napier' (nectarine)

still thrive in the wild. Some adventurous trader must have brought them from China to Persia about a century before the birth of Christ. From there, they travelled to Rome, where they were extensively cultivated.

Wherever they could be grown, their popularity was assured.

Planning the crop

Peach trees will thrive only in a sheltered, sunny position. In this country they do best when fan-trained against a south-facing wall or fence; or, if this is not possible, one facing west or south-west.

In some favourable parts in the south they can be grown as bush trees in sunny, sheltered gardens.

Peaches and nectarines do well under glass, but before planting a tree in a large greenhouse you should consider whether the space could be used more economically for short-term crops, such as tomatoes. In a lean-to greenhouse, however, a tree can be fan-trained against the back wall and other crops grown in front of it.

Peaches succeed only in well-drained soil. If the soil is heavy, dig a trench 6 ft (1.8 m.) long, 3 ft (1 m.) wide and 3 ft deep along the

wall where the tree is to be fan-trained. Place a layer of broken bricks or mortar at the bottom, cover this with chopped turves, and fill with good-quality loam. Add Nitro-chalk to the loam at the rate of 1 oz. to the square yard (30 g. to the square metre).

Before planting, secure horizontal wire supports to the wall or fence at 6 in. (150 mm.) spacings. Secure the wires with vine eyes, obtainable at garden shops and centres.

How many to grow A single tree will provide enough fruit for the average family. Both peaches and nectarines are self-fertile – that is, each flower can be fertilised from another on the same tree – so the presence of a second tree is not required.

Varieties of peaches For growing outdoors in the south choose varieties that ripen by the first half of September; in the north, plant those ripening by mid-August.

'Duke of York': hardy; large fruits with greenish-white flesh; ripens mid-July.

'Hale's Early': hardy; fruits with pale yellow flesh; ripens late July to early August.

'Peregrine': hardy; crimson fruits with yellowish-white flesh; ripens early August.

'Rochester': hardy; large, fine-flavoured fruits with yellow flesh; ripens early August.

'Bellegarde': large fruits; rich flavour; pale yellow flesh; ripens early to mid-September.

Varieties of nectarines As the nectarine is less hardy than the peach, few varieties have proved successful in this country – and then only against a sunny wall in the south. It is not recommended for the north unless grown in an unheated greenhouse.

'Early Rivers': rich flavoured; pale yellow flesh; ripens mid-July.

'Lord Napier': large, rich-flavoured fruits with pale green flesh; ripens early August.

How to grow peaches and nectarines

Plant peaches, or nectarines in favourable districts, between late October and January, but the earlier the better. Space fans 12–15 ft (3.6–4.5 m.) apart and bushes 15 ft apart.

Dig a hole so that the roots can be well spread out, and plant to the same depth as the trees grew in

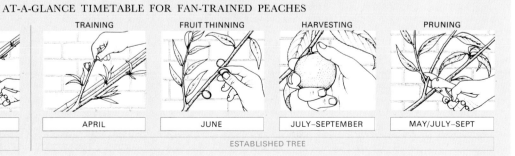

AT-A-GLANCE TIMETABLE FOR FAN-TRAINED PEACHES

PLANTING	PRUNING	TRAINING	FRUIT THINNING	HARVESTING	PRUNING
OCTOBER–JANUARY	FEBRUARY	APRIL	JUNE	JULY–SEPTEMBER	MAY/JULY–SEPT
YOUNG TREE		ESTABLISHED TREE			

225

FAN-TRAINING A YOUNG TREE

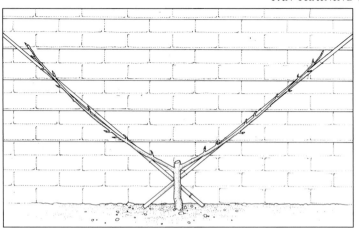

SECURING THE SIDE BRANCHES In February, before growth begins, cut both the side branches back to 12–18 in. (305–455 mm.), making each cut just above a growth bud. Secure the canes to the wires at about 40 degrees and tie the branches to these.

SECURING ADDITIONAL SHOOTS During the summer after planting, tie in the shoots that will grow from each end bud. Allow two well-spaced shoots to grow upwards from each branch, and one from the lower side. Tie these to canes and rub out other buds.

the nursery. This can be seen by the soil mark on the stem. Set the stem about 9 in. (230 mm.) from the wall and incline it slightly inwards.

In late January each year feed with 1 oz. of sulphate of potash per square yard (30 g. per square metre). Every third year add 2 oz. of superphosphate per square yard (60 g. per square metre).

In March give 1 oz. of Nitro-chalk per square yard (30 g. per square metre), and mulch with well-rotted manure or compost.

Pollination is essential to ensure a good crop, but often the flowers open before insects are about in sufficient numbers to pollinate them. In such conditions, and always when growing under glass, artificial pollination is necessary.

To pollinate peach blossoms, dab each flower with a camel-hair paint brush about noon every day during the flowering period. Pro-

tect the flowers against frost by covering the trees with small-mesh netting, but remove this during the day so that pollinating insects can reach the flowers.

Keep the ground moist all through the growing season. The ground near a wall dries out quickly, and after a hot summer's day at least 30 gallons (136 l.) of water may be needed by a mature tree carrying a full crop.

Start thinning the fruits when they are about the size of a marble. Reduce clusters to single fruits, and remove all fruits growing towards a wall and any that have insufficient room to develop properly. Thin the fruits out to a final spacing of 9 in. (230 mm.) when they are about the size of a golf ball. Space nectarines 6 in. (150 mm.) apart.

Formative pruning

A two-year-old tree trained at a

nursery will have at least two side branches, or ribs. After planting, cut these back to 12–18 in. (305–455 mm.), making the cut just above a growth bud.

Tie the ribs to canes with soft string and secure the canes to the support wires at an angle of about 40 degrees. During the summer, tie extension shoots from the end buds to the canes.

Select two evenly spaced shoots on the upper side of each branch, and one on the lower, to train on as ribs. Rub out all other shoots. As the selected shoots grow, tie them to canes and space them out evenly.

In the following winter prune the leader (last year's summer growth) of each of the eight ribs back to a triple bud, leaving about 2–2½ ft (610–760 mm.) of well-ripened wood. A triple bud is easily recognised because it has one growth bud, which is pointed,

accompanied by two blossom buds, which are round.

This pruning will stimulate the

tree into producing more strong shoots that can be trained on to form additional ribs and so fill the available wall space.

A three-year-old fan tree bought from a nursery will have about the same number of ribs, and should be pruned in the same way after planting.

Pruning a mature tree

Established trees need pruning twice each year – first in spring and summer, and again after the fruit has been harvested.

Spring and summer pruning consists of rubbing out, pinching back and tying in. As growth begins, usually in April, rub out shoots growing outwards or towards the wall.

Last year's laterals, carrying blossom, should have a number of growth buds. Select one or two of these at the base of the laterals to form replacement shoots for the

FINAL SHAPING OF A YOUNG TREE

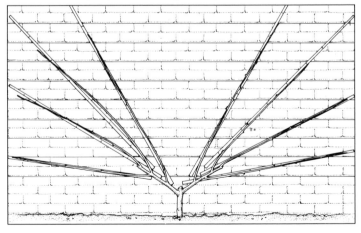

During the second winter, prune each of the eight branches or ribs back to a triple bud, leaving 2–2½ ft (610–760 mm.) of well-ripened wood. This will encourage more ribs to develop, so providing even growth over the whole wall space covered by the tree.

following year. Pinch back all others to one leaf. Leave the leader unpruned at this stage.

In the early summer, usually in May, thin out the many new laterals which will be produced along the extension growth so that the remainder are 4–6 in. (100–150 mm.) apart along the upper and lower sides of the ribs. These shoots will become next year's fruiting laterals.

Next, pinch back to six leaves the present fruit-carrying laterals, unless they are required as additional framework branches.

Pinch back replacement shoots to about ten leaves. Tie shoots, especially the fruit-carrying laterals, to supporting wires.

Carry out the second part of annual training after the fruits have been harvested, from mid-July to mid-September according to the variety. Cut back laterals that have fruited – unless they are wanted as part of the framework – to the replacement shoots which are tied in.

After this pruning the ribs, radiating out parallel to the wall, should carry shoots spaced out about 4–6 in. (100–150 mm.) apart, all tied securely to the wires.

Growing from a stone

Peaches are among the few fruits that can be grown successfully from seed.

In September or October set the stones singly in 5 in. (130 mm.) pots of John Innes No. 1 potting compost. Plant the resultant seedlings in the garden when they are about 6 in. (150 mm.) high.

In the second winter plant them in their permanent positions, dealing with them in the same way as for a grafted tree.

Pests and diseases Pests most likely to affect peaches and nectarines are APHIDS (p. 282), CATERPILLARS (p. 282), GLASS-HOUSE RED SPIDER MITES (p. 283) and SCALE INSECTS (p. 285).

The principal diseases and disorders of peaches and nectarines are BACTERIAL CANKER (p. 286), BROWN ROT (p. 286), CHLOROSIS (p. 287), HONEY FUNGUS (p. 288), PEACH LEAF CURL (p. 289), POWDERY MILDEW (p. 289), SHOTHOLE (p. 290), SILVER LEAF (p. 290) and SPLIT STONE (p. 290).

TRAINING REPLACEMENT AND FRUITING SHOOTS

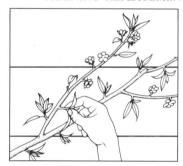

APRIL. Pinch back growth buds on last year's laterals to one leaf – leaving one or two buds at the base to provide replacement shoots.

MAY Thin out new laterals on the upper and lower sides of ribs to 4–6 in. (100–150 mm.) apart. These will fruit next year.

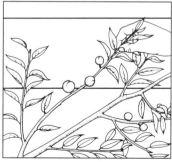

MAY Pinch back fruit-bearing laterals to six leaves, unless needed as replacements. Pinch back replacement shoots to ten leaves.

AFTER HARVESTING Cut out fruited laterals, unless needed as part of the framework, to the replacement shoots already tied in.

Harvesting and storing

Peaches and nectarines are ready for picking when the flesh around the stalk yields to gentle pressure from the fingers. Pick the fruits very carefully by gripping them in the palm of the hand.

For the many uses to which peaches and nectarines may be put, see bottling (p. 309); chutneys (p. 335); drying (p. 343); freezing (p. 294); fruit cheeses and butters (p. 323); jams (p. 314); pickles (p. 328) and wine-making (p. 357). 🍑🍑

Preparing & serving peaches

These luscious, juicy fruits are at their most enjoyable when served fresh as a dessert. Like the related nectarines, they need no peeling.

Peaches can, however, also be used fresh in fruit salads, and as a fresh purée can form the basis for ice creams and sweet soufflés. Peach slices, lightly poached in a sugar syrup, are excellent as fillings for pies and flans and associate particularly well with raspberries.

For cooked desserts, peaches should be peeled. To make this easier, dip them first in a bowl of boiling water for 1–2 minutes and then immerse them in cold water. Peel the skins downwards in strips, using a small knife.

Cut the peaches into halves along the indentations of the flesh, twist the two halves apart and remove the stones.

---◇---

PEACH MELBA

2 large peaches
½ lb. (250 g.) raspberries
2 oz. (50 g.) sugar
¾ pint (450 ml.) vanilla ice cream

Peel the peaches, cut them into halves and remove the stones. Rinse the raspberries and drain them thoroughly, then rub them through a fine sieve and sweeten the purée to taste with sugar.

Place two scoops of ice cream in each of four serving glasses. Set a peach half, rounded side up,

over the ice cream and spoon the raspberry purée over it.
Serving Serve at once, before the ice cream begins to melt.
Variation Instead of ice cream, stir 4 oz. (100 g.) of cream cheese until smooth, and sweeten to taste with vanilla sugar. Fold in 5 fl. oz. (150 ml.) of whipped cream and chill slightly before assembling the sweet like the peach melba.

---◇---

CURRIED PEACHES

4 peaches
1½ oz. (40 g.) butter
1 oz. (25 g.) demerara sugar
1 teaspoon curry powder

COOKING TIME: 15–20 minutes
OVEN TEMPERATURE: 180°C (350°F) – gas mark 4

Peel the peaches, cut them into halves and remove the stones. Cut the peach halves into narrow slices and arrange them, cut sides up, in an ovenproof dish buttered with half the butter.

Mix the demerara sugar with the curry powder, and sprinkle over the peaches. Dot with flakes of the remaining butter and bake in the oven for about 15 minutes, or until the sugar has melted and the peaches are golden-brown.
Serving Curried peaches are an unusual accompaniment for roast pork or any savoury dish that includes rice.

Continued . . .

Peach recipes (continued)

STUFFED PEACHES

4 peaches
Lemon juice
4 oz. (125 g.) Mycella, or other mild
  blue cheese
2–3 tablespoons cream
Garnish : lettuce leaves ; walnut halves

CHILLING TIME: 1 hour

Chill the peaches in the refrigerator for 1 hour.

Wipe the peaches clean, cut them into halves along the indentations, remove the stones and enlarge the cavities slightly with a pointed teaspoon. Sprinkle the cut surfaces with lemon juice.

Stir the cheese with the cream until smooth, and pile this mixture into the halved peaches.
Serving Arrange the stuffed peaches on individual plates, in each case setting two halves on a bed of crisp lettuce ; garnish with walnut halves and serve with cream crackers.
Photograph on pages 142–3.

—————◦⟩◦—————

PEACH COMPÔTE

4 peaches
4 oz. (125 g.) caster sugar
1 small lime
5 fl. oz. (150 ml.) whipping cream
2 oz. (50 g.) small macaroons

COOKING TIME: 15–20 minutes
CHILLING TIME: 2 hours

Put the peaches in a bowl of boiling water for 1 minute, then lift them out and remove the skins. Cut the peaches into halves and take out the stones.

Put the sugar in a pan with ½ pint (300 ml.) of water, the pared rind of the lime and the juice. Bring to the boil over low heat until the sugar has dissolved, then add the peach halves – rounded sides down.

Poach gently for about 10–15 minutes, depending on ripeness. The peaches should be tender, but still retain their shape. Lift them out and leave to cool.

Turn up the heat, and boil the syrup rapidly until it has reduced and thickened. Be careful not to let it caramelise. Set aside to cool.

Cut the cooled peach halves into three or four segments and chill in the refrigerator for 2 hours.
Serving Just before serving, whisk the cream until it retains its shape. Fold in 2 tablespoons of the cooled syrup and the roughly crushed macaroons. Spoon a layer of the cream into four individual serving glasses, arrange the peach slices on top and decorate with a swirl of cream.

—————◦⟩◦—————

PEACH AND RASPBERRY FLAN

4 large peaches
6 oz. (175 g.) caster sugar
½ vanilla pod
8 in. (200 mm.) flan case
4 oz. (125 g.) raspberries
5 fl. oz. (150 ml.) double cream

COOKING TIME: 15 minutes

Put the sugar and vanilla pod with ½ pint (300 ml.) water in a pan, bring to the boil and simmer for 5 minutes. Keep the syrup at simmering point, add the wiped whole peaches and poach in the syrup for 5–10 minutes, depending on ripeness. Remove the peaches and leave to cool slightly, then strain off the syrup.

Peel the peaches, cut them into halves and remove the stones. Cut the fruits into ½ in. (12 mm.) slices.

Bring the strained syrup back to the boil, and continue boiling rapidly until it has thickened and reduced. Brush the base and sides of the flan case with the warm glaze and arrange the peach slices on top, in overlapping rows. Brush a little more of the glaze over the top, and set the flan aside to cool.
Serving Just before serving, decorate the flan with the rinsed and drained raspberries, laying them along the rows of peaches. Whip the cream, and pipe it round the edge of the flan.

—————◦⟩◦—————

Pears

Espalier   *Dwarf pyramid*

Pears, which are native to Europe and western Asia, have been cultivated since the earliest times. By the 16th century, 232 varieties were available in Italy. Of these, 209 were served to the Grand Duke Cosmo III during a single year.

Nowadays, there are probably three times that number of varieties in existence, though not more than a dozen are generally available from nurseries.

Wherever apples grow, pears will grow too, but they need slightly different conditions and treatment. Since their blossoms open earlier than those of apples, when there are fewer flying insects to pollinate them, they should, if possible, be planted in a less-exposed position.

Pears also need watering more frequently during dry spells, since they are less able than apples to withstand drought.

Few pears are self-fertile ; therefore, when buying trees it is necessary to purchase two different varieties which will flower at the *same time. Plant bush trees within 12–15 ft (3.6–4.5 m.) of each other; half standards, 15–20 ft (4.5–6 m.); cordons, 2½–3 ft (760 mm.–1 m.); espaliers, 12–15 ft; dwarf pyramids, 4–5 ft (1.2–1.5 m.).*

Space permitting, by choosing early, mid-season and late varieties it is possible to have pears from August until the New Year.

Planning the crop

Plant pears in a sunny, sheltered position, preferably in deep, loamy soil that will retain moisture in summer. If the soil is free-draining and sandy, dig two or three buckets of peat into the planting area.

Before planting, fork in general fertiliser at the rate of 3 oz. per square yard (90 g. per square metre).

During subsequent years, in late January feed with 1 oz. of sulphate of potash per square yard (30 g. per square metre).

In March apply 1–1½ oz. of sulphate of ammonia per square yard (30–45 g. per square metre). Every third year add 1½–2 oz. (45–60 g.) of superphosphate to the sulphate of ammonia dressing.

How many to grow Yields of pears may vary each year according to the weather – that is, the incidence of spring frosts and the amount of rainfall. About 3–5 lb. (1.5–2.5 kg.) may be expected from an established cordon; 5–6 lb. (2.5–3 kg.) from a dwarf pyramid; 20–25 lb. (10–12 kg.) from a three-tier espalier, and 40–50 lb. (18–23 kg.) from a bush tree.

A tree planted when three years old should fruit within two or three years, depending on weather and position.

Varieties Although all the following are dessert varieties, any may be cooked if used while still firm and not completely ripe.

'William's Bon Chrétien': pick in late August to ripen in September; generally regarded as the best-flavoured September pear, but keeps only a short time; pollinated by 'Conference' and 'Joséphine de Malines'.

'Louise Bonne of Jersey': pick in late September for eating in October; pollinated by 'Joséphine de Malines'.

'Conference': pick the fruits in September for eating in October and November; a regular cropper which is excellent for bottling; suitable pollinators are 'William's Bon Chrétien' and 'Joséphine de Malines'.

'Fertility': pick in September for eating in October; a heavy cropper; pollinated by 'Doyenné du Comice' and 'Winter Nelis'.

'Doyenné du Comice': this is generally considered the best-flavoured pear; needs a sheltered position with rich soil and regular mulching; pick early October for eating from late October to early December; excellent for bottling; pollinated by 'Fertility' and 'Winter Nelis'.

'Joséphine de Malines': a good late pear which is picked in October to ripen at a temperature of 16°C (61°F) during December or January; pollinated by 'Louise Bonne of Jersey', 'William's Bon Chrétien' and 'Conference'.

'Winter Nelis': pick in mid-October to ripen in a temperature of 16°C (61°F) in December; pollinated by 'Doyenné du Comice'.

How to grow pears

Plant your pear trees between November and March. November planting gives the best start.

Before planting a bush tree, drive a stake at least 2 ft (610 mm.) deep into the soil so that the tree can be tied to it by plastic strap

ties. Plant to the same depth as it was in the nursery – as indicated by the soil mark on the stem. Ensure that the union between stock and scion is above soil level.

Spread the roots out evenly and firm the soil as it is put back.

During the winter, firm any trees that have been lifted by frost. In the spring, water the trees during dry weather to help them to become established. Throughout the tree's life, water during dry spells, giving not less than 4 gallons per square yard (18 l. per square metre). Mulch with peat or well-rotted compost or manure.

Generally, pear fruitlets need less thinning than those of apples. In a good year, however, reduce each cluster to one or two fruitlets just at the time they begin to turn downwards.

Pruning and training Prune and train pear trees in the same way as apples (see pp. 64–68). Established bush pear trees can, however, be cut back harder than apples, so do not hesitate to remove overcrowded branches, particularly in the centre of the tree, during winter pruning.

Summer pruning of cordons, espaliers and dwarf pyramids is earlier than for apples, starting when the summer growth matures – usually in early July in the south, but later in the north.

As the tree matures it will produce fruiting spurs more freely than apples, and these should be thinned in winter.

Pests and diseases Among the pests that may attack pear trees are APHIDS (p. 282), CATERPILLARS (p. 282), CODLING MOTH (p. 283), FRUIT TREE RED SPIDER MITES (p.

283), PEAR LEAF BLISTER MITE (p. 284), PEAR SUCKER (p. 284) and TORTRIX MOTHS (p. 285).

The principal diseases and disorders are BORON DEFICIENCY (p. 286), BROWN ROT (p. 286), FIRE BLIGHT (p. 288), HONEY FUNGUS (p. 288), SCAB (p. 290), SPLITTING (p. 290) and STONY PIT (p. 291).

Spraying Although affected by many of the same pests and diseases as apples, pears tend to be more resistant. Adapt the spraying programme outlined on p. 69 in the light of local experience.

Harvesting and storing

Most varieties of pears ripen off the tree. Harvest early varieties, such as 'William's Bon Chrétien', by cutting the stalk when the fruit is mature but still hard.

Pick mid-season fruits (for eating in October or November) and late varieties (for use from December) when the stalk parts easily from the spur after a gentle twist.

Store the fruit in a cool room or shed at a temperature of 2–4°C (36–40°F). Do not wrap them, but lay them on a tray or shelf in a single layer. Make sure the fruits do not touch each other.

Check frequently, and when they approach maturity – which is shown by a slight softening of the flesh close to the stalk – bring them into a temperature of about 16°C (61°F) for two or three days to finish off the ripening.

Pears can be put to many uses. See bottling (p. 309); chutneys (p. 335); drying (p. 343); freezing (p. 294); fruit cheeses and butters (p. 323); jams (p. 314); pickles (p. 328) and wine-making (p. 357).

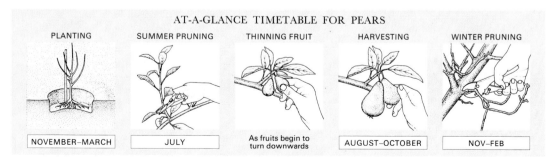

AT-A-GLANCE TIMETABLE FOR PEARS

PLANTING	SUMMER PRUNING	THINNING FRUIT	HARVESTING	WINTER PRUNING
NOVEMBER–MARCH	JULY	As fruits begin to turn downwards	AUGUST–OCTOBER	NOV–FEB

PEAR VARIETIES

Provided they are still firm and not fully ripe, any of the dessert varieties illustrated below may be cooked. Suitable pollinators – that is, varieties with overlapping blossoming periods – are suggested on p. 229.

'Conference'

'Louise Bonne of Jersey'

'William's Bon Chrétien'

'Fertility'

'Doyenné du Comice'

'Joséphine de Malines'

'Winter Nelis'

Preparing & cooking pears

Dessert pears, which should be just ripe, may be served as a dish on their own, as part of a fresh fruit salad or as an accompaniment to the cheese-board. They may also be cooked – preferably poached in a sugar syrup and served chilled with, for example, a chocolate or custard sauce.

Prepare pears for cooking by first peeling them with a stainless-steel knife to prevent discoloration. If they are to stand for any length of time before cooking, brush them with lemon juice to prevent browning.

Pears may be poached whole, first removing the blossom end but leaving the stalk intact and scraping it clean with a knife. Alternatively, cut the peeled pears into halves and use a pointed teaspoon to scoop out the centre cores and the woody filaments running towards the stalk ends.

blossom ends. Scoop out the cores.

Put the sugar, water and vanilla pod in a pan, stirring over moderate heat until the sugar has dissolved. Simmer the syrup for 2–3 minutes, then add the pear halves and poach them over gentle heat for about 10 minutes, or until just tender.

Lift the pears out and leave to drain and cool in a colander. Use the strained syrup in a fruit salad or a boiled fruit dessert.

Meanwhile, put the egg yolks, caster sugar, wine and lemon juice in the top half of a double boiler or in a bowl set over a pan of boiling water. Beat the mixture constantly until it begins to thicken enough to coat the back of a wooden spoon. It must not be allowed to boil.

Serving Arrange the pear halves, rounded sides up, on individual plates, and spoon the wine custard over them.

Variation Sprinkle the pear halves with the demerara sugar and cover with equal amounts of red wine and water. Poach in the oven at 180°C (350°F) – gas mark 4 for about 45 minutes, or until tender. Serve the pears with the reduced liquid poured over them.

PEARS IN WINE SAUCE

4 pears
4 oz. (125 g.) sugar
4 fl. oz. (100 ml.) water
1 vanilla pod
4 egg yolks
2 oz. (50 g.) caster sugar
8 fl. oz. (250 ml.) dry white wine
1 tablespoon lemon juice

COOKING TIME: 35–40 minutes

Peel the pears, cut them into halves and remove the stalks and

CINNAMON PEARS

4 dessert pears
4 oz. (125 g.) sugar
1 cinnamon stick
5 fl. oz. (150 ml.) double cream
2 tablespoons rum
1 oz. (25 g.) flaked almonds

COOKING TIME: 20 minutes

Peel the pears, cut them into halves and remove cores, stalks and base ends. Put the sugar in a pan with ½ pint (300 ml.) water and the cinnamon stick. Bring to the boil and simmer for 5 minutes, then add the pear halves and poach them in the syrup over gentle heat, rounded sides down, for 15 minutes or until just tender.

Lift the pear halves from the syrup and leave them to drain, keeping them warm.

Whisk the cream until stiff. Stir in the rum, together with the flaked almonds toasted under the grill until golden-brown.
Serving Arrange the pear halves on four individual plates and serve them while still warm, with the cream in a separate bowl.
Variation Replace the rum with brandy or curaçao, and blend with chopped glacé cherries instead of almonds.
Photograph on pages 214–15.

PEARS AND PEPPERS WITH YOGHOURT

2–3 ripe pears
2 tablespoons lemon juice
2 red peppers
5 fl. oz. (150 ml.) natural yoghourt
1 teaspoon French mustard
Sugar, salt and white pepper
Garnish : paprika

CHILLING TIME: 30 minutes

Wash and wipe the pears, but peel them only if the skin is bruised and tough. Cut them into halves, remove the stalks and blossom ends and scoop out the cores.

Cut the pears into ½ in. (12 mm.) chunks and sprinkle these with lemon juice.

Wash and dry the peppers: remove the stalk base, seeds and membranes. Cut each pepper in half, and each half into thin slices.

Mix the peppers and pears, together with the lemon juice, in a bowl. Add the mustard to the yoghourt and season to taste with sugar, salt and white pepper. Stir this dressing into the pears and peppers, blend thoroughly and chill in the refrigerator.
Serving Spoon the salad on to individual plates, sprinkle lightly with paprika and serve as a side salad with cold, lean meat. It may also be served as a light lunch dish on its own, accompanied with crusty bread.
Photograph on pages 210–11.

CROÛTES AUX POIRES

4 dessert pears
4 oz. (125 g.) sugar
½ vanilla pod
4 slices of fruit loaf
4 oz. (125 g.) unsalted butter
5 fl. oz. (150 ml.) double cream
2 tablespoons rum (optional)
Garnish : cocktail cherries

COOKING TIME: 25 minutes

Peel the pears with a stainless-steel knife, cut them into halves and remove the cores. Bring the sugar and ½ pint (300 ml.) water to the boil, then add the vanilla pod and the pear halves – rounded sides down.

Poach the pears gently in the syrup for 15 minutes.

Lift out the pear halves with a perforated spoon and keep them warm. Remove the vanilla pod, then turn up the heat and boil the syrup until it has reduced to a few spoonfuls. Let it cool slightly.

Trim the crusts from the bread slices and fry them in the butter until golden on both sides. Keep the bread warm with the pears. Whip the cream until it holds its shape; flavour with the reserved syrup and, if you wish, the rum.
Serving Set the hot bread slices on individual plates and arrange two pear halves on each, rounded sides up. Pipe the cream on top, and decorate with drained cocktail cherries.
Photograph on pages 208–9.

Peas

'Kelvedon Wonder' (First early)

'Onward' (Second early)

Sugar peas, or mangetout

Peas are among the most difficult and yet the most rewarding of vegetable crops.

On the debit side they need a good deal of attention, are prone to a number of pests and diseases, and give a comparatively small yield for the space they take up.

In compensation, the flavour of freshly picked garden peas is much finer than that of either fresh or frozen field-grown peas – one of the great treats of the vegetable-grower's year.

In a small kitchen garden it is generally best to grow only one or two rows of early peas to be harvested with the first carrots, French beans and turnips. As soon as the peas are finished, the ground can be used for growing leeks or cabbages.

On a larger plot, peas can be grown in succession for picking from

May to October if the right varieties are sown at the right time.

There are two main types of peas. Hardy, round-seeded peas are sown in late autumn and early spring for picking in late May and June; the wrinkled type, which have a sweeter flavour, can be sown only from March to July for harvesting from June onwards.

In addition, there are sugar peas – also known as mangetout – which are grown in the same way as garden peas but are picked when the seeds have only just begun to develop. They are cooked and eaten whole.

Depending on variety, peas grow to heights varying from $1\frac{1}{2}$ ft (455 mm.) to 6 ft (1.8 m.).

Planning the crop

Peas grow best on rich, well-drained soil. Good drainage is particularly important for early varieties, as the seeds will rot in cold, wet soil.

Dig the plot at least three or four weeks before sowing, working in two buckets of compost or well-rotted manure to the square yard. A week before sowing, rake in a top-dressing of general fertiliser at 2–3 oz. per square yard (60–90 g. per square metre).

How much to grow A packet of seed is usually sufficient to sow a row 15 ft (4.5 m.) long, but the yield from this will vary, depending on the height of the plant and growing conditions.

A row of dwarf early peas, for example, may provide a family of four with only enough helpings for four meals, whereas three times this yield may be expected from a tall, maincrop variety.

Varieties First-early round-seeded varieties for sowing in early November (late October in the north) or February–March: 'Feltham First', $1\frac{1}{2}$ ft (455 mm.); 'Meteor', $1\frac{1}{2}$ ft (455 mm.); 'Kelvedon Viscount', 2 ft (610 mm.); 'Pilot', $3\frac{1}{2}$ ft (1.1 m.).

First-early wrinkled varieties for sowing in March: 'Kelvedon Wonder', $1\frac{1}{2}$ ft (455 mm.); 'Little Marvel', $1\frac{1}{2}$–2 ft (455–610 mm.); 'Progress No. 9', also known as 'Early Bird', $1\frac{1}{2}$–2 ft (455–610 mm.); 'Early Onward', 2 ft (610 mm.); 'Gradus', 4 ft (1.2 m.).

Second-early wrinkled varieties for sowing in late March and April: 'Onward', 2 ft (610 mm.); 'Hurst Green Shaft', 2–$2\frac{1}{2}$ ft (610–760 mm.); 'Chieftain', $2\frac{1}{2}$ ft (760 mm.); 'Kelvedon Monarch', also known as 'Victory Freezer', $2\frac{1}{2}$ ft (760 mm.); 'Jof', 3 ft (1 m.); 'Miracle', $4\frac{1}{2}$ ft (1.4 m.), and 'Achievement', $4\frac{1}{2}$ ft (1.4 m.).

Maincrop varieties, for sowing in April and May: 'Lord Chancellor', 3–4 ft (1–1.2 m.); 'Gladstone', 4 ft (1.2 m.); 'Alderman', 5 ft (1.5 m.).

Late crops, for sowing in June and July for picking in September and October: 'Kelvedon Wonder'; 'Progress No. 9'.

Sugar peas, for sowing from March to June: 'Dwarf Sweet Green', 3 ft (1 m.); 'Sugar Dwarf De Grace', 3–4 ft (1–1.2 m.). Petit pois, small-seeded peas for sowing from March to June: 'Gullivert', 3 ft (1 m.); good crop, small pods.

How to grow peas

If a number of rows of peas are to be grown, allow 2 ft (610 mm.) between varieties that will reach $1\frac{1}{2}$ ft (455 mm.) high; 3 ft (1 m.) between those 4 ft (1.2 m.) high, and so on.

In a small garden where only one row of peas is to be grown, a reasonable distance must be allowed between peas and the neighbouring crop. Onions, beetroot or lettuces, for example, can be grown successfully on the southerly or sunny side only 18 in.

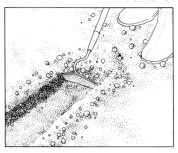

DRAWING A DRILL With a draw hoe, form a drill 4 in. (100 mm.) wide. Use short, smooth motions and keep the depth even.

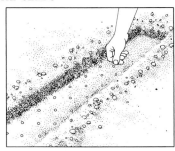

SPACING THE SEEDS Place the seeds 2–3 in. (50–75 mm.) apart in three rows – or, in autumn, rather closer to allow for losses.

(455 mm.) from a row of tall maincrop peas. But about double this space is needed on the shaded side, especially when the taller varieties of peas are grown.

When sowing, use a swan-neck hoe or a short-handled onion hoe to draw a flat-bottomed drill 4 in. (100 mm.) wide and $1\frac{1}{2}$–2 in. (40–50 mm.) deep. In spring and summer sow the seeds 2–3 in. (50–75 mm.) apart in three staggered rows in the drills. Sow overwintering varieties rather more thickly to compensate for any losses in bad weather.

Reduce the risk of disease in overwintered crops by shaking the seeds in a bag containing a proprietary chemical seed dressing, such as Murphy's Combined Seed Dressing.

To level the surface after sowing, draw the soil over the drills with a rake.

Immediately after sowing, protect the seed from birds by covering the rows with netting, black cotton stranded from sticks close to the ground, or with clusters of twigs.

Overwintered crops are more

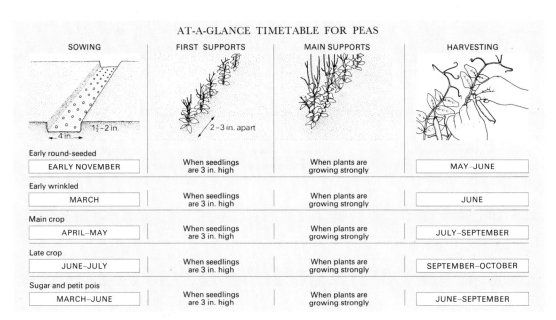

AT-A-GLANCE TIMETABLE FOR PEAS

	SOWING	FIRST SUPPORTS	MAIN SUPPORTS	HARVESTING
Early round-seeded	EARLY NOVEMBER	When seedlings are 3 in. high	When plants are growing strongly	MAY–JUNE
Early wrinkled	MARCH	When seedlings are 3 in. high	When plants are growing strongly	JUNE
Main crop	APRIL–MAY	When seedlings are 3 in. high	When plants are growing strongly	JULY–SEPTEMBER
Late crop	JUNE–JULY	When seedlings are 3 in. high	When plants are growing strongly	SEPTEMBER–OCTOBER
Sugar and petit pois	MARCH–JUNE	When seedlings are 3 in. high	When plants are growing strongly	JUNE–SEPTEMBER

(sowing diagram labels: 4 in. — $1\frac{1}{2}$–2 in. — 2–3 in. apart)

SUPPORTING THE PEAS

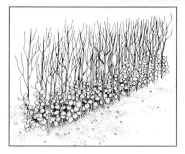

Short, twiggy sticks will start the peas climbing, and so discourage slugs and snails, when they are about 3 in. (75 mm.) high.

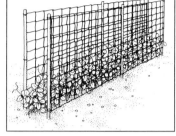

Later, provide taller sticks, wires or well-supported plastic mesh to suit the height of the variety that is being grown.

likely to succeed if protected with cloches until the following spring.

As soon as the seedlings are through, hoe on each side of the rows to get rid of weeds. When the seedlings are 3 in. (75 mm.) high, push in small, twiggy sticks to encourage the plants to climb.

Do not delay in giving this support because plants left to straggle on the ground may be attacked by slugs.

Once the plants are growing strongly, put in the final supports at least as high as the ultimate height of the variety being grown. These final supports can be long, twiggy branches, wire criss-crossed between bamboo stakes, or netting tied to posts.

Make sure the peas get a constant supply of moisture. Water regularly during dry spells and give the rows a mulch of damp peat, leaf-mould or garden compost.

Pests and diseases APHIDS (p. 282), BEAN SEED FLY (p. 282), PEA MOTH (p. 284) and PEA THRIPS (p. 284) are among the most trouble-some pests.

Likely diseases and disorders include DAMPING OFF (p. 287), FOOT ROT (p. 288), MANGANESE DEFICIENCY (p. 289) and SOIL-BORNE DISEASES (p. 290).

Harvesting and storing

When the pods seem to have reached their full length, check daily to feel if the peas are swelling inside. Aim to pick the pods when the seeds are well developed but before they are fully mature.

To harvest your crop, pull the pod upwards with one hand while holding the stem with the other.

Harvest sugar peas when the pods are about 2 in. (50 mm.) long and the seeds only just beginning to develop inside. If insufficient of these small pods are available at a single gathering, keep the first gathering in the refrigerator until more can be gathered.

Immediately the plants are cleared of pods, cut the haulms down to ground level and put them on the compost heap.

For the various methods of storing peas, see freezing (p. 294) and salting (p. 346).

Preparing & cooking peas

Top and tail mangetout peas as for French beans. They should not require stringing. Wash them in cold water and cook for no more than 5 minutes in boiling, lightly salted water, or in butter.

The tiny petit pois, like other garden peas, are shelled from their pods.

Do not throw the pods out, as they can be used for vegetable stocks; or, if quite young and fresh, as a vegetable on their own. After shelling, break the pod near the blossom end and pull off the thin waxy covering. Cook the pods in butter for about 10 minutes, or until tender but still crisp.

Petit pois may be boiled in salted water, but they are much tastier if only par-boiled and then finished off in butter, under a cover, and sprinkled with chopped mint.

Shell full-sized peas and cook them in boiling, lightly salted water with a sprig of mint, 1 teaspoon of sugar and a little lemon juice to preserve the fresh green colour. Boil for 15–20 minutes, depending on size. Serve them tossed in butter and sprinkled with mint, parsley, dill or basil.

Use cold, cooked or tiny fresh peas as an ingredient in mixed salads, particularly rice salads or moulds. Or arrange buttered peas in grilled or fried mushroom caps and serve as an edible garnish with fish, meat or poultry.

SUMMER VEGETABLE CABARET

½ lb. (250 g.) young peas (prepared weight)
½ lb. (250 g.) baby carrots
½ lb. (250 g.) young turnips
1 small cauliflower
4 oz. (100–125 g.) mushrooms
Bouillon
2 oz. (50 g.) butter
3 tablespoons flour
Salt and pepper
Garnish : chopped chervil

COOKING TIME: 25–30 minutes

Shell the peas, trim and scrape the carrots, peel the turnips and cut them into quarters. Divide the cauliflower into florets. Trim the stalks and edges of the mushrooms and cut into thick slices.

Make up the bouillon from boiling water and stock cubes and cook the peas and carrots in one pan of bouillon (do not add the salt), the turnips in another pan, and the cauliflower florets in a third. Simmer the vegetables until tender, drain thoroughly in a colander and arrange them in groups on a deep serving dish.

Set the cooking liquid aside and keep the vegetables warm.

Melt the butter in a pan, add the mushrooms and cook for 5 minutes, then stir in the flour and cook through. Gradually add the reserved cooking liquid until the sauce has the required consistency. Season to taste with salt and pepper, and

simmer for 3 minutes.
Serving Pour the mushroom sauce over the vegetables and sprinkle with chopped chervil. Serve as a dish on its own, or with lamb, veal or chicken.
Photograph on pages 140–1.

BUTTERED MANGETOUT

1 lb. (500 g.) mangetout peas
Salt
2 oz. (50 g.) butter
1 dessertspoon mixed parsley and mint

COOKING TIME: 10 minutes

Top and tail the peas, string if necessary, then wash thoroughly. Put the pods in a pan with a small amount of boiling, lightly salted water and cook for 4–5 minutes. Drain thoroughly in a colander.

Melt the butter in a pan without letting it brown, add the pods and cover with a lid. Cook over a gentle heat for 5 minutes, shaking the pan frequently to prevent sticking and to ensure that the peas are evenly coated with butter. Stir in the mixed, finely chopped herbs.
Serving Spoon the pods and the cooking liquid into a dish and serve with grilled or baked fish, veal, lamb or poultry.
Variation Cook small, finely chopped onions in the butter before adding the mangetout.

Continued . . .

233

Pea recipes (continued)

PEASE PUDDING

1½ lb. (750 g.) old, floury peas
1 dessertspoon finely chopped mint
1 teaspoon sugar
Salt and pepper
1–2 oz. (25–50 g.) butter
2 egg yolks

COOKING TIME: 1¾ hours

Pease pudding with boiled bacon or pork is a traditional English dish that dates back to medieval times. Split peas can be used instead of fresh, old peas, but should first be soaked overnight in cold water. Pease pudding is cooked in a pudding cloth, together with the bacon.

Shell the peas and put them, with the chopped mint and sugar, in a greased pudding cloth. Tie this up, leaving room for the peas to swell during cooking. Add the peas to the simmering bacon for the last 1½ hours.

Remove the pudding cloth from the bacon broth; rub the peas through a coarse sieve, or blend to a purée in the liquidiser. Heat the pease pudding through in a pan, season to taste with salt and pepper, and stir in the butter and egg yolks until the pudding is creamy.
Serving Serve pease pudding instead of potatoes with the carved meat.

CREAMED PEA SOUP

¾ lb. (375 g.) young peas (prepared weight)
1 oz. (25 g.) butter
2 tablespoons flour
1 pint (600 ml.) white stock
Salt and pepper
Sugar
4 tablespoons double cream
Garnish: chopped mint

COOKING TIME: 25 minutes

Put the shelled peas in a pan with the butter; simmer, covered with a lid, for 5 minutes. Blend in the flour and cook through, then gradually add the stock. Bring to the boil, season to taste with salt and pepper, and simmer gently for 10 minutes.

Rub the soup through a sieve or blend in a liquidiser. Return the soup to the pan and add the sugar to taste. Heat the soup through and stir in the cream, but do not let the soup reach boiling point again.
Serving Pour into soup bowls and sprinkle with finely chopped mint. Offer a separate bowl of crisp bread croûtons.
Variations A less-rich version of pea soup is made as above, but omitting the cream. Chopped lettuce or spinach may be cooked and puréed with the peas for extra colour.

Peppers and chillis

Sweet pepper

Chilli

Sweet peppers, or capsicums, are usually grown under glass in Britain, although in a good summer they will succeed outdoors in the south and west of England.

The fruits can be eaten when green, or allowed to ripen to yellow, or red, according to variety.

Chillis, a form of capsicum, are related to sweet peppers and are grown in exactly the same way.

The hot-flavoured fruits are used in curries, pickles and sauces.

Planning the crop

Grow indoor plants in 9 in. (230 mm.) pots of potting compost, or plant them in the greenhouse border after digging in a moderate dressing of well-rotted manure.

In the garden, prepare a bed against a south-facing wall or fence by digging in manure or compost – a bucketful to the square yard – some weeks before planting. Rake in 2 oz. per square yard (60 g. per square metre) of a general fertiliser before planting.

How many to grow Even outdoors you should be able to pick at least three peppers from each plant – more in a good summer – and perhaps twice as many indoors. Between four and six outdoor plants or two or three greenhouse plants, should be sufficient.

Varieties 'Canape' (F1 hybrid): an early variety that does well outdoors and under glass.

'New Ace' (F1 hybrid): early and high yielding; best grown in a greenhouse.

'Worldbeater': heavy cropper; succeeds outdoors in warm summers.

Growing under glass

Sow a few seeds in a pan of seed compost during March at a temperature of 16–18°C (61–64°F). When the seedlings are large

AT-A-GLANCE TIMETABLE FOR PEPPERS

	SOWING	PRICKING OUT	TRANSPLANTING	HARVESTING
Under glass	MARCH	When large enough to handle	Into 9 in. pots or greenhouse border	JULY–AUGUST
For growing outdoors	MARCH	When large enough to handle	LATE MAY–JUNE	AUGUST–SEPTEMBER

enough to handle, prick them out individually into 3 in. (75 mm.) pots of potting compost. Grow the pepper plants at an average day-time temperature of 16–27°C (61–81°F), with a night-time minimum of 7°C (45°F). Make a final potting in 9 in. (230 mm.) pots of John Innes No. 3 potting compost.

Alternatively, transplant them from the 3 in. (75 mm.) pots directly into the greenhouse border, setting them 18 in. (455 mm.) apart.

Insert 3 ft (1 m.) canes into the pots or soil, and secure the growing plants to them with string. Shade the glass during hot weather.

Syringe the plants daily during the flowering period. Apply liquid fertiliser every ten days after the first fruits appear.

Growing outdoors

Sow and prick out into individual pots as for growing under glass. In April, harden the plants off in a cold frame before planting out 18 in. (455 mm.) apart in late May or early June. Tie to a cane.

After the first fruits set, give a liquid feed every ten days.

Pests and diseases CATERPILLARS (p. 282) are the pests most likely to occur. The plants are liable to attack by GREY MOULD (p. 288).

Harvesting and storing

Green peppers are ready for picking in July or August in the greenhouse, and in August or September outside. If yellow or red peppers are required, leave them to turn colour.

See also chutneys (p. 335); freezing (p. 294); pickles (p. 328) and sauces, ketchups and relishes (p. 339).

Preparing & cooking sweet peppers

In spite of their common name, the large red, green or yellow vegetable peppers have a sweet rather than a spicy flavour. Use them as soon as possible after harvesting, before they become limp, and remove the seeds before cooking and serving.

Peppers are ideal ingredients for salads, their crunchy texture giving body and substance to softer vegetables.

In cooking, peppers combine well with aubergines and tomatoes and are essential ingredients of such classic dishes as Hungarian goulash, ratatouille, caponata and peperonata. They are also excellent for stuffing and baking.

Prepare peppers by first washing and drying them. Slice off the stalk, complete with a sliver of the base – which may be reserved and used as a lid for stuffed peppers – and pick out the seeds with a teaspoon.

Use a small knife to cut out the pale membranes inside, taking care not to break the skin if the peppers are to be stuffed. The peppers can now be cut crossways into slices.

Red and green chillis are used mainly for flavouring chutneys, spicy marinades, meat stews and casseroles.

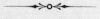

PEPPERS AND TUNA FISH SALAD

2–3 green peppers
1 large onion
4 tomatoes
12 stuffed olives
1 large tin tuna fish
5 tablespoons olive oil
2 tablespoons garlic vinegar
Salt and pepper
Garnish : chopped parsley

CHILLING TIME: 30 minutes

Trim the stalk bases off the peppers, remove the seeds and membranes and wash the peppers. Cut them into narrow rings and arrange in a salad bowl. Peel the onion, chop it finely and slice the tomatoes. Add these two ingredients to the peppers, together with the thinly sliced olives.

Drain the tuna fish and set the oil aside. Break up the fish with a fork and add to the salad bowl.

Make a dressing from the reserved tuna-fish oil, the olive oil and the vinegar, and season to taste with salt and pepper. Toss with the salad ingredients. Chill for 30 minutes.

Serving Sprinkle the salad with finely chopped parsley just before serving with hot bread.

Variation Dice the peppers instead of slicing them and substitute chopped anchovies for the tuna fish. Serve with thin brown bread and butter.

Photograph on pages 210–11.

COLD STUFFED PEPPERS

4 green or red peppers
¾ lb. (375 g.) cooked chicken
4 sticks celery
4 salad onions
5 fl. oz. (150 ml.) mayonnaise
2½ fl. oz. (75 ml.) double cream
1 tablespoon tomato paste
Salt and pepper
Tabasco sauce
Garnish : grated orange rind

Slice off the stalk base from the peppers and remove the seeds and membranes. Blanch the peppers in boiling water for 5 minutes, then leave them upside-down to drain and cool.

Remove the skin and bones from the chicken and dice the flesh into tiny pieces. Scrub the celery sticks and chop them finely ; clean and slice the salad onions. Blend the mayonnaise with the cream and tomato paste, and season to taste with salt and pepper and a few drops of tabasco.

Fold the chicken, celery and salad onions into the mayonnaise mixture, and spoon this stuffing into the drained peppers.

Serving Sprinkle the stuffing with finely grated orange rind and serve the peppers as a light, main course with a salad of dressed watercress.

Photograph on pages 206–7.

COCKTAIL PEPPERS

2 peppers (red or green)
3 oz. (75 g.) cream cheese
3 oz. (75 g.) grated Parmesan cheese
1 tablespoon cream
2 tablespoons mayonnaise
2 teaspoons chopped chives
Lemon juice
Salt and paprika

CHILLING TIME: 2 hours

Cut the stalk ends from the peppers, and remove the seeds and membranes. Cover the peppers with boiling water and leave to blanch for 5 minutes, then stand them upside-down to drain and cool.

Stir the cream cheese until smooth, and blend with the grated Parmesan cheese. Stir in the cream and mayonnaise until the mixture is perfectly smooth and of a consistency suitable for spreading.

Fold in the finely chopped chives and season to taste with lemon juice, salt and paprika. Spoon the stuffing into the peppers. Wrap the peppers in foil and chill in the refrigerator for a couple of hours.

Serving Cut the stuffed peppers crossways into thin slices with a very sharp knife. Serve on cream crackers as an appetiser with drinks, or with wholemeal rye bread as part of a cheese-board.

Perpetual spinach : see **Spinach**

Plums and gages

'Victoria'

'Denniston's Superb'

Plums, introduced from France and Italy in the 15th century, were a staple fruit in Britain until the Second World War. Then, unaccountably, the popularity of the plum suddenly declined, and many acres of orchards were turned over to other crops. The result of this slump is that plums are now comparatively expensive and, therefore, well worth growing in a garden.

The home gardener with only a small plot must, however, plan carefully where to plant and what variety to grow.

A bush or half-standard tree may have a spread of 15 ft (4.5 m.) or more, and many varieties also require a nearby tree of a different variety for cross-pollination.

The answer for the gardener with restricted space is to plant either a pyramid, that can be restricted by pruning to 9 ft (2.7 m.) high, with a spread of 8–10 ft (2.5–3 m.), or a fan-shaped tree.

In this country dessert plums and gages – the latter a fine-flavoured but less hardy form of plum – grow best against a sunny wall.

If there is space for only one tree, choose a variety that is self-fertile – that is, capable of setting fruit without being pollinated by another tree.

Prune between March and July. During autumn and winter, there is a risk that silver leaf disease may enter the pruning cuts.

Planning the crop

Both plums and gages grow best in full sun. It is essential to avoid frost pockets, as plums flower early.

They succeed in most well-drained soils, but on very acid soils top-dress with carbonate of lime at the rate of 8 oz. per square yard (240 g. per square metre) after planting.

How many to grow Provided you choose a self-pollinating variety, a single tree should yield sufficient fruit for an average family.

An established pyramid may produce 30–75 lb. (13.5–34 kg.) of fruit, according to the variety. If more than one is to be planted, space the trees 10–12 ft (3–3.6 m.) apart.

A fully grown, fan-trained tree will produce an average of 25–30 lb. (12–13.5 kg.) of plums, and much more in a good year. Plant fans 15–18 ft (4.5–5.5 m.) apart.

Where space is plentiful, plant bush trees 12–15 ft (3.6–4.5 m.) apart. Each tree, when established, will produce an average of 50–100 lb. (23–45 kg.), according to the variety.

Varieties If only one plum or gage tree is to be grown, choose from the following self-fertile varieties:

'Early Transparent Gage': apricot yellow; August.

'Laxton's Gage': large, golden-yellow fruits; heavy yielder; August. 'Denniston's Superb': greenish-yellow dessert plum; late August.

'Victoria': bright red plum suitable for bottling, jam and dessert; susceptible to silver leaf; late August.

'Marjorie's Seedling': purple plum for cooking and bottling; late September.

If there is room for more than one plum tree, so that there can be cross-pollination, choose from these varieties:

'Early Rivers': small fruits from a small, compact tree; pollinator 'Victoria'; August.

'Kirke's': purple-black dessert plum; pollinator 'Early Transparent Gage' or 'Laxton's Gage'; mid-September.

How to grow plums and gages

Plum trees can be planted at any time from November to March, but the earlier the better.

To plant (see also p. 42) dig a hole slightly wider than the spread of the roots. Make it sufficiently deep to allow the soil mark on the stem of the tree to be level with the surrounding soil after planting.

When planting a bush or dwarf pyramid, first hammer in a support stake and place the tree

Pyramid　　　*Bush*　　　*Fan-trained*

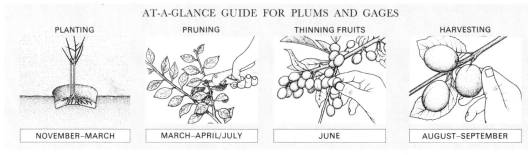

AT-A-GLANCE GUIDE FOR PLUMS AND GAGES

PLANTING — NOVEMBER–MARCH

PRUNING — MARCH–APRIL/JULY

THINNING FRUITS — JUNE

HARVESTING — AUGUST–SEPTEMBER

against it. Secure the trunk to the stake with a proprietary tree tie, or with soft string tied round a piece of cloth to protect the bark from chafing.

Before planting a fan tree, prepare the wire supports on walls as for peaches (p. 225). Place the trunk about 9 in. (230 mm.) from the wall and slope it slightly inwards while replacing the soil. Spread out the ribs of the fan evenly and tie them to the support wires with soft string.

Every April apply sulphate of ammonia at the rate of $\frac{1}{2}$ oz. per square yard (15 g. per square metre) plus a similar amount of sulphate of potash.

Every third year add a dressing of superphosphate at the rate of 2 oz. per square yard (60 g. per square metre).

After applying the fertiliser, mulch with well-rotted compost or manure at the rate of a bucketful to the square yard. Apply both the compost mulch and the dressings of fertiliser to the soil covered by the spread of the branches.

When weeding, be careful not to disturb the roots, or the tree will throw up suckers. If suckers do appear, pull them up rather than cut them off.

Training a fan tree Prune as for fan-trained peaches (p. 226) for the two or three years after planting. This will establish the framework of the tree.

Thereafter, the treatment differs because plums, unlike peaches, fruit on both old wood and on shoots produced in the previous summer.

As soon as growth begins in the spring, rub out all buds that point towards or away from the wall.

PRUNING A FAN-TRAINED PLUM TREE

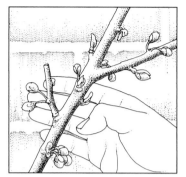

RUBBING OUT BUDS In spring, as soon as growth begins, rub out all buds that are growing towards or away from the wall.

PINCHING OUT SHOOTS In July, pinch out the tips of side-shoots not needed to form new branches. They will have six or seven leaves.

SHORTENING THE SHOOTS After the crop has been harvested, shorten by half the side-shoots that were pinched out in July.

Early in July pinch out the tips of side-shoots not needed for new branches. These shoots will have produced six or seven leaves.

Shorten these shoots by half after the crop has been picked. Cut out dead wood and prune back any unwanted shoots flush with the wood from which it springs. Brush the wounds with a bituminous tree paint.

Tie down any vertical-growing shoots so that they are trained horizontally.

Training a pyramid If you decide to train a pyramid from a maiden or one-year-old tree, cut back the stem to 5 ft (1.5 m.) above the ground in the late March after planting. Cut off flush with the stem any branches lower than 18 in. (455 mm.) from the ground. Prune back any other branches to half their length.

In the third week of July shorten branch leaders to 8 in. (200 mm.) to a downward or outward-facing bud. At the same time, prune laterals to 6 in. (150 mm.).

If you do not want to spend time on this early training you can plant a two-year-old tree in November.

In either case, future care of the tree is the same.

In the following April, and in subsequent years, shorten the central leader by two-thirds, cutting back to just above a bud. Cut out any shoots that are competing with the leader.

PRUNING AN ESTABLISHED PYRAMID

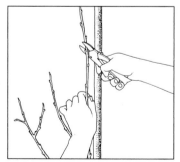

SPRING PRUNING Each April, cut back the central leader by approximately two-thirds. Make the cut just above a bud.

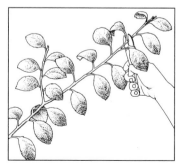

SUMMER PRUNING In July, shorten the growth on branch leaders to eight leaves. Cut back laterals to six leaves.

In July prune new growth as in the previous summer.

When the tree reaches a height of 9 ft (2.7 m.) shorten the last year's growth on the central leader to about 1 in. (25 mm.) each May. Try to keep branches at a maximum length of 4–5 ft (1.2–1.5 m.), pruning back in July.

Training a bush tree Nurserymen generally sell bush plum trees as either two or three-year-olds.

After planting a two-year-old tree, prune each of the four or five primary leaders by half to an outward-facing bud in late March or early April.

A three-year-old tree will have six to eight leaders. Prune these in late March or early April by one-third to an outward-facing bud. Repeat this treatment in the next two years.

Thereafter, restrict pruning to the cutting out of dead wood and

PRUNING A BUSH TREE

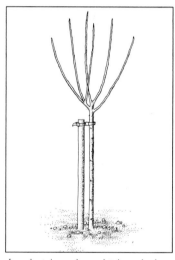

In early spring, reduce each primary leader on a newly planted two-year-old tree by half. Cut to an outward-facing bud.

shoots crossing each other. Do this as soon as possible after the crop has been harvested, and always well before leaf-fall.

Thinning the crop Plum-tree branches are often brittle. If they snap under the weight of fruit, silver leaf or other diseases may enter the wound.

To avoid this, start thinning a heavy crop in early June, but do not complete the final thinning to 2–3 in. (50–75 mm.) apart until after the natural June drop.

When thinning, curl a finger round the stalk and snap off the fruitlet with your thumbnail, leaving the stalk on the tree.

If branches are still overladen, support them by tying to stakes driven into the ground.

Pests and diseases Common pests of plums and gages are APHIDS (p. 282), CATERPILLARS (p. 282), FRUIT TREE RED SPIDER MITES (p. 283) and PLUM SAWFLY (p. 284).

The diseases most likely to occur are BACTERIAL CANKER (p. 286), BROWN ROT (p. 286), HONEY FUNGUS (p. 288), RUST (p. 290), SCALD (p. 290), SHOTHOLE (p. 290) and SILVER LEAF (p. 290).

Harvesting and storing

Pick plums for cooking, bottling (p. 309) or freezing (p. 294) before they are quite ripe. If plums are intended for eating, leave them on the tree as long as possible so that they ripen.

Go over the tree a number of times, choosing only the plums that are ready at each picking.

In wet weather pick gages before they are quite ripe or their skins are likely to split. Pick plums and gages so that the stalk comes away with the fruit.

For the various methods of preserving plums, see bottling (p. 309); chutneys (p. 335); freezing (p. 294); fruit cheeses and butters (p. 323); jams (p. 314); jellies (p. 320); pickles (p. 328) and wine-making (p. 357).

Preparing & cooking plums and gages

Sweet, juicy plums are excellent as fresh dessert fruits. They are also, together with cooking varieties, used for cooked desserts.

Wash plums and greengages, and wipe them dry before serving. Serve them whole as dessert fruits, but remove the stones before cooking. Cut along the indentations on the flesh, twist the halves apart and remove the stones with the tip of a knife.

Use halved plums and greengages in fresh fruit salads, for compôtes, as fillings for pies, flans and turnovers, and in steamed, sweet suet dumplings.

BAKED PLUM CUSTARD

1 lb. (500 g.) plums
3 eggs
3 oz. (75 g.) sugar
Grated rind of ½ lemon
7 fl. oz. (200 ml.) single cream
Pinch of baking powder

COOKING TIME: 45 minutes
OVEN TEMPERATURE: 180°C (350°F) – gas mark 4

Wash and dry the plums, cut them into halves and arrange in a lightly buttered ovenproof dish. Sprinkle 1–2 tablespoons of the sugar over them.

Separate the eggs, and beat the yolks with the remaining sugar and the lemon rind until light and fluffy. Heat the cream to just below boiling point and

pour it slowly over the creamed eggs, stirring all the time.

Strain this custard back into the pan and heat carefully until it thickens, without letting it boil. Remove from the heat. Whisk the egg whites with a pinch of baking powder until very stiff, then fold into the custard.

Pour the custard over the plums, set the dish in a roasting tin with about 1 in. (25 mm.) of cold water and bake for about 35 minutes, or until the custard is set. *Serving* For preference, serve this custard pudding warm.

COMPÔTE OF GAGES

1 lb. (500 g.) greengages
3–4 oz. (75–100 g.) sugar
½ pint (300 ml.) water
Vanilla pod

COOKING TIME: 15 minutes

Put the sugar, water and vanilla pod in a pan and set over low heat until the sugar has dissolved. Bring to the boil and simmer the syrup for 2 minutes.

Wash and dry the gages, cut them into halves and remove the stones. Add the gage halves to the syrup and bring back to the boil. Cover with a lid and simmer gently for about 10 minutes. Leave to cool, then remove pod. *Serving* Compôtes may be served lukewarm or cold, with a jug of cream or custard sauce.

ALSATIAN GREENGAGE TART

1 lb. (500 g.) greengages
4 tablespoons ginger wine
1 oz. (25 g.) sugar
½ lb. (250 g.) sweet shortcrust pastry
½ pint (300 ml.) milk
1 tablespoon caster sugar
2 egg yolks
1 teaspoon cornflour
1 tablespoon ground almonds

COOKING TIME: 35 minutes
OVEN TEMPERATURE: 180°C (350°F) – gas mark 4

Wash and wipe the greengages, cut them into halves and remove the stones. Dissolve the 1 oz. (25 g.) of sugar in the ginger wine and pour over the greengages.

Meanwhile, make up the shortcrust pastry, using ½ lb. (250 g.) flour. Roll it out and use it to line an 8 in. (200 mm.) flan ring set on a baking sheet. Prick the base closely with a fork and leave to chill in the refrigerator.

Make a custard from the milk, sugar and egg yolks, and thicken with the cornflour stirred in a little cold milk. Fold the ground almonds into the custard sauce.

Drain the greengages and arrange, rounded sides up, over the pastry base. Pour the custard over the greengages and bake in the centre of the oven for about 35 minutes, or until the custard has set and the pastry is golden. *Serving* Remove the ring from the baked flan, leave to cool slightly but serve while still warm.

PLUMS IN RED WINE

1½ lb. (750 g.) 'Victoria' plums
2 oz. (50 g.) sugar
5 fl. oz. (150 ml.) water
½ pint (300 ml.) red wine
6 whole cloves
2 tablespoons flaked almonds

COOKING TIME: 20 minutes

Wash and dry the plums, cut them into halves along the indentations, twist the halves apart and ease out the stones.

Put the sugar and water in a pan, bring to the boil and simmer gently until the sugar has dissolved. Stir in the red wine, then add the cloves and the halved plums.

Cover the pan with a lid and remove from the heat. Leave the plums to steep in the syrup for 10 minutes.

Lift out the plums with a perforated spoon, put them in a serving bowl and keep them warm. Return the syrup to the heat, and boil rapidly until it has reduced by about one-third and thickened slightly. Strain the syrup and pour it over the plums.

Toast the flaked almonds under a medium grill until golden-brown. *Serving* Sprinkle the toasted almonds over the plums and serve while still warm, accompanied with a jug of cream. *Photograph* on pages 208–9.

Potatoes

POPULAR VARIETIES

'King Edward'
(Maincrop)

'Majestic'
(Maincrop)

'Kerr's Pink'
(Second early)

'Home Guard'
(First early)

'Golden Wonder'
(Maincrop)

Despite the legends, it seems unlikely that Sir Walter Raleigh had much to do with the introduction of the potato to England, though he may well have planted some on his Cork estates in 1588, the year of the Armada.

There is some evidence, though it is not conclusive, that the potato was brought to England some two years earlier in the holds of Sir Francis Drake's ships, fresh from their profitable raids on South America, where the vegetable originated.

Surprisingly, more than 150 years were to pass before the British regarded the potato as anything more than a novelty or as cattle food. Only since the Irish and Scottish famines of the 18th century, when its true value was realised, has it become the second most important food crop in Britain.

Because potatoes were traditionally cheap in the shops, a couple of rows of an early variety were considered sufficient by most gar-

deners until a year or two ago. More recently, startling increases in price have led the owners of even small gardens to grow both early and maincrop varieties.

Unless space is at an absolute premium, it is a good idea to grow at least a few potatoes – preferably of an early variety. Apart from being a basic part of the family diet, the frequent moving of the soil during their cultivation helps to clear the plot of annual weeds.

Ground from which early potatoes have been harvested can be used for planting late crops such as cabbages, leeks and even peas.

Planning the crop

Potatoes grow best in an open position. If grown in shade, the haulm, or green top, becomes lank and spindly as it reaches upward for the light.

Potatoes grow reasonably well in most soils, but the best results are obtained from land that has been well manured. Dig the

ground in the autumn or winter, working in compost or well-rotted manure at the rate of a bucketful to the square yard.

A fortnight before planting, dress the ground with a mixture of 2 parts superphosphate, 1 part sulphate of ammonia and 1 part sulphate of potash, using the mixture at the rate of 4 oz. per square yard (120 g. per square metre). Alternatively, apply a general fertiliser at 2–3 oz. per square yard (60–90 g. per square metre).

How much to grow Potatoes take up a lot of space, so much depends on how valuable you feel these vegetables to be to the family economy. A bed 20 × 20 ft (6 × 6 m.) for example, might produce about 4 cwt (200 kg.) of maincrop potatoes, which could keep a family of four supplied for six months or more.

A bed of this size, however, is as big as the whole vegetable plot in many gardens, and such a yield would depend on good manuring

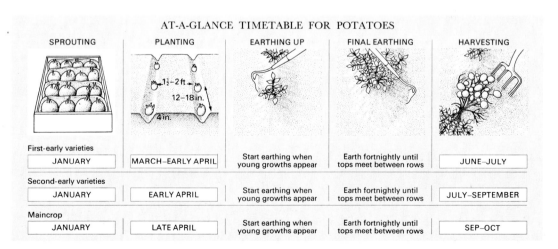

AT-A-GLANCE TIMETABLE FOR POTATOES

	SPROUTING	PLANTING	EARTHING UP	FINAL EARTHING	HARVESTING
First-early varieties	JANUARY	MARCH–EARLY APRIL	Start earthing when young growths appear	Earth fortnightly until tops meet between rows	JUNE–JULY
Second-early varieties	JANUARY	EARLY APRIL	Start earthing when young growths appear	Earth fortnightly until tops meet between rows	JULY–SEPTEMBER
Maincrop	JANUARY	LATE APRIL	Start earthing when young growths appear	Earth fortnightly until tops meet between rows	SEP–OCT

and cultivation. Early potatoes give a much smaller yield, but are dug in June and July when prices are still comparatively high.

Varieties Not all potatoes are suitable for every district, so seek local advice before settling on a particular variety. It is advisable to buy seed potatoes, which are grown in an area free from disease-carrying aphids, and not to plant those sold for eating.

First-early varieties (for harvesting in early summer):

'Arran Pilot': a potato with a somewhat floury texture.

'Home Guard': round tubers; good on heavy soil.

'Pentland Javelin': early; white, firm flesh; good flavour.

'Sutton's Foremost': produces heavy crops; firm texture when cooked.

'Ulster Chieftain': often the first variety to appear; this, too, has a floury texture.

Second-early varieties (for harvesting in mid-summer):

'Ben Lomond': a floury and flaky potato.

'Craig's Royal': smooth, waxy texture.

'Kerr's Pink': excellent for growing in heavy soil.

Maincrop varieties (for harvesting in early autumn):

'Desirée': a heavy cropper with a fine flavour.

'Golden Wonder': perhaps the best-flavoured potato; moderate cropper; excellent roasted or chipped.

'King Edward': pink eyes; heavy cropper; good cooker.

'Majestic': will grow almost anywhere; smooth, waxy texture.

'Pentland Crown': large crops; excellent whether boiled, baked,

mashed or fried; scab resistant.

'Pentland Dell': produces good crops; resistant to blight and mosaic virus.

Preparing seed potatoes for planting

Buy seed potatoes in January and at once take them from their bags and put in a cool, well-ventilated room. At the end of the month set them in seed trays with their 'eyes', from which the sprouts will grow, uppermost.

Place the trays in a cool room or greenhouse. In four or five weeks the sprouts should be sturdy and, ideally, $\frac{1}{2}$–1 in. (12–25 mm.) long.

Sprouted in this way, the potatoes have a longer growing season and produce a heavier crop.

How to grow potatoes

Plant first-early potatoes between mid-March and early April in the south of England; but in the north and in more exposed parts of the country it is best to wait until mid-April. Plant second-earlies in early April, and maincrop varieties towards the end of the month.

Use a draw hoe to make drills 4 in. (100 mm.) deep and 18 in. (455 mm.) apart for early potatoes, and 2 ft (610 mm.) apart for maincrop varieties. Alternatively, plant the potatoes 4 in. (100 mm.) deep with a trowel.

Select well-sprouted tubers and set them at the bottom of the drills or trowel holes – 12 in. (305 mm.) apart for early varieties and 18 in. (455 mm.) apart for maincrop potatoes. Place them carefully so that the sprouts are uppermost.

The ideal seed potato is about the size of a hen's egg and has at least two sprouts. A larger tuber

may be cut in half before planting, leaving at least one sprout on each piece.

Return the soil to the drill, or fill each hole, and draw up a little more soil from between the rows to make a slight ridge over the line of planted potatoes.

When the first shoots appear draw soil over them with a hoe, increasing the height of the ridge, as protection from late frosts.

Earth up the plants again when they are about 9 in. (230 mm.) high, and again a fortnight or so after that.

Continue earthing at intervals until the foliage meets between the rows.

During a dry spring, water early potatoes frequently during May and early June to ensure that the crop matures while shop prices are still high.

Potato blight may infect maincrop potatoes between May and August if a spell of warm weather coincides with high humidity. June and July are the main danger months. Regular spraying (see p. 289) will prevent infection.

Pests and diseases APHIDS (p. 282), POTATO CYST EELWORM (p. 284), SLUGS AND SNAILS (p. 285) and WIREWORM (p. 285) are common pests of the potato.

The diseases most likely to occur are BLACK LEG (p. 286), GANGRENE (p. 288), POTATO BLIGHT (p. 289), POWDERY SCAB (p. 289), SCAB (p. 290), SPRAING (p. 291) and WART DISEASE (p. 291).

Harvesting and storing

Potato-lifting time varies considerably from one part of the country to another, depending on prevailing climatic conditions. In the

south-west, and in other sheltered areas, the earliest varieties may be ready for harvesting at the beginning of June, while in other districts they may not come to maturity until several weeks later.

As a rough guide, you should be able to gather a few new potatoes when about 12–14 weeks have elapsed since planting.

To gather a few early potatoes before the crop as a whole is ready for digging, brush away a little soil from the sides of a ridge and remove any potatoes that have grown to the size of a hen's egg.

Replace the soil over the smaller tubers and leave them to grow. They should at least double in size during the next two or three weeks, after which the crop can be lifted as required.

When lifting potatoes, insert the fork at least 6 in. (150 mm.) away from the stems to avoid impaling the tubers. Push it well into the side of the ridge so that the plant can be lifted and thrown between the rows in a single action.

Maincrop potatoes, on the other hand, take at least 20 weeks to come to full maturity – that is, to be ready for storing.

Some may be dug a few weeks earlier, but they will have to be used immediately since the skins will not yet have set.

Before lifting the entire crop, test one or two potatoes by rubbing the skin with your thumb. If the skin of the tuber does not rub off, the crop is ready for storing.

Store potatoes in a dry, cool, but frost-free place. Place them in light-proof but ventilated containers such as boxes or hessian sacks, or pile them on a dry floor and cover with straw.

See also freezing (p. 294). ✍✍

Home-grown new potatoes have unequalled flavour and a firm texture. They should be scrubbed or scraped – never peeled – or boiled in their skins. They are excellent served cold in salads, but are probably most delicious when boiled whole in lightly salted water, with a sprig of mint, until just tender. Serve them tossed in butter, and sprinkled with chopped parsley, dill, chives or coarse salt.

Maincrop potatoes should be scrubbed free of dirt, peeled, and any eyes cut out, then cut into even-sized pieces. Place in cold water and boil for about 20 minutes.

Potatoes of even size may also be boiled without peeling, and the skins removed after cooking and draining. This method reduces wastage due to peeling.

Boiled potatoes can be mashed with a fork or a potato masher, or rubbed through a coarse sieve to make 'potato snow'. Mashed potatoes may be creamed with butter, milk or cream, eggs and seasoning. Add a touch of green by folding in chopped parsley, chives, freshly chopped kale or spinach, or brighten the dish with roughly chopped tomato or crisp-fried onions.

Duchesse potatoes are made from creamed potatoes enriched with egg. Pipe the potato into small heaps about 2 in. (50 mm.) high on a baking tray, or place them as a border round a

Preparing & cooking potatoes

cooked dish, and bake in a hot oven for about 25 minutes, or until golden.

For fried or sautéed potatoes, boil the potatoes until almost tender, cut them into $\frac{1}{4}$ in. (5 mm.) thick slices, and shallow-fry in hot fat over moderate heat until golden-brown and crisp. Serve sprinkled with coarse salt, parsley, chopped marjoram or chives.

To make chips, peel the potatoes, cut them into $\frac{1}{4}$–$\frac{1}{2}$ in. (5–12 mm.) slices and cut these into $\frac{1}{4}$–$\frac{1}{2}$ in. strips.

Heat fat in a deep-fryer to smoking point – 196°C (385°F) – and lower the basket with a single layer of chips into the hot fat for 4–6 minutes. Drain thoroughly on absorbent paper, but just before serving fry the chips again for 1–2 minutes.

Matchstick chips are cut into tiny strips and fried for about 3 minutes. Game chips – cut into very thin rounds – should also be fried for 3 minutes.

For roasting, peel the potatoes and cut them into even sizes, then par-boil for 5 minutes before placing round a roasting joint for 50–60 minutes. Baked potatoes in their jackets need at least 1 hour in a hot oven.

Anna potatoes are made with new or old potatoes. After peeling, cut them into thin slices and arrange them in overlapping layers in a buttered, ovenproof dish. Sprinkle with salt, dot with butter and bake, covered, in the oven for an hour at 190°C (375°F) –gas mark 5.

BAKED POTATOES

4 large, even-sized potatoes
2 oz. (50 g.) butter

COOKING TIME: 1$\frac{1}{4}$ hours (approx.)
OVEN TEMPERATURE: 200°C (400°F) – gas mark 6

Scrub the potatoes thoroughly to remove all dirt, then dry them and prick all over with a fork. Use a sharp knife to make a small cross through the skin on the upper side, then set the potatoes on a baking tray and bake near the top of the oven for 1–1$\frac{1}{4}$ hours.

Open up the cross on the potatoes, top with a good knob of butter and serve at once.
Photograph on pages 212–13.

Variations For baked, stuffed potatoes, scoop out the flesh carefully from the baked potatoes, mash it and mix with any of the following ingredients, then pile the stuffing back into the potato skins and return to the oven for another 15 minutes to heat through. Baked stuffed potatoes make a complete snack on their own.

For four large baked potatoes, blend the mashed potato with any of the following:

1 oz. (25 g.) butter
1 lightly beaten egg
2 oz. (50 g.) diced, cooked ham
Salt, pepper and chopped parsley

3 oz. (75 g.) butter
1 flaked, smoked haddock or mackerel
Salt and pepper
Milk

2 teaspoons mixed, freshly chopped herbs
1 oz. (25 g.) butter
1 egg
4 tablespoons breadcrumbs
Milk

8 rashers of bacon, diced and fried crisp
1 finely chopped onion
Milk

8 tablespoons soured cream
Finely chopped chives

POTATO SALADS
Salads based on potatoes may be served hot or cold – hot with grilled or fried chops, cutlets, sausages and frankfurters; cold with cold meats and poultry and with other salads. For four persons, allow 1 lb. (500 g.) of new potatoes, which should be scrubbed clean and boiled in salted water for about 20 minutes, until tender but still firm.

Peel the cooked potatoes, cut them into $\frac{1}{4}$ in. (5 mm.) slices and make into a hot salad as follows:

Melt 1 oz. (25 g.) of butter in a pan. Add 2 sliced onions and cook for 5 minutes, then add 4 tablespoons of water, 4 tablespoons of vinegar, salt, pepper and 1 tablespoon of sugar. Add the potato slices, turn them in the marinade, cover with a lid and heat through gently.

Alternatively, heat the potato slices in a dressing of 4 tablespoons of tomato purée and 4 tablespoons of cream, and flavour with thyme.

Another method is to dice 6–8 bacon rashers and fry until crisp,

then add 1 finely chopped onion and fry lightly for 5 minutes.

Mix 1 tablespoon of flour with 3 tablespoons of vinegar and 6 tablespoons of water, and add to the pan. Put the sliced potatoes into the sauce, with half a sliced cucumber and 6 sliced radishes. Heat through and sprinkle with freshly chopped dill.
Photograph on pages 138–9.

Alternatively, heat the potato slices through in a creamy white sauce seasoned with freshly grated horseradish and sugar.

For a cold potato salad, turn the slices in 2$\frac{1}{2}$ fl. oz. (75 ml.) of mayonnaise mixed with a little cream and finely chopped chives or parsley. Or toss the potatoes in a French or oil-vinaigrette dressing, or in a soured-cream dressing.

Cold sliced potatoes can also be mixed with cooked French beans and diced celeriac, and tossed in a French dressing. Or they may be mixed with chopped hard-boiled eggs or salami, finely chopped raw onion, and diced red or green pepper, before dressing with mayonnaise thinned with cream, vinegar and mustard.
Photograph on pages 140–1.

BULGARIAN POTATO PIE

2 lb. (1 kg.) potatoes
6 tablespoons oil
1 large onion
4 tablespoons tomato paste
6 fl. oz. (175 ml.) dry white wine
Salt, pepper and paprika
2 tablespoons fine white breadcrumbs

COOKING TIME: 1$\frac{1}{4}$ hours
OVEN TEMPERATURE: 180°C (350°F) –gas mark 4

Peel the potatoes and cut into $\frac{1}{2}$ in. (12 mm.) slices; dry thoroughly on absorbent kitchen paper. Heat 5 tablespoons of the oil in a pan and fry the potato slices for 2 minutes. Lift out with a perforated spoon and drain on kitchen paper.

Add the finely chopped onion to the pan and fry for 3 minutes, then stir in the tomato paste and the wine. Bring to the boil, and continue boiling rapidly until the liquid has reduced by one-third.

Spoon half the potato slices into a buttered ovenproof dish, sprinkle with salt, pepper and paprika, and pour half the sauce over them. Add the remaining potatoes and the rest of the sauce.

Top with the breadcrumbs and sprinkle the last tablespoon of oil over them. Cover with a lid and bake in the lower half of the oven for 1 hour. Remove lid for the last 15 minutes.
Serving The pie may be served as a dish on its own, with a bowl of soured cream and a salad.

Continued...

Potato recipes (continued)

POTATO NESTS

1 lb. (500 g.) potatoes
Salt and pepper
2 egg yolks
3 tablespoons butter
2 tablespoons grated Cheddar cheese
1 egg

COOKING TIME: 35–40 minutes
OVEN TEMPERATURE: 200°C (400°F) –
gas mark 6

Peel the potatoes and cut them into even pieces. Put in a pan with water and 1 teaspoon of salt and cook for about 20 minutes, or until tender. Drain, and press through a coarse sieve.

Beat the egg yolks, butter and cheese into the potato mixture, blending thoroughly and seasoning to taste with salt and pepper. Shape about two-thirds of the mixture into round cakes, each about 3 in. (75 mm.) across. Set them on a greased baking sheet and brush the surfaces with the lightly beaten egg.

Spoon the remaining potato mixture into a forcing bag fitted with a broad, fluted nozzle and pipe the mixture round the edge of the potato cakes. Bake the potato nests in the oven for about 15 minutes, or until golden-brown.
Serving Potato nests can be served just as they are. They are also attractive when filled with tiny buttered peas, creamed mushrooms or bits of left-over meat in a cream sauce.
Photograph on pages 206–7.

POTATO SOUP

1½ lb. (750 g.) potatoes
1 large onion
2 leeks
2 carrots
2 oz. (50 g.) butter
2 pints (1 l.) white stock
1 bouquet garni
Salt and pepper
2 oz. (50 g.) cooked ham
Garnish : chopped chives

COOKING TIME: 40 minutes

Peel the potatoes and chop them roughly. Peel the onion and chop it finely, and trim the roots and upper green leaves from the leeks. Wash the leeks thoroughly, then cut cross-ways into narrow slices. Peel and chop the carrots.

Melt the butter in a pan, add the onion and cook gently for about 5 minutes, until soft but not coloured. Add the potatoes, leeks and carrots and cook until all the vegetables are coated.

Add the stock and bouquet-garni. Season with salt and pepper, cover, and simmer for about 20 minutes, or until the vegetables are tender and the potatoes are breaking up. Put the soup through a coarse sieve.

Re-heat the soup, adding milk to give the required consistency. Dice the ham, stir it into the soup and correct the seasoning.
Serving Pour the soup into bowls, and sprinkle with finely chopped chives.

Pumpkins and squashes

Pumpkins, squashes and edible gourds occur in one form or another in most tropical regions. They have certain basic similarities, and the pumpkins and squashes are closely related to the more familiar vegetable marrow. However, ornamental gourds are not suitable for eating.

There are two types of plants – bushes and trailers. Though interesting as novelties, both occupy a good deal of space. Therefore, if you have only a small vegetable plot, you should perhaps consider whether it is worth growing pumpkins at all.

Planning the crop

Pumpkins thrive in full sun in rich, well-drained soil. The top of a compost heap would be ideal.

Otherwise, dig holes about 15 in. (380 mm.) square and fill with well-rotted compost, leaving a shallow depression at the top.

How many to grow Two or three plants should be adequate.

Varieties 'Gold Summer Crook-neck' and 'Prolific Straight Neck' are both bush types that produce small pumpkins in early summer.

'Noodle' is a trailing variety.

'Hundredweight', 'Large Yellow' and 'Mammoth' are all large-fruited, bush varieties.

How to grow pumpkins

Sow one or two seeds in 3 in. (75 mm.) pots of seed compost in late April or early May. Germinate at a temperature of 18–21°C (64–70°F) and harden off the seedlings in a cold frame. Transplant to the final growing positions in late May or early June, setting the plants at least 3 ft (1 m.) apart.

Pinch out the growing point of each plant when it has about five leaves.

Larger fruits may be grown by heaping soil over the axis of fruit-bearing laterals, the point where they emerge from the main stem. Roots will then be sent out to obtain more food and moisture.

Water copiously in dry spells.

Pests and diseases APHIDS (p. 282), GLASSHOUSE RED SPIDER MITES (p. 283) and GLASSHOUSE WHITE-FLY (p. 283) are the principal pests.

Possible diseases include CUCUMBER MOSAIC VIRUS (p. 287), POWDERY MILDEW (p. 289) and SOIL-BORNE DISEASES (p. 290).

Harvesting and storing

Cut small-fruited varieties as they mature in summer. Leave large-fruited types on the plants until late autumn. Store for winter use in a frost-free shed.

AT-A-GLANCE TIMETABLE FOR PUMPKINS

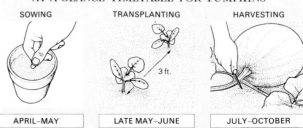

SOWING	TRANSPLANTING	HARVESTING
APRIL–MAY	LATE MAY–JUNE	JULY–OCTOBER

Preparing & cooking pumpkins and squashes

Both vegetables belong to the same family as marrows and courgettes. The smaller varieties, which often have crooked necks, may be cooked like courgettes after the thin skin has been removed.

Young, ripe squashes are also suitable for steaming in butter or for baking whole with a savoury filling. Another way is to mix the mashed pulp with creamed spinach for stuffing aubergines.

Pumpkins, which are a large type of squash, mature in early autumn. They are an extremely popular vegetable in America, where they are associated with hallowe'en and used in two classic dishes – pumpkin pie and pumpkin soup.

They can also be used as an accompanying vegetable. For this purpose, cut the pumpkin in half crossways, and remove the seeds and stringy bits. Put in a roasting tin, shell side up, round a joint of meat and bake in the oven at a temperature of 160°C (325°F) – gas mark 3 – for about an hour, or until the flesh is tender. Scrape the pulp from the shell, mash to a purée and cream with butter and seasoning.

Pumpkins may also be cut into small chunks, peeled and divested of seeds, and boiled in lightly salted water for 20–30 minutes. Serve with a cheese sauce.

PUMPKIN SOUP

2 lb. (1 kg.) pumpkin
Salt, pepper and cayenne
4 oz. (100 g.) butter
1 large onion
2 pints (1 l.) milk
Sugar
5 fl. oz. (150 ml.) cream (optional)
Garnish : finely chopped dill or chervil

COOKING TIME: 45–50 minutes

Cut the pumpkin into small chunks. Cut off the peel and remove the seeds and stringy parts. Put the pumpkin in a pan containing just enough boiling, lightly salted water to cover the chunks. Bring to the boil and simmer for about 15 minutes, or until the pulp is tender.

Drain, and either rub the pumpkin pulp through a coarse sieve or mash it in a liquidiser.

Melt the butter in a pan and fry the peeled and finely chopped onion for about 5 minutes, or until soft and transparent. Add the pumpkin purée and heat through for 10 minutes, stirring frequently to prevent burning. Gradually add the hot milk, and season to taste. Heat the soup through.

Strain the soup through a sieve. Return it to the pan and heat again. Correct the seasoning and blend in the cream (if used) without letting the soup reach boiling point.
Serving Pour into soup bowls and sprinkle with the herbs.

PUMPKIN PIE

1 lb. (500 g.) pumpkin purée
½ lb. (250 g.) shortcrust pastry
½ pint (300 ml.) cream
3 eggs
1 tablespoon grated lemon peel
5 oz. (150 g.) caster sugar
½ teaspoon salt
1 teaspoon ground ginger
½ teaspoon each of ground cinnamon and ground cloves

COOKING TIME: 1¼ hours
OVEN TEMPERATURE: 180°C (350°F) – gas mark 4

Make the purée by cutting the pumpkin into chunks, removing the skin and seeds and boiling in lightly salted water until tender. Drain, rub through a sieve, then set aside to cool.

Roll out the pastry and use it to line a 9–10 in. (230–255 mm.) flan ring set on a baking sheet. Bake this blind in the oven, at a temperature of 200°C (400°F) – gas mark 6 – until brown.

Beat the cream lightly with the eggs, lemon peel and sugar. Stir this mixture into the pumpkin purée and add the salt, ginger, cinnamon and ground cloves. Combine thoroughly, then spoon the filling into the pie shell and bake until set and brown.
Serving This Thanksgiving Day pie is served cold with a bowl of whipped cream, or the cream may be piped on to the pie and garnished with walnut halves or crystallised violets.
Photograph on pages 208–9.

Quince

The quince has been grown in Europe for so long that its place of origin has been forgotten, though it probably derived from somewhere in central Asia.

The tree lives to a great age and, as it matures, puts out wide, contorted branches. These, and the large white or pale rose flowers that are produced in June, make the tree a picturesque backdrop for any large garden.

Quinces require a good deal of space. Even in bush form they grow to a height of 10–12 ft (3–3.6 m.) with a spread of 10 ft, while as standard trees they may reach 15 ft (4.5 m.) with a spread of 15 ft.

Planning the crop

Quinces will succeed in any good garden soil, but do best in a moist loam and in an open, sunny situation.

In the north, however, they require some protection, such as a sunny corner bounded by two walls. Unless grown in such a sheltered place, it is unlikely that the fruits will ripen on the tree.

How many to grow Quinces are self-fertile, so it is unnecessary to grow more than a single tree.

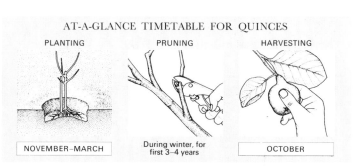

AT-A-GLANCE TIMETABLE FOR QUINCES

PLANTING	PRUNING	HARVESTING
NOVEMBER–MARCH	During winter, for first 3–4 years	OCTOBER

Varieties At least some of the following are usually stocked by the bigger shrub nurseries:

'Champion', 'Meech's Prolific', 'Portugal' and 'Vranja' ('Bereczeki'). The fruits of 'Champion' are apple-shaped. The others are pear-shaped.

How to grow quinces

Buy two-year-old plants for bushes, and three or four-year-olds for standards. Plant between November and March (see p. 42).

Each February apply bonemeal at the rate of 4–5 oz. per square yard (120–150 g. per square metre) to the area beneath the branches. In May, apply a mulch of compost over the same area.

For the first three or four years, winter-prune the one-year-old growths by half. In following years no pruning is necessary, except to cut out diseased wood or badly placed branches.

Pests and diseases The pests most likely to occur are APHIDS (p. 282), CAPSID BUGS (p. 282), CATERPILLARS (p. 282), CODLING MOTH (p. 283) and FRUIT TREE RED SPIDER MITES (p. 283).

The most likely disease is POWDERY MILDEW (p. 289).

Harvesting and storing

Pick the fruits in October and store in a cool, dry, frost-proof place. Fruits continue to ripen after harvesting, and generally last for six to eight weeks.

Keep them away from other fruits, such as apples and pears, which may become tainted by the strong aroma of the quinces.

See also freezing (p. 294); fruit cheeses and butters (p. 323); jams (p. 314) and jellies (p. 320). 🐌🐌

Preparing & cooking quinces

This hard fruit, which is ready for picking in the autumn, is not suitable for eating raw. For this reason it is usually made into a sparklingly clear, rose-pink jelly which is an ideal accompaniment to fatty meats and roast game. Because of their high pectin content, quinces also make excellent jams.

Quinces require long, slow cooking – about 1½ hours – to reduce them to a pulp for jam and jelly-making, but only about half that time for use as pie fillings. They combine particularly well with apples, but need a lot of sweetening in the form of sugar or honey.

Quince honey is a form of confectionery favoured by the ancient Greeks. To make it, boil chopped quinces until pulpy, rub them through a sieve, and add 1½ lb. (750 g.) sugar to every 2 lb. (1 kg.) of quince purée.

Bring to the boil and simmer for about 15 minutes, until quite thick, as for making fruit cheeses (see p. 323). Pour the mixture on to a flat, wet dish and leave to dry in a warm place for about a week; then cut into squares and roll in crushed lump sugar. Store in air-tight tins.

QUINCE AND APPLE PIE

½ lb. (250 g.) quinces (prepared weight)
¾ lb. (375 g.) apples (prepared weight)
1 oz. (25 g.) honey
1 oz. (25 g.) butter
2 oz. (50 g.) sugar
6 oz. (175 g.) shortcrust pastry

COOKING TIME: 1¼ hours (approx.)
OVEN TEMPERATURE: 200°C (400°F) – gas mark 6

Peel the quinces, cut them into small chunks and remove the cores. Melt the honey and butter in a heavy-based pan and stir in about 4 fl. oz. (100 ml.) of water.

Add the quinces, cover with a lid and simmer over a gentle heat until the quinces are just tender. This will take about 45 minutes, depending on ripeness. Leave to cool.

Peel and core the apples and cut them into chunks. Mix the apple and quince pieces and arrange in a pie dish. Sprinkle with the sugar and add 4 tablespoons of either the quince cooking liquid or water.

Cover the pie with the rolled-out pastry, decorate with the pastry trimmings, brush with milk and sprinkle lightly with sugar. Make a slit in the pastry top and bake in the oven for 35–40 minutes.
Serving Serve, either warm or cold, with a jug of cream.

Radishes

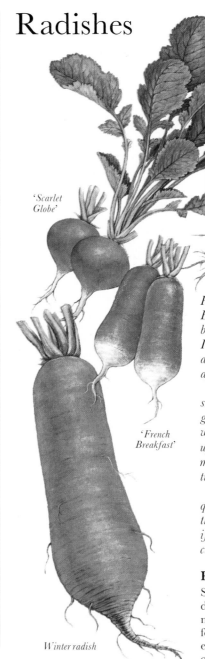

'Long White Icicle'

'Scarlet Globe'

'French Breakfast'

Winter radish

Radishes were grown by the ancient Egyptians, and were probably brought to Britain by the Romans. In Shakespeare's day the radish was a favourite dish to stimulate the appetite.

There are two main types: the small, summer varieties that are grown for salads; and the large, winter radishes, whose roots weigh up to ½ lb. (250 g.) or more and may be eaten raw or cooked like turnips.

Summer radishes are among the quickest-maturing vegetables, and they may be grown all the year round if given the protection of frames and cloches during the winter.

Planning the crop

Summer radishes do not need deeply dug soil because they are not in the ground for more than a few weeks, but they grow best – especially in hot weather – if sifted compost or sedge peat is worked into the top 3–4 in. (75–100 mm.) at the rate of a bucketful to the square yard.

Well-drained soil is needed for the first sowings under glass in January and February.

Winter radishes, like other root crops, grow best in soil that was manured for a previous crop.

In spring, sow radishes in a sunny but sheltered spot. In summer, choose a position in partial shade to help prevent the plants going to seed prematurely.

How much to sow For a continuous supply of summer radishes, sow a row 8 ft (2.5 m.) long every three weeks.

When sown thinly, an average packet of seed should be enough for three sowings.

Varieties For sowing in a frame or under cloches:

'Round Scarlet Forcing': the earliest of the round radishes.

'Saxerre': an early, round-rooted variety.

For outdoor sowing between March and September:

'French Breakfast': tender, with a mild flavour; long-rooted.

'Long White Icicle': the best of all white radishes.

'Scarlet Globe': a brilliant red radish, with delicate white flesh.

Note that some seedsmen sell packets of mixed varieties, which are useful for adding interest to a salad.

Winter radishes:

'Black Spanish Long' and 'Black Spanish Round': both varieties have black skin and white flesh.

'China Rose': long, blunt-ended roots; rose-coloured skin.

How to grow summer radishes

Make the first sowings in a cold frame or under cloches in January and February. Put cloches in position a fortnight before sowing, to help warm the soil and prevent excessive wetness.

Sow thinly in drills ¼ in. (5 mm.) deep and about 6 in. (150 mm.) apart.

Do not sow thickly or the plants will produce foliage at the expense of the roots. Instead, aim at sowing about ½–1 in. (12–25 mm.) apart in the drills.

If you do this, and subsequently thin out any crowded plants, the crop will get away to the best possible start.

Keep the soil moist so that the radishes grow quickly.

From March onwards, sow outdoors at the spacings advised for early crops. Frequent sowings will ensure a continuous supply of tender young radishes. If left for more than a week or two when mature, they will become woody and lose their flavour.

Since radishes are in the ground for such a short time they make an admirable catch-crop. The first row, for instance, can be sown between two rows of parsnips; the second between rows of peas; and so on.

How to grow winter radishes

Sow the large-rooted winter varieties from June to August in drills 12 in. (305 mm.) apart, and thin the plants to 6 in. (150 mm.) spacings when large enough to handle.

Keep the soil moist during dry weather, otherwise the plants will not make sufficient growth by autumn.

Pests and diseases Radishes may be attacked by FLEA BEETLE (p. 283).

They are generally disease-free.

Harvesting and storing

Pull as many summer radishes as needed when they are young and tender. Throw any plants not required on to the compost heap.

The roots of winter radishes may be left in the ground until required. Alternatively, lift them in late October and store in boxes of sand in a cool, airy place.

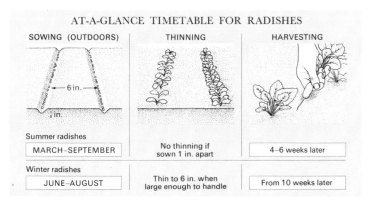

AT-A-GLANCE TIMETABLE FOR RADISHES

SOWING (OUTDOORS)	THINNING	HARVESTING
Summer radishes MARCH–SEPTEMBER	No thinning if sown 1 in. apart	4–6 weeks later
Winter radishes JUNE–AUGUST	Thin to 6 in. when large enough to handle	From 10 weeks later

Preparing & serving radishes

Both red and white radishes, whether round or tapering, may be used in salads or served with cheese or as a garnish.

Trim the roots and tops off completely if used in salads, but leave ½–1 in. (12–25 mm.) of the tops when served with cheese. Wash and dry the radishes, and cut away any blemishes on the skins.

For mixed salads, cut large radishes into slices; otherwise, leave them whole and serve with a hunk of cheese, coarse rye bread, ice-cold butter and coarse salt.

Use sliced radishes in sandwich fillings – where they are particularly good with smoked fish, such as buckling and mackerel – or with cold chicken or chopped hard-boiled eggs turned in a little mayonnaise.

Prepare large radishes and winter radishes as above, leave them whole and cook in boiling, lightly salted water for about 10 minutes. Serve with parsley sauce.

RADISH GARNISHES

Attractive garnishes can be made from fresh radishes to decorate cold savoury dishes, sandwiches, salads and hors-d'oeuvres.

For radish roses, choose round radishes, trim off the roots and make six to eight cuts lengthways from the root end towards the stalk. Put the radishes in a bowl of iced water with a few ice cubes, and leave in the refrigerator until the cuts open out like flower petals.

Long radishes can be cut almost through along their length, and left in iced water until they open like a concertina.

BRIE AND RADISH MOUSSE

8 oz. (250 g.) ripe Brie
½ pint (300 ml.) double cream
Celery salt, white pepper
¾ oz. (20 g.) powdered gelatine
14–16 radishes
Garnish: radish roses

CHILLING TIME: 3–4 hours

Remove the rind from the Brie and stir it smooth with a little of the cream. Season to taste with celery salt and white pepper.

Whisk the remaining cream fairly stiff and fold into the cheese mixture. Dissolve the gelatine in a little water and blend thoroughly into the creamed mixture.

Remove the tops and roots from the radishes; wash and dry them well, then chop them roughly. Blend the radishes into the cheese mixture and spoon it into a lightly oiled mould. Chill in the refrigerator for 3–4 hours, or until set.

Serving Turn the mould out on to a serving dish, garnish with radish roses and serve with cheese biscuits.

Raspberries

Among the most delicious of summer fruits, raspberries are grown throughout the cooler parts of Europe. A site in full sun will produce the best crops, but the canes will also thrive in partial shade and will yield well even during a cool, damp summer.

For the space they occupy, raspberries give a higher yield than any fruit other than strawberries. As they also freeze well, retaining almost all their flavour, they warrant a place in most gardens.

There are two kinds of raspberries: summer-fruiting varieties that produce fruit on the previous season's shoots during July and August, and the lighter-cropping autumn varieties that fruit on current season's growth from mid-September onwards.

Birds will make heavy inroads unless the canes are protected by a fruit cage (see p. 45), or at least by draping muslin or netting over them while the fruits ripen.

Like strawberries, raspberries taste best when served fresh with sugar and cream. They can also be used to make a wide range of other desserts, including a refreshing water ice, and are excellent for jam.

Planning the crop

Choose a sunny site if possible, or one that is in shade for a few hours each day, but not exposed to strong winds. Raspberries need a moisture-retaining but well-drained soil. Ideally, it should be slightly acid.

Prepare the bed a few months before the canes are to be planted. Dig in a generous layer of well-rotted manure, compost or alternative sources of humus (see p. 17). This is particularly necessary if the soil is alkaline.

Rake in a surface dressing of 2 oz. of general fertiliser per square yard (60 g. per square metre).

How many to grow A 12 × 9 ft (3.6 × 2.7 m.) plot will support three rows of seven canes, which should eventually yield over 20 lb. (10 kg.) of berries in a season – plenty for the average family to eat fresh and to freeze.

Varieties Among the best summer-fruiting varieties are 'Glen Clover': early; heavy cropper; small to medium fruits.

'Lloyd George': early to mid-season; heavy cropper but subject to virus infection.

'Malling Admiral': late; heavy cropper; good flavour.

'Malling Jewel': early to mid-season; heavy cropper; excellent flavour.

'Malling Promise': early; heavy cropper; fair flavour.

The following autumn-fruiting raspberries are recommended:

'September': medium-sized berries; good flavour.

'Zeva': dwarf habit; large, good-flavoured fruits.

How to grow raspberries

Raspberries are highly susceptible to virus diseases, and it is important to start by purchasing one-year-old canes, certified disease-free, from a reputable nursery.

If possible, plant the canes in November. Otherwise, plant at any time up to March.

For each row dig a trench about

PLANTING THE CANES

Set the canes 15–18 in. (380–455 mm.) apart, depending on variety, in a spade-width trench 3 in. (75 mm.) deep. Spread the roots.

9 in. (230 mm.) wide and 3 in. (75 mm.) deep. Set the canes in this, 18 in. (455 mm.) apart, with their roots well spread out. The exception is 'Malling Jewel', which may produce fewer canes and should be planted 15 in. (380 mm.) apart.

Cover the roots with soil, and firm this down with your heel. Space rows 6 ft (1.8 m.) apart.

After planting, cut down each cane to 12 in. (305 mm.) above soil

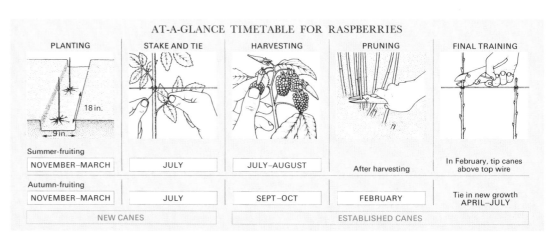

AT-A-GLANCE TIMETABLE FOR RASPBERRIES

	PLANTING	STAKE AND TIE	HARVESTING	PRUNING	FINAL TRAINING
Summer-fruiting	NOVEMBER–MARCH	JULY	JULY–AUGUST	After harvesting	In February, tip canes above top wire
Autumn-fruiting	NOVEMBER–MARCH	JULY	SEPT–OCT	FEBRUARY	Tie in new growth APRIL–JULY
	NEW CANES		ESTABLISHED CANES		

(18 in. / 9 in.)

WIRE SUPPORTS

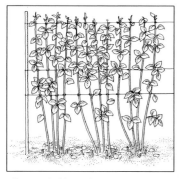

Summer-fruiting varieties need three supporting wires, autumn varieties only two. In each case, secure the wires to stout end posts.

level. This will prevent fruit being borne the following summer, but the vigour of the plant will be increased to ensure better fruiting in following years.

Apply a mulch of peat, well-rotted lawn mowings or compost around the plants each April to help feed them and to conserve moisture (see p. 36). You can also improve yields by applying 1 oz. of sulphate of potash per square yard

(30 g. per square metre) in January, and ½ oz. of sulphate of ammonia per square yard (15 g. per square metre) in March.

Control unwanted suckers, as well as weeds, by shallow hoeing or by smothering with rotted straw or compost.

Give the plants plenty of water in summer.

The first July after planting, insert an 8 ft (2.5 m.) post into the ground at both ends of each row, sinking the posts 2 ft (610 mm.). For summer-fruiting varieties, space three 12–13 gauge galvanised wires 2½ ft, 3½ ft and 5½ ft (760 mm., 1.1 m. and 1.7 m.) from the ground, and stretch them between each pair of posts. Tie the canes to the wires with soft string.

Each summer, after picking summer-fruiting varieties, remove the canes that have carried berries by severing them just above soil level. Select the strongest current-year canes and tie to the wires, spacing them 3–4 in. (75–100 mm.) apart. Cut out the remaining new shoots; pull out suckers well away from the rows.

In February, cut off the top of each cane to a good bud a few inches above the top wire.

Autumn-fruiting canes do not grow as tall as summer varieties. Space two parallel support wires, 2½ ft and 4 ft (760 mm. and 1.2 m.) from the ground, and set cross-ties every 12 in. (305 mm.) so that the canes are supported without being tied.

Cut down the canes of autumn-fruiting plants in February.

Raising new plants If the canes are virus-free, take suckers in November to increase the area of the bed. Generally, they begin to deteriorate from the eighth year and it is then better to buy in new stock. Burn the old plants. Set out new plants on a fresh site.

Pests and diseases The commonest pests are APHIDS (p. 282), LEAFHOPPERS (p. 283) and RASPBERRY BEETLE (p. 285).

The most troublesome diseases are CANE BLIGHT (p. 287), CANE SPOT (p. 287), CHLOROSIS (p. 287), CROWN GALL (p. 287), GREY MOULD (p. 288), HONEY FUNGUS (p. 288), MOSAIC (p. 289), SPUR BLIGHT (p. 291) and VIRUS DISEASES (p. 291).

Harvesting and storing

Pick raspberries when they are well-coloured all over. At this stage they will come away easily from the stalk, leaving the core behind.

Raspberries do not keep well, so eat or freeze them as soon as possible after picking, meanwhile keeping them in the cool.

See also bottling (p. 309); freezing (p. 294); fruit cheeses and butters (p. 323); jams (p. 314); jellies (p. 320) and wine-making (p. 357).

TRAINING SUMMER-FRUITING CANES

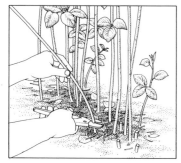

PRUNING After harvesting the crop, cut down to ground level the canes that have fruited. Also remove any spindly new growths.

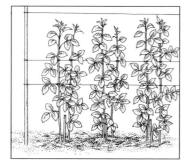

TYING IN Use soft string to tie the new canes to the wires, in place of those that have fruited. Space the canes evenly.

Preparing & cooking raspberries

Like strawberries, raspberries are at their most enjoyable when served fresh with plenty of cream and sugar.

Use them as soon as possible after picking. The fruits bruise easily, so, if washing is needed, place in single layers in a colander and immerse in cold water.

Drain thoroughly before rinsing and serving. Hull the berries by removing the flower calyces.

For most desserts, raspberries are made into a purée in order to remove the pips. One way is to rub the berries through a nylon sieve, pressing the fruits down with a wooden spoon. This can be a lengthy process, and it is easier to purée the raspberries in a liquidiser, then sieve to remove the pips.

RASPBERRIES WITH SOURED CREAM

1 lb. (500 g.) raspberries
4 tablespoons sweet sherry
5 fl. oz. (150 ml.) soured cream
2 tablespoons demerara sugar

CHILLING TIME: 1 hour

Hull, rinse and drain the raspberries. Arrange them in four individual serving glasses, spoon 1 tablespoon of sherry over each portion and chill in the refrigerator for 1 hour.

Spoon the soured cream over the raspberries and sprinkle the

top with demerara sugar.
Serving Just before serving, heat a metal skewer until glowing and draw it through the demerara sugar in a criss-cross pattern to caramelise it.

BAVARIAN RASPBERRY TARTLETS

8 small tartlet cases
½ lb. (250 g.) raspberries
2 oz. (50 g.) sugar
1 teaspoon lemon juice
1 teaspoon powdered gelatine
5 fl. oz. (150 ml.) whipping cream

CHILLING TIME: 1 hour

Set 16 of the finest raspberries aside. Put the rest in the liquidiser or rub them through a sieve to make a purée. Sweeten the purée with the sugar, and sharpen with lemon juice.

Dissolve the gelatine in 1 tablespoon of hot water and stir this into the raspberry purée. Fold in the lightly whipped cream as the purée begins to set. Chill in the refrigerator until fairly firm.

Spoon the raspberry cream into the tartlet cases.
Serving Decorate the filled cases with the reserved raspberries. Serve as a dessert course, or with afternoon tea.

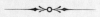

Continued . . .

Raspberry recipes (continued)

RASPBERRY FLAN

¾ *lb. (375 g.) raspberries*
3 tablespoons sugar
1 miniature bottle of Cointreau
2 oz. (50 g.) gooseberry jam
1 flan case – 10 in. (255 mm.)
½ *pint (300 ml.) double cream*

CHILLING TIME: 30 minutes

Hull the raspberries, rinse
carefully in a colander and drain
thoroughly. Put the fruits in a
shallow dish, sprinkle the sugar
and Cointreau over them and
leave in a cool place for a couple
of hours while the sugar dissolves.

Heat the gooseberry jam until
runny, then spread it over the
base of the flan case. Set aside
to cool.

Drain the raspberries. Whisk
the cream with the raspberry
juice until thick, then spread
two-thirds of the mixture over
the gooseberry jam. Arrange the
raspberries on top, and chill in
the refrigerator for 30 minutes.
Serving Just before serving,
pipe the remaining cream round
the inside edge of the flan.
Photograph on pages 142–3.

PANCAKES WITH RASPBERRY CREAM

½ *pint (300 ml.) pancake batter*
¾ *lb. (375 g.) raspberries*
5 fl. oz. (150 ml.) double cream
½ *lb. (250 g.) cream cheese*
Sugar
2 tablespoons Kirsch (optional)

CHILLING TIME: 2 hours
COOKING TIME: 20 minutes

Prepare the raspberry cream
first.

Hull, rinse and drain the
raspberries, and rub them
through a sieve. Stir the cream
cheese smooth with a little of the
cream, fold in the raspberry
purée and sweeten to taste with
sugar. Add the Kirsch if used.

Whisk the cream fairly stiff
and fold it into the raspberry
mixture. Chill in the refrigerator
for about 2 hours.

Make eight pancakes from the
batter, sprinkle with sugar and
keep warm in the oven.
Serving Serve the pancakes
hot, each rolled round a filling of
the chilled raspberry cream.
Variation Serve the raspberry
cream in a bowl, with hot waffles.
Photograph on pages 136–7.

RASPBERRY ICE CREAM

½ *lb. (250 g.) raspberries*
*Juice of ½ lime, or 1 teaspoon lemon
juice*
3 oz. (75 g.) icing sugar
5 fl. oz. (150 ml.) single cream
5 fl. oz. (150 ml.) double cream
Red food colouring

FREEZING TIME: 8 hours

Hull the raspberries, if necessary,
then rinse and drain them
thoroughly. Put the berries and
the lime juice in the liquidiser
and blend to a fine purée. Rub
this through a fine sieve to get rid
of the pips.

Alternatively, simply rub the
raspberries through a fine sieve
and stir in the lime juice.

Sweeten the purée to taste
with the sifted icing sugar. Mix
the two creams and whisk them
until thick, but not stiff. Fold in
the raspberry purée and add a
few drops of red food colouring.

Spoon the mixture into a
plastic freezing container, cover
with a lid and leave to freeze
overnight, or for about 8 hours.
Serving Remove the ice cream
from the freezer 2 hours before
serving, and put it in the
refrigerator to thaw. Scoop into
glasses and serve.
Variation After blending in the
cream, but before freezing, fold
2 tablespoons of finely grated
dark chocolate into the mixture.

Red currants : see **Currants, Red and white**

Rhubarb

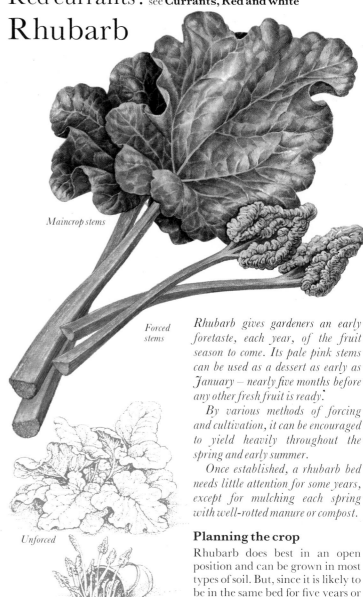

Maincrop stems

Forced stems

Unforced

Forced

*Rhubarb gives gardeners an early
foretaste, each year, of the fruit
season to come. Its pale pink stems
can be used as a dessert as early as
January – nearly five months before
any other fresh fruit is ready.*

*By various methods of forcing
and cultivation, it can be encouraged
to yield heavily throughout the
spring and early summer.*

*Once established, a rhubarb bed
needs little attention for some years,
except for mulching each spring
with well-rotted manure or compost.*

Planning the crop

Rhubarb does best in an open
position and can be grown in most
types of soil. But, since it is likely to
be in the same bed for five years or
more, correct preparation of the
ground is vital. Rhubarb roots
penetrate deeply, so work in well-

rotted manure or compost to about twice the depth needed for most vegetables.

A month or two before planting, dig a hole 2 ft square (610 × 610 mm.) where each root is to be planted. Fork a bucketful of well-rotted manure or compost into the soil at the bottom of the hole. Spread a further bucket of manure or compost and return the topsoil.

If more than one root is to be planted, space the prepared holes 3 ft (1 m.) apart and mark each with a stake.

How much to grow Three or four plants will provide sufficient stems for an average family.

Varieties 'Hawke's Champagne': reliable cropper with red stems.

'The Sutton': large maincrop variety that rarely runs to seed.

'Timperley Early': thin-stemmed variety suitable for forcing; matures early.

How to grow rhubarb

March is the best time for planting rhubarb, though February is satisfactory provided the ground is not frozen. Rhubarb may also be planted in October or November.

In the prepared ground, earlier

PLANTING RHUBARB

Set each crown so that the roots are covered but the new shoots just protruding. Replace the soil and firm with your feet.

marked with a stake, dig a hole deep enough to take the whole of the woody part of the rootstock, leaving any new shoots just protruding. Tread the soil round the roots, and water freely.

Mulch the bed with peat or well-rotted manure, and water freely in dry spells. Feed regularly through the summer with a general liquid fertiliser. Cut off any flowering spikes at once.

At the end of July dress the ground with a general fertiliser at the rate of 4 oz. per square yard (120 g. per square metre).

Forcing rhubarb After the rhubarb has been growing for three years, some of the clumps can be selected for forcing.

For a very early crop, use a spade to lift one or two strong plants in November and turn them over to expose their roots to frost. This has the effect of producing a false 'winter', to make the plants dormant.

In December, put the plants the right way up in boxes, cover with moist peat and place the boxes in a dark shed. If the shed is not dark, cover the boxes with black polythene.

Alternatively, place the boxes under a greenhouse bench, using a sheet of black polythene as a curtain to keep them dark. Rhubarb forced in this way can be re-planted, but will take two or three years to crop heavily again.

For a second-early crop, force one or two of the crowns outdoors, without moving them, by covering with a barrel or large bucket in early February. Bank straw or leaves round the box for extra protection.

For a third crop, cover rhubarb in the permanent bed with straw, which will advance it a week or two ahead of the main crop.

GROWING EARLY RHUBARB

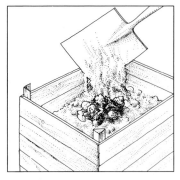 

FORCING INDOORS In December, put crowns in peat after exposing to frost. Place in the dark, or cover with black polythene.

FORCING OUTDOORS In early February, place a bucket or barrel over a mature crown and bank straw or leaves round the outside.

Raising new plants With regular feeding a rhubarb bed may be left undisturbed for years.

However, when new plants are needed, dig up a clump in late February or early March. Divide the roots with a spade, leaving at least one growing point on each, and re-plant the pieces.

Plants can also be raised by sowing seeds outdoors in April.

Pests and diseases Among pests attacking rhubarb are STEM AND BULB EELWORMS (p. 285) and caterpillars of the SWIFT MOTH (p. 285).

The diseases most likely to occur on rhubarb are CROWN ROT (p. 287), HONEY FUNGUS (p. 288) and LEAF SPOT (p. 288).

Harvesting and storing

Do not pull any of the stems in the first year. In the second and third years pick only a few stems. In following years, pull fully grown stems as needed.

To pull rhubarb, place your thumb inside the stem as far down

as possible and, with a twisting motion, pull it from the crown.

Cut off the leaves, which are poisonous, and put them to rot on the compost heap.

See also bottling (p. 309); freezing (p. 294); fruit cheeses and butters (p. 323); jams (p. 314); pickles (p. 328); sauces, ketchups and relishes (p. 339); syrups and juices (p. 326) and wine-making (p. 357). ✿✿

HARVESTING

Pull the largest stems from each plant, grasping them close to the base and pulling away from the crown with a twisting motion.

AT-A-GLANCE TIMETABLE FOR RHUBARB

PREPARING THE GROUND	PLANTING	FORCING (OUTDOORS)	HARVESTING

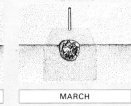  

JANUARY	MARCH	FEBRUARY	From MARCH/APRIL
FIRST YEAR		SUBSEQUENT YEARS	

Preparing & cooking rhubarb

The tender, pink rhubarb forced for use in late winter and early spring has a more delicate, less acid flavour than the thicker and coarser maincrop stalks.

The acidity of rhubarb can be diminished by blending it with ginger, cinnamon and the juice and rind of an orange. Its clean taste makes rhubarb an ideal dessert to follow fatty or stodgy main courses.

Apart from its uses in cooked desserts, rhubarb is also an excellent filling for pies and baked puddings and as a base for fools and other creamed desserts. It is also used for jams, either on its own or in combination with soft fruits such as red currants and raspberries.

Prepare young, forced rhubarb simply by trimming off the leafy tops and the pale pink root slivers at the base of the stalks. Wash and dry carefully.

Older rhubarb often develops a stringy covering which must be peeled off, together with any bruised or damaged parts, as the stems are being cut into pieces.

When cooked, stems often have a pale, uninteresting colour, but this is easily improved by adding a few drops of cochineal.

RHUBARB MERINGUE

1¼ lb. (625 g.) rhubarb
½ lb. (250 g.) caster sugar
1 orange
2 egg whites

COOKING TIME: 45 minutes
OVEN TEMPERATURE: 180°C (350°F) – gas mark 4

Trim and wash the rhubarb, cut the stalks into 1 in. (25 mm.) pieces, and at the same time remove any stringy bits. Put in an ovenproof dish in alternate layers with half the sugar.

Sprinkle with the juice and the grated rind of the orange. Cover with a lid or foil and bake in the oven for 30 minutes.

Meanwhile, beat the egg whites stiff with the remaining sugar. Remove the rhubarb from the oven and spread the meringue mixture over the top. Return the dish, uncovered, to the lower part of the oven, set to 150°C (300°F) – gas mark 2. Remove after about 20 minutes, or when the meringue is golden-brown.

Serving Serve warm, rather than hot or cold, with a jug of cream or scoops of vanilla ice cream.

RHUBARB CRUMBLE

1½ lb. (750 g.) rhubarb
6 oz. (175 g.) sugar
2 tablespoons orange juice
3 oz. (75 g.) butter
6 oz. (175 g.) flour
½ teaspoon ground ginger

COOKING TIME: 35–40 minutes
OVEN TEMPERATURE: 190°C (375°F) – gas mark 5

Trim the root ends and leafy tops from the rhubarb stalks, and wash thoroughly. Remove any stringy bits from maincrop rhubarb. Chop into ½ in. (12 mm.) pieces, and put in a deep, buttered, ovenproof dish, sprinkling the fruit with half the sugar. Spoon the orange juice over the rhubarb.

Cut the butter into small pieces and rub it into the flour until the mixture resembles fine breadcrumbs. Blend in the remaining sugar, mixed with the ground ginger.

Spoon the crumble mixture over the rhubarb, pressing it down well with the back of a spoon. Bake in the centre of the oven for 35 minutes, or until the topping is brown and crisp.

Serving Fruit crumbles are usually served warm, accompanied with cream or custard sauce, but are also suitable as a cold dessert.

Photograph on pages 136–7.

RHUBARB AND BANANA FOOL

1 lb. (500 g.) young rhubarb
Juice of ½ lemon
4 bananas
4 oz. (100–125 g.) sugar
5 fl. oz. (150 ml.) whipping cream
2 oz. (50 g.) small macaroons

COOKING TIME: 15 minutes
CHILLING TIME: 1 hour

Trim the roots and tops from the rhubarb, wash the stems and cut them into small pieces. Put in a pan with the lemon juice, and simmer over a gentle heat for about 15 minutes, until the rhubarb is quite tender and pulpy.

Rub the rhubarb through a sieve and, if necessary, thicken the purée by boiling it to evaporate some of the liquid.

Peel three of the bananas and mash them finely with a fork. Mix the rhubarb purée and mashed bananas, and sweeten the mixture to taste.

Whisk the cream lightly until it just holds its shape. Crush the macaroons with a rolling pin and fold them into the cream. Blend the cream into the rhubarb mixture, spoon it into glasses and chill in the refrigerator for 1 hour.

Serving Just before serving, peel and slice the remaining banana and arrange on top of the rhubarb fool.

Photograph on pages 214–15.

POACHED RHUBARB

1 lb. (500 g.) rhubarb
4 oz. (100–125 g.) sugar
2 tablespoons orange juice
½ cinnamon stick
Peel of ½ orange

COOKING TIME: 25 minutes

Trim the tops and roots off the rhubarb. Cut out any stringy pieces and blemishes, and wash the stalks. Cut into 1 in. (25 mm.) lengths.

Put the sugar in a pan, with 3 tablespoons of cold water, the orange juice, cinnamon stick and orange peel. Bring to the boil over gentle heat, stirring until the sugar has dissolved. Cover the pan with a lid, remove from the heat and leave for 10 minutes to allow the flavours to blend. Strain this syrup into a pan, add the rhubarb and simmer gently, uncovered, for about 10 minutes, or until tender.

Serving Poached rhubarb may be served warm or cold, with either a jug of cream or custard sauce.

Variations Thicken the rhubarb with a little cornflour stirred smooth in cold water, and if necessary add a few drops of red food colouring. Poached rhubarb may also be used as the filling for summer pudding (see p. 155).

RHUBARB MOUSSE

1 lb. (500 g.) rhubarb
Sugar
Cochineal
3 eggs
½ teaspoon ground cinnamon
2 teaspoons powdered gelatine
Garnish : split toasted almonds

COOKING TIME: 15 minutes
CHILLING TIME: 2–3 hours

Remove the roots, tops, stringy bits and any damaged parts from the rhubarb. Wash the stalks and cut them into ½ in. (12 mm.) pieces.

Put in a pan with 6 tablespoons of water, and bring to the boil over a gentle heat. Simmer for about 10 minutes, or until the rhubarb is quite soft. Strain through a sieve and muslin to obtain a perfectly clear juice, which should measure about ¾ pint (450 ml.).

Bring the juice to the boil and sweeten to taste with sugar. Add a few drops of cochineal, if necessary, to improve the colour. Set aside to cool.

Separate the eggs, and beat the egg yolks with the cinnamon and 1 tablespoon of sugar until light and fluffy. Blend in the cooled rhubarb juice, mixing thoroughly, then add the gelatine dissolved in 2 tablespoons of water. Stir to combine thoroughly, and set aside.

Meanwhile, whisk the egg whites until stiff, but not dry. When the rhubarb mixture begins to set, fold in the egg whites. Spoon into a serving dish and chill in the refrigerator.
Serving Garnish the top of the rhubarb mousse with blanched and split toasted almonds. Serve with a bowl of lightly whipped cream.

RHUBARB PIE

1½ lb. (750 g.) young rhubarb
4 oz. (100–125 g.) sugar
Rind and juice of ½ orange
½ lb. (250 g.) sweet shortcrust pastry

COOKING TIME: 35–40 minutes
OVEN TEMPERATURE: 200°C (400°F) – gas mark 6

Trim the roots and leafy tops from the rhubarb, wash the stalks and cut them into ½ in. (12 mm.) pieces. Mix the rhubarb with the sugar and the finely grated rind from the orange. Put a pie funnel in a deep pie dish and arrange the rhubarb round it.

Make up the pastry from ½ lb. (250 g.) flour, and roll out to fit the pie dish. Make a slit in the pastry for the steam to escape, brush the pastry with the orange juice and sprinkle with sugar.

Bake in the oven for 35–40 minutes, or until golden. If the pastry browns too quickly, cover it with a double layer of moistened greaseproof paper.
Serving Serve the pie warm, with a jug of custard or cream.

Rosemary

Rosemary, a hardy, evergreen shrub, originally came from the shores of the Mediterranean, where it is still collected for use in medicines and ointments. It is sometimes planted as a hedge.

In the kitchen, its sweetly fragrant leaves are used, fresh or dried, to flavour roast lamb, pork, chicken, veal, rabbit stews, and grilled fish.

The blue flowers, which appear from March to September, make a fragrant garnish for a fruit cup.

Planning the crop

Rosemary thrives in any well-drained soil in a sunny position, given shelter from cold winds.

How much to grow Since rosemary can grow up to 7 ft (2.1 m.) high – although it is usually shorter – one bush is sufficient to provide a supply of leaves throughout the year.

How to grow rosemary

Sow the seeds in seed compost in a 3 in. (75 mm.) pot or in a steel pan under glass in March. When the seedlings have grown large enough to handle, prick them out individually into pots of potting compost.

Set the plants out in their permanent positions in May or June. If more than one plant is to be grown, space them 3 ft (1 m.) apart, or 15 in. (380 mm.) if you are growing a hedge.

Alternatively, sow the seeds ¼ in. (5 mm.) deep in an outdoor seed bed in April. Thin to 2 in. (50 mm.) spacings when they are large enough to handle, and plant out in their permanent positions in June or July.

Raising new plants Take 4 in. (100 mm.) cuttings of half-ripe shoots between June and September, and insert them in equal parts (by volume) of peat and sand in a cold frame.

Shade the frame until the cuttings root, then pot them in 3 in. (75 mm.) containers of potting compost. Plant them in their permanent positions during the following May.

Hardwood cuttings, 6–8 in. (150–200 mm.) long, can be planted in September or October in the positions where the plants are to grow.

Pests and diseases Rosemary is generally trouble-free.

Harvesting and storing

Pick the young leaves and stems fresh for immediate use. To dry the leaves for winter use, or sprigs for a bouquet garni, see p. 346.

AT-A-GLANCE TIMETABLE FOR ROSEMARY

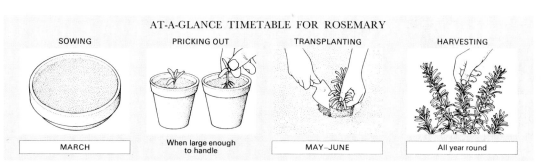

SOWING	PRICKING OUT	TRANSPLANTING	HARVESTING
MARCH	When large enough to handle	MAY–JUNE	All year round

Cooking with rosemary

This evergreen Mediterranean herb is used freely in Italian cooking to flavour almost any kind of savoury dish.

Small sprigs of rosemary give an aromatic flavour when inserted into small slits cut in lamb, pork or veal that is to be roasted. Alternatively, use fresh rosemary sprigs in stuffing.

ROSEMARY POTATO PIE

2 lb. (1 kg.) potatoes
1 lb. (500 g.) onions
1 oz. (25 g.) flour
Salt and pepper
Rosemary sprigs
3 oz. (75 g.) butter
½ pint (300 ml.) milk (approx.)

COOKING TIME: 1½ hours
OVEN TEMPERATURE: 180°C (350°F)
– gas mark 4

Peel the potatoes and onions, and slice thinly. Arrange them in layers in a buttered, deep, ovenproof dish, sprinkling each layer with flour, salt, pepper and chopped rosemary, and dotting with flakes of butter. Finish with a layer of potatoes, and pour enough milk into the dish to come halfway up the sides.

Cover the dish with a lid or foil and bake in the oven until the milk has been absorbed and the potatoes are tender.
Serving Serve with cold boiled bacon or ham.

PORK CHOPS WITH ROSEMARY

4 thick pork chops
Rosemary sprigs
Salt and pepper
2 oz. (50 g.) butter
2 oz. (50 g.) lean bacon rashers
1 small onion
5 fl. oz. (150 ml.) bouillon
2 tablespoons tomato paste
Paprika
4 tablespoons soured cream

COOKING TIME: 20–25 minutes

Trim the chops and wipe dry. Make small incisions in the meaty parts with the point of a sharp knife and insert a small sprig of rosemary in each cut. Season the chops with salt and pepper; fry in half the butter until tender, turning once.

Meanwhile, melt the remaining butter in a pan and add the diced bacon. Fry over a moderate heat until crisp, then add the finely chopped onion and fry for another 5 minutes.

Stir in the bouillon and tomato paste, heat through and season to taste with salt and paprika. Simmer over a gentle heat for 10 minutes, and stir in the soured cream at the last moment.
Serving Arrange the chops on a serving dish, pour the sauce over them and serve with mashed or baked potatoes and a salad.

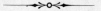

Runner beans:
see **Beans, Runner**

Sage
(see also pp. 28–29)

The wrinkled, grey-green leaves of the hardy sage can be picked all the year round for making stuffing to flavour such rich meats as pork, duck and goose.

The attractive evergreen plants, growing up to 2 ft (610 mm.) high, produce spikes of small, violet-blue flowers in June and July. Sage is therefore suitable for growing in the flower border as well as in the herb garden.

Planning the crop

Sage grows best in a warm, dry position. It thrives in any well-drained garden soil, except the most acid.

How much to grow One or two plants will provide more than sufficient leaves for the kitchen all through the year, although you may choose to grow more for their decorative value.

How to grow sage

Sow the seeds in a pan of seed compost in a cold frame or greenhouse in March, just covering the seeds with sifted compost. Prick the seedlings out when the first true leaves show, placing them singly in 3 in. (75 mm.) pots. Plant them out 12 in. (305 mm.) apart when the roots fill the pots.

Alternatively, sow the seeds outdoors in April or May. Prick out the seedlings into a nursery bed, and transfer them to their final positions in the autumn.

Raising new plants Take 3 in. (75 mm.) heeled cuttings (see p. 29) between June and September, and insert in equal parts (by volume) of peat and sand in a cold frame. When the cuttings have rooted put them singly in 3–4 in. (75–100 mm.) pots of potting compost and overwinter them in the frame.

Nip out the growing tips, and plant out in March or April.

Alternatively, 6–8 in. (150–200 mm.) hardwood cuttings, similar to those of gooseberries and currants (see p. 47), may be planted in September or October in their final growing positions.

Pests and diseases CAPSID BUGS (p. 282) sometimes attack the leaves and young shoots.

GREY MOULD (p. 288) is the disease most likely to attack sage.

Harvesting and storing

Pick the fresh leaves when needed. They have the best flavour in midsummer, just before flowering.

Sage can be dried (see p. 343) but, since the leaves can be picked all the year, it is hardly worth the trouble.

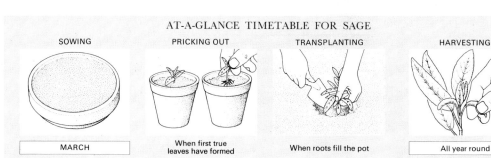

AT-A-GLANCE TIMETABLE FOR SAGE

SOWING	PRICKING OUT	TRANSPLANTING	HARVESTING
MARCH	When first true leaves have formed	When roots fill the pot	All year round

Cooking with sage

This is one of the few herbs to have been in fairly constant use in English cookery since the Middle Ages. Today, however, sage is chiefly an ingredient of stuffings for fatty meat and poultry, and sometimes in country-style pork sausages. It is much favoured by German and Norwegian cooks to counteract the richness of oily fish.

The finely chopped leaves give a distinctive flavour to meat loaves and similar dishes made from pork, ham or sausage-meat.

Mix them into the covering for Scotch eggs, or sprinkle the chopped leaves over liver when frying or grilling.

Add sage to cream cheese, omelettes, meat and vegetable soups, stews and casseroles, to bouillon for oily fish and marinades for hare and venison.

SAGE-AND-ONION STUFFING

4 onions
2 oz. (50 g.) dripping or butter
4 oz. (100–125 g.) fresh white breadcrumbs
1 tablespoon freshly chopped sage leaves
Salt and pepper
1 egg (optional)

Peel the onions, and chop finely. Fry them in melted dripping for about 5 minutes, or until soft but not brown. Remove from the heat and mix with the breadcrumbs and the freshly chopped sage leaves. Season to taste with salt and pepper.

The stuffing may be used as it is, or a lightly beaten egg may be mixed in for a looser, richer forcemeat.

Use the stuffing with roast pork, chicken or goose. For the latter, blend the finely chopped goose liver into the stuffing.

As a variation, substitute finely chopped cooking apples for half the onions, and mix with fresh thyme as well as the chopped sage.

Salsify

Salsify is also known as the vegetable oyster, or the oyster plant, because of the flavour of its long, fleshy roots. This makes it a distinctive vegetable for use in late autumn and winter.

It has the disadvantage on a small vegetable plot, however, of taking up space over a long growing period. A gardener with space problems could compromise by growing only a short row, and catch-cropping with lettuces or radishes during the early spring (see p. 28).

Planning the crop

Salsify grows best in light loam, although it will succeed in any soil except the heaviest clay. Do not grow on recently manured soil.

In autumn or winter, dig a trench where the salsify is to grow and break up the soil at the base.

Varieties Only two varieties are usually obtainable:
'Mammoth': long-tapering roots, sweet flavour.
'Sandwich Island': vigorous grower, large roots.

How to grow salsify

Sow the seeds thinly about the middle of April in drills ½ in. (12 mm.) deep. If more than one row is grown, allow 12 in. (305 mm.) between them. Thin the seedlings to allow 9 in. (230 mm.) between the plants.

Hoe lightly between the rows, drawing the soil up to the plants rather than away from them.

Pests and diseases Salsify is generally free of pests.

One of the few diseases to attack it is WHITE BLISTER (p. 291).

Harvesting and storing

The roots are ready from mid-October. They are hardy and can be left in the ground until needed.

When lifting, avoid damaging the roots or they will bleed like beetroot. To prevent this, break up the soil on each side of the row with a fork, then ease it away to expose the roots. Be sure to insert the fork to its full depth.

Leave some roots in the ground to produce the tender shoots, called chards, that will be ready for picking in March or April. These can be blanched, for eating raw in salads, by drawing soil over them as they grow.

Alternatively, they can be left unblanched and cooked as a green vegetable.

Recipes on next page

AT-A-GLANCE TIMETABLE FOR SALSIFY

SOWING	THINNING	HARVESTING
½ in.	9 in.	
APRIL	When large enough to handle	MID-OCTOBER

Preparing & cooking salsify

The chief difference between salsify and scorzonera is the colour of their skins. Both are long, slender vegetables, salsify having a light brown soft skin and scorzonera a black skin. Both have soft, white, sweet flesh, that of salsify having a faint oyster flavour.

Prepare both vegetables by brushing the soil off under cold running water. Cut off the base of the roots and the leafy tops, and remove the skin by peeling thinly or scraping. Rinse quickly and cut into 1–2 in. (25–50 mm.) lengths.

Put in a pan with just enough boiling, lightly salted water to cover the vegetables and add 1 tablespoon of lemon juice or white wine vinegar to preserve the white colour. Boil for 20–30 minutes, or until tender.

The rinsed and dried, finely chopped leaves may also be used fresh in salads or cooked like spinach. The white shoots, known as chards, produced by salsify towards the end of the winter, can be cooked like asparagus.

Both salsify and scorzonera roots are also excellent for winter salads. Clean the roots, grate them on the coarse blade of a grater, sprinkle with lemon juice and fold into a dressing of mayonnaise, soured cream or oil-vinaigrette.

All recipes for salsify and scorzoneras (see facing page) are interchangeable.

SALSIFY WITH CHEESE

1 lb. (500 g.) salsify
Salt
1 tablespoon lemon juice
3 oz. (75 g.) butter
Nutmeg
2 oz. (50 g.) finely grated cheese

COOKING TIME: 30 minutes

Wash the salsify, trim off the tops and root ends and peel the roots thinly. Cut into 2 in. (50 mm.) pieces and put in a pan of boiling, lightly salted water to which the lemon juice has been added. Simmer gently for 25–30 minutes, or until tender. Drain thoroughly and keep warm.

Melt the butter in a large pan, add the salsify and toss quickly until thoroughly coated. Sprinkle with nutmeg. Spoon the buttered salsify into a serving dish, and cover with the finely grated cheese.
Serving Serve at once, as an accompaniment to any kind of grilled meat, ham or bacon.
Variation Flavour a white sauce with the nutmeg and cheese and fold the cooked, drained salsify into this.
Photograph on pages 134–5.

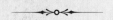

SALSIFY WITH MOUSSELINE SAUCE

1 lb. (500 g.) salsify
Salt and pepper
Juice of 1 lemon
2 egg yolks
4 oz. (100 g.) butter
4 tablespoons double cream

COOKING TIME: 30–45 minutes

Rinse the salsify roots, then cut off the tops, root ends and the outer skin. Cut the roots into 1–2 in. (25–50 mm.) pieces and put in a pan of lightly salted water with 1 tablespoon of lemon juice. Simmer gently for 25–30 minutes, or until tender. Drain well and keep warm.

Meanwhile, put the remaining lemon juice with 1 tablespoon of cold water in a bowl. Stir in the lightly beaten egg yolks and set the bowl over a pan of simmering water.

Add $\frac{1}{2}$ oz. (15 g.) of butter and whisk the mixture until it thickens. Remove the bowl from the pan and gradually whisk in knobs of the remaining butter, beating thoroughly between each addition. Season to taste with salt and pepper, and fold in the lightly whipped cream. Heat the sauce through over the pan of simmering water.
Serving Arrange the salsify in a serving dish, pour over the Mousseline sauce, and serve at once with roast or grilled meat, fish or poultry.

Savory

Summer   *Winter*

Two types of savory are grown for their spicy-flavoured leaves – which are excellent as a flavouring for stuffing, or, like mint, may be used sparingly with peas and beans.

Summer savory is an erect bushy annual which grows to a height of about 12 in. (305 mm.). Its leaves, when dried, are generally considered to have a better flavour than those picked fresh from winter savory.

Winter savory is a hardy, evergreen perennial which grows to about the same height as summer savory but has a more spreading habit.

Its base becomes so woody that plants need to be replaced every two or three years.

Planning to grow savory

Grow summer and winter savory in a sunny position in any fertile, well-drained soil.

How much to grow Three or four plants of summer savory, and one or two of winter savory, should supply plenty of leaves all the year round for most families.

AT-A-GLANCE TIMETABLE FOR SAVORY

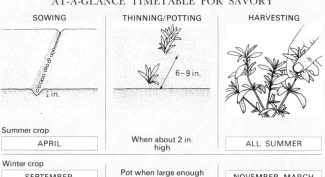

SOWING	THINNING/POTTING	HARVESTING
Summer crop	When about 2 in. high	
APRIL		ALL SUMMER
Winter crop	Pot when large enough to handle	
SEPTEMBER		NOVEMBER–MARCH

How to grow savory

For a summer supply of either type of savory, sow the seeds in drills ¼ in. (5 mm.) deep in April. When the seedlings are about 2 in. (50 mm.) high, thin them to 6–9 in. (150–230 mm.) apart.

For a winter supply of summer savory, sow a few seeds in a pot or seed pan in September. When the seedlings are large enough to handle, prick them out into 3 in. (75 mm.) pots of potting compost and grow on either indoors, or in a greenhouse heated to 7–10°C (45–50°F).

Pests and diseases Savory is generally trouble-free.

Harvesting and storing

Pick fresh leaves and young shoots as needed.

For drying (see p. 343) pick the shoots of summer savory in August. The leaves and shoots may also be frozen (see p. 294).

Pick the leaves of winter savory as needed. 🌿🌿

Cooking with savory

Fresh savory, both the summer and the winter types, should be picked while quite young. They may be used, sparingly, to flavour peas or beans in the same manner as mint.

The leaves of both types dry well, losing little of their sharp flavour.

The dried leaves may be used like sage to flavour stuffings and sausage-meat and to give a distinctive flavour to a variety of meat dishes.

Scorzoneras

Scorzoneras – hardy, winter vegetables grown for their black-skinned, delicately flavoured roots – are believed to have been named after 'scurzon', the Catalonian for serpent. It is known for certain that scorzoneras were at one time used in Spain in the treatment of snakebite.

Planning the crop

Scorzoneras thrive in any fertile, well-drained soil, in a sunny, open position. Choose ground manured for a previous crop because fresh manure may make them fork, or split up into a number of separate roots.

In shallow soil, dig a trench during the previous winter in the position where they are to grow, and break up the soil at the bottom with a fork. Do not bring the subsoil to the surface.

How much to grow Scorzoneras take up ground for a long period, so a single row – say 20 ft (6 m.) long – may have to suffice where space is limited. This would provide sufficient roots for about five meals for an average family.

Variety 'Russian Giant' is an established variety, and is obtainable from most seedsmen.

How to grow scorzoneras

Sow the seeds in April or May in drills ½ in. (12 mm.) deep. If more than one row is to be grown, draw the drills 15 in. (380 mm.) apart. Thin the seedlings in two or more stages until they are 8–12 in. (200–305 mm.) apart.

Alternatively, sow the seeds in groups of two or three, 8–12 in. apart, and remove all but the strongest seedling in each group.

Hoe regularly to keep down weeds.

Water thoroughly in dry spells or there is a risk of the plants running to seed.

Pests and diseases Scorzoneras are generally free of pests.

WHITE BLISTER (p. 291) is one of the few diseases that may occur.

Harvesting and storing

The roots are ready in October. Lift them as needed, as scorzoneras are very hardy and may be left in the ground throughout the winter.

When digging them up be careful not to snap the slender roots. Break up the soil on each side of the row with a fork and ease the roots out of the ground by inserting the fork to full depth alongside the plants. 🌿🌿

AT-A-GLANCE TIMETABLE FOR SCORZONERAS

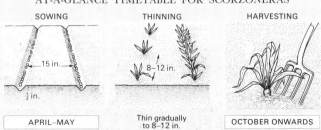

SOWING	THINNING	HARVESTING
15 in. ... ½ in.	8–12 in.	
APRIL–MAY	Thin gradually to 8–12 in.	OCTOBER ONWARDS

Cooking scorzoneras

This winter root vegetable is similar to salsify, and prepared and cooked in the same way (see facing page). Recipes for scorzoneras and salsify are interchangeable.

CRISP-FRIED SCORZONERAS

1½ lb. (750 g.) scorzoneras
Salt
1 egg
Breadcrumbs
2 oz. (50 g.) butter
Garnish: lemon twists, chopped parsley

COOKING TIME: 35 minutes

Brush the dirt off under running water. Cut off the tops and root ends and peel the roots. Cut them into 4 in. (100 mm.) lengths and put in a pan of boiling, lightly salted water.

Bring back to the boil and simmer for 25 minutes, or until barely tender. Drain, and dry on absorbent paper.

Beat the egg lightly and dip the scorzoneras in this, then coat with the breadcrumbs. Melt the butter in a pan and fry the scorzoneras until crisp and golden-brown.

Serving Lift the scorzoneras on to a dish and garnish with lemon twists and chopped parsley. Serve with baked or poached fish, or with poultry.

Seakale

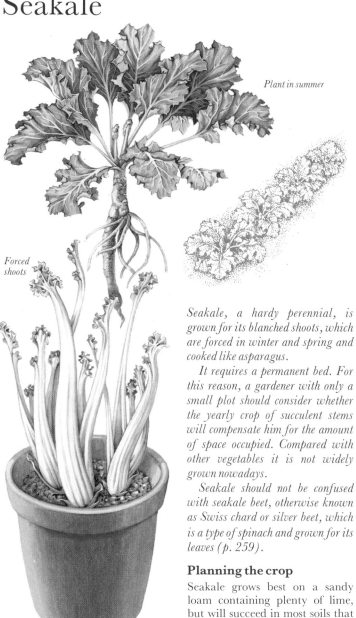

Plant in summer

Forced shoots

Seakale, a hardy perennial, is grown for its blanched shoots, which are forced in winter and spring and cooked like asparagus.

It requires a permanent bed. For this reason, a gardener with only a small plot should consider whether the yearly crop of succulent stems will compensate him for the amount of space occupied. Compared with other vegetables it is not widely grown nowadays.

Seakale should not be confused with seakale beet, otherwise known as Swiss chard or silver beet, which is a type of spinach and grown for its leaves (p. 259).

Planning the crop

Seakale grows best on a sandy loam containing plenty of lime, but will succeed in most soils that are suitably prepared. It is worth going to some trouble, since the crop will occupy the same piece of ground for some years.

Dig the ground deeply in autumn, working in a bucketful of well-rotted manure or compost to each square yard.

Leave the ground rough and give a dressing of carbonate of lime at the rate of 2–4 oz. per square yard (60–120 g. per square metre).

In spring, apply a top-dressing of general fertiliser at 4 oz. per square yard (120 g. per square metre).

How much to grow A double row 20 ft (6 m.) long will provide an average family with sufficient for one meal a week from the end of December until April, provided successive methods of forcing are adopted to ensure a continuing supply.

Varieties 'Lily White', a heavy cropper with pure white, well-flavoured shoots, is the variety most commonly available.

How to grow seakale

Thongs – sometimes available at good nurseries – can be planted during the winter, but March is the best time.

Set them 2 ft (610 mm.) apart in rows 2 ft apart. Plant so that the

Use a trowel to plant the thongs 2 ft (610 mm.) apart in each direction. Set them with their tops 2 in. (50 mm.) below the surface.

tips are 2 in. (50 mm.) below soil level.

Water and feed the plants liberally. Mulch with peat or well-rotted, strawy manure in May. In June, add a top-dressing of agricultural salt at the rate of 1 oz. per square yard (30 g. per square metre).

Remove all flowering stems as soon as they appear because they reduce the plants' strength unnecessarily and tend to diminish the crop.

To raise plants from seed, sow the seeds $\frac{1}{2}$ in. (12 mm.) deep in March or April. Thin to 6 in. (150

mm.) spacings and leave the plants to grow for a year.

The following spring, re-plant them 2 ft (610 mm.) apart. In the autumn, dress the bed with well-rotted compost and leave the plants for a further year before forcing them.

Forcing the shoots There are three ways to provide blanched shoots through the winter and early spring: by digging up roots and bringing them indoors for the early pickings; by forcing them outdoors under flower pots – although this depends on having a supply of fresh manure; and by blanching plants in their permanent bed to provide a later crop.

For early shoots, lift some roots in November after the leaves have withered.

Cut off the pencil-thick side roots, or thongs, for planting the following spring (see facing page for method).

Pack the main roots for forcing in boxes or large pots of soil, leaf-mould or peat and keep them in a dark place, such as a cellar or shed, at a temperature of about 7°C (45°F) as forcing proceeds. Do not exceed 16°C (61°F).

In December and January start off more roots in the same way to

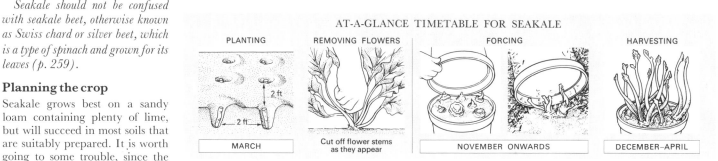

AT-A-GLANCE TIMETABLE FOR SEAKALE

PLANTING	REMOVING FLOWERS	FORCING	HARVESTING
2 ft / 2 ft	Cut off flower stems as they appear		
MARCH		NOVEMBER ONWARDS	DECEMBER–APRIL

FORCING SEAKALE SHOOTS

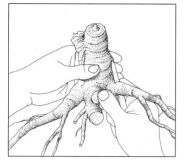

TRIMMING THE ROOTS Lift roots from November, trimming off the side roots or thongs. These can be kept for planting.

POTTING THE ROOTS Pack the main roots, which are to be forced, in boxes or pots of soil, leaf-mould or peat and keep in the dark.

FORCING AND HARVESTING With gentle warmth – about 7°C (45°F) – the forced shoots will be ready in seven weeks, or less.

FORCING OUTDOORS Alternatively, force shoots by placing a pot over the roots. Cover first with leaves, then with rotting manure.

get a steady succession of shoots.

Alternatively, force the plants in the open by covering them with 9–10 in. (230–255 mm.) flower pots in autumn and piling leaves around them. In January, raise the temperature by replacing the leaves with fresh, rotting manure packed in a 12 in. (305 mm.) layer round and over the pots.

Forced shoots will be ready for picking in six or seven weeks during the winter, but this period becomes progressively shorter as spring approaches.

By March, only about three weeks is needed.

For a final crop, to be cut in April, prepare the bed in the autumn as soon as the foliage has died down, by piling soil from the side of the rows to a depth of 8 in. (200 mm.) on the remaining plants in the permanent bed.

Raising new plants When preparing the roots for forcing in autumn, select the best of the thongs, or side roots. Cut them into pieces 5–6 in. (130–150 mm.)

long, making a straight cut at the upper end, nearest the main root, and a slanting one at the other as a guide to subsequent re-planting.

Tie the thongs in bundles and place them under about 3 in. (75 mm.) of sand or soil in a cold frame for the winter.

By the spring the thongs will have developed buds at the end that was cut straight. Keep the strongest bud to form the new shoot and rub out the rest with your thumb.

Plant the thongs in the same way as the parent crowns, straight end uppermost, just covering the bud or developing shoot.

Pests and diseases Seakale is subject to the same pests as other brassicas – CABBAGE ROOT FLY (p. 282), CABBAGE WHITEFLY (p. 282), CATERPILLARS (p. 282) and FLEA BEETLE (p. 283).

CLUB ROOT (p. 287) and VIOLET ROOT ROT (p. 291) are the diseases most likely to occur.

Harvesting seakale

Cut the shoots when they are about 6 in. (150 mm.) high. When all the blanched shoots have been cut, discard roots forced indoors as they will not grow again satisfactorily if re-planted.

Outdoors, fork the ground around roots that have cropped and allow them to grow again.

They can be forced outdoors, year after year, if the ground is kept well manured.

Use the shoots as soon as possible after cutting as they soon lose both texture and flavour.

The leaves from any stems that have not been forced can also be gathered for eating raw or cooked.

Preparing & cooking seakale

This vegetable can be used in two quite different ways. Cook and serve the blanched leaf shoots in the same way as celery; use the fresh leaves from unforced stems in salads, or cook them like spinach.

To use unforced leaves, wash and dry them before shredding, then toss in a lemon or oil-vinaigrette dressing.

Alternatively, put the washed leaves in a pan with the absolute minimum of boiling, lightly salted water and simmer for about 10 minutes. Drain thoroughly, chop the leaves finely and re-heat with a little butter or cream.

To prepare the blanched or forced stalks for cooking, trim off the roots and tops, wash in cold water and tie the stems in small bundles with soft string.

Put in a pan of boiling, lightly salted water, adding a little lemon juice to preserve the white colour. Boil gently for 25 minutes, or until tender.

Drain, and serve with melted butter, chopped parsley or with a white sauce.

SEAKALE SALAD

¾–1 lb. (375–500 g.) seakale
6 oz. (175 g.) mayonnaise
2 teaspoons chopped parsley
1 teaspoon chopped chives
1 teaspoon chopped mint
1 teaspoon chopped chervil
1 teaspoon chopped tarragon
1 tablespoon lemon juice
Salt and pepper

COOKING TIME: 25 minutes
CHILLING TIME: 30 minutes

Trim the roots and tops off the seakale. Wash the stalks, tie them in bundles and put in a pan of boiling, lightly salted, water with a little lemon juice. Simmer for 25 minutes, then drain thoroughly through a colander and leave to cool completely. Cut the stalks into 2 in. (50 mm.) lengths.

Prepare the dressing while the seakale is cooking: put the mayonnaise in a bowl and blend in all the finely chopped, fresh herbs. Add the lemon juice, and salt and pepper to taste. If necessary, add a little fresh or soured cream to give a pouring consistency.

Arrange the drained seakale in a serving dish, spoon the mayonnaise dressing over it and chill in the refrigerator for 30 minutes.

Serving This novel salad is excellent with poached fish or cold lean meat.

Continued...

Seakale recipes (continued)

SEAKALE WITH EGG SAUCE

1 lb. (500 g.) seakale stalks
White stock or bouillon
1 tablespoon lemon juice
Salt and pepper
1 oz. (25 g.) butter
1 oz. (25 g.) flour
½ pint (300 ml.) milk
2 hard-boiled eggs

COOKING TIME: 25 minutes

Trim the roots and tops off the seakale stalks. Wash them and tie in small bundles. Put in a pan with stock, bouillon or lightly salted water, adding 1 tablespoon of lemon juice. Bring to the boil, cover with a lid and simmer gently for 25 minutes. Drain thoroughly.

While the seakale stalks are cooking, prepare a white sauce from the butter, flour and milk, thinning if necessary with a little of the seakale cooking liquid. Season to taste with salt and pepper. Separate the hard-boiled egg whites from the yolks, chop the whites finely and add to the white sauce.

Serving Arrange the hot seakale stalks on a dish, pour the white sauce over them and rub the egg yolks through a coarse sieve over the sauce as a garnish. The vegetable is excellent with baked or grilled fish, and with roast or grilled meat.

BRAISED SEAKALE

1 lb. (500 g.) seakale stalks
1 oz. (25 g.) butter
½ pint (300 ml.) milk
Salt and pepper
Garnish: chopped parsley

COOKING TIME: 25 minutes

Trim the roots and tops off the seakale, wash the stalks in cold water and cut into 4 in. (100 mm.) lengths.

Melt the butter in a heavy-based pan and add the seakale. Toss to coat evenly with the butter, but without browning them. Pour the milk into the pan, bring to the boil and season with salt and pepper.

Cover with a lid and simmer over a gentle heat for about 25 minutes, by which time the seakale stalks should be tender and the cooking liquid reduced to a glaze.

Serving Spoon the seakale and liquid into a dish and garnish with finely chopped parsley. Serve with poached fish, or with grilled or roast meat.

Variations Cook the seakale stalks in milk and use this as a base for a Béchamel or cheese sauce. Bearnaise sauce also goes well with seakale.

Seakale beet:
see **Spinach**

Shallots

In France, many cooks consider the flavour of shallots to be finer than that of onions. In Britain, the bulbs are used mostly for pickling, but there is a compromise that should suit the cook, the gardener and the gourmet. This is to use the largest bulbs as a substitute for onions, medium-sized bulbs as seed for the following year, and the smallest for pickling in spiced vinegar.

After planting, each shallot splits up to form a cluster of bulbs. Their final size depends largely on the richness of the soil. The biggest shallots may be 1–1½ in. (25–40 mm.) across – an excellent size for cooking.

How many to grow

Seed merchants sell shallots by weight, and there are 20–30 bulbs to the pound. Thirty shallots planted in a 15 ft (4.5 m.) row will produce a crop of 4–5 lb. (2–2.5 kg.) – or more on a rich soil.

When grown for pickling, about ½ lb. (250 g.) of shallots will fill a 1 lb. (500 g.) jam-jar.

Varieties Most seedsmen sell only one or two varieties. The most popular are 'Giant Yellow', 'Red Dutch' and 'Yellow Dutch'.

'Hâtive de Niort' is a large variety popular with exhibitors.

How to grow shallots

Plant shallots in February or March in a sunny position on land previously manured for another crop. Like onions, shallots grow best on firm soil.

On light soil, push the bulbs firmly into the soil so that they are three-quarters buried. On firmer soils, make a hole with the tip of a trowel or draw a drill with a hoe. In each case leave only the tip of the bulb protruding. Allow 6 in. (150 mm.) between the bulbs and 12 in. (305 mm.) between rows.

After a week or two, re-plant any bulbs that have become dislodged. Hoe regularly throughout the spring and early summer.

Pests and diseases ONION EELWORM (p. 284) and ONION FLY (p. 284) are the principal pests of shallots.

The most likely diseases are DOWNY MILDEW (p. 288), NECK ROT (p. 289) and WHITE ROT (p. 291).

Harvesting and storing

When the foliage dies back in July, lift the clusters of shallots and lay them to dry for a few days.

When the foliage has withered completely, split the clumps into single bulbs and leave them to ripen for a few days longer. Finally, store them in a net or a basket in a cool, dry place.

AT-A-GLANCE TIMETABLE FOR SHALLOTS

PLANTING | HARVESTING | DIVIDING AND STORING

6 in. — 12 in.

FEBRUARY–MARCH | JULY | When tops have withered

Cooking with shallots

These small onions are used for flavouring rather than as a vegetable. Their mild flavour enhances stocks, soups and marinades.

Prepare shallots by peeling away the outer layers of dry skin, then dicing the bulb or cutting it crossways into thin rings.

Soya beans : see **Beans, Soya**

Spinach

Summer spinach

New Zealand spinach

Perpetual spinach

Even before Popeye the Sailor was called into being to boost the sales of the US spinach crop, most people in the Western world were aware of the high nutritional value of the leaves.

In fact, there are two types of true spinach – the round-seeded, which is generally harvested in summer; and the hardier, prickly seeded variety that is grown for use in winter and spring.

In addition, there are three other vegetables that resemble spinach, and are cooked in exactly the same way, though none is a true spinach.

New Zealand spinach, a native of Australasia, is a branching, mat-forming plant that withstands drought and will do quite well on poor, dry soils where other kinds are a failure. But it is killed by frost.

Spinach beet, which is also known as perpetual spinach, produces a succession of fresh leaves over a long period. This is perhaps the easiest to grow of all the spinach-type crops, although it is not truly perpetual and will run to seed during the spring of its second year.

The leaves of seakale beet, or Swiss chard (silver beet), are eaten like spinach, although the midribs are cooked like seakale.

By planting at least some of these crops you can enjoy fresh spinach, or indistinguishable substitutes, through most of the year. If you grow only one or two types, surplus leaves can be frozen for use when the outdoor crop is finished.

Planning the crop

As summer spinach needs to be grown quickly in order to produce large, succulent leaves, sow the seeds in soil that has recently been dressed with manure or compost. The crop takes only a few weeks from sowing to harvesting, so it is a good idea to grow some between rows of other vegetables.

Summer spinach will also benefit from the shade cast by the leaves of neighbouring plants.

Spinach beet, New Zealand spinach and seakale beet, however, remain in the ground for considerably longer and must therefore be allocated a place in the cropping plan. They, too, need well-manured soil.

Two weeks before sowing any type of spinach, rake a general fertiliser into the soil at the rate of 2 oz. per square yard (60 g. per square metre).

How much to grow Sow a 12–15 ft (3.6–4.5 m.) row of round-seeded summer spinach every three weeks if you want a succession of pickings throughout the summer.

One 20 ft (6 m.) row of spinach beet, New Zealand spinach or seakale beet will be sufficient to provide an average family with regular pickings over many weeks.

Grow one or two rows of winter spinach, according to its popularity in the family.

Varieties Round-seeded: 'Long Standing Round'; quick-growing with dark leaves.

'Sigmaleaf'; does not run to seed as quickly as most other varieties.

Prickly seeded: 'Long Standing Prickly'; quick-growing and slow to run to seed.

Perpetual spinach, New Zealand spinach and seakale beet are sold under these names.

How to grow spinach

Make the first sowing of round-seeded spinach in early March in the south and late March in the north. Continue sowing at three-week intervals until early July.

Sow seeds of the winter varieties

AT-A-GLANCE TIMETABLE FOR SPINACH

	SOWING	THINNING	HARVESTING
Summer spinach	MARCH–JULY	When large enough to handle	JUNE–OCTOBER
New Zealand spinach	APRIL (in groups)	Leave strongest seedling in each group	JUNE–SEPTEMBER
Spinach beet	APRIL: JULY	When large enough to handle	Most months
Seakale beet	MAY	When large enough to handle	AUG–NOV: APRIL–JULY

(Sowing diagram: 12–15 in. width, 1 in. depth; Thinning diagram: 12 in.)

during August and September, for harvesting between October and April.

Sow spinach beet in April and again in July, New Zealand spinach in April and seakale beet in May.

Sow the seeds of all but New Zealand spinach in drills 1 in. (25 mm.) deep and 12–15 in. (305–380 mm.) apart. As soon as the seedlings are large enough to handle, thin them to 6 in. (150 mm.) apart, and finally to 12 in. (305 mm.). The second thinnings can be used in cooking.

Sow seeds of New Zealand spinach 1 in. (25 mm.) deep, in groups of two or three, with 2 ft (610 mm.) between groups and 3 ft (1 m.) between rows. Remove the weakest seedlings in each group.

Water all spinach plants liberally, especially during dry spells, to reduce the risk of the plants running to seed. This is one of the main hazards of the crop during spells of hot weather.

Pests and diseases Spinach may be attacked by APHIDS (p. 282).

CUCUMBER MOSAIC VIRUS (p. 287), DOWNY MILDEW (p. 288), LEAF SPOT (p. 288) and SHOTHOLE (p. 290) are the most likely diseases.

Harvesting and storing

With all types of spinach, pick the leaves when they are ready. Even when not required in the kitchen, the leaves of spinach beet, New Zealand spinach and seakale beet should be picked regularly to encourage further growth.

When picking New Zealand spinach, gather the young shoot tips, each with two or three leaves.

See also freezing (p. 294).

Preparing & cooking spinach

Spinach deteriorates quickly after picking and should be used as quickly as possible, while still crisp.

Pick the spinach just before cooking, strip the leaves from the stalks, and if the midribs are coarse remove these as well.

Immerse the leaves in a large bowl of cold water, lift them out and repeat with fresh water – once or twice more – until the water is quite clear of sand and grit.

As spinach has a high water content, it does not need additional water for cooking. It is sufficient to put the leaves in a large pan with only the water that adheres to the leaves from the last rinsing.

Sprinkle lightly with salt, cover with a lid and cook over gentle heat for 7–10 minutes, until soft. Drain the spinach thoroughly, squeezing out as much water as possible with a potato masher.

CRISP BUTTERED SPINACH

1 lb. (500 g.) spinach
Salt, pepper and nutmeg
1 oz. (25 g.) butter
4 tablespoons coarse breadcrumbs
Garnish : poached eggs

COOKING TIME: 10–15 minutes

Strip the spinach from the leaf stalks and midribs, wash thoroughly and put in a large

pan with a sprinkling of salt. Cover with a lid and cook over gentle heat for 7 minutes, or until soft. Drain through a colander and chop roughly.

Melt the butter in a pan, add the spinach and toss evenly. Stir in sufficient breadcrumbs, a little at a time, to absorb all the liquid from the spinach and butter. Season to taste with salt, pepper and nutmeg.

Serving Spoon the spinach into a shallow dish and top with four poached eggs. Serve as an accompaniment to baked fish or grilled chicken, or as a light lunch or supper dish on its own. *Photograph* on pages 134–5.

SPINACH MOULD

1 lb. (500 g.) spinach
Salt, pepper and nutmeg
4 eggs
½ pint (300 ml.) cream

COOKING TIME: 45 minutes
OVEN TEMPERATURE: 180°C (350°F) – gas mark 4

Strip the leaves from the stalks and remove all midribs. Wash the spinach thoroughly and put in a pan without any extra water. Cover with a lid and simmer for 7–8 minutes, or until tender. Drain the spinach thoroughly, then chop the leaves finely with a sharp knife.

Beat the eggs with a pinch of salt, pepper and ground nutmeg and gradually beat in the cream

to a smooth, well-blended mixture. Fold in the chopped spinach and spoon into a well-buttered ring-mould.

Set the mould in a roasting tin with 1 in. (25 mm.) of hot water and bake in the oven for 35 minutes, or until the spinach mixture is set and firm.

Serving Turn the mould out upside-down and fill the centre with mushrooms in a cream sauce, glazed carrots, or cooked flaked haddock in a cheese sauce. *Photograph* on pages 140–1.

SPINACH AND ANCHOVY QUICHE

½ lb. (250 g.) spinach
½ lb. (250 g.) shortcrust pastry
1 small onion
1 oz. (25 g.) butter
Salt and pepper
Sugar and grated nutmeg
3 eggs
5 fl. oz. (150 ml.) cream
5 fl. oz. (150 ml.) milk
Small tin of anchovy fillets

COOKING TIME: 1 hour
OVEN TEMPERATURE: 190°C (375°F) – gas mark 5

First make up the pastry from ½ lb. (250 g.) flour, roll it out and use to line an 8 in. (200 mm.) flan ring set on a baking sheet. Bake this 'blind' for 15 minutes at a temperature of 200°C (400°F) – gas mark 6 – until the pastry is dry. Remove from the oven.

Meanwhile, strip the spinach from the stalks and wash thoroughly in several lots of cold water. Put the spinach, without any extra water, in a pan and cook gently for about 5 minutes, until soft. Drain thoroughly, squeezing out as much water as possible, then chop the spinach finely.

Peel the onion, chop it finely, and fry in the butter for a few minutes, until soft. Add the spinach and continue cooking until all the water has evaporated, stirring well all the time. Season to taste with salt and pepper, sugar and nutmeg. Remove from the heat.

Beat the eggs with the cream and milk, and gradually incorporate the spinach mixture. Spoon this into the pastry case and level the top. Drain the anchovy fillets, rinse them in cold water to remove excess salt, pat them dry and lay in a criss-cross pattern over the spinach.

Bake the quiche in the oven for 25–30 minutes, or until the filling is firm.

Serving This quiche is best served warm, as a filling main course, perhaps accompanied by buttered or creamed potatoes.

CREAM OF SPINACH SOUP

1 lb. (500 g.) spinach
2 oz. (50 g.) butter
1 onion
2 carrots
4 sprigs parsley
Bouquet garni
Salt, pepper and nutmeg
1½ pints (850 ml.) white stock
5 fl. oz. (150 ml.) cream
Garnish : bread croûtons

COOKING TIME: 40 minutes

Strip the spinach from the leaf stalks and discard any coarse midribs. Wash the spinach in several lots of water and chop the leaves roughly.

Melt the butter in a pan and add the roughly chopped onion, the carrots and the spinach. Cook gently for about 5 minutes, then add the stock, parsley sprigs and bouquet garni.

Bring to the boil, season with salt and pepper and simmer gently for 30 minutes, or until all the vegetables are tender. Blend the soup in a liquidiser.

Return the soup to the pan, heat through and correct the seasoning with salt, pepper and nutmeg. Adjust the consistency, if necessary, by adding milk, and at the last minute stir in the cream. Do not boil.
Serving Pour the soup into bowls or a soup tureen, and serve a separate bowl of crisp croûtons sprinkled with nutmeg.
Photograph on page 216.

SPINACH SALAD

1 lb. (500 g.) young spinach
6 oz. (175 g.) cooked ham or gammon
1 green pepper
1 tablespoon chopped chives
6 tablespoons olive oil
2 tablespoons white wine vinegar
1 garlic clove
French mustard
Salt and pepper
2 hard-boiled eggs

Use only absolutely fresh young spinach leaves for this salad. Strip the leaves from the stalks, wash them carefully and dry in a salad basket or on a soft cloth.

Arrange the spinach leaves in a salad bowl. Dice the ham. Remove the stalk base, seeds and membranes from the pepper and cut it into narrow slices. Mix these two ingredients with the chopped chives and arrange in the centre of the bowl.

Mix up a dressing from the oil, vinegar and crushed garlic clove, seasoning to taste with mustard, salt and pepper. Pour the dressing over the salad.
Serving Garnish with slices of hard-boiled eggs and serve the salad as a light lunch dish on its own, with crusty bread, or as a side salad.
Photograph on pages 210–11.

Spinach beet:
see **Spinach**

Sprouting seeds

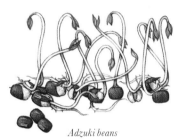
Adzuki beans

Alfalfa

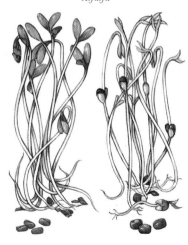
Fenugreek   *Mung beans*

Sprouting seeds were possibly the first true crops harvested by man. Some 5,000 years ago, long before the Great Wall of China was built, a Chinese emperor, writing a book on plants, made special mention of 'health-giving sprouts'.

Even so long ago, the remarkable quality of food plants at this particular state of their growth was recognised, though perhaps not understood. Only in recent years has research affirmed that many seeds, shortly after germination, contain a wealth of vitamins, minerals and protein.

As an easy-to-grow, cheap and nutritious food crop, sprouting seeds can hardly be bettered. They are also delicious, both in their subtleties of flavour and in the wide range of dishes they enhance.

The most familiar of edible sprouting seeds are, of course, mustard and cress (see p. 203), while the ever-growing number of Chinese restaurants has done much to popularise bean shoots.

But almost all vegetable and cereal sprouts are edible, and may be utilised in any one of a hundred recipes. Among the few exceptions are tomato and potato sprouts, both of which are poisonous.

Sprouting varieties of wheat, chick peas, kidney beans, lentils and buckwheat are available from most health-food shops, while one or two seedsmen offer fenugreek, mung beans, alfalfa and adzuki.

Methods and equipment

One of the advantages of growing sprouts is that, having bought the seeds, there is almost no further expense. Depending on the method used, all you need is a few jam-jars or trays, paper towelling, muslin and elastic bands.

Most seeds will germinate at living-room temperature and may be grown in the kitchen. Some, however, need a few days in the airing cupboard, and some require 'greening' to achieve their full flavour.

Those benefiting from the slightly higher temperature are buckwheat, fenugreek, lentils, sunflowers, triticale and wheat.

Whichever method you choose, there are two basic rules to follow:

First, wash the seeds well and soak them overnight in a bowl of lukewarm water, using four cups of water to one cup of seeds.

Second, drain off the water, rinse the seeds thoroughly and place them in the sprouting container. During the ensuing few days, rinse the seeds again, once or more daily, depending on variety and the dryness of the weather.

Jar method You will require a jam-jar, a square of muslin or nylon cut from an old pair of tights, and an elastic band. Put the soaked seeds into the jar and cover the opening with the muslin or nylon, holding it in place with the elastic band.

Lay the jar in a bowl with the open end slightly downwards to aid drainage, and place it in a dark corner or airing cupboard, according to the temperature required. Rinse the seeds daily (see chart on p. 262) until the sprouts grow to the required length.

If they require 'greening', leave them on a shady window-sill. Further growth can be arrested by placing them in the refrigerator for up to a week.

Tray method In some ways this is the easiest method, but it is not suitable for every type of seed. The only equipment required is an oven tray and several lengths of paper towelling.

Simply dampen a thick layer of towelling, place it in the tray, and scatter the soaked seeds over it. Cover with a further layer of damp towelling and place in a dark, warm cupboard. Keep the paper moist until the seeds sprout.

If the sprouts require 'greening', place the tray on a shady window-sill for a day or two.

SPROUTING SEEDS IN A TRAY

Scatter the seeds on damp paper towelling and cover them with similar material. Remove the top paper when the seeds sprout ; keep the base damp until the shoots have reached the required length.

SPROUTING SEEDS IN A JAM-JAR

1 Place the soaked seeds in a jar and secure muslin over the top. Place the jar on its side, in a bowl, in a warm room.

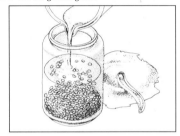

2 Rinse the seeds at least once daily (see chart). To do this, remove the muslin and half fill the jar with water.

3 Replace the muslin, swill the seeds gently and drain through the cover. Continue rinsing until the sprouts are long enough.

4 If the sprouts require 'greening', place on a window-sill for a day or two. After emptying from the jar, rinse in a colander.

HOW TO GROW TEN KINDS OF SPROUTING SEEDS

	Method	*Rinsing*	*Sprouting time*
Adzuki beans Crisp, sweet, nutty shoots ; often used in oriental cooking	Jam-jar Tray	Four times daily, or damp when necessary	3–4 days. Harvest when 1 in. (25 mm.) long
Alfalfa Fresh green sprouts ; ideal for winter salads	Jam-jar	Twice daily	3–6 days, including 'greening'. Harvest when 1–2 in. (25–50 mm.) long
Buckwheat Originating in Siberia, this versatile plant may be used in breads, soups and salads, or as a cooked vegetable	Jam-jar Tray	Once daily	2–3 days. Harvest when $\frac{1}{2}$ in. (12 mm.) long
Chick peas A Mediterranean plant, frequently used as an accompaniment to curries	Jam-jar	4–5 times daily	3–4 days. Harvest when $\frac{1}{2}$ in. (12 mm.) long
Fenugreek A classic ingredient of curries. Also good in salads and soups. Requires 'greening'.	Jam-jar	Once or twice daily	4–7 days, including 'greening' time. Harvest when 3 in. (75 mm.) long
Lentils A staple vegetable in many countries. May be eaten raw or cooked	Jam-jar	2–3 times daily	3–4 days. Harvest when 1 in. (25 mm.) long
Mung (Chinese bean sprouts) White, crisp shoots ; a favourite dish in Chinese restaurants	Jam-jar Tray	Three times daily, or damp when necessary	4–5 days. Harvest when 2–3 in. (50–75 mm.) long
Sunflower The shoots are delicious, but become strong-flavoured if grown too long	Jam-jar	Twice daily	2–3 days. Harvest when $\frac{1}{2}$ in. (12 mm.) long
Triticale A hybrid of wheat and rye. Excellent for soups and salads	Jam-jar	2–3 times daily	2–3 days. Harvest when 2–3 in. (50–75 mm.) long
Wheat Wheat sprouts will add a fresh flavour and texture to soups and salads	Jam-jar	2–3 times daily	2–5 days. Harvest when $\frac{1}{2}$ in. (12 mm.) long

The young sprouts of beans and other seeds need minimum preparation, except for a final rinsing.

They can be added, raw, to mixed salads to give a crunchy texture, or served on their own as a salad with an oil-vinaigrette or sour-cream dressing.

Sprouted seeds make an excellent addition to soups, stews, and main dishes, adding a welcome new flavour and texture.

They can also be quick-fried or steamed, and served as a side-dish vegetable.

Where a recipe specifies bean sprouts, either mung beans or adzuki beans may be used. Fenugreek is suitable for curries, salads and soups. Buckwheat, triticale and wheat may be added to bread dough, as well as being used to flavour soups and salads.

Mung beans, or Chinese bean sprouts, are the basis for much oriental cooking and are probably the most versatile of the sprouting seeds, either on their own or in combination with other foods.

In Chinese cookery, bean sprouts are cooked by the method known as stir-frying, whereby the bean sprouts are added to a pan of very hot vegetable oil and fried quickly, being turned over constantly, until cooked through but still crisp.

They must be served at once, otherwise the crunchy texture will be lost.

Cooking & serving sprouted seeds

BEAN SPROUTS WITH NOODLES

½ *lb. (250 g.) bean sprouts*
½ *lb. (250 g.) egg noodles*
½ *lb. (250 g.) beef (fillet or rump)*
3 tablespoons oil
1 onion
2 garlic cloves
6 salad onions
2 sticks celery
1 teaspoon ground ginger
4 tablespoons beef stock or bouillon
2 tablespoons soy sauce
Salt
Garnish : omelette strips, prawns or lemon

COOKING TIME: 35 minutes

Bring a pan of lightly salted water to the boil and drop in the noodles. Bring back to the boil and cook over moderate heat for 10 minutes. Drain thoroughly.

Cut the meat into very thin strips, 2 in. (50 mm.) long. Heat the oil in a large pan, add the meat and fry to seal for 1 minute. Stir in the finely chopped onion, crushed garlic, finely chopped salad onions (including the green parts), and the celery.

Add the ginger, stock and soy sauce and fry all the ingredients over moderate heat for about 15 minutes, stirring frequently, until the meat is tender. Season to taste. Add the drained noodles and the bean sprouts and heat through, stirring well.
Serving For the garnish of omelette strips, make a thin omelette from two eggs beaten with water. Bake it on both sides and cut into narrow strips. Spoon the bean-sprout mixture into a large, shallow dish ; garnish with the omelette strips in a lattice pattern, the peeled prawns, or the lemon wedges.
Photograph on pages 138–9.

⊰⊹⊱

BEAN SPROUTS WITH MUSHROOMS AND CHICKEN

½ *lb. (250 g.) bean sprouts*
2 onions
2 young leeks or 8 salad onions
½ *lb. (250 g.) uncooked chicken meat*
½ *lb. (250 g.) mushrooms*
2–3 tablespoons vegetable oil
2 tablespoons soy sauce
1 tablespoon sherry
Salt and white pepper

COOKING TIME: 15 minutes

In Chinese cooking, the actual cooking time is minimal whereas the preparations can be lengthy, depending on the number and nature of the ingredients in a dish. All the components are finely shredded, and are stir-fried in an order that is determined by the amount of cooking needed. Thus, onions and meat are fried before soft vegetables, and bean sprouts are added last.

Heat the oil in a large pan, and add the finely chopped onions, and leeks. If you are using salad onions, add the green parts as well. Stir-fry for 2–3 minutes, then add the skinned, boned and finely diced chicken meat.

Continue stir-frying for 7–10 minutes until the chicken is tender, then add the finely sliced mushrooms and fry for a further 2 minutes before adding the bean sprouts, soy sauce and sherry.

Stir-fry briskly for 2–3 minutes and season with salt and pepper.
Serving This is a light, crisp dish – a complete meal on its own. Serve at once, with a small bowl of extra soy sauce.
Variation Chopped prawns may be used instead of chicken.

⊰⊹⊱

MIXED SPROUT SALAD

Use a selection of sprouts of your own choice to make this easy salad.
4 oz. (100 g.) mung bean sprouts
2 oz. (50 g.) alfalfa sprouts
2 oz. (50 g.) adzuki bean sprouts
1 large carrot
2 sticks celery
½ *onion*
2 dessert apples
2 oz. (50 g.) raisins
Mayonnaise

Rinse the sprouts; peel and grate the carrot, onion and apples. Chop the celery. Add the raisins and enough mayonnaise to coat the ingredients.
Serving Serve as a side-salad.
Variation Use an oil-vinaigrette dressing instead of the mayonnaise.

Squashes : see **Pumpkins and squashes**
Strawberries

Strawberries are an essential ingredient of both great and small summer treats – whether a lunch at Royal Ascot races or a birthday party in the back garden. Yet they are by no means difficult to grow.

Strawberries also give a quicker return than any other fruit, because plants set out in late summer will provide a crop the following June.

In a large garden, strawberries can be picked from May to October if a number of selected varieties are planted, and cloches are used to extend the growing season.

There are two types – those that carry a single crop in June and July, and 'perpetual', or remontant, varieties that begin to crop slowly in June, reach a peak in August, but then continue until October.

Planning the crop

Strawberries need a rich, well-drained soil in a sunny position. They do best in slightly acid soils,

Alpine strawberry

263

but they can be grown successfully in almost any well-drained land.

A soil can hardly be too rich for them. Before planting, dig in well-rotted manure or compost at the rate of at least a bucketful to the square yard. Do not, however, leave any organic material on the surface as this will encourage slugs and snails.

Afterwards, fork into the surface 2 oz. of general fertiliser per square yard (60 g. per square metre).

Buy only plants that are certified free from disease.

How many to grow A 12 × 5 ft (3.6 × 1.5 m.) plot will support 27 plants – enough for most average families.

Varieties Recommended varieties setting a single crop are, in order of fruiting:

'Grandee': large fruits of fine flavour; may produce up to 3½ lb. (1.75 kg.) per plant; early June.

'Cambridge Rival': richly flavoured; mid-June.

'Gorella': good flavour; mid-June.

'Royal Sovereign': very fine flavour; light cropper; mid-June.

'Cambridge Favourite': heavy cropper; flavour fair; late June.

'Redgauntlet': heavy cropper; fair-flavoured fruit; thrives in cold areas; fruits early July but can produce a second crop in autumn, if protected by glass or polythene.

'Cambridge Late Pine': fine-flavoured fruit but only a moderate cropper; late July.

Perpetual varieties that will crop into autumn include:

'Gento': large, good-flavoured fruits produced June to October; succeeds on chalky soils.

'Sans Rivale': heavy cropper; fruits of only fair flavour; August to October.

'St Claude': good flavour; almost continuous cropping from July to October.

How to grow strawberries

Plant as early as possible – from July to the first week in September – if the plants are to be protected by cloches from November for an early crop, or if a good crop is expected in the open in the first season.

If planting must be delayed until March or April, remove the flowers so that the plants get

PLANTING STRAWBERRIES

Form a small mound in each planting hole. Spread the roots over this, with the base of the plant level with the surface.

established to crop the following year.

Plant perpetuals no later than August; otherwise wait until March or April. Remove the first flowers from those planted in spring.

Set the plants 18 in. (455 mm.) apart in rows 2½ ft (760 mm.) apart. For each plant, dig a hole about 1½ in. (40 mm.) deeper than the root system. Then make a mound at the bottom of the hole and spread the roots over this so that the base of the plant is level

with the surface as you replace the soil over the roots.

Water the plants in, and keep watering during dry weather.

In early February, place glass or polythene cloches in position if you are aiming for an early crop.

When the berries start to develop – during May for single crop varieties – scatter slug pellets between the rows and tuck fresh straw under each plant to keep the berries off the ground. Alternatively, use black polythene or the strawberry mats sold by most horticultural suppliers.

At the same time, protect ripening fruit from birds by covering with netting supported by canes.

When all the fruit on single-cropping varieties has been picked, loosen the straw round the plants and set light to it, provided there is no risk of the fire spreading to other dry growth or timber fencing. This will destroy pests, and both old and diseased leaves.

Rake off any unburned debris and lightly fork between the rows.

Do not burn perpetual varieties, or the new growth will be killed. Instead, remove some of the old leaves and burn them on a bonfire.

In late September or early October, cover perpetual plants with cloches to provide a late crop.

In January, add sulphate of potash to the soil at the rate of ½ oz. per square yard (15 g. per square metre). On light soils, give a dressing of sulphate of ammonia at ½ oz. per square yard in early April.

Raising new plants Layering runners is the simplest method of propagation.

In July or August, small plants will appear as runners from the

mother plants. If you want to increase your stock, choose four of the strongest runners from each plant and peg them into the soil with pieces of bent wire. If the soil is dry or of indifferent quality, sink 3 in. (75 mm.) compost-filled pots into the soil and insert the plants in these.

Pinch off the outer end of the runner extending from each pegged plant, but do not sever the new plant from its parent until it is well-rooted – after four to six weeks. Once it is growing strongly on its own roots, sever the runner and set the new plant in its permanent position.

The vigour and yield of strawberry plants soon decrease, and all plants – including those raised from runners – should be renewed at least every five years, with the new plants set on a fresh site. Burn old plants.

Pests and diseases The most common pests attacking strawberries are APHIDS (p. 282), CUTWORMS (p. 283), GLASSHOUSE RED SPIDER MITES (p. 283), LEAF EELWORM (p. 283), SLUGS AND SNAILS (p. 285), STRAWBERRY BEETLE (p. 285) and STRAWBERRY MITE (p. 285).

The disorders most likely to occur are FROST DAMAGE (p. 288), GREY MOULD (p. 288), LEAF SPOT (p. 288), POWDERY MILDEW (p. 289) and VIRUS DISEASES (p. 291).

Harvesting and storing

Pick strawberries by the stalk to avoid bruising. Eat them as soon as possible after picking. See also bottling (p. 309); freezing (p. 294); fruit cheeses and butters (p. 323); jams (p. 314) and syrups and juices (p. 326).

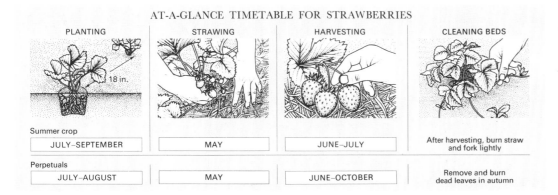

AT-A-GLANCE TIMETABLE FOR STRAWBERRIES

PLANTING	STRAWING	HARVESTING	CLEANING BEDS
18 in.			After harvesting, burn straw and fork lightly
Summer crop			
JULY–SEPTEMBER	MAY	JUNE–JULY	
Perpetuals			Remove and burn dead leaves in autumn
JULY–AUGUST	MAY	JUNE–OCTOBER	

RAISING NEW PLANTS

PEGGING RUNNERS During the summer, use bent wire to peg strong runners directly to the soil or to compost-filled pots set in the soil.

TRIMMING THE END Pinch off the outer end of the runner, but do not sever the stem that joins the new plant to the parent plant.

SEVERING THE RUNNER After 4–6 weeks, when the plant is rooted, sever the runner and set the plant in its permanent bed.

Alpine strawberries

Although seeds of the true wild strawberry are obtainable, Alpine varieties are much more widely grown and both seeds and plants are stocked by many seedsmen and nurserymen.

The flowers and fruits of the Alpine strawberry are much smaller than the usual cultivated varieties. The fruits are somewhat tedious to pick, but gourmets who enjoy their sweet, rich flavour will consider the effort worthwhile.

Although the Alpine is a perennial, the plants deteriorate after the first year. It is, therefore, better to grow plants from seed each year. Alternatively, plants can be bought from nurseries in April and May. One of the best varieties is 'Baron Solemacher'.

Alpines thrive in rich soil in a sunny position, although they will tolerate a little shade. They need not take up space in the fruit garden. Plants can be grown in the front of a flower border.

How to grow Alpine strawberries

During the winter before planting, prepare the site by digging in well-rotted manure or compost at the rate of a bucketful to the square yard. About three weeks before planting in April or May, rake into the surface 3 oz. of general fertiliser to the square yard (90 g. per square metre).

Sow the seeds in pots or pans of seed compost in September. Sprinkle the very fine seeds on the surface, cover with a dusting of compost and press down lightly. Cover the pans with glass and paper until the seeds germinate.

Germination is erratic, but the seedlings should be ready for pricking out into trays of potting compost by the end of October. Overwinter them in a cold greenhouse or frame for planting out in late April or May.

Alternatively, sow the seeds in pots under glass in February, March or April for planting out in late April or May.

Set the plants 12 in. (305 mm.) apart, in rows the same distance apart. Protect autumn-sown plants with cloches if there is a likelihood of frost when they start flowering in May. Keep the soil moist at all times. The plants will stop cropping if the roots dry out.

Alpine strawberries fruit over a comparatively long period. Leave the fruits to ripen fully as they will then have the most flavour. Pick regularly to encourage more fruit to set.

AT-A-GLANCE TIMETABLE FOR ALPINE STRAWBERRIES

SOWING	TRANSPLANTING	HARVESTING
	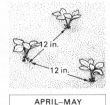 12 in. / 12 in.	
SEPT: FEB–APRIL	APRIL–MAY	JULY–OCTOBER

Preparing & serving strawberries

Undoubtedly, strawberries are at their most enjoyable when served fresh with sugar and thick cream; but they are also excellent, again used fresh, as fillings for tartlets and cream cakes. They are also easily made into ice creams or as a mousse, or cooked for a compôte.

Serve strawberries whole unless they are very large, in which case cut them into halves with a stainless-steel blade to prevent discoloration. The green flower calyx is attractive and may be left on the berry, but usually strawberries are 'hulled' by removing this and the soft centre stalk.

Rinse the berries carefully in a colander in cold water, and drain thoroughly before serving.

A small number of strawberries can be made to go further by sprinkling them with sugar, and perhaps a dash of liqueur or sweet wine, and chilling lightly in the refrigerator until the sugar has melted.

Arrange the berries in tall glasses on a bed of vanilla ice cream or sweetened whipped cream.

STRAWBERRY MOUSSE

6–8 oz. (175–250 g.) strawberries
3 tablespoons sugar
3–4 tablespoons rum
4 eggs
2 oz. (50 g.) caster sugar
¾ oz. (20 g.) powdered gelatine
½ pint (300 ml.) double cream

CHILLING TIME: 2 hours

Hull, rinse and drain the strawberries. Cut the berries into thick slices and put them in a bowl, sprinkling with sugar and rum. Set aside in a cool place until the sugar has dissolved.

Beat the eggs with the caster sugar until they are creamy, fluffy and pale yellow. Dissolve the gelatine in 3 tablespoons of water and stir it quickly into the egg mixture. Whip the cream lightly and fold most of it, together with the liquid drained from the strawberries, into the eggs when these begin to set.

Spoon the mixture into a serving dish and leave in the refrigerator until set.

Serving Just before serving, arrange the sliced strawberries in a thick layer on the cream mousse and decorate with the remaining piped cream.

Variation Simmer 1 lb. (500 g.) of whole, rinsed strawberries in 1 pint (600 ml.) of water until soft. Thicken with a little cornflour and sweeten to taste. Serve chilled, with cream.

Continued . . .

Strawberry recipes (continued)

STRAWBERRY CREAM

¾ *lb. (375 g.) strawberries*
4 oz. (100–125 g.) sugar
Lemon or lime juice
½ *pint (300 ml.) double cream*
3 teaspoons powdered gelatine

CHILLING TIME: 2–3 hours

Hull, rinse and thoroughly drain the strawberries. Cut them into small pieces and blend to a purée in a liquidiser or rub them through a sieve. Stir the sugar, with a squeeze of lemon or lime juice, into the strawberry purée. Fold in the lightly beaten cream.

Dissolve the gelatine in 3 tablespoons of water and blend it into the strawberry cream, stirring all the time until the mixture begins to thicken. Spoon into a wetted mould, and chill.
Serving Turn the mould out, upside-down, and decorate with whole, hulled strawberries.
Photograph on pages 142–3.

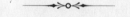

STRAWBERRY MERINGUE CAKE

½–¾ *lb. (250–375 g.) strawberries*
4 egg whites
½ *lb. (250 g.) caster sugar*
1 teaspoon white wine vinegar
Vanilla essence
½ *pint (300 ml.) vanilla ice cream*

COOKING TIME: 1–1¼ hours
OVEN TEMPERATURE: 140°C (275°F)
– gas mark 1

Hull and rinse the strawberries, and leave to drain. Whisk the egg whites stiff, fold in half the sugar, add the vinegar and continue whisking until the whites stand in firm peaks. Whisk in the remaining sugar and flavour the meringue mixture with a few drops of vanilla essence.

Line a baking sheet with non-stick paper and draw on it a circle about 8 in. (200 mm.) wide.

Spread two-thirds of the meringue in an even layer over the circle, levelling the top with a broad-bladed knife. Spoon the remaining meringue into a forcing bag fitted with a large, fluted nozzle. Pipe two layers of meringue round the edge of the circle, one layer on top of the other to form a raised edge.

Bake the meringue basket in the lower half of the oven for about 1¼ hours, or until the meringue is firm and dry and comes clean away from the paper.
Serving Fill the cooled meringue case with slices of vanilla ice cream and lay the strawberries on top. Serve at once.
Variations Replace the strawberries with other soft fruit, such as loganberries or raspberries.

STRAWBERRY TRIFLE

1 lb. (500 g.) strawberries
4 oz. (100–125 g.) macaroons
2 tablespoons sherry
1 tablespoon caster sugar
3 egg yolks
2 oz. (50 g.) sugar
½ *vanilla pod*
½ *pint (300 ml.) single cream*
1 teaspoon cornflour

COOKING TIME: 20 minutes

Break up the macaroons roughly and put them over the base of a glass dish. Pour the sherry over them and leave to soak.

Hull, rinse and drain the strawberries. Set 8–10 berries aside, cut the rest into pieces and mash to a rough purée. Stir in the tablespoon of sugar and spoon over the macaroons.

Beat the egg yolks with the sugar. Bring the cream, with the vanilla pod, to the boil, cover, and leave for 10 minutes.

Remove the vanilla pod and gradually whisk the cream into the egg yolks. Strain back into the pan and bring back to just under boiling point, whisking constantly to prevent the custard curdling. Remove from the heat and stir in the cornflour, first blending it with a little cold milk.

Leave the custard to cool, sprinkling the top with sugar to prevent a skin forming, then pour it over the strawberries.
Serving Decorate with the reserved berries.

Swedes

A fairly open plot is needed to grow swedes successfully. Although worth trying in any position other than one that is shaded, they are essentially a field crop and seem to do best where fences or walls do not restrict the flow of air.

If conditions are right, however, the mild, turnip-flavoured roots, which are extremely hardy, can be left in the ground for using as required during the winter.

Planning the crop

Swedes will grow well in any fertile soil except one that is acid. Even this can be brought into condition by giving a top-dressing of carbonate of lime at 6 oz. per square yard (180 g. per square metre) after

AT-A-GLANCE TIMETABLE FOR SWEDES

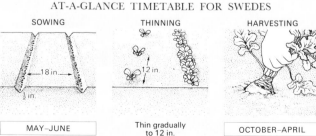

SOWING	THINNING	HARVESTING
MAY–JUNE	Thin gradually to 12 in.	OCTOBER–APRIL

digging the soil in preparation for the crop.

Grow swedes in ground that was well manured for a previous crop, not in freshly manured ground.

How many to grow A row 20 ft (6 m.) long will provide about 30 lb. (13.5 kg.) of roots – ample to last most families through the winter.

Varieties 'Acme': quick growing; excellent for eating young and for storing.

'Chignecto': a purple-top swede which is resistant to club root (see p. 287).

How to grow swedes

Sow the seeds where the crop is to grow, in late May in the south and in early June in the north. Sow thinly in drills $\frac{1}{2}$ in. (12 mm.) deep and 18 in. (455 mm.) apart.

Thin the plants as they grow, spacing them finally at intervals of 12 in. (305 mm.) to allow them plenty of room to develop.

Except for hoeing to keep down weeds, little attention is required after thinning.

Pests and diseases The crop may be attacked by APHIDS (p. 282) CUTWORMS (p. 283), FLEA BEETLE (p. 283) and caterpillars of the SWIFT MOTH (p. 285).

Diseases and disorders include BORON DEFICIENCY (p. 286), CLUB ROOT (p. 287) and SPLITTING (p. 290).

Harvesting and storing

Lift the roots as required from autumn until spring. A few may be lifted as a reserve, and kept in a cool, airy place such as a garage or shed, for use when the soil is frozen.

Preparing & cooking swedes

Although swedes may be cooked and served like turnips, they are even better mashed with butter and cream and seasoned with ground nutmeg or ginger. Mashed swedes may also be blended with mashed potatoes, giving the potatoes a sweet flavour which can be further emphasised by adding ginger and butter to the mixture.

Add quartered swedes to meat and vegetable stews and casseroles. They are especially good with fatty meats, such as lamb and mutton.

Prepare swedes by cutting a thick slice off the top and trimming the root end until the yellow flesh is revealed. Cut off the tough peel in a thick layer.

Wash peeled roots in cold water, cut them into quarters or large cubes and boil in slightly salted water for 30–40 minutes, or until soft. Drain, and serve tossed in butter.

Alternatively, par-boil quartered swedes for about 10 minutes, drain them and add to a roasting joint for the last 30 minutes, as for parsnips.

SWEDES WITH BACON

1 lb. (500 g.) swedes
Salt and pepper
2 oz. (50 g.) butter
Milk
4 oz. (100–125 g.) bacon

COOKING TIME: 40 minutes

Trim the tops and root ends off the swedes and peel them thickly. Wash the peeled roots and cut into small chunks. Put in a pan of boiling, lightly salted water, cover with a lid and simmer for 35 minutes, or until quite tender.

Drain through a colander, then mash thoroughly with a potato masher. Return to the pan, and cream the mashed swedes with half the butter and a little milk. Season to taste with salt and pepper.

Meanwhile, remove any rind and gristle from the bacon, dice the flesh and fry in the remaining butter until crisp. *Serving* Spoon the mashed swedes into a dish, shaping it into a dome. Make a deep depression in the top and pour into this the crisp bacon and butter. Serve with grilled or fried sausages, or liver.

Variation Omit the bacon and fold a little cream and plenty of chopped parsley into the mashed swedes.

Sweet corn

Also known as maize, corn-on-the-cob and Indian Corn, sweet corn is believed to have been introduced to Europe from America by Christopher Columbus at the end of the 15th century. It was once considered an unsuitable crop for Britain, but in the last 30 years plant breeders have developed varieties suited to our climate, producing reasonable crops even in poor summers.

With its fine foliage and loose, feathery flowers, the plant makes a decorative addition to the garden. It is not difficult to grow, as some people believe, and fresh, home-grown cobs are extra delicious.

Planning the crop

Sweet corn needs a sunny, sheltered position.

It will grow in any soil, but for good-quality crops enrich the bed with well-rotted compost or manure, at the rate of a bucketful to the square yard, during the winter before planting.

Just before sowing or planting, apply a general fertiliser at the rate of 2 oz. per square yard (60 g. per square metre).

When preparing the bed, remember that sweet corn does best when grown in a block rather than in a long row. This provides the best chance for the light, air-borne pollen to fall from the male flowers at the top of the plants on to the silky female flower tassels which hang from the tops of the immature cobs.

How much to grow Fifteen plants set in a block measuring about 6×15 ft (1.8×4.5 m.) will provide 15 to 25 cobs, depending on the soil and the weather during the summer.

Varieties Among varieties suited to our climate are:

'Earliking' (F1 hybrid): large, broad cobs of excellent quality.

'First of All' (F1 hybrid): medium-size cobs; matures very early and is therefore ideal for northern areas.

'Golden Bantam': excellent flavour, medium-size.

'John Innes Hybrid' (F1 hybrid): early ripening, compact.

'Kelvedon Glory' (F1 hybrid): heavy yields; good flavour.

'North Star' (F1 hybrid): reliable; especially suitable for northern areas.

How to grow sweet corn

Sweet corn can be grown directly in the open ground in late May, but success is more assured if seeds are given an early start, whether by sowing in pots under glass in April and setting the plants out later, or by sowing under cloches.

To raise seedlings under glass, sow the seeds two at a time and ½ in. (12 mm.) deep in 2½ in. (65 mm.) peat pots filled with moist seed compost. Alternatively, sow the seeds in 3 in. (75 mm.) earthenware or plastic pots.

Cover the pots with newspaper and glass until the seeds germinate. If you are raising them indoors, enclose the pots in plastic bags and place them in a warm airing cupboard. As soon as the seeds have germinated, discard the weaker of the two seedlings and place the pots in full light.

When the seedlings are about 6 in. (150 mm.) tall, harden them off (see p. 34). Plant them out in late May. Set the plants 15 in. (380 mm.) apart in rows 2 ft (610 mm.) apart.

A sowing can be made under cloches in mid-April. Place the cloches in position a week before sowing to warm up the soil. Sow the seeds ½ in. (12 mm.) deep in groups of three, spacing the groups 15 in. (380 mm.) apart in the rows, with the rows 2 ft (610 mm.) apart.

When the young plants appear, remove the two weakest from each group.

Leave the cloches in position until the plants touch the top.

An outdoor sowing can be made in mid-May, placing the seeds in the same way as under cloches. Net the plot against birds.

Give all plants a regular and plentiful supply of water and a weekly feed of liquid fertiliser. Hoe to keep down weeds, and on windy

sites tie young growths to canes.

Remove any side-shoots that grow from the base of a plant, pinching them out when they are about 6 in. (150 mm.) long.

Pests and diseases BEAN SEED FLY (p. 282) and FRIT FLY (p. 283) are the only common pests. Sweet corn is usually disease-free.

Harvesting and storing

Cobs are ready for picking about six weeks after the silky tassels have appeared at their tops. These will shrivel and turn brown as the seeds develop.

Test by pulling back part of the cob's sheath and pressing one of the seeds with your thumbnail.

If it exudes a creamy liquid, the cobs should be picked and used. If the liquid is watery, the cob is not yet ready. If there is no liquid, the cob is well past its prime.

Colour is also a useful guide. The cob is ready to use when the seeds start to turn pale yellow.

Twist the cobs from the plants or snap them outwards, just before they are needed, as they become dry and lose their flavour if they are stored.

See also freezing (p. 294) and sauces, ketchups and relishes (p. 339).

Preparing & cooking sweet corn

Corn-on-the-cob is most succulent when the cobs are picked just before the kernels become fully mature, woody and deep yellow. Strip the outer husks from the cobs in a downward direction, trim the stalk close to the cob and pull off the silky tassels from the top.

Corn cobs are often overcooked. They need, at the most, 8 minutes in boiling water, and salt should not be added until the cobs are half-cooked, otherwise the kernels will become tough.

Test the tenderness of the cobs by inserting the prongs of a fork in the corn. When they are ready, drain the cobs thoroughly and serve with a liberal quantity of butter.

Special corn-cob skewers are available for inserting into either end of the cooked corn. The cobs are held by these, and the kernels chewed off. Alternatively, use forks.

Photograph on pages 140–1.

The kernels of cooked corn may also be stripped off the cobs with the aid of a fork, or the kernels may be cut from the fresh cobs. The kernels can then be mixed with cream and butter, or folded into a well-flavoured cream sauce and served as an accompanying vegetable.

Deep-fried corn fritters are a popular American dish.

CORN FRITTERS

1 lb. (500 g.) corn kernels
2 eggs
4 oz. (125 g.) flour
2 teaspoons baking powder
½ teaspoon salt
Pinch of nutmeg
5 fl. oz. (150 ml.) milk
Butter for frying

COOKING TIME: 20 minutes

Strip the kernels from the cooked cobs and mash them to a pulp with a potato masher, or turn them into a purée in the liquidiser. Beat the eggs lightly and stir them into the mash or purée.

Sift the flour and baking powder, add the salt and nutmeg, and gradually beat in the milk to make a smooth, fairly thick batter. Fold in the corn mixture, blending thoroughly.

Melt some butter in a frying pan and, when hot, add spoonfuls of the corn-fritter batter. Fry for 1–2 minutes, turning once, until the fritters are golden-brown on both sides.
Serving Serve the fritters sizzling hot, with maple syrup, as a snack. They may also be served with a mushroom sauce, or as an accompaniment to fried chicken or sausages.

AT-A-GLANCE TIMETABLE FOR SWEET CORN

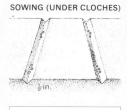

SOWING (UNDER CLOCHES)

APRIL

THINNING

15 in.

2 ft.

Remove weakest seedlings
from each group

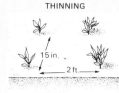

REMOVING SIDE-SHOOTS

Remove any basal shoots
when 6 in. long

HARVESTING

AUGUST–SEPTEMBER

SWEET-CORN TOASTS

½ lb. (250 g.) corn kernels
2 tablespoons corn oil
1 onion
2 tablespoons flour
4 fl. oz. (100 ml.) mixed milk and
   cream
1 teaspoon French mustard
Tabasco sauce
Salt and pepper
½ lb. (250 g.) cooked ham
8 slices Gruyère cheese
8 slices bread (for toasting)

COOKING TIME: 30 minutes

Strip the kernels from the cooked
corn cobs. Heat the oil in a pan
and add the finely chopped
onion. Fry over moderate heat
for 5 minutes.

Stir in the flour and cook
through, then gradually add the
milk and cream, stirring all the
time until the sauce is smooth
and free from lumps. Add
mustard, tabasco, salt and
pepper to taste.

Fold the corn kernels and
diced ham into the sauce, and
simmer for 5–10 minutes. Make
the toast and spread the corn
mixture over each slice, topping
it with a thin slice of cheese. Set
the slices under a hot grill until
the cheese is bubbling-brown.
Serving Serve the toast at once,
as a complete meal.
Variations Substitute crisp,
crumbled bacon, diced chicken
or smoked haddock for the ham.
Photograph on pages 212–13.

SWEET-CORN AND LEEK SOUP

1 lb. (500 g.) corn kernels
2 leeks
3 oz. (75 g.) butter
4 tablespoons flour
1 pint (600 ml.) water
1 pint (600 ml.) dry white wine or
   milk
Salt, pepper and nutmeg
5 fl. oz. (150 ml.) cream
Garnish: bread croûtons

COOKING TIME: 40 minutes

Boil the corn cobs for 6–7
minutes, drain them and strip off
the kernels. Trim the roots and
upper leafy parts from the leeks,
cut them in half lengthways and
wash thoroughly. Chop finely.

Melt the butter in a pan, add
the leeks and cook over a gentle
heat for 5 minutes, or until soft.
Stir in the flour and cook through
before gradually blending in the
water and wine. Add the corn
kernels and bring to the boil.
Season to taste and simmer for
15 minutes.

Blend the soup in the liquidiser
or rub it through a sieve. Return
to the pan and re-heat,
correcting the seasoning if
necessary. Blend a little of the hot
soup with the cream, stir back
into the pan and heat through
without boiling.
Serving Pour into soup bowls
and offer a separate bowl of crisp
bread croûtons.
Photograph on pages 210–11.

CREAMED SWEET CORN

1½ lb. (750 g.) corn cobs (approx.)
Salt and paprika
1 oz. (25 g.) butter
1 oz. (25 g.) flour
5 fl. oz. (150 ml.) milk
5 fl. oz. (150 ml.) cream
1 egg yolk
Garnish: crumbled bacon

COOKING TIME: 30 minutes

Strip the husks and tassels from
the corn cobs, trim the stalks and
put the cobs in a pan of boiling
water. Bring back to the boil and
cook for 7–8 minutes, or until the
kernels are tender. Add a
teaspoon of salt halfway through
cooking. Drain the cobs.

Strip the kernels from the cobs,
using a fork and working from
the stalk end towards the tip.

Melt the butter, stir in the
flour and let it cook through.
Gradually add the milk and
cream, stirring all the time until
the sauce is smooth.

Fold in the corn kernels and
simmer for 10 minutes. Beat the
egg yolk lightly, mix it with a
little of the sauce and return it to
the pan. Heat through to thicken
slightly, and season to taste with
salt and paprika.
Serving Spoon into a dish and
sprinkle the top with crumbled,
crisp-fried bacon. Serve as an
accompanying vegetable with
grilled or roast meat, or with
baked fish.

Sweet peppers:
see **Peppers and chillis**

Tarragon

*Tarragon, a hardy perennial herb,
is grown for its sweetly aromatic
leaves which are used to flavour fish
and meat dishes, and soups. The
leaves are also an essential ingredient of fines herbes and are used to
make tarragon vinegar (p. 343).*

*Tarragon is easy to grow and
needs very little attention once
established.*

Planning the crop
The herb grows best in a sunny
position in light, well-drained soil.

If the soil is heavy, dig in peat or
well-rotted manure or compost at
the rate of a bucketful to the
square yard in the autumn before
planting.

How much to grow A tarragon
plant grows to the height of 2 ft
(610 mm.), with a spread of 12 in.
(305 mm.) or more, so one plant
should supply the needs of the
average family.

Varieties French tarragon
(*Artemesia dracunculus sativa*),
which has smooth, dark green
leaves, is generally regarded as
having a better flavour than
Russian tarragon (*Artemesia
dracunculus inodora*), which is a
fresher green and has less-smooth

AT-A-GLANCE TIMETABLE FOR TARRAGON

PLANTING — OCTOBER–MARCH

PINCHING OUT — When flowering stems appear

HARVESTING — JUNE–SEPTEMBER

269

leaves. However, not all seedsmen and nurseries distinguish between the two.

How to grow tarragon

Since generally only a single plant is needed, the simplest plan is to buy this from a nursery. October or March are the best months for planting, the latter being best on heavy soils.

Keep the plant well-watered during dry spells and pinch out the flowering stems as they appear.

Raising new plants Once established, tarragon will keep growing for years. However, it is better to divide and re-plant old stock every two or three years.

To do this, dig up a plant in March or April and pull apart – but do not cut – the underground runners. Re-plant these 2–3 in. (50–75 mm.) deep and 15 in. (380 mm.) apart.

Pests and diseases Tarragon is usually trouble-free.

Harvesting and storing

Pick fresh leaves from mid-June until the end of September. Sprigs can be dried (p. 343) or frozen (p. 294), but these have less flavour than fresh tarragon.

Cooking with tarragon

This is one of the classic herbs and features particularly in French cuisine as a flavouring for chicken and other white meats. With its bitter-sweet flavour, tarragon is much used in the production of vinegar, to which it adds a dis-tinctive taste that comes to the fore in salad dressings.

It is a traditional herb in sauce Bearnaise, and one of the important ingredients in omelettes aux fines herbes.

The fresh, aromatic leaves make a good flavouring for cream sauces to accompany fish, for herb butters and as an addition to creamed vegetable soups.

Use the finely chopped leaves, too, sprinkled over green salads and in stuffings for poultry. Sprinkle them over sole fillets prior to baking or grilling, and use them as a flavouring for creamed, stuffed eggs.

Add new flavours to tomato juice, and to prawn and other shellfish cocktails, with chopped tarragon. Sprinkle the chopped leaves on hot or cold broccoli spears and beans, and add them to scrambled eggs and green vegetables in a cream sauce.

Pound fresh tarragon with parsley, chives and coarse salt and add to a good wine sauce, with extra butter, for serving with chicken, veal or baked fish.

A favourite tarragon-flavoured dish consists of chicken pieces browned in butter and then cooked in dry white wine, in the same pan, for 30 minutes, with salt, pepper and sprigs of tarragon added.

Serve the cooked pieces with chilled tarragon butter.

To make this, blanch a handful of tarragon leaves in boiling water for 1 minute, then drain them and pat dry. Pound the leaves to a paste and blend with 4 oz. (100 g.) of butter.

Shape into a sausage, wrap in greaseproof paper and chill in the refrigerator until firm.

Thyme

Lemon thyme   *Common thyme*

Although wild thyme grows profusely on chalk downs in Britain, the common thyme used in cooking is a native of Mediterranean countries.

The ancient Greeks enjoyed its mild, slightly sweet spiciness, and in this country the evergreen plant has been used since the Middle Ages to flavour soups, casseroles and stuffings for rich meats and fish.

The wiry-stemmed common thyme grows to a height of 8 in. (200 mm.), with a spread of 12 in. (305 mm.). Once established, it can be left for three or four years.

Lemon thyme, which grows to a height of 12 in. and has a similar spread, is cultivated in the same way as common thyme.

Planning to grow thyme

Thyme will grow well in a sunny position in well-drained soil.

How much to grow Two or three plants will supply leaves for the average family all the year.

How to grow thyme

Sow the seeds in a pan of seed compost in a cold frame in March or April. When the seedlings are large enough to handle, prick them off into 3 in. (75 mm.) pots of potting compost. Plant out in September.

Raising new plants Propagate thyme by taking cuttings of lateral shoots with a heel (see p. 29) in May or June. Insert the cuttings in equal parts (by volume) of peat and sand in a cold frame.

Pot the rooted cuttings singly in 3 in. (75 mm.) pots of potting compost and plant out in September.

Alternatively, divide the roots of established plants in spring and re-plant the pieces individually.

Pests and diseases Thyme is generally trouble-free.

Harvesting and storing

Pick the sprigs of leaves when needed. As they are evergreen, there is little to be gained by drying or freezing them.

Cooking with thyme

This is one of the classic herbs and fruit juices, salads and salad dressings, to savoury cream sauces, to all types of vegetable and meat soups, and to stews. Use thyme also to flavour baked, grilled or poached fish. Rub the leaves on meat before roasting it, or insert small sprigs in the skin.

This highly aromatic herb is one of the essential ingredients in a classic bouquet garni, and it is one of the most useful herbs in everyday cooking.

Used with discretion, a little finely chopped thyme adds aroma and flavour to fruit juices, salads and salad dressings, to savoury cream sauces, to all types of vegetable and meat soups, and to stews. Use thyme also to flavour baked, grilled or poached fish. Rub the leaves on meat before roasting it, or insert small sprigs in the skin.

Add thyme to stuffings for poultry, to tomato sauces and soups and to pâtés, terrines and marinades.

A refreshing and health-giving herb tea can be made from the leaves of lemon thyme infused with boiling water for 10 minutes.

AT-A-GLANCE TIMETABLE FOR THYME

SOWING   PLANTING   HARVESTING

| MARCH–APRIL | SEPTEMBER | Pick when the leaves are needed |

Tomatoes

'Moneymaker'

'Big Boy'

'Golden Sunrise'

Tomatoes, grown under glass or in the open, are the gardener's most consistent money-saver.

In an unheated greenhouse ripe tomatoes can be picked from the end of June until autumn, provided the plants are fed correctly, tended daily and sprayed against pests and diseases.

In the open, good crops ripen in August and September in warm summers, but even in cooler years plants produce a worthwhile crop of ripe tomatoes. Any remaining green fruits can be ripened indoors or made into chutney.

Tomatoes can also be grown successfully in pots and containers, or in bags of specially prepared compost, in sunny, sheltered spots, such as on a patio or balcony.

In the open, bush varieties, which need no de-shooting or staking, produce large numbers of relatively small fruits. Bush tomatoes are excellent for growing under cloches to produce an early crop of high-quality fruits.

Planning the crop

Outdoor tomatoes grow best in a sunny, sheltered position. The soil, whether in the open or greenhouse border, must be rich and moisture-holding. In the winter dig in well-rotted compost or manure at the rate of at least a bucketful to the square yard.

Before planting, rake in a dressing of general fertiliser at the rate of 3 oz. per square yard (90 g. per square metre).

How much to grow An outdoor plant with four trusses of fruit will yield about 4 lb. (2 kg.) or more of tomatoes, depending on the summer and the amount of feeding. A greenhouse plant developing six trusses will produce at least 6 lb. (3 kg.) of fruit.

Varieties Except for bush varieties, most tomatoes are suitable for growing in greenhouses. But only certain types crop reliably outdoors.

The fruits of different varieties vary in colour, size, flavour, thickness of skin and earliness, and some are disease-resistant.

The following varieties are suitable for growing either outdoors or under glass:

'Ailsa Craig': noted for its outstanding flavour; has a tendency to 'greenback' (see p. 288).

'Alicante': smooth-skinned, with exceptionally fine flavour; an early variety.

'Carter's Fruit': reliable cropper; produces exceptionally thin-skinned fruits.

'Golden Sunrise': suitable for growing indoors or outdoors; sweet, yellow fruits.

'Moneymaker': one of the most popular and reliable tomatoes for growing under a wide range of conditions.

'Outdoor Girl': one of the earliest tomatoes to ripen.

Varieties which need greenhouse protection include:

'Big Boy': fruits weigh up to 2 lb. (1 kg.).

'Davington Epicure': a large, well-flavoured tomato.

'Eurocross': a heavy-cropping, disease-resistant variety; does best in a heated house.

Among the best outdoor bush varieties are:

'Amateur': early and heavy-cropping.

'Sigmabush': outstanding for the earliness and quality of its fruits.

'Tiny Tim': a compact plant with marble-size fruits.

How to grow tomatoes

Although plants can be bought from nurseries, it is cheaper to raise

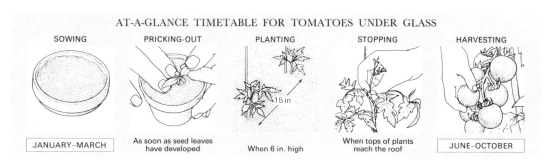

AT-A-GLANCE TIMETABLE FOR TOMATOES UNDER GLASS

SOWING	PRICKING-OUT	PLANTING	STOPPING	HARVESTING
JANUARY—MARCH	As soon as seed leaves have developed	When 6 in. high	When tops of plants reach the roof	JUNE—OCTOBER

SUPPORTING AND TYING

TYING TO A CANE Pass the string twice round the cane and once round the plant's stem. Leave space for the stem to expand.

GREENHOUSE METHOD Tie string beneath one of the lower leaves, and the upper end to a roof strut. Twist the growing stem round it.

your own tomato plants from seed.

For growing plants in a heated greenhouse sow in January; for an unheated house, sow in late March; and for planting outside, sow in early April.

Sow the seeds about 1 in. (25 mm.) apart in a pan of seed compost. Sift compost to a depth of $\frac{1}{4}$ in. (5 mm.) over the top and water in with a fine rose.

Ideally, place the pan, covered with a sheet of paper, in a propagator. Alternatively, put it in a polythene bag and place in an airing cupboard.

After about four days keep checking for germination. As soon as the seedlings begin to break the surface put the pan in the light.

When the seed leaves are fully developed, the seedlings are ready for pricking out into 3 in. (75 mm.) pots of potting compost. They can remain in these pots until planting time.

Greenhouse cultivation Stand the pots in their planting positions for a day or two before setting the

plants in the soil. This gives a gradual transition from the warmer conditions on the greenhouse staging. Tomatoes are ready for planting when about 6 in. (150 mm.) tall.

Set the plants at least 15 in. (380 mm.) apart. On a broad border, two staggered rows 2 ft (610 mm.) apart can be planted.

Support each plant with a tall cane or with string tied under a leaf joint near the base of the stem and taken up to a hook screwed into a roof glazing bar. If canes are used, tie the developing stems to them loosely every 12 in. (305 mm.) or so with strings – simply twist them round the plant's stem.

Keep the plants on the dry side for a week or two after planting, but then gradually increase the amount of water to ensure steady growth. Daily watering may be needed in warm weather.

Nip off the side-shoots that appear in the leaf axils.

Begin weekly feeding with a high-potash fertiliser as soon as the tomatoes on the lowest trusses

begin to develop. Pinch·out the tops of the stems when they are nearly up to the roof.

Outdoor cultivation Plant outdoors when danger of frost is past – usually the last week of May in the south of England and a week or two later in the north.

Planting time can, however, be advanced by two or three weeks if cloches are used.

Set the plants 18 in. (455 mm.) apart, allowing $2\frac{1}{2}$ ft (760 mm.) between rows. Make the planting hole deep enough for the soil ball to be at least $\frac{1}{2}$ in. (12 mm.) below ground level.

Insert a 5 ft (1.5 m.) stake or bamboo alongside each single-stem plant just outside the soil ball. Tie the plants to the supports at intervals throughout the summer.

Remove side-shoots regularly from the leaf axils of single-stem plants, water the plants frequently in dry weather and apply a liquid tomato fertiliser weekly once the fruits have started to develop. Pinch out the tops of the plants when four fruit trusses have formed, leaving two leaves above the top truss.

Do not stake or remove side-shoots from bush varieties, but spread black polythene, straw or

REMOVING SIDE-SHOOTS: PINCHING OUT

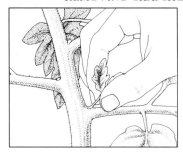

REMOVING SIDE-SHOOTS Pull off the small shoots which grow from the leaf joints. Wait until they are about 1 in. (25 mm.) long.

PINCHING OUT Remove the tips of outdoor plants when four trusses have formed. Indoors, remove the tip at roof height.

peat underneath to keep the ripening fruits off the ground.

Ring culture This method of growing tomatoes prevents the plants' roots from coming into contact with the greenhouse soil – an advantage when there is a known risk of the soil carrying disease organisms.

Rings are simply bottomless pots, generally made of bituminous felt, in which compost is placed and the tomatoes are planted. The rings are placed on a bed of fine aggregate.

The tomatoes send down roots into the aggregate, which is given a daily drenching once the root

system is well established, together with a weekly liquid feed.

To set up a ring culture bed, dig a trench 6 in. (150 mm.) deep in the greenhouse floor and line it with polythene. Pierce a drainage hole every 3 ft (1 m.) and spread the aggregate evenly on top to a depth of 6 in.

Rings can be bought, or they can be made at home by stapling together the ends of pieces of lino or roofing felt. They should be 9–10 in. (230–255 mm.) in diameter and at least 8 in. (200 mm.) deep. Stand the rings 18 in. (455 mm.) apart on the aggregate.

Growing tomatoes in pots A sunny patio or balcony is ideal for growing tomatoes in 10 in. (255 mm.) pots or deep boxes filled with John Innes No. 3 compost, or with a mixture of 2 parts loam to 1 part peat (parts by volume).

Leave a 4 in. (100 mm.) space between the compost and the top of the container to allow for a top-dressing with similar compost when the fruits appear.

Support, remove side-shoots and feed the plants as for tomatoes

AT-A-GLANCE TIMETABLE FOR OUTDOOR TOMATOES

PLANTING — 18 in. — **LATE MAY–JUNE**

STOPPING — Pinch out top when four trusses form

HARVESTING — **AUGUST–OCTOBER**

SETTING UP A RING-CULTURE BED

Dig a trench 6 in. (150 mm.) deep and about 12 in. (305 mm.) wide, allowing 18 in. (455 mm.) for each plant to be grown. Line with polythene, piercing drainage holes every 3 ft (1 m.). Fill with weathered ash, clinker or crushed stone and stand the rings on top. Plant the tomatoes in John Innes No. 3 compost.

grown in the soil. They will need more water, however – perhaps even a drenching twice daily during hot weather. Give double the amount of liquid feed recommended by manufacturers for plants growing in the open.

Growing in plastic bags Garden shops supply plastic bags filled with a mixture of peat-based compost and fertiliser in which two or three plants can be grown. This method is suitable for both indoor and outdoor crops.

After planting, keep the compost moist but do not saturate. Apply liquid fertiliser weekly after the first fruits have set.

Pests and diseases Tomatoes are liable to be attacked by APHIDS (p. 282), GLASSHOUSE WHITEFLY (p. 283), POTATO CYST EELWORM (p. 284) and WIREWORM (p. 285).

Diseases and disorders to which the crop is subject are BLOSSOM END ROT (p. 286), BLOTCHY RIPENING (p. 286), DAMPING OFF (p. 287), FOOT ROT (p. 288), GREENBACK (p. 288), GREY MOULD (p. 288), MAGNESIUM DEFICIENCY (p. 288), SCALD (p. 290), SOIL-BORNE DISEASES (p. 290), SPLITTING (p. 290), SPRAY DAMAGE (p. 291), TOMATO BLIGHT (p. 291) and VIRUS DISEASES (p. 291).

Harvesting and storing

Fruits can be left to ripen fully on the plant (which tends to increase their flavour) or removed when they start to change colour.

Hold the tomato in your hand and press the stalk with your thumb to break it neatly at the joint just above the fruit.

At the end of September or beginning of October, ripening of fruits that are already turning colour can be completed under cloches. Place straw along the row, lay the stems horizontally, and cover with the cloches.

Remove green fruits, wrap them separately in newspaper and place in a drawer or boxes indoors. Remove fruits as they ripen.

See also bottling (p. 309); chutneys (p. 335); freezing (p. 294); fruit cheeses and butters (p. 323); pickles (p. 328); sauces, ketchups and relishes (p. 339) and syrups and juices (p. 326).

Preparing & cooking tomatoes

Strictly fruits, but classified as vegetables because of their use in savoury dishes, tomatoes are one of the most worthwhile crops for gardeners. These luscious red or golden-skinned love apples, as they used to be called, can be enjoyed fresh in numerous ways – as sandwich fillings or thirst quenchers; thinly sliced and turned in a good oil-vinaigrette dressing, sprinkled with chopped parsley or chives, or served with finely chopped onion and a touch of garlic.

Tomatoes are also used as a garnish for salads, vegetable and cheese flans, or for fried or grilled fish and meat.

Serrated, or 'vandyked', tomatoes, which look so attractive, can be filled with tiny cooked peas, with variously flavoured mayonnaises or with salad creams. Use a small, sharp knife to make 'V'-shaped indentations round the centres of firm tomatoes. Pull the halves apart and use them as they are, or remove the pulp and substitute with the chosen filling.

Form tomato flowers by making four cross cuts, almost but not quite to the base of the tomato, open out the eight petals carefully and remove the pulp. Set half a hard-boiled egg yolk, rounded side up, in the centre on a few small sprigs of parsley to represent leaves.

In cooking, tomatoes are used for what is many people's favourite soup. They are added to casseroles for extra flavour and juice, folded into omelettes, and served grilled – cut into halves, topped with a knob of butter and seasoning and grilled for 5–10 minutes. Cooked in this way they go with scrambled eggs, bacon, grilled meat and baked fish.

Tomatoes may also be baked on their own for 15 minutes, after brushing with oil, or stuffed with any number of savoury fillings and served as first courses, light snacks or complete meals. The pulp removed from the tomatoes may be added to soups and casseroles.

Many recipes call for skinned tomatoes. Skins are easily removed by placing tomatoes in a bowl of boiling water for 1 minute, then cooling them in cold water and peeling off the skin, beginning at the stalk end.

Alternatively, hold the tomato on a fork over an open flame, turning it slowly until the skin cracks and can be pulled off.

Both green and ripe tomatoes make excellent chutneys. Imperfect or over-ripe tomatoes are ideal for making juices and sauces (see pp. 328 and 340).

TOMATO MOULD

14 fl. oz. (400 ml.) tomato juice
½ oz. (15 g.) powdered gelatine
Juice of ½ lemon
Worcester sauce
Salt and pepper

CHILLING TIME: 3 hours

Dissolve the gelatine in 3 tablespoons of hot tomato juice and season the remainder to taste with strained lemon juice, Worcester sauce, salt and pepper. Stir in the dissolved gelatine and pour the mixture into a wetted ring mould. Chill in the refrigerator for 3 hours, or until set.

Serving Turn the mould out, upside-down, on to a bed of lettuce and fill the centre with diced ham, cucumber, green pepper and celery, and serve with mayonnaise sharpened with lemon juice and curry, or mixed with grated horseradish.

Alternatively, stir a blue cheese with cream to a sauce-like consistency, and season to taste.

Variations Set the mixture in small dariole moulds. When turned out, garnish with sardines, hard-boiled egg wedges and lemon slices. Alternatively, fold 5 fl. oz. (150 ml.) of whipped cream and chopped prawns into the mixture as it is beginning to set.

Continued . . .

Tomato recipes (continued)

CREAMED TOMATO SOUP

1½ *lb. (750 g.) tomatoes*
1 onion
1 garlic clove
2 oz. (50 g.) butter
½–*1 pint (300–600 ml.) beef stock*
Bicarbonate of soda
Salt, pepper and sugar
5 fl. oz. (150 ml.) double cream
Garnish : 2 tablespoons chopped basil

COOKING TIME: 30 minutes

Skin the tomatoes and chop roughly; peel the onions and garlic and chop finely. Melt the butter in a pan and fry the onion and garlic for 5 minutes, or until soft. Add ½ pint (300 ml.) of stock, a pinch of bicarbonate of soda and the chopped tomatoes.

Bring the soup to the boil, then cover with a lid and simmer for 15 minutes. Blend the soup in a liquidiser and strain it through a sieve back into the pan.

Re-heat the soup, adding more stock to give the desired consistency. Season to taste with salt, pepper and sugar. Bring the cream almost to boiling point in a separate pan, stir it into the soup and remove from the heat.
Serving Pour the soup into bowls and sprinkle with basil.
Variations 2–3 oz. (50–75 g.) of rice may be cooked with the soup, which will then need extra stock. Finely grated cheese may be used instead of herbs as a garnish.
Photograph on pages 210–11.

STUFFED TOMATOES

8 large tomatoes
Salt and pepper
1 onion
1 tablespoon chopped parsley
1 tablespoon chopped marjoram
1 tablespoon chopped chives
2 oz. (50 g.) grated Parmesan cheese
5 fl. oz. (150 ml.) soured cream
Garnish : lemon wedges ; parsley

COOKING TIME: 15–20 minutes
OVEN TEMPERATURE: 190°C (375°F)
– gas mark 5

Cut a top slice from the washed and dried tomatoes and scoop out the pulp with a teaspoon. Sprinkle the inside of the tomato shells with salt and leave upside-down for 30 minutes.

Peel the onion, grate it finely, and mix with the finely chopped parsley, marjoram and chives.

Set the tomatoes in a buttered ovenproof dish and divide the cheese between them. Cover with the herb mixture and sprinkle with salt and pepper. Spoon the soured cream into the tomatoes and bake in the oven.
Serving Arrange the stuffed tomatoes on each plate and garnish with a lemon wedge and parsley sprigs. Serve with crusty bread as a lunch or a supper dish.
Photograph on pages 206–7.

Variations Tomatoes can also be filled with chopped prawns turned in a little mayonnaise flavoured with lemon juice and curry, and served cold.

Alternative fillings are tuna fish, chopped hard-boiled eggs, chives or finely chopped onion – all bound with a little mayonnaise or soured cream.
Photograph on pages 141–2.

◆◇◆

TOMATO AND MEAT SAUCE

4 large tomatoes
1 large onion
1 garlic clove
1 tablespoon olive oil
1 tablespoon butter
1 lb. (500 g.) minced beef
2–3 sticks celery
Salt, pepper and paprika
1 teaspoon mixed herbs
5 fl. oz. (150 ml.) cream

COOKING TIME: 30 minutes

Peel the onion and the garlic and chop finely. Heat the oil and butter in a pan, add the onion and garlic and fry for about 5 minutes, until transparent. Skin the tomatoes, chop them roughly and add to the pan. Crumble in the minced beef and stir until it has browned and separated into grains.

Clean the celery, chop it finely and add to the other ingredients, with salt, pepper and paprika to taste, and also the herbs. Cover, and simmer gently for about 20 minutes. Stir in the cream.
Serving This is a quick tomato and meat sauce to serve with spaghetti or a rice mould.

Triticale:
see **Sprouting seeds**

Turnips

Globe-shaped turnip

Flat-rooted turnip

Although the turnip has been a favourite since Roman times, its popularity has little to do with its nutritional value. The root consists of about 90 per cent water, with some sugar and pectin – a jelly-like substance which helps jams to set. Nevertheless, it adds a fresh flavour to a dish of vegetables, particularly when accompanied by the season's first peas and carrots.

Turnips can provide a space-saving bonus for the gardener with a small plot. Since they grow quickly and are picked young, they may be sown between rows of slow-growing crops such as parsnips. The small turnips are harvested before the parsnips develop fully.

AT-A-GLANCE TIMETABLE FOR TURNIPS

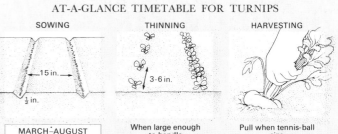

SOWING	THINNING	HARVESTING
←15 in.→ ½ in.	3–6 in.	
MARCH–AUGUST	When large enough to handle	Pull when tennis-ball size

Different varieties of turnip can be grown to provide roots during most of the year.

Planning the crop

Turnips grow best on a light, fertile loam, but they will succeed on most garden soils in an open, sunny position. Do not sow on freshly manured ground, or the roots may split into a number of fangs.

Before sowing, rake in a general fertiliser at the rate of 2 oz. per square yard (60 g. per square metre).

On an acid soil give a top-dressing of carbonate of lime at the rate of 7 oz. per square yard (210 g. per square metre) during the winter before sowing.

How much to grow Because turnips grow quickly and are picked young, sow little and often. A row 10 ft (3 m.) long can be expected to yield 10–12 lb. (5–5.5 kg.) of roots.

Sow every three to four weeks from March to July for a continuous supply, and again in late August for winter use.

Varieties 'Golden Ball': much hardier than white turnips and stores well; round roots with yellow flesh.

'Jersey Navet': for early crops in frames or under cloches; cylindrical, white roots.

'Manchester Market': mild flavour; fairly hardy; white flesh.

'Purple Top Milan': very early; flat, white roots with purple tops.

'Snowball': quick-growing; round roots with white flesh and mild flavour.

'White Milan': fast-growing; medium-size; delicate flavour; ivory-white flesh and skin.

How to grow turnips

A February sowing of 'Jersey Navet' may be made under cloches or in a frame, provided there are no hard frosts and the soil is dry enough for a tilth to be created.

Make the first outdoor sowing in a sunny, sheltered bed in mid-March in the south, or two weeks later in the north.

Sow again in April and May for summer supplies. For autumn and winter crops, sow in mid-July and late August.

Sow the seed in drills ½ in. (12 mm.) deep, with 15 in. (380 mm.) between rows. Thin the seedlings as soon as they are large enough to handle, first to about 3 in. (75 mm.) apart, then two or three weeks later to 6 in. (150 mm.).

Keep the ground well-watered or the turnips may go to seed and the roots will become stringy.

Pests and diseases CUTWORMS (p. 283), FLEA BEETLE (p. 283) and caterpillars of the SWIFT MOTH (p. 285) are the principal pests.

Diseases and disorders that may occur are BORON DEFICIENCY (p. 286), CLUB ROOT (p. 287) and SPLITTING (p. 290).

Harvesting and storing

Pick the turnips regularly, never allowing them to become larger than a tennis ball. Turnips larger than this may be stringy and will have a less pleasant flavour.

Summer-harvested turnips may be frozen (p. 294). Pull winter turnips when needed, or lift a few and store in a shed for use during spells when the soil is frozen.

Preparing & cooking turnips

Turnips are at their best in spring and summer if the small, globe-like roots are pulled when about six weeks old. At this stage they will be about the size of tennis balls.

Prepare turnips by cutting off a slice from the leafy top and trimming off the fibrous roots. Peel young turnips thinly, maincrop turnips thickly, and on the latter also cut out any woody parts. Wash them well, leaving small turnips whole but cutting winter turnips into rough chunks.

Cook young, whole turnips in boiling, lightly salted water for 20–30 minutes. Cook maincrop turnips for 30–40 minutes in boiling, salted water – or, preferably, in white stock to improve the flavour.

Serve young boiled turnips tossed in butter and chopped parsley, or coated with a white or parsley sauce. Maincrop turnips can be served in the same way, but are more often mashed, creamed with butter and cream and seasoned with salt, pepper, mace and lemon juice.

Cooked in this way they are the traditional accompaniment to Scottish haggis.

BUTTERED TURNIPS

½ lb. (250 g.) young turnips
½ lb. (250 g.) young carrots
3 oz. (75 g.) butter
2 fl. oz. (50 ml.) dry white wine
Salt and pepper
Garnish : 2 tablespoons chopped parsley

COOKING TIME: 20 minutes

Trim the tops and roots from the turnips and carrots. Peel the turnips thinly and scrape the carrots. Wash both vegetables in cold water and cut them, crossways, into ¼ in. (5 mm.) slices.

Melt the butter in a pan, add the wine, the turnips and the carrots and sprinkle with salt and freshly ground black pepper. Stir to combine thoroughly, then cover with a lid and simmer for about 20 minutes, or until tender.

Serving Spoon the turnips and carrots, together with the liquid, into a serving dish. Sprinkle with finely chopped parsley.

Photograph on pages 134–5.

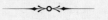

GLAZED TURNIPS

1 lb. (500 g.) young turnips
1 oz. (25 g.) butter
1 oz. (25 g.) sugar
5 fl. oz. (150 ml.) white stock
Salt and pepper

COOKING TIME: 35–40 minutes

Trim the roots and tops from the turnips, peel them thinly, and rinse. Leave the turnips whole if they are of even size; otherwise cut them into pieces of about equal size. Melt the butter in a pan, add the sugar and stir until dissolved. Then blend in the stock, and add salt and pepper to taste.

Add the turnips to the pan, bring to the boil and cover with a lid. Simmer over very gentle heat for about 30 minutes, by which time the turnips should be tender and the liquid reduced to a glaze. Otherwise, increase the heat and reduce the liquid by fast boiling.

Serving Serve the turnips in the glaze as an accompaniment to roast or grilled meat or poultry. They may also be served with baked or poached fish.

Variation Turnips may be parboiled for 15 minutes, sliced, and then baked in a moderate oven – in milk – for about 40 minutes. A crisp topping can be added by sprinkling breadcrumbs over the turnip slices.

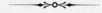

Watercress

Although the natural environment of watercress is a running stream, it can easily be grown in the garden.

Under these conditions its main need is copious watering.

There are two types of watercress, one a bronze-green and the other dark green, both of which are native to this country. The bronze-green cress is hardier and has a slightly more pungent flavour.

Planning the crop

Grow watercress either in a trench in the vegetable plot or in shallow boxes. Fruit boxes from a greengrocer are ideal.

If you use a box, cover the bottom and sides with a sheet of polythene to ensure that moisture is retained.

Fill the box with garden soil or potting compost.

In the garden, dig a trench 9 in. (230 mm.) wide and 2 ft (610 mm.) long. Mix a bucketful of well-rotted manure or garden compost with the soil in the base of the trench, leaving this about 3 in. (75 mm.) below the surrounding soil level.

How to grow watercress

In April or early May remove 4 in. (100 mm.) shoots from plants bought from a greengrocer and plant them 6 in. (150 mm.) apart in the prepared trench.

Keep the trench well-watered and the plants will root readily.

In a box, cover with a polythene bag to increase the humidity. Keep out of direct sunshine.

Alternatively, sow by broadcasting seeds in the trench or box in late March or April. Thin the plants to 6 in. apart when they are large enough to handle.

Remove flower heads as soon as they appear. If the soil has been well prepared, watercress needs no extra feeding. If, however, the leaves are getting very small towards the end of the season, feed them with general liquid fertiliser to encourage sturdier growth.

A second planting can be made in August for a late crop to be covered with a frame or cloches. Whenever possible, remove the covering to give the plants air.

Pests and diseases Watercress is usually free of pests.

Plants may sometimes be attacked by VIRUS DISEASES (p. 291).

Harvesting watercress

Start picking as soon as the plants are established. Sometimes this can be as early as three or four weeks after planting.

The more the tops are picked, the more new branches will be thrown up to provide a fresh supply.

Picking can go on into the autumn, when boxed plants can be brought indoors or placed in a cold greenhouse to extend the season.

Fresh, bright-green watercress is used chiefly to garnish savoury dishes. Wash the stems in cold running water, shake them dry and separate into small sprigs. Trim the stalks short and pick off any wilting or yellowing leaves.

Chopped watercress can be mixed into green salads or white sauces to accompany vegetables or poultry.

It is also excellent blended into mayonnaise, salad cream or soft sandwich spread.

Use small bunches of watercress to hide the crop end of roast game birds, chicken and duck.

Finally, watercress is used to make one of the oldest of English soups – delicious when served chilled on a hot summer's day – and for light, delicate stuffings.

WATERCRESS SOUP

2 good handfuls of watercress
¾ lb. (375 g.) potatoes
1 onion
2 pints (1 l.) brown stock or bouillon
1½ oz. (40 g.) butter
1 bay leaf
Salt and pepper
3 tablespoons double cream
Garnish : watercress

COOKING TIME: 45 minutes
CHILLING TIME: 2 hours

Wash the watercress thoroughly in cold water, and remove the stalks and any wilting leaves. Peel the potatoes and onion, and slice thickly. Put the watercress, potatoes, onion, stock, butter and bay leaf in a large pan, and season with salt and pepper.

Bring to the boil, cover with a lid and simmer the soup for about 30 minutes, until the potatoes and onion are quite soft. Remove the bay leaf, and either blend the soup in the liquidiser or rub it through a sieve.

Return the soup to the pan, correct the seasoning and heat through. Stir in the cream without letting the soup reach boiling point. Leave the soup to cool, then chill in the refrigerator for 2 hours.

Serving Spoon the chilled soup into individual bowls, float a few fresh watercress leaves on top and serve with crisp Melba toast.

AT-A-GLANCE TIMETABLE FOR WATERCRESS

PLANTING

2 ft.
3 in.
9 in.

APRIL—MAY

DISBUDDING

Remove flower heads as they appear

HARVESTING

From about four weeks after planting

A Food-Grower's Calendar

Correct timing is vital for the successful cultivation of fruit and vegetables. Use this month-by-month reminder of what to do in conjunction with the Growing and Cooking guide (pp. 61–276). This gives details of the varieties to sow or plant, the way to prune, the fertiliser to use, and general hints on cultivation. As explained on p. 61, the timings advised in the guide are based on an 'average' year in the south of England. Further north, and in East Anglia, sowing and planting must be delayed by up to three or four weeks, and some autumn tasks advanced by a similar period. It is also necessary to take into account the vagaries of the particular season.

January

VEGETABLES
Complete digging if the weather is suitable.

Prepare CELERY trenches, if not completed in December.

Force CHICORY and SEAKALE in fortnightly batches.

Blanch Batavian-type ENDIVES.

Place seed POTATOES in a tray to sprout.

In the greenhouse, sow CAULIFLOWERS, ONIONS and TOMATOES (for growing on in heat).

Sow RADISHES under cloches, and LETTUCES in a cold frame or under cloches for planting out in March.

FRUITS
Prepare a bed for planting RHUBARB in March. For an early picking of established plants, cover the crowns with a bucket or box.

Plant (unless the soil is frozen or waterlogged) APPLES, APRICOTS, MEDLARS, outdoor GRAPE vines (although March is preferable), PEARS and PLUMS; also BLACKBERRIES, BLACK, RED and WHITE CURRANTS, BLUEBERRIES, GOOSEBERRIES and RASPBERRIES.

Prune BLUEBERRIES and GOOSEBERRIES. Apply fertiliser to APPLES, CHERRIES, PEACHES, PEARS. Top-dress the rooting area of greenhouse GRAPE vines.

Apply tar-oil wash to APPLE and PEAR trees every third year, if this was not done in December.

HERBS
Sow CHERVIL in the greenhouse.

February

VEGETABLES
Put cloches in position to warm the soil for early CARROTS.

Plant GARLIC, JERUSALEM ARTICHOKES and SHALLOTS.

Force CHICORY in batches.

In the greenhouse, sow AUBERGINES, CAULIFLOWERS and, at the end of the month, frame CUCUMBERS.

In the open, sow round-seeded PEAS.

FRUITS
Plant (unless the soil is frozen or waterlogged) APPLES, APRICOTS, BLACKBERRIES, BLACK, RED and WHITE CURRANTS, BLUEBERRIES, GOOSEBERRIES, MEDLARS, outdoor GRAPE vines (although March is preferable), PEARS, RASPBERRIES and RHUBARB.

Prune BLUEBERRIES, GOOSEBERRIES, RASPBERRIES, and RED and WHITE CURRANTS.

Cut down the canes of autumn-fruiting RASPBERRIES.

Apply fertiliser to GRAPE vines in the open.

Protect APRICOT trees with netting against frost.

HERBS
Sow CHERVIL in the greenhouse.

March

VEGETABLES
Prepare the greenhouse bed for CUCUMBERS, and fix support wires.

Thin Japanese varieties of ONIONS, harden off January-sown onion seedlings, and plant maincrop onions sown in August.

Harden off CAULIFLOWERS sown under glass, and plant out.

Plant GARLIC, HORSERADISH, JERUSALEM ARTICHOKES, early POTATOES and SHALLOTS.

In the greenhouse, sow CELERIAC, CELERY, frame CUCUMBERS, PEPPERS and TOMATOES (for growing under cold glass). *Continued...*

March (continued)

Sow CARROTS in a frame or under cloches.

Outdoors, sow globe BEETROOT, BROAD BEANS, early BRUSSELS SPROUTS, CALABRESE, CAULIFLOWERS, CORN SALAD, HAMBURG PARSLEY, KOHL-RABI, LAND CRESS, LEEKS, LETTUCE, ONIONS, PARSNIPS, first-early wrinkled PEAS, early POTATOES, SHALLOTS, SPINACH and TURNIPS.

Apply fertiliser to spring CABBAGES.

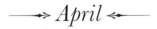 FRUITS

Plant APPLES, APRICOTS, FIGS, MEDLARS, outdoor GRAPE vines and PLUMS; also BLACKBERRIES, BLACK, RED and WHITE CURRANTS, BLUEBERRIES, GOOSEBERRIES, RASPBERRIES and RHUBARB.

Prune BLUEBERRIES, acid CHERRY trees and fan-trained PLUMS.

Apply fertiliser to APPLES, sweet CHERRIES, PEACHES and PEARS; also to BLACKBERRIES, CURRANTS, GOOSEBERRIES and RASPBERRIES.

Spray APPLE trees at bud-burst.

Pollinate PEACH blossom with a camel-hair brush.

HERBS

Sow BURNET, CHERVIL, COMMON FENNEL, DILL, LOVAGE, MARJORAM, PARSLEY, ROSEMARY, SAGE and THYME.

Raise new plants of LOVAGE by division of roots.

Plant BAY trees and TARRAGON.

⟶ *April* ⟵

VEGETABLES

Prepare ground and fix stakes for RUNNER BEANS.

Harden off CAULIFLOWERS sown under glass, and plant out.

Plant ASPARAGUS, GLOBE ARTICHOKES, ONIONS sown in January, ONION SETS, POTATOES (second-early at the beginning of the month, maincrop at the end) and red CABBAGES.

Sow ridge CUCUMBERS and TOMATOES (both for growing outdoors) in the greenhouse.

Sow CELERY in a cold frame; FRENCH BEANS and SWEET CORN under cloches–all in mid-month.

Outdoors, sow BROAD BEANS, maincrop BRUSSELS SPROUTS, summer and autumn CABBAGES, CARDOONS, CARROTS, CAULIFLOWERS, CORN SALAD, globe BEETROOT, KALE, KOHL-RABI, LETTUCE, second-early PEAS, PUMPKINS, RADISHES, SALSIFY, SCORZONERAS, SPINACH, SPINACH BEET, NEW ZEALAND SPINACH, SEAKALE BEET, SPROUTING BROCCOLI and TURNIPS.

Apply fertiliser to SEAKALE.

FRUITS

Prune PEACH trees.

Apply fertiliser to BLACKBERRIES, LOGANBERRIES and PLUMS.

Give a top-dressing of Epsom salts to GRAPE vines grown in the open. In the greenhouse, select the strongest vine shoot from each spur and rub out others. Close ventilators and spray vines with water twice a day.

Thin APRICOTS.

Spray APPLE trees, before the flowers open fully. Mulch established FIG trees and RASPBERRIES. Gradually remove winter protection from FIG trees.

Sow MELONS in the greenhouse.

HERBS

Sow ANGELICA, BALM, BORAGE, BURNET, CHERVIL, CORIANDER, DILL, FLORENCE FENNEL, HYSSOP, pot MARJORAM, SAGE and summer SAVORY.

Plant BAY trees.

 *May* ⟵

VEGETABLES

Prepare the cold frame for frame CUCUMBERS, and sow seeds in pots in the frame. Prepare outside beds for COURGETTES, MARROWS and ridge CUCUMBERS.

Plant summer CABBAGES. Harden off CELERIAC and TOMATOES and plant out towards the end of the month.

Plant AUBERGINES in the greenhouse or under cloches.

Mulch GLOBE ARTICHOKES and SEAKALE.

In the greenhouse or under cloches, sow CELERY, COURGETTES, MARROWS and SOYA BEANS early in the month. Plant out at the end of the month or in early June.

Outdoors, sow ASPARAGUS PEAS, long-rooted BEETROOT, winter CABBAGES, CARROTS, FRENCH and RUNNER BEANS, CAULIFLOWERS, CHICORY, KOHL-RABI, LETTUCES, RADISHES, SAVOYS, SPINACH, SWEDES, SWEET CORN and TURNIPS.

FRUITS

Plant ALPINE STRAWBERRIES.

Complete summer pruning of PEACH trees. Prune leaders of mature cordon, espalier and dwarf pyramid APPLE and PEAR trees.

Spray APPLE trees.

In the greenhouse, tie up laterals of GRAPE vines and begin liquid feeding.

Plant MELONS under cloches or in the greenhouse.

HERBS

Harden off BASIL and MARJORAM in mid-month and plant a fortnight later.

Sow CHERVIL, DILL, pot MARJORAM and SAGE.

June

VEGETABLES

Plant frame CUCUMBERS in a cold frame.

Outdoors, plant BRUSSELS SPROUTS, CAULIFLOWERS, CELERY, LEEKS, PUMPKINS, ridge CUCUMBERS, SPROUTING BROCCOLI, SWEET PEPPERS and TOMATOES.

Sow CARROTS, CHICORY, CHINESE CABBAGES, curly-leaf ENDIVE, FRENCH BEANS, KOHL-RABI, LETTUCES, PEAS, RADISHES and SPINACH.

Spray RUNNER BEANS with water to help the flowers set.

Feed TOMATOES with a liquid fertiliser when the first fruits set. Nip out side-shoots.

Top-dress SEAKALE with agricultural salt.

FRUITS

Prune RED and WHITE CURRANT bushes. Pinch back the side-shoots of FIGS. Rub out shoots of fan-trained sweet CHERRIES that are growing towards or away from the wall.

Spray APPLE trees and thin the crop after the natural June drop.

Apply sulphate of ammonia to APRICOT trees. In the greenhouse, thin GRAPES and reduce watering. Outdoors, restrict the number of branches according to the age of the vine.

HERBS

Sow CHERVIL and DILL in seed beds outdoors.

July

VEGETABLES

Plant KALE, LEEKS and white CABBAGES.

Sow curly-leaf ENDIVE, KOHL-RABI, LETTUCES, PEAS, RADISHES, RAPE KALE, SAVOYS, SPINACH and TURNIPS.

Lift SHALLOTS, and ripen on a path before storing.

Spray RUNNER BEANS against aphids.

Feed PEPPERS and TOMATOES with liquid fertiliser when the first fruits form.

FRUITS

Plant STRAWBERRIES to ripen under cloches in the spring.

Layer runners of established plants.

Prune back growing tips of new shoots on CHERRY trees. Prune cordon, dwarf pyramid and espalier APPLE and PEAR trees.

Prune BLACK CURRANTS after fruiting, and prune fan-trained PLUM trees.

After pruning fan-trained PEACH trees, tie in replacement shoots.

Cut back to just above soil level LOGANBERRY and RASPBERRY canes that have fruited.

Tie autumn-fruiting RASPBERRIES to support wires.

Spray APPLE trees against codling moth.

HERBS

Sow CHERVIL, DILL and PARSLEY.

August

VEGETABLES

Sow CARROTS (to be covered with cloches in October), CORN SALAD, Batavian ENDIVE, ONIONS (Japanese varieties in a permanent bed and maincrop varieties in a seed bed), spring CABBAGES and TURNIPS.

Feed PEPPERS and TOMATOES with liquid fertiliser.

Earth up trench-grown CELERY.

At the end of the month, lift self-blanching CELERY.

FRUITS

Plant STRAWBERRIES. Layer runners of established plants.

Prepare ground for growing GRAPE vines outdoors. Train fruiting laterals of GRAPE vines growing in the open through support wires, and prune.

Prune PEACH trees after fruiting and tie in replacement shoots.

Cut back RASPBERRY canes, after fruiting, to just above soil level.

HERBS

Sow CHERVIL in a seed bed outdoors.

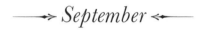

September

VEGETABLES

Sow CAULIFLOWERS under cloches or in a cold frame.

Outdoors, sow CORN SALAD, LAND CRESS, overwintering LETTUCES and red CABBAGES.

Remove any side leaves from CELERIAC. Earth up CELERY.

Blanch CARDOONS and curly-leaf ENDIVE.

Harvest and store MARROWS and TOMATOES when the first frost warnings are given.

FRUITS

Sow seeds of ALPINE STRAWBERRIES.

Continued...

September (continued)

Prepare ground for planting APPLES, LOGANBERRIES and PEARS.

Prune any secondary growth on APPLE and PEAR trees. Cut away dead wood on sweet CHERRY trees and shorten shoots pinched back in June.

Remove immature FIGS at the end of the month.

Cut down fruited BLACKBERRY canes to ground level.

Close greenhouse ventilators to raise the temperature until the last GRAPES are picked.

 *HERBS*

Plant RUE and THYME.

Outdoors, sow ANGELICA and LOVAGE; under glass sow summer SAVORY.

Gather FENNEL seed-heads for drying.

Root SAGE cuttings in a cold frame.

→ *October* ←

VEGETABLES

Prepare a bed for planting SEAKALE in March.

Sow CAULIFLOWERS and LETTUCES under cloches or in a cold frame.

Blanch curly-leaf ENDIVE.

Start lifting trench-grown CELERY.

Cut down ASPARAGUS ferns to within 1 in. (25 mm.) of the soil.

Lift and store maincrop CARROTS and CHICORY when the leaves die down; also JERUSALEM ARTICHOKES.

FRUITS

Plant DAMSON, MEDLAR and PEACH trees; also

GOOSEBERRIES, RED and WHITE CURRANTS and RHUBARB. Plant outdoor GRAPE vines (although March is preferable).

Propagate BLACK, RED and WHITE CURRANTS.

Protect FIG trees from frost with straw, bracken or lengths of matting.

HERBS

Raise new plants of BALM by division.

Plant TARRAGON.

Sow CHERVIL under glass for a winter supply.

 → *November* ←

VEGETABLES

Sow BROAD BEANS and round-seeded PEAS for late spring crops.

Blanch curly-leaf ENDIVE.

Force CHICORY in batches. Begin forcing SEAKALE, keeping side-shoots for raising new plants in spring.

Lift and store long-rooted BEETROOT and any remaining CELERIAC.

Cut GLOBE ARTICHOKE stems almost to ground level and draw soil around them.

FRUITS

Plant APPLE, APRICOT, DAMSON, HAZEL, MEDLAR, PEACH, PEAR, PLUM and QUINCE trees; also BLACKBERRIES, BLACK, RED and WHITE CURRANTS, BLUEBERRIES, GOOSEBERRIES, outdoor GRAPE vines (although March is preferable), LOGANBERRIES, RASPBERRIES and RHUBARB.

Prune BLACKBERRIES and GOOSEBERRIES.

Prune GRAPE vines in the open. In the

greenhouse, prune the vines, treat the rods with winter wash, scrub down the house and replace the top layer of soil.

Begin forcing RHUBARB by lifting one or two plants and exposing their roots to frost to make the plants dormant.

HERBS

Sow CHERVIL under glass for a winter supply.

→ *December* ←

 *VEGETABLES*

Dig ground where BEANS and PEAS are to be sown next year, incorporating well-rotted manure or compost.

Prepare CELERY trenches.

Force CHICORY and SEAKALE in batches.

Blanch Batavian-type ENDIVES.

FRUITS

Plant APPLE, APRICOT, MEDLAR, PEAR, PLUM and QUINCE trees; also BLACKBERRIES, BLACK, RED and WHITE CURRANTS, BLUEBERRIES, GOOSEBERRIES, GRAPE vines (although March is preferable), LOGANBERRIES and RASPBERRIES.

Prune BLUEBERRIES.

Feed and mulch CURRANT bushes.

Every third year apply tar-oil wash to fruit trees and bushes.

Force RHUBARB by putting roots lifted in November in boxes of moist peat.

HERBS

Sow CHERVIL under glass for a winter supply.

PESTS AND DISEASES

How to identify and combat common plant disorders

The following pages explain how to deal with the plant pests and diseases referred to in Growing and Cooking that starts on page 61. Though the list appears daunting, many of these troubles will be avoided if the soil is fed and limed adequately, so that the plants grow vigorously.

GARDEN HYGIENE Rubbish and dead growth harbour pests and diseases, so put fallen leaves on the compost heap and keep the garden free from debris. It is better to burn diseased growth rather than make compost of it.

USING FUNGICIDES AND PESTICIDES Follow the manufacturer's instructions to the letter, especially with regard to the interval between spraying and

harvesting. If a particular pesticide does not seem to work, try another; the pests in your area may have developed an immunity.

Do not spray plants or trees indiscriminately, or you run the risk of destroying the insect predators that are doing half your work for you.

SAFETY RULES Keep all chemicals locked up and out of reach of children. Make sure that the bottles are correctly labelled, and do not transfer the contents into, for instance, lemonade bottles. If possible, spray on dull, still days.

Wash all implements in detergent. Ideally, keep a separate set for use with chemicals. Wash your hands and face after using pesticides and fungicides.

Pests

Aphids

Known by various names –
blackfly, greenfly, cabbage
aphids, etc. – they cause much
damage by feeding on the sap of
young shoots. Many species
transmit viruses.
SYMPTOMS Clusters of small,
variously coloured, round-
bodied insects on leaves and
stems. Distortion of young
growth; galls or sticky
honeydew on foliage.
DANGER PERIOD Warm, dry
spells in spring and summer
outdoors; any time in the
greenhouse.
TREATMENT Spray with
malathion, nicotine or
bioresmethrin if the colonies are
accessible; systemic insecticides
such as dimethoate or
formothion if the aphids are in
protected positions, or dust with
propoxur. Kill overwintering
eggs on dormant fruit trees with
tar oil or DNOC/petroleum.

Apple sawfly

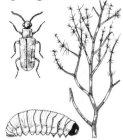

Caterpillars of this small, flying
insect eat into the hearts of
young apples.
SYMPTOMS Young fruitlets drop
prematurely; superficial
scarring on mature fruit.
DANGER PERIOD May and June.
TREATMENT Spray with HCH
dimethoate or fenitrothion
immediately after petal-fall.

Asparagus beetle

Reddish-yellow beetle, which
has black, yellow-marked wing
cases, that lays eggs on
asparagus in late spring. Dark
grey grubs cause damage in
summer.
SYMPTOMS One-sided, injured
shoots; brown patches on
foliage.
DANGER PERIOD Growing
season.
TREATMENT Spray with derris.

Bean seed fly

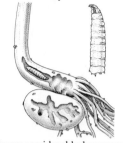

Causes considerable damage to
germinating seeds of beans,
peas, sweetcorn and other
vegetables.
SYMPTOMS Small, white
maggots eat into the seeds.
DANGER PERIOD Spring.
PREVENTION Dress seeds with
HCH/thiram before sowing.

Black bean aphid

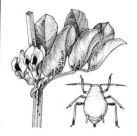

Attacks many plants, but is
particularly damaging to broad
beans.
SYMPTOMS Colonies of small,
black aphids appear on young
shoots, from which they draw
sap and so reduce the vitality of
the plant.
DANGER PERIOD May to July.
TREATMENT Spray with
insecticides such as pirimiphos-
methyl, dimethoate or
formothion before plants come
into flower.

Black-currant gall mite

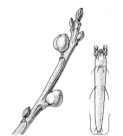

The most serious of all black-
currant pests, not only for the
direct damage it does but also
because it transmits reversion
virus (see p. 290).
SYMPTOMS Infested buds swell
and fail to develop, forming
characteristic 'big buds'.
DANGER PERIOD February and
March.
TREATMENT Remove and burn
infested buds, and spray with
lime-sulphur as the first flowers
open. Repeat three weeks later.
Destroy plants infected by
reversion.

Black-currant leaf midge

Maggots of this pest feed upon
the young leaves of black
currants.
SYMPTOMS Tightly twisted
leaves at the tips of shoots fail to
open. Severe attacks may check
growth.
DANGER PERIOD April to
September.
TREATMENT Spray with
dimethoate or formothion just
before flowering, and repeat
three weeks later.

Cabbage root fly

The maggots of this fly attack
the roots of recently
transplanted cabbages, Brussels
sprouts and other brassicas.
SYMPTOMS Young plants
collapse.
DANGER PERIOD April to
September.
PREVENTION Protect transplants
by mixing bromophos or
diazinon granules in the surface
soil around the plants, or by
watering in a spray-strength
solution of diazinon or
trichlorphon.

Cabbage whitefly

A pest on cabbages, Brussels
sprouts and other brassicas.
Often active in winter.
SYMPTOMS Small whiteflies take
off from undersides of leaves
when plants are disturbed.
Leaves are discoloured and
sticky; plant growth is checked.
DANGER PERIOD May to
September.
TREATMENT Spray with
malathion, pyrethrum or
bioresmethrin.

Capsid bugs

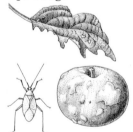

Several species cause similar
damage to a wide range of
plants, including apples and
currants. As well as feeding on
sap, they inject toxic saliva.
SYMPTOMS Ragged holes in
younger leaves; mis-shapen
and discoloured fruits.
DANGER PERIOD April to
August.
PREVENTION Good garden
hygiene (see p. 281) plus winter
sprays of DNOC/petroleum on
dormant apples and currants.

Carrot fly

Maggots burrow into the edible
roots of carrots, parsley,
parsnips and celery.
SYMPTOMS Young plants die off.
Mature roots are spoiled by
tunnels.
DANGER PERIOD June to
October.
PREVENTION Sow dressed seed
thinly in May. When thinning,
destroy discarded seedlings and
scatter bromophos or diazinon
granules along the row, or water
in a spray-strength solution of
diazinon.

Caterpillars

The larval stage of moths and
butterflies. Most eat leaves, but
some eat roots, stems or fruit.
SYMPTOMS Ragged holes in
leaves. Plants may be destroyed.
DANGER PERIOD March
onwards outdoors. Any time in
greenhouses.
TREATMENT Remove by hand,
if practicable, or spray with
HCH, derris, malathion,
trichlorphon or bioresmethrin.
(See also Codling moth,
Cutworms, Pea moth, Swift
moth and Tortrix moth.)

Celery fly

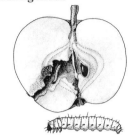

Maggots burrow into leaves of celery and parsnips.
SYMPTOMS Brown blotches on leaves. Checked growth or death of severely infected plants.
DANGER PERIOD April onwards.
TREATMENT Spray young plants with dimethoate, malathion or trichlorphon.

Codling moth

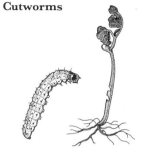

The caterpillars are the major cause of 'maggoty' apples, and may also atttack pears and other fruits.
SYMPTOMS Hollow, brown and rottted cores, often with caterpillars inside.
DANGER PERIOD July and August.
TREATMENT Spray with fenitrothion or permethrin in mid-June, and again three weeks later, before the young caterpillars enter the fruit.

Cutworms

Name given to the caterpillars of various species of moth that attack a number of plants, including root vegetables and lettuces.
SYMPTOMS Fat green or grey-brown caterpillars in soil. Plant stems cut through at ground level.
DANGER PERIOD Spring and summer.
PREVENTION Keep weeds in check. Work bromophos or diazinon granules into the soil around susceptible plants.

Flea beetle

A pest of seedling cabbages, radishes, swedes, turnips and related plants.
SYMPTOMS Young leaves pitted with very small holes.
DANGER PERIOD Dry, sunny weather in April and May.
PREVENTION Good garden hygiene (see p. 281). Dust susceptible seedlings with derris or HCH, or dust or spray with carbaryl.

Frit fly

A serious pest on sweet-corn seedlings.
SYMPTOMS Leaves become striped and tattered. Growth is checked and central shoot may die.
DANGER PERIOD Warm weather in late May and early June.
PREVENTION Avoid outdoor sowing in the first half of May. Instead, sow earlier, under cloches or in greenhouses; or later, when the danger has passed.

Fruit tree red spider mites

Microscopic mites that feed on the sap of apple, pear and plum leaves.
SYMPTOMS Older leaves turn yellow-bronze, wither and fall.
DANGER PERIOD May to September.
TREATMENT Spray in winter with DNOC/petroleum to kill eggs, or spray immediately after flowering with derris, dimethoate or malathion.

Glasshouse red spider mites

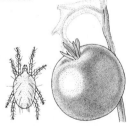

A serious pest not only of greenhouse and house plants, but also of outdoor peaches, cucumbers and strawberries.
SYMPTOMS Mottling of upper leaf surfaces, followed by general yellowing. Severely infested plants are covered by a silky webbing.
DANGER PERIOD Any time under glass; late summer outdoors.
TREATMENT Maintain humidity. Spray with derris, dimethoate or malathion.

Glasshouse whitefly

Affects many greenhouse plants, especially tomatoes and cucumbers.
SYMPTOMS Small whiteflies take off from the undersides of leaves when plants are disturbed. Leaves are discoloured and sticky; plant growth is checked.
DANGER PERIOD All year in a heated greenhouse.
TREATMENT Spray with malathion or pyrethrum. Greenhouses may be fumigated with HCH or dichlorvos.

Gooseberry sawflies

Various species of sawfly caterpillar cause severe damage to gooseberries and currants.
SYMPTOMS Leaves stripped to skeletons; entire bush may be defoliated.
DANGER PERIOD April to August.
TREATMENT Spray with derris, malathion or nicotine in late spring, or when symptoms appear.

Leaf eelworm

Attacks a wide range of plants, including strawberries and other soft fruits.
SYMPTOMS Brown or yellow discolorations between main leaf veins.
DANGER PERIOD Wet summers and autumns.
PREVENTION Remove and burn affected leaves; destroy severely infested plants.

Leafhoppers

Related to aphids, these small creatures also feed on the sap of a wide range of plants, both indoors and out.
SYMPTOMS Green insects leap from undersides of disturbed foliage. White mottled leaves, to which insect skins may be attached.
DANGER PERIOD April to October outdoors; any time indoors.
TREATMENT Spray with malathion or nicotine, repeating at 14 day intervals.

Leatherjackets

Larvae of craneflies (daddy-longlegs) feed on the roots of a wide range of plants.
SYMPTOMS Grey-brown, legless grubs in the soil. Plants wilt and occasionally die.
DANGER PERIOD April to June.
TREATMENT Before planting, dig deeply to expose grubs to birds. Protect individual plants by scattering bromophos or diazinon granules in the soil around them. Dust or spray with carbaryl.

Mealy bugs

A serious greenhouse pest, especially on grape vines.
SYMPTOMS Stunted foliage covered with patches of mealy wax threads, beneath which are colonies of bugs or yellow egg clusters.
DANGER PERIOD Any time, particularly late summer and autumn.
TREATMENT Spray with diazinon or malathion before the fruit swells, and/or apply tar oil to dormant vines in the winter.

Millipedes

Pest in greenhouses and on root crops. Distinguished from centipedes (which are beneficial) by greater number of legs, grey-black colouring and slower movement.
SYMPTOMS Tunnels in potato tubers and other root crops.
DANGER PERIOD Late summer and autumn.
PREVENTION Good garden hygiene. Deep cultivation, especially in damp, well-manured soil.

Mushroom flies

Maggots of several species of fly eat into the stalks and caps of mushrooms, rendering them inedible.
SYMPTOMS Clusters of small, adult flies on mushrooms; tunnels created by maggots.
DANGER PERIOD Growing season.
TREATMENT Spray infested beds with nicotine or malathion.

Nut weevil

Grubs of this weevil hatch in hazelnuts and eat the kernels.
SYMPTOMS Holes through which the grubs have left the nuts. Adults – golden-brown flying insects with long proboscises – lay eggs in soft, young nuts.
DANGER PERIOD May.
TREATMENT Dust nut trees with derris or HCH at the end of May, and repeat three weeks later.

Onion eelworm

A pest on onions, shallots and garlic.
SYMPTOMS Bloated, swollen leaves, stems and bulbs.
DANGER PERIOD June to August.
PREVENTION Dig up infested plants and burn them. Do not grow onions or related crops on the same site for at least two years.

Onion fly

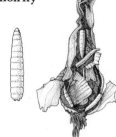

Maggots are a major pest of onions, leeks and shallots.
SYMPTOMS Mushy bulbs, on whose rotting tissues small, white maggots feed.
DANGER PERIOD May to August.
PREVENTION Apply calomel dust to the soil before sowing, and spray with trichlorphon two or three times during May and June. Bromophos granules in the soil also give some protection. Avoid thinning onions in areas where the fly is prevalent.

Pea moth

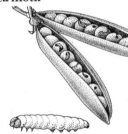

The 'maggots' often discovered in garden peas are in fact the caterpillars of this small moth.
SYMPTOMS Tiny, pale yellow caterpillars eat the peas in the pod.
DANGER PERIOD June to August.
PREVENTION Spray with fenitrothion or permethrin when the flowers first open. Alternatively, grow early-maturing varieties.

Pea thrips

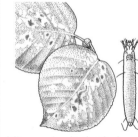

Minute, elongated insects that feed upon the leaves of peas.
SYMPTOMS Silver mottling of leaves and pods. Severe attacks result in stunted growth and few flowers.
DANGER PERIOD Hot, dry summers.
TREATMENT At first appearance of symptoms, spray with dimethoate or fenitrothion.

Pear leaf blister mite

Microscopic mite that feeds upon young leaves of pears.
SYMPTOMS Yellow pustules on leaves gradually turn brown.
DANGER PERIOD April to August.
TREATMENT Pick off and burn infested leaves, or spray with lime-sulphur at the end of March.

Pear sucker

Related to aphids, these creatures feed on the sap of pear shoots.
SYMPTOMS Clusters of tiny insects with flattened bodies, large eyes and prominent wing buds. Sticky excretions on young growth, which becomes distorted.
DANGER PERIOD Spring.
TREATMENT Spray with dimethoate, formothion or malathion shortly after petal-fall.

Plum sawfly

Caterpillars tunnel into fruits, causing serious reduction in yields.
SYMPTOMS Holes in plums exuding a sticky, black ooze. Infested fruits drop prematurely.
DANGER PERIOD Spring and summer.
PREVENTION In areas where the pest is prevalent, spray with dimethoate, fenitrothion or formothion shortly after petal-fall.

Potato cyst eelworm

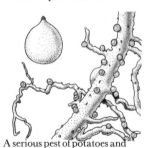

A serious pest of potatoes and tomatoes.
SYMPTOMS Pinhead-size yellow or brown cysts develop on roots, causing wilting and death of plants.
DANGER PERIOD July to September.
PREVENTION Rotate crops so that neither tomatoes nor potatoes are grown too frequently on the same sites. Where infestation is severe, do not plant either crop on that site for at least five years.

Raspberry beetle

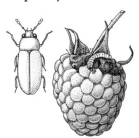

Grubs of this small beetle tunnel into fruits of the raspberry, loganberry and blackberry.
SYMPTOMS Distorted, grub-infested fruits.
DANGER PERIOD June to August.
PREVENTION Spray with derris, fenitrothion or malathion as the first fruits turn pink.

Root aphids

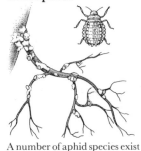

A number of aphid species exist in the soil, where they live on the roots of a wide range of plants.
SYMPTOMS Colonies of white, waxy aphids on roots; yellowing, wilting leaves.
DANGER PERIOD Summer and autumn.
TREATMENT Water round infested plants with a spray-strength solution of diazinon, malathion or nicotine.

Scale insects

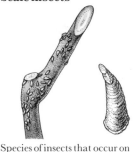

Species of insects that occur on vines, peaches and other greenhouse plants; also on apples.
SYMPTOMS Flat or rounded, yellow or brown scales, usually on the undersides of leaves beside the veins.
DANGER PERIOD Any time.
TREATMENT Whenever the insects are active, spray with malathion or nicotine. Systemic insecticides such as dimethoate or formothion may also be used on some plants.

Slugs and snails

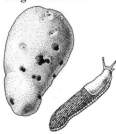

Some six species of slugs attack many different kinds of plants, both above and below ground. Snails cause similar, but less extensive, damage.
SYMPTOMS Large holes torn in foliage; tubers and roots eaten. Slime trails can be seen.
DANGER PERIOD Spring and autumn in mild, moist weather.
TREATMENT Scatter proprietary slug pellets around affected plants. Baits based on methiocarb give best results, but metaldehyde baits are also effective.

Stem and bulb eelworm

These affect a number of plants, including rhubarb, onions and strawberries. A large number of other plants, garden weeds among them, also act as hosts to the several species of this microscopic pest.
SYMPTOMS Infested bulbs and plants become soft, rotten and distorted. Plants collapse and die.
DANGER PERIOD Mainly in spring.
PREVENTION Dig up and destroy infested plants. Do not re-plant susceptible species on the same site for at least three years afterwards.

Strawberry beetle

These attack ripening strawberries in a manner that may be confused with bird damage.
SYMPTOMS Shiny, black beetles seen scuttling beneath fruit trusses and under straw.
DANGER PERIOD Early summer.
PREVENTION Good garden hygiene, and effective weed control.

Strawberry mite

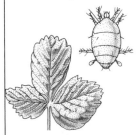

One of a group of minute creatures – hardly visible to the naked eye – that attack a number of plants, including strawberries.
SYMPTOMS Brittle leaves with curled-down margins; terminal buds are killed.
DANGER PERIOD Spring and summer.
TREATMENT Spray with dicofol, or dust with sulphur or lime-sulphur.

Swift moths

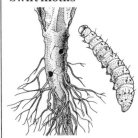

The caterpillars of these moths feed on the roots of many cultivated plants.
SYMPTOMS Dirty-white caterpillars with brown heads; usually seen when the soil is cultivated.
DANGER PERIOD Growing season.
PREVENTION Good garden hygiene and weed control. Plants may be protected by working bromophos or diazinon granules into the surrounding soil.

Tortrix moths

The caterpillars of these moths feed upon many plants, including pears and apples.
SYMPTOMS Holes in leaves, which are also drawn together by silk threads; fruits sometimes tunnelled. Small caterpillars wriggle backwards when disturbed.
DANGER PERIOD May and June.
TREATMENT Remove caterpillars by hand, or spray forcibly with derris, fenitrothion or trichlorphon.

Winter moths

Caterpillars of this species cause considerable damage to the foliage, flowers and embryo fruits.
SYMPTOMS Leaves holed or spun together; green caterpillars often present.
DANGER PERIOD Spring.
TREATMENT Spray with derris, fenitrothion, malathion or trichlorphon as buds open and leaves develop.

Wireworm

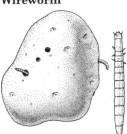

Larvae of click beetles that feed in the soil on the tubers, roots and stems of potatoes, lettuces and tomatoes.
SYMPTOMS Tough-skinned, yellow-brown, worm-like creatures among plant roots.
DANGER PERIOD March to September.
TREATMENT Newly cultivated land, especially, should be dug thoroughly before planting. Control weeds, and apply HCH, bromophos or diazinon to the soil around susceptible plants.

Woolly aphid

A common pest on many trees, especially apples.
SYMPTOMS Tufts of white, waxy wool on twigs and branches. Neglected trees develop woody galls.
DANGER PERIOD April to September.
TREATMENT On cordons and dwarf pyramids, brush spray-strength solution of gamma-BHC or malathion into cracks. On larger trees, spray with similar solutions before bud-burst and again after petal-fall.

Diseases

American gooseberry mildew

A fungal disease that attacks leaves, shoots and fruits of gooseberries. Also black currants late in the season.
SYMPTOMS A white, powdery coating on fruits, shoots and leaves. Tips of diseased shoots are distorted.
DANGER PERIOD Throughout the growing season.
PREVENTION Prune bushes to permit free circulation of air.
TREATMENT Destroy all diseased shoots in late summer. Spray with dinocap or lime-sulphur (except yellow-fruited varieties), or with a weak solution of washing soda. Spray just before the flowers open, again as the fruit is setting, and then every fortnight.

Anthracnose

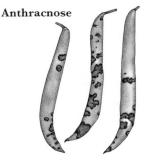

A fungal disease of dwarf beans and, occasionally, runner beans.
SYMPTOMS Dark brown, sunken patches on pods; brown spots on leaves and stems.
DANGER PERIOD Throughout the growing season – especially in cool, wet summers.
TREATMENT Destroy all affected plants; sow fresh seed in a new area.

Apple canker

A fungus that attacks the trunks and branches of apple trees and, less frequently, pears.
SYMPTOMS Elliptical cankers that cause the bark to shrink until the inner wood is exposed.
DANGER PERIOD Any time.
TREATMENT Destroy infected spurs and small branches. Pare away diseased material on larger branches, and seal.
In severe cases, spray young trees with benomyl mixture at leaf-fall, and again as buds open.

Bacterial canker

A serious disease of cherries, plums, gages and damsons.
SYMPTOMS Elongated, flattened cankers exude gum on dying shoots. Leaves wither.
DANGER PERIOD Autumn and winter, but symptoms do not appear until spring or summer.
PREVENTION Prune in summer.
TREATMENT Cut out infected branches; treat with wound-sealing paint. Spray with Bordeaux mixture in mid-August, mid-September and mid-October.

Bitter pit

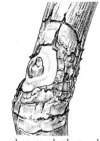

An apple disease that appears on mature fruits.
SYMPTOMS Brown spots on the skin and throughout the flesh.
DANGER PERIOD Throughout the growing season, but not apparent until harvest time.
PREVENTION Feed and mulch the tree. Never let the soil dry out. In mid-June, spray with calcium nitrate at a rate of 8 tablespoons to 5 gallons (22.7 l.) of water. Repeat at three-weekly intervals.

Black leg

A common disease of potatoes, particularly on poorly drained soil. Avoid wet land, or drain it.
SYMPTOMS A black rot develops at the base of a stem. The leaves yellow; the stem softens and dies.
DANGER PERIOD June.
TREATMENT Destroy all affected plants, and re-plant with healthy tubers.

Black root rot

A fungal disease that attacks many plants, indoors and out. Occurs most frequently where crops of the same type are grown in the same place for several years in succession, permitting a build-up of the infection.
SYMPTOMS Rotting black roots and crown tissues.
DANGER PERIOD Throughout the growing season.
PREVENTION Rotate crops regularly (see pp. 26–27) so that the same vegetables are not grown on the same part of the plot in successive years. Partial control may be obtained by watering at three-weekly intervals with a captan solution.

Blossom end rot

Tomato damage caused by drought.
SYMPTOMS Brown or black patches at the blossom end of the fruits.
DANGER PERIOD As the young fruits develop.
PREVENTION Water the plants regularly, and apply garden lime if the soil is acid.

Blotchy ripening

A disorder of greenhouse tomatoes caused by irregular feeding and watering, and periods of over-high temperatures.
SYMPTOMS Light patches on the fruits that fail to ripen.
DANGER PERIOD As the fruits develop.
PREVENTION Ensure regular feeding and watering, and maintain even temperatures.

Bolting

Premature flowering. Lettuces and endives are particularly prone to this; also Chinese cabbages if sown too early in the season.
SYMPTOMS The plants put out long stems, which if left will bear flowers and seeds that are bitter and useless for eating.
DANGER PERIOD Growing season, especially during hot weather.
PREVENTION Avoid late transplanting and overcrowding. Keep the plants well watered, especially at the seedling stage, so that they do not suffer a check in growth.

Boron deficiency

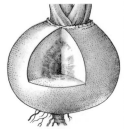

A disorder that afflicts beets, swedes, turnips and celery.
SYMPTOMS Edible roots turn brown within; brown cracks on celery stalks.
DANGER PERIOD Growing season.
TREATMENT Apply 1 tablespoon of borax, mixed with fine sand for easier distribution, to every 20 sq. yds (17 sq. m.) of soil.

Brown rot

A fungus that attacks most tree fruits and nuts.
SYMPTOMS Brown patches and concentric rings of white fungus spores appear on the fruit.
DANGER PERIOD Summer, and in store.
TREATMENT Discard all damaged or withered fruits, and remove any dead shoots during pruning. Late spraying with thiophanate-methyl helps prevent fruit rotting in store.

Bud-drop

A disorder that afflicts many plants. In the vegetable garden, runner beans are particularly susceptible. The condition is generally due to unsuitable cultural conditions, such as too dry soil at the time that the buds are forming.
SYMPTOMS Buds or partly open flowers drop before pollination, causing a total failure of the crop.
DANGER PERIOD As buds develop, though symptoms are not apparent until the flowers begin to open.
PREVENTION Good soil preparation and regular watering.

Cane blight

Raspberries are often afflicted by this fungal disease. It is particularly rife in the north-east and in Kent, though it does occasionally occur in other areas as well.
SYMPTOMS Leaves wilt and wither in summer; canes discolour and snap off at ground level.
DANGER PERIOD Growing season.
TREATMENT Cut diseased canes below ground level and burn them. Spray new canes with Bordeaux mixture. Spray in early and mid-May with fenitrothion to control cane midge. The damage caused by the midge allows blight spores to enter cane tissue.

Cane spot

A common fungal disease of raspberries and loganberries.
SYMPTOMS Purple spots on the canes enlarge into white spots with purple borders. These eventually split down the cane. Leaves and fruits become spotted and distorted
DANGER PERIOD May to October.
TREATMENT Destroy badly infected canes. At 14 day intervals, between bud-burst and blossoming, spray plants with benomyl, thiram or dichlofluanid.

Chlorosis (lime induced)

A condition affecting raspberries and other acid-loving plants growing in an alkaline soil.
SYMPTOMS Yellowing of the leaves between the veins.
DANGER PERIOD Growing season.
TREATMENT Improve the acidity of the soil by digging in peat and by using acid fertilisers. Add chelated iron (sequestrene) at the rate recommended by the manufacturers.

Chocolate spot

A fungal disease, seldom serious, of broad beans.
SYMPTOMS Dark brown spots on leaves and stems.
DANGER PERIOD December or January on overwintered plants; June or July on spring-sown beans.
PREVENTION Sow thinly, and encourage strong growth with lime and a potash fertiliser.
TREATMENT In serious cases, spray with copper fungicide.

Club root

A serious fungal infection of turnips and brassicas.
SYMPTOMS Swollen, distorted roots; yellowing, sickly foliage.
DANGER PERIOD Growing season.
PREVENTION Improve drainage, especially on acid soils, and rotate the crops. Apply 8 oz. of hydrated lime to each sq. yd of soil (240 g. per sq. m.) and put 4% calomel dust in planting holes or dip roots in benomyl.
TREATMENT Destroy infected plants.

Coral spot

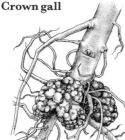

This fungus, normally found on dead wood, may also enter living tissue and destroy entire bushes, especially red currants.
SYMPTOMS Red, cushion-like masses of spores on dead twigs.
DANGER PERIOD Any time.
PREVENTION Cut out and burn all dead wood and treat the cuts with wound-sealing paint.
TREATMENT Cut diseased shoots back to 6 in. (150 mm.) below the infected area; treat with wound-sealing paint.

Crown gall

A bacterial disease occurring on fruits, vegetables and other plants.
SYMPTOMS Large galls, hard or soft, develop on roots. Plants may appear stunted.
DANGER PERIOD Growing season.
PREVENTION Bacteria enter through wounds, so avoid damaging roots. Burn diseased plants. The roots of new plants destined for the same site should be dipped in copper fungicide.

Crown rot

A bacterial disease of rhubarb, encouraged by wet soil conditions.
SYMPTOMS Discoloration of leaves, followed by progressive rotting of stalks and crowns.
DANGER PERIOD Growing season.
PREVENTION Improve drainage and avoid damage to crowns.
TREATMENT Destroy infected plants. Do not plant rhubarb in the same position again.

Cucumber mosaic virus

Afflicts not only cucumbers, but also marrows and other related plants. Usually transmitted by aphids, it may also be carried on the hands and garden tools.
SYMPTOMS Greenish-yellow mottling of leaves and fruit. Plants become stunted and fruits puckered.
DANGER PERIOD Growing season.
PREVENTION Control aphids by spraying. Destroy infected plants at first sign of symptoms.

Damping off

A fungal disease of seedlings; in the vegetable garden, young lettuces are especially susceptible.
SYMPTOMS Plants rot and collapse at soil level.
DANGER PERIOD Germination.
PREVENTION Avoid overcrowding and over-watering. Use clean pots and sterilised compost.
TREATMENT Water with Cheshunt compound, captan or zineb.

Die-back

A condition of trees and shrubs which may be due to disease, frost damage or simply to poor cultural conditions.
SYMPTOMS Withering of young shoots followed by the death of larger branches.
DANGER PERIOD Any time.
TREATMENT Cut back to healthy tissue and treat cuts with wound-sealing paint to prevent further infection.
Where disease is the cause, apply appropriate treatment; if no disease is apparent, improve growing conditions.

Downy mildew

A disease, caused by fungi, that attacks brassicas, lettuces, onions and spinach.
SYMPTOMS Furry coating on undersurfaces of leaves; yellow patches on upper surfaces.
DANGER PERIOD Spring and autumn.
PREVENTION Good cultural conditions.
TREATMENT Spray brassicas, spinach and onions with zineb; dust onions with Bordeaux powder; use thiram on lettuces.

Fig canker

A serious fungal disease that enters fig trees through wounds in branches or twigs.
SYMPTOMS Cankerous growths on branches.
DANGER PERIOD Growing season.
TREATMENT Carefully remove diseased branches and paint the cut surfaces with wound-sealing paint.

Fire blight

A serious bacterial disorder of pears, apples and other trees.
SYMPTOMS Leaves brown and wither; shoots die back and develop cankers at the base.
DANGER PERIOD Flowering time.
TREATMENT The Ministry of Agriculture, Fisheries and Food must be informed, and will advise on treatment.

Foot rot

A disorder of tomatoes, peas and beans, due to fungal attacks and other causes.
SYMPTOMS Discoloration and rotting of stem bases, usually leading to the death of the plant.
DANGER PERIOD Growing season.
PREVENTION Rotate crops and use sterile compost in peat pots and seed trays. Water young plants with captan, zineb or Cheshunt compound.

Frost damage

SYMPTOMS May include silvering of tomato leaves; cracked tree trunks; puckered, distorted leaves; browned or blackened flowers and buds; and die-back of shoots.
DANGER PERIOD Spring.
TREATMENT When danger of frost has passed, cut out damaged shoots to prevent attack by fungi.

Gangrene

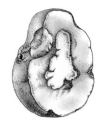

A fungus that enters potatoes through wounds, generally at lifting time, and appears when the tubers are in store.
SYMPTOMS A slight depression on the skin that enlarges until the tuber is decayed and shrunken.
DANGER PERIOD Winter and spring.
PREVENTION Handle tubers carefully and store them in an airy, frost-free place. Burn infected tubers. Start again with clean seed potatoes from a reliable source.

Greenback

A condition of greenhouse tomatoes that is brought about by too high a temperature.
SYMPTOMS Stalk end of fruit fails to ripen.
DANGER PERIOD Summer.
TREATMENT Keep the greenhouse ventilated, and shade the glass in hot weather. Grow resistant cultivars, such as 'Moneymaker'.

Grey mould

A fungal blight on many plants. Raspberries, strawberries and other soft fruits are particularly susceptible.
SYMPTOMS Rotting fruit covered by a soft, grey mould.
DANGER PERIOD Flowering time, but symptoms apparent only at fruiting.
PREVENTION Spray with benomyl, dichlofluanid or thiophanatemethyl as the first flowers open. Repeat at 14 day intervals. Another method is to fumigate with tecnazene.

Halo blight

A seed-borne disease that attacks French and runner beans.
SYMPTOMS Brown spots – surrounded by a halo – on pods, leaves or stems. Infected seeds show raised blisters.
DANGER PERIOD Growing season, especially in wet weather.
PREVENTION AND TREATMENT Do not plant infected seeds. Some control can be established by spraying with copper fungicide.

Honey fungus

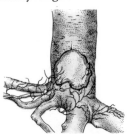

A widespread parasitic disease on many types of plant.
SYMPTOMS Honey-coloured mushrooms growing from dead wood; white, fanned-out, fungal growths beneath bark; black threads on roots.
DANGER PERIOD Any time.
PREVENTION Destroy diseased plants. Sterilise soil with 1 pint of formaldehyde to 6 gallons of water (600 ml. to 27 l.) applied at 5 gallons (23 l.) per square yard, or use a proprietary phenolic compound.

Leaf spot

Condition caused by various bacteria and fungi, each specific to one type of plant and unlikely to spread to others.
SYMPTOMS Small brown or black spots of different shapes and sizes. Occasionally, premature leaf-fall.
DANGER TIME Growing season.
PREVENTION Remove diseased leaves and burn them. Remove all autumn leaves to the compost heap. Spray diseased plants with fungicides such as captan, maneb or zineb.

Magnesium deficiency

Affects the chlorophyll balance of plants, particularly apples and tomatoes.
SYMPTOMS Orange and brown bands between leaf veins. Occasionally, premature withering.
DANGER PERIOD Growing season, and after applications of potash.
TREATMENT Spray with magnesium sulphate – 8 tablespoons to 2½ gallons (12 l.) of water – plus a few drops of liquid detergent.

Manganese deficiency

Often occurs in sandy and alkaline areas, affecting many plants.
SYMPTOMS Premature yellowing between veins of older leaves.
DANGER PERIOD Growing season.
TREATMENT Spray with manganese sulphate – 2 tablespoons to 2½ gallons (12 l.) of water – adding a few drops of detergent.

Mosaic

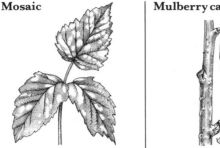

A virus infection of raspberries, marrows and many other plants.
SYMPTOMS A yellow blotching of the leaves, which sometimes become distorted.
DANGER PERIOD Growing season.
TREATMENT The plants should be dug up and destroyed. Buy raspberries that are certified virus-free.

Mulberry canker

A fungal disease that attacks the young shoots of mulberry trees, especially those growing in exposed gardens.
SYMPTOMS Die-back and destruction of young shoots.
DANGER PERIOD Damp, cold springs and summers.
TREATMENT Remove and burn diseased shoots. Paint the wounds with protective paint.

Mushroom diseases

Several bacterial and fungal diseases affect mushrooms; but unless you are growing the plants on a commercial scale it is unlikely they will cause much damage to your crop.
SYMPTOMS The most serious disease – bacterial blotch – causes mushrooms to become discoloured and sticky. Similar symptoms are produced by other mushroom diseases.
DANGER PERIOD Any time if the crop is grown under cover.
TREATMENT Most disorders are caused by too high a temperature, over-moist conditions or inadequate ventilation, and can be cured by correcting these faults. Water with solutions of sodium hypochlorite, or dust with zineb or quintozene.

Neck rot

Occurs in stored onions.
SYMPTOMS Grey, velvety mould on the neck of the onion, which then rapidly rots.
DANGER PERIOD Growing season, but symptoms not apparent until the onions are in store.
PREVENTION Sow treated seed. Store only ripened, healthy onions in a well-ventilated, frost-free place. Destroy diseased onions.

Papery bark

Condition of apple trees caused by poor cultural conditions, especially waterlogging.
SYMPTOMS Papery-thin bark peels off in pale brown sheets. Die-back occurs as shoots become girdled.
DANGER PERIOD Growing season.
TREATMENT Improve cultural conditions. Cut out dead shoots, and remove rotting tissue beneath peeling bark on the trunk. Paint all wounds with wound-sealing paint.

Parsnip canker

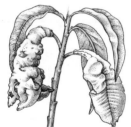

Name given to several fungal diseases affecting parsnips.
SYMPTOMS Brown, orange-brown or black cankers on the edible root, causing rot to different degrees.
DANGER PERIOD Growing season.
PREVENTION Sow seeds early and thinly in deep, limy loam, adding a balanced fertiliser. Rotate crops regularly (see pp. 26–27) and grow resistant varieties, e.g. 'Avonresister'. Destroy diseased plants.

Peach leaf curl

A fungal disease of peaches and nectarines.
SYMPTOMS Leaves with red blisters that turn white then brown. Leaves fall prematurely.
DANGER PERIOD Before bud-burst.
TREATMENT Remove and burn diseased leaves. Spray with lime-sulphur or Bordeaux mixture in January, repeating a fortnight later and again just before leaf-fall.

Petal blight

A serious disease on several plants; in the vegetable garden it may particularly affect globe artichokes.
SYMPTOMS Dark, saturated spots on petals. Flowers eventually rot.
DANGER PERIOD Flowering time, especially in chilly summers.
PREVENTION Spray with zineb before the flowers open, repeating weekly. Destroy diseased flowers.

Potato blight

The most serious of potato diseases; also attacks tomatoes.
SYMPTOMS Leaves develop yellow-brown patches and shrivel up in dry weather. White fungal threads appear on the underside of leaves in wet weather. Haulms and tubers rot.
DANGER PERIOD May to August.
PREVENTION In a wet season especially, spray at 10–14 day intervals with maneb, zineb or Bordeaux mixture, starting before the tops meet in the rows.

Powdery mildew

General term applied to a number of fungi that produce similar symptoms on a wide variety of plants.
SYMPTOMS White, powdery coating on leaves, shoots and flowers.
DANGER PERIOD Growing season.
PREVENTION Spray regularly with benomyl, dinocap or thiophanate-methyl. Remove diseased shoots in autumn. Dust with sulphur, except on sulphur-shy varieties, or fruit for processing.

Powdery scab

A fungal disease of potatoes.
SYMPTOMS Raised scabs that later burst into a brown, powdery mass of spores.
DANGER PERIOD Growing season.
PREVENTION Dig up and destroy affected plants. Do not plant potatoes on the same site for several years. Work in plenty of organic matter at planting time.

Reversion

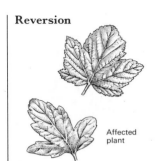

Affected plant

A disease of black currants transmitted by the black-currant gall mite.
SYMPTOMS Small leaves with fewer lobes than usual. Poor crops.
DANGER PERIOD Mid-summer.
PREVENTION Spray with lime-sulphur to control black-currant gall mite. Dig up and burn diseased plants, and re-plant with bushes certified virus-free.

Root rot

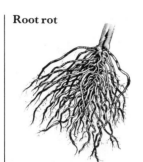

Any type of plant may be affected. The cause may be soil that is too wet or too dry, or fungal diseases such as black root rot and violet root rot.
SYMPTOMS Foliage discoloration; premature leaf-fall; die-back of shoots; collapse of plants.
DANGER PERIOD Growing season.
PREVENTION Destroy infected plants and improve soil conditions. Regular crop rotation is beneficial.

Rust

Parasitical diseases that in the kitchen garden particularly affect mint and plums.
SYMPTOMS Brown, orange or yellow spore masses gather on leaves and stems.
DANGER PERIOD Growing season for mint; late summer for plums.
TREATMENT Cut out and burn diseased mint shoots in spring. Remove and burn dead stalks and debris in autumn. Plums: improve growing conditions; spray with maneb or zineb.

Scab

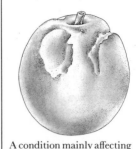

Fungal diseases of pears and apples.
SYMPTOMS Olive-green blotches on leaves, which fall prematurely. Brown-black scabs on fruit, whose skins may crack.
DANGER PERIOD Growing season.
TREATMENT Spray regularly – from the appearance of the first flower buds until July if necessary – with benomyl, captan, thiophanatemethyl or thiram. Burn diseased leaves.

Scald

A condition mainly affecting fruits in overheated greenhouses. It may also occur on outdoor fruits in hot summers.
SYMPTOMS Discoloured, sunken patches on grapes, tomatoes, plums and gooseberries.
DANGER PERIOD Hot weather.
PREVENTION Remove damaged fruits. Shade and ventilate the greenhouse, and damp it down early in the day.

Sclerotinia disease

A fungal disease that attacks many plants, including root crops in store.
SYMPTOMS Fungus appears on stems as a white, fluffy mass containing black lumps of resting spores. Stems rot and collapse. Stored roots soften and decay.
DANGER PERIOD Spring and summer.
PREVENTION Burn all rotting material before the spores enter the soil. Store sound roots only.

Shanking

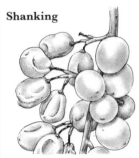

Grape disorder caused by an inadequate root system or over-cropping.
SYMPTOMS Dark spots and rings on berry stalks. Berries fail to ripen, turning red on black varieties. White grapes stay green.
DANGER PERIOD Growing season.
TREATMENT Feed the vines and never let the soil dry out. Do not over-crop. Remove affected grapes as the disorder appears.

Shothole

Holes in leaves of plums, peaches and cherries, also spinach and horseradish. May be due to either bacterial or fungal diseases.
SYMPTOMS Brown patches on leaves develop into holes.
DANGER PERIOD Growing season.
TREATMENT Good feeding and watering. If the disease persists, spray fruit trees with half-strength copper fungicide in summer, and full-strength as the leaves fall in autumn.

Silver leaf

A fungal disease that attacks many trees, especially plums.
SYMPTOMS Leaves become silvered and their upper surfaces peel off easily. An infected branch, cut across and moistened, will show a brown or purple stain. Make this test before treating.
DANGER PERIOD Sept. to May.
TREATMENT Cut off affected branches to a point 6 in. (150 mm.) below the stain and apply sealing paint. Water and feed regularly.

Soil-borne diseases

A wide variety of disorders, transmitted through the soil by fungi or bacteria. Plants particularly susceptible are beans and peas, cucumbers, melons, pumpkins, squashes and tomatoes.
SYMPTOMS These vary according to the particular disease and the plants affected. (See also Black root rot, Foot rot and Root rot.) They include the rotting of the roots and tissues at the crowns of all types of plants, and blackening and rotting at the base of stems.
DANGER PERIOD Growing period.
PREVENTION AND TREATMENT This also varies, but control can be achieved by good garden hygiene and crop rotation. Where disease is persistent, use seed dressings of captan or thiram; or water with captan, Cheshunt compound or zineb.

Split stone

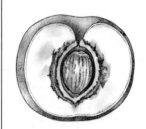

A disorder of peaches and nectarines.
SYMPTOMS The stone splits, causing the fruit to crack open at the stalk end.
DANGER PERIOD Growing season.
TREATMENT Feed and mulch the tree; water regularly and add lime if the soil is acid. Pollinate the flowers by hand.

Splitting

A condition affecting the skins of tomatoes and some root crops.
SYMPTOMS The skin splits, often from the shoulder downwards.
DANGER PERIOD As the fruit or root develops.
PREVENTION Maintain even growth by regular feeding and watering.

Spraing

A serious potato disease.
SYMPTOMS Brown, curving stains in the potato's flesh.
DANGER PERIOD Growing season.
PREVENTION Destroy infected tubers and do not re-plant potatoes in the same site for some years.

Spray damage

Scorching and distortion of plants caused by careless use of garden sprays. Apples, tomatoes, cabbages and other brassicas are especially susceptible.
SYMPTOMS Apples: roughened skins on fruit. Tomatoes, cabbages, cauliflowers and other brassicas: cup-shaped leaves with parallel vein patterns; spiral twisting of shoots.
DANGER PERIOD After spraying with weedkillers or insecticides.
PREVENTION Avoid spraying on windy days. Keep separate watering cans for sprays, or wash them thoroughly after use.
TREATMENT Most plants will outgrow spray damage. However, put affected cauliflowers and other brassicas on the compost heap.

Spur blight

Fungal disease of raspberries and loganberries.
SYMPTOMS Canes show purple blotches, fading to silver spotted with black. Spurs die back.
DANGER PERIOD Spring and summer.
TREATMENT Cut out infected canes after fruiting and remove superfluous young shoots early. Spray with benomyl, dichlofluanid, thiram or captan when new canes are a few inches high, and repeat three or four times at fortnightly intervals.

Stony pit

A disease affecting old pear trees.
SYMPTOMS Deformed, pitted fruit whose flesh is stony and inedible. The disease spreads gradually over a number of years until the entire tree is infected.
DANGER PERIOD Any time.
TREATMENT None, beyond destroying the tree.

Tomato blight

A serious disorder of outdoor tomatoes.
SYMPTOMS A soft, brown patch spreads rapidly across the fruit, which then shrivels and rots.
DANGER PERIOD Wet summers.
TREATMENT In damp weather, especially, spray at roughly fortnightly intervals with Bordeaux mixture, maneb or zineb.

Violet root rot

A fungal disease on many plants. Asparagus is especially prone.
SYMPTOMS Roots are covered with violet threads that kill the plant.
DANGER PERIOD Any time.
PREVENTION Lift and destroy all infected plants, and isolate the plot by sinking pieces of corrugated iron or plastic 12 in. (305 mm.) deep into the soil. Do not grow asparagus again on the same site.

Virus diseases

A wide variety of disorders caused by minute organisms that enter plant tissues through wounds in the outer skin. Some are transmitted through handling the plants, but most are spread by insects such as aphids.
SYMPTOMS These vary according to the plant affected; the same virus will produce different symptoms on different plants. Typical among them are colour changes in leaves and stems, wilting and stunting, the development of outgrowths and the killing of tissues.
DANGER PERIOD Any time.
PREVENTION Destroy badly diseased plants and re-plant with stock that is certified virus-free. Maintain good garden hygiene and keep pests under control with insecticides.

Wart disease

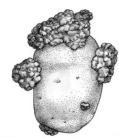

A fungal disease of potatoes. Its presence must be reported to the Ministry of Agriculture, Fisheries and Food.
SYMPTOMS Large warty growths on the tubers, causing them to disintegrate.
DANGER PERIOD Growing season.
PREVENTION Plant varieties that are certified immune from the disease. The Ministry will order the destruction of diseased plants.

Whiptail

A deficiency disorder of cauliflowers and broccoli.
SYMPTOMS Reduction of the leaf blade to the midrib, giving a whip-like appearance.
DANGER PERIOD Growing period, particularly in acid soils.
TREATMENT Water with a solution of sodium molybdate at a rate of 1 tablespoon to 2 gallons (9 l.) of water for each 10 sq. yds (8 sq. m.).

White blister

Fungal diseases, not usually fatal, that attack horseradish, scorzonera, salsify and brassicas.
SYMPTOMS Blisters, filled with white, powdery spores, on leaves and stems.
DANGER PERIOD Growing season.
TREATMENT Remove and destroy diseased leaves and stems.

White rot

A fungal disease of onion, leeks, shallots and garlic.
SYMPTOMS White fungus on the edible roots, which quickly rot.
DANGER PERIOD Growing season. Spring onions are most susceptible.
PREVENTION Dust seed drills with 4% calomel dust. Destroy diseased plants and do not sow onions, leeks, etc., on the same site for at least eight years.

Wire stem

A disease that affects many young plants, especially cauliflowers and other brassicas.
SYMPTOMS Browning and shrinking of stem bases, causing death or stunting of the plant.
DANGER PERIOD Early growth.
PREVENTION Raise seedlings in sterilised compost, or rake quintozene into the soil before planting outdoors.

PESTICIDES

Chemical	Trade names
BIORESMETHRIN	**Aerosol** Cooper's Garden Spray.
BROMOPHOS	**Granules** pbi Bromophos.
CARBARYL	**Dust** Murphy Sevin Dust.
DERRIS	**Dusts** Boots Derris Dust; Murphy Derris Dust; UGS Derris Dust. **Sprays** Bugges Liquid Derris; UGS Liquid Derris; pbi Liquid Derris.
DIAZINON	**Spray** Gesal Vegetable Insecticide. **Granules** Gesal Root Guard.
DICHLORVOS	**Fumigant** Vapona Strips.
DIMETHOATE	**Sprays** Boots Systemic Greenfly Killer; Murphy Systemic Insecticide; Fison's Combat Garden Insecticide (with malathion and HCH).
DNOC	**Sprays** Cresofin DNC Winter Wash; Murphy Ovamort Special.
FENITROTHION	**Spray** Murphy Fentro.
FORMOTHION	**Sprays** Topgard Systemic Liquid; Toprose Systemic Spray.
HCH	Also known as gamma-HCH, Gammexane or Lindane. **Dusts** Boots Ant Destroyer; ICI Rootfly and Wireworm Dust; Murphy Gamma-HCH Dust; New Ant Doom. **Sprays** Murphy Lindex Garden Spray; Abol-X (with menazon); Fison's Combat Garden Insecticide (with malathion and dimethoate). **Fumigants** Fumite HCH Cones; Fumite Smoke Pellets; Murfume HCH Smoke.
LIME-SULPHUR	**Spray** Murphy Lime-Sulphur.
MALATHION	**Dusts** Murphy Malathion Dust; UGS Malathion Dust. **Sprays** Boots Greenfly Killer; Murphy Liquid Malathion; pbi Malathion Greenfly Killer. **Aerosol** Murphy Greenhouse Aerosol.
METALDEHYDE	**Spray** Murphy Slugit Liquid. **Slug baits** Boots Slug Destroyer Pellets; Carter's Slug Killer Pellets; ICI Slug Pellets; Murphy Slugit Pellets.
METHIOCARB	**Slug baits** Draza Slug Killer; pbi Slug Gard.
NICOTINE	**Sprays** Campbell's Nico Soap; XL All Liquid Insecticide. **Fumigant** Darlington's Autoshreds.
PERMETHRIN	**Spray and smoke Bio** Flydown; Fumite Whitefly Insecticide; Murphy Permethrin; Picket; Picket G.
PIRIMICARB	**Spray** ICI Rapid Greenfly Killer.
PIRIMIPHOS-METHYL	**Spray** ICI Pestkiller for Fruit and Vegetables.
PYRETHRUM	**Sprays** Py Spray Concentrate; Plant Pest Killer; Bio Sprayday. **Aerosol** Py Spray Garden Insect Killer.
SLUG PELLETS	See Metaldehyde and Methiocarb.
TAR OIL	**Sprays** Carbo-Craven; Bugges Standard Tar Oil Winter Wash; Mortegg Tar Oil Winter Wash; Para-Carbo (with petroleum).
TRICHLORPHON	**Spray** May and Baker Dipterex, pbi Crop Saver (with malathion).

FUNGICIDES, etc.

Chemical	Trade names
BENOMYL	pbi Benlate.
BORAX	Borax or sodium tetraborate.
BORDEAUX MIXTURE	**Powder** Murphy Bordeaux Powder. **Liquid** Bugges Wetcol '3'.
CALCIUM NITRATE	From a chemist.
CALOMEL DUST	**4% dusts** Boots Calomel Dust; M & B Cyclosan; pbi Calomel dust; ICI Club Root Control; Murphy Calomel Dust.
CAPTAN	**Wettable powders** Murphy Orthocide; Captan Fungicide. **Dust** Murphy Orthocide Captan Dust.
CAPTAN WITH BHC	Murphy Combined Seed Dressing.
CHELATED COMPOUNDS	Gesal Sequestrene; Murphy Sequestered Iron.
CHESHUNT COMPOUND	pbi Cheshunt Compound; Boots Cheshunt Compound.
COPPER FUNGICIDE	**Liquid** Murphy Liquid Copper Fungicide.
DICHLOFLUANID	Bayer Elvaron Black Spot Spray.
DINOCAP	**Wettable powders** Bugges AM62 Fungicide; Murphy Dinocap Mildew Fungicide. **Dust** Murphy Dinocap Dust. **Liquids** Synchemicals XL All Mildew Wash. **Smoke** Murfume Dinocap Smoke Cone.
FORMALDEHYDE	Murphy Formaldehyde Soil Steriliser.
FRITTED TRACE ELEMENTS	Fortone E.
LIME-SULPHUR	Murphy Lime-Sulphur.
MAGNESIUM SULPHATE	Epsom Salts.
MANEB	Bugges Maneb 80% Wettable Powder; Nutilis Maneb.
MANEB WITH DINOCAP	**Aerosol** Murphy Combined Pest and Disease Spray.
PHENOLIC COMPOUND	Armillatox.
QUINTOZENE	**Dust** ICI Botrilex.
SODIUM HYPOCHLORITE	From a chemist.
SODIUM MOLYBDATE	From a chemist.
SULPHUR	**Wettable powder** Bugges Microsulf. **Liquid** Bentley's Mildew Specific No. 2. **Dusts** Corry's Sulphur Powder; Bentley's Green Sulphur.
TECNAZENE	Fumite TCNB Smoke Pellets.
THIOPHANATE-METHYL	Murphy Systemic Fungicide.
THIRAM	ICI General Garden Fungicide; also with BHC and derris in pbi Hexyl Plus.
WOUND-SEALING PAINT	pbi Arbrex.
ZINEB	Bugges Dyblite Wettable Powder; pbi Dithane.
ZINEB WITH SULPHUR	**Dust** Murphy Combined Pest and Disease Dust.

CHOOSING A SPRAYER

Each type of sprayer is suited to a particular purpose, so consider your main needs before buying. For maximum convenience you may decide to buy two – one for big jobs, such as spraying fruit trees, and another for small plants.

Following are the four main categories:

Syringes The simple design of this traditional sprayer should ensure a long and trouble-free life. Many are still made of brass; cheaper versions are of plastic. Some of the more expensive models, fed by tube from a bucket, have a two-way continuous action.

Syringes are more versatile than most sorts of sprayers, particularly if fitted with adjustable or interchangeable nozzles.

Trigger-action sprayers These inexpensive plastic-bodied sprayers are excellent for small plants or for spraying isolated colonies of pests. Each squeeze of the trigger releases a mist-like spray. Most models have a 1–2 pints (600 ml.–1 l.) capacity.

Small compression sprayers Pressurised by pump action, sprayers of this type are useful for more continuous action than simple, trigger-action sprayers. However, their small size – about 2 pints (1 l.) – makes them more suitable for greenhouse work or vegetables rather than for fruit trees.

Large compression sprayers A capacity of 4–14 pints (2–8 l.) makes these the best choice for major spraying jobs, especially as they are supplied with a lance for long reach and easy control. Some are fitted with a sling for easy carrying, but the container can generally be placed on the ground while the sprayer is in use.

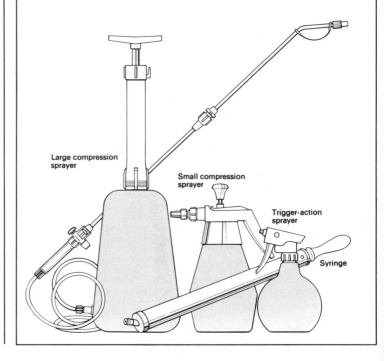

Large compression sprayer

Small compression sprayer

Trigger-action sprayer

Syringe

HOME PRESERVING

Enjoying summer's plenty throughout the year

Drying and salting – among the earliest ways of preserving food – are both employed to this day. Alongside these time-honoured techniques – which also include the making of delectable jams and fruit jellies, chutneys and relishes – are more recent methods, such as bottling and freezing. These allow a much wider range of fruits and vegetables to be preserved for winter use.

All these techniques, which are fully explained in the following pages, can be used for storing garden produce. As well as preventing waste and helping to fill any gaps between fresh crops, they ensure that

favourite foods from the garden can be enjoyed out of their normal season.

With this in mind, some gardeners plan deliberately for a surplus of summer vegetables for eating during winter. For instance, peas, runner beans and sweet corn may be preferred to the usual winter diet of Brussels sprouts, cabbages and broccoli.

Like the fresh produce from which they are made, home-preserved foods provide a delightful change from the often bland and predictable flavours of commercial products and they are, of course, free from preservatives and other artificial additives.

How preservation works

Like all living things, food plants grow, die and decay. The object of preserving is to arrest this process at the point where the fruit or vegetable is at its best, and to keep it that way rather than let it undergo the changes that make it unfit for human consumption.

Such changes are brought about by a number of chemicals and microscopic organisms that must be destroyed or inactivated if the food is to be preserved. Among them are:

Enzymes *The term covers a group of complex chemicals essential for various biological processes. One example of enzymic action is the browning of cut fruit when exposed to the air, leading eventually to decay.*

This action is halted by freezing, and totally stopped by high temperatures. Therefore, blanch vegetables before you freeze them; this reduces the enzymic effect that

takes place both after picking and when thawing begins.

Bacteria *Apart from spoiling food in store, bacteria can in some cases cause food poisoning. Most are destroyed by temperatures around boiling point, but some produce spores that will survive up to 115°C (240°F). In such cases, you will have to use a pressure cooker.*

Freezing inhibits the growth of bacteria; but, as with enzymes, they are reactivated when the food is thawed. Acid, too, arrests bacterial growth and assists their destruction by heat. For this reason, foods low in acids require longer cooking at higher temperatures. High salt or sugar concentrations will also halt the growth of bacteria.

Yeasts *These cause fermentation in sugar. They are destroyed by heat and inactivated by freezing, or where more than 60% of a preserve consists of sugar.*

Moulds *The presence of these fungal bodies becomes obvious when they settle as a green deposit on foods inadequately prepared or processed. Most are destroyed by heat and, like yeasts and bacteria, are inhibited by freezing.*

Sealing and storage

Whether these chemicals and micro-organisms are destroyed by sterilising, or their action halted by freezing or by packing the fruit or vegetables in salt, sugar or vinegar, remember that the correct sealing and storage of foods is as vital to successful preservation as careful processing. Inadequate sealing, the storage of jars in a too-warm or light cupboard, or one in which they are constantly disturbed can reactivate harmful bodies and spoil your preserves.

A word of caution: if, when opened, the jars smell musty or the contents look slimy or mushy, throw them away without tasting.

RULES FOR SUCCESSFUL FOOD PRESERVING

- *Ensure that all work surfaces are clean and use only clean, undamaged utensils.*

- *Prepare and preserve your produce as soon as possible after harvesting.*

- *When freezing or bottling, use only prime quality produce; damaged, wind-fallen, or over-ripe fruits are suitable only for syrups or jellies.*

- *Where heat processes are recommended, follow the directions exactly.*

- *Label each jar or package with a description of the contents and the date of preserving.*

- *Store your preserves in a place that is cool, dry, dark and frost-free, where they will remain undisturbed until required for use.*

Freezing—the easy path to home preserving

Freezing has two advantages over other methods of preserving fruits and vegetables at home. In the first place, it is simpler and quicker than heat preservation – than bottling, for instance, or making jams, jellies or chutneys. Secondly, freezing makes it possible to store small quantities of food that it would be impractical to store by other means.

In most cases, too, more of the true flavour, colour and appearance of the food is retained by freezing than by other methods of preservation.

However, the cost of running the freezer must be taken into consideration. A 10 cu. ft (280 l.) freezer uses an average of 15 units of electricity a week. Some of this can be offset by purchasing foods in bulk, but the biggest saving of all is to freeze garden produce.

Both soft fruits and tree fruits (see p. 300) can be frozen either on their own, or in sugar or syrup.

Most vegetables (see p. 302) freeze well after blanching. The chief exceptions are salad vegetables, whose high water content makes them unsuitable for freezing. Even tomatoes can be frozen, though whole fruits will not retain their shape and texture when thawed.

It is possible to freeze several types of herbs (see p. 305).

Choosing a freezer

When buying a freezer, first decide what type and size will best suit your family's needs, whether you have sufficient space, and how much money you can allocate to keep the freezer stocked.

Domestic freezers and refrigerators are made in several sizes, whose capacity is measured in either cubic feet or litres. As a guide, 1 cu. ft equals approximately 28 litres; therefore, freezers whose stated capacities are either 10 cu. ft, or 280 l., will hold the same amount of foods.

When deciding what size of freezer to buy, it helps to know that one of 10 cu. ft (280 l.) capacity will hold about 280 lb. (127 kg.) of frozen food. However, large quantities of stored joints and poultry, which do not stack compactly, will reduce this figure.

The smallest available freezer is 3.5 cu. ft (100 l.), and the largest 20.8 cu. ft (582 l.), with food capacities, respectively, from 100 lb. (45 kg.) to 578 lb. (262 kg.).

As well as deciding how much total space you are likely to need, remember that only a certain amount of unfrozen food can be added to the freezer at any one time.

Not more than one-tenth of the total capacity of a freezer should be occupied by unfrozen food during a 24 hour period, so a 3.5 cu. ft (100 l.) freezer will take only 10 lb. (5 kg.) of unfrozen food in a day. This is sufficient for small batches of home-grown produce, but the total capacity of such a freezer is quite inadequate for most families.

A 14 cu. ft (400 l.) freezer can take up to 30 lb. (13.6 kg.) of unfrozen food a day, and has overall storage space to meet most families' needs.

Space availability is another determining factor when choosing a freezer. The two basic designs are the upright cupboard type, with outward-opening doors, and the chest cabinet with a lid cover.

Upright freezers occupy less floor space. They are fitted with shelves and baskets and often have additional shelves in the door. Stacking and removal is easy, and the contents can be seen at a glance.

They are a little more expensive to run, however, because cold air escapes every time the door is opened. In chest freezers the cold, and therefore heavy, air sinks to the bottom.

Chest freezers use less electricity

and the lid makes an additional working surface. But they take up more floor space, and it is more difficult to stack and remove frozen foods than in the upright type.

For home freezing on a small scale, a single upright cabinet combining separate freezer and refrigerator sections may be sufficient. There are separate doors to each of the two sections, so no cold air is lost from the freezer by opening the refrigerator.

However, such an arrangement is too small for most families, and would be inadequate for even the smallest household where the intention is to freeze regular batches of garden produce.

Where to put the freezer

The kitchen is not necessarily the best place for a freezer, since it will use more electricity to maintain its low temperature in these warm surroundings. The ideal place for a freezer is a cool position where it

will cost less to run. In a centrally heated house, the landing or the hall are often the coolest places, though remember that no freezer is completely silent. Other good situations include the garage or garden shed, or a purpose-built outhouse.

Freezers can be purchased with fitted locks, which are certainly advisable if there are young children in the house. Lights or bells can be fitted in the house and connected to the freezer outside to

THREE MAIN TYPES OF FREEZER

COMBINED REFRIGERATOR/FREEZER Use the upper part of the freezer compartment for fast freezing. Sliding baskets give easy access to contents, which for convenience can be grouped into fruit, meat, etc.

UPRIGHT FREEZER The upper shelves are for fast freezing, but can also be used for normal storage. Place often-used items as close as possible to eye level. Use door storage, if provided, for items in frequent use.

CHEST FREEZER Fast freezing compartment is at one end. Use the baskets for small, delicate packs, such as patés, bacon, cakes and flans. Place joints and chickens on the bottom. Stack soft-fruit containers at one end.

295

warn of failures or power cuts.

However, if you do put the freezer in a garage or outhouse, make sure that the electric cables and fittings are sound, and adequate for the load. A freezer usually runs off a normal ring circuit. Follow the manufacturer's advice, and if in doubt consult a qualified electrician.

The building must also be absolutely dry, otherwise parts of the machine will corrode.

It is a good idea to have a permanently wired connection rather than a plug and socket, so that it cannot be turned off by mistake. If the freezer is connected to a socket, never use a multiple adaptor as this increases the risk of accidental disconnection.

If you have to use a switched socket, cover the switch with sticky tape as a safeguard. Whether or not there is a switch, stick tape over the plug, or pin a warning notice on the wall.

Finally, before choosing a freezer, check that narrow doors or awkward bends will not prevent you putting it where you want it. Remember, too, that a freezer full of food is extremely heavy, so the floor must be strong enough to take the weight. If in doubt, ask a builder to check.

Getting the freezer ready

Before using a new freezer, wash out the inside with a solution of 4 teaspoons of bicarbonate of soda dissolved in 2 pints (1 l.) of warm water. Dry the freezer thoroughly, switch it on and let it run for a few hours to see that it works satisfactorily.

Study the manufacturer's leaflet to make sure that you use the machine correctly. Some freezers

must be turned to a low temperature some time before freezing, and then turned up when the food is frozen. Others have a separate switch for the fast freezing of fresh food, and there are some with a separate compartment for freezing food before transferring it to the main body of the machine.

Do not add more than the permitted quantity of unfrozen food in any 24 hour period.

Unfrozen food will freeze more quickly if stacked loosely and packed in small quantities. Do not let it touch any frozen food already in the freezer, as this may lead to temperature variations which could spoil food that is already frozen.

Most foods freeze solid in eight hours, after which they can be transferred to the storage section and stacked with the other contents of the freezer.

Looking after your freezer

It is necessary to defrost a freezer only once or twice a year, provided that the loose frost that forms inside is removed regularly. Follow the manufacturer's recommendations as to when to defrost. Upright freezers need defrosting more often than chest-type freezers.

To defrost, remove the food from the freezer and stack it in several layers of newspaper and a blanket. Put the papers and the blanket in the freezer for a few hours in advance to make them cold.

When the contents have been removed and wrapped, switch off the current and put bowls of hot water in the freezer to speed defrosting. Remove as much frost and ice as possible with a wooden

scraper to reduce the amount of mopping up incurred as defrosting progresses.

Mop up the water as the frost and ice thaw, and finally wash the inside with a solution of 4 teaspoons of bicarbonate of soda, dissolved in 2 pints (1 l.) of warm water. If any smell lingers, wash the interior again with a solution of 3 tablespoons of vinegar to 2 pints (1 l.) of warm water.

Dry the cabinet thoroughly, switch on the current and close the freezer. After about an hour the freezer should be cold enough for the food to be replaced.

Work quickly, so that defrosting and cleaning are completed within a couple of hours. The outside of the freezer can be wiped down and polished before you return the contents.

Breakdowns and power cuts

When you buy a freezer, find out what service facilities are available in your area. In case of emergencies, note the telephone numbers of your local electricity board and the nearest freezer service centre. (Both may be found in the Yellow Pages of your local telephone directory.) Once the freezer is installed and working, check it daily to see that it is operating satisfactorily.

If it is fitted with an alarm system, check it occasionally. Freezer alarms are battery-operated and need new batteries from time to time. If the red light – fitted to some freezers to show they are working – goes out, discover whether the bulb, rather than the freezer, has failed before calling in expert help. Use a thermometer to detect any rise in temperature

and, if the freezer is definitely out of action, check the fuse.

If you are unable to put things right, get in touch at once with the nearest service organisation and, meanwhile, keep the freezer closed.

Frozen food will not suffer any damage for at least 12 hours following power failure – the exact period depends on the type of food, and the temperature outside the freezer. If expert help arrives within reasonable time, no further action need be taken.

If the freezer needs emptying to carry out repairs, remove the contents and wrap as for defrosting. Do not, however, open the cabinet first to chill newspapers or blankets.

When a power cut occurs, try to find out from the local electricity board how long it will last. If it is expected to last over 12 hours, or if service is not at hand in the event of a mechanical breakdown, emergency action is necessary to save the contents of the freezer.

If at all possible, ask a friend living outside your immediate area if you can transfer the food in your freezer into hers for the duration of the power cut. Some service centres have facilities to store contents of domestic freezers in emergencies.

Alternatively, use dry ice – frozen carbon dioxide – to maintain a freezing temperature, although it is not always easy to find. Look up 'Carbon dioxide manufacturers' in the Yellow Pages to locate your nearest supplier. Find out if they will deliver dry ice at short notice, or whether you can collect some.

Cover the food in the freezer with cardboard or several layers of

newspaper, and put the chopped dry ice on top. Do not close the freezer, or pressure will build up – which could be dangerous. Wear thick gloves to prevent frost burn, and top up with more dry ice every day or two until the freezer has been repaired or power has been restored.

In theory, 8 lb. (4 kg.) of dry ice will keep the contents of a 3.5 cu. ft (100 l.) chest frozen for two or three days.

What to do if the food does thaw

Foods that have not been thawed for too long, and still feel cold, can be thoroughly cooked and then re-frozen in the cooked state. On no account should they be re-frozen raw.

Cooked dishes, even if they still seem very cold, should never be re-frozen. They can, however, be eaten after thorough re-heating. If in doubt, destroy the food.

Holidays and house removals

Do not switch off the electric current at the mains when you go on holiday. Get a neighbour to come in and check your freezer once a day while you are away. Alternatively – and this would be impracticable in most households – use the contents before you go away, and leave the freezer defrosted and clean. In this case, leave the lid or door open so that fresh air can circulate.

When moving house there is no need to run down frozen food stocks. As food will not be harmed by a power cut of about 12 hours, a freezer full of food can generally be moved without difficulty.

Switch off the freezer at the last

minute, have it loaded on to the removal van just before setting off, and then have it unloaded and switched on at the next destination as soon as possible. Check beforehand that the removal firm will be able to handle a freezer full of food.

Freezer insurance

For an annual premium the contents of a freezer can be insured. This is worth considering, particularly if you intend keeping your freezer well stocked with a wide variety of food whose value could easily amount to £100 or more. Consult your dealer or insurance broker for advice on a suitable policy.

Packaging materials

Frozen food must be packaged correctly to guard against various forms of deterioration. Packaging should be vapour-proof, so that the food will not dry out, and thick enough both to retain the aroma and flavour of each particular food and prevent them from tainting others. In practice, this means buying purpose-made bags and containers rather than using make-shift packaging that may be inadequate.

Oxygen can cause frozen food, especially meat and fruit, to deteriorate, so exclude as much air as possible from bags when packing food for freezing.

Polythene bags These are widely used for packaging frozen foods, being suitable for all foods except liquids. They are available in a variety of sizes and thicknesses, but those with a gauge of 120–150 are particularly recommended.

Polythene bags are useful for odd-shaped, bulky objects such as

poultry and joints of meat, since they can be wrapped tightly round the food to exclude air. They may also be used for loose items, such as sprouts or beans. However, these are likely to freeze into awkward shapes which are difficult to pack.

A way round this problem is to put the bag inside a carton and fill it with vegetables before freezing. When the food has frozen solid the carton can be removed, and the resulting rectangular block will be easy to stack.

Polythene bags also make useful liners for cartons or tubs made from cardboard or other absorbent materials.

Overwrapping Ideally, wrap large, bulky, or awkwardly shaped items – such as poultry with protruding joints, whole fish or cooked pies – in foil or stockinette after being frozen in polythene bags. This minimises the danger of tears in the bags.

Alternatively, leave the frozen bags in cardboard boxes.

Plastic boxes Boxes with air-tight lids, sold in a variety of shapes and sizes, are ideal for frozen fruits, vegetables, sauces, liquids and cooked foods.

Avoid using very large boxes, even for bulky items, as too much air is likely to be enclosed. Round plastic boxes are not a good idea as they waste space when stacked. It is important when filling containers to leave the amount of space recommended in the instructions for the particular food between the contents and the top of the container.

Aluminium foil This material can be used to wrap such foods as

sausages, bacon or cooked dishes that will not readily pack into polythene bags.

Foil sold for general kitchen use is too thin to use in the freezer, and a heavy-gauge material is sold for this purpose. If thin kitchen foil does have to be used, protect it with an overwrap of strong paper or polythene.

Never allow foil to come into contact with acid foods, such as rhubarb and beetroot.

Trays and dishes made of aluminium are useful for freezing cooked dishes, pies, pâtés, puddings and complete meals. Though such containers slow down the thawing process, they can afterwards be put straight in the oven for re-heating, preferably on a baking tray.

Waxed cartons Waxed boxes, cartons and tubs – many with fitted lids and some with polythene liners – are sold in a range of shapes and sizes. They are ideal for cooked dishes, gravies, fruits and vegetables, purées and soups, and for such fragile items as cakes and biscuits.

Line waxed containers with bags if the contents are liable to stain. Provided this is done, waxed containers can be used several times. Tubs and containers saved from yoghurt, sour cream and margarine can be used after cleaning, provided they have an adequate wax lining or are lined with polythene.

Never pour hot foods into waxed containers, as the heat will melt the wax and render the containers porous.

Glass Containers made of glass are not really ideal for use in a freezer,

POLYTHENE BAGS Generally made of 120–150 gauge polythene, these are excellent containers for non-liquid frozen foods. When freezing loose vegetables, however – such as sprouts or beans – put the bag into a rectangular plastic or cardboard box before packing. When freezing is complete, remove the box, leaving an easy-to-stack pack.

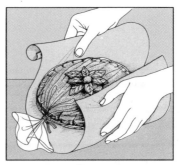

OVERWRAPPING Bulky items, such as poultry, joints and pies, should be frozen in polythene bags before being given a protective overwrapping of foil or stockinette.

PLASTIC BOXES A wide variety of plastic containers, with fitted lids, is available. These make ideal freezing packs, but remember to leave headspace above the food.

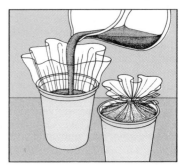

ALUMINIUM FOIL Use this, as wrapping or shaped containers, for freezing pies, puddings or pre-cooked meals. Heavy-gauge foil is more suitable than the thin kitchen type.

WAXED CARTONS Use yoghourt, margarine or sour-cream tubs as storage receptacles for gravies, purées and soups. If lined with polythene, they can be re-used.

as they become increasingly brittle at low temperatures. There is a danger of jars being crushed by the freezer lid if a chest has been over-filled, and it is necessary to thaw the contents before they can be removed.

However, most brands of oven glassware will withstand freezing. Allow the contents to cool down before putting the containers in the freezer.

Sealing containers

Polythene bags can be sealed with wire ties. If these are covered with paper or plastic they will not damage the bag, which can be re-used.

Alternatively, heat-seal the bag with a special sealing-iron or an ordinary domestic iron.

If using a domestic iron, set the iron to 'cool', as for ironing nylon, and make sure that the opening of the filled bag is clean. Press out as much air as possible and lay a thin sheet of paper on either side of the opening. Run the iron along the edge of the bag, on the paper.

When opening the frozen bag, cut off the seal as narrowly as possible so that the bag can be used again.

Make sure that polythene bags are sound before re-using. Wash the bags thoroughly after empty-ing and turn them inside-out to dry.

Packages for freezing, whether wrapped in aluminium foil, poly-thene, waxed paper or cloth, can also be sealed with tape. Ordinary sticky tapes come unstuck when frozen, but special freezer tape is available.

As well as making containers air-tight, tape is useful for securing labels on packs.

Labelling and coding frozen food

Every packet in the freezer should have a label, stating what it contains – including the amount or number of portions, the date on which it was frozen and the date by which it must be eaten.

It is time-wasting and possibly damaging to open sealed packages to find out if they contain for instance, peas or blueberries.

Use special freezer labels that stick to packages. Tie non-stick labels on firmly, or stick them on with freezer tape. Write on the labels with a pencil, felt pen or freezer pen – not a fountain-pen or ball-point.

Apart from the obvious in-formation on contents, weight and date of freezing, it is also useful to note how much sugar, if any, the food contains if this will affect its subsequent cooking. These and similar details are sure to have been forgotten by the time the food is used.

Include any other information you may find useful when you come to use the food, such as the amount of cream or the time needed for re-heating.

Colour coding can be a great help in identifying various types of food in the freezer. Use labels of one colour for fresh vegetables, another for cooked vegetables, a third for fruits, and so on. Alter-natively, group foods of similar types in baskets, trays or string bags.

Keep a record or log-book of everything that goes into the freezer, and cross out the items as they are removed. In this way you can see at a glance how much is in the freezer and which items should be used by a given date.

A log-book will also tell you how much of each food you have used in the course of the year and enable you to adjust next year's stocks accordingly.

Packing the freezer

When food has been prepared, packaged, sealed and labelled, it is ready to go into the freezer. Remember that an amount equalling not more than one-tenth of the freezer's total capacity should be frozen at any one time.

Foods for freezing must be quick-frozen before being stored in the main body of the freezer. Quick-freezing causes small ice crystals to form which can be retained within the cell structure, whereas slow freezing results in large crystals which damage the cell walls and reduce the food value, which is further lost in thawing.

For the initial freezing, follow the freezer manufacturer's recom-mendations. Set the gauge to the given temperature several hours in advance.

Some freezers have a special quick-freezing compartment or shelf. In others it is necessary to move some of the contents so that fresh foods can be quick-frozen against the base or sides of the freezer.

Once the foods have frozen solid, return the freezer to its normal running temperature and stack the newly frozen food.

Arrange the frozen packages compactly to leave as little air space as possible between them, following whichever coding system you have adopted. Avoid stacking foods at the bottom or back of the freezer if you intend to use them within a short time.

RULES FOR SUCCESSFUL FREEZING

- *Freeze only fresh food in perfect condition.*

- *Freeze fruits and vegetables as soon as possible after gathering and initial preparation.*

- *Pick only as much produce at one time as can be prepared and frozen without delay.*

- *Blanch vegetables prior to freezing.*

- *Cool hot foods quickly before freezing.*

- *Pack the prepared food into moisture-proof and vapour-proof bags or containers.*

- *Use meal-size packs whenever possible.*

- *Exclude as much air as possible from the packs.*

- *Label the packs and keep a freezer record.*

- *Freeze packs solid in the coldest part of the freezer.*

- *Follow the manufacturer's instructions on setting the temperature gauge.*

- *Thaw fruits slowly ; cook most vegetables straight from the frozen state.*

- *Eat or cook food soon after removing from the freezer.*

- *Never re-freeze food without cooking it first.*

- *Defrost the freezer when necessary.*

- *Memorise emergency action in the event of a breakdown or power cut.*

- *Keep the freezer fully stocked and, to save electricity, never open it for longer than necessary.*

FREEZING CALENDAR FOR HOME-GROWN FRUITS AND VEGETABLES

The following is a summary of the months during which fresh produce is in peak condition and most suitable for freezing. Some crops, such as cabbages and cauliflowers – according to variety – and perpetual spinach, can be frozen at most times of the year.

JANUARY
FRUIT
Rhubarb *forced*

VEGETABLES
Brussels sprouts
Cabbages
Cauliflowers
Celery
Leeks
Mushrooms
Parsnips
Spinach
Swedes
Turnips

FEBRUARY
FRUIT
Rhubarb *forced*

VEGETABLES
Brussels sprouts
Cabbages
Cauliflowers
Celery
Leeks
Mushrooms
Parsnips
Spinach
Swedes
Turnips

MARCH
FRUIT
Rhubarb

VEGETABLES
Broccoli *sprouting*
Cauliflowers
Leeks
Mushrooms
Spinach
Swedes
Turnips

APRIL
FRUIT
Rhubarb

VEGETABLES
Cabbages
Cauliflowers
Leeks
Mushrooms
Spinach
Swedes
Turnips

MAY
FRUIT
Rhubarb

VEGETABLES
Asparagus
Beans: broad, French
Broccoli *sprouting*
Cabbages
Cauliflowers
Herbs
Kohl-rabi
Mushrooms
Spinach

JUNE
FRUITS
Cherries
Currants: black, red
Gooseberries
Rhubarb
Strawberries

VEGETABLES
Artichokes, globe
Asparagus
Beans: broad, French
Beetroot
Carrots
Cauliflowers
Herbs
Kohl-rabi
Mushrooms
Peas
Potatoes
Spinach

JULY
FRUITS
Apricots
Blueberries
Cherries
Currants: black, red, white
Gooseberries
Peaches and nectarines
Raspberries
Rhubarb
Strawberries

VEGETABLES
Artichokes, globe
Aubergines
Beans: broad, French, runner
Beetroot
Carrots
Cauliflowers
Kohl-rabi
Marrows and courgettes
Mushrooms
Onions
Peppers, sweet
Potatoes
Tomatoes

AUGUST
FRUITS
Apples
Apricots
Blackberries
Blueberries
Currants, black
Figs
Gooseberries
Loganberries
Melons
Peaches and nectarines
Pears
Plums and gages
Raspberries
Strawberries

VEGETABLES
Aubergines
Beans: broad, French, runner
Beetroot
Cabbages
Cauliflowers
Celery
Herbs
Kohl-rabi
Marrows and courgettes
Mushrooms
Onions
Peas
Peppers, sweet
Potatoes
Spinach
Swedes
Sweet corn
Tomatoes
Turnips

SEPTEMBER
FRUITS
Apples
Blackberries
Blueberries
Cherries
Damsons
Figs
Melons
Mulberries
Peaches and nectarines
Plums and gages
Pears
Raspberries
Strawberries

VEGETABLES
Aubergines
Beans: French, runner
Beetroot
Brussels sprouts
Cabbages
Cauliflowers
Celery
Fennel
Herbs
Kohl-rabi
Marrows and courgettes
Mushrooms
Onions
Parsnips
Peas
Peppers, sweet
Potatoes
Swedes
Sweet corn
Tomatoes

OCTOBER
FRUITS
Apples
Damsons
Figs
Pears
Raspberries
Strawberries
Quince

VEGETABLES
Aubergines
Beans, runner
Beetroot
Brussels sprouts
Cabbages
Carrots
Cauliflowers
Celeriac
Celery
Fennel
Kohl-rabi
Marrows and courgettes
Mushrooms
Parsnips
Peas
Potatoes
Spinach
Swedes
Tomatoes
Turnips

NOVEMBER
FRUIT
Apples

VEGETABLES
Brussels sprouts
Cabbages
Cauliflowers
Celeriac
Celery
Leeks
Mushrooms
Parsnips
Spinach
Swedes
Turnips

DECEMBER
VEGETABLES
Brussels sprouts
Cabbages
Cauliflowers
Celery
Leeks
Mushrooms
Parsnips
Spinach
Swedes
Turnips

FREEZING HOME-GROWN FRUITS

Most kinds of fruit will freeze well, though some varieties, because of their colour or size, are more suitable than others.

Methods of freezing, too, vary considerably with the type of fruit. Some soft fruits, for instance, may be frozen whole with no addition other than a little sugar; others, however, must be cooked or puréed before they are worth allocating valuable freezer space. Similarly, a number of tree fruits – among them apricots, peaches and plums – require special treatment before freezing.

But whatever method is chosen, it is vital that as little time as possible is lost between harvesting and freezing. Pick the fruit in prime condition, rejecting any damaged produce.

If some delay cannot be avoided, store the fruit in a cool, dark place until you are ready to prepare it for freezing.

Preparation

Select the fruit carefully, and prepare it as though for cooking – by hulling, removing stalks, peeling and slicing.

Use only cold water when washing the fruit; drain and dry before freezing.

Methods of freezing fruits

Choose the freezing method best suited to the particular fruit, bearing in mind the final use to which it will be put – whether it will be eaten whole, used as a filling for pies or puddings, in sauces or purées, or perhaps to give added attraction to fruit salads or fruit flans.

1. Dry-freezing This method is particularly suitable for berry fruits, such as blackberries, loganberries, raspberries and strawberries.

Spread the prepared, dry fruit in single layers on clean trays and freeze for about 1 hour until firm, then pack.

2. Sugar-freezing In common with dry-freezing, this method is suitable for soft berry fruits, including currants, and can also be used for blueberries, cherries and gooseberries.

Fruit frozen in this way is best used in cooked desserts, such as pies and puddings.

Freeze the cleaned fruit in rigid containers in alternate layers with sugar. Allow 4–6 oz. of caster sugar to 1 lb. of fruit (100–175 g. sugar to 500 g. fruit).

3. Syrup-freezing Though a little more trouble, freezing in syrup is an excellent means of bringing out the flavours of such fruits as damsons, figs, grapes, melons and peaches, and for fruits without much natural juice.

The syrup solution varies from light to heavy according to the type of fruit (see chart). Make up a light syrup solution from 1 lb. of sugar to 2 pints of water (500 g. sugar to 1 l. water) and chill it. Two pints of liquid syrup will cover approximately 3 lb. (1.5 kg.) of fruit. For a heavy syrup, use double the quantity of sugar to the same amount of water.

Pack the fruit in rigid containers, pour the syrup over it, and keep the fruit fully immersed with a ball of crumpled greaseproof or waxed paper beneath the lid. Allow at least ½ in. (12 mm.) headspace between the fruit and the lid to allow for the expansion that takes place during freezing.

4. Poaching The skins of such larger fruits as apricots, plums and peaches will harden during freezing unless the fruits are first poached. Do this by simmering them, stoned and halved, for a few minutes in a heavy syrup – 1 lb. (500 g.) sugar to 1 pint (600 ml.) water – before allowing them to cool and packing into containers.

5. Purées Over-ripe but sound fruit of any kind may be frozen in this way. For fresh purées, rub the fruit through a fine sieve and sweeten with sugar before freezing or, later, when cooking.

For cooked purées, simmer the fruit in a very little water, rub through a sieve and sweeten if necessary. Pack when cold.

Preventing fruit from becoming discoloured

As is well known, apples and some other tree fruits turn brown when peeled and exposed to the air. While freezing inhibits this, some browning may still occur in frozen fruits such as apples and pears.

This can be prevented by adding lemon juice to the syrup solution. But as fruit treated in this way often absorbs too much lemon flavour, a solution of ascorbic acid – which does not have an effect on the flavour – can be used instead.

Dissolve crystals of ascorbic acid in a little cold water and add to the syrup. If you are unable to find a chemist selling the crystals use vitamin C tablets instead, first dissolving them in water. Follow the manufacturer's instructions.

FIVE METHODS OF FREEZING FRUITS

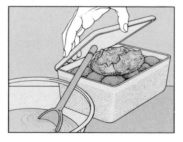

1. Dry-freezing *Especially suitable for the softer berry fruits. Spread single layers on trays lined with waxed paper; freeze for about 1 hour until firm, then pack.*

2. Sugar-freezing *For soft fruits that will later be cooked in pies and other desserts. Place the prepared fruit in containers and freeze with alternate layers of sugar.*

3. Syrup-freezing *Freeze delicately flavoured fruits by placing them in containers and covering with syrup. Keep them immersed with crumpled greaseproof paper.*

4. Poaching *Preserve the larger hard-skinned fruits, halved and stoned, by simmering in syrup for a few minutes before freezing. Allow to cool, pack into containers and freeze.*

5. Purées *Over-ripe but sound fruits may be rubbed – cooked or uncooked – through a sieve. Sweeten the purée, pack and freeze. Alternatively, sweeten the fruits when cooking.*

Packaging fruit for freezing

Small packs containing only a few portions are generally the most convenient. These can be combined if larger amounts are required, but it is difficult to remove two portions from a six-portion pack without first thawing the whole contents.

Pack dry-frozen fruit in heavy polythene bags, and seal. Fruit frozen by any other method – dry sugar, syrup, poaching or purées – must be packed in rigid containers.

Leave headspace of about ½ in. (12 mm.) below the lid to allow for the expansion that will occur when the contents freeze.

Seal, label and code the containers, and freeze solid in the coldest part of the freezer before placing them in the storage compartment.

If matching containers are used, they can be stacked together to save storage space.

Freezing fruit for making jam

If you are too busy to make jam at harvest time, there is no reason why you should not freeze the fruit until you have more time at your disposal. The fruit can be frozen dry, or packed in sugar (not syrup). Sugar-freezing helps to retain the colour, an essential feature of well-made jam.

Note the amount of sugar used with the fruit, so that this may be deducted when the jam is eventually made.

As a rough guide to quantity, pack the fruit in about one-fifth its weight of sugar.

The pectin content of fruit decreases in frozen storage. To counteract this, freeze and eventually use about one-tenth more fruit than specified in a given recipe, otherwise it may fail to set adequately.

To use the frozen fruit, place it, still frozen, in the preserving pan with very little water – or none at all for soft fruit. Heat gently until the juices run, and proceed as for fresh-fruit jams (see p. 314).

The temperature of a freezer should be maintained at –18°C (0°F). At this temperature, dry, frozen fruit will store satisfactorily for 6–8 months, and fruit frozen in sugar or syrup for 9–12 months. Purées have a storage life of some 4–6 months, and fruit juices can be stored for the same length of time.

Storing and thawing frozen fruit

Whatever freezing method is used, all fruit should be thawed, unopened, in the package in which it was frozen.

This is especially important for soft fruits.

Fruits to be served as a dessert should be thawed only to the chilled state. The best method is to leave them overnight in the refrigerator.

Alternatively, they can be left at room temperature for 3–4 hours, or in an emergency left in cold water for about 1 hour.

Fruit which is likely to discolour – apples, pears, peaches – should be kept submerged in its syrup while thawing.

Fruit for stewing and jam-making can be heated gently while still frozen.

Fruit used for pie fillings should be thawed before the pastry is put on, or the covering is likely to become soggy.

AT-A-GLANCE GUIDE TO FREEZING FRUIT	
FRUIT	METHODS OF FREEZING
Apples	DRY, WITH OR WITHOUT SUGAR Peel, core and cut into thick slices. Blanch in boiling water for 1–2 minutes, and cool in chilled water. Alternatively, drop into water with ascorbic acid to prevent discoloration, then drain and dry. Pack in rigid containers, with or without sugar, leaving ½ in. (12 mm.) headspace, and freeze. Thaw in containers and use for pies and puddings.	IN SYRUP Cover prepared slices with light sugar syrup, adding 1½ tablespoons of lemon juice to every 2 pints (1 l.). Pack in rigid containers and keep the slices immersed. Allow 1 in. (25 mm.) headspace, and freeze. Use, thawed, in cooked desserts. PURÉED Cook slices to a pulp in very little water. Sieve, and pack when cold in rigid containers. Leave ½ in. (12 mm.) headspace, and freeze.
Apricots	IN SUGAR Wash, cut in half and remove stones. Scald in boiling water for 1–2 minutes to prevent them becoming tough during freezing, and drop into water with ascorbic acid. Drain and dry. Pack in dry sugar in rigid containers, leaving ½ in. (12 mm.) headspace, and freeze. Use as a pie filling. IN SYRUP Pack either unpeeled halves, or peeled and sliced apricots, into rigid containers. Cover with a	light sugar syrup, adding 1½ tablespoons of lemon juice to every 2 pints (1 l.). Keep the apricots immersed, with 1 in. (25 mm.) headspace, and freeze. Use in fresh or cooked desserts. PURÉED Use over-ripe apricots. Peel, stone and slice the fruit before sieving. Sweeten to taste, and pack cold in containers, leaving ½ in. (12 mm.) headspace. Freeze.
Blackberries	DRY-FROZEN As for blueberries. IN SUGAR As for blueberries. IN SYRUP Cover the fruit with heavy sugar syrup and pack in rigid containers, leaving 1 in. (25 mm.) headspace. Freeze. Use in cooked desserts.	POACHED Simmer the cleaned fruit in a very little syrup for a few minutes. When cold, pack into rigid containers with ½ in. (12 mm.) headspace. Freeze, and use as pie fillings, and for fools and mousses.
Blueberries	DRY-FROZEN Pick over the fruit; wash and dry if necessary. Dry-freeze on trays, pack into heavy-duty polythene bags, seal, and store in the freezer. IN SUGAR Layer the prepared fruit with sugar in	rigid containers, leaving ½ in. (12 mm.) headspace. Freeze. Best used in pies and puddings. IN SYRUP Cover with light sugar syrup, pack with 1 in. (25 mm.) headspace, and freeze. Use in desserts.
Cherries	DRY-FROZEN Use red rather than black varieties. Make them firm by leaving in chilled water for 1 hour, then drain, dry and remove the stones. Pack in rigid containers – preferably made of plastic – with ½ in. (12 mm.) headspace, and freeze. Use freshly thawed.	IN SUGAR Pack cleaned, stoned fruit in plastic containers, layered with sugar. Leave ½ in. (12 mm.) headspace, and freeze. Use as pie fillings. IN SYRUP Freeze in light sugar syrup with the addition of 1½ tablespoons of lemon juice to every 2 pints (1 l.). Freeze, and use for pies and puddings.
Currants (black, red, white)	DRY-FROZEN Strip from the stalks, rinse and drain thoroughly. (A few sprigs of red currants may be frozen whole for use as garnishing.) Freeze in single layers on trays; when solid, pack in heavy-duty polythene bags. Use for fresh desserts, and in mousses and fools. Alternatively, pack in containers without any sugar. Freeze, leaving ½ in. (12 mm.) headspace. Use	for fresh desserts, fools, ices or cooked puddings. IN SUGAR Pack with dry sugar, leaving ½ in. (12 mm.) headspace. Freeze, and use in pies and puddings. PURÉED Cook black currants to a pulp, and sweeten. Pack in rigid containers, with ½ in. (12 mm.) headspace, and freeze. Use for sweet sauces, in puddings and in ices.
Damsons	DRY-FROZEN Wash in chilled water, cut into halves and remove the stones. The skins tend to toughen with freezing, so counteract this by using ascorbic acid in the chilling water. Dry, and pack in rigid containers with dry sugar. Leave ½ in. (12 mm.) headspace, freeze, and use for stewed desserts or pies. IN SYRUP Pack the prepared fruit halves in rigid	containers. Cover with cold, light sugar syrup, adding ½ teaspoon ascorbic acid to every 2 pints (1 l.). Leave 1 in. (25 mm.) headspace, freeze, and use cooked. PURÉED Cook in a little water, rub through a sieve and sweeten. Pack the purée in containers, leaving ½ in. (12 mm.) headspace, and freeze. Use for pies and fools. *Continued...*

AT-A-GLANCE GUIDE TO FREEZING FRUIT (continued)

FRUIT	METHODS OF FREEZING		
Figs	DRY-FROZEN Wash carefully, cut off stalks and dip the figs in chilled water. Avoid bruising when drying. Freeze, unpeeled, on trays and pack in heavy-duty	polythene bags. Thawed figs, peeled or unpeeled, may be served as a dessert. IN SYRUP Peel, pack into rigid containers and cover	with cold, light sugar syrup. Add 1½ tablespoons of lemon juice to every 2 pints (1 l.). Leave 1 in. (25 mm.) headspace. Freeze, and serve as a dessert in syrup.
Gooseberries	DRY-FROZEN Top and tail the berries, wash in chilled water and dry thoroughly. Place on trays and pack into polythene bags or containers, without sugar, and freeze. Use in pies. IN SUGAR Pack the prepared fruit in rigid containers,	layered with dry sugar and leaving ½ in. (12 mm.) headspace. Freeze, and use as pie fillings. IN SYRUP Pack in rigid containers, covered with cold sugar syrup made from 1 lb. (500 g.) sugar to 1 pint (600 ml.) water. Leave 1 in. (25 mm.) headspace, and	freeze. Use in cooked desserts. PURÉED Cook to a pulp in very little water; sieve and sweeten. Pack, when cold, in rigid containers with ½ in. (12 mm.) headspace, and freeze. Use for sauces, fools and mousses.
Grapes	Strip from the stalks, and freeze seedless varieties whole. Varieties with seeds, however, should be cut in	half and the seeds removed. Pack in rigid containers and cover with cold, light sugar syrup, leaving 1 in.	(25 mm.) headspace. Freeze, and use in fruit salads and jellies.
Greengages	As for damsons.		
Loganberries	DRY-FROZEN Rinse the fruit in chilled water, drain and dry. Freeze on trays, and pack in polythene bags. Use in fresh desserts. IN SUGAR Pack the prepared fruit in rigid containers	with dry sugar. Leave ½ in. (12 mm.) headspace. Freeze, and use as dessert fruits and in salads. IN SYRUP Pack in rigid containers. Cover with heavy sugar syrup, leaving 1 in. (25 mm.) headspace, and	freeze. Use in cooked desserts. PURÉED Rub the fruit through a fine nylon sieve, and sweeten the resulting purée to taste. Pack in rigid containers and freeze. Use for fools and mousses.
Melons	Peel, cut in half and remove the seeds. Cut into cubes or scoop into balls, and pack in rigid containers.	Cover with cold, light syrup, leaving 1 in. (25 mm.) headspace, and freeze. Use in fruit salads.	
Mulberries	As for loganberries.		
Peaches and nectarines	IN SUGAR Prepare quickly, as the fruits discolour fast. To facilitate peeling, drop them into hot water for 1 minute, peel, cut into halves and remove the stones. Leave in halves or slice; brush with lemon juice or drop into water with ascorbic acid. Drain, and dry on absorbent paper.	Pack in layers of sugar in rigid containers, and freeze. Use, nearly thawed, in fresh or cream desserts. IN SYRUP Pack halves or slices in rigid containers. Cover with cold, light sugar syrup, adding ½ teaspoon of ascorbic acid or 1½ tablespoons of lemon juice to every 2 pints (1 l.) of syrup. Leave 1 in. (25 mm.)	headspace, and freeze. Use in pies. PURÉED Simmer peeled halves in very little water, rub through a sieve and add 1 tablespoon of lemon juice to every 1 lb. (500 g.) of purée. Sweeten to taste, pack into rigid containers leaving ½ in. (12 mm.) headspace, and freeze. Use for sauces and soufflés.
Pears	Not really recommended for freezing as they discolour badly and become squashy. If frozen at all, prepare and pack as for apples in syrup.		
Plums	As for apricots. Thaw in closed containers and use at once, as the colour is quickly lost.		
Quinces	Peel, core and slice. Simmer until tender in water flavoured with orange and lemon juice. Lift out, drain	and dry. When cool, pack in rigid containers and cover with cold, heavy sugar syrup made from the	simmering liquid. Leave 1 in. (25 mm.) headspace, and freeze. Use with other fruits in pies and puddings.
Raspberries	DRY-FROZEN Hull, rinse, drain and dry the fruit. Freeze on trays and pack in rigid containers or polythene bags. Use in fresh desserts.	IN SUGAR Pack the prepared fruit in containers with dry sugar, and freeze. This is the best method; thawed fruit can be used cooked or uncooked.	IN SYRUP Pack the prepared fruit in rigid containers. Cover with cold, light sugar syrup, leaving 1 in. (25 mm.) headspace. Freeze, and use for cream desserts.
Rhubarb	DRY-FROZEN Wash, trim and cut stalks into 1 in. (25 mm.) lengths. Blanch in boiling water for 1–2 minutes. Drain, dry, pack in containers without sugar, and freeze. Use for stewed fruit and pies.	IN SYRUP Pack the prepared fruit in rigid containers and cover with cold, heavy sugar syrup. Leave 1 in. (25 mm.) headspace, and freeze. Use in pies, fools and crumbles.	PURÉED Cook, pulp and sweeten if liked. Pack in containers, leaving ½ in. (12 mm.) headspace, and freeze when cold. Use for sauces.
Strawberries	As for raspberries. Ripe berries may also be made into uncooked purée and packed in rigid containers. Leave ½ in. (12 mm.) headspace. Use for mousses and ice creams.		

FREEZING GARDEN VEGETABLES

Most summer vegetables can be frozen without too much trouble. Pick them when young and in prime condition, and process them as soon as possible. Among the few exceptions are salad vegetables, whose high water content makes them unsuitable for freezing.

All vegetables should be prepared in the same way as for cooking. They must then be blanched before freezing.

Blanching

Blanching is essential, as it inhibits the action of enzymes which would otherwise affect the colour, flavour and nutritional value.

Time it carefully – though over-blanching does less harm than too little – and blanch only 1 lb. (500 g.) of prepared vegetables at a time. Use boiling, lightly salted water to preserve the colour, and change it for every 6 lb. (3 kg.) of vegetables blanched.

To blanch a batch of vegetables, bring 6 pints (3 l.) of lightly salted water to the boil in a large pan. Put the prepared vegetables in a wire basket or muslin bag and plunge them into the pan. The heat should be high enough for the water to return to the boil in less than 1 minute. Cover the pan, and leave the vegetables in the boiling water for the recommended time (see pp. 303–5).

Lift out immediately, and transfer to a large bowl of cold water until cool – at least the same length of time as for blanching. Drain the vegetables thoroughly, and dry on kitchen paper or clean towels.

Pack the blanched, drained and dried vegetables either in rigid

BLANCHING VEGETABLES

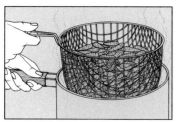

Plunge the basket or muslin bag containing the prepared vegetables into a large pan of boiling, lightly salted water.

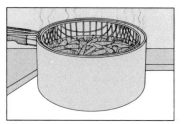

The heat must be high enough to bring the water back to the boil in 1 minute. Cover the pan, and boil for the recommended period.

Take the vegetables from the pan and transfer to a bowl of cold water. Leave to cool for at least as long as the boiling period.

Drain the vegetables thoroughly, and dry them on absorbent paper or towels before packing them in containers or polythene bags.

containers or in polythene bags. Remove as much air as possible from the bags, either by squeezing them before sealing or by gathering them at the top and sucking the air out through a straw.

Allow an average of 4 oz. (100 g.) per portion and pack the vegetables in two, four or six portions. Seal and label the packets and enter the details in the log-book.

Storing and cooking frozen vegetables

Most frozen vegetables will keep for 10–12 months in a domestic freezer. Cauliflowers should be used within six months and mushrooms within three months.

Most vegetables should be cooked while still frozen. Put them in a small amount of boiling, lightly salted water and bring back to the boil.

Many vegetables can also be steamed, but it is advisable to thaw them until they can be separated. They should also be partly thawed and separated for baking in the oven. Put the vegetables in a buttered ovenproof dish, with knobs of butter, and cook at 190°C (375°F) – gas mark 5 – for about 30 minutes.

Thaw sweet corn completely before cooking. Put the cobs in boiling water, and cook for 5–10 minutes after the water returns to the boil. Add salt when the cobs are half cooked.

Courgettes and mushrooms should be partially thawed, and fried gently in oil or butter.

Thaw potatoes, and warm through in hot water. Chips can be fried from the frozen state, but the amount of spluttering will be reduced if they are thawed first.

AT-A-GLANCE GUIDE TO FREEZING VEGETABLES

VEGETABLE	PREPARATION AND PACKING		BLANCHING TIME	COOKING TIME
Artichokes, Globe	Cut off the coarse outer leaves and the stems; trim off the tops and remove the chokes (see p. 79). Wash thoroughly, and	blanch with a few drops of lemon juice in the water. Cool and drain upside-down; pack in rigid containers.	5–7 minutes	Cook frozen for about 10 minutes, or until the leaves pull out easily.
Artichokes, Jerusalem	Not recommended for freezing as vegetables. Make them into	soup, freeze, and store as other cooked dishes.		
Asparagus	Wash thoroughly, cut off woody parts, and grade according to thickness. Trim to even lengths. Blanch, cool and drain. Tie in	bundles and pack in rigid containers, laying adjacent bundles tips to stalks. Separate the layers with waxed paper.	Thin stems: 2 minutes Thick stems: 4 minutes	Cook frozen for 5–8 minutes, depending on thickness.
Aubergines	Peel and cut into slices about 1 in. (25 mm.) thick. Blanch, cool, and dry thoroughly. Pack	in rigid containers, keeping the layers separate with waxed paper.	4 minutes	Cook frozen for 5 minutes.
Beans, Broad	Remove from the pods, grading to size and discarding old and	shrivelled beans. Blanch, cool and dry. Pack in bags or containers.	3 minutes	Cook frozen for 7–8 minutes.
Beans, French	Top and tail, wash and blanch. Cool, drain and dry. Grade	according to size, and cut large beans in half. Pack in bags.	2–3 minutes	Cook frozen for 7–8 minutes if whole; for 5 minutes if cut.
Beans, Runner	Top, tail and string. Wash, and cut into $\frac{1}{2}$ in. (12 mm.) pieces.	Blanch, cool, drain thoroughly and dry. Pack in polythene bags.	2 minutes	Cook frozen for 5 minutes.
Beetroot	Freeze only young, small beetroot about 3 in. (75 mm.) across. Wash carefully without breaking the skins and boil in water until tender. Cool under	cold running water; rub off the skins. Slice or dice and pack in rigid, lined containers with $\frac{1}{2}$ in. (12 mm.) headspace.		Store for no more than eight months. Thaw in containers and drain. Serve, dressed, with cold meats or salads.
Broccoli	Trim off the leaves and woody stems and wash thoroughly in salted water. Divide into sprigs. Blanch, cool, drain and dry.	Pack in cartons, tops to tails, and separate the layers with waxed paper.	3–4 minutes	Cook frozen for 5–8 minutes.
Brussels sprouts	Choose small, firm heads of uniform size. Remove the outer leaves, wash and blanch. Cool,	drain and dry. Pack in polythene bags.	3–4 minutes, according to size	Cook frozen for 8 minutes.
Cabbages (green and red)	Freeze only young, crisp cabbages. Trim off the outer leaves, wash, and cut into rough	shreds. Blanch, cool, drain and dry. Pack in polythene bags.	1½ minutes	Use within six months. Boil, frozen, for 8 minutes.

Continued . . .

AT-A-GLANCE GUIDE TO FREEZING VEGETABLES *(continued)*

VEGETABLE	PREPARATION AND PACKING	BLANCHING TIME	COOKING TIME
Carrots	Young carrots are best for freezing. Remove the tops, trim the roots, and wash. Blanch whole, cool, peel if necessary, drain and dry. Pack the whole carrots in polythene bags; or either slice or dice them and place in rigid containers with ½ in. (12 mm.) headspace.	4 minutes	Cook frozen for 8 minutes.
Cauliflowers	Freeze only firm, white cauliflowers. Break into small sprigs of uniform size, wash and blanch – add several drops of lemon juice to the water to preserve the colour. Cool, drain and dry thoroughly. Pack in rigid containers, separating the layers with waxed paper.	3 minutes	Use within six months of freezing. Cook frozen for 8–10 minutes.
Celeriac	Trim off the roots and tops. Scrub and cook in water until almost tender. Peel, cut into slices or sticks; cool, drain and dry. Pack into rigid containers, with waxed paper between the layers, allowing ½ in. (12 mm.) headspace.		Cook frozen for 8–10 minutes; or thaw in containers and use, dressed, as a salad.
Celery	May be frozen for cooking, but not for salads or eating raw. Cut off the roots and leaves; trim crisp stems, removing any strings. Scrub, and cut into 1 in. (25 mm.) pieces. Blanch, cool, drain and dry, retaining the blanching water. Pack in small bags or in rigid containers and cover with the strained blanching water. Leave ½ in. (12 mm.) headspace.	3 minutes	Thaw before cooking and add to soups and stews; or boil in the blanching liquid for 10 minutes and serve as a vegetable dish.
Chicory	Not suitable for freezing.		
Corn salad	Not suitable for freezing.		
Courgettes	Trim the ends from firm, young courgettes, wash and cut into ½ in. (12 mm.) thick slices. Blanch, cool, drain and dry. Alternatively, fry the slices in a little butter and cool quickly. Pack into rigid containers, separating the layers with waxed paper. Leave ½ in. (12 mm.) headspace.	1 minute	Thaw partially and fry in butter.
Cress	Not suitable for freezing.		
Cucumber	Not suitable for freezing.		
Endive	Not suitable for freezing.		
Fennel, Florence	Trim off the roots, wash, and cut into 1–2 in. (25–50 mm.) lengths. Blanch, setting the liquid aside. Cool and drain, pack into rigid containers and cover with the blanching water. Leave ½ in. (12 mm.) headspace.	3 minutes	Use within six months of freezing. Cook frozen in the blanching water for 30 minutes.

VEGETABLE	PREPARATION AND PACKING	
Kale	Not recommended for freezing.	
Kohl-rabi	Freeze small roots, no more than 2–3 in. (50–75 mm.) across. Trim off the root ends and tops, peel, dice large roots but leave small roots whole. Blanch, cool, drain and dry.	Pack whole kohl-rabi in polythene bags; pack diced kohl-rabi in rigid containers, leaving ½ in. (12 mm.) headspace.
Leeks	Remove the outer leaves; cut off the root ends and most of the green tops. Wash thoroughly and cut into 1 in. (25 mm.) lengths. Blanch, drain, cool and dry. Pack in small quantities in rigid containers.	
Lettuce	Not suitable for freezing.	
Marrows *(see also Courgettes)*	Not really suitable for freezing, unless quite young and tender. Peel, cut into ¾ in. (20 mm.) slices and blanch. Cool, drain and dry. Pack in rigid containers.	
Mushrooms	Freeze only freshly picked mushrooms. Wipe them clean and trim the roots. Leave whole or cut into slices, and fry lightly in butter. Cool quickly and pack into small, rigid containers with ½ in. (12 mm.) headspace.	
Onions	Although hardly worth freezing, they may be peeled, finely chopped or sliced and packed in small containers. Wrap the containers well to avoid the smell affecting other foods. Tiny onions may be peeled, blanched whole, cooked and dried. Pack in polythene bags.	
Parsnips	Trim the roots and tops of young parsnips. Peel and cut into slices, ½ in. (12 mm.) wide, or dice. Blanch, cool and drain. Pack in rigid containers with ½ in. (12 mm.) headspace.	
Peas	Shell young, sweet-tasting peas and grade according to size. Blanch, cool quickly, drain and dry. Leave mangetout peas in pods, and blanch. Pack garden peas in polythene bags; pack mangetout peas in rigid containers with ½ in. (12 mm.) headspace.	
Potatoes	Freeze small, new potatoes only, either raw or cooked. Scrape the potatoes, blanch (unless cooked), cool quickly, drain and dry. Pack in polythene bags. For chips, peel and wash firm potatoes, cut into uniform chips and part-fry in deep fat for about 3 minutes. Drain thoroughly and cool quickly. Pack in polythene bags.	

BLANCHING TIME	COOKING TIME
Whole: 3 minutes Diced: 1½ minutes	Cook frozen for 10 minutes.
minutes	Use within six months. Thaw in the container and use to flavour soups and stews.
minutes	Partially thaw in the container and steam until tender, or fry in oil
	Use within three months. Partially thaw in the containers; fry in butter, or grill.
Whole: 4 minutes	Use chopped raw onions, just thawed, in salads. Whole onions may be cooked frozen. Serve with a sauce, or add to stews.
minutes	Cook frozen for 10 minutes.
–2 minutes Mangetout: 2–4 minutes)	Cook frozen for 7 minutes.
3–4 minutes	Cook frozen (if blanched) for 15 minutes, or heat (if already cooked) in hot water. Partially thaw chips; fry for 3 minutes.

VEGETABLE	PREPARATION AND PACKING		BLANCHING TIME	COOKING TIME
Pumpkins and squashes	Not suitable for freezing.			
Radishes	Not suitable for freezing.			
Salsify and scorzonera	Not recommended for freezing, as they both discolour badly.			
Spinach	Trim stalks from young leaves, wash thoroughly and drain. Blanch in small portions, cool quickly and squeeze out surplus	moisture. Pack in rigid containers with ½ in. (12 mm.) headspace.	2 minutes	Cook frozen, with butter for 7 minutes.
Swedes	Not recommended for freezing.			
Sweet corn	Freeze only young cobs, with pale yellow kernels. Strip off the husks and tassels and trim the stalks close. Blanch a few at a time. Cool, drain and dry. Wrap each cob in foil or	freezer paper, pack in bags or containers, and freeze. Alternatively, scrape the kernels from the blanched cobs, and pack in rigid containers with ½ in. (12 mm.) headspace.	Small: 4 minutes. Medium: 6 minutes	Thaw completely, and boil for 5–10 minutes.
Sweet peppers	Keep green and red peppers separate. Wash, cut off stalk ends, de-seed, and remove membranes. Cut in half lengthways, for stuffing, or into narrow slices. Blanch, cool,	drain and dry. Pack in rigid containers, separating the sliced layers with waxed paper. Leave ½ in. (12 mm.) headspace.	Halves: 3 minutes. Slices: 2 minutes	Thaw halved peppers to be stuffed. Use slices, unthawed, to flavour stews and casseroles.
Tomatoes	May be frozen whole, but only for cooking afterwards. Best frozen as purée or juice. To freeze whole, wipe small, firm, ripe tomatoes and pack in polythene bags. For purée, wash the tomatoes. quarter them, simmer for 5 minutes, and rub through a nylon sieve. Cool and pack in	rigid containers with ½ in. (12 mm.) headspace. To prepare juice, wipe and core the tomatoes, cut in quarters and simmer for 10 minutes. Put through a sieve, season with salt. Peel, and pack in rigid containers with ½–1 in. (12–25 mm.) headspace.		Thaw whole tomatoes in the containers, slip off the skins and use in cooked dishes. Use frozen purée in sauces, soups and casseroles, thaw the juice in the containers and serve chilled.
Turnips	May be frozen fresh or cooked. Trim the roots and tops from young turnips. Peel, dice and blanch. Alternatively, cook the peeled and quartered turnips until tender, then drain and	mash. Cool, and pack in rigid containers with ½ in. (12 mm.) headspace.	2 minutes	Cook whole turnips without thawing for 8 minutes. Heat partially thawed, mashed turnips in a double boiler with butter.
Watercress	Not suitable for freezing.			

FREEZING FRESH HERBS

Home-grown herbs can be frozen, although they have a storage life of only six months. Also, since they become limp on thawing, they are unsuitable for garnishing.

Use them to flavour soups and stews by simply crumbling the frozen herbs into the dish to be cooked. There is no need to thaw them first.

Evergreen herbs are not worth freezing, as they are better used fresh. Some smaller herbs can be grown throughout the winter in pots on the kitchen window-sill, though you may choose to keep a small supply of frozen herbs in case the pot-grown herbs fail.

In general, freeze only those herbs that are most often required for cooking, such as basil, chives, mint, parsley and tarragon. Pick the herbs fresh, and keep them separate to prevent them imparting their flavours to one another. Wash, drain and dry thoroughly.

It is unnecessary to blanch herbs. Instead, divide them into sprigs and pack in polythene bags.

Herbs may also be frozen on trays, and packed in small portions to be used separately as required.

Yet another method is to chop the herbs finely and pack, with a little water, into ice-cube trays and freeze solid. Remove the frozen cubes and pack in bags in convenient portions. Use the cubes for flavouring while still frozen.

All herbs should be wrapped and sealed carefully to prevent other foods in the freezer taking up their scent or flavour.

As an extra precaution, store the packs of herbs in a container with a tight-fitting lid.

Using the freezer as a store cupboard

As well as storing fresh garden produce for later use, the freezer provides an ideal way to store cooked dishes, such as vegetable gratins and casseroles, fruit pies and fruit crumbles.

Left-overs can be made into purées by rubbing them through a sieve or blending them in the liquidiser. Use them later for making soups and sauces.

Cooked vegetables may be coated with a sauce, packed in rigid containers and frozen for later use. Leave ½ in. (12 mm.) headspace for expansion. If you are spending a whole day cooking, it is worthwhile to make extra quantities and store the surplus – when cold – in the freezer.

Home-made bread, wrapped and frozen as soon as it is quite cool, will taste newly baked when thawed.

Since most frozen fruits are intended to be used as pie fillings, it is a good idea to freeze both fruit and pastry together. Line aluminium-foil plates with pastry, and sweeten the fruit to taste with sugar. Add a little cornflour to prevent the pastry from becoming soggy.

If you are using very soft, juicy fruit, brush the pastry base with a little melted butter before adding the fruit. Cover with the top crust, wrap in strong freezer film and foil, and freeze.

To cook the frozen pie, first leave it to thaw at room temperature for 2–4 hours before slitting the top crust and baking.

The following recipes are only a small selection of the many fruit and vegetable dishes that can be cooked in advance and frozen.

RECIPES
for
quick-frozen fruit dishes

APPLE CHEESE CAKE

2 large cooking apples
12 oz. (350 g.) shortcrust pastry
½ lb. (250 g.) caster sugar
4 oz. (125 g.) butter
2 eggs
Juice and grated rind of 2 lemons

Line two foil flan cases, 8 in. (200 mm.) in diameter, with the pastry. Cream the sugar and butter, and mix with the beaten eggs. Chop and coarsely grate the peeled, cored apples, and add, with the butter and egg mixture, to the lemon juice and rind.

Fill the flan cases. Bake at 200°C (400°F) – gas mark 6 – for 20 minutes, then lower the heat to 180°C (350°F) – gas mark 4 – until set, which will take about 30 minutes. Cool, wrap in foil or polythene, and freeze.

BLACKBERRY FLAN

½ lb. (250 g.) rich shortcrust pastry
¾ lb. (375 g.) blackberries
6 oz. (175 g.) sugar
2 tablespoons cornflour

Roll out the prepared pastry. Fit it into an 8 in. (200 mm.) flan ring lined with foil. Prick the pastry base and bake blind at 200°C (400°F) – gas mark 6 – for about 25 minutes. Remove from the oven and leave to cool, then wrap the flan, still in its foil case, in plastic film and foil, and then freeze.

Hull and rinse the blackberries, put them in a pan with the sugar and just under ½ pint (300 ml.) of water. Bring to the boil and simmer for 10–15 minutes, or until the berries are soft but not broken up. Stir the cornflour with a little of the juice, and blend into the blackberries. Simmer gently until thickened.

Cool the berries quickly, then pack into a rigid container, leaving ½ in. (12 mm.) headspace. Wrap and freeze.

Both the pastry case and filling will store in the freezer for up to six months. To use, thaw the flan case in its wrapping, at room temperature; then fill with the blackberries, gently heated, and put in the oven for 15–20 minutes at 200°C (400°F) – gas mark 6 – to heat through. Serve with cream.

CHERRY FLAN

5 oz. (150 g.) plain flour
3 oz. (75 g.) softened butter
1 egg yolk
8 oz. (250 g.) stoned black cherries
4 oz. (125 g.) ground almonds
4 oz. (125 g.) icing sugar
2 eggs

To make the pastry, put the flour in a bowl. Make a well in the centre, add the butter and egg yolk, and work together with your fingertips to a smooth paste.

Leave the pastry to relax for 15 minutes, then roll out and line an 8 in. (20 cm.) flan ring.

Prick the pastry case, and fill with the stoned cherries. Mix the ground almonds and sugar together. Beat the eggs, and add

them to the almonds and sugar. Pour over the cherries.

Bake for 30 minutes at 200°C (400°F) – gas mark 6. Cool, and freeze when cold.

EVE'S PUDDING

1½ lb. (750 g.) cooking apples
Juice of 1 lemon
3 oz. (75 g.) demerara sugar
Almond essence
3 oz. (75 g.) caster sugar
3 oz. (75 g.) butter
2 eggs
3 oz. (75 g.) flour
Salt

Peel, core and thinly slice the apples, and brush with lemon juice. Put the apple slices in a greased 2 pint (1 l.) pudding basin and sprinkle with demerara sugar, mixing it thoroughly with the apple slices. Add a few drops of almond essence.

Cream the caster sugar and butter until fluffy, then gradually beat in the lightly beaten eggs and finally fold in the flour, sifted with a pinch of salt. Spoon this mixture over the apples. Tie the pudding basin down with greaseproof paper, foil and string, allowing room for expansion. Freeze until solid and store for up to six months.

To use, steam the pudding from the frozen state for about 2 hours, turn out and serve.

Gooseberries, stoned apricots, damsons and plums can be prepared, frozen, and steamed in the same way, although a true Eve's pudding is always made with apples.

PEACH CRÈME BRULÉE

6 peeled peaches
Caster sugar
Whipped cream
Soft brown sugar

Slice the peeled peaches and sweeten to taste with caster sugar. Arrange in a foil dish and cover with whipped cream. Freeze and wrap.

To serve, leave to thaw for about 4 hours at room temperature, or for 6 hours in the refrigerator. Sprinkle the cream thickly with brown sugar and place under a hot grill for a few minutes, until the sugar has melted.

RASPBERRY CREAM

1 lb. (500 g.) raspberries
Juice of ½ lime
4 oz. (100–125 g.) sugar
½ pint (300 ml.) double cream
2 tablespoons icing sugar

Rub the raspberries through a sieve and mix in the lime juice and sugar, stirring until this has dissolved.

The raspberry purée may be mixed with cream before freezing, but this reduces the storage time. It is a better idea to freeze the purée in a rigid container, when it will keep for at least six months.

To use, thaw the purée at room temperature. Whip the cream with the icing sugar until fairly stiff. Blend in the raspberry purée, spoon into glasses and chill for 1 hour. Decorate with toasted hazelnuts before serving.

RASPBERRY JAM, UNCOOKED

2 lb. (1 kg.) raspberries
4 lb. (2 kg.) caster sugar
1 bottle commercial pectin
4 tablespoons lemon juice

Crush the fruit and stir in the sugar. Leave for about 1 hour in a warm room, stirring the mixture until the sugar has dissolved. Add the pectin and lemon juice, and stir for 2 minutes. Pour into small pots and cover with lids or foil. Leave in a warm place for two days and then freeze.

Thaw for use as required, but once opened use within a few days.

STRAWBERRY ICE CREAM

1 lb. (500 g.) strawberries
4 oz. (125 g.) icing sugar
2 teaspoons lemon juice
Double cream

Stalk the strawberries, wash if necessary, and drain well. Rub them through a nylon sieve, measure the purée. Stir in the icing sugar and lemon juice. Whisk an even quantity of double cream until floppy, and fold into the strawberry purée.

Freeze, stirring occasionally during the first 2 hours.

Best stored in a plastic container in the freezer.

RECIPES
for
quick-frozen vegetable dishes

ARTICHOKES À LA GRÈCQUE

4–6 globe-artichoke fonds (see p. 79)
5 fl. oz. (125–150 ml.) olive oil
Juice of 1 small lemon
Bouquet garni
8 coriander seeds
8 peppercorns
Salt

Put 2 pints (1 l.) of water in a pan, with the oil, lemon juice, bouquet garni, spices and salt. Bring to the boil and simmer for 5 minutes. Add the quartered artichoke fonds and cook for 20 minutes. Cool, and freeze in cartons with ½ in. (12 mm.) headspace.

Serve these pickled artichokes as a chilled hors-d'oeuvre. Thaw in the containers, strain, and arrange on small plates.

Sprinkle with paprika.

ASPARAGUS VOL-AU-VENTS

1 lb. (500 g.) prepared puff pastry
1 egg white
6 oz. (175 g.) cooked asparagus tips
½ pint (300 ml.) Béchamel sauce

Roll out the pastry, ½ in. (12 mm.) thick, cut into 3 in. (75 mm.) rounds and hollow out the centres. Set the cases on a moist baking sheet, brush with beaten egg white and bake for 20 minutes at 230°C (450°F) – gas mark 8. Leave the pastry cases to cool, then pack

in rigid containers, interlaced with waxed paper, and freeze.

Fold the asparagus tips into the Béchamel sauce; cool and freeze separately in a plastic container.

Thaw the vol-au-vent cases in their containers at room temperature for about 4 hours, then heat through in the oven. Heat the frozen asparagus filling over gentle heat, correct the seasoning and spoon into the cases. Snip a little parsley over the top.

BAKED CUCUMBER

2 cucumbers
Salt
Juice of 1 lemon
1 tablespoon sugar
1 tablespoon finely chopped parsley, chives or basil
2 oz. (50 g.) butter

Peel the cucumbers, cut in half lengthways, scoop out the seeds and cut the flesh into cubes. Sprinkle with salt, lemon juice and sugar and leave for 1 hour.

Drain, and place in an ovenproof dish. Sprinkle with the herbs, add knobs of butter and bake at 220°C (425°F) – gas mark 7 – for 30 minutes, turning from time to time. Cool, and freeze in cartons with ½ in. (12 mm.) headspace.

To serve, thaw before heating at 180°C (350°F) – gas mark 4.

BASIC ONION SAUCE

1 lb. (500 g.) onions
2 level tablespoons cornflour
½ pint (300 ml.) milk
½ chicken stock cube

Peel the onions and chop finely. Place in a saucepan and cover with water. Bring to the boil, then drain. Return the onions to the pan, cover with fresh water, and simmer until tender. Drain, and reserve ½ pint (300 ml.) of the liquid. Mix the cornflour with milk to make a smooth paste.

Place the remaining milk, the onion water, and the crumbled stock cube in a saucepan and bring to the boil. Pour on to the cornflour paste, stirring at the same time, return to the saucepan. Add the drained onions, and cook for 2–3 minutes, stirring all the time.

Allow to cool, covering the surface with a dampened circle of greaseproof paper.

Pour into containers and freeze. Add extra seasoning, if needed, when re-heating for use.

BEAN AND BACON POT

8 oz. (250 g.) broad beans, shelled
8 oz. (250 g.) potatoes
1 large parsnip
2 carrots
2 medium onions
8 oz. (250 g.) bacon
½ pint (300 ml.) tomato juice, fresh or tinned
Salt and pepper
2 tablespoons Worcestershire sauce – optional

Place the beans in a casserole, and add the peeled and diced potatoes, parsnip and carrots. Add the peeled and sliced onions. Dice the bacon and fry briskly for 1 or 2 minutes to seal. Add to the casserole with the tomato juice, and salt and pepper to taste. Cover and cook at 180°C (350°F) – gas mark 4 – for 1¼ hours. Cool and freeze. When thawed and re-heated, add the Worcestershire sauce.

BRUSSELS SPROUTS AU GRATIN

6 lb. (3 kg.) Brussels sprouts
2 pints (1 l.) white sauce

Cook the prepared sprouts and drain thoroughly. Arrange in foil dishes and cover with sauce, leaving ½ in. (12 mm.) headspace. Freeze when cool.

To serve, warm through in the oven, then brown under the grill after topping with grated cheese and knobs of butter.

CELERY AND LEEK CASSEROLE

2 large heads of celery
8 leeks
½ lb. (250 g.) chopped bacon
4 oz. (125 g.) butter
2 oz. (50 g.) flour
2 pints (1 l.) white stock
Salt and pepper

Prepare the celery and leeks and cut both into 1 in. (25 mm.) pieces.

Continued . . .

Quick-frozen vegetable dishes (continued)

Fry the leeks and bacon in the butter until golden, stir in the flour and cook for about 5–10 minutes. Gradually add the stock, bring to the boil and simmer until smooth.

Blend in the celery and season with salt and pepper. Cook in a foil-lined casserole for 45 minutes in the oven at 180°C (350°F) – gas mark 4. Cool and freeze.

COURGETTES PROVENÇALE

3 lb. (1.5 kg.) courgettes
Salt and pepper
Seasoned flour
6–7 tablespoons cooking oil
1½ lb. (750 g.) onions
2½ lb. (1.25 kg.) tinned tomatoes
Juice of 1 lemon
4 oz. (125 g.) grated Parmesan cheese

Cut the washed but unpeeled courgettes into 1 in. (25 mm.) slices, sprinkle with salt and leave for 5 minutes. Wipe dry, and coat with seasoned flour.

Fry in 4 tablespoons of the oil until golden, then drain. Fry the sliced onions in the rest of the oil.

Put layers of courgettes, onions and sliced tomatoes in a foil-lined casserole, seasoning each layer and sprinkling with lemon juice; finish with a layer of tomatoes. Cover and freeze overnight; remove from casserole, wrap and seal.

To cook, set the foil mould in the original casserole and bake in the oven at 190°C (375°F) – gas mark 5 – for 1¼ hours. Sprinkle with the cheese; brown under the grill.

LEEKS PROVENÇALE

4 lb. (2 kg.) leeks
1 tablespoon olive oil
1 lb. (500 g.) tomatoes
4 oz. (125 g.) black olives
Juice and grated rind of 2 lemons

Clean the leeks and cut into 1–2 in. (25–50 mm.) lengths. Fry in the oil for 10 minutes, then add the peeled and chopped tomatoes, stoned olives, lemon juice and rind. Season to taste and cook for a further 10 minutes. Cool and freeze in rigid containers, leaving ½ in. (12 mm.) headspace.

To serve, thaw in the containers and serve chilled as an appetiser.

ONIONS IN WHITE SAUCE

2 lb. (1 kg.) pickling onions
2 oz. (50 g.) butter
2 oz. (50 g.) cornflour
1 pint (600 ml.) white stock
½ pint (300 ml.) milk
Salt and pepper

Make a white sauce from the butter, cornflour, stock and milk. Season with salt and pepper.

Blanch the onions in boiling water for 2 minutes and refresh in cold water. Put them back in the pan with cold water to cover, bring to the boil and simmer until tender. Drain, and add to the white sauce. Cool, and freeze in waxed cartons or plastic boxes.

Thaw at room temperature in the containers and heat through gently before serving.

PANCAKES STUFFED WITH MUSHROOMS

4 oz. (100–125 g.) plain or self-raising flour
Salt and pepper
1 egg
½ pint (300 ml.) milk
1 oz. (25 g.) butter
1 tablespoon flour
8 fl. oz. (225 ml.) single cream
1 tablespoon sherry
1 tablespoon chopped parsley

Make up a batter from the flour – sifted with a pinch of salt – the egg and the milk, and bake eight pancakes. Leave the pancakes flat, to cool, interspersed with waxed paper.

Trim the mushrooms and slice thinly. Melt the butter and fry the mushrooms lightly, then stir in 1 tablespoon of flour and gradually blend in the cream. Bring to the boil and season lightly with salt and pepper. Remove from the heat and stir in the sherry and parsley.

Spread the mushroom filling over the pancakes, roll them up and arrange in a rigid container or an ovenproof dish. Double wrap with foil, and freeze. Store for up to two months.

To use, heat the pancakes from the frozen state for about 1¼ hours at 200°C (400°F) – gas mark 6. After 1 hour, sprinkle the pancakes with finely grated cheese and return to the oven until golden-brown.

Pancakes can also be filled with creamed spinach, asparagus, cauliflower or broccoli in a rich velouté sauce.

PIPERADE

1 lb. (500 g.) tomatoes
2 onions
4 peppers
3 tablespoons oil
Salt and pepper

Peel and slice the onions, de-seed the peppers and cut them into

PASTA SAUCE

1 lb. (500 g.) minced beef
1 large onion
2 tablespoons olive oil
6 large tomatoes
1 small green pepper
4 oz. (125 g.) mushrooms
½ pint (300 ml.) beef stock
5 fl. oz. (150 ml.) red wine
2 tablespoons tomato paste
2 tablespoons oregano or basil
Salt and pepper

Fry the beef and finely chopped onion in the oil for 5 minutes, or until the meat has browned and separated into grains. Add the peeled and chopped tomatoes, the de-seeded pepper and the chopped mushrooms, together with the stock and red wine. Bring to the boil over gentle heat, stir in the tomato paste and oregano and season with salt and pepper.

Simmer for about 45 minutes, then cool and spoon into rigid containers. Wrap, and freeze solid, and store for up to three months.

To use, cook slowly from the frozen state, adding a little more stock if necessary and, if you wish, seasoning with crushed garlic and more herbs. Use as a meat sauce with pasta dishes.

strips, and skin the tomatoes. Heat the oil in a heavy pan, add the onions and fry them gently until golden. Add the peppers and cook for about 15 minutes, until soft.

Add the tomatoes, cover the pan and cook for a further 30 minutes, stirring often to prevent sticking. Leave to cool, then pour into rigid containers, seal, label and freeze.

Piperade is delicious with pasta. Or, add 2 beaten eggs per person and cook in the same way as scrambled eggs.

POTATO AND CUCUMBER PIE

1 lb. (500 g.) potatoes
8 oz. (250 g.) cucumber
1 oz. (25 g.) butter or margarine
1 oz. (25 g.) flour
½ pint (300 ml.) milk
Salt
Large pinch cayenne pepper
2 or 3 eggs
4 oz. (125 g.) grated cheese

Thinly peel and dice the potatoes and cucumber. Cook in salted water for 5 minutes until just tender, and drain well.

Make a sauce with the butter, flour and milk, season to taste with salt and add the pepper. Hard boil the eggs, shell and chop roughly. Add the potatoes, cucumber and chopped eggs to the sauce and simmer gently for 5 minutes. Turn out into a greased heat-proof dish and cool before freezing.

To serve, thaw, cover with the cheese. Heat through, then flash under the grill to brown the top.

PUMPKIN SOUP

1 lb. (500 g.) pumpkin
2 large leeks
1 lb. (500 g.) tomatoes
2 oz. (50 g.) butter
2 tablespoons vegetable oil
2 pints (1 l.) chicken stock
Salt and pepper

Peel and dice the pumpkin. Wash the leeks thoroughly and slice thinly. Skin the tomatoes and slice them.

Melt the butter in a saucepan and add the oil. Add all the vegetables, and cook slowly for 10 to 15 minutes, stirring occasionally. Add the stock, and continue cooking slowly until vegetables are tender. Liquidise or sieve, then cool and freeze in cartons.

Season to taste when re-heating for use.

RATATOUILLE

2 lb. (1 kg.) tomatoes
Salt and pepper
1 large or 2 medium marrows
8 small aubergines
2 red or green peppers
4 chopped onions
2 or 3 garlic cloves
Bacon fat

Skin the tomatoes, halve, sprinkle with salt and drain – cut side down. Cut the peeled marrow into large chunks, discarding the seeds. Cut the aubergines in half lengthways and slice across.

Trim the bases off the peppers, remove the seeds and membranes, and slice.

Fry the onions with the crushed garlic in a little bacon fat. Add all the vegetables, season highly and simmer, covered, for about 30 minutes, until tender. Cool, pack in rigid containers with ½ in. (12 mm.) headspace, and freeze.

To serve hot, partially thaw and heat through gently.

To serve cold, thaw in the refrigerator for 4 hours.

SAVOURY BEETROOT

2 oz. (50 g.) butter
1 large onion
1 lb. (500 g.) beetroot
1 large cooking apple
¾ lb. (375 g.) potatoes
Salt and pepper
3 tablespoons wine vinegar
1 heaped teaspoon sugar

Melt the butter in a frying pan, add the peeled, finely chopped onion. Cook gently until soft.

Peel the raw beetroot and grate into the pan. Peel the apple and grate into the pan. Stir around in the butter, then add the peeled and diced potatoes.

Season to taste, then add the vinegar and sugar. Stir, then cover the pan and cook *slowly* until the mixture is tender. Stir or shake the pan occasionally.

Cool before freezing.

TOMATO PROVENÇALE

2 lb. (1 kg.) tomatoes
Salt and pepper
½ tablespoon finely chopped basil or parsley

4 garlic cloves
4 finely chopped onions
4 heaped tablespoons of breadcrumbs
2 tablespoons olive oil

Cut the tomatoes in half and sprinkle with salt and pepper. Mix the herbs, crushed garlic and onions with the breadcrumbs. Cover each tomato half with the mixture and sprinkle with a little oil. Grill for 20 minutes. Wrap, pack in containers and freeze.

To serve, cook frozen for 30 minutes in the oven at 190°C (375°F) – gas mark 5.

VEGETABLE PIE

1 onion
1 turnip
2–3 carrots
2 leeks
3 sticks of celery
2 oz. (50 g.) butter
¾ pint (450 ml.) parsley sauce
1 small can of butter beans
8 oz. (250 g.) shortcrust pastry

Chop the prepared vegetables. Melt the butter in a pan, add the vegetables and cook gently for 10 minutes; the vegetables should be soft, but not browned. Make the parsley sauce (see p. 222) and season well. Stir in the vegetables, juices and butter beans.

Put the mixture into a 1½ pint (850 ml.) pie dish and top with pastry or mashed potato. Freeze until hard, place in a polythene bag, seal and label. Return to the freezer, use within 2 months.

VEGETABLE SOUP

2 leeks
2 carrots
½ celeriac
1 small cauliflower
2 oz. (50 g.) butter
1 oz. (25 g.) flour
1 pint (600 ml.) white stock or bouillon
Salt and pepper

Prepare the cleaned vegetables, cutting the leeks, carrots and celeriac into narrow slices and dividing the cauliflower into florets.

Melt the butter in a pan and sweat the vegetables until soft, then stir in the flour and cook to a roux. Gradually blend in the stock.

Simmer, covered, until the vegetables are tender, season lightly with salt and pepper and leave to cool. Blend the soup in the liquidiser until smooth and creamy, and leave to cool completely.

Pour the soup into rigid plastic containers, leave ½–¾ in. (12–20 mm.) headspace, and seal. Freeze solid and store for up to three months.

To use, heat the frozen soup gently, adding milk to the required consistency, and correct the seasoning.

WINTER SOUP

3 to 4 heads of celery
8 oz. (250 g.) parsnips
8 oz. (250 g.) turnips
8 oz. (250 g.) onions
4 pints (2 l.) chicken stock
6 black peppercorns
1 bay leaf
4 oz. (125 g.) mushrooms – optional

Prepare the celery, and slice thinly. Peel the parsnips and turnips, and cut into dice. Peel and slice the onions. Put the stock and all the vegetables in a large saucepan and add peppercorns and bay leaf tied in muslin.

Bring to the boil, then simmer for 30 minutes. Add the cleaned and thinly sliced mushrooms, and simmer for a further 10 minutes.

Cool, and remove the muslin bag. Freeze in cartons, allowing ½ in. (12 mm.) head space.

Makes a filling supper dish when served with croutons.

Preserving summer fruit by bottling

Apart from freezing, bottling is the only method of preserving food in which the natural taste and texture of the produce are retained almost intact. The process, which is not a difficult one, is basically that of packing fruit into bottling jars, covering the contents with water, syrup or brine, sterilising them at high temperatures, then sealing the jars while still hot to prevent the entry of bacteria.

Good results depend upon careful adherence to the rules – especially those concerned with cleanliness – and upon using the correct equipment and selecting high-quality produce.

Equipment

Bottles While good results can sometimes be achieved with improvised equipment, special preserving bottles with tops held on by screw-bands or spring-clips are strongly recommended. They are available in sizes ranging from 1–4 lb. (0.5–2 kg.).

Whether held in position by a screw-band or by a spring-clip, the tops of both types consist of metal or glass discs to which rubber gaskets are attached. When placed on top of the bottles the tops form an air-tight seal, whose purpose,

once the air has been driven from the bottle by heating, is to create a germ-proof vacuum.

The slightest flaw in the rubber, or fault in a metal top, will destroy this effect, so spoiling the contents of the jar.

For this reason, the tops cannot be used more than once; and even then they should be inspected carefully. Additional tops may be purchased separately from the jars. If these are stored they should be kept in air-tight boxes, with a little talcum powder rubbed into the gaskets to keep them supple.

The modern jam jars which have twist-on tops with integral gaskets can also be used. These are useful if small quantities of fruit are required, and they have the advantage of fitting easily into an ordinary deep saucepan or pressure cooker. New lids should be used each time. The lids are placed on loosely, and tightened down after processing, except in the oven method when they are fitted afterwards.

Closures for ordinary rimmed jam jars, consisting of preserving caps with replaceable gaskets, are also available, sold under various trade names.

Sterilising pans A large, deep pan is needed for the processing of bottled fruit. Purpose-built sterilisers, complete with false bottoms, thermometers and lids, can be bought, but they are expensive.

Any deep vessel – such as a galvanised bucket or a large preserving pan – will serve equally well for the purpose. Whatever the vessel used, it should be deep enough to incorporate a false bottom – a grill pan or a thick layer of newspaper – and at the same time contain sufficient water to reach the level of the liquid in the jars.

Taking the temperature If you use the slow water-bath method of sterilising, it is necessary to use a thermometer. The best, specially made for bottling and jam-making, registers up to 110°C (230°F).

Packing Wooden bottling spoons with long handles and small bowls may be used to pack the produce into the containers. But smooth, clean, round-ended sticks will serve just as well.

Handling the bottles A pair of bottling tongs – non-slip grips attached to a steel spring – are almost indispensable when removing the heated bottles from the sterilising pan.

Checking and preparing the bottles

Before using either type of bottle, check the rim carefully for chips, as even the smallest will prevent an efficient seal.

See that metal lids are not distorted or scratched, and that the screw-bands are not too loose or the spring-clips weakened. Discard any rubber rings that show signs of drying or cracking. They will not make an efficient seal.

Test the jars and lids by filling the jars with water, putting on the lids and turning the jars upside-down.

If there is any sign of leakage after 10 minutes, the bottle or fittings are suspect.

Wash the jars thoroughly, and boil them for 5 minutes in a pan which has either a built-in false bottom or contains a grid or a thick pad of newspaper. Invert the jars to drain; but do not dry them, since it is easier to pack fruit into wet bottles.

Soak the rubber rings in warm water for 15 minutes, then dip them in boiling water immediately before putting them on. This will make the rings more supple.

BOTTLING FRUIT

Bottling is one of the best methods of storing fruit, since in most cases it will preserve the colour and flavour almost unimpaired. Success, however, depends on strict adherence to the rules.

STEP 1
Preparing the fruit

The fruit should be fresh and just ripe, and free from the slightest sign of disease or decay. The importance of inspecting the produce for bottling cannot be overstressed. All types of fruit are suitable for storing in this way, provided they are prepared correctly before being packed into bottles.

Apples Peel, core and slice, and put straight into lightly salted water to prevent discoloration. Rinse before packing; or blanch for 2–3 minutes in boiling water until pliable, then pack.

Apricots Either bottle the fruits whole, or cut them into halves and remove the stones. Bottle quickly after preparing, and include a few kernels.

These will help to bring out the flavour.

Cherries Bottle whole fruits, or stone them first, and add any juice to the syrup. As sweet cherries are low in acid, add ¼ teaspoon citric acid to every 1 pint (600 ml.) of syrup.

Damsons, plums As a general rule, bottle these and other stone fruits whole after washing them. However, very large plums may be halved and stoned if preferred.

TWO KINDS OF JARS FOR BOTTLING

SCREW-TOP JARS *The metal lid, with rubber gasket attached, is held in place with a screw-top. Jars are made in several sizes.*

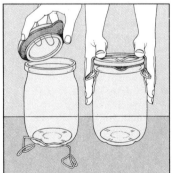

CLIP-ON JARS *In this type, the glass top with detachable rubber ring is secured by a spring until the vacuum has been formed.*

Figs These may be peeled or left with their skins on. Add ½ teaspoon citric acid to every 1 pint (600 ml.) of syrup, and use equal amounts of syrup and fruit.

Gooseberries Only unripe gooseberries are suitable for bottling. Top and tail with scissors.

Peaches Halve and stone the peaches, blanch, and peel off the skins. Pack without delay.

Pears Peel, halve and core dessert varieties, putting them straight into cold, lightly salted water with 1 teaspoon of citric acid. Rinse and pack quickly.

Treat cooking pears and quinces similarly, but simmer in syrup until soft before packing.

Rhubarb Cut trimmed rhubarb into 2 in. (50 mm.) pieces. This fruit will pack better if soaked overnight in hot syrup.

Soft fruits Fruits such as black-berries, currants, loganberries, mulberries and raspberries should be picked over, hulled or stripped from the stalks. Rinse if necessary, and drain well.

Strawberries are not always successful, but their flavour can be improved by soaking them over-night in warm bottling syrup (see Step 2), and the appearance improved by adding a few drops of red food colouring to the syrup.

Tomatoes Tomatoes are bottled in the same way as fruits.

Clean the ripe, firm tomatoes and bottle in a brine solution made from ½ oz. (15 g.) salt to 2 pints (1 l.) cold water. Tomatoes may also be peeled and packed tight without liquid, but sprinkled with 1 teaspoon of salt and ½ teaspoon of sugar for every 1 lb. (500 g.) of fruit.

STEP 2
Making the syrup

Although water can be used for bottling, syrup gives a better flavour and colour. The strength of the syrup varies according to the type of fruit, averaging about 7–8 oz. (200–250 g.) of sugar to every 1 pint (600 ml.) of water.

Add the sugar, preferably granulated, to half the water and boil for 1 minute before adding the rest of the water.

Sometimes the syrup is poured cold over the fruit and sometimes it is used hot; if the latter, put a lid on the pan.

Honey or golden syrup can be substituted for sugar, but they will impart their own flavours to the fruit. Strain all types of syrup before using.

STEP 3
Packing the fruit

Pack the prepared fruit carefully into the wet bottles. Try to choose fruits of uniform size, and use a bottling spoon or stick to pack them in tightly without damaging them. A 1 lb. (500 g.) bottle will hold about 10–12 oz. (275–350 g.) of most types of fruit.

If syrup is to be added before processing it can be poured in when the bottle is full of fruit. It is easier, however, to pack the fruit and syrup in layers. Release any air bubbles by inserting a steri-lised knife blade down one side of the bottle, or by jerking the jar. Top up with syrup until the fruit is covered.

STEP 4
Sterilising the fruit

There are four methods of sterilising bottled fruit:

The slow water-bath – the most reliable method, but a thermo-meter is required.

The quick water-bath method is a good second choice, and there is no need to use a thermometer.

The oven method – no special equipment is needed, but it is difficult to gauge the correct temperature, and this may result in some failures.

Pressure-cooking is a quick and economical method, but it is easy to overcook the fruit.

Slow water-bath method Slacken screw-bands off a quarter of a turn to allow steam to escape during processing. Spring-clips are designed to permit this to happen without being loosened.

Place the bottles on the false bottom – a wire grill or thick layer of newspaper – and put folded cloth or newspaper between the bottles to prevent them touching as the water boils.

Fill the pan with cold water until the bottles are completely submerged, cover with a lid and heat the pan slowly. After 1 hour the water should just be reaching 55°C (130°F). After a further 30 minutes the water should reach the recommended temperature (see chart).

At all stages, check the tem-perature regularly with a thermo-meter.

When the bottles have been kept at the correct temperature for the exact time, remove them from the pan with bottling tongs, or bale out sufficient water to enable

BASIC STEPS IN BOTTLING FRUIT

Continued . . .

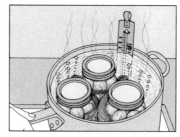

1. Preparing the fruit *Carefully select blemish-free fruits. Wash them scrupulously; then peel, core and chop them as advised for the fruits you are bottling.*

2. Making the syrup *For an average syrup, add ½ lb. (250 g.) of sugar to each ½ pint (300 ml.) of water used. Boil for 1 minute, then add the same amount of water again.*

3. Packing the fruit *Place fruits in wet jars, pour syrup over them and release any air bubbles with a carefully inserted knife. Top up with syrup and loosely screw on lids.*

4. Sterilising the fruit *Place the bottles on the false bottom of the pan, keeping them separate with newspapers or cloth. Pour cold water into the pan to cover the bottles.*

5. Testing the seal *Screw down lids and leave to cool overnight. Test vacuum by removing screw bands and lifting by the sealed lids. If lid comes away, use contents at once.*

WATER-BATH METHOD

Tongs are useful when removing the bottles from the bath. Otherwise, the boiling water must be bailed out before lifting them.

you to pick them out with a cloth. As each jar is removed, place it on a dry, wooden surface – it is liable to crack on a metal surface – and tighten the screw-bands at once. Check the tightness as the bottles cool, and screw down further if necessary.

The table of processing temperatures and times is for 2 lb. (1 kg.) bottles, which are the most practical. For 4 lb. (2 kg.) bottles add 5 minutes, and for bottles

---

Bottling fruit (continued)

6. Storing bottled fruit Coat the inner sides of the screw-bands with oil and replace them. Wipe any stickiness from the jars, label them and store in a cool, dark cupboard.

---

holding up to 6 lb. (3 kg.) add 10 minutes.

Solid-packed tomatoes are a special case. Give 4 lb. (2 kg.) bottles an extra 10 minutes, 6 lb. (3 kg.) bottles an extra 20 minutes.

Quick water-bath method Fill the warm bottles with prepared fruit and pour in hot syrup up to the brim. Cover the bottles and place them in a pan in which a false bottom has been created with a wire grill or with thickly folded sheets of newspaper. Pack further layers of newspaper or cloth between the bottles to prevent them banging together.

Add warm water to cover the jars, and heat the water slowly so that it reaches simmering point after 30 minutes. Continue simmering for 2–50 minutes (see chart).

Remove the bottles and tighten screw-tops.

Pressure-cooker method A suitable pressure cooker can be used

---

EQUIPMENT

Bottles and tops
Bottling tongs or thick cloth
Screw-bands or spring-clips
Wooden spoon
Asbestos mat (oven method)
Pressure cooker (pressure-cooker method)
Thermometer (slow water-bath method)
Steriliser (optional, for water-bath methods)
Sterilising pan (water-bath methods)

---

for bottling fruit, provided it is deep enough to take the bottles together with the same kind of improvised false bottom described above.

The cooker must also be able to maintain a steady pressure of 5 lb. per sq. in. (low).

Pack the fruit into warm bottles and cover with boiling syrup to within ½ in. (12 mm.) of the top. Put on the tops, leaving the screw-bands slightly loose. Pour about 1 in. (25 mm.) of boiling water into the pressure cooker and add a little vinegar to prevent staining. Set the bottles on the false bottom, and separate them with cloth or newspaper.

Fasten the lid and heat gently with the vent open until steam jets out in a steady stream. Close the vent and bring up the pressure to 5 lb. per sq. in. (low). The time taken from the start of heating until pressure is reached should not be less than 5 minutes, nor more than 10 minutes.

For apples, rhubarb, all soft fruits, cherries, damsons, greengages and plums, hold the pressure for 1 minute. Extend this to 3–4 minutes in the case of apples if these are tightly packed, and also for halved apricots and plums.

Figs, pears and whole tomatoes need 5 minutes; solid-packed tomatoes, 15 minutes.

Remove the pressure cooker from the heat, but leave it for 10 minutes before opening the vent. The sterilising process is still continuing during this time. Lift the bottles on to a dry wooden surface and tighten screw-bands.

Oven method – dry pack Pack the prepared fruit into the jars and cover them with saucers or plates.

BOTTLING FRUIT BY WATER-BATH METHODS
TIME CHART

The following times and temperatures are those recommended for 2 lb. (1 kg.) bottles. If 4 lb. (2 kg.) bottles are used, add 5 minutes. For 6 lb. (3 kg.) bottles, add 10 minutes. Double these times if tomatoes are being processed.
Whether by the slow or quick method, sterilising times are reckoned from the moment the water reaches simmering point.

FRUIT	TEMPERATURE	STERILISING TIME in minutes	
		Slow method	Quick method
Apples, packed solid	82°c (180°F)	15	20
Apples, sliced	74°c (165°F)	10	2
Apricots, whole and halved	82°c (180°F)	15	10
Blackberries	74°c (165°F)	10	2
Cherries, whole and stoned	82°c (180°F)	15	10
Currants	74°c (165°F)	10	2
Damsons, whole	82°c (180°F)	15	10
Figs	88°c (190°F)	30	40
Gages, whole	82°c (180°F)	15	10
Gooseberries, dessert	82°c (180°F)	15	10
Gooseberries, green	74°c (165°F)	10	2
Loganberries	74°c (165°F)	10	2
Mulberries	74°c (165°F)	10	2
Nectarines, halved	82°c (180°F)	15	20
Peaches, halved	82°c (180°F)	15	20
Pears	88°c (190°F)	30	40
Plums, halved and stoned	82°c (180°F)	15	20
Plums, whole	82°c (180°F)	15	10
Raspberries	74°c (165°F)	10	2
Rhubarb	74°c (165°F)	10	2
Strawberries	74°c (165°F)	10	2
Strawberries, syrup-soaked	82°c (180°F)	15	20
Tomatoes, solid pack	88°c (190°F)	40	50
Tomatoes, whole	88°c (190°F)	30	40

Do not add any syrup or fit on the lids, screw-bands or spring-clips.

Place the bottles in the centre of an oven heated to 120°C (250°F) – gas mark ½, on a mat of asbestos, thick cardboard or newspaper. Leave 2 in. (50 mm.) between the bottles, and between the sides of the oven and the bottles. Process for the time indicated on the chart.

If different fruits are being processed at the same time, set jars with large fruits near the sides of the oven, jars with smaller fruits in the centre.

Remove the bottles one at a time, topping up from one bottle if any shrinkage has occurred; pour boiling syrup over immediately, filling the bottles to the brim.

Dip the lids in boiling water and place them immediately on the

BOTTLING FRUIT IN THE OVEN
TIME CHART

The lower range of processing times (in minutes) is for quantities of up to 4 lb. (2 kg.), and the higher range for larger quantities of up to 10 lb. (5 kg.).

FRUIT	WET PACK in minutes	DRY PACK in minutes
Apple rings	30–40	Not recommended
Apples, solid packed	50–60	Not recommended
Apricots, halved	50–60	Not recommended
Apricots, whole	40–50	Not recommended
Blackberries	30–40	45–55
Cherries, whole	40–50	55–70
Currants	30–40	45–55
Damsons, whole	40–50	55–70
Figs	60–70	80–100
Gages, whole	55–70	Not recommended
Gooseberries, green	45–60	60–75
Loganberries	45–60	60–75
Mulberries	45–60	60–75
Nectarines, halved	65–80	Not recommended
Peaches, halved	65–80	Not recommended
Pears	60–70	Not recommended
Plums, halved	65–80	Not recommended
Plums, whole	55–70	Not recommended
Raspberries	45–60	60–75
Rhubarb, dessert	40–50	55–70
Rhubarb (for pies)	45–60	60–75
Strawberries, soaked	50–60	Not recommended
Tomatoes, solid-packed	70–80	Not recommended
Tomatoes, whole	60–70	80–100

THE OVEN METHOD

The advantage of this method is that, apart from a sheet of asbestos laid over the oven shelf, no special equipment is required.

bottles. Screw down the retaining bands or apply the spring-clips, and leave the bottles to cool on a warm, dry surface.

Success with this method depends on filling the bottles and sealing them as quickly as possible after taking them from the oven.

Oven method – wet pack Pack the prepared fruit into warm jars and fill to within 1 in. (25 mm.) of the brim with boiling syrup. Put on the lids, but not the bands or clips.

Place in the oven as for the dry-pack method and sterilise at 150°C (300°F) – gas mark 2, for the time advised in the table. Remove the bottles and fit the screw-bands or spring-clips immediately.

Leave the bottles to cool on a wooden surface.

STEP 5
Testing the seal

Whatever method is used, allow the bottles to cool completely – preferably overnight. Remove the screw-bands or spring-clips and test each bottle by picking it up with your fingertips, holding it by the lid only.

If the seal works, the vacuum inside the bottle will hold the lid securely. If the seal is faulty, the lid will come away.

Should the lid give way, examine the bottle to discover the cause. Chipped jars, distorted tops or perished rubber seals may all give rise to trouble; such damaged articles should be rejected.

STEP 6
Storing bottled fruit

If the seal is perfect and a vacuum has been created, it is hardly necessary to replace either screw-bands or spring-clips. These can be used in further bottling operations. Spring-clips should not be replaced, since it will weaken them; screw-bands may be, but if this is done the inner surface should first be lightly coated with oil.

Wipe off any sticky marks and label the bottles to show the type of fruit, the date of bottling and the covering liquid used. Store in a cool, dry, dark and well-ventilated place.

To open bottled fruit, stand the jar in hot water for a few minutes and gently prise off the lid with the tip of a knife.

Bottling fruit pulps and purées

Mis-shapen but otherwise sound fruits can be preserved in pulp form for use as pie or pudding fillings. This is a highly economical method of storing fruit for winter use, since quite large quantities will reduce to a comparatively small bulk.

Pick over and prepare the fruit according to type; simmer in a little water until thoroughly cooked. Pour into hot bottles while the fruit is still boiling hot; seal at once, using lids and gaskets dipped in boiling water immediately beforehand.

Sterilise the bottles by the quick water-bath method. Bring the water to the boil, and hold at boiling point for 5 minutes. When cold, check that the seal is air-tight, using the method already described.

Alternatively, make fruit purées by rubbing the cooked pulp through a nylon sieve and sweetening them to taste.

Bottle and process in the same way as for fruit pulps.

Grated lemon rind adds flavour to apple purée. Season tomato purée to taste with salt, and sterilise for 10 minutes.

Bottling fruit in brandy

The most popular fruits for this treatment are cherries, small plums, damsons, peaches and pears. Prepare them as for the water-bath method, and prick firm-skinned fruit with a stainless-steel fork so that the syrup is able to permeate the flesh.

Make a fairly heavy syrup from 1 lb. (500 g.) of sugar to 2 pints (1 l.) of water. Cook the syrup until thick, measure it, and when it is cool add an equal quantity of brandy.

Pack the fruit into bottles and fill up with the cold brandy syrup, then process by the slow water-bath method.

The dry-pack oven method can also be used, but to prevent evaporation the brandy must be added to the boiling syrup immediately before pouring it over the fruit.

Things that can go wrong

Over-heating, or too-rapid heating at the beginning of processing, may cause the fruit to rise or sink in the bottles. The same faults may occur if over-ripe fruit is used, or the contents of the bottles are packed too loosely. When fruit rises in the bottles, this may indicate that the syrup is too heavy.

Air bubbles will appear in newly bottled fruit if they have not been released before processing. This is sometimes difficult to avoid, but the bubbles can be dislodged by knocking the jar several times against the palm of the hand.

Mould is due to insufficient or too-quick sterilising, or to a poor seal. Fermentation occurs in over-ripe fruit and may also take place in fruit that has not been sterilised sufficiently.

Fruit spoiling in storage may also be due to insufficient heat, too short a heating period, or to an ill-fitting seal.

Bad flavour or colour is usually due to processing unripe fruit, or to over-cooking.

Making jams from garden fruits

Despite the advent of freezers, jam-making is still far and away the most popular means of preserving fruit. Few occupations in the kitchen are more absorbing or satisfying, and there are fewer still in which the end product is so much better than any that can be bought from a shop.

Though the price of sugar has risen sharply in recent years, jams made from your own garden produce are also much cheaper.

Jams have so many uses that it is well worth making them in large quantities. As well as being the traditional accompaniment to bread and butter, home-made scones and pancakes, they also provide the fillings for sponge cakes, sweet omelettes, tartlets and biscuits. Baked and steamed puddings, trifles and ice-cream sauces are given new interest by home-made jams.

Jam-making is not difficult; but to achieve the finest clarity, colour and consistency, while retaining the true fruit flavour, needs strict adherence to the rules.

Above all, choose the fruit carefully. It is upon this that success or failure really depends.

Equipment

Jam can be made using only the tools and utensils found in the average kitchen. However, if you intend making it in large quantities – and to continue doing so each year – you will find it more convenient to buy the correct equipment. This can be used not only for jams, but also when making jellies, pickles, chutneys and other kinds of preserves.

Preserving pans The most useful piece of equipment is a preserving pan. A heavy-based saucepan can be used for small amounts of fruit, but a good-quality preserving pan will hold larger quantities and, once bought, will last for a lifetime.

Pans made of heavy aluminium or stainless steel are best. Tin-lined copper, unchipped enamel and Monel-metal preserving pans may also be used, but not iron or zinc pans. Copper or brass pans are suitable for most jams and jellies, but as these metals are affected by acids, they cannot be used for pickles and chutneys.

The pan should be heavy-based to prevent burning the contents, wide for effective evaporation, and deep enough to prevent the fruit boiling over.

Bowls and basins Both will be needed for the prepared fruit. Earthenware, enamel or plastic receptacles are all suitable.

Sieves and strainers These, too, are necessary. Nylon or hair sieves are preferable to those made of metal.

A measuring jug An essential item, which ideally should be of heat-proof glass with fine gradations. Most jugs now have both imperial and metric markings. Enamel and stainless-steel jugs are also useful, but plastic jugs should be used only for cool and non-acid liquids.

Measuring cups and spoons It is useful to have a small measure such as a plastic measuring cup for mixing baby food, or the standard 5 ml. spoon that is often provided with medicines.

Cutlery spoons vary in capacity, although both British Standard and metric standard sizes are available.

Scales Next to a good preserving pan, accurate scales are the most important tool in the jam-maker's kit of equipment.

The scale dial, preferably in dual imperial and metric markings, should be set to zero before the ingredients are weighed.

Some preserving recipes specify very small amounts – of spices, for example. Scales for measuring minute quantities can be bought, but in most cases the exact amount is not critical. As a guide, a level standard teaspoon equals 5 ml., or 2.5–3.5 g., of most spices in powder form.

In using any recipe which gives dual quantities – that is, both metric and imperial – it is essential to follow either one or the other – not to mix them. Thus, if the equipment has imperial markings and gradations, use only imperial weights and measures – and vice versa for metric markings.

This is because conversions are always approximate, making it inadvisable to use a mixture of imperial and metric quantities.

Spoons A long-handled wooden spoon is needed for stirring the contents of the preserving pan, and a slotted stainless-steel spoon is ideal for removing scum from the cooked jam.

If you use knives and peelers with stainless-steel blades the fruit will not become discoloured. In addition, there are special tools for coring apples and pears, removing the stones from cherries, and pulping fruit for purées.

A wide-necked funnel This piece of equipment makes it easy to fill jam-jars without splashing, and also to transfer dry ingredients

BASIC STEPS IN JAM-MAKING

1. Preparing the fruit *Select firm fruit that is only just ripe. If necessary, mix fully ripened fruit with it, but avoid over-ripe fruit. Wash, trim and remove stalks and cores.*

2. Softening the fruit *Add water as necessary. Bring to the boil and simmer gently until fruit is reduced to a pulp. If necessary, add acid fruit juice or citric acid.*

3. Adding pectin *Remove the pan from the heat and test the pectin content (see p. 316). If this is low, add pectin-rich fruit juice or commercial pectin to ensure a good set.*

4. Adding the sugar *Warm the sugar and add it to the fruit, using exact amount stated in recipe. Stir in sugar and heat to boiling point. Continue boiling for 3–20 minutes.*

from packets to other containers.

Special jam-jar fillers, made in metal or heatproof glass, are sold. They are designed so that the jam can be scooped up without burning the fingers.

Thermometers A sugar thermometer is useful for gauging the correct setting point.

This metal-cased instrument, which clips on to the side of the pan, should be warmed in hot water before being placed in the hot jam. Most jams have reached setting point when the thermometer registers 105°C (220°F).

Jam-jars and covers Jars specially made for bottling can be used for jam, but jars which previously contained honey, coffee or jam are suitable provided they are scrupulously cleaned – and, preferably, sterilised in boiling water – before use.

For covering the jars, packs containing waxed sealing discs, Cellophane covers and rubber

bands are sold. But as the bands may gradually become slack it is better to secure the Cellophane covers with fine string.

Alternatively, use air-tight, lined screw-caps, Porosan preserving skins, or greaseproof paper dipped in egg white.

STEP 1
Preparing the fruit

Select fresh, firm and just-ripe fruit. A mixture of under-ripe and ripe fruit can be used to make up the quantities for a recipe, but avoid using over-ripe fruit since it will have lost much of its pectin content.

This substance, which is found in the cell walls of fruit, forms a jelly when boiled with sugar and causes the jam to set. According to the type of fruit, the cells also contain varying amounts of acid, which help in releasing the pectin.

Wash and pick over the fruit, and discard any that are decayed, squashy or over-ripe.

Remove the stems and cores

PREPARING FRUIT FOR JAM-MAKING

 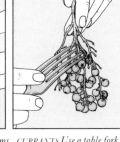 

SOFT BERRIES Remove stems and cores from soft fruits, such as strawberries.   *CURRANTS Use a table fork to strip currants and elderberries from the stalks.*   *APPLES AND PEARS For jam-making, these fruits must be peeled, cored and quartered.*

CHERRIES Remove stones with either a sharp knife or with a patent stone remover.   *STONE FRUITS Cut apricots, peaches and plums into halves and remove stones.*   *HIPS Remove the seeds from halved rose-hips with the handle of a teaspoon.*

from soft berries such as strawberries and blackberries. Top and tail gooseberries. Strip currants and elderberries from the stalks, and peel, core and quarter apples and pears.

Cherries may be left whole, or the stones removed before or after cooking. Halve and stone plums, apricots and peaches.

Some people like the nutty taste of fruit kernels, and a few stones may be split, the kernels extracted and cooked with the fruit – allowing six per pound of jam.

STEP 2
Softening the fruit

After this initial preparation, the next step is to pre-cook the fruits in order to soften their skins, evaporate some of the moisture and break down the cell walls. Water is generally added, depending on the juiciness of the fruit, the type of pan and stove being used, and the amount of fruit being processed.

As a rough guide, no water is necessary with juicy fruits such as strawberries, raspberries, blackberries, loganberries, red currants and rhubarb.

But other fruits do require water in varying amounts. Weigh the fruit, and to plums and apples add half their weight of water. Pears and quinces need an equal weight. Evaporation is quicker in wide or shallow pans, so use more water and extra acid.

Bring the fruit to the boil and simmer gently until it has reduced to a pulp, and diminished by about one-third. Do not stir the fruit during cooking.

Fruit in a deep pan or in a thick layer needs a slightly longer cooking time, as does fruit that is unripe or wet.

5. *Testing for setting point* *Boil for a few minutes, remove from heat and test for setting (see p. 316). If necessary, return to heat and test again a few minutes later.*

6. *Removing the scum* *Once setting point is reached, remove jam from heat, leave to stand for a few minutes, then gently remove any scum with a perforated spoon.*

7. *Potting and storing* *With a cup or jug pour jam into warmed jars and cover immediately with a waxed disc and a Cellophane cover, secured with a rubber band.*

> ### EQUIPMENT
> *Preserving pan*
> *Bowls or basins*
> *Sieves and strainers*
> *Measuring jug and spoons*
> *Scales*
> *Long-handled wooden spoon*
> *Knives and peelers*
> *Perforated spoon*
> *Jam-jar filler*
> *Wide-necked funnel*
> *Thermometer*
> *Jam-jars and covers*

If the stove gives a low heat intensity, this must also be allowed for during cooking.

Adding acid The acid contained in the fruit cells is released during the preliminary cooking, but some fruits – sweet apples, bilberries, blackberries, cherries (except 'Morello' cherries), peaches, pears, quinces, raspberries and strawberries – are low in acid.

Add acid to these fruits by any of the following methods:

To every 2 lb. (1 kg.) of fruit add 3 fl. oz. (90 ml.) red-currant or gooseberry juice, or 1 fl. oz. (30 ml.) lemon juice (which roughly equals 2 tablespoons), or ½ teaspoon citric acid.

STEP 3
Adding pectin

Before the sugar is added, but after the fruit has been reduced, it is necessary to determine the pectin content of the pulp. You may have to add further pectin before achieving a perfect set in the finished jam.

To test for pectin, take 1 teaspoon of fruit juice from the pan, and put it in a glass to cool. Add 3 teaspoons of methylated spirit and shake the mixture well.

After 1 minute, pour it gently into another glass.

If the jam juice has formed a single, large clot it contains a high amount of pectin; a few, smaller clots indicate a sufficient or fair pectin content, while a large number of small clots shows that the fruit needs added pectin.

After some experience, you will know in advance which fruits are naturally low and high in pectin, and you can therefore take the necessary action before you begin cooking the fruit. This involves adding either lemon juice, or a high-pectin fruit, to fruit in which pectin is scarce.

Cooking apples are high in pectin, and combine well with low-pectin fruits such as cherries and blackberries. Red currants, too, have a high pectin content and are often mixed with raspberries and strawberries, which are unlikely to set on their own.

If it becomes obvious, after carrying out the pectin test on softened fruit, that the jam has a low pectin content, pectin stock or commercially prepared pectin – in liquid or powder form – can be added.

Pectin stock is made from apple, red-currant or gooseberry juice. Place the prepared fruit in a pan with about ¾ pint (450 ml.) of water to every 2 lb. (1 kg.) of fruit, and simmer until tender. Strain, and set the juice aside.

The following day, cook the pulp again with half the original amount of water. Simmer for about 1 hour and strain.

Mix the two batches of juice together. Bottle and sterilise the

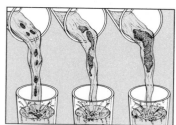

TESTING FOR PECTIN

Low pectin is shown by a large number of very small clots (left). A few small clots (centre) show that it is adequate; a single large clot that pectin is high.

pectin stock if it is not needed for immediate use. To sterilise, fill heated preserving jars with boiling juice and immerse in boiling water for 5 minutes.

Commercially prepared pectin should be added according to the manufacturer's instructions. Do not be tempted to add too much, or the flavour of the jam will be spoiled.

In general, use 4–8 fl. oz. (125–250 ml.) of liquid pectin, or ½ oz. (15 g.) powdered pectin, to every 2 lb. (1 kg.) of fruit.

STEP 4
Adding the sugar

Always use exactly the amount of sugar specified by the recipe. Too little sugar will result in the jam setting poorly; too much will have the same effect, as well as ruining the fruit flavour.

The type of sugar used in jam-making is unimportant, and there is little difference between results obtained with preserving, caster, lump or granulated sugar. (Brown sugars, however, will flavour the jam.)

Lump and preserving sugar cause less scum. Preserving sugar dissolves more quickly than granulated, but is more expensive.

The amount of sugar needed for setting depends on the amount of pectin present. For fruits with plenty of pectin, allow one-and-a-half times the amount of sugar to fruit. For example, with 2 lb. (1 kg.) black currants, use 3 lb. (1.5 kg.) sugar.

If the test shows that there is just enough pectin, use equal amounts of sugar and fruit. Add pectin to low-pectin fruits.

The best combination of flavour, setting and keeping qualities is obtained in a jam which contains 60% of added sugar. Thus, 10 lb. (5 kg.) of jam should use up 6 lb. (3 kg.) of sugar.

If 6 lb. (3 kg.) of sugar is used and the end result is more than 10 lb. (5 kg.) of jam, fermentation may result.

Before the sugar is added to the softened fruit it should be heated gently in the oven, to avoid lowering the temperature of the jam. Stir the jam constantly while gradually adding the sugar, and continue stirring until it has dissolved completely. Increase the heat, and bring the jam rapidly to boiling point.

Keep the jam boiling quickly until setting point is reached – after 3–20 minutes, according to the type of fruit. Do not stir more than is necessary to prevent the jam at the bottom of the pan from burning.

The heat should be high enough to keep the jam bubbling while being stirred.

On the other hand, too much stirring will mix the rising scum into the jam. If this happens, a knob of butter or a few drops of glycerine added to the jam will help to reduce the scum.

Boil only until setting point is reached. If boiled too little the jam will not set; if boiled too much it will become sticky and dark and lose much of its flavour.

STEP 5
Testing for setting point

To test for setting, remove the pan from the heat a few minutes after the jam reaches boiling point. There are several ways of testing for setting: the flake test, the cold-saucer test and the temperature test being the most practicable.

Flake test Stir the jam and scoop a little on to a wooden spoon. Allow a moment to cool the jam, and then turn the spoon on its side to allow the jam to run off.

If the jam has been boiled enough to set, drops of jam will run together and fall off in large flakes. If several thin flakes run off the spoon in quick succession, the jam has not been boiled enough.

Cold-saucer test Spoon a little jam on to a cold saucer and leave to cool. If setting point has been reached, a skin will form over the surface and should wrinkle when pushed.

In hot weather, placing the saucer in the refrigerator for a minute or two will speed the setting process.

Temperature test Heat a sugar thermometer in hot water, then put it in the jam. Stir the jam gently with the thermometer for a moment or two to ensure an accurate reading.

If the temperature reads 105°C (220°F), the jam has probably reached setting point. But to be on the safe side, carry out one of the other tests as well as a double check.

STEP 6
Removing the scum

The jam is ready for potting when it has reached setting point. Take the pan from the heat and leave the jam to settle for 10–15 minutes; do not stir it during this time.

Afterwards, remove scum with a perforated spoon, then drop in a walnut-size knob of butter to get rid of any traces that still remain.

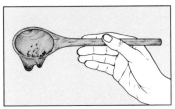

FLAKE TEST Scoop a little jam on to a spoon (top picture), allow it to cool, then turn the spoon on its side. If the jam is setting, it will run together and fall in large flakes.

SAUCER TEST Allow a little jam to cool on a cold saucer. If setting point is reached, a skin will form on the jam's surface. This will wrinkle when pushed with the finger.

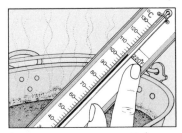

TEMPERATURE TEST Heat a thermometer in hot water and dip it in the jam. Setting generally occurs at 105°C (220°F). Double-check with a different test.

STEP 7
Potting and storing

Having given the hot jam a final stir, pour it into clean, warm and dry jars, filling them right to the top. A wide-necked funnel is useful to minimise drips and spills. Wipe off any jam on the outside of the jars and cover the surface immediately with a waxed disc – wax side down. Make sure that it lies level.

Wipe the rims of the jars and cover while still hot with Cellophane, greaseproof paper or parchment, folded down over the neck and tied securely. To ensure an air-tight seal, the cover must be put on while the jam is hot.

Label each jar with the name and date. For large-scale jam-making, it is helpful to keep a log-book of each batch and to identify the batch on the labels. If something should go wrong in storage, you will then be able to check on the amounts of sugar and fruit used in that group.

When potting whole fruit, such as strawberries, the fruit should remain evenly distributed – neither floating to the top nor settling on the bottom. Even distribution is more likely if the jam is allowed to cool in the pan until a skin forms.

Correct storage conditions are essential. The ideal store is dry, dark, cool and well ventilated, but protected from frost.

Low-sugar jams

Jams with less than the usual amount of sugar can be made from fruits with good setting qualities. The proportions are 1½ lb. sugar to 2 lb. fruit (750 g. to 1 kg.). The jam will keep for only a few weeks unless stored in air-tight jars, and

once opened will remain in good condition for only ten days to a fortnight. The set will be less firm than usual.

Make the jam as already described, and test for setting by either the flake or the cold-saucer test. Pot at once in clean, hot jars and seal.

If bottling jars are used, the keeping quality of the jam can be improved by sterilising the jars in boiling water for 5 minutes.

Jams from preserved fruit

Bottled fruit (see pp. 309–12) that has become mis-shapen or discoloured, or whose preserving fluid is losing its clarity, can be used for making jam, though you may not obtain so good a set as with fresh fruit. This, however, can be corrected by adding commercial pectin.

Pour the fruit and preserving liquid together into a pan and, by fast boiling, reduce the amount of fluid by half. Add roughly 50% of the sugar specified in the recipe for making jam from fresh fruit, and

continue boiling until the sugar is dissolved.

Test for setting after a few minutes and, if there is no sign of this taking place, add the commercial pectin according to the manufacturer's instructions on the bottle.

Though excellent results can be obtained in this way, jams made from bottled fruits are unsuitable for storing; so use them straight away.

Home-frozen fruit can also be made into jam, although the pectin content of soft-setting fruits, such as strawberries, may have diminished, and it is advisable to pay special attention to the pectin test.

Allow for any pectin deficiency by using 10% more fruit than specified, or use the same amount of fruit with 10% less sugar to give a lower yield. Alternatively, add pectin stock.

Things that may go wrong

However, in spite of careful attention to every stage of jam-

POTTING AND COVERING JAM

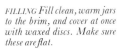

FILLING Fill clean, warm jars to the brim, and cover at once with waxed discs. Make sure these are flat.

COVERING While still hot, cover the jars with Cellophane or parchment. Secure with string or a rubber band.

LABELLING Trim the covers, wipe the jars, and fix labels stating the type of jam and the date it was made.

making, the finished jam may sometimes be disappointing.

By identifying the cause, the same mistake can be avoided next time you make jam.

Mould Possible causes are insufficient cooking at the preliminary stage, resulting in too little sugar in proportion to fruit. The jam may have been stored in a damp or warm place.

Mould may also occur if the jam was sealed while only warm, not hot, or if the cover was loose.

Fermentation Tiny bubbles in the jam show that it is fermenting. This indicates that there is too little sugar; that the jam was stored in a warm place; or that the pots were loosely sealed.

Crystallisation This is generally a sign that the jam is lacking in acid, or contains too much sugar. Crystallisation is caused by cooking the jam too little or too much after adding the sugar; or by adding the acid after the sugar has been added.

Poor setting Probably due either to insufficient pectin in the fruit or ineffective release of the pectin. This may happen if the fruit is not reduced sufficiently before the sugar is added, or if the jam is over-cooked or under-cooked afterwards.

Alternatively, the jam may contain too much sugar in relation to its acid and pectin content; or the vital acid may have been omitted.

Shrinkage This is due to evaporation caused by loose covering or storage in a warm place.

RECIPES
for
home-made jams

Recipes containing 6 lb. (3 kg.) each of fruit and sugar yield about 10 lb. (5 kg.) of jam. Where smaller amounts of these ingredients are used, yields will be reduced in proportion.

APPLE JAM

6 lb. (3 kg.) sharp cooking apples
2 pints (1 l.) water
2 level tablespoons citric acid
12 cloves
6 lb. (3 kg.) sugar
Red colouring (optional)

Wash, dry and slice the apples, but do not peel or core. Simmer to a pulp, with the citric acid and cloves tied in a muslin bag.

Remove the cloves; sieve and weigh the pulp. Return to the pan, with 1½ lb. of sugar to every 2 lb. of pulp (750 g. to 1 kg.).

Stir until dissolved, and boil rapidly to setting point. Add a few drops of colour, if required; pot and cover.

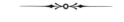

APPLE AND DATE JAM

To every 1 lb. (500 g.) of peeled, cored and sliced cooking apples, add 6–8 oz. (175–250 g.) of stoned dates, 1 lb. (500 g.) of sugar and the juice and grated rind of 1 lemon.

Place the apples in a pan with the rind and lemon juice, and cook gently until soft. Add the sugar and stir until dissolved. Add the chopped dates, simmer gently until thick, then pot in warmed jars and cover while hot.

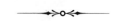

APPLE GINGER JAM

6 lb. (3 kg.) apples
2 pints (1 l.) water
2 oz. (50 g.) ground ginger
Grated rind and juice of 4 lemons
1 lb. (500 g.) crystallised ginger
6 lb. (3 kg.) sugar

Peel, core and slice the apples. Put the peel and cores in a large muslin bag and place, with the apples, in the preserving pan, adding the ground ginger and the lemon rind and juice.

Simmer until tender, then remove the muslin bag. Add the finely chopped ginger and sugar. Stir until the sugar has dissolved, then boil rapidly to setting point. Pot and cover.

APRICOT JAM

6 lb. (3 kg.) apricots
1 pint (600 ml.) water
6 lb. (3 kg.) sugar

Wash, halve and stone the apricots. Remove a few kernels and blanch in boiling water. Simmer the apricots with the water and kernels until the fruit is tender and the contents have reduced by about half. Add sugar, stir until dissolved and boil to setting point.
Variation To make jam from dried apricots, soak 2 lb. (1 kg.) of fruit in 6 pints (3 l.) of water for 24 hours. Simmer the apricots in the water in which they were soaked for about 30 minutes before adding 1 teaspoon of citric acid and 6 oz. (175 g.) of blanched almonds. Stir in 6 lb. (3 kg.) of sugar and boil to setting point.

BLACKBERRY JAM

6 lb. (3 kg.) blackberries
5 fl. oz. (150 ml.) water
Juice of 2 lemons, or 1 teaspoon citric acid, or ½ pint (300 ml.) apple-pectin stock
6 lb. (3 kg.) sugar

Hull and pick over the berries; rinse and drain carefully. Put in a pan with the water, lemon juice or citric acid. If pectin stock is used, add it with the sugar after the preliminary cooking.

Simmer until the berries are soft, then add the sugar and stir until dissolved. Boil rapidly to setting point.

BLACKBERRY AND APPLE JAM

4 lb. (2 kg.) blackberries
1½ lb. (750 g.) peeled and cored cooking apples
½ pint (300 ml.) water
6 lb. (3 kg.) sugar

Simmer the cleaned blackberries in half the water until soft, and simmer the chopped apples separately in the remaining water. Mash both to a pulp. Mix the two fruits, add the sugar and stir until dissolved. Boil rapidly to setting point.

For seedless jam, strain the blackberry pulp before mixing the juice and purée with the softened apples. Use 25% less sugar than for whole-fruit jam.

BLACKBERRY AND ELDERBERRY JAM

3 lb. (1.5 kg.) cultivated or wild blackberries
3 lb. (1.5 kg.) elderberries (prepared weight)
6 lb. (3 kg.) sugar
½–¾ pint (300–450 ml.) water

Simmer the stemmed and washed elderberries in the water until soft and pulpy; rub through a sieve to remove the seeds. Return the pulp to the pan, with the hulled and rinsed blackberries, and simmer for about 10 minutes or until soft.

Add the warmed sugar, stir until dissolved, then boil rapidly until setting point is reached.

BLACK-CURRANT JAM

4 lb. (2 kg.) black currants
3 pints (1.5 l.) water
6 lb. (3 kg.) sugar

Stem the currants, wash and drain carefully, put the fruit in a pan with the water and simmer until reduced by almost half. Stir frequently to avoid burning.

Add the sugar, stirring until dissolved; boil rapidly until setting point is reached.

CHERRY JAM

5 lb. (2.5 kg.) stoned, red cherries
Juice of 2–3 lemons, or 1 teaspoon citric acid
3½ lb. (1.75 kg.) sugar

Simmer the cherries for 30 minutes with the juice or citric acid, and with some stones tied in a muslin bag. Remove the stones, add the sugar and stir until dissolved. Boil rapidly to setting point.

CHERRY AND RED-CURRANT JAM

4 lb. (2 kg.) dark cherries (weight after stoning)
2 lb. (1 kg.) red currants
½ pint (300 ml.) water
6 lb. (3 kg.) sugar

Wash and stone the cherries, strip the currants from the stalks and rinse them. Simmer both with the water for 30 minutes, or until soft. Stir in the sugar; when dissolved, boil rapidly to setting point.

DAMSON JAM

5 lb. (2.5 kg.) damsons
1½–2 pints (850 ml.–1 l.) water
6 lb. (3 kg.) sugar

Wash and dry the damsons; put in a pan with the water and simmer until pulpy. Remove the stones. Stir occasionally. Add the sugar, and when dissolved boil quickly until setting point is reached.

GOOSEBERRY JAM

4½ lb. (2.25 kg.) gooseberries
1½ pints (850 ml.) water
6 lb. (3 kg.) sugar

Top and tail the gooseberries, then wash and drain them thoroughly. Put in a pan with the water and simmer gently until the skins burst and the fruit has reduced to a pulp.

Add the sugar, stirring until dissolved, then boil to setting point.
Variation Add a dozen elderflower heads, tied in a muslin bag, to the simmering fruit. Remove before adding the sugar.

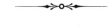

GREENGAGE JAM

6 lb. (3 kg.) greengages
1 pint (600 ml.) water
6 lb. (3 kg.) sugar

Wash, halve and stone the gages; crack a dozen stones and blanch the kernels. Simmer the fruit and kernels with the water for about 30 minutes, or until the gages are soft. Stir in the sugar until it has dissolved, then boil rapidly to setting point.

Alternatively, leave the gages whole and remove the stones as they float to the top while the fruit is simmering.

LOGANBERRY JAM

6 lb. (3 kg.) loganberries
6 lb. (3 kg.) sugar

Simmer the cleaned berries over a very low heat for 15–20 minutes or until reduced to a pulp, stirring constantly. Add the sugar, stirring until dissolved, then boil until setting point is reached.

MARROW AND APRICOT JAM

2 lb. (1 kg.) prepared marrow (peeled, seeded and cut into small chunks)
1 lb. (500 g.) fresh apricots or ½ lb. (250 g.) dried apricots
3 lb. (1.5 kg.) sugar
2 lemons
1¼ pints (725 ml.) water

If the apricots are dried, soak them overnight in 1 pint (600 ml.) of water, then simmer until tender. If the apricots are fresh, wash, halve and cook them gently in a little water until soft, removing the stones as they rise to the surface.

In another pan, cook the prepared marrow in a little water until tender, then mash to a pulp. Combine the marrow and apricots in one pan; add the lemon juice, grated rind and sugar.

Bring to the boil, stirring until the sugar has dissolved. Boil fast, stirring occasionally for 15 minutes, or until the jam has thickened. Pot into warmed jars and cover while hot.

MARROW AND GINGER JAM

6 lb. (3 kg.) marrow (prepared weight)
2 oz. (50 g.) root ginger
Juice and grated rind of 4 lemons
6 lb. (3 kg.) sugar

Peel the marrows and remove the seeds; cut the flesh into tiny cubes and steam until just tender.

Bruise the ginger, tie in a muslin bag and place in a pan with the steamed marrow and the juice and rind of the lemons. Bring to the boil, stir in the sugar until it has dissolved, then boil rapidly to setting point.

For a pronounced ginger flavour, double the quantity of root ginger and leave the steamed marrow cubes, sprinkled with sugar, to stand for 24 hours. Put in the pan with the ginger, lemon juice and rind, and heat carefully until the sugar has dissolved and the marrow cubes are transparent.

Test for setting with the saucer or flake test. Pot at once.

PEACH JAM

3 lb. (1.5 kg.) yellow peaches
½ pint (300 ml.) water
Juice and peel of 2 lemons
2 lb. (1 kg.) sugar

Cover the peaches with boiling water, leave for 1 minute, then peel off the skins, quarter the fruits and remove the stones. Put the peaches in a pan with the water, the lemon juice and the peel; simmer gently until reduced to a pulp. Remove the lemon peel. Stir in the sugar and boil rapidly until

setting point has been reached.
Variation Simmer 12 kernels for 1–2 minutes, then peel. Mix with the peach flesh, and simmer.

PEACH AND PEAR JAM

2 lb. (1 kg.) peaches
2 lb. (1 kg.) pears (they must not be over-ripe)
4 lb. (2 kg.) sugar
4 lemons
5 fl. oz. (125 ml.) water

Peel and stone the peaches; peel and core the pears. Chop both fruits roughly, place in a pan with the water and simmer gently until they are tender, but not mushy.

Add the lemon juice, grated rind and sugar, and stir until the sugar has dissolved. Bring to the boil, then boil fast, stirring occasionally until set (about 20 minutes). Pot into warm jars and cover while hot.

PLUM JAM

6 lb. (3 kg.) plums
1½–2 pints (850 ml.–1 l.) water
6 lb. (3 kg.) sugar

Wash and dry the plums; cut in half and remove the stones. Crack 12–24 stones, extract the kernels and blanch them. Put the plums, kernels and water in a pan and simmer until reduced by half.

Add the sugar, stirring until dissolved, then increase the heat and boil rapidly until setting point is reached.

QUINCE JAM

4 lb. (2 kg.) quinces (prepared weight)
2–4 pints (1–2 l.) water
6 lb. (3 kg.) sugar
Juice of 2 lemons

Peel and core the fruit; cut the flesh into small cubes or grate on a coarse grater. Put in the pan with the water, cover with a lid and simmer for 30 minutes, or until tender.

Take off the lid and continue simmering until reduced. Add the sugar and lemon juice, stirring until the sugar has dissolved completely. Boil rapidly to setting point.

RASPBERRY JAM
(see also p. 306)

6 lb. (3 kg.) raspberries
6 lb. (3 kg.) sugar

Put the cleaned berries in a pan and cook gently until the juice begins to run, then simmer until soft. Stir in the sugar and boil rapidly to setting point.

A better-flavoured jam, but not of such good setting quality, can be obtained by using 5 lb. (2.5 kg.) of fruit to the same amount of sugar. Boil for 10 minutes, stir in the sugar and boil rapidly for 2 minutes.

Continued...

Jam recipes (continued)

RHUBARB AND GINGER JAM

3 lb. (1.5 kg.) rhubarb (prepared weight)
3 lb. (1.5 kg.) sugar
Juice of 3 lemons
1 oz. (25 g.) root ginger

Wash and trim the rhubarb and cut into small chunks. Place in alternate layers with the sugar in a deep bowl, add the lemon juice and leave for about eight hours.

Put the contents of the bowl into a pan, with the bruised ginger tied in a muslin bag. Bring to boiling point, and boil rapidly until setting point is reached.

ROSE-PETAL PRESERVE

2 oz. (50 g.) red or pink rose petals
½ lb. (250 g.) sugar
2 fl. oz. (50 ml.) water
1 tablespoon lemon juice
1 tablespoon orange juice
Cochineal (optional)

For this preserve, use old-fashioned species or wild roses. Hybrid tea and floribunda roses are not really suitable unless highly scented.

Cut away the leafy matter and the white or yellow part at the base of each rose petal, rinse and drain thoroughly. Bring the sugar, water, and lemon and orange juice to the boil to make a syrup. Add the rose petals and simmer over the lowest possible heat, stirring all the time. Cook for about 30 minutes, or until thick.

Add a few drops of red cochineal to improve the colour, and pot at once in small jars or moulds, brushed inside with a little glycerine. Use the preserve as toppings for vanilla and strawberry ice cream, trifles and cream parfaits.

STRAWBERRY JAM

7 lb. (3.5 kg.) strawberries
Juice of 2 lemons
6 lb. (3 kg.) sugar

Hull, wash and drain the strawberries thoroughly; put in a pan with the lemon juice and simmer until soft, stirring frequently to prevent burning. Add the sugar and stir while it dissolves. Boil rapidly to setting point.

Remove the scum and leave the jam to cool until a skin has formed. Stir and pot.

WHOLE STRAWBERRY JAM

6 lb. (3 kg.) strawberries
6 lb. (3 kg.) sugar
¾ pint (450 ml.) pectin stock

Heat the prepared strawberries and sugar gently in a pan until all the sugar has dissolved. Add the pectin stock and boil rapidly to setting point. Cool the jam slightly, then stir and pot.

Jellies that capture summer's essence

Of all the ways in which the subtle flavours of summer may be preserved for winter enjoyment, fruit jellies are paramount. This attraction is enhanced by their clear, glowing colours.

In principle, jelly and jam-making are closely akin, though the former requires rather more time and care. To make the perfect jelly, all traces of pulp, skin or pips must be completely eliminated, leaving only the richly coloured and flavoured juices.

This calls for considerably more fruit than is needed in making jam, and the choice of fruit is more limited. Only distinctively flavoured fruits such as red currants, quinces, black currants, blackberries, elderberries, plums and greengages are really suitable, though these are often combined with apples to give a better set.

Incidentally, the pulp remaining in the jelly bag can be used to make fruit cheeses (see pp. 323–5).

In this way, both the jellies and the cheeses become more worthwhile, as they otherwise require large quantities of fruit for the amount of preserve that you are likely to obtain.

Equipment

The equipment and tools recommended for jam-making are equally suitable for jellies.

Jelly bag In addition to a good preserving pan, scales, measuring jugs and a thermometer, you will need a jelly bag for straining the fruit pulp. Thick flannel jelly bags, sold separately or attached to special drip-stands, can be obtained from kitchen-equipment shops, but it is cheaper to make your own.

A home-made jelly bag can easily be improvised from a square of cotton or flannel, or from two or three layers of butter muslin or cheesecloth. But whether you use a bag or cloth, it should be thoroughly scalded before use.

AN IMPROVISED JELLY BAG

Make your own jelly bag by tying the corners of a square of cotton, or several layers of cheesecloth or muslin, to the legs of an upturned kitchen stool. The cloth must be scalded before use.

For a stand, tie each corner of the cloth to the legs of an upturned kitchen stool.

Place a bowl or basin – earthenware, glass or plastic – beneath the jelly bag to catch the juice as it drips through.

Jars Ordinary jam-jars are suitable for jellies, provided they are clean and unchipped. Small glass jars, such as those which previously contained fish and meat paste, mustard and other relishes, are ideal for jellies if first sterilised. Filled with glowing jelly, their attractive shapes permit them to be set directly on the table.

STEP 1
Preparing the fruit

Fruits with distinctive flavours and colours are preferable, and they should contain enough pectin and acid to ensure a good set. Wild fruits or inexpensive varieties of cultivated fruits are ideal, since you will need quite a lot of them to make a worthwhile quantity. The yield of jelly from a given amount of fruit is considerably less than the yield of jam.

Suitable fruits, which must be fresh and just ripe, include crab and cooking apples, bilberries, blackberries, black currants, gooseberries, loganberries, quinces and red currants.

Used on their own, cooking apples tend to be insipid and so are usually mixed with other fruits. They are also used with wild berry fruits to improve the setting quality of jellies.

Successful jelly cannot be made from cherries, pears, marrows or strawberries, because the additional pectin and acid needed would overpower the fruit flavour.

Before cooking, pick over the fruits and discard any that are over-ripe or of doubtful quality. Wash and drain thoroughly and chop large fruits into chunks, cutting out any bruised parts. There is no need to hull or stalk berries, or to peel and core apples, as the fruit pulp will later be strained.

STEP 2
Softening the fruit

Simmer the fruit in the preserving pan with the correct amount of water. Very little water will be needed with juicy fruits such as loganberries and blackberries, but hard fruits such as apples and quinces need enough water to cover the fruit in the pan.

Testing for pectin Carry out a pectin test at this stage (see p. 316). If the pectin content is low, simmer the juice further to evaporate more of the water, or add previously prepared pectin-rich juice.

STEP 3
Straining the pulp

As soon as the fruit has cooked to a pulp and the juices are running freely, strain the contents of the pan.

Tip them into the scalded jelly bag, having first placed a wide basin underneath to catch the juice as it strains through.

Leave the pulp to drain for several hours, or until there is no juice dripping through.

Do not squeeze the bag to extract the juice, since this will make the jelly cloudy.

If the fruit is rich in pectin, as is the case with apples, gooseberries and red currants, you can take two

extracts of juice. For the initial softening of the fruit, use two-thirds of the recommended amount of water, then drain in the jelly bag for about 15 minutes. Return the pulp to the pan with the rest of the water and simmer for 30 minutes; drain the pulp again, this time for several hours.

Mix the two batches of juice, which will exceed the amount of juice you would have obtained from a single extraction, and process into jelly at once.

STEP 4
Measuring the juice

When the pectin test is satisfactory, measure the volume of juice obtained, return it to the pan and bring to the boil.

STEP 5
Adding the sugar

A pectin-rich juice will need 1–1¼ lb. of sugar added for every pint of juice (1 kg. to 1 l.).

Do not add more than ¾ lb. sugar per pint (750 g. to 1 l.) of juice with a low pectin content.

Add the warmed sugar to the simmering juice, stirring constantly until fully dissolved.

STEP 6
Test for setting

Continue boiling rapidly for about 10 minutes, when setting point is normally reached. Prolonged boiling at this stage results in a rubbery jelly.

The flake test (see p. 316) is the best way to determine the setting point of jelly.

When boiling is nearly finished, reduce the heat so that boiling is less vigorous, though still steady, to avoid the risk of trapping air bubbles in the jelly.

BASIC STEPS IN JELLY-MAKING

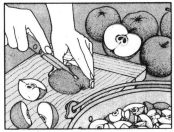

1. Preparing the fruit *Choose ripe, pectin-rich fruit. Wash it well and cut large fruits into chunks. As the pulp will be strained there is no need to core, peel or remove stalks.*

2. Softening the fruit *Simmer fruit slowly until juice is extracted. Carry out pectin test (see p. 316) and, if pectin is low, simmer for a further period or add more pectin.*

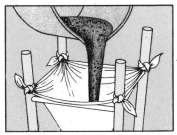

3. Straining the pulp *Make a strainer from an upturned stool and some muslin. Pour in pulp and leave to drip into a basin. Do not squeeze the pulp, otherwise the jelly will be cloudy.*

4. Measuring the juice *When pulp has stopped dripping, take the juice from the basin and measure it. Return the juice to a clean pan and bring back to the boil.*

5. Adding the sugar *Measure the sugar carefully, following the instructions on this page; warm it and then stir into the heated juice until it has completely dissolved.*

6. Test for setting *Boil rapidly for about 10 minutes, slightly reducing heat towards the end to avoid trapping air bubbles. Test the juice for setting (see pp. 316–17).*

7. Removing the scum *As setting point is reached, lift pan from heat and remove scum quickly with a perforated spoon, or by straining through linen into a warm bowl.*

8. Potting and storing *Gently pour jelly into warmed jars, tilting them to prevent air bubbles forming. Cover with waxed discs and seal with Cellophane. Store when set.*

EQUIPMENT

Preserving pan
Bowls and basins
Measuring jug
Ladle
Scales
Perforated spoon
Wooden spoon
Drip-stand and jelly bag; or use a square of muslin and a kitchen stool
Small jam-jars
Wax discs and covers

STEP 7
Removing the scum
As soon as setting point is reached, lift the pan away from the heat and quickly remove any scum. This can be done with a perforated spoon, dipped into boiling water and then shaken.

Alternatively, the jelly can be strained through a piece of scalded, fine linen.

Speed is important, as the jelly must be potted before it sets.

STEP 8
Potting and storing
Pot the jelly in clean, warm jars, pouring it gently down the inside of the tilted jar to avoid creating air bubbles.

Cover the jelly surface at once with a disc, waxed side down, and seal securely with Cellophane covers and string. Avoid moving the jars until the jelly has set. Store in a cool, dry, dark place.

Things that may go wrong
Faults in fruit jellies are basically the same as those that may occur with jams. But, in addition to the general rules, remember to simmer the fruit gently before straining, otherwise it may not have broken down completely to release the maximum amount of juice.

Always bring the juice to boiling point before adding the sugar, and pot the jelly as quickly as possible after it has reached setting point.

Avoid disturbing the jars until the jelly is completely set.

Cloudy jelly may result from the pulp being squeezed during straining.

It is as well, too, not to leave the strained juice for more than 24 hours before adding the sugar to finish the jelly.

RECIPES
for home-made jellies
———◆◇◆———

Yields of jellies cannot be given, as these depend partly on the type of fruit used and on the amount of juice extracted. On average 10 lb. (5 kg.) of jelly can be expected for every 6 lb. (3 kg.) of sugar used.

———◆◇◆———

APPLE JELLY

6 lb. (3 kg.) cooking apples
Ginger root or whole cloves
Juice of 1 lemon
Sugar

Wash the apples, cut them into chunks and put them in the preserving pan with water to cover.

Apple jelly can be somewhat insipid unless the fruit has a distinctive flavour, but a bruised ginger root, or half-a-dozen whole cloves, can be added to the simmering fruit for extra flavour.

Strain the fruit pulp, measure, and return the juice to the clean pan. Bring to boiling point and add warm sugar at the rate of 1 lb. for every pint (750 g. to 1 l.). Boil to setting point.
Variation Essence of cloves or lemon, or strained lemon juice, may be used for flavouring instead of spices; add these just before setting point is reached. The colour of apple jelly can be improved by simmering a few blackberries, cranberries, loganberries, raspberries or red currants with the apples.

———◆◇◆———

BILBERRY JELLY

4 lb. (2 kg.) bilberries
½ pint (300 ml.) water
1 teaspoon citric acid
Pectin stock
Sugar

Put the cleaned berries in a pan with the water and citric acid, and simmer gently. Strain the pulp for at least 1 hour, then test for pectin and add sufficient pectin (apple juice) for a satisfactory test result.

Measure the juice, bring to the boil in a clean pan and add ¾ lb. of sugar for every pint (750 g. to 1 l.). Boil until setting point is reached.

———◆◇◆———

BLACKBERRY JELLY

4 lb. (2 kg.) blackberries
¾ pint (450 ml.) water
Juice of 2 lemons, or 1 teaspoon citric acid
Sugar

Rinse and drain the berries, put in a pan with the water and either lemon juice or citric acid. Simmer until soft, strain, and bring the extracted juice to boiling point. Stir in the sugar, allowing 1 lb. of sugar to each pint of measured juice (750 g. to 1 l.).

———◆◇◆———

BLACKBERRY AND APPLE JELLY

4 lb. (2 kg.) blackberries
2 lb. (1 kg.) cooking apples
2 pints (1 l.) water
Sugar

Rinse and drain the berries, wash and chop the apples and put both in a pan with the water. Simmer until soft, then strain the pulp and measure the juice.

Return to the pan, with 1 lb. of sugar for every pint of juice (750 g. to 1 l.). Boil until setting point is reached.

———◆◇◆———

BLACK-CURRANT JELLY

4 lb. (2 kg.) black currants
2 pints (1 l.) water
Sugar

Simmer the rinsed berries with two-thirds of the water until soft; strain for 15 minutes, then re-boil the pulp with the remaining water. Strain again for 3–4 hours and mix the two batches of juice. Measure the juice and bring to the boil, adding 1–1¼ lb. sugar for each pint (1 kg. to 1 l.). Boil to setting point.

———◆◇◆———

CRAB-APPLE JELLY

6 lb. (3 kg.) crab apples
Juice of 1 lemon
Sugar

Scrub the crab apples clean, especially round the blossom ends, and remove the stalks. Quarter the fruits and put in the pan with the lemon juice and enough water – about 4 pints (2 l.) – to cover them. Simmer over gentle heat until completely tender, then strain and measure the juice. Bring this to boiling point, add 1 lb. of sugar for each pint (750 g. to 1 l.) and boil until set.

———◆◇◆———

GOOSEBERRY JELLY

4 lb. (2 kg.) gooseberries
2 pints (1 l.) water
Sugar

There is no need to top and tail the gooseberries. After washing them, put the fruit in a pan with two-thirds of the water, simmer until quite soft, then strain for 15 minutes. Simmer the gooseberry pulp for a further 30 minutes with the remaining water; strain.

Mix and measure the two batches of juice, boil, and stir in 1–1¼ lb. of sugar for each pint of juice (1 kg. to 1 l.). Boil until setting point is reached.

———◆◇◆———

LOGANBERRY JELLY

4 lb. (2 kg.) loganberries
1 pint (600 ml.) water
Sugar

Simmer the berries in the water for about 1 hour. Strain the pulp and measure the juice. Bring to the boil, adding 1 lb. of sugar for every pint of juice (750 g. to 1 l.).

QUINCE JELLY

4 lb. (2 kg.) quinces

Juice of 2 lemons, or 2 teaspoons citric acid

6 pints (3 l.) water

Sugar

Scrub the quinces, cut into small pieces and put in a pan with the lemon juice, or citric acid, and two-thirds of the water.

Simmer until quite tender, then strain for 15 minutes. Return the pulp to the pan with the remaining water, and simmer for another 30 minutes. Strain and mix the two batches of juice.

Measure the juice and bring to the boil, stirring in 1 lb. of sugar to every pint of juice (750 g. to 1 l.). Boil until setting point is reached.

RED-CURRANT JELLY

6 lb. (3 kg.) red currants

2 pints (1 l.) water

Sugar

Take two extracts from the pulp, using just over half the water for the first extract. Blend and measure, bring to the boil and add 1 lb. of sugar to each pint of juice (750 g. to 1 l.).

For a jelly with a stronger flavour, simmer the fruit gently without any water, strain and measure the juice. Boil, and stir in 1¼ lb. of sugar for each pint (1 kg. to 1 l.). The yield will be smaller, although tastier, than when two batches of juice are extracted.

ROSE-PETAL JELLY

2 lb. (1 kg.) cooking apples

1 oz. (25 g.) dark red rose petals

1 pint (600 ml.) water

Juice of ½ lemon

Sugar

Wash and roughly chop the apples, and put in a pan with the water and lemon juice. Bring to the boil and simmer gently until soft and pulpy. Strain through a jelly bag.

Remove the pale bases from old-fashioned, scented rose petals, rinse carefully and dry thoroughly on absorbent kitchen paper or in a soft towel.

Pound the dried petals with 2 teaspoons of sugar until well broken up, put in a pan with ¼ pint (150 ml.) water and simmer, covered, for about 15 minutes. Strain through a fine sieve, muslin or coffee filter.

Mix the apple and rose-petal juices, measure, and bring to the boil. Add 1 lb. of sugar for each pint (750 g. of sugar to 1 l.), stir until dissolved, then boil rapidly until setting point. A drop of red colouring may be added, although this should be unnecessary with dark red petals.

SLOE AND APPLE JELLY

2 lb. (1 kg.) sloes

4 lb. (2 kg.) cooking apples

Juice and peel of 1 lemon

Sugar

Wash and drain the sloes. Frost helps to break down the tough flesh, but if the sloes have been picked before the first autumn frosts, prick them with a silver fork. Put in a pan with the lemon juice and peel, and barely enough water to cover, and simmer until pulpy.

Wash and chop the apples, then simmer in a separate pan, with water to cover, until soft and pulpy. Strain the two fruit pulps and measure the juice.

Bring the juice to the boil, add the sugar at the rate of 1 lb. to each pint of juice (750 g. of sugar to 1 l.) and stir until dissolved. Boil to setting point.

TOMATO JELLY

3 lb. (1.5 kg.) ripe tomatoes

3 lb. (1.5 kg.) sugar

1 cup vinegar, preferably white

1 pint (600 ml.) water

About 6 cloves

½ stick cinnamon

Place the spices, enclosed in a muslin bag, in the water. Stew gently with the tomatoes, until soft. Remove the spice bag and rub the pulp through a sieve. Return to the pan, adding the vinegar and sugar, stir until the sugar has dissolved, then boil rapidly until setting point is reached.

Delicacies of yesterday – fruit cheeses and butters

Fruit cheeses and butters were as indispensable to teas on Victorian and Edwardian lawns as were cucumber sandwiches and gentleman's relish. They were used in place of dairy cheese, as accompaniments to bread and butter, and as fillings in cakes and trifles.

In these busier and less expansive days they have lost something of their appeal, chiefly because they require a certain amount of trouble to make and have a relatively low yield in relation to the amount of fruit and sugar used. But as a treat for special occasions, or as a means of recapturing the era of Mrs Beeton, these preserves can hardly be bettered.

Equipment

The basic equipment for making fruit cheeses and butters is the same as that for jam (see p. 314); but, in addition, you will need a fine sieve. This should be made of nylon or plastic, but not of metal.

STEP 1
Preparing the fruit

Almost any type of fruit is suitable for these preserves – that is, both berries and tree fruits – and also some vegetables. Apples are often spiced with ginger, cinnamon, cloves or nutmeg; marrow can be flavoured with raspberries or strawberries; rhubarb with oranges or lemons; pears with ginger or cloves, and melon with ginger.

Wash and pick over the fruits, discarding any that are diseased, and cutting out any bruised areas. Cut up large fruits, but do not waste time on stemming, coring, stoning or peeling.

STEP 2
Softening the fruit

Place the fruit in a preserving pan with just enough water to cover. Fruits low in acid, such as dessert apples, peaches and pears, will require the addition of 2 tablespoons of lemon juice or ½ teaspoon of citric acid to every 2 lb. (1 kg.) of fruit.

Simmer the fruit gently over a low, steady heat until it is thoroughly softened.

STEP 3
Sieving the fruit

Once the fruit is soft, take it from the pan and rub it through a fine nylon or plastic sieve. Carefully weigh the sieved pulp and return it to a clean pan.

STEP 4
Cooking the mixture

a. *Making fruit cheeses* Allow equal amounts of sieved fruit pulp and sugar. If the pulp is runny, reduce it by fast boiling until thick – before adding the sugar.

Evaporation is an important part of the process, so do not cover the pan when reducing the fruit.

Stir the mixture until the sugar is completely dissolved, then simmer it gently for about 1 hour. Stir constantly during cooking.

b. *Making fruit butters* In their finished state, these are less solid than cheeses and so should contain no more than half to three-quarters as much sugar as pulp.

Stir the sugar into the pulp until dissolved, and add whatever spicy flavourings that are required at the same time.

Simmer the mixture, stirring frequently, until it becomes smooth and creamy.

STEP 5
Testing for setting

Fruit cheeses are ready for potting when a wooden spoon, drawn over the base of the pan, leaves a clean-cut line. Remove butters from the heat when the last liquid evaporates and the surface is creamy.

STEP 6
Potting and storing

Fruit cheeses were originally potted in moulds, but the cheeses can be turned out equally well from small glass jars or pots.

The containers should be warm, and brushed inside with a little glycerine. Seal the hot surface with a waxed disc, wax side down, and cover the container.

Fruit butters are potted in warm jars. They do not keep well, however, and should be air-tight and, ideally, sterilised by boiling in water for 5 minutes.

Cheeses often improve with age, and should preferably mature for two months before using. Butters generally have a storage life of only a few weeks, and once opened should be eaten within a few days.

*RECIPES
for
fruit cheeses and butters*

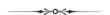

The yield of these preserves is small, on average amounting to just half of the total amount of fruit and sugar.

BLACKBERRY CHEESE

2 lb. (1 kg.) blackberries
1 lb. (500 g.) cooking apples
½ pint (300 ml.) water
Sugar

Wash and chop the apples; wash and drain the blackberries. Place the fruit in a pan with water, and cook until soft and mushy. Rub through a sieve, then return the pulp to the pan, adding 1 lb. (500 g.) of sugar to every 1 pint (600 ml.) of pulp.

Stir until the sugar has dissolved, then bring to the boil and cook until thick, stirring occasionally.

The pulp from blackberry jelly can be used for this recipe. In this case, simmer the apples until tender, add the blackberry pulp and a little water, cook for a few minutes, then sieve and proceed as above.

BASIC STEPS IN MAKING FRUIT CHEESES AND BUTTERS

1. *Preparing the fruit* Clean and roughly chop large fruits, discarding any that are bruised or diseased and removing any bruised parts. Small fruits may be used whole.

2. *Softening the fruit* Place the fruit in the preserving pan and just cover with cold water. Simmer until soft, adding lemon juice or citric acid to fruits low in acid.

3. *Sieving the fruit* Rub the softened fruit through a sieve made of nylon or plastic, so producing a fine pulp. Weigh the pulp and pour it into a clean preserving pan or saucepan.

4a. *Making fruit cheese* Add a similar weight of sugar to the pulp and stir until dissolved. Simmer for 1 hour or until the cheese thickens, stirring the mixture constantly.

4b. *Making fruit butter* Boil the pulp until thick, then stir in half the pulp's weight of sugar, plus spices if required. Simmer until the mixture is thick and creamy.

5. *Testing for setting* Fruit cheese is ready when a spoon drawn across the pan leaves a clean line. Fruit butter is ready when no free liquid is visible and the surface is creamy.

6. *Potting and storing* Pour cheeses into pots or moulds painted inside with glycerine. Pour fruit butters into warm jars, as when making jam. Cover both preserves immediately.

EQUIPMENT

Preserving pan
Bowls or basins
Measuring jug, spoons and cups
Scales
Long-handled wooden spoon
Knives and peelers
Perforated spoon
Jam-jar filler
Wide-necked funnel
Fine nylon or plastic sieve
Jars, pots, waxed discs,
covers and string

DAMSON CHEESE

6 lb. (3 kg.) damsons
½ pint (300 ml.) water
Sugar

Wash the fruit and simmer with the water in a covered pan until soft; rub through a fine sieve and weigh the pulp. Reduce the pulp by simmering until thick, then add an equal amount of sugar to the sieved pulp, stirring until the sugar has dissolved completely. Boil until quite thick.

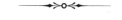

MEDLAR CHEESE

2 lb. (1 kg.) medlars
2 lemons
½ pint (300 ml.) water
½ teaspoon ground cinnamon
Sugar

Wash and quarter the medlars; wash the lemons, and slice or chop them. Place the prepared medlars and lemons, and ½ pint (300 ml.) of water, in a pan. Simmer gently until tender. Rub through a sieve then return the pulp to the pan, adding 12 oz. (350 g.) of sugar and ½ teaspoon of cinnamon to every pint of pulp.

Bring slowly to the boil, stirring until the sugar has dissolved, then simmer gently until thick.

QUINCE CHEESE

4 lb. (2 kg.) ripe quinces
Water
Sugar

Pick over the fruit, scrub and chop roughly. Put in a pan with enough water to just cover; put a lid on the pan and simmer until soft. Sieve and weigh the pulp, thicken the pulp by simmering to reduce its volume, then add the same weight of sugar as that of the sieved pulp.

Stir until the sugar dissolves, then boil until the cheese is thick.

Alternatively, peel and core the quinces and cook in water until soft. Pulp with a vegetable masher, and weigh before adding an equal weight of sugar.

RHUBARB CHEESE

2 lb. (1 kg.) rhubarb
Juice of 1 lemon
Sugar

Trim the rhubarb and cut into small chunks; simmer in a covered pan with the lemon juice until soft. Sieve and weigh the pulp. Reduce pulp until it has thickened, stir in an equal amount of sugar and boil until thick enough to leave a trail over the base of the saucepan.

It is advisable to carry out the pectin test before sieving and, if necessary, to add pectin stock or commercial pectin (see p. 316) to the mixed pulp before reducing it.

APPLE BUTTER

6 lb. (3 kg.) crab or windfall apples
2 pints (1 l.) water
2 pints (1 l.) cider
Sugar

Wash the apples, chop into large pieces and cook gently, in a covered pan, with the water and cider until soft. Rub through a fine sieve and weigh the pulp; allow ¾ lb. of sugar for every 1 lb. of pulp (375 g. sugar to 500 g. pulp).

Simmer the pulp until it has reduced by about one-third, and thickened. Stir in the sugar, and simmer until creamy.

Variation For spiced apple butter, add 1 teaspoon ground cloves and 1 teaspoon ground ginger, with the sugar.

APRICOT BUTTER

3 lb. (1.5 kg.) apricots
Sugar
Lemons
Cinnamon and cloves (optional)

Wash and halve the fruit, place in a pan with half a cup of water and simmer gently until really soft. Rub through a sieve, then return the pulp to the pan.

Allow 8 oz. (250 g.) of sugar, and the juice and grated rind of 1 lemon, to each pint of pulp. Add spices, if required, at the rate of ½ teaspoon each of ground cinnamon and cloves to every pint of pulp.

Bring to the boil stirring until the sugar has dissolved, then simmer gently until thick.

BLACK-CURRANT BUTTER

4 lb. (2 kg.) black currants
4 pints (2 l.) water
Sugar

Wash the fruit and simmer in the water until soft. Rub through a sieve and weigh the pulp. Allow ½–¾ lb. sugar for each 1 lb. of pulp (250–375 g. sugar for 500 g. pulp). Boil the pulp until thick, add the sugar and stir until dissolved. Simmer to the desired consistency.

GOOSEBERRY BUTTER

4 lb. (2 kg.) ripe gooseberries
¾ pint (450 ml.) water
Sugar

Wash the gooseberries, then simmer the whole, ripe fruits in the water, rub through a sieve and weigh. Add ¾ lb. sugar for every 1 lb. of pulp (375 g. sugar to 500 g. pulp). Stir to dissolve the sugar, and continue simmering until the pulp is thick and creamy.

MARROW BUTTER

Marrow
Sugar

Wash and dry the marrow, cut into large pieces and simmer gently, without any water, to soften. Rub through a sieve and weigh the pulp; allow ½–¾ lb. sugar for each 1 lb. of pulp (250–375 g. sugar to 500 g. pulp).

Boil until thickened, then add the sugar and stir until dissolved;

flavour with the juice of 1 lemon for each 1 lb. (500 g.) of pulp. Boil to the correct consistency.

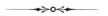

PLUM BUTTER

2 lb. (1 kg.) plums
Sugar

Plums need not be stoned, but a few may be cracked open and the blanched kernels cooked with the fruit. Simmer gently, with a little added water if the plums are under-ripe, until soft. Rub through a fine sieve and weigh the pulp, allowing ½–¾ lb. sugar to 1 lb. of pulp (250–375 g. sugar to 500 g. pulp).

Simmer the pulp until it has thickened, stir in the sugar and boil to the required consistency.

TOMATO BUTTER

2 lb. (1 kg.) ripe tomatoes
Juice of 2 lemons
Sugar

Quarter the tomatoes and simmer gently with the lemon juice. When soft, rub through a fine sieve and weigh the pulp, allowing ½–¾ lb. sugar to 1 lb. of pulp (250–375 g. sugar to 500 g. pulp). Stir until dissolved.

Simmer the pulp until it has reduced and thickened, then add the sugar and boil to the required consistency.

Home-made syrups and juices

Summer weekends and school holidays will be less expensive if you use surplus garden produce to make fruit juices and syrups. Syrups are especially versatile; not only can they be used to flavour jellies and puddings, but diluted with water or milk they can also be turned into delicious drinks as well. They can also be mixed with equal quantities of water, and frozen to make superb iced lollies.

Basically, syrups consist of a concentrated solution of fruit juice and sugar; while juices, which are drunk undiluted, contain only a little sugar. The same kinds of fruit are best for both purposes – black and red currants, blackberries, gooseberries, loganberries and strawberries, either singly or in combination. Excellent syrups can also be made from hedgerow fruits, such as rose-hips and elderberries, while apple juice makes a refreshing summer drink.

Make sure the fruits are ripe. Unripe fruits contain too little juice.

Equipment

This varies considerably according to the method chosen. For the basic, hot-preparation method you will require a saucepan big enough to accommodate a large earthenware bowl.

If you are using the quick, hot method, you will need only a large pan. For cold methods, earthenware jars will be necessary. Whichever method you choose, make sure that no iron, zinc or copper utensil comes in direct contact with the fruit.

Other essential items of equipment are a wooden spoon or pulper, and either a jelly bag or some butter muslin that can be attached to the upturned legs of a kitchen stool to act as a strainer.

The bottles you use should be able to withstand moderate pressure, and be fitted either with screw-tops or with new corks.

You will also need a sugar thermometer, and a broad pan. The pan must be deep enough to heat the bottles when placed on a grid, or wad of folded newspaper, to protect them from direct heat. They should also be separated from each other by further wads of the same material.

STEP 1
Preparing the fruit

Select ripe, juicy fruits and wash them gently in cold water. Fruits too ripe for jam are ideal for syrups and juices, but discard any that are unripe or going bad.

STEP 2
Breaking down the fruit

Fruit juices are prepared only by hot methods. Though these are also the easiest ways of making syrups, cold methods give better flavours. Syrups, once prepared, are preserved by heating and sterilising, or by the addition of chemical preservatives.

Basic hot method Place the fruits in a large earthenware basin and mash them with a wooden spoon. If you are using black currants, add 1 pint of water to every 2 lb. (600 ml. to 1 kg.) of fruit. For blackberries, add 4 fl. oz. of water to every 2 lb. (100 ml. to 1 kg.). With most other fruits, there is no need to add water.

Fill a large pan with water, put the basin of fruit over it and heat until the juices flow, topping the pan up with water as necessary to prevent it burning. Mash the fruit again when the juice is flowing freely.

Quick, hot method An alternative method is to put the fruits in a large pan, together with any water required, and bring rapidly to the boil. Continue boiling for 1 minute, crushing any whole fruits with a wooden spoon.

This is a fast means of breaking up the fruits, but the first method avoids the risk of overcooking. If this takes place, it may easily spoil the flavour or the colour of the finished product.

Cold method (syrups only) Put the fruits in an earthenware jar and crush them thoroughly with a wooden spoon. Cover the jar with a thin cloth and leave it in either a warm room or a cupboard until fermentation takes place.

With most fruits, this happens within 24 hours, though black currants may need as long as four or five days.

The signs of fermentation are tiny bubbles of gas forming on the surface.

STEP 3
Straining the pulp

Whatever the method of preparation, the pulp must now be strained to obtain the juice. Ideally, this would be done with a fruit press, but equally good results may be obtained by allowing the pulp to drain overnight through a jelly bag, or a few layers of muslin or cheesecloth attached to the upturned legs of a kitchen stool.

Next morning, thoroughly squeeze the bag of pulp to extract the last remaining drops of juice.

STEP 4
Adding the sugar

When making syrup, add ¾ lb. of sugar to 1 pint of juice (375 g. to 600 ml.). For fruit juices, add only

BASIC STEPS IN MAKING SYRUPS AND JUICES

1. *Preparing the fruit* *Select only ripe fruits. If unripe, they have little flavour or juice. Wash the fruits and reject any that are damaged or starting to go bad.*

2. *Breaking down the fruit* *Mash the fruit in a bowl, heat over a pan of water until the juice runs, then mash again. Fruits for syrups can be broken down by fermentation.*

3. *Straining the pulp* *Strain the pulp through a jelly bag. Allow it to drain overnight, and on the following day squeeze the bag to extract the remaining juice.*

4. *Adding the sugar* *Measure juice and add sugar – for syrups, about ¾ lb. to 1 pint of juice (375 g. to 600 ml.); for juices, 3 oz. (75 g.) per pint. Stir until dissolved.*

3 oz. per pint (75 g. to 600 ml.). In each case, stir the mixture without heating until the sugar is dissolved.

STEP 5
Straining the syrup
At this point, syrups should be strained again through a clean jelly bag or muslin. Fruit juices do not require straining again.

STEP 6
Bottling
Pour the juice or the strained syrup into bottles. Clean, unchipped sauce bottles with screwtops are ideal, but any sound, cork-stoppered bottle is suitable so long as new corks are provided. Boil both tops and corks for 15 minutes immediately before use.

Fill the bottles to within an inch or so of the tops, put the screw-tops on or drive home the corks and secure them with wire to prevent them blowing out during sterilisation. Make a false bottom in the sterilising pan with a wire grid or a thick pad of newspaper.

STEP 7
Sterilising the bottles
Stand the bottles on the false bottom and keep them separate with further pads of paper. Fill the pan with water up to the necks of the bottles, so that the contents are below the surface.

Slowly raise the temperature of the water to 77°C (170°F), and keep it there for 30 minutes. Alternatively, speed the process by raising it to 88°C (190°F) for 20 minutes. Do not exceed the times suggested, or you may spoil the flavour.

STEP 8
Sealing the bottles
Grip the bottles with a thick cloth and remove them carefully from the pan. Seal the bottles by screwing the tops hard down or driving the corks well in. Give cork-stoppered bottles added protection with paraffin wax.

When the bottles have cooled, brush melted wax over the cork and the top of the bottle.

Preserving syrups with chemicals
For an alternative means of preserving syrup, carry out Steps 1 to 3, and to 1 pint of extracted juice, add 1 lb. of sugar (600 ml. to 500 g.). Stir until the sugar is fully dissolved.

At this point, too, correct the low acid content of strawberry syrups by adding 1 teaspoon of citric acid to each pint (600 ml.) of juice. Clarify these and other syrups by straining them.

The best chemical preservative for this purpose is sulphur dioxide, usually added in tablet form. Known as Campden tablets, they may be obtained from most chemists and wine-making supply shops.

Add one tablet, crushed and dissolved, in 1 tablespoon of warm water, to each pint (600 ml.) of juice. Since sulphur dioxide causes the colour of syrup to fade, a little artificial colouring may also be added at this stage.

Sterilise the stoppers and corks as described in Step 6 and, just before filling the bottles, sterilise them by boiling for a few minutes. After boiling, turn them upside-down to drain.

Pour the syrup into the bottles, filling those with screw-caps to within ½ in. (12 mm.) of the top and those with corks to within 1 in. (25 mm.). Having filled them, screw the caps on hard and push the corks home immediately.

Vegetable juices
Delicious and health-promoting drinks can be made from a wide range of vegetables. Carrots, celery, spinach, beetroot and cucumbers, for example, can all be used in this way, either singly or in combination.

Though juices can be made by more old-fashioned methods, it is simpler to use a liquidiser.

Scrub, peel and grate root vegetables, and chop the others before putting them raw into the machine. Add a little orange juice to preserve the colour. Bottle the vegetable juices without heating and put them in the refrigerator. Serve, chilled, within a few days.

Storing
If you intend to keep fruit juices or syrups for any length of time, make sure that the seals are air-tight and that the corks or stoppers are perfectly sterilised. Few will survive long contact with the air, and even those preserved by chemicals will, when opened, last no more than a week or so. Store in a cool, dark place.

Things that may go wrong
Mould on the juice or cork may be due to a number of causes: insufficient processing time; inadequate depth of water; ill-fitting corks, or corks that were insufficiently sterilised.

Cloudiness in the syrup is caused by shaking the bottle before serving.

Stomach upsets can be caused by using iron, zinc or copper implements during processing.

5. Straining the syrup *Syrups should be strained again at this point through a jelly bag or muslin in order to clarify the liquid, but this is unnecessary with juices.*

6. Bottling *Screw-top bottles are best, but those with corks may be used. Sterilise bottles and tops by boiling, and fill to the level indicated. Replace tops tightly to ensure a good seal.*

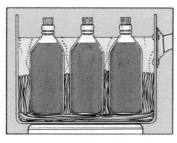

7. Sterilising the bottles *Do this by simmering the filled bottles in boiling water. Stand them on pads of folded paper, packing further pads between them to keep them apart.*

8. Sealing the bottles *Remove bottles from the pan, using a thick cloth to grasp them, and screw the tops home. Seal cork-stoppered bottles with a layer of paraffin wax.*

> *EQUIPMENT*
>
> *Scales*
> *Large pan*
> *Jelly bag*
> *Measuring jug and ladle*
> *Funnel*
> *Bottles with screw-tops or corks*
> *Brush*
> *Paraffin wax*
> *Earthenware bowl (hot method)*
> *Earthenware cask and square of cotton or muslin (cold method)*

RECIPES
for
syrups and juices

Most fruit syrups, especially those made from soft berry fruits, are prepared by the methods described in the preceding pages. There are, however, a number of unusual and interesting variations, some of which are given here.

BLACKBERRY SYRUP

6 lb. (3 kg.) ripe blackberries
Sugar
½ pint (300 ml.) water
Brandy

Wash and clean the fruit, and discard any berries that show signs of grub infestation. Put the water and berries together in a large earthenware bowl, and break up the fruits by the basic hot method described in Step 2.

Strain the pulp through muslin or a jelly bag and to each pint (600 ml.) of juice, add ¾ lb. (375 g.) of sugar.

Put the sweetened mixture into a pan and simmer for 10 minutes. Allow to cool slightly and add a wineglass of brandy. Pour into clean, warmed bottles, then sterilise and seal by the methods described in Steps 7 and 8.

ELDERBERRY SYRUP

6 lb. (3 kg.) ripe elderberries
Sugar
½ pint (300 ml.) water
6 cloves and a piece of root ginger or 2 oz. (50 g.) cinnamon and 1 level teaspoon allspice

Strip the elderberries from the stalks, wash them and discard any that are shrivelled. Put the water and berries together in a large earthenware bowl and break up the fruits, using the basic hot method described in Step 2. Strain the pulp through muslin or a jelly bag and to each pint (600 ml.) of juice, add ¾ lb. (375 g.) of sugar.

Put the sweetened mixture into a pan and simmer for 10 minutes, adding, during this period, either the cloves and ginger or the cinnamon and allspice. Pour into clean, warmed bottles, sterilise and seal – using the methods described in Steps 7 and 8.

NETTLE SYRUP

2 lb. (1 kg.) young nettle tops
White sugar
3 pints (1.5 l.) water

Gather the nettle tops only when they are young, tender and a delicate olive-green in colour. Wash and drain them, place them in a pan and simmer in the water for 1 hour. Strain through muslin and add 1 lb. (500 g.) of sugar to each pint (600 ml.) of liquid.

Return to the pan and simmer for 5 minutes, stirring until the sugar is dissolved. Pour into bottles, sterilise and seal –

following the methods described in Steps 7 and 8.

This old country recipe for a blood-purifying drink is especially delicious when diluted with soda water.

ROSE-HIP SYRUP

2 lb. (1 kg.) ripe rose-hips
6 pints (3 l.) water
1 lb. (500 g.) sugar

Gather the hips from the wild or dog rose, or from the cultivated *Rosa rugosa*. These are the easiest to clean.

Wash the hips, remove the stalks and calyces, and put the hips through the coarse blade of a mincer. Add them to a pan containing 4 pints (2 l.) of boiling water, bring back to the boil, and remove the pan from the heat.

Allow to stand for 15 minutes, then strain through a jelly bag. Extract as much juice as possible.

Return the pulp to the pan with a further 2 pints (1 l.) of boiling water. Bring back to the boil and remove from the heat. Leave for 10 minutes, then strain through a clean jelly bag.

Mix the two juice extracts, and boil in a clean pan until reduced to about 2 pints (1 l.).

Add the sugar, stirring until dissolved. Bring to the boil and keep at boiling point for 5 minutes.

Pour into clean, warm bottles and seal at once with sterilised stoppers or corks. Use small bottles, if possible, for the syrup does not keep long once opened. Sterilise as described in Step 7.

CARROT JUICE

4 lb. (2 kg.) carrots
1 tablespoon orange juice

Scrub the carrots, but do not skin them. Grate to a pulp and sprinkle with orange juice before putting through the liquidiser. Strain, bottle and place in the refrigerator.

This weight of carrots will yield approximately 3 pints (1.5 l.) of juice, which should be drunk within a day or so.

Not only is carrot juice delicious by itself; blended with the juices of other vegetables – spinach, lettuce or celery for example – it also provides the basis for a wide range of refreshing breakfast drinks.

TOMATO JUICE

Tomatoes
Caster sugar
Salt
Black pepper
Water

Wash the tomatoes, cut them into halves and cook gently until soft. Rub the tomatoes through a sieve and to each pint (600 ml.) of sieved pulp, add ¼ pint (150 ml.) of water, ½ oz. (15 g.) of caster sugar, 1 teaspoon of salt and 1 teaspoon of freshly ground black pepper.

Re-heat the juice, pour into bottles and sterilise.
Tomato cocktail Mix equal quantities of tomato juice and apple juice, and add 1 teaspoon of honey to each pint (600 ml.).

Pickles round the year

No one witnessing the rush upon the produce stalls at village fêtes can fail to be impressed by the enormous popularity and range of home-made pickles. Onions and eggs, red cabbage and beetroot, piccalilli and peaches, cherries and cucumbers glow invitingly in their jars, offering colours and flavours that no commercially produced pickle can imitate.

Despite their exotic appearance, they are made, apart from vinegar and a few spices, entirely from garden fruits and vegetables. Consequently, with only a little trouble and expense, it is quite easy to create a range of pickles that for months to come will turn casual snacks into feasts.

All four types of pickle – raw and cooked vegetable, sweet vegetable and fruit – are preserved by the action of the acetic acid in vinegar, to which different combinations of spices are added to produce flavours that will match or enhance those of the basic materials. Generally, it is best to prepare the vinegars a month or so in advance in order to give the spices sufficient time to permeate them thoroughly.

Pickles are therefore prepared in three basic stages: making the vinegar; adding the vinegar to the vegetables or fruit; bottling, sealing and storing. Keep all pickles for at least a month before using.

Equipment

The most important rule when making either pickles or chutneys is that utensils made of copper or brass must never be used, since vinegar will react upon them and spoil the preserve. Use only enamel, stainless-steel or aluminium pans, nylon sieves and wooden spoons.

In addition, you will need deep bowls or earthenware casseroles in which to salt the vegetables before bottling them, and some butter muslin in which to wrap spices.

Bottling jars, either with clip-on lids or screw-tops, are particularly recommended for pickles, though care must be taken to ensure that the metal tops do not come in contact with the corrosive vinegar. Fit discs of ceresin paper, obtainable from most chemists, within the metal lids, or use plastic-coated tops instead.

Ordinary jam-jars are not really suitable, since even with Cellophane tops they cannot be made completely air-tight. Lack of an air-tight seal permits the vinegar to evaporate, and causes the pickle to dry out.

It is better to use large coffee or fruit-juice jars of the type with plastic lids. But if jam-jars are the only type available, cover the tops with preserving skins to prevent evaporation.

STEP 1
Preparing the vinegar

Most pickles are preserved in spiced vinegars, whose contents and flavours vary enormously according to the recipe and to individual taste.

The vinegar itself must be of the best possible quality; those most suitable are the bottled malts, brown or white distilled. The more expensive white wine and cider vinegars can also be used, but their delicate flavours tend to become lost in those of the pickles.

A number of exceptions include a few fruit pickles, whose recipes require a more subtle base.

Spiced vinegars are at their best when they are allowed to mature for one or two months before being added to the pickle. Use whole, rather than ground, spices, and adjust the amounts according to whether you want a hot or mild pickle.

Spices should not be placed directly in the vinegar. Tie them instead in a muslin bag and allow them to steep in a vinegar-filled, closed jar, shaking occasionally.

For mild pickles
2 pints (1 l.) malt vinegar (brown or white distilled)
¼ oz. (7 g.) each of cinnamon bark, whole cloves, whole mace, allspice and white peppercorns

For hot pickles
2 pints (1 l.) malt vinegar (as above)
1 oz. (25 g.) each of mustard seed and allspice
½ oz. (15 g.) each of cloves and black peppercorns
¼ oz. (7 g.) whole, crushed chillies

For fruit and sweet pickles
2 pints (1 l.) malt vinegar (brown or white distilled)
10 oz. (275 g.) brown sugar
Pinch of salt
½ teaspoon each of whole mixed spice and white peppercorns
4 whole cloves

Dissolve the brown sugar in the vinegar and add the pinch of salt. Tie the spices in a muslin bag and leave to steep for one or two months, shaking occasionally.

BASIC STEPS IN MAKING PICKLES

1. Preparing the vinegar *Recipes for spiced vinegar vary according to the fruit or vegetable to be pickled. If possible, prepare vinegars one or two months in advance.*

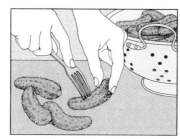

2. Preparing for pickling *Select young vegetables or just-ripe fruit in perfect condition. Clean, cut into chunks, or prick skins as required by the particular recipe.*

3. Salting vegetables *Most vegetables, but not fruit, should be soaked in brine or packed in salt before pickling. Keep them immersed with an upturned plate while soaking.*

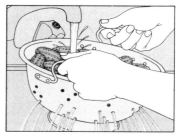

4. Rinsing the vegetables *Steep the vegetables in salt or brine for 12–48 hours, then drain off the brine, wash them thoroughly in cold water and allow them to drain.*

5a. Cold pickling *To retain the crisp texture of raw vegetables, pack them into clean, dry jars, leaving 1 in. (25 mm.) headspace, and cover with cold, spiced vinegar.*

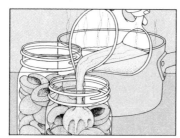

5b. Hot pickling *For soft pickles, such as those made from apricots or marrows, pack the cooked ingredients into heated jars and cover at once with boiling spiced vinegar.*

6. Sealing the bottles *Make sure covers are completely air-tight. Use plastic-coated covers, or insert discs of ceresin paper before sealing if metal covers are used.*

EQUIPMENT

Large jars or bottles
Butter muslin
Large saucepan
Large, deep bowls
Jars with air-tight lids
Preserving skins or ceresin discs
Bottling spoon
Bottling tongs
Funnel
Ladle
Scales

All the preceding recipes are intended for your guidance only. Quantities may be increased or lessened, and other spices, such as crushed garlic, ginger and horse-radish added.

Ready-mixed pickling spices are also available.

Quick-spiced vinegar If you have not prepared the spiced vinegar in advance, make a sufficient supply for your pickle by the hot, quick method instead. Put the vinegar and spices together into a bowl, cover with a lid or plate and stand the bowl over a pan of cold water. Bring to the boil, remove from the heat, but leave the bowl in the water for 2 hours.

Strain the vinegar in order to remove the spices.

STEP 2
Preparing for pickling

Use only young, firm vegetables, and sound fruits that are only just ripe. Peel, wash and drain the vegetables, rejecting any that are unsound.

Chop, shred or leave them whole, as required by the recipe you are following.

Among the many fruits suitable for pickling are apples and crab apples, apricots, currants, damsons, gooseberries, grapes, peaches, pears and plums. Pick over the fruits, discarding any that are over-ripe or under-ripe or otherwise unsound.

If whole fruits are to be pickled, prick them with a silver or stainless-steel fork to prevent shrinkage.

STEP 3
Salting vegetables

Vegetables – though not fruit – are greatly improved by being salted before they are pickled. Immerse the prepared vegetables in a brine solution of 4 oz. of coarse salt to 2 pints water (125 g. to 1 l.). Alternatively, place the vegetables in layers in a bowl or casserole, liberally sprinkling each layer with salt.

Whichever method is chosen, it is important that coarse or block salt should be used. Avoid using table salt, as this contains chemicals that may cloud the pickle.

Dry salting is recommended only for watery vegetables, such as marrows and cucumbers. Others, with a few exceptions for particular recipes, should be saturated in brine.

When doing this, keep the vegetables submerged in the brine by pressing them down into the bowl with an upturned plate.

STEP 4
Rinsing the vegetables

Leave the vegetables to salinate for about 24 hours. Drain off the brine or remove them from the dry salt, wash them thoroughly in cold water and drain.

STEP 5
Bottling the pickles

a. *Cold pickling* Pack raw, salted vegetables – such as onions, beans, cauliflowers, cucumbers or cabbages – into clean jars, leaving a headspace of about 1 in. (25 mm.). Drain off any water that falls to the bottom of the jar and fill up with spiced vinegar, covering the vegetables by at least ½ in. (12 mm.).

Make the jars completely airtight with screw-on plastic lids, or else with metal tops protected by ceresin paper.

b. *Hot pickling* A few pickles (see recipes in this section) involve the use of cooked vegetables. Some are salted, some not; but almost all should be packed, immediately after cooking, into hot jars, covered with spiced vinegar and sealed.

c. *Fruit pickles* For each 4 lb. (2 kg.) of fruit, dissolve 2 lb. (1 kg.) sugar in 2 pints (1 l.) of vinegar – either malt or wine according to the recipe. Add the spices, tied in a muslin bag, cover the pan and bring to the boil. Simmer the fruit until tender, but not mushy.

Carefully strain off the spiced vinegar into a bowl or jug, remove the muslin bag, and pack the fruit into hot, clean jars, leaving about 1 in. (25 mm.) headspace.

Boil the vinegar rapidly in an uncovered saucepan until it is reduced to a thick syrup and pour it over the fruits, making sure they are covered by at least ½ in. (12 mm.) of liquid to allow for evaporation. Cover the jars, seal them, and store in a dry, cool, dark place. They will be ready for use in six to eight weeks.

STEP 6
Sealing the bottles

As a general rule, all pickles should be covered and sealed immediately, whether using hot or cold vinegar. Remember that metal lids, unprotected by ceresin paper or a plastic coating, will quickly corrode.

Storing

Most uncooked pickles should be left to mature for about two months. An exception is pickled cabbage, which is ready for eating within a week.

Most cooked pickles are ready for the table after about a week. They generally store well – with the exception of pickled beetroot, which should be used within two months.

Once matured, your pickles can be put to many uses. Pickled onions need no introduction as the ideal companion of strong British cheese and bread, while pickled cucumbers, beetroot, red cabbage and piccalillis are the equally traditional garnishings of cold meats and salads.

Some of the sweet and fruit pickles, however, are not so familiar, and require a certain degree of enterprise when serving them.

Try pickled peaches, apricots and pears with cream as the basis of a winter fruit salad; or a small bowl of pickled black currants or blackberries may be served with a board of British and continental cheeses.

Things that may go wrong

Shrunken pickles May be caused by poor packing or sealing, or storing the bottles in a too-warm cupboard.

Cloudy vinegar Perhaps due to inadequate salting, stale spices or poor-quality vinegar.

Poor colour This may occur throughout the jar, or in the top layer only.

If evenly distributed, over-long cooking after adding the sugar may be the cause, or you may have used the wrong vinegar.

If only the top layer is affected, the pickle may have been under-cooked, the storage place may be too warm or the cover of the jar may not be quite air-tight.

RECIPES
for
raw-vegetable pickles
➤○◄

PICKLED CABBAGE

1 large red or white cabbage
Spiced vinegar
Coarse salt

Choose firm, good-coloured cabbages. Remove the outer leaves, wash, cut into quarters, and discard the tough inner cores. Shred finely, layer with coarse salt, and leave to stand for 24 hours.

Drain and rinse thoroughly, pack into bottles and cover with cold vinegar. Seal at once.

Both red and white cabbage are ready for use after a week. Red cabbage will store for two or three months; white cabbage for two months only.

➤○◄

PICKLED CAULIFLOWER

4–6 cauliflowers
Spiced vinegar
Sugar (optional)
Coarse salt

Choose firm, close-knit heads and break into small florets. Steep in a brine solution of 1 lb. salt to 1 gallon of water (500 g. to 4 l.) for 24 hours. Rinse and drain thoroughly, and pack into jars. Cover with cold vinegar, and seal.

For a slightly sweeter pickle, add 2–3 teaspoons of sugar to every pint (600 ml.) of spiced vinegar a few days before pickling.

PICKLED CUCUMBER

3 cucumbers : total weight approx. 2 lb.
(1 kg.)
Coarse salt
Spiced vinegar

Wash the cucumbers, wipe them dry, but do not peel. Cut in half lengthways and chop into slices ½ in. (12 mm.) thick. Layer with the salt in a deep dish and leave for 24 hours.

Drain off the liquid, rinse the cucumber in cold water and drain thoroughly again. Pack the cucumber into clean jars, cover with hot, spiced vinegar and seal at once. The pickle will be ready for eating after a week.

PICKLED GHERKINS

2 lb. (1 kg.) gherkins
Coarse salt
Spiced vinegar
Sugar (optional)

Miniature cucumbers, known as gherkins, are excellent for pickling. Prick well with a silver or stainless-steel fork before soaking in brine for 72 hours. Drain, pot, and cover with hot vinegar.

Keep in a warm place for 24 hours, then drain off the vinegar and bring it to the boil. Pour the hot vinegar back over the gherkins, seal and keep it in a warm room for another 24 hours.

Repeat this process until the gherkins are an overall green. Top with more vinegar, if necessary, and seal at once. Pickled gherkins will be ready for eating in a month.

PICKLED NASTURTIUM SEEDS

Ripe nasturtium seeds
Coarse salt
Spiced vinegar

Nasturtium seeds can be used instead of capers, but do not confuse them with the seeds of the caper spurge (*Euphorbia lathyrus*), which are poisonous. Pick the seeds on a dry day, wash, and steep in a brine solution of 2 oz. salt to 1 pint water (50 g. to 600 ml.).

Drain, and pack into small jars to within 1 in. (25 mm.) of the top. Cover with cold, spiced vinegar and seal. Use in salads after about a month.

PICKLED ONIONS

6 lb. (3 kg.) pickling onions
Coarse salt
2 pints (1 l.) spiced vinegar

Steep the small, unpeeled onions in a brine solution for 12 hours. Drain, peel and soak in fresh brine for 24–36 hours.

Rinse and drain well, pack into jars and cover with cold vinegar. Leave for two or three months before using.

Small shallots can be pickled in the same way as onions.

PICKLED WALNUTS

2 lb. (1 kg.) green walnuts
Coarse salt
Spiced, or sweet, spiced vinegar

Use only immature, green walnuts, picked in June or July. Wear rubber gloves throughout the pickling process, since walnuts stain almost ineradicably.

Prick the walnuts all over with a large needle. Discard the nut if there is any hardness at the end opposite the stalk, where the shell begins to develop.

Soak the walnuts in a brine solution of 6 oz. salt to 2 pints water (175 g. to 1 l.) for 48 hours. Drain, and steep in fresh brine for a further week.

Drain again, and leave exposed to the air for a day or two. The walnuts will turn black.

Pack the nuts into clean jars and cover with cold, spiced vinegar. Seal at once.

For a sweet walnut pickle, use a sweet, spiced vinegar, as for fruit pickles.

Pickled walnuts are ready for eating in about six weeks.

ONION AND APPLE PICKLE

4 lb. (2 kg.) onions
2 lb. (1 kg.) cooking apples
Spiced vinegar

Peel the onions and cut into thin slices. Peel and core the apples and slice, or cut into cubes. Mix the two ingredients quickly or the apples will turn brown.

Pot at once in clean jars, cover with hot vinegar, and seal.

This pickle can be eaten the following day, as neither the onions nor the apples have been salted, but it improves with keeping.

ONION, CAULIFLOWER AND CUCUMBER PICKLE

6 lb. (3 kg.) altogether of pickling
onions, cauliflowers and cucumbers
Coarse salt
Spiced vinegar
Dried red chillies

Peel the onions, break the washed cauliflowers into small florets and chop the washed cucumbers into ½ in. (12 mm.) pieces.

Mix thoroughly, layer with coarse salt and leave to stand for 24 hours.

Drain, rinse in cold water and drain again. Pack into jars, cover with cold, spiced vinegar and add one red chilli to each jar.

The pickle is ready for eating in about two months.

ONION, CAULIFLOWER, BEAN AND MARROW PICKLE

6 lb. (3 kg.) altogether of pickling
onions, cauliflowers, dwarf beans and
marrow
Coarse salt
Spiced vinegar

Peel the onions, separate the cauliflowers into tiny florets and chop the beans into 1 in. (25 mm.) lengths. Peel the marrow, remove the seeds and chop the flesh into 1 in. (25 mm.) cubes.

Steep the onions, cauliflowers and beans in brine, and layer the marrow with salt. Leave for 24 hours, drain, rinse and drain again.

Pot in jars and cover with cold vinegar.

Leave for about two weeks before eating.

ONION AND CUCUMBER PICKLE

2 lb. (1 kg.) onions
2–3 cucumbers
Coarse salt
Spiced vinegar

Peel and slice the onions; wash and dry the cucumbers and cut into ½ in. (12 mm.) slices. Mix thoroughly and place in layers with the salt in a deep bowl.

Leave for 24 hours, drain, and rinse in cold water. Drain well and pot in clean jars.

Cover with spiced vinegar and seal at once.

The pickle is ready for eating in about two weeks.

Continued...

RECIPES
for
cooked vegetable pickles

PICKLED BEETROOT

4 lb. (2 kg.) uncooked beetroot
Spiced vinegar

Wash the beetroot carefully without damaging the skin, then boil in lightly salted water for about 1½ hours, until tender. Leave to cool, rub off the skins and then cut into slices ¼ in. (5 mm.) thick.

Pack into jars and cover with cold vinegar. If a sweeter pickle is preferred, a little sugar may be added.

This pickle must be used within two months. However, a beetroot pickle with a rather longer storage life can be made by dicing the beetroot instead of slicing it, packing the pieces loosely into jars and covering with boiling, spiced vinegar.

PICKLED CARROTS

2 lb. (1 kg.) small carrots
1¼ pints (725 ml.) distilled white vinegar
½ lb. (250 g.) sugar
2 oz. (50 g.) pickling spice
¼ pint (150 ml.) water

Trim and scrape the carrots, simmer for 15–20 minutes in slightly salted water until just tender, then drain.

Boil the vinegar and water, together with the pickling spices in a muslin bag, for 10 minutes.

Remove the spices, add the sugar and the carrots, and boil until tender. Pack into hot jars and cover with the vinegar. Seal at once.

PICKLED CAULIFLOWERS

1 large cauliflower
Spiced vinegar
2 teaspoons marjoram
A pinch each of salt and ground white pepper
1 red pepper
Olive oil

Clean the cauliflower and break into florets. Boil in lightly salted water for 5 minutes, drain, and cover with boiling vinegar. Steep for 24 hours, drain, and reserve the vinegar for use as the pickling liquid.

Pack the florets into jars – sprinkling each layer with marjoram, a pinch each of pepper and salt, and the blanched, de-seeded, finely chopped red pepper.

Mix the cooled vinegar with olive oil in the proportion of 1 part vinegar to 2 parts oil; pour over the cauliflower and seal at once.

The pickle can be used in three or four weeks.

PICKLED EGGS

12 new-laid eggs
2–2½ pints (1–1.25 l.) white wine or cider vinegar
12 cloves
1 oz. (25 g.) mixed pickling spice
2 blades of mace
Peel of ½ orange

Hard-boil the fresh eggs and leave in cold water. Put the vinegar in a pan and add the cloves, spice, mace and orange peel, all tied in muslin. Cover with a lid, bring to the boil and simmer for 10 minutes. Leave to cool and remove the muslin bag.

Pour half the vinegar into a wide-necked jar with a tight-fitting top, and add the shelled eggs. Fill up with vinegar and seal. The eggs will be ready for eating in about six weeks.

PICKLED MARROW

2 lb. (1 kg.) marrow
4 oz. (125 g.) coarse salt
1 teaspoon ground ginger
1 teaspoon curry powder
1 oz. (25 g.) mustard
6 peppercorns
4 oz. (125 g.) sugar
¾ pint (450 ml.) vinegar

Peel the marrow, remove the seeds and chop into small cubes. Sprinkle with the salt and leave overnight. Add the ginger, curry powder, mustard, peppercorns and sugar to the vinegar, bring to the boil and boil for 5 minutes.

Add the rinsed and drained marrow cubes. Simmer until tender, and pack into jars. Seal at

once. The pickle can be used in three to four weeks.

PICKLED MUSHROOMS

1 lb. (500 g.) mushrooms
Malt or distilled vinegar
1 small onion
2 blades of mace
½ teaspoon each of ground ginger, salt and ground white pepper

Peel and trim the mushrooms. Put in a pan with enough vinegar to cover, and add the peeled, sliced onion, mace, ginger, salt and pepper. Cover with a lid and simmer until the mushrooms are tender and shrunken. Pack into the jars and cover with strained vinegar. Seal at once.

Leave for a month before eating.

CELERY AND CUCUMBER PICKLE

2½ cucumbers
1 large onion
4 long sticks of celery
1½ oz. (40 g.) coarse salt
1 teaspoon of turmeric
3 oz. (75 g.) plain flour
2 oz. (50 g.) dry mustard
4 oz. (125 g.) sugar
½ pint (300 ml.) cider vinegar

Peel and cube the cucumbers, peel and finely chop the onion, and scrub and dice the celery. Mix well and add the salt, leave for 30 minutes, then drain. Add the turmeric, flour, mustard and sugar to the vinegar and simmer for 2–3 minutes.

Add the vegetables and cook over gentle heat for 30 minutes, stirring occasionally. Pack in hot bottling jars, seal and sterilise (see Bottling, p. 309). The pickle can be used in three or four weeks.

MIXED PICKLE

3 cucumbers
1½ oz. (40 g.) coarse salt
1 pint (600 ml.) water
1 large carrot
1 green pepper, 2 red peppers or 1 lb. (500 g.) French or runner beans
¾ pint (450 ml.) cider vinegar
1½ lb. (750 g.) sugar
1 oz. (25 g.) each of mustard seed, celery seed and turmeric

Wash the cucumbers and cut into pieces about 2 in. (50 mm.) long and ¼ in. (5 mm.) wide. Sprinkle with three-quarters of the salt, cover with the water and leave overnight. Rinse and drain.

Scrape or peel the carrot and cut into similar pieces. Boil for 5 minutes in lightly salted water, then drain.

Remove the stalk base and seeds from the green and red peppers; chop finely. Put the vinegar in a pan with the sugar, and the spices tied in muslin. Add the vegetables and bring to boiling point.

Remove from the heat and pack in hot jars. Pour the strained vinegar over the vegetables and seal at once. Keep for six to eight weeks before eating.

MUSTARD PICKLE

¾ *lb. (375 g.) peeled cucumber*
¾ *lb. (375 g.) peeled onions*
1 lb. (500 g.) cauliflower florets
½ *lb. (250 g.) green tomatoes*
1½ *lb. (750 g.) green peppers, or 1 lb.*
(500 g.) French or runner beans
1 lb. (500 g.) gherkins
½ *lb. (250 g.) coarse salt*
5 pints (2.75 l.) water
3 pints (1.5 l.) distilled vinegar
1 lb. (500 g.) sugar
1½ *oz. (40 g.) mustard seeds*
2 oz. (50 g.) plain flour
Pinch of turmeric
1 oz. (25 g.) dry mustard

Put the cucumber, onions, cauliflower, tomatoes and de-seeded peppers through the medium blade of the mincer. Slice the gherkins thickly. Mix the vegetables and soak overnight in the salt and water.

Put most of the vinegar in a pan with the sugar, mustard seeds and well-drained vegetables, and bring to the boil.

Make a paste with the remaining vinegar, flour, turmeric and dry mustard and add to the vegetable mixture. Bring back to the boil, uncovered, and simmer for about 20 minutes, stirring occasionally, until tender. Pot in hot jars and seal at once.

Keep for about four to six weeks before eating.

PICCALILLI

6 lb. (3 kg.) mixed vegetables
(prepared weight)
1 lb. (500 g.) coarse salt
8 pints (4 l.) water
For a hot, sharp piccalilli:
   3 teaspoons turmeric
   8 teaspoons dry mustard
   8 teaspoons ground ginger
   6 oz. (175 g.) sugar
   1 oz. (25 g.) cornflour
   2 pints (1 l.) distilled vinegar
For a mild, sweet piccalilli:
   3 teaspoons turmeric
   4 teaspoons dry mustard
   4 teaspoons ground ginger
   10 oz. (275 g.) sugar
   2 oz. (50 g.) cornflour
   3 pints (1.5 l.) distilled vinegar

This popular pickle is made from fresh, crisp vegetables, such as beans (dwarf, broad or runner), red or white cabbage, cauliflowers, cucumbers, celery, gherkins, marrows, onions, shallots, peppers and green tomatoes.

Prepare the vegetables as for cooking, and cut into uniform small pieces. Keep the vegetables immersed in a brine solution of the salt and water, or spread them on a large dish and sprinkle with the dry salt. Leave overnight, then rinse and drain the vegetables thoroughly. Whether you choose a sharp or sweet piccalilli, proceed as follows:

Blend the turmeric, mustard, ginger and sugar with all but 2–3 tablespoons of the vinegar. Put in a large pan with the vegetables, bring to the boil and simmer for about 20 minutes, according to the degree of crispness or tenderness you prefer. Carefully lift out the vegetables with a slotted spoon

and put at once into hot jars.

Blend the cornflour with the remaining vinegar and stir in the hot syrup. Boil for 2–3 minutes, stirring occasionally, then pour over the vegetables to cover. Seal at once and store for four to six weeks before using.

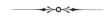

PIMENTO PICKLE

18–24 pimentoes
1 pint (600 ml.) spiced vinegar
2 oz. (50 g.) coarse salt
4 oz. (125 g.) sugar

Wash the pimentoes, cut them into quarters and remove the seeds, membranes and stalks. Set these aside. Pour boiling water over the pimentoes and leave for 20 minutes.

Put the pimento stalks and seeds in the vinegar with the sugar and salt, bring to the boil and simmer for 10 minutes. Drain the pimentoes, and pack into jars, cover with the strained, hot vinegar, and seal.

This pickle is ready after a couple of days, but do not keep for more than a month.

GREEN TOMATO PICKLE

6 lb. (3 kg.) green tomatoes
Coarse salt
Spiced vinegar
Sugar
1 large onion

Wash and dry the tomatoes, quarter or cut into slices. Layer with the salt and leave overnight.

Drain off the liquid, put the tomatoes in a pan and cover with vinegar in which sugar has been dissolved at the rate of 1 oz. to each pint (50 g. to 1 l.).

Add the thinly sliced onion, bring to the boil and simmer for about 30 minutes, until tender. Pour into warm jars and seal.

Keep for a month before using.

RED TOMATO PICKLE

6 lb. (3 kg.) small tomatoes
Spiced vinegar

Choose small barely ripe tomatoes. Cover with boiling water for 1–2 minutes, then peel off the skins.

Put the tomatoes in an ovenproof dish, and pour over enough vinegar to cover. Put foil or a lid over the dish and cook in the oven at a temperature of 180°C (350°F) – gas mark 4 for 30 minutes. Pack the whole tomatoes carefully into hot jars, cover with hot vinegar and seal. Keep for a month before using.

SWEET PICKLE

2 lb. (1 kg.) mixed vegetables
1 oz. (25 g.) pickling spice
1 pint (600 ml.) malt or distilled
vinegar
2 oz. (50 g.) plain flour, or 1 oz.
(25 g.) cornflour
6 oz. (175 g.) sugar
5 oz. (150 g.) sultanas
Coarse salt

Cut the prepared vegetables – such as cauliflowers, marrows, onions, cucumbers, small green tomatoes

and beans – into small pieces. Soak overnight in brine. Rinse well in cold water and drain.

Tie the spices in a muslin bag, place in the vinegar and boil, reserving 2 tablespoons of vinegar to make a paste with the flour and sugar. Stir this into the hot vinegar, and remove the spices.

Simmer until the mixture begins to thicken, then add the vegetables and sultanas and boil for 5 minutes. Pot in hot jars and seal at once.

Keep for four to six weeks before using.

SWEET APPLE AND CUCUMBER PICKLE

2 lb. (1 kg.) dessert apples (prepared
weight)
2 cucumbers
4 onions
½ *pint (300 ml.) vinegar (unspiced)*
½ *lb. (250 g.) granulated sugar*
1 teaspoon celery seeds
½ *teaspoon each of ground ginger and*
turmeric
¼ *teaspoon ground white pepper*

Peel and core the apples and chop finely. Peel and dice the cucumbers; peel the onions and chop finely.

Put the vinegar in a pan with the sugar, celery seeds and spices. Bring to the boil, stirring until the sugar has dissolved, then add the apples, cucumbers and onions. Bring back to the boil and simmer for 20–30 minutes.

Pot the pickle in hot jars, and seal. Keep for a month before using.

Continued . . .

RECIPES for fruit pickles

APPLE PICKLE

2 lb. (1 kg.) cooking apples
2 lb. (1 kg.) sugar
1 pint (600 ml.) sweet, spiced vinegar

Dissolve the sugar in the hot vinegar in a large pan.

Peel, core and slice the apples and add at once to the vinegar in the pan. Bring to the boil and simmer gently until tender.

Lift out and pack the apples into hot jars. Increase the heat and boil the syrup rapidly until it has reduced by half. Pour over the apples and seal. The pickle can be used in two or three weeks.

APRICOT PICKLE

2 lb. (1 kg.) apricots
2–3 lb. (1–1.5 kg.) sugar
¾ pint (450 ml.) sweet, spiced, white wine vinegar

Cut the apricots into halves and remove the stones. Put the apricots in an ovenproof dish and cook, covered, in the oven at a temperature of 180°C (350°F) – gas mark 4, for 15–20 minutes, or until the skin is peeling off.

Remove from the oven, take off the skin and pack the apricots in hot jars. Dissolve the sugar in the hot, spiced vinegar and pour over the apricots. Seal at once, and leave for a month before eating.

BLACKBERRY PICKLE

2 lb. (1 kg.) blackberries
1 lb. (500 g.) sugar
½ pint (300 ml.) white vinegar (wine or malt)
1½ teaspoons each of whole cloves, allspice and cinnamon

Dissolve the sugar in the vinegar, and add the spices tied in a muslin bag. Bring to the boil and add the cleaned and hulled blackberries. Cover, and simmer until tender.

Remove the spices, pour off the vinegar and pack the blackberries into hot jars. Reduce the syrupy vinegar by half through fast boiling, and pour it over the blackberries. Seal at once, and leave for a month before eating.

Black currants may be pickled in exactly the same way.

PICKLED CHERRIES

2 lb. (1 kg.) stoned 'Morello' cherries
½ pint (300 ml.) distilled vinegar
1 lb. (500 g.) sugar
2 cloves
1½ teaspoons cinnamon bark
1–2 pieces bruised root ginger

Heat the vinegar and dissolve the sugar, add the spices in a muslin bag and bring to the boil. Add the stoned cherries and cover the pan. Cook until soft.

Remove the spices, lift out the cherries with a slotted spoon and pack into hot jars. Boil the vinegar rapidly until it has reduced by half, then pour over the cherries.

Seal at once, and leave for a month before eating.

CRAB-APPLE PICKLE

3 lb. (1.5 kg.) crab apples
¼ lemon
1 pint (600 ml.) malt vinegar
2 lb. (1 kg.) sugar
2 cloves
2 pieces bruised root ginger
1 cinnamon stick

Choose small, unblemished fruits, remove the stalks, wash thoroughly and dry. Put the crab apples and lemon in a pan with enough water to cover. Bring to the boil and simmer, covered, until almost tender. Carefully lift out the apples and leave to drain.

Measure ½ pint (300 ml.) of the apple cooking liquid and put in a pan with the vinegar. Add the sugar and stir until dissolved, then add the spices tied in muslin.

Bring to the boil, return the apples to the pan and simmer, covered, until tender but still whole. Lift out the apples and pack into hot jars. Reduce the syrup by half and pour over the whole apples.

Seal at once, and leave for a month before using.

DAMSON PICKLE

4 lb. (2 kg.) damsons
2 lb. (1 kg.) sugar
1 pint (600 ml.) sweet, spiced, white vinegar (malt or wine)
½ lemon

Wash and dry the damsons. Prick them thoroughly all over with a stainless-steel or silver fork.

Dissolve the sugar in the vinegar, stirring all the time, then add the damsons and sliced lemon.

Cover the pan and simmer gently until just tender. Lift out the damsons and pack into warm jars. Boil the syrup rapidly until reduced by half, pour it over the damsons and seal at once.

Leave for two months before using.

GOOSEBERRY PICKLE

5 lb. (2.5 kg.) green gooseberries
3 lb. (1.5 kg.) sugar
2 pints (1 l.) sweet, spiced, white wine vinegar

Top and tail the gooseberries, rinse and drain. Dissolve the sugar in the vinegar, add the gooseberries and simmer, covered, over very gentle heat until just soft. Lift out the gooseberries and leave to drain.

Reduce the syrup until thick. Pack the gooseberries into warm jars, pour the syrup over them and seal at once.

Store for two or three months before using.

PEACH PICKLE

2 lb. (1 kg.) peaches
2–3 lb. (1–1.5 kg.) sugar
¾ pint (450 ml.) sweet, spiced, white vinegar

Follow the method for apricot pickle.

PICKLED PEARS

4 lb. (2 kg.) pears
2 lb. (1 kg.) sugar
1 pint (600 ml.) sweet, spiced, white vinegar

Choose cooking pears or firm, barely ripe dessert pears. Peel, quarter and core unless the pears are quite small, in which case they may be left whole. Dissolve the sugar in the vinegar and bring to the boil. Add the pears and cover the pan with a lid.

Simmer gently until the pears are soft, lift out and drain, then pack into hot jars. Boil the syrup until it has reduced to a thick consistency, pour over the pears and seal at once. The pears can be eaten after a month.

PICKLED PLUMS

2 lb. (1 kg.) plums
2 lb. (1 kg.) sugar
1 pint (600 ml.) sweet, spiced, white vinegar
Juice and rind of ½ lemon

For this pickle, select firm, medium-sized plums such as 'Victoria' or 'Kirke's'. Wash and dry the plums, and prick them thoroughly.

Boil the sugar and vinegar to a syrup. Add the plums and simmer, covered, until tender. Remove and drain the plums, put in warm jars, and reduce the syrup by boiling until thick. Pour over the plums. Cover at once, and store for two or three months before using.

Rich chutneys from garden produce

In pickling, one of the main objectives is to preserve the colour, shape and texture of the original fruit or vegetables. In chutneys, however, these are chopped, cooked, mixed with spices and other ingredients, and reduced to a smooth pulp in which only the flavour of the produce is recognisable.

The character of a good chutney depends on the careful blending of the ingredients, so that they balance and complement each other. This can be achieved only by long, slow cooking, followed by a lengthy period of maturation in the jar.

Both fruit and vegetable chutneys improve considerably with keeping. If properly stored, they will remain in good condition for years.

Equipment

Use the same equipment for chutney-making as for pickles. It is important that cooking should be done in a heavy-based pan of stainless steel or well-scoured aluminium. Sieves should be of fine nylon, hair, or stainless steel.

STEP 1
Preparing the ingredients

Wash and prepare the ingredients by peeling, coring, topping and tailing, as appropriate. Ensure the smooth texture of the chutney by finely chopping or mincing the fruit and vegetables, especially in the case of onions.

STEP 2
Softening tough vegetables

If tough fruit or vegetables are included in the recipe, you will find it quicker, and more economical on fuel, to soften them first. Do this by placing them in a pan with a little of the vinegar and cooking them gently, covered by a lid, until soft. Then add the remaining ingredients, including the vinegar.

Certain ingredients, such as blackberries, require sieving. Do this after the chutney has been simmering in an open pan for 1 hour. Remove the pan from the heat, rub the contents through a sieve and return them to the pan. Continue simmering until the chutney thickens.

STEP 3
Cooking

Use ground spices, rather than whole, if available. If this is not possible, use whole spices, bruised and tied in a muslin bag.

Remove the bag from the pan

BRUISING SPICES

If preferred, or if ground spices are unavailable, whole spices may be used. Bruise, or half crush them with the back of a spoon, before tying them in muslin.

when you have finished cooking.

Many recipes specify the use of ginger – ground, whole root or crystallised. These are interchangeable, provided you remember that 1 unit of ground ginger is equivalent to $1\frac{1}{2}$ units of root ginger or 4 units of crystallised ginger.

Dark-coloured chutneys are made by cooking the sugar with the other ingredients over a long period, or by using brown sugar.

For light-coloured chutneys, add the sugar when the other ingredients are well softened, and use white sugar rather than brown.

With a few exceptions, good-quality malt vinegar is recommended for chutneys. Savings can be made on the amounts of vinegar needed by using just enough to cover the fruit or vegetables at the beginning of cooking, and adding the rest towards the end.

With the exceptions of sugar and vinegar, cook all the ingredients for the same length of time, otherwise the texture will be rougher and the flavour of late-added ingredients will dominate. If sugar and vinegar are added late in the cooking, first dissolve the sugar in the vinegar.

Simmer chutneys for an average of 1–2 hours, until they reach a jam-like consistency. Evaporation is an important part of the process, so always cook them uncovered.

If the mixture becomes too thick, add a little more vinegar. Chutneys thicken as they cool.

BASIC STEPS IN CHUTNEY MAKING

1. Preparing the ingredients *Wash, peel, core and finely chop or mince the fruit or vegetables, according to the recipe. In a few cases, produce should be coarsely cut.*

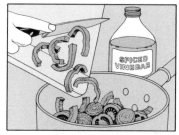

2. Softening tough vegetables *To save fuel, put any tough fruit or vegetables into a pan with a little of the vinegar, cover, and cook them gently until softened.*

3. Cooking *Add remaining vinegar, sugar and ground spices (or whole spices in a muslin bag). Simmer for 1–2 hours, uncovered, until the chutney has thickened to a jam-like consistency.*

4. Potting and storing *Pour the hot chutney into warmed jars, and cover immediately with plastic-coated screw-tops. Alternatively, cover with cloth lids dipped in paraffin wax.*

> ### EQUIPMENT
> *Small knife and peeler*
> *Mincer*
> *Large, heavy-based, stainless-steel or aluminium pan*
> *Muslin for wrapping whole spices*
> *Wooden spoon*
> *Nylon, stainless-steel, or hair sieve*
> *Funnel*
> *Ladle*
> *Jars with screw-tops, or waxed cloth covers*
> *Measuring jug and scales*

STEP 4
Potting and storing

Pot chutney at once, while still hot, in clean, warm jars. Screw-cap jars are the most likely to give an air-tight seal. Metal lids must be provided with vinegar-proof linings of ceresin paper, plastic or cork.

Preserving skin can be used, but should be tied down tight or the chutney will shrink and harden in storage.

If screw-capped jars are not available, use ordinary jam-jars and lay greaseproof-paper discs on the chutney, covering the jars with a clean cloth dipped in melted paraffin wax.

Once the chutney has cooled completely, store the jars in a dry, cool, dark cupboard or larder until they are eaten.

Leave chutneys for two or three months before serving. They generally improve as they mature and, provided they are properly potted and stored, should remain in good condition for up to three years.

Things that may go wrong

The most common failing of chutneys in store is that they dry out and shrink to two-thirds or less of their original bulk.

This drying and shrinking is due to inadequate covering and the lack of an air-tight seal.

The same cause may lead to contamination, whose symptoms are either a dark layer at the top of the jar, or the darkening of the entire contents.

These symptoms may also arise from over-long storage, from storage in too warm a place, or because brown sugar or brown vinegar was used instead of white.

RECIPES
for
fruit and vegetable chutneys

Unless you are certain of your family's preference for mild or hot chutneys, make a small trial batch before beginning large-scale chutney-making.

Chutneys taste spicy when freshly made, but usually become mellow in storage. The amount of spices may be reduced or increased, but always use the recommended quantities of sugar and vinegar.

APPLE CHUTNEY I
Approx. yield 8 lb. (4 kg.)

6 lb. (3 kg.) cooking apples
2 lb. (1 kg.) onions
½ pint (300 ml.) water
1½ oz. (40 g.) salt
1½ oz. (40 g.) ground ginger
2 tablespoons ground cinnamon
¼ teaspoon cayenne
2 pints (1 l.) vinegar
2 lb. (1 kg.) sugar (brown or white)
1 lb. (500 g.) golden syrup

Simmer the peeled and finely chopped apples, and the peeled onions, for 20 minutes in the water before adding the salt, spices and half the vinegar.

Cook until soft, then add the sugar, syrup and the rest of the vinegar. Simmer until smooth and thick. Pot and cover.

APPLE CHUTNEY II
Approx. yield 8 lb. (4 kg.)

7 lb. (3.5 kg.) cooking apples
2–3 garlic cloves
2 pints (1 l.) vinegar
3 lb. (1.5 kg.) brown or white sugar
1 lb. (500 g.) sultanas
8 oz. (250 g.) crystallised ginger
1 teaspoon each of mixed spice, cayenne and salt

Simmer the peeled and finely chopped apples with the crushed garlic in almost a quarter of the vinegar until soft. Add the sugar, sultanas, ginger and spices, and cook for a further 20 minutes.

Stir in the remaining vinegar and simmer until thick. Pot in hot jars and seal.

APPLE AND RED-PEPPER CHUTNEY
Approx. yield 2 lb. (1 kg.)

2 large cooking apples – approx. 1 lb. (500 g.)
4 red peppers
2 aubergines
8 oz. (250 g.) onions
2 garlic cloves
6 oz. (175 g.) stoned raisins
1–2 teaspoons curry powder
Pinch of saffron powder (optional)
6 chillis
1 piece of root ginger
2 oz. (50 g.) brown sugar
1 pint (600 ml.) spiced vinegar

Peel and core the apples, cut the base from the peppers and remove the seeds and membranes. Peel the aubergines, onions and garlic. Thinly slice the apples, peppers, aubergines and onions. Chop the raisins and put all the ingredients

in a pan with the crushed garlic.

Mix the curry powder and saffron (if used) with a little vinegar, and add to the pan with the bruised chillis and ginger, tied in muslin, and half the vinegar. Simmer until soft, then add the sugar and remaining vinegar and continue cooking until the chutney is smooth and thick. Pot at once.

APPLE AND TOMATO CHUTNEY
Approx. yield 5 lb. (2.5 kg.)

2 lb. (1 kg.) apples
2 lb. (1 kg.) red tomatoes
1 lb. (500 g.) onions
1 garlic clove
8 oz. (250 g.) sultanas
1 tablespoon mustard seeds
1 lb. (500 g.) demerara sugar
1 oz. (25 g.) salt
2–3 teaspoons curry powder
Pinch cayenne
2 pints (1 l.) malt vinegar

Peel and core the apples, slice thinly and cook in a little water until tender. Peel and slice the tomatoes; peel the onions and chop finely. Add these ingredients to the pan with the crushed garlic, the chopped dried fruit, and the mustard seeds tied in a muslin bag.

Stir in the salt, curry powder, cayenne and half the vinegar.

Bring to the boil and simmer until soft, then add the sugar and the remaining vinegar and cook until smooth and thick. Remove the muslin bag; pot at once.

APRICOT CHUTNEY
Approx. yield 2 lb. (1 kg.)

8 oz. (250 g.) dried apricots
4 oz. (125 g.) stoned raisins
4 oz. (125 g.) sultanas
2 crushed garlic cloves
Juice and grated rind of 1 lemon
2 teaspoons pickling spice
1 teaspoon salt
1 pint (600 ml.) white vinegar
1 lb. (500 g.) brown sugar
1 lb. (500 g.) apples

Wash the apricots and cut into small pieces. Soak for 3 hours, drain, and put in a pan with the chopped raisins, sultanas, garlic, lemon juice and rind, the pickling spice tied in a muslin bag, the salt and half the vinegar. Bring to the boil and simmer for 30 minutes.

Stir in the sugar, the grated apples and the remaining vinegar. Simmer to a jam-like consistency. Remove the muslin bag before potting and sealing.

BEETROOT CHUTNEY
Approx. yield 4 lb. (2 kg.)

2 lb. (1 kg.) uncooked beetroot
1 lb. (500 g.) onions
1½ lb. (750 g.) cooking apples
1 lb. (500 g.) seedless raisins
3 tablespoons ground ginger
2 lb. (1 kg.) granulated sugar
2 pints (1 l.) malt vinegar

Peel and grate the beetroot; peel the onions and chop finely; peel, core and chop the apples. Put in a pan with the raisins, ginger, sugar and vinegar. Bring to the boil. Simmer until thick, then pot.

BLACKBERRY AND APPLE CHUTNEY
Approx. yield 8 lb. (4 kg.)

6 lb. (3 kg.) blackberries
2 lb. (1 kg.) cooking apples
2 lb. (1 kg.) onions
1 oz. (25 g.) salt
2 oz. (50 g.) dry mustard
2 oz. (50 g.) ground ginger
2 teaspoons ground mace
1 teaspoon cayenne
2 pints (1 l.) malt vinegar
2 lb. (1 kg.) brown sugar

Wash and drain the hulled blackberries and simmer for 20 minutes, then rub through a sieve. Peel, core and chop the apples, and peel and chop the onions. Put all ingredients, except sugar, in a pan.

Simmer for 1 hour then add the sugar and cook until thick. Pot the chutney at once.

CRANBERRY AND APPLE CHUTNEY
Approx. yield 4–5 lb. (2–2.5 kg.)

2 lb. (1 kg.) cranberries
2 lb. (1 kg.) cooking apples
1 lb. (500 g.) onions
1½–2 lb. (750 g.–1 kg.) brown sugar
1½–2 teaspoons ground ginger
2 teaspoons ground allspice
Pinch each of ground cloves, nutmeg, dry mustard, cayenne
1 oz. (25 g.) salt
Juice and grated peel of 2 oranges
2 pints (1 l.) malt vinegar

Place the cranberries in a pan with the peeled, cored and chopped apples and the peeled and chopped onions.

Add all the other ingredients

and bring to the boil, then simmer the chutney until all the liquid has evaporated. Pot at once.

DAMSON CHUTNEY
Approx. yield 7–8 lb. (3.5–4 kg.)

7 lb. (3.5 kg.) damsons
4 onions
1 lb. (500 g.) stoned raisins
8 oz. (250 g.) stoned dates
2 garlic cloves
2 oz. (50 g.) ground ginger
Pinch of ground allspice
1 oz. (25 g.) salt
3 lb. (1.5 kg.) brown sugar
5¼ pints (2.75 l.) malt vinegar

Wash, rinse and dry the damsons; chop the peeled onions, the raisins and the dates, and crush the garlic. Place the fruits, onions, garlic, spices and salt in a pan with the sugar and vinegar. Simmer until quite soft and thick. Remove the damson stones before potting.

GOOSEBERRY CHUTNEY
Approx. yield 4 lb. (2 kg.)

3 lb. (1.5 kg.) gooseberries
8 oz. (250 g.) onions
6 oz. (175 g.) stoned raisins
12 oz. (350 g.) granulated sugar
½ teaspoon mixed spice
1 teaspoon crushed mustard seeds
1 oz. (25 g.) salt
1 pint (600 ml.) white vinegar

Chop the peeled onions and cook in a little water until tender. Drain. Put the washed, topped and tailed gooseberries into a pan with the onions, raisins and remaining ingredients.

Simmer gently for about 1 hour until the chutney has thickened, then pot at once.

INDIAN CHUTNEY
Approx. yield 5–6 lb. (2.5–3 kg.)

2 lb. (1 kg.) cooking apples
1 lb. (500 g.) onions
8 garlic cloves
2 pints (1 l.) malt vinegar
2 lb. (1 kg.) soft brown sugar
2 oz. (50 g.) salt
1 lb. (500 g.) stoned raisins
4 oz. (125 g.) dry mustard
5 oz. (150 g.) ground ginger
4 teaspoons cayenne

Peel, core and slice the apples, peel and chop the onions, and crush the garlic.

Simmer the apples in the vinegar with the onions, garlic, sugar and salt until soft.

Rub through a fine sieve and return to a clean pan. Add the chopped raisins and stir in the mustard, ginger and cayenne pepper.

Leave the mixture overnight, covered with a cloth, in a warm room or an airing cupboard before potting.

MARROW AND APPLE CHUTNEY
Approx. yield 6 lb. (3 kg.)

4 lb. (2 kg.) marrow
3 oz. (75 g.) coarse salt
2 lb. (1 kg.) cooking apples
1 lb. (500 g.) shallots
1 lb. (500 g.) granulated sugar
Mixed bruised ginger, chillis and black peppercorns
2 pints (1 l.) white vinegar

Peel the marrow, remove the seeds and cut the flesh into small chunks. Place in a bowl, sprinkling each layer with salt, and leave overnight. Wash and drain thoroughly.

Put in a pan with a little vinegar, the finely chopped, peeled and cored apples, the peeled, chopped shallots and the spices tied in a muslin bag. When soft, add the remaining vinegar and sugar, and simmer until thick. Remove the spices before potting.

MIXED-FRUIT CHUTNEY
Approx. yield 3–4 lb. (1.5–2 kg.)

3 lb. (1.5 kg.) mixed apples, pears, damsons and ripe tomatoes
4 oz. (125 g.) stoned dates
1 lb. (500 g.) onions
2 garlic cloves
8 oz. (250 g.) brown sugar
Salt
1 oz. (25 g.) mustard seeds
1 teaspoon each of ground pepper, allspice, cloves and ginger
1 pint (600 ml.) malt vinegar

Peel and core the apples and pears, stone the damsons and skin the tomatoes. Put through the mincer

with the dates, the peeled onions and the garlic. Mix thoroughly and blend in the sugar and a pinch of salt.

Cook the spices in the vinegar, together with the mustard seeds tied in muslin, for 15 minutes, then add the fruit mix. Simmer gently to the required consistency, stirring occasionally. Remove the muslin bag and pot the chutney.

MIXED-FRUIT CHUTNEY, CHINESE STYLE
Approx. yield 6 lb. (3 kg.)

2 lb. (1 kg.) plums
2 lb. (1 kg.) fresh, ripe apricots
1 large or 2 small pineapples
2 lb. (1 kg.) brown sugar
1 pint (600 ml.) white wine vinegar

Skin and halve the plums and apricots, remove the stones and chop the flesh finely. Peel the pineapple, discard the hard central core, and cut the flesh into small pieces.

Put the fruit in a pan with the sugar and about half of the vinegar. When the sugar has dissolved, taste the chutney to determine whether it needs more vinegar or sugar. Simmer until quite soft and thick, stirring frequently. Pot at once.

Continued...

Chutney recipes (continued)

PEACH CHUTNEY
Approx. yield 3 lb. (1.5 kg.)

3 lb. (1.5 kg.) small ripe peaches
1 lemon
2 garlic cloves
8 oz. (250 g.) seedless raisins
1 oz. (25 g.) stem or crystallised ginger
1 green pepper
1 lb. (500 g.) brown sugar
1 teaspoon cayenne
2 pints (1 l.) cider vinegar
Salt

Peel and stone the peaches and cut into chunks. Place in a pan with the minced lemon, crushed garlic, chopped raisins, ginger and pepper, having first removed the seeds from the pepper.

Add the sugar, cayenne and vinegar and simmer until soft and thick. Season to taste with salt before potting.

PEAR AND GINGER CHUTNEY
Approx. yield 4 lb. (2 kg.)

3 lb. (1.5 kg.) pears
1 lb. (500 g.) onions
1 orange
1 lemon
4 oz. (125 g.) seedless raisins
8 oz. (250 g.) granulated sugar
Large pinch ground cloves
1 tablespoon ground ginger
¼ teaspoon salt
3 black peppercorns
½ pint (300 ml.) malt vinegar

Chop the peeled and cored pears and the peeled onions. Grate the peel from the orange and lemon and extract the juice. Place these

ingredients in a pan with the raisins, sugar, spices and salt, and the peppercorns tied in muslin.

Add the vinegar and simmer until the consistency is soft and thick. Remove the peppercorns before potting.

PEAR AND LEMON CHUTNEY
Approx. yield 4 lb. (2 kg.)

3 lb. (1.5 kg.) pears
5 shallots
3 garlic cloves
1 large lemon
4 oz. (125 g.) stem ginger
4 oz. (125 g.) sultanas
4 oz. (125 g.) seedless raisins
1 lb. (500 g.) brown sugar
1 pint (600 ml.) white wine vinegar
1 teaspoon each of turmeric, cinnamon, pepper, salt and coriander

Dice the peeled and cored pears, chop the peeled shallots and crush the garlic. Cut the lemon into thin slices, discarding the pips, and chop the stem ginger.

Put these ingredients in a pan with the sultanas, raisins (whole), sugar, spices and vinegar. Simmer gently until all the ingredients are soft and the chutney has a firm consistency. Pot at once.

PEPPER CHUTNEY
Approx. yield 3 lb. (1.5 kg.)

3 red peppers ; 3 green peppers
1 lb. (500 g.) ripe tomatoes
12 oz. (350 g.) onions
1 lb. (500 g.) cooking apples
1 teaspoon each of ground allspice and mustard seeds
2 teaspoons peppercorns
8 oz. (250 g.) demerara sugar
16 fl. oz. (475 ml.) malt vinegar

Cut the base from the peppers and remove the seeds ; mince or chop finely. Peel and quarter the tomatoes, peel and chop the onions, and peel, core and chop the apples.

Simmer these ingredients for about 1½ hours with the vinegar and sugar, together with the allspice, peppercorns and mustard seeds in a muslin bag. Pot when the required consistency is obtained.

PLUM CHUTNEY
Approx. yield 4½ lb. (2.25 kg.)

2 lb. (1 kg.) stoned plums
1 lb. (500 g.) apples
1 lb. (500 g.) shallots or onions
1 lb. (500 g.) stoned raisins
6 oz. (175 g.) brown sugar
1 oz. (25 g.) salt
1 teaspoon each of ground ginger and allspice, dry mustard and nutmeg
1 pint (600 ml.) vinegar

Chop the stoned plums, the peeled and cored apples, the peeled shallots and the raisins. Place in a pan with the sugar, salt, spices and vinegar. Bring to the boil; simmer until soft and thick. Pot at once.

PUMPKIN CHUTNEY
Approx. yield 4 lb. (2 kg.)

2½ lb. (1.25 kg.) pumpkin (prepared weight)
1 lb. (500 g.) red tomatoes
8 oz. (250 g.) onions
2 oz. (50 g.) sultanas
1½ lb. (750 g.) soft brown sugar or 12 oz. (350 g.) each of caster sugar and soft brown sugar
2 garlic cloves
2 teaspoons each of ground ginger, black pepper and ground allspice
2½ tablespoons salt
1 pint (600 ml.) tarragon vinegar

Cut the peeled pumpkin flesh into small pieces ; slice the peeled tomatoes and peeled onions. Put these ingredients in a pan with the sultanas, sugar, crushed garlic, spices, salt and vinegar.

Bring to the boil and simmer gently until soft, and the chutney is of the consistency of jam. Pot at once.

RHUBARB CHUTNEY
Approx. yield 6 lb. (3 kg.)

5 lb. (2.5 kg.) rhubarb
2 lb. (1 kg.) onions
2 pints (1 l.) white vinegar
2 lb. (1 kg.) granulated sugar
½ teaspoon salt
2 tablespoons ground ginger
3 teaspoons mixed spice

Cut the washed and dried rhubarb into small chunks ; mince the peeled onions. Place in a pan with one-third of the vinegar, the sugar, salt, ginger and spice, and simmer gently until the rhubarb is soft.

Add the remaining vinegar and simmer to the required

consistency, stirring frequently.

For a hot chutney, use 3 teaspoons of curry powder instead of the mixed spice. Pot at once.

TOMATO CHUTNEY
Approx. yield 5–6 lb. (2.5–3 kg.)

6 lb. (3 kg.) ripe tomatoes
1 lb. (500 g.) onions
½ pint (300 ml.) spiced vinegar
1 oz. (25 g.) salt
1½ teaspoons paprika
Large pinch of cayenne
12 oz. (350 g.) granulated sugar

Peel and chop the tomatoes and put in a pan with the peeled, minced onions. Simmer until reduced to a thick pulp. Pour in half the vinegar, the salt and the spices and continue cooking until thick.

Add the remaining vinegar, after dissolving the sugar in it.

Cook until the chutney has attained the required consistency, then pot and cover.

Piquant sauces, ketchups and relishes

Sauces, ketchups and relishes – so rich and diverse in flavour and texture – can quite easily be made from the produce of your garden. They can be used as accompaniments to hot curries, as side-dishes with a cheese-board or as flavourings in soups and stews.

All are made from the same kinds of fruits and vegetables as chutneys, and many are made with the same kinds of spices and vinegars. The ingredients of both sauces and ketchups are first either finely chopped or minced and are then cooked, sieved and generally re-cooked to the consistency of thick cream.

The difference between the two – though not a hard-and-fast rule – is that ketchups are usually made from the juice of not more than two kinds of vegetables or fruits. Ketchups are highly concentrated and seasoned, and have one predominating flavour.

The flavours of sauces tend to be more subtle, as the result of blending a larger number of ingredients.

Relishes differ from both of these in that they consist of coarsely chopped vegetables or fruit, which are seasoned with spices and pickled in vinegar. Some are cooked, others are not; in some instances they are made with hot vinegar; in others it is added cold.

Consequently, a relish may be anything between a richly flavoured, chunky sauce and a colourful, fine-textured pickle.

Because of the wide variation between the three condiments – and between individual recipes – they have few basic steps in common. When making them, therefore, apart from noting the general instructions on equipment, bottling and so on, simply follow the recipe of your choice.

Equipment

Since relishes, sauces and ketchups are made with vinegar, which is a mild acid, use only heavy-based pans of aluminium or stainless steel, never iron or copper. For the same reason, use only sieves made from stainless steel or nylon. Apart from these, you will need:

Small knife or peeler
Mincer
Muslin for wrapping spices
Wooden spoon
Scales
Funnel
Ladle
Measuring jug
Bottles with screw-tops or corks
Large preserving pan or saucepan
Newspaper
Ceresin papers and paraffin wax

The finished sauces should be potted in clean, warm bottles and sealed with sterilised caps or corks. The seals must be completely airtight.

Bottling and sterilising

Some of these preserves tend to ferment in storage – especially those made with mushrooms and ripe tomatoes, which have a low acid content.

This can be overcome by sterilising, as for fruit syrups (see p. 327), immediately after bottling.

Tie down corks to prevent them blowing out during sterilising. Secure screw-caps loosely. Set the bottles on a false bottom in a pan deep enough to hold them upright, and do not allow them to touch each other or the sides of the pan.

Pour in warm water to cover the contents of the bottles, heat to a temperature of 77°C (170°F) and maintain this temperature for 30 minutes; or heat to 88°C (190°F) and maintain this for 20 minutes. After sterilising, tighten screw-caps, or seal corks with melted paraffin wax.

Storing

Once opened, sauces that have been sterilised must be used up quickly. But most ketchups and relishes can be opened and re-covered as the need arises, and will keep for several months.

Things that may go wrong

If the preserves shrink after a few months in store, this is almost certainly due to evaporation caused by a faulty seal. This can also lead to the contamination of the contents of the bottle.

A dark layer at the top of the bottle, which should be removed before serving, is probably due to the storage place being too warm.

Mould on the preserve or cork may be due to insufficient processing time; to the water in the preserving pan not being deep enough; or to corks that were not sufficiently sterilised.

RECIPES
for
fruit and vegetable sauces

APPLE SAUCE

2 lb. (1 kg.) apples
1 tablespoon sugar
½ pint (300 ml.) water
1 oz. (25 g.) butter
6 cloves
1 teaspoon ginger

Chop the washed, unpeeled apples finely. Put in a pan with the sugar, spices, water and butter, and simmer, uncovered, over a low heat until soft and pulpy.

Rub through a sieve, pour into clean, warm bottles and cover with screw-caps or corks. Sterilise in a hot water-bath.

DAMSON SAUCE

4 lb. (2 kg.) damsons
8 oz. (250 g.) onions
¼ teaspoon each of ground ginger,
  allspice, mace and dry mustard
4 oz. (125 g.) stoned raisins
1–2 chillies
12 peppercorns
8 oz. (250 g.) sugar
1½ oz. (40 g.) salt
2 pints (1 l.) white vinegar

Wash the damsons. Peel and slice the onions. Put in a pan with the spices, chillies, peppercorns, half the vinegar and the raisins. Simmer, uncovered, over a gentle heat until tender. Sieve, and add the sugar, salt and remaining vinegar.

Return to a clean pan and cook very gently until the sauce has the consistency of thick cream. Bottle while hot, and cover at once.

Make plum sauce in the same way, but use currants instead of raisins.

MAKING DAMSON SAUCE

Wash the damsons; peel and slice the onions. Put the fruit and vegetables in a pan with half the vinegar and simmer until tender.

Rub the mixture through a sieve. Add sugar, salt and the remaining vinegar, pour the pulp into a clean pan and return to heat.

Cook the sauce until it reaches the consistency of thick cream. Pour it into bottles while still hot and cover at once.

Continued ...

Fruit and vegetable sauces (continued)

RHUBARB SAUCE

5 lb. (2.5 kg.) rhubarb
5 lb. (2.5 kg.) onions
1 oz. (25 g.) salt
20 peppercorns
1 chilli
1–2 teaspoons each of dry mustard and curry powder
1 oz. (25 g.) bruised root ginger
3 pints (1.5 l.) malt vinegar
3 lb. (1.5 kg.) brown sugar

Wash and trim the rhubarb, but do not peel. Cut into chunks. Peel and chop the onions. Put in a heavy-based pan with the salt, peppercorns, chilli, spices and vinegar. Simmer, uncovered, stirring frequently, for 2 hours.

Rub through a sieve and return to the pan with the sugar. Boil until the sauce is like thick cream. Bottle and seal at once.

GREEN TOMATO SAUCE

3 lb. (1.5 kg.) green tomatoes
1½ lb. (750 g.) cooking apples
2 small shallots or onions
8 oz. (250 g.) sugar
½ teaspoon each of ground pepper and dry mustard
1 tablespoon salt
½ pint (300 ml.) malt vinegar
1 teaspoon ground pickling spice
Gravy browning (optional)

Wash the tomatoes, peel and core the apples and peel the shallots. Cut into small pieces and put in a pan with all the other ingredients. Simmer, uncovered, for about 1 hour, or until soft.

Add a few drops of browning, if

necessary, to improve the colour. Sieve and bottle while still hot. Cover at once.

RED TOMATO SAUCE

6 lb. (3 kg.) ripe tomatoes
8 oz. (250 g.) sugar
½ pint (300 ml.) spiced white vinegar (see p. 342)
2 tablespoons tarragon vinegar
1 tablespoon salt
Pinch of cayenne pepper
½ teaspoon paprika

Slice the washed tomatoes and cook, uncovered, over a low heat until soft and the skins are coming off. Rub the pulp through a fine sieve and put in a clean pan with the other ingredients. Simmer to the consistency of thick cream.

Bottle and sterilise in a hot water-bath. Screw the caps tight or seal the corks.

TOMATO AND APPLE SAUCE

2 lb. (1 kg.) ripe tomatoes
2 lb. (1 kg.) cooking apples
4 onions
½ pint (300 ml.) vinegar
4 chillies
8 oz. (250 g.) sugar
24 peppercorns
16 cloves
1 oz. (25 g.) bruised root ginger
1 oz. (25 g.) salt

Wash and cut up the tomatoes, peel, core and chop the apples and peel and chop the onions. Cook these together in a covered pan over low heat until soft.

Add the vinegar, chillies, sugar, spices and salt; simmer, covered, for 30 minutes. Sieve, and cook until it resembles thick cream. Pour into hot bottles and seal.

RECIPES
for
fruit and vegetable ketchups

BLACKBERRY KETCHUP

5 lb. (2.5 kg.) blackberries
Spiced white vinegar
Sugar

Wash the fruit and simmer, uncovered, without any extra water over gentle heat until soft. Rub through a sieve and measure the resultant purée.

For every 1 pint (600 ml.) of blackberry purée allow ½ pint (300 ml.) of vinegar and 2 oz. (50 g.) of sugar. Simmer the sauce to the consistency of thick cream. Pour into hot bottles, sterilise and seal.

GRAPE KETCHUP

Follow the recipe for blackberry ketchup, using grapes instead of blackberries and doubling the amount of sugar.

MUSHROOM KETCHUP

3 lb. (1.5 kg.) mushrooms
3 oz. (75 g.) salt
1 pint (600 ml.) vinegar
1 teaspoon each of peppercorns and allspice
½ teaspoon each of ground mace and ginger
¼ teaspoon each of ground cloves and cinnamon

Trim the mushrooms and break into small pieces. Sprinkle with the salt and leave overnight. Rinse them well and mash with a wooden spoon.

Simmer in the vinegar, with the spices, for 30 minutes in a covered pan. Sieve, pour into hot bottles and seal. Sterilise for 30 minutes.

TOMATO KETCHUP

4 lb. (2 kg.) ripe tomatoes
1 large onion
2 large apples
2 teaspoons pickling spices
¾ pint (450 ml.) vinegar
Large pinch of cayenne or paprika
6 oz. (175 g.) sugar
Salt

Slice the washed tomatoes; peel the onion and the apples. Boil the pickling spices in the vinegar for 10 minutes, and strain.

Cook the apples, onion and tomatoes to a thick pulp, stirring frequently. Sieve the pulp and simmer gently with the vinegar, cayenne and sugar until thick and creamy. Add salt to taste. Pot at once in hot bottles and seal.

TOMATO AND GREEN PEPPER KETCHUP

7 lb. (3.5 kg.) ripe tomatoes
8 large onions
2 oz. (50 g.) bruised root ginger
2 level tablespoons whole cloves
8 green peppers
4 pints (2 l.) distilled vinegar
5 teaspoons salt
8 oz. (250 g.) demerara sugar
2 tablespoons whole allspice
4 in. (100 mm.) stick of cinnamon

Skin and chop the tomatoes and onions. Cut the base off the peppers, remove the seeds and membranes and chop the flesh. Put in a pan with the vinegar, salt and sugar, and the spices tied in a muslin bag.

Bring to the boil and simmer, uncovered, for 1 hour, stirring frequently. Remove the spices and rub the pulp through a sieve. Simmer again until the ketchup has a creamy consistency, then pour into hot bottles, seal and sterilise.

STERILISING KETCHUPS

To prevent fermentation in storage, place the filled bottles in a pan of water and heat them for 20–30 minutes.

RECIPES
for
vegetable relishes

BEETROOT RELISH

1 lb. (500 g.) cooked beetroot
1 lb. (500 g.) white cabbage
8 oz. (250 g.) sugar
1 pint (600 ml.) white vinegar
1 tablespoon fresh or dried grated horseradish
1 teaspoon salt
1 teaspoon pepper

Chop the beetroot roughly, and the cabbage very finely. Place in a pan with the other ingredients, and stir until the sugar has dissolved. Cook gently for 20 minutes. Pot into warm jars and cover.

CELERY RELISH

2 green peppers
2 red peppers
1 lb. (500 g.) onions
3 tablespoons salt
1¼ lb. (625 g.) sugar
4 tablespoons mustard seeds
Large pinch turmeric
½ pint (300 ml.) distilled vinegar
5 tablespoons water
5 celery sticks

Remove the base, seeds and membranes from the peppers and peel the onions. Finely chop the peppers and onions. Mix the dry ingredients and blend into the vinegar and water.

Bring to the boil and add the diced celery with the peppers and onion. Simmer in a covered pan

for 3 minutes and pot in hot jars, covering the vegetables with the hot liquid. Seal air-tight.

CORN RELISH

6 corn cobs
½ small white cabbage
2 onions
2 small red peppers
2 teaspoons salt
2 teaspoons flour
½ teaspoon turmeric
6 oz. (175 g.) sugar
2 teaspoons dry mustard
1 pint (600 ml.) distilled vinegar

Boil the corn for 3 minutes and strip from the cobs. Prepare and mince the cabbage, onions and peppers, and put in a pan with the corn. Bring to the boil. Mix the dry ingredients thoroughly and gradually blend in the vinegar.

Add to the vegetables and simmer for 30 minutes, stirring occasionally. Pot in hot jars, and seal.

PEPPER RELISH

1 small cucumber
2 large onions
2 cooking apples
10 chillies
1 tablespoon salt
7 oz. (200 g.) sugar
½ pint (300 ml.) white vinegar

Peel the cucumber and onions and peel and core the apples. Mince them, drain if necessary, and mix in a bowl. Add the crushed chillies.

Mix together the salt, sugar and vinegar and stir into the contents of

MAKING PEPPER RELISH

Peel the cucumber and onions, and peel and core the apples. Chop them roughly.

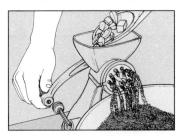

Mince the fruit and vegetables and put them in a bowl. Crush and add the chillies.

Mix the salt, sugar and vinegar together and stir them into the other ingredients.

No cooking is required, so pot the relish straight from the bowl into sterilised jars.

the bowl until the sugar has dissolved. Pot, without cooking, in sterilised jars and seal.

MUSTARD RELISH

3 lb. (1.5 kg.) apples
1 lb. (500 g.) onions
1 tablespoon mustard seeds
2 pints (1 l.) vinegar
8 oz. (250 g.) sultanas
1 lb. (500 g.) sugar
2 teaspoons dry mustard
1 tablespoon salt

Core the peeled apples and chop the peeled onions. Simmer, until soft, with half the vinegar, and with the mustard seeds in a muslin bag. Add the other ingredients, blending the remaining vinegar with the mustard.

Stir to dissolve the sugar and boil to the required thickness, stirring occasionally. Remove the mustard seeds, pot and seal.

TOMATO RELISH

4 lb. (2 kg.) ripe tomatoes
3 large onions
1 oz. (25 g.) salt
3 large celery sticks
1 red pepper
1 lb. (500 g.) sugar
1 tablespoon mustard seeds
¾ pint (450 ml.) vinegar

Skin and finely chop the tomatoes and onions. Mix in a bowl, sprinkle with the salt and leave overnight. Drain through a colander for 5 or 6 hours.

Finely chop the cleaned celery and de-seeded pepper, and mix in

a bowl with the sugar, mustard seeds and vinegar. Stir in the tomatoes and onions and mix well. Pot in sterilised jars and seal.

TOMATO AND HORSERADISH RELISH

4 lb. (2 kg.) ripe tomatoes
1 large onion
2 large apples
¾ pint (450 ml.) vinegar
2 teaspoons pickling spices
2 teaspoons salt
½ teaspoon cayenne pepper or paprika
1 lb. (500 g.) sugar
3 tablespoons grated horseradish

Skin the tomatoes; peel and chop the onion; peel, core and chop the apples.

Cook to a thick pulp, stirring at first to prevent burning. Meanwhile, boil the vinegar and pickling spices together for 10 minutes, strain, and add the vinegar, salt and cayenne to the tomatoes.

Boil to reduce to a thick, creamy texture, then stir in the sugar and horseradish. Cook for 10 minutes. Pour into hot bottles, seal and sterilise.

Flavoured vinegars for exciting dishes

Flavoured vinegars are not now so widely used as they were a hundred years ago, in the golden era of Mrs Beeton. Then, no salad was thought complete without its accompanying bottles of celery, cucumber or tarragon vinegar. Cold meats were dressed with horseradish vinegar, while chilli vinegars made a spirited addition to soups, stews and curries.

Fruit vinegars, too, were widely used – as flavourings for steamed puddings, as soothing draughts for sore throats or simply, when diluted with water, as cooling summer drinks.

Their passing must be regretted, for apart from being simplicity itself to make, they are an inexpensive and delightful way of using up small quantities of surplus garden produce.

The only expense is the vinegar itself. Wine vinegar is best for most of the recipes, since its flavour, less harsh than that of malt vinegar, will not obliterate the delicate flavours imparted by the additional ingredients.

Among the exceptions are condiments containing such strong-tasting ingredients as chillis and horseradish. For these, the cheaper malt vinegars will suffice.

Equipment

Apart from bottles, only standard items of kitchenware are needed:
Large, glazed earthenware or glass bowl
Wooden spoon
Sharp kitchen knife
Bottles, with screw-tops or new corks
Scales
Paraffin wax

Fruit vinegars

These are made from soft fruits such as raspberries, blackberries and black currants. Put the fruits in a bowl, bruise them with a wooden spoon and to each 2 lb. (1 kg.), add 2 pints (1 l.) of good-quality wine vinegar.

Cover the bowl with a cloth and leave it to stand for three or four days, stirring twice a day.

Strain the juice through clean muslin, put it into a pan and boil for 10 minutes.

Pour the fruit vinegar into warmed bottles, and either screw on the tops or drive home the corks and seal them with paraffin wax.

For a sweet vinegar, add 2 lb. (1 kg.) of granulated sugar to each 2 pints (1 l.) of strained liquid, just before boiling. Some older recipes also recommend the addition of a glass of brandy to each bottle of fruit vinegar.

Use the vinegars, diluted, as a summer drink or, undiluted, as a flavouring for puddings.

Vegetable vinegars

These are made from delicately flavoured vegetables such as cucumbers and celery, or strong-tasting roots and fruits like horseradish, peppers and chillis. The

MAKING FRUIT VINEGAR

Place fruit in a bowl and bruise with a wooden spoon. Add wine vinegar.

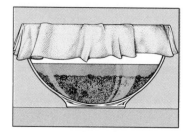

Cover the bowl with a cloth and leave to stand, stirring occasionally.

Strain juice through clean muslin into a pan. Boil for 10 minutes.

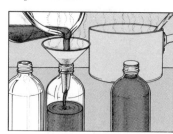

Pour into warm, sterilised bottles; cork, seal with paraffin wax, and label.

former can be used to flavour fish and salads, while the latter make a fiery accompaniment to grills and barbecues.

Chop, grate or split the vegetables, according to the recipe. Place them in a large jar and cover with good-quality vinegar. Cover the jar and leave it to stand for the specified period, stirring or shaking occasionally. Strain the vinegar through muslin, and bottle.

Herb vinegars

Made with garden herbs such as tarragon, thyme, mint, basil or marjoram – singly or in combination – they can be used to flavour dressings and sauces. Pick the herbs just before they flower and put the leaves and tender parts of the stalks into a large jar.

Bruise the herbs with a wooden spoon, cover them with wine vinegar and leave to stand for six to eight weeks. If a clear glass jar is used, stand it in a dark cupboard to prevent loss of colour.

After this period, strain the vinegar through muslin and bottle it, first placing a sprig or two of the particular herb in each bottle.

MAKING HERB VINEGAR

Add a sprig of herbs, stalk first, to the finished vinegar before corking and labelling.

RECIPES for vinegars

CELERY VINEGAR

Finely chop a large head of washed celery – leaves, stalks and all – and place in a jar. Pour over white wine vinegar and leave, covered, for two weeks. Strain and bottle. Use to dress cold chicken.

CHILLI VINEGAR

Use about 2 oz. (50 g.) of red chillies, split in half and steeped in 2 pints (1 l.) of wine or malt vinegar. Steep, covered, for four to six weeks. Strain and bottle.

CUCUMBER VINEGAR

Peel and finely chop 8 small cucumbers and 3 onions. Steep for a week in 2 pints (1 l.) of white wine vinegar, shaking occasionally. Bottle the strained vinegar, and use in dressings for summer salads and cold fish dishes.

FRUIT VINEGARS

Cover 1 lb. (500 g.) of soft fruit, such as currants or raspberries, with 1 pint (600 ml.) of white vinegar. Leave to stand for about four days, stirring occasionally, then strain.

Place the liquid in a pan with 8 oz. (250 g.) of sugar to each pint of liquid, bring to the boil, and boil for 10 minutes. Bottle and seal.

GARLIC VINEGAR

Peel 2 oz. (50 g.) of garlic and chop thinly. Add it to 1 pint (600 ml.) of vinegar and leave for two weeks. Strain into a clean bottle.

HORSERADISH VINEGAR

Steep 3 oz. (75 g.) of grated horseradish and 1 oz. (25 g.) of finely chopped shallot, in 2 pints (1 l.) of malt or white vinegar for about a week. Shake frequently, strain and bottle the vinegar. It is best used in dressings.

After straining, the horseradish can be squeezed and used for sauce with roast beef.

LAVENDER VINEGAR

Method as for Tarragon vinegar. The lavender flavour makes a pleasant change in salad dressings, and the vinegar can also be used on a cloth pad to relieve headaches.

Use white vinegar.

MINT VINEGAR

Pick fresh, healthy mint leaves, strip the leaves from the stalks, wash and dry. Pack 4–6 oz. (100–175 g.) of mint into a jar, pour 2 pints (1 l.) of wine vinegar over it, cover and steep for three weeks.

Strain, and use in oil-vinaigrette dressings and freshly made mint sauce.

ONION VINEGAR

Add 4 oz. (125 g.) of finely chopped onions to 2 pints (1 l.) of white wine vinegar. Steep for two weeks, shaking often. Strain and bottle.

Use in dressings for beetroot and green salads.

ROSE-PETAL VINEGAR

Fill a 2 pint (1 l.) jar half full with clean, dark, rose petals, preferably from old-fashioned, scented roses. Press the petals well down and top up the jar with white wine vinegar. Leave, covered, for two or three weeks, then strain and bottle.

This rose-coloured, delicately flavoured vinegar is ideal with summer salads.

TARRAGON VINEGAR

Half fill a 2 pint (1 l.) jar with fresh young tarragon leaves. Top up with good white wine vinegar and leave, covered, for four weeks. Strain and bottle, adding a sprig of tarragon to each bottle after straining. Use in salad dressings and white sauces.

Other herbs, such as dill, thyme and marjoram, may be treated in the same way.

VIOLET VINEGAR

Follow the method for rose-petal vinegar, using violet petals.

Drying – the economical way to preserve

For thousands of years, drying was the only known method – apart from salting – of preserving food. To this day, in tropical climates, fruits such as figs, dates and grapes are still dried in the sun, while in northern Europe, drying fish by sun, wind or smoke remains a thriving industry.

In Britain's more variable climate, surplus garden produce is better dried indoors where a steady temperature can be guaranteed. The process is simple, if somewhat lengthy, and the

MAKING A DRYING RACK

Make a rack by stretching muslin over a cake tray and securing it with pins.

expense negligible. There are two principal requirements; these are correct temperature and adequate ventilation.

Food to be dried is laid on trays or racks, which can be made by stretching muslin over a wooden frame and fixing it in place with tacks. When drying small quantities, use a wire cake tray covered with muslin.

Methods of drying

Drying by artificial heat can be carried out in a single operation in a cool oven over a period of several hours. The correct temperature is 50–65°C (120–150°F) – gas mark ¼. Alternatively, it can be spread over several days by using the residual heat of the oven after cooking. An oven thermometer is useful for gauging the low temperatures needed.

A rack over the boiler or in the airing cupboard can also be used for drying, provided the food is protected from dust and there is adequate ventilation.

Fruits and vegetables that have been dried correctly will keep for many months. The flavour and texture are restored by soaking before cooking.

DRYING FRUIT

Stone fruits, such as apricots, peaches and plums, are excellent for drying. So, too, are apples, grapes and pears. The fruits should be sound and just ripe.

Wash the fruits, then halve, slice, or leave them whole – according to type. Lay them on muslin-covered trays and dry at a temperature of 50–65°C (120–150°F) – gas mark ¼. The temperature must not rise above

Lay prepared fruit on the muslin-covered rack or tray, spacing evenly.

Dry in the oven at 50–65°C (120–150°F) until the juices have evaporated.

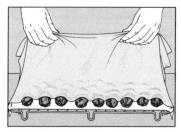
Remove tray from the oven, cover fruit with a cloth and leave to cool for 12 hours.

When cool, pack fruit in boxes lined with greaseproof paper and store in a dry place.

343

50°C (120°F) for the first hour, or the fruit will harden and the skins may burst.

The temperature may then be allowed to rise gradually to 65°C (150°F) for a further three to six hours, depending on the type and size of fruit.

Dried fruits should feel springy and soft, not brittle, and should not exude moisture when pressed. Leave them to cool at room temperature for 12 hours; cover them with a cloth to exclude light, which may affect the colour. Pack them in boxes lined with grease-proof or waxed paper.

The cover need not be completely air-tight, but the boxes must be stored in a dry place.

Apples In the 16th century, whole apples, peeled and cored, used to be dried in the chimney. Today, they are dried as rings, which take up less storage space.

Choose firm, crisp, juicy apples. Peel, core and cut them crossways into even slices about ¼ in. (5 mm.) thick. Drop the slices immediately into a bowl of lightly salted water – 1 teaspoon of salt to 2 pints (1 l.) of water – to prevent them going brown.

Dry the rings and thread them on to bamboo canes cut to fit the oven width. Hang the canes in the oven, set to the correct cool temperature, and leave the oven door slightly ajar.

Drying should be complete in four to six hours, when the apple rings will look like chamois leather. Cool for 12 hours before packing.

Apricots, peaches and plums As stone fruits shrink during drying, use large, firm, ripe fruits. Use

DRYING APPLES

Peel, core and cut apples into rings. Drop these into lightly salted water.

Remove excess moisture and thread rings on to canes cut to fit into the oven.

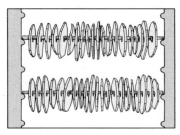

Place canes in the oven, set to correct temperature, and leave the door ajar.

When dry, remove rings from oven and leave to cool for 12 hours before packing in jars.

dark-coloured varieties of plums; these may be left whole, but apricots and peaches should be halved and stoned.

Place the fruit in single layers on covered trays, cut surfaces uppermost to prevent the juices from dripping down.

Dry slowly at a temperature of 50°C (120°F) – gas mark ¼ – in a cool oven or airing cupboard, with the door left open. Maintain this temperature until the skins begin to shrivel, then raise it to 65°C (150°F).

Whole fruit may take up to two days to dry; halved stoned fruit about a day. Drying is complete if no juice flows, and the skin remains unbroken, when the fruit is gently squeezed. Leave the fruits to cool for 12 hours before packing and storing.

Grapes Home-grown grapes, preferably the seedless varieties, may be dried and used as a substitute for sultanas in cakes and puddings. Pick ripe grapes, separate them into single berries and wash them. Remove excess moisture with a towel, and spread the grapes on covered trays.

Dry them in an airing cupboard, with the door left open, or in a cool oven, at a temperature gradually rising to 65°C (150°F), for about eight hours. Cool overnight at room temperature, then pack and store.

Pears Peel, core and quarter the fruits and drop them into lightly salted water – 1 teaspoon of salt to 2 pints (1 l.) of water – to prevent discoloration during the preparation period. Dry the pears on muslin trays for four to six hours, with the cut surfaces uppermost.

Cooking with dried fruit

Failures with dried fruits are usually due to insufficient soaking before use, or to adding sugar at too early a stage.

Soak all dried fruits in cold water to plump them up before cooking. Soak stone fruits for at least 24 hours; apples and pears for about 12 hours. Cook them in the water in which they were soaked, and use as fillings for pies and puddings.

Bring to the boil very slowly and simmer gently until tender. Do not add sugar until the fruits have almost finished cooking.

DRYING VEGETABLES

Root vegetables can be stored in boxes of peat or sand, so drying is unnecessary. Most other vegetables are better preserved by freezing or bottling, but young peas, French and runner beans, mushrooms and onions can be dried with reasonable success.

Prepare peas and beans for drying as for cooking, then blanch them in boiling water for about 5 minutes before rinsing them in cold water. Soak up surplus moisture with a towel, then dry on trays in a cool oven or airing cupboard until quite hard. Allow to cool, pack in air-tight containers and store in a cool, dry place.

To cook, soak the dried beans or peas for 12 hours in cold water mixed with 1 teaspoon of bicarbonate of soda to improve the colour. Strain and rinse, then cook in salted water until tender.

Mushrooms Flat cap or field mushrooms are the most suitable for drying. Pick them fresh, trim

DRYING MUSHROOMS

Wipe and trim freshly picked mushrooms and remove stalks. Retain stalks for cooking.

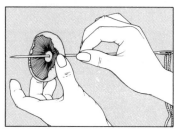

With a poultry needle, thread mushrooms on a string. Large mushrooms may be halved.

Tie a knot between each mushroom and hang them to dry in a warm, airy place.

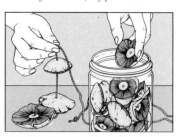

Hang the strung mushrooms in the kitchen for easy access, or store them in jars.

any ragged edges, and peel them if dirty; otherwise wipe them clean with a soft, damp cloth.

Remove the stalks – which can be used in soups, sauces or for vegetable stock – and cut large mushrooms into halves or quarters.

Thread them on string, using a poultry or packing needle to push through the centre.

Tie a thick knot between each mushroom, allowing 2 in. (50 mm.) between them so that they do not touch when hung up. Thread about a dozen mushrooms on each string.

Hang the strings up to dry in a warm, airy place, such as over the boiler or in the airing cupboard with the door ajar. They take a couple of days to dry and will then have the colour and texture of chamois leather.

Store dried mushrooms in jars in a dry cupboard; or leave the strings hanging in the kitchen, away from dust and steam.

Dried mushrooms can be used to flavour soups, stews, casseroles and sauces, and need no soaking beforehand. Simply break them off the string and add to the pan.

To fry or grill dried mushrooms, soak them first for about an hour in cold water or milk. Dry carefully before cooking.

Onions Whole onions are usually stored in nets or tied in strings, but it is useful to have a handy supply of onion rings in the kitchen. These can be left until the supply of whole onions is finished, or until the bulbs start to deteriorate in late winter or spring.

Peel and cut medium-sized onions into $\frac{1}{4}$ in. (5 mm.) slices. Separate these into single rings

Peel the onions, slice, and separate into rings. Use centres for immediate cooking.

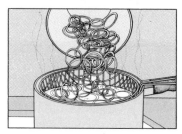
Blanch the rings in boiling water for 30 seconds, rinse in cold water and drain.

Alternatively, cook the rings in a solution of sugar and salt until they become soft.

Dry on a muslin-covered rack in a moderate oven, with the door ajar. Pack in jars.

and discard the centre circles, using these the same day in salads, cheese sandwiches or for cooking.

Blanch the rings chosen for drying in boiling water for 30 seconds, strain through a colander and rinse in cold running water. Drain, and spread them out on kitchen paper or a cloth to absorb the excess moisture.

As an alternative to blanching, mix the onion rings with salt and sugar – 1 tablespoon of cooking salt and 1 teaspoon of sugar to 2 lb. (1 kg.) onions. Heat slowly in a heavy-based pan, stirring carefully until the rings have softened. This method helps to crisp the rings as they dry.

Spread the blanched and dried, or softened, rings in single layers on muslin-covered trays, and dry in a cool oven with a maximum temperature of 65°C (150°F) – gas mark $\frac{1}{4}$ – with the door left ajar until the rings are crisp and dry. This will take about three hours. Those softened with sugar and salt will dry more quickly.

Leave the rings to cool completely before packing them into jars and storing in a cool, dry place. To use the onions, soak them in warm water for 30 minutes and add them to stews and casseroles.

DRYING HERBS

Herbs, like any other garden produce, are at their best when freshly picked. But, since most are annuals or deciduous perennials, it is not always possible to have fresh herbs to hand.

A supply of some types can be maintained throughout the year by growing them in pots on the kitchen window-sill for picking as

required. Basil, chives, mint and parsley are especially suitable (see pp. 28 and 29).

Evergreen herbs such as bay, rosemary and thyme can be picked fresh at any time of the year, and there is therefore no need to preserve them.

The great majority of herbs, however, must be preserved for winter use, and drying is the best method. The exceptions are those that can be frozen (see p. 305) or preserved by other means.

Picking the herbs

It is important to harvest herbs at the right time. In most cases, it is the leaves that are used for flavouring, and these should be picked while still young, in early to midsummer, before the flowers develop and the leaves become tough.

Choose warm, dry days for harvesting. Mornings are best, after the dew has evaporated and before the sun scorches the leaves. Pick one variety of herb at a time and prepare it for drying. The process is quite lengthy, and some patience is needed in dealing with the smaller herbs.

Examine each branch or shoot carefully, and pull off and discard any damaged or diseased leaves. Strip large-leaved herbs, such as sage and mint, from their stalks, but leave small and feathery herbs, such as chervil and fennel, on the stalks until drying is complete.

Drying methods

Drying depends on abundant dry, fresh air rather than on heat, so artificial warmth is not essential. An airing cupboard a well-ventilated larder or a garden shed are suitable, even if it takes longer

Tie freshly picked herbs into bunches, and dip them briefly into boiling water.

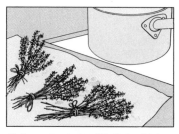
Shake excess moisture off the herbs, then leave them to drain on absorbent paper.

Put the bunches, leaves down, into paper bags and hang them up to dry in an airy place.

Discard twigs and leaf ribs, and crumble the dried leaves into air-tight jars or pots.

to dry them there than in an oven or over a radiator.

Tie the herbs in small bunches and dip them in boiling water for a few seconds. In addition to cleaning them, this also helps to preserve their colours.

Shake off excess moisture and leave to dry on absorbent kitchen paper.

Method 1 Hang the bunches up to dry, leaves downwards, wrapped loosely in muslin or thin paper bags to keep the dust out. Do not use plastic bags, which may cause moulds to develop.

The time needed to dry fresh herbs depends on the size of the branches and the humidity of the place where they are hung. On average, allow between seven and ten days.

Method 2 Drying can be speeded by placing the blanched herbs, well spaced out, on a tray.

Place the tray in an airing cupboard, over a radiator, or in the warming drawer of a cooker, and turn the leaves or stalks frequently to ensure even drying. They should be dry in two or three days.

Method 3 Herbs can also be dried in an oven. Leaves of sage, mint and parsley, stripped from their stalks, are particularly suitable for this.

Place blanched leaves, well spaced, on a muslin-covered tray in an oven set to the lowest possible temperature.

Leave the door ajar to allow the moisture to escape.

Turn the leaves over after 30 minutes to ensure even drying; they will be quite dry after about

an hour. Leave in the oven until they are quite cool.

Storing herbs

The process of packing and storing is identical, whichever method of drying is chosen.

Crumble the dried herbs through your fingers, and discard the hard leaf stalks and midribs. Store in small, air-tight containers, preferably made of pottery or opaque glass. If glass containers are used, store them in a dark place so that the herbs do not lose colour.

Using dried herbs

Use fresh herbs for flavouring, garnishing and in cold drinks. Dried herbs are suitable only for cooked foods, and even then need using with care.

As the flavours are concentrated, a smaller amount is needed than with fresh herbs. For instance, where a recipe requires 1 teaspoon of fresh, chopped herbs, substitute half the amount of dried herbs.

Do not shake dried herbs from their containers into foods that are cooking. The rising heat and steam may result in moulds growing in the herb jar. Remove the required amount with a spoon, and close the jar immediately.

Bouquet garni

This consists of a sprig of parsley, another of thyme and a bay leaf, tied in a small muslin bag. It is used to flavour stocks, soups, sauces and casseroles.

If you are drying these herbs, it is a good idea to prepare a number of bouquets garnis and store them in an air-tight, screw-top jar for use as required.

Preserving vegetables and nuts in salt

Salting is a very ancient method of food preservation. It was the standard means of preserving meat and fish in pre-Christian times. During the Middle Ages, vegetables – beans especially – were also successfully salted down for winter use.

In Chaucer's day the provident housewife would salt down her beans in late summer, and in autumn would lay down barrels of salted pork. These were the staples of the family's winter diet, with a bought-in supply of salted herrings and stockfish for eating on days of abstinence, when no meat might be eaten.

Refrigeration has largely replaced salting as a means of preserving meat. The salt-fish industry, too, has dwindled considerably, while bottling, pickling and freezing are generally used for home preserving. But as an alternative and cheap method, salting still has advantages.

Types of salt

Vegetables and nuts are dry salted – unlike meat, which is salted in brine. The liquid content of the vegetables and the salt, however,

combine to make their own brine, so the salt used must be readily soluble.

Table salt is not suitable, as it is relatively expensive and contains chemicals that form a scum on top of the vegetables. Also, as it is so fine, there is a tendency to use too much of it.

Coarse-grained sea salt is ideal, but it is also more expensive than other types.

Coarse cooking salt is the best type, especially if it is purchased in block form and grated by hand. When buying, allow 1 lb. (500 g.) salt to 3 lb. (1.5 kg.) vegetables.

Equipment

Unglazed earthenware jars, available in sizes up to 7 lb. (3.5 kg.) are the most suitable. Enamelled containers may be used, provided the enamel is not chipped. Large glass preserving jars can also be used, so long as the neck is wide enough to admit your hand.

On no account must salt come into contact with metal, so always use a wooden spoon.

Preparation

Select only best-quality produce. Wash, top and tail, string or slice the vegetables, as for cooking. Remove the husks and outer skins from nuts.

Packing and storing

It is unnecessary to fill a large jar in one operation. As surplus produce becomes available, it can be prepared and packed in layers of salt into the same jar, always finishing with a layer of salt.

Until the jar is full, place a light weight, such as an upturned saucer, on the vegetables to keep them immersed.

As the salt dissolves to a brine, the contents of the jar will compress and sink.

Keep the jar loosely covered with greaseproof or waxed paper until full. Leave it for a couple of days, then tie down securely to exclude air with a double layer of greaseproof paper and fine string. Store in a cool, dark place for up to six months.

Cooking salted vegetables

Take as many vegetables from the jar as you require. Having done so, replace the top, tie it down firmly and put the jar back into cool storage.

Put the vegetables in a colander, rinse them under cold running water and leave them to steep – again in cold water – for a couple of hours to draw out the salt. If they are left longer than this, the vegetables are likely to reabsorb the salted water.

Give a final rinse in cold running water and cook as usual – except that there is no need to add salt to the water.

SALTING BEANS IN A JAR

Starting with a layer of salt, top up with layers of salt and beans. Compress the mixture with an inverted saucer.

RECIPES
for
salting vegetables and nuts

SALTED BEANS

3 lb. (1.5 kg.) beans (French or runner)
1 lb. (500 g.) cooking salt

Use freshly picked, sound young beans. Wash, top and tail and dry the beans, and string runner beans. French beans may be left whole if small, or cut in half; cut runner beans into about 1 in. (25 mm.) lengths.

Put a $\frac{1}{2}$ in. (12 mm.) layer of salt in a clean, dry jar and cover with a 1 in. (25 mm.) layer of beans. Repeat these layers until the jar is full or the beans used up, finishing with a layer of salt.

Press each layer well down and put a lightly weighted saucer over the top to keep the beans immersed in the salt. Cover the jar loosely with waxed paper and leave for two or three days while the beans settle in the salt.

Add a further layer of prepared beans and a last layer of salt, and replace the weight for a couple of days until the beans are fully submerged in the salt. Remove the weight and seal with waxed paper.

SALTED CUCUMBERS

4 cucumbers
1 lb. (500 g.) coarse salt (approx.)

Choose straight, uniformly shaped cucumbers. Wash well and dry, but do not peel. Cut them crossways into thin slices.

Put the cucumber slices in layers in a shallow dish, and sprinkle with half the salt. Press lightly with a plate and leave in a cool place for 24 hours.

At the end of this time, the cucumbers will have produced a great deal of liquid. Drain, and pat as dry as possible in a clean cloth.

Put a shallow layer of the remaining salt in a 2 lb. (1 kg.) container, cover with a layer of cucumber slices and continue like this until all the cucumbers are used up. Finish with a layer of salt. Seal the jar; store in a cool place.

To use, remove cucumber slices as required, rinse in cold running water and leave to soak in a bowl of cold water for about an hour. Dry the cucumbers and sprinkle them with a dressing made from lemon juice or white wine vinegar, seasoned with pepper and sugar but no salt.

Serve as a side salad with roast meat or cold roast chicken.

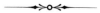

HAZELNUTS IN SALT

Hazelnuts, ready for gathering in September and October, do not usually store well, as they tend to shrivel up inside their shells. They can be salted, however.

To do so, first spread the nuts out to dry. Discard any that show signs of disease or worm attack. Rub off the outer husks, scrub the nuts in cold water, and dry thoroughly in a cool oven.

Pack the nuts closely into a wide-necked container and sprinkle them with cooking salt. Knock the jar against the edge of the table so that the salt trickles down between the nuts, and add more salt as necessary. Finish with a $\frac{1}{2}$ in. (12 mm.) layer of salt. Seal with waxed or greaseproof paper and store in a cool place.

Take as many nuts as you require at a time. Seal again before storing the remainder.

SALTED HAZELNUTS

1 lb. (500 g.) hazelnuts
5 tablespoons olive or salad oil
2 tablespoons sea salt

Hazelnuts can be stored in salt, as described in the previous column, or they can be oiled, salted and served with drinks in the same way as peanuts.

Shell the ripe nuts (the shells account for about half the weight) and place the kernels on a grill pan. Grill for a few minutes, after which the skins will rub off easily.

Heat some olive oil in a heavy-based frying pan, add the nuts and cook gently until golden-brown, stirring all the time until the nuts have absorbed most of the oil. Stir in the salt and continue cooking over low heat until the nuts are thoroughly coated.

Turn on to greaseproof paper and shake the nuts gently to make sure they are evenly coated. Leave until quite cold, then store in air-tight containers.

SALTED PARSLEY

Preserving parsley in salt is an alternative, and sometimes preferred, means of obtaining a winter supply of the herb. It is less trouble than drying, and the leaves keep their shape and colour better.

Use freshly picked parsley and divide into small sprigs, but do not strip from the stalks. Pack into small earthenware jars, with layers of salt, and tie down with waxed paper. Remove as required and rinse thoroughly under cold running water.

Parsley preserved in this way can be used in stews, soups or chopped for garnishing. Remember to take the extra salt into account in cooked dishes.

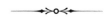

SALTED PEAS

This recipe is only to be recommended when you have grown considerably more peas than you can use in their fresh state, and if you do not possess a freezer. However, they do make a useful addition to winter soups and stews.

Use only young, freshly shelled peas and layer them with coarse salt in an earthenware jar in the same way as for beans. Press each layer well down, and put a lightly weighted saucer over the top layers to keep the peas immersed. After a couple of days, remove the weight, cover the jar with waxed paper, tie down with string and store.

To use salted peas, soak them in cold water for a couple of hours, rinse, and cook with a little sugar in the water.

SAUERKRAUT

This has been a staple dish of eastern Europe ever since it was introduced – together with yoghourt and tea – by invading Mongol hordes.

Basically, it is salted cabbage; but it must also go through a process of fermentation.

To make sauerkraut, finely shred the hearts of fresh cabbages and, having placed them in a wooden or glazed earthenware bowl, mix thoroughly with coarse salt at the rate of $\frac{1}{2}$ oz. of salt to 1 lb. of cabbage (15 g. to 500 g.).

Put a saucer or plate on top, making sure it covers the cabbage entirely. Compress further by putting weights on the plate.

Store the bowl for two or three weeks at a temperature of about 24°C (75°F). After a few days, the plate should be covered with brine; when this happens, remove the scum that rises to the surface.

If, after a week or so, the plate is no longer covered by brine, add more, at the rate of 1 tablespoon of salt to $2\frac{1}{2}$ cups of water.

The sauerkraut may now be used as an accompaniment to frankfurters, or to ham and pork dishes of many kinds. It can also be stored by draining off the brine, bringing it to the boil, and then returning the cabbage, simmering the two together for a few minutes.

Pack the hot sauerkraut into warmed jars, cover, and stand the jars in a deep pan containing a false bottom of folded newspaper.

Pour in boiling water up to the level of the contents of the jars, and simmer for 30 minutes. Seal the sterilised jars tightly and store them in a cool, dark place.

Easter eggs at Christmas

Everyone who keeps chickens is aware that both the supply and price of eggs vary considerably at different times of the year. Birds that lay half-a-dozen eggs a week in spring may produce only three or four in winter, and none at all during the autumn moult.

Thrifty poultry-keepers discovered the answer to the problem long ago. By preserving surplus eggs into seasons of scarcity, an even supply is made available throughout the year.

There are several methods of achieving this, all of which arrest decay by sealing the pores of the egg-shell. All are effective if properly carried out, but it should be remembered they are not intended to preserve the eggs indefinitely.

Nine or ten months is as much as can be reasonably expected.

(See also freezing eggs, p. 370.)

Selecting the eggs

Though eggs for preserving must be fresh, they should not be taken straight from the nest. Ideally, leave for between one and three days before preserving them.

It is inadvisable, therefore, to preserve eggs bought from a shop, since their age will be unknown. They may of course be bought from a farm, but even then you should check that they are not more than a day or two old.

Large, standard, or small eggs will preserve equally well. Choose thick-shelled eggs, if possible. Avoid cracked or rough-shelled eggs.

Preparation

The eggs must be clean. If there is any nest dirt on them, remove it with a brush or steel wool. Do not wash the eggs, as this will make them porous.

Whichever means of preservation you choose, it is vital that the eggs should be kept cool. Before you start, stand them in cold water; and if you are preserving them in liquid make sure it is cold and that, afterwards, the eggs are stored in a cool place.

Methods of preserving eggs

Materials for preserving eggs are inexpensive and easy to obtain. Of the methods suggested, dry preserving is probably the simplest.

Preserving in waterglass *(sodium silicate)* Best known as an agent for sizing interior walls before decorating, this may be bought at most do-it-yourself shops. Follow the instructions on the packet to make a solution, and fill a clean bucket or large earthenware jar about three-quarters full. Place the cooled eggs, pointed ends downwards, in the pickling solution. This keeps the yolks in the middle of the eggs.

While zinc, enamel or plastic buckets are all suitable for use as containers, plastic buckets are the easiest to clean afterwards, as inevitably there will be a deposit of waterglass after use.

More eggs may be stacked in the solution as they become available, but always be sure they are completely covered by the liquid. It is advisable to wear rubber gloves when packing or removing eggs from the waterglass solution.

Store the container in a cool place and keep it covered to prevent evaporation. Should this take place, leaving the top layer of eggs exposed, add cold water until the original level is reached. However, a fall in the level due to the removal of eggs should be made good only by the addition of more waterglass solution of the same strength as the original.

Try to store your buckets or containers of eggs where they will be disturbed as little as possible, as movement may cause hairline cracks in the shells.

Preserving in lime water This is a slightly cheaper method than preserving in waterglass, but it involves rather more trouble. The general rules are the same, but in this case the solution is composed of slaked lime and water.

Slaked, or hydrated, lime can be bought in handy packs from a garden shop. Mix 4 parts of lime with 20 parts of water (parts by volume) and stir the solution each day for a week, adding 1 part of coarse salt on the fourth or fifth day.

Pack the eggs into a clean bucket or glazed earthenware container and pour the lime water over them, making sure that all sediment is left behind. Cover the container, and after a time a crust will form on the surface. This will prevent evaporation.

Dry preserving This method is particularly suitable for storing small quantities of eggs – say three or four dozen. Simply rub the eggs all over with white petroleum jelly – Vaseline – or some other fine, odourless grease, using the palms of your hands. Take care that the shells are completely covered.

Pack the eggs into egg boxes so that they do not touch each other, and store the boxes in a cool place.

Using preserved eggs

Preserved eggs are best used for frying, poaching or for cooking. Boiled eggs taste better if newly laid, though preserved eggs may be hard-boiled for salads.

When using eggs preserved by the waterglass or lime water methods, wash them under running cold water before use, to remove preservative.

Break each egg into a cup or container, never directly into the mixture, as the shell may have a pinhole or hairline crack. This may allow preserving liquid to seep into the egg.

If the recipe calls for the separation of white and yolk, do this very carefully, as the skin covering the yolk becomes delicate with age.

Recipes such as marrow or lemon curd may require the addition of an extra yolk to produce the correct texture when made with preserved eggs. The same applies when making an egg custard or a recipe with a custard base.

If you hard-boil the eggs for use in salads or as a garnish, plunge them straight into really cold water as soon as they are cooked. This prevents the ugly black line around the yolks.

THREE WAYS OF PRESERVING EGGS

WATERGLASS A solution of sodium silicate used to size walls, but also useful as an egg preserver. Place the eggs, point down, in a vessel filled with the liquid.

LIME WATER Slaked lime, bought from a garden shop and mixed with salt, makes an excellent egg-preserving solution, though rather more troublesome than waterglass.

DRY PRESERVING Rub petroleum jelly – Vaseline – or any other odourless grease into the pores of each shell before packing the eggs into boxes and storing in a cool place.

FOOD FROM THE COUNTRYSIDE

Fruits, greenfood and fungi
to pick and enjoy

The wild foods described in the following pages are all still plentiful, and little harm will ensue if you use them in a reasonable manner. Take them sparingly, however; even the humble nettle provides food for butterflies and insects, while many species of birds and animals depend on nuts and berries for winter survival. Spread your gathering over as wide a range as possible, rather than denuding a small area and so depriving local wildlife.

In addition, many plants are to some degree protected by law. All land in Britain belongs to someone, and while owners may not object to your removing a few leaves or berries, they might prosecute if you dig up or remove the plant itself.

Fungi, however, are exempted from this rule. Provided you do no damage to private land in the process, and you do not offer the plant for sale, you may pick almost anywhere – that is, apart from on land owned by the National Trust or nature reserves.

For your own safety, it is inadvisable to eat wild foods gathered from the verges of major roads – where they may have been contaminated by exhaust fumes – or from places where they might have been affected by agricultural chemicals.

FRUITS & NUTS

Hedgerow, wood and moorland provide a rich autumn harvest for animals, birds – and man

Elder It is difficult to understand why this attractive tree, found in almost every hedgerow, should have such a sinister reputation. Yet this is reflected in its many local names: devil's tree, witch tree, judas tree – this last because it was said to be the tree on which Judas Iscariot hanged himself.

To approach an elder after dusk was to place yourself at the mercy of witches. But, somewhat bewilderingly, to plant one at your cottage door was a sure defence against enchantment.

In fact, few trees provide a finer harvest. Elderflower wine and elderberry port are among the best of home-made brews. (See p. 364 for the recipes.)

Elderberries may be gathered from August to October. To save time, cut whole sprays rather than pick individual berries. Having washed them, strip them from the stalks with a fork.

Not only are they good for wine-making; they can also be added whole to apple or blackberry and apple pies and crumbles, or used to impart a new flavour to crab-apple and other jellies (see p. 320).

The frothy white flowers of the elder that appear in early summer also have a wide range of uses. Add them, tied in a muslin bag, when making gooseberry jam (see p. 319) to impart a new and spicy fragrance. Elder pancakes, an old country dish, are made by dipping flower heads into pancake batter and serving them with sugar.

A more unusual recipe is that for elder milk. Simmer two flower heads in 2 pints (1 l.) of milk for 10 minutes, remove the flowers and thicken the milk with 1 teaspoon of cornflour. Add sugar and salt to taste, together with the yolks of two eggs. Whip the egg whites with sugar and float them on the milk. Serve cold.

Sweet chestnut John Evelyn, the 17th-century diarist, described this traditional Christmas accompaniment as 'a lusty and masculine food for rusticks . . . a robust food, that makes women well-complexion'd . . .' and he should have known, for he laid out a great avenue of the trees in London's Greenwich Park.

Sweet chestnuts were probably introduced to this country by the Romans, who valued them as a food crop. The trees are now well distributed throughout Britain, growing as far north as the Highland Line.

Chestnuts are at their best in October and November, when the ripe fruits fall to the ground. Break the husks open by treading them underfoot, and wear heavy gloves to extract the polished brown nuts from the spiny shells.

The most popular way of cooking them is, of course, to roast them. Their delicate aroma is the very breath of Christmas. Make a slit in the skins of all the chestnuts, except one. When this explodes, the others are ready.

It is best to roast chestnuts in an open fireplace; in an oven, the exploding nut may make a mess.

But chestnuts are far more versatile than this. They can be pickled, boiled whole with onions or Brussels sprouts, used as a stuffing, or mashed and served as an alternative to potatoes. To do this, peel the nuts and boil until soft in vegetable stock.

Rub them through a fine sieve and add milk to make a thick purée. Return to the heat for a few minutes, add a knob of butter and a pinch of salt, and serve.

When peeling chestnuts, cut a cross in the shells and boil them for a few minutes. The shells and skins will then come off more easily.

Rose-hip Loveliest of all the casual flowers that grow in our hedgerows is the dog-rose – *Rosa canina* – Rupert Brooke's 'English unofficial rose'. Despite the savage cutting inflicted annually upon the hedges, this national emblem survives, inextricably entwined with hawthorn, elder, and all the many other plants that go to make up our field boundaries.

The pink and white, delicately perfumed flowers – ideal for rose jams and jellies (see pp. 320 and 323) – appear in June and July. The fruits, 1 in. (25 mm.) long, glow orange-red among the fading leaves of autumn.

Though served as a dessert as long ago as the Middle Ages, it was not until the 1930s that the greatest value of these fruits was discovered.

Rose-hips contain more vitamin C than any other fruit or vegetable – 20 times more than the same weight of oranges.

This interesting fact went largely unremarked until the Second World War, when the pressures upon shipping caused a serious shortage of fruit and vegetables.

A national campaign was organised, and hundreds of tons of rose-hips were collected each autumn by volunteers.

After processing, the syrup was sold at cost price to the public.

Though the need for it is less acute in these more bountiful days, the syrup still makes a valuable and delicious addition to the diet of growing children. It is cheap and easy to make (see p. 328) and it can also be used as a flavouring in a range of jams, jellies, drinks and puddings.

Sweet chestnut
Castanea sativa

Elder
Sambucus nigra

Rose-hip
Rosa canina

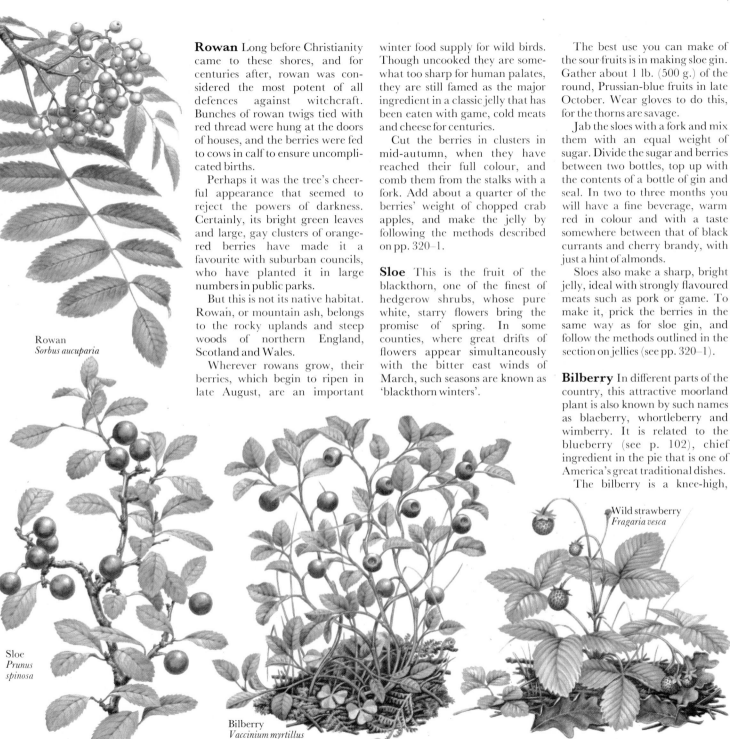

Rowan Long before Christianity came to these shores, and for centuries after, rowan was considered the most potent of all defences against witchcraft. Bunches of rowan twigs tied with red thread were hung at the doors of houses, and the berries were fed to cows in calf to ensure uncomplicated births.

Perhaps it was the tree's cheerful appearance that seemed to reject the powers of darkness. Certainly, its bright green leaves and large, gay clusters of orange-red berries have made it a favourite with suburban councils, who have planted it in large numbers in public parks.

But this is not its native habitat. Rowan, or mountain ash, belongs to the rocky uplands and steep woods of northern England, Scotland and Wales.

Wherever rowans grow, their berries, which begin to ripen in late August, are an important winter food supply for wild birds. Though uncooked they are somewhat too sharp for human palates, they are still famed as the major ingredient in a classic jelly that has been eaten with game, cold meats and cheese for centuries.

Cut the berries in clusters in mid-autumn, when they have reached their full colour, and comb them from the stalks with a fork. Add about a quarter of the berries' weight of chopped crab apples, and make the jelly by following the methods described on pp. 320–1.

Sloe This is the fruit of the blackthorn, one of the finest of hedgerow shrubs, whose pure white, starry flowers bring the promise of spring. In some counties, where great drifts of flowers appear simultaneously with the bitter east winds of March, such seasons are known as 'blackthorn winters'.

The best use you can make of the sour fruits is in making sloe gin. Gather about 1 lb. (500 g.) of the round, Prussian-blue fruits in late October. Wear gloves to do this, for the thorns are savage.

Jab the sloes with a fork and mix them with an equal weight of sugar. Divide the sugar and berries between two bottles, top up with the contents of a bottle of gin and seal. In two to three months you will have a fine beverage, warm red in colour and with a taste somewhere between that of black currants and cherry brandy, with just a hint of almonds.

Sloes also make a sharp, bright jelly, ideal with strongly flavoured meats such as pork or game. To make it, prick the berries in the same way as for sloe gin, and follow the methods outlined in the section on jellies (see pp. 320–1).

Bilberry In different parts of the country, this attractive moorland plant is also known by such names as blaeberry, whortleberry and wimberry. It is related to the blueberry (see p. 102), chief ingredient in the pie that is one of America's great traditional dishes.

The bilberry is a knee-high, bushy shrub with bright green leaves, found on heaths and moors from one end of Britain to the other, except in East Anglia. The round, black fruits that appear in late summer formed part of the diet of our Celtic ancestors, though few accorded it as much reverence as did the Clan MacLaine, who adopted the bilberry plant as their war-badge.

Raw bilberries are sharp but refreshing if eaten with sugar and cream. They are delicious in pies, tarts and crumbles, and contribute to fine jams and jellies, particularly when combined with apples.

Wild strawberry Garden strawberries, delicious though they may be, can never approach in sweetness or delicacy of taste the tiny wild fruits that grow in woodland or under hedgerows in July and August.

Wild strawberries are not very easy to find. Like their garden relatives, the fruits lie hidden beneath the trefoil leaves of the ground-hugging plants, additionally camouflaged by bracken and tangled grasses. A further complication is created by the so-called barren strawberry, a completely different species with hard, inedible fruits, that resembles the wild strawberry and is often found in the same habitat.

Very occasionally, most likely in heathland, you may come across wild strawberries in sufficient numbers to make it worth while soaking them in wine or making them into jam. But, as a rule, you will only find enough for yourself and perhaps one other person. Then the fruits should be eaten as quickly as possible after picking, accompanied by sugar and cream.

Rowan
Sorbus aucuparia

Sloe
Prunus spinosa

Wild strawberry
Fragaria vesca

Bilberry
Vaccinium myrtillus

351

SALADS & GREENS

*Some of yesterday's food crops are today's garden nuisances;
ancient recipes tell you how to make the best of weeds*

Ground elder It is good to know that this curse upon all tidy-minded gardeners is of some use after all. The weed's other name, Herb Gerard, refers to the old story that it was first given by St Gerard to a monastery whose brethren prayed that they might be delivered from the gout that afflicted them all.

An infusion . of the leaves brought them instant relief and, in consequence, ground elder became an established plant in the herb gardens of medieval monasteries. It can often be seen growing among their ruins to this day.

Long after its reputation as a cure for gout faded, it was still being grown as a vegetable. As early as the 16th century, however, its most familiar characteristic was noted by another Gerard, the botanist John Gerard, who wrote that 'where once it hath taken roote, it will hardly be gotten out again . . . getting every yeere more ground, to the annoying of better herbes'.

Despite this, when cooked like spinach with a knob of butter, ground-elder leaves make a pleasant green vegetable with a tangy, aromatic flavour.

Stinging nettle For thousands of years the nettle has been man's constant companion. Indeed, because of its fondness for broken and nitrogen-rich soil – the latter resulting from the inadequate sanitary arrangements of our ancestors – its presence often acts as a signpost for archaeologists in search of ancient dwelling places.

Not even the oceans could bar it. In their first spring in the New World, the Pilgrim Fathers discovered that they had inadvertently brought the nettle with them.

Most modern gardeners will ruthlessly exterminate nettles wherever they are found; yet, once, they were regarded as a valuable crop. Samuel Pepys enjoyed a dish of nettle porridge. Mary, Queen of Scots, found sheets of nettle linen superior to those of flax. And Sir Walter Scott reported that nettles grown under glass were an excellent substitute for spring kale.

Old herbals tell of nettle tea and nettle beer, and give detailed instructions for the making of nettle puddings – nettles, onions, sprouts and rice all boiled together in a bag.

Probably only the most fervent of wild-food enthusiasts would go so far nowadays. All the same, young nettles are among the finest of the free green vegetables available to us.

Wear gloves to gather the tender tops in spring, when the plants are no more than 8 in. (200 mm.) high. Wash them, and cook them gently – without water – in a pan for 20 minutes. Chop finely, rub through a sieve and serve at once or re-heat with a little butter, pepper and salt as an accompaniment to poached eggs.

Nettle soup, too, is excellent. Cook the nettle tops with butter over a slow heat, rub through a sieve, and add 1 tablespoon each of butter and flour. Stir the mixture into a roux and re-heat gently, adding ½ pint (300 ml.) of milk, and salt and pepper to taste.

This obliging weed also provides a highly nutritious plant food. Soak bunches of nettles in water for a month and put the resulting liquor around your vegetables.

Fat hen This is only one of many names given to the plant to which the human race owes a considerable debt of gratitude.

This coloniser of dung heaps and newly broken ground, undistinguished in appearance with its dull green leaves and tiny green flowers, may well have been one of the first plants ever harvested by man.

Its ground seeds, probably used to make gruel or bread, have been found in Stone Age settlements. Tollund Man – whose 2,000-year-old, perfectly preserved corpse was found in a Danish peat bog in 1950 – had eaten porridge containing a large proportion of fat-hen seeds shortly before he was ritually strangled and buried.

Its Saxon name, *melde*, is reflected in East Anglian village names such as Meldreth and Melbourne, lasting memorials to the gratitude of long-ago settlers who found a crop of free food in those places.

Until supplanted by spinach in the 16th century, fat hen was among the most popular of green vegetables, and is in fact more nutritious.

The leaves can be boiled like those of spinach. Afterwards, chop them finely, adding a large lump of butter and seasoning with salt, pepper and nutmeg.

A chopped, fried onion may also be included. Stir the purée and serve hot as a vegetable or as an accompaniment to poached eggs.

Sorrel Sorrel looks very much like a small dock. Its pointed, spear-shaped leaves are among the first green growths of spring, while its deep red flowers lend colour to road verges and hedgerows from early to late summer.

For centuries, the cool, acid flavour of the leaves was familiar to farmworkers who chewed them to slake their thirst in the hot harvest fields. It is this sharp taste, too, that makes one or two leaves, finely chopped, a welcome and interesting addition to a salad.

As is so often the case with wild foods, it was the French who exploited the full potential of sorrel. As well as using it to flavour

Ground elder
Aegopodium podagraria

Stinging nettle
Urtica dioica

heavy soups, such as potato and lentil, they also make a soup based on the plant itself.

This is done by chopping two large handfuls of leaves together with an onion and a sprig of rosemary. Simmer the mixture in ½ pint (300 ml.) of water for a few minutes, then add 2 pints (1 l.) of milk blended with two eggs that have been well beaten.

Heat the soup thoroughly, but do not allow it to boil. Season with salt, pepper and mace.

The classic use for sorrel, however, is as a sharp, green sauce to accompany fish or veal. Purée a handful of chopped leaves in butter, and gradually stir in the contents of a small carton of cream. Rub through a sieve and serve. The mixture, unsieved, also makes an excellent stuffing for trout and other river fish.

Dandelion Odd as it may seem, there was a time when the vegetable gardens of all great houses used to contain a row or two of dandelions carefully mulched and coaxed by skilled hands to giant size. Some were blanched like chicory. Others had their leaves, roots and flowers chopped into the sumptuous salads beloved by the Elizabethans.

Dandelions are still grown commercially in France, where their virtues as salad vegetables are more widely appreciated than they are here. The usual combination is to garnish the leaves with chives, parsley and garlic and serve them with a dressing of oil and lemon juice. Another method is to serve them raw with crisp, fried bacon.

They are also excellent with tomatoes, and a distinctive side salad can be made from equal proportions of cress and dandelion leaves sprinkled with French dressing.

Dandelion leaves are at their best in spring, before the plant comes into full flower. After June they tend to become coarse and bitter, so pick the leaves when they are young and pale green.

It is a good idea to blanch a plant or two in the winter. Choose a couple in an unobtrusive corner of the garden, cover them with flower pots and pile manure over the pots. This will provide you with salad vegetables in early spring, as well as imparting a particularly delicate flavour to the leaves.

Dandelion leaves can also be cooked like spinach. Boil them for an hour or so with a little melted butter, and serve with butter and fried onions. If the leaves are too bitter for your taste, mix them with an equal quantity of spinach; part-cook the dandelions first, however, since they require longer preparation than the spinach.

Chickweed The Tudor botanist John Gerard praised chickweed as a means of encouraging 'little birdes in cadges . . . that loathe their meate'. It is still sold for this purpose in some pet shops today. Otherwise, it is regarded as a pest by gardeners who grub it up and burn it each year.

This is something of a pity, for chickweed was at one time sold in bundles in city streets, not only as a green vegetable but also as a cure for an awesome range of diseases. Made into an infusion it was, reputedly, an infallible potion to assist slimming.

As is only too well known, chickweed will grow almost anywhere and has a particular fondness for cultivated ground. Though its fine roots have only the slightest hold in the earth, it flourishes all the year round and its white, star-like flowers may be seen even in winter.

The pale green, soft, oval leaves grow in pairs on the stems, which have single lines of fine hairs running up them.

Whatever their virtue in poultices and eye-lotions, the leaves are probably most appreciated nowadays as a substitute for, or even as an improvement upon, cress.

Since the leaves are far too small to be picked, it is best to strip them off the stem with a fork. It does not particularly matter if portions of the stem are included, since they are equally tender. Serve chickweed in sandwiches of thinly cut, buttered bread.

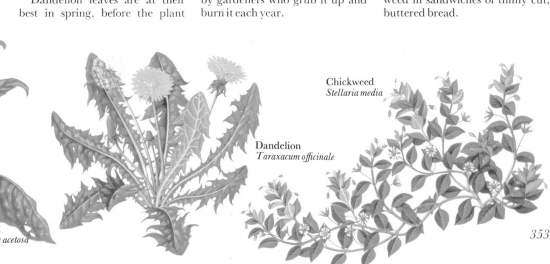

Chickweed
Stellaria media

Dandelion
Taraxacum officinale

Sorrel
Rumex acetosa

Fat hen
Chenopodium album

353

FIELD & WOODLAND MUSHROOMS

Despite their bizarre appearance, many of our wild fungi are delicious. Here is a guide to the best of them

Morel The delicate, aromatic flavour of this fungus has been widely appreciated since classical times. Fresh or dried, it can be used in soups, stews and risottos, as well as being served, stuffed, as a meal in itself.

Unusual among fungi in that they grow only in spring, morels are generally found on light soil near trees and hedgerows, and grow best on damp, warm days. They seem to have a preference for broken, burned ground, and are said to have grown thickly on the First World War battlefields in France.

They have been likened in appearance to knobs of honeycomb growing on short, stout stalks. The shapes of the pitted caps, about 3–4 in. (75–100 mm.) wide, vary considerably, but are roughly conical. The colouring, too, may lie anywhere between pale yellow and dark grey.

Pick morels only when they are young and firm, and wash them thoroughly. It is also advisable to boil them in order to get rid of any grit, mould or insects.

Once cleaned, stuff the hollow interiors of large morels with mince or seasoned scrambled egg and fry them in deep fat. Serve with fried bread or toast. Smaller specimens can be hung on strings to dry (see p. 344), to be used later, crumbled or powdered, as flavouring in soups.

Parasol mushroom The parasol is one of the most easily recognised of edible fungi. Its dry, scaly cap grows first as an egg-shape attached to the tall stem by a white ring. Later, the ring descends, permitting the cap to extend, like an opening umbrella, into a round plate. This may measure as much as 7 in. (180 mm.) across, and in its open state is dark brown at the centre. Parasols are generally found in colonies on the edges of woods, in grassy clearings and on roadsides, from July to November.

Young parasols are delicious if cooked in butter and oil like field mushrooms, or if stuffed with sage and onions or mince and baked for 30 minutes. They can also be dipped in egg and breadcrumbs and fried.

The shaggy parasol (*Lepiota rachodes*) grows in similar places and closely resembles its relative, except that it is shorter and sturdier and the open cap has no boss. This variety, too, is delicious, especially when fried or grilled.

Shaggy cap, or shaggy ink cap These mushrooms more often favour areas of mown grass rather than meadowland, and can be found from June to November on road verges, ancient lawns, playing fields and even the approaches to rubbish tips.

They should only be picked when young, when the short, white, cylindrical caps, covered with shaggy, woolly scales, are still closed. Later, the gills blacken and dissolve into an inky liquid.

Young shaggy caps, however, are delicious. As an interesting side dish, casserole the caps in cream for 2 hours, or fry them like mushrooms. For an unusual ketchup, pack young caps into an earthenware jar, sprinkling each layer with salt. Cover, and simmer for $1\frac{1}{2}$–2 hours in a medium oven, then rub the mixture through muslin. Add 1 oz. (25 g.) of black pepper and a pinch of nutmeg to each 2 pint (1 l.) of fluid, pour it into a clean saucepan and bring to the boil. Pour into sterilised bottles and seal. Once opened, use the ketchup within a few days.

Note: to avoid unpleasant side effects, do not drink alcohol when eating these fungi.

Blewit Also known as blue legs, the name derives from the blue-violet stems. They have long been famed in England, and are still sold in the more old-fashioned market-places and grocery stores in the Midlands.

The most popular is the meadow or field blewit (*Tricholoma*

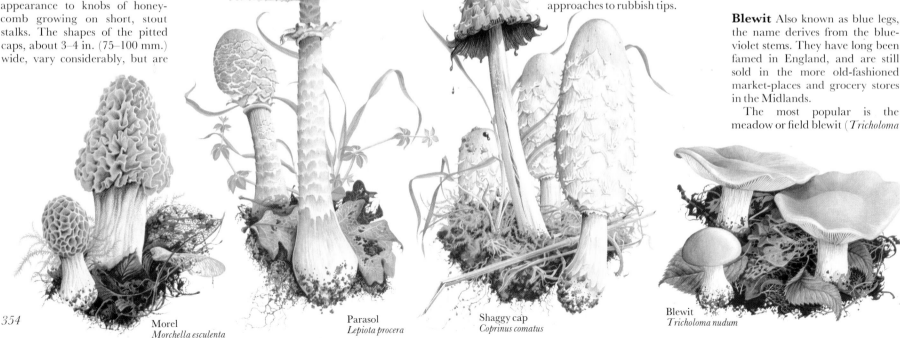

Morel
Morchella esculenta

Parasol
Lepiota procera

Shaggy cap
Coprinus comatus

Blewit
Tricholoma nudum

saevum) which can be found growing in clusters in rough pasture at any time from October to well after the early frosts. The caps are irregular and flattish, curling under at the edges, pale brown to violet-grey in colour and from 2–5 in. (50–130 mm.) across. Though dry to the touch, the flesh is slightly jelly-like and translucent. The white, or greyish pink gills grow close together, and the stems are sometimes swollen at the base.

The flavour of this particular variety is somewhat uninteresting, and some people consider it suitable only to give body to soups and stews. Traditionally, however, it was regarded as a very acceptable substitute for tripe, and was cooked in the same way. To do this, gather the blewits on a dry day, clean them, chop off the stems and put the caps in a pan.

Slice the stems finely, add the same quantity of chopped sage and onions together with a little bacon fat and pack the mixture round the caps.

Just cover with milk, and simmer for 30 minutes. Drain, and make a sauce from the liquid with butter and flour. Pour this back over the fungi and serve with mashed potatoes and apple sauce.

Those who prefer less robust fare may like to try the wood blewit (*Tricholoma nudum*) that grows in coniferous and deciduous woods at about the same time as its field relation. It is slighter and more delicate, but its colouring – violet cap, gills and stalk – is more pronounced. Fry in its own juice with butter and parsley.

Wood hedgehog This, the most common of the *Hydnum* family, belongs to the only group of fungi that possesses spines instead of gills; hence the countryman's name for it.

It flourishes in most kinds of woodland from August to November. The irregularly shaped cap, with undulating curves, measures 2–4 in. (50–100 mm.) across and is covered by a pinkish-buff skin resembling fine leather. The tiny white spines are on the underside of the fungus, which is supported on a short, sturdy stem.

Wood hedgehogs should be gathered when they are young. To get rid of their slightly bitter taste, chop them and stew them for a few minutes in boiling water. Drain, and cook them in milk or stock for 20 minutes before adding a dash of sherry and serving on toast.

Cep, or Cèpe de Bordeaux For centuries, continental housewives have regarded ceps as being among the most useful of edible fungi – a notion that is gradually gaining ground in this country through the enterprise of delicatessens that sell dried continental ceps to British gourmets.

This is a case of taking coals to Newcastle, for ceps grow readily in this country, where they flourish in woodland clearings from August to November.

The caps closely resemble old-fashioned buns – a smooth, dry, polished brown disc 2–6 in. (50–150 mm.) across.

The underside is a yellowish mass of pores like sponge rubber and the stem is short, swollen and fawny-white.

Ceps are chiefly famed as the principal ingredient of Cèpes à la Bordelaise. As with all recipes for these fungi, remove the pores with a spoon before, in this instance, cutting the ceps into finger-thick slices. Season with salt and pepper, drop them into a deep pan of boiling olive oil and cook them to a deep golden-brown. Drain, reheat with a little melted butter, parsley and garlic, and serve as a starter or snack.

Ceps can also be made into soup or dried, strung in the kitchen, as a standby for flavouring such dishes as omelettes.

The old-wives' tale that colour changes in fungi denote poison is actually true in the case of *Boletus*. When picking ceps, break a small piece off each cap. If the flesh remains firm and white, they are true ceps. But if any colour change occurs, you have probably gathered another species of the same genus.

Some of these are inedible, and one, devil's boletus (*Boletus satanas*), is poisonous.

However, this is also distinguished by a blood-red stripe at the base, and pores of a similar colour when the plant is mature, so there should be no confusion.

Chanterelle Also known as the egg mushroom, from the vivid, egg-yolk colouring of its flesh, this, in many continental countries, is one of the most popular of all edible fungi. It flourishes from June to October in mixed and coniferous woodland, in both of which it is most commonly associated with firs.

Though local soil conditions can produce either dwarfs or giants, the horn-shaped chanterelles are generally ¾–3 in. (20–75 mm.) in diameter. The gills flare upwards and outwards like fan tracery from halfway up the stem to the lip of the horn.

Perhaps the most distinctive feature of this attractive fungus is its scent, which is closely akin to that of ripe greengages or apricots. The flavour, too, resembles that of apricots. Chanterelles are slightly tough, so steep them in boiling water for a few minutes before cooking them in omelettes or with scrambled eggs.

Wood hedgehog
Hydnum repandum

Cep
Boletus edulis

Chanterelle
Cantharellus cibarius

WILD FLOWERS
FOR FLAVOUR

*Spring flowers add colour to your cooking, but pick them sparingly;
other people enjoy them in the hedgerows*

Primrose The story goes that
as the 19th-century statesman
Benjamin Disraeli lay dying, he
was much cheered to receive a box
of primroses, the first of the season,
picked by Queen Victoria's own
hands at Osborne. In a gracious
accompanying note, Her Majesty
wrote: 'His favourite flower.' For
primroses were the flowers that
Prince Albert, her late consort,
had loved above all.

Disraeli's secretary inquired
whether he would like the Queen
to visit him. The old statesman
waved a weak hand: 'No, No,' he
said, 'she would only want me to
take a message to Albert'.

The Queen's note, clear enough
to Disraeli – who understood well
enough the depth of her devotion
to Albert – conveyed a different
impression to some of his friends.
The idea arose that primroses were
Disraeli's own favourite flower.
This in turn led to the formation of
the Primrose League, a body
dedicated to his ideas of Empire,
and a consequent decimation – so
it is said – of the primrose population around his Buckinghamshire
home by devoted pilgrims.

Whether the story is true in all
its details or not, primroses remain
among the best loved of our spring
flowers. Many appear before sufficient insects are abroad to pollinate them – hence Shakespeare's
'pale primroses that die un-
married'. However, their life can
be extended by crystallising the
flowers, using the following
ingredients:

1 saltspoon of gum tragacanth
(buy this from a good chemist or
health-food store)

2 tablespoons of triple-strength
rose-water (which may be purchased from the same sources)

Caster sugar

Mix the gum and rose-water in a
screw-top jar and leave in a warm
place for 24 hours. Cut a bunch of
primrose flowers, leaving sufficient
stalk to hold them by, and, using a
fine brush, coat each petal with the
mixture. Dip the flowers in the
caster sugar and leave them to dry.

Having snipped off the stems,
store the primroses in a jar and use
them to decorate chocolate cakes.

Pick primroses only where they
are plentiful – and then sparingly.

Violet To the Greeks and the
Romans, the violet was the flower
of love and fertility. Consequently,
it was used in cosmetics and as a
flavouring in confectionery.

In Britain, about the same
period, Celtic ladies mingled violets with goats' milk as a skin food.
Later, monks grew them in their
physic gardens as cures for in-
somnia and constipation.

Sweet violets – the variety used
in ancient remedies and modern
recipes – appear in early spring
under hedgerows and in shady
woods. The flowers may be white
or purple. Sweet violets are often
found growing in association with
the dog violet, but may be distinguished from it by their sweet scent
and by their hairy stalks.

The young, tender leaves impart a delicate flavour to soups and
salads. The flowers may be crystallised (see Primrose) or steeped in
either syrup or hot, white vinegar
as a flavouring for drinks or
puddings.

Broom This dark green and gold
plant was once the badge of a
mighty dynasty of English kings,
who also adopted its medieval title
– *Planta genista* – as their family
name. Carved sprigs of broom
decorate the effigy of the tragic
King Richard II – Richard Plan-
tagenet – which lies beside that of
his queen in Westminster Abbey.

In contrast, the shrub's more
usual name is applied to one of the
humblest of domestic tools. Bound
together in bunches, the tough,
springy twigs were for centuries
used to sweep floors.

Equally at home, therefore, in
cottage and castle, the 'bonnie
yellow broom' makes an early
summer blaze on sandy heath-
lands throughout Europe.

The flowers have been used for
many purposes: as an emblem of
love, for instance, and as the base
of a traditional country wine. In
Yorkshire, they were mashed with
lard to make an ointment for cuts
on fishermen's hands.

A recipe of perhaps more
general usefulness is to gather the
buds in spring and pack them into
jars with vinegar or salt. Thus
pickled, they can be served in
salads as an alternative to capers.

Infused, dried broom flowers
also make a refreshing tea. Henry
VIII considered this an excellent
'remedy for surfeits'.

Broom
Sarothamnus scoparius

Primrose
Primula vulgaris

Sweet violet
Viola odorata

MAKING YOUR OWN WINE

Delicious and inexpensive drinks from garden produce

The ancient tradition of country wine-making – which began long before the Romans brought the grape to these shores – has never died out. Indeed, in the past few years it has attracted an ever-growing group of enthusiasts whose links with the soil are usually confined to their own gardens.

There are many reasons for this. Apart from being able to entertain friends at a fraction of the cost of buying commercial wines, there is the pleasure of acquiring a creative and satisfying hobby and of finding additional uses for garden produce.

The principles of wine-making are very simple and it is unnecessary to buy a great deal of expensive equipment. Many of the items you need can be found in a well-equipped kitchen, and the remainder bought from a chemist or ironmonger or from one of the ever-growing number of shops specialising in home-brewing and wine-making.

The results of your efforts should be at least as drinkable as the less expensive commercial wines, and will certainly offer much more variety. With experience and a little care, you could soon be producing a range of beverages with really distinctive flavour and character.

Making your own wine

In spite of the many concentrates and kits sold for home wine-making, it is still cheaper and more satisfying to use produce grown in your garden or gathered in the countryside. No greater skill is needed and, with a little care, good results are assured.

Main ingredients

Almost all garden fruits and vegetables, many wild hedgerow plants and even the petals of scented flowers can provide the basis for delicious wines, each with a distinctive flavour. Apart from the plants themselves, the principal ingredients are yeast, sugar and water.

All 'country' wines, made from these homely ingredients, are improved by the addition of grapes, whose ideal balance of acids, mineral salts, tannin and vitamins, aids fermentation and makes up for any deficiencies in the basic fruit, flower or vegetable. Raisins, sultanas or concentrated grape juice may be used instead of fresh grapes for this purpose.

Yeast Fermentation – the process by which sugar is converted into alcohol and carbon dioxide – is brought about by the enzymes secreted by yeast cells. These tiny vegetable cells, invisible to the naked eye, grow on most fruit skins – especially those of grapes.

However, since the wild strains produced on fruits in Britain are unsuitable for making wine of good quality, yeast must be added.

Bakers' or brewers' yeasts are unsuitable. Wine yeasts, which provide both a stronger wine and a firmer sediment, may be bought in tablet, granular or liquid forms.

Sachets of 'super yeast' are particularly useful for the beginner, since they also contain the correct amounts of nutrient salts. This yeast starts fermenting extremely quickly, falls cleanly to the bottom of the jar and promotes a good flavour in the wine.

For those who like to experiment, there are special yeasts produced in the great wine-growing districts – Sauternes, Burgundy, Bordeaux and so on. When added to the must of a wine of similar type – a Graves yeast to rhubarb, for example – they help to impart their characteristic flavour.

Whatever type is chosen, it is always better to add activated, rather than dormant, yeast to the must. This ensures prompt fermentation and helps to avoid infection by micro-organisms. As the sachets contain dormant yeast, it is necessary to activate it before adding it to the must.

Starter bottles

To activate yeast, place it in a sterilised bottle containing a few spoonsful of boiled and cooled fruit juice that has been slightly sweetened. Grape juice is ideal, but the juice of any sharp-tasting fruit, such as oranges, will do.

Leave plenty of air space in the bottle, plug the neck lightly with cotton wool, and leave it in a warm place for several hours or overnight. A stream of bubbles indicates that the yeast is active and ready to be added to the must. In the case of 'super yeast', this may occur within four or five hours. Other types, however, take up to two days.

Some of the remarkable qualities of yeast are reflected in the fact that if you wish to make several batches of wine within a short time, you need use only three-quarters of the contents of the bottle and replace the amount taken out with fresh fruit juice, cold boiled water and sugar. Within two days, you will have another large colony of yeast cells.

Water Use tap water – hard or soft – or water from a spring or well. Rainwater is unsuitable, unless first filtered and boiled.

Sugar Alcohol in wine is produced exclusively from sugar, either from that contained in the basic fruit or vegetable or from the extra sugar that you add to the must. Grapes and honey apart, all musts require some additional sugar.

Ordinary white granulated sugar is the most suitable – except when making Madeira-type wines, when brown sugar should be used. Chemicals such as saccharin are non-fermentable, and are therefore suitable only for sweetening finished wine.

Wine-makers often ask whether a particular fruit will produce dry or sweet wine. The answer is that any wine will be as dry or sweet as you make it, for this depends on the amount of sugar you use – not the type of fruit. The more sugar you use, the longer the wine will take to ferment and the stronger it will be.

Bear in mind that the natural sugar content of fruit and vegetables may vary from year to year, so the quantities of sugar recommended in the recipes on pp. 362–4 are only approximate.

Though you can produce good wines simply by following the recipes, perfectionists should measure the natural sugar content of the must with a hydrometer and add only enough sugar to produce the amount of alcohol required.

Secondary ingredients

In addition to the basic materials used for wine-making, various additives are needed to ensure reliable fermentation and a good-tasting wine.

Nutrient Like all living things, yeast requires feeding in order to function properly. All the elements it needs are present in pure grape juice and also in some other fruits, but are lacking in vegetables, herbs, flowers and honey.

Therefore, to ensure good fermentation in wines made from fruits and vegetables, it may be necessary to add nutrient to the yeast. This is sold as crystals and added to the wine at the rate of half a level teaspoonful per gallon.

Acid Yeast can flourish only in an acid solution, and wine, too, requires acid to assist in the development of a good bouquet and flavour. Citric-acid crystals are best, but tartaric or malic acid may also be used, or a combination of all three.

Almost every must will require some acid; the amount depends on the natural acidity of the basic material. Some musts – those made from honey, flowers, herbs or vegetables, for instance – will require the full dose of $\frac{3}{4}$ oz. per gallon (5 g. per litre) while others, such as rhubarb and red currants, need considerably less.

Tannin Tannin gives red wine its bite and character and is also beneficial in white wines, though to a lesser extent. Half a level teaspoonful of grape tannin – a brown powder – is sufficient for six bottles of wine.

Some wine-makers, however, prefer to use cold tea instead. Half a cup is usually enough, depending on the strength of the tea.

Campden tablets These are the wine-maker's cure-all. One, dissolved in a pint (600 ml.) of cold water, is the perfect sterilising agent for wine-making equipment. Each item must first be washed in this solution.

One tablet dissolved in a gallon of must, or of finished wine, will prevent oxidation and the growth of spoilage organisms.

Add two tablets to sweet wines after racking, to stabilise them and prevent further fermentation.

Pectin-destroying enzyme Added to all fruit wines, the enzyme improves both juice extraction and flavour by breaking down the pectin contained in the fruits. It also reduces the risk of haziness in the finished wine.

Add the enzyme at an early stage, before sugar is added to the must. A rounded teaspoonful per gallon should be enough for most types of fruit.

UNDERSTANDING THE TERMS USED IN WINE-MAKING

Acid Essential for fermentation. Citric, tartaric and malic acids are all suitable and may be obtained in crystal form from a chemist's. (See also Ingredients, on opposite page.)

Airlock A device that excludes airborne bacteria and other sources of infection from the must during fermentation, but allows gas to escape. It works in much the same way as the U-trap under a sink.

Body A word used to describe the density of a wine. Some wines taste thin and watery, while others are 'full-bodied'.

Campden tablet A small white tablet used for sterilising ingredients and equipment. (See also Ingredients, on opposite page.)

Carbon dioxide A gas formed during fermentation, which must be allowed to escape through the airlock.

Decant To pour wine from a bottle into a glass container suitable for table use, leaving any sediment behind in the bottle. Hold the bottle against the light, and decant the wine slowly, so that you can stop pouring when the sediment reaches the neck of the bottle.

Dry The term used to describe a wine with no trace of sweetness.

Fermentation The process whereby sugar is converted by yeast into alcohol and carbon dioxide.

Fermentation lock: see Airlock.

Finings Substances such as isinglass and bentonite that are sometimes stirred into wine to help it clear.

Hydrometer An instrument for measuring the specific gravity in a liquid. It is used in wine-making to measure the sugar content.

Lees A sediment, composed of dead yeast and pulp tissue, that collects in the bottom of the jar while the wine is fermenting.

Maturation The mellowing of a new wine by storage to the point when it is ready to drink.

Must The term used to describe the mixture of ingredients before they have been fermented to make wine.

Nutrient Ammonium phosphate and other vitamins fed to yeast to promote growth and development. They are required in the making of most wines in the home, except those made from grape juice. (See also Ingredients, on opposite page.)

Pectin-destroying enzyme A white powder or brown liquid used to break down the pectin in fruit. (See also Ingredients, on opposite page.)

Racking The removal of clear wine from a vessel containing lees. Each wine needs at least two rackings to get rid of all sediment.

Siphon A plastic or rubber tube used for racking and bottling wine.

Specific gravity In wine-making terms, the amount of sugar contained in a must or wine.

Tannin A substance extracted from the skins of grapes, some other fruits, cold tea and oak. It is used to give the wine 'bite' and character. (See also Ingredients, on opposite page.)

Yeast A tiny vegetable cell, invisible to the naked eye, that causes fermentation. Yeast is essential in the making of wine.

Equipment

Though increasing expertise may lead you to buy certain refinements such as a press, a juice extractor and a corking tool, the basic equipment for wine-making is both inexpensive and long-lasting.

Bottle brush Essential for cleaning fermentation jars as well as bottles.

Bottles Use only orthodox wine bottles – dark for red wine, clear for white. Champagne bottles are essential for sparkling wines.

Corks Always use undamaged corks. Pierced corks are unsuitable. Sterilise all corks before use.

Fermentation and storage jars One-gallon glass jars are generally used to contain the wine during fermentation and storage. Start with two jars.

Fermentation lock or airlock This essential item of equipment prevents the admission of air and spoilage organisms during fermentation. A bored cork or rubber bung is needed to fit eack lock on to a jar.

Hydrometer and testing jar Not absolutely essential, but the best means of controlling the sugar and alcohol content of your wine.

Large saucepan For preference, use one made of stainless steel or unchipped enamel.

Long-handled wooden spoon For macerating flowers, and for stirring all types of must.

Nylon straining bag and sieve The bag is an additional aid when straining pulp.

Polythene funnel Useful when pouring the must into a fermentation jar.

Polythene mashing bin An uncoloured polythene bin with a tight-fitting lid is best. Coloured plastic buckets may contaminate the wine.

Polythene tubing You will need about 4½ ft (1.4 m.) for siphoning the wine from one container to another.

EQUIPMENT NEEDED FOR HOME WINE-MAKING

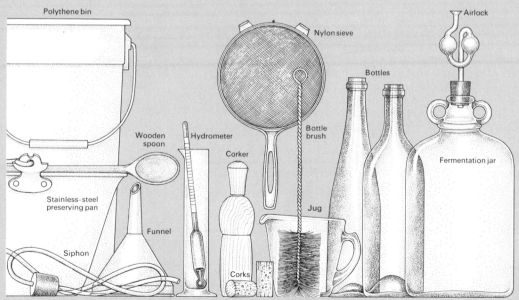

Polythene bin
Nylon sieve
Airlock
Bottles
Wooden spoon
Hydrometer
Bottle brush
Corker
Fermentation jar
Stainless-steel preserving pan
Funnel
Jug
Siphon
Corks

Some of the items needed for home wine-making – such as a wooden spoon, a strainer and a plastic bucket – are standard kitchen equipment. The rest can be bought at shops specialising in home-brewing equipment or at branches of multiple chemists.

STEP-BY-STEP GUIDE TO WINE-MAKING

Making your own wine can be as simple or as complicated as you wish – a pleasant pastime for a wet afternoon, or a deeply absorbing hobby. But as nothing is more encouraging to the beginner than early success, here is a step-by-step guide to making your first half-dozen bottles – i.e. 1 gallon, or about 4 litres of wine.

Preparing the must

As a rough guide, use 3–4 lb. (1.5–2 kg.) of vegetables or fruit for each gallon of wine, depending on the strength of the material's flavour. Methods of extracting the juice – such as pressing, soaking or using a domestic extractor – depend on the fruits or vegetables used.

Vegetables Clean and prepare vegetables as for cooking (coarse, end-of-season vegetables may be used), cut them into small pieces and simmer until tender. When cool, strain the liquor into a bin, stir in the concentrated grape juice if included in the recipe, and add the sugar, acid, tannin, nutrient and yeast.

Pour the must into a fermentation jar, top up with cold water and fit an airlock.

Flowers Carefully comb the petals or blossoms from the stalks with a fork. Place the petals in a bin – making sure that all stems and leaves are excluded – pour hot water over them, and macerate to a soft consistency with the back of a wooden or plastic spoon.

Stir in one teaspoonful of citric acid and one crushed Campden tablet, cover the bin and leave it to stand in a temperature of about 21°C (70°F).

Macerate the petals again on each of the following three days. Strain and press them to extract the liquor. Stir in the concentrated grape juice, together with the sugar, tannin, nutrient and yeast.

Pour into a fermentation jar and top up with cold water, and fit an airlock to prevent possible infection from airborne spores.

Fruit Wash the fruits and remove any damaged portions. (Windfalls and bruised fruits are quite suitable for wine-making.) Then either pass them through a juice extractor or ferment the fruits on the pulp.

If you extract the juice, dilute it and make it into wine in the same way as vegetable and flower liquors. If you ferment the fruit on the pulp, first crush it and then drop it into a bin containing water in which a Campden tablet, some pectin-destroying enzyme and a little citric acid have been dissolved. Cover the bin and leave it in a warm room.

After 24 hours add raisins, sultanas or concentrated grape juice, together with activated yeast. Re-cover the bin and return it to its warm position for a further four or five days.

Keep the floating pulp moist by pushing it beneath the surface of the liquid twice a day.

Strain and press the pulp, add the sugar to the liquid and stir until it is dissolved. Pour the must into a fermentation jar, top up with cold water, and fit an airlock.

Mead Despite its association with our distant ancestors, mead is an acquired taste. Also, since it takes

BASIC STEPS IN MAKING WINE WITH VEGETABLES

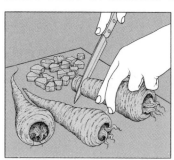

1 Clean the vegetables and cut them into small pieces to reduce cooking time.

2 Cover the vegetables with water and simmer them until they are tender.

3 Strain the resultant liquid into a bucket, using a sieve to remove the pulp.

BASIC STEPS IN MAKING WINE WITH FLOWERS

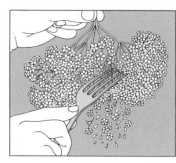

1 Use a fork to comb the petals off the stalks, or pick the petals off by hand.

2 Pour hot water over the petals; press with a spoon to a soft consistency.

3 Strain off the liquid three days after adding citric acid and a Campden tablet.

BASIC STEPS IN MAKING WINE WITH FRUIT

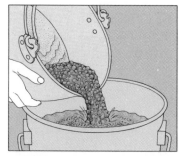

1 Clean the fruits, remove damaged parts, then press them with a rolling pin.

2 Mix the fruit with the other ingredients. Cover, and leave in a warm room.

3 One day later, add the activated yeast, and raisins or grape juice. Re-cover the bin.

4 After straining, add grape juice, sugar, acid, tannin and the other ingredients.

5. Pour the mixture into a fermentation jar, top up with cold water and fit an airlock.

4 Strain, then add grape juice, yeast, sugar, tannin and nutrient.

5 Empty the liquor into a fermentation jar; top up with cold water and fit an airlock.

4 Four or five days later, strain and press the pulp and stir the sugar into the liquid.

5 Empty the must into a fermentation jar, top up with water and fit an airlock.

3 lb. (1.5 kg.) of honey to make six bottles of dry table mead, it can be rather expensive.

On the other hand, it is very easy to make. Simply dissolve the honey in warm water and pour it into a fermentation jar.

When cool, add the acid, tannin, nutrient and yeast and top up with cold water.

Fermentation

Whatever the basic ingredients, the yeast will now be working in the must and an airlock must be fitted to the fermentation jar. Make sure that the pierced cork is of the right size, insert the tube of the airlock in the cork, put a few drops of water in the airlock and seal the jar with the cork.

The end of the tube should only just protrude through the cork and must be above the liquid.

Tie a label on the jar stating its contents, the quantities used and the date when it was made.

Stand the jar in a warm place. An average living room, with a temperature of 21°C (70°F), is ideal. Avoid excessive heat as this may kill the yeast and, in consequence, halt fermentation.

Too low a temperature may prevent or slow down fermentation but will not harm the yeast. Fermentation will start again if the jar is moved to a warmer place.

Do not expect any sudden and spectacular change, as signs of fermentation may not appear for a day or two. By then, and probably sooner, you should see bubbles of carbon dioxide rising in the must and forcing their way through the water in the airlock.

For a week or so, fermentation will be extremely vigorous, before settling down to a steady rhythm.

FERMENTING THE WINE

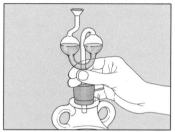

FITTING AN AIRLOCK Push the stem of the lock into the hole in the cork or bung. Half fill the airlock with water.

PLACING THE JAR Stand the jar where it will be warm but not too hot. Normal living-room temperature is ideal for fermentation.

RACKING

Position the jars so that the top of the empty one is lower than the base of the jar containing wine. Tilt the upper jar.

The particles of pulp and dead yeast cells will then slowly begin to form a sediment.

Prolonged fermentation When making strong dessert wines – about 16% alcohol – it is advisable to begin with only about half the sugar needed, and to add the rest gradually as fermentation proceeds. In this way, the alcoholic tolerance of the yeast can be built up and a really strong wine produced.

If all the sugar is added at the outset, it is sometimes too much for the yeast and fermentation may stop prematurely.

This results in a sweet, low-alcohol wine.

Dissolve the sugar in a little wine before adding it to the fermentation jar. Dry sugar will simply lie on the bottom of the jar and impede the action of the yeast.

Racking

When bubbles cease to rise in the jar, and there is no movement of gas through the water in the airlock, it is time to rack the wine from its sediment even though it is not perfectly clear. The time this takes varies considerably, depending on the sugar content and temperature, but even with a light, dry wine it may take a month.

It is important to remove the wine from the sediment as soon as fermentation is finished because the pulp and dead yeast soon start to decompose and this imparts an unpleasant flavour to the wine.

It is also important to leave as much of the sediment behind in the original jar as you can. The best way to rack a wine is to siphon the clearing wine into another jar.

First sterilise a storage jar and place it on the floor. Set the jar of wine on a table above the storage jar and remove the airlock. Place one end of a polythene or rubber tube into the wine just above the level of the sediment and gently suck the other end of the tube until it is filled with wine.

Squeeze this end to prevent the wine escaping until you have placed it in the storage jar, then release the pressure. Gravity will pull the wine from the jar above to the one beneath.

Carefully tilt the upper jar so that the end of the siphon remains clear of the sediment until the last of the wine has been removed. Discard the sediment, wash and sterilise the jar and airlock, dry them and put them away until next required.

Top up the jar of wine with cool, boiled water or some weak, cold tea. Add one Campden tablet, fit a bung, tie on a descriptive label and store the jar in a cool place.

Maturing

After six or eight weeks a further sediment will be seen and by this time the wine may be quite bright. It now needs to be racked again in the same manner as before.

Bottling

Light and medium wines require up to eight months' storage in the jar before bottling. Heavy and strong wines may need two years, or even longer.

The beginner's commonest mistake is over-eagerness to see the wine in the bottle.

If it is bottled too soon, fermentation may start again, especially in hot weather. The wine will then become hazy and fizzy. The bottle might blow its cork, or, in extreme conditions, it might burst.

Sterilise the bottles thoroughly and use new corks. Soak the corks in hot water to make them supple and to get rid of the 'corky' flavour they might impart.

Before using them, give a final rinse or soak them in a solution made up with a Campden tablet.

Carefully siphon the wine from the jar into the bottles and drive the corks well home.

Softened cylindrical corks can be thrust home by hand, or, more efficiently, with a corker.

If T-shaped stoppers are used, they should be fastened on with string or wire before laying the bottles down.

Do not overfill the bottles or the air will be so compressed when the corks are fitted that it will push them out a little, leaving them unsightly and the wine at risk.

Store the bottles on their sides so that the corks remain wet and do not dry out and shrink.

Leave the bottles in store for at least a month, and preferably much longer. A red wine kept for a year or more will well reward your patience.

White wines should be put in the refrigerator for an hour before drinking. Red wines, however, should be drunk at room temperature. They also benefit by removing the cork half an hour or so before drinking, to allow them to 'breathe'. Even better, pour them into a decanter or carafe.

Things that may go wrong

Stuck fermentation The commonest problem in wine-making is that of fermentation stopping too soon. It may happen for a number of reasons:

1. The yeast has converted as much sugar as it can and has reached the limit of its alcohol tolerance. The remaining sugar just sweetens the wine.

If it is too sweet, try blending it with a dry wine.

2. The yeast is lacking acid or nutrient. Add some and stir the wine well.

3. The must is too hot or too cold and the yeast is inhibited. Move the jar to a different position; overheating, however, may have killed the yeast.

4. The must needs to 'breathe'. Splash it into another jar to release the carbon dioxide, but don't expect any immediate results. It may be a day or two before the bubbles start rising again.

5. The yeast colony has died and needs replacing. Start fresh yeast in a large jar and add the stuck must in stages, making sure that the previous batch is fermenting before adding more.

Using the hydrometer before fermentation has started, and after it is stopped, will indicate the amount of sugar converted and therefore the amount of alcohol produced. This information will help you identify why the fermentation has stuck.

Excessive dryness If, when fully fermented, the wine has too dry a taste, sweeten it with saccharin. If sugar is used, fermentation may start again.

Clearing If a wine fails to clear naturally, use wine finings – consisting of isinglass, gelatin or bentonite – in accordance with the instructions on the packet. Filtering is very rarely necessary and is recommended only as a last resort.

Vinegary taste A wine or must imperfectly corked or left open to the air is likely to develop a vinegary smell. There is no cure for this, and any wine so infected should be thrown away.

RECIPES
for
home-made wine

Inquiring how to make a certain kind of wine is like asking the best way to cook an egg. Elderberry wine, for example, may be made in 20 different ways and each of them could be successful. For this reason the following recipes are simply suggestions, but all are based on the basic methods described on the preceding pages.

It is best to err on the low side when using strong-tasting vegetables, fruits or flowers.

The amount of sugar used is more critical. Though it is unnecessary to adhere slavishly to the recipe, bear in mind that low sugar gives quick results, a dry wine and low alcohol content; high sugar means slow results, and a sweet, strong wine.

APPLE WINE

*7½ lb. (3.5 kg.) mixed apples
(windfalls will do)
9 oz. (250 g.) sultanas
1¾ lb. (875 g.) sugar
5½ pints (3 l.) water
1 teaspoon citric acid
1 Campden tablet
1 teaspoon pectin-destroying enzyme
Hock yeast and nutrient*

Pour the water into a bin and add the citric acid, the pectin-destroying enzyme and a crushed Campden tablet.

Wash the apples, crush them into a mash or cut them up and drop them into the bin. Cover the

THE FINAL STAGES

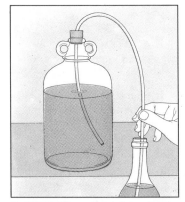

BOTTLING After racking twice, and storing for from eight months to two years, siphon the wine into sterilised bottles.

CORKING Drive the corks home by hand or with a corker. Store the bottles on their sides to prevent the corks drying out.

bin and leave it in a warm place for 24 hours.

Activate the yeast in a starter bottle (see p. 358). Add the sultanas, nutrient and yeast to the mash, re-cover the bin and place it in the warm for 4–5 days.

Press and strain the pulp and add the sugar, dissolving this first in warm water.

Pour the strained must into a fermentation jar, top up with cold water and fit an airlock to the jar. Tie on a label describing the contents and store the jar at room temperature until fermentation is complete.

BEETROOT WINE

4½ lb. (2.25 kg.) scrubbed, diced beetroot
9 oz. (250 g.) concentrated red grape juice
2¼ lb. (1 kg.) sugar
½ oz. (15 g.) citric acid
¼ teaspoon grape tannin
7 pints (4 l.) water
Bordeaux yeast and nutrient

Simmer the diced beetroot until tender. When cool, strain the liquor into a bin.

Activate the yeast and add it to the liquor, together with the concentrated grape juice, the acid, tannin, nutrient and sugar dissolved in warm water.

Pour the must into a fermentation jar and proceed as for apple wine.

BILBERRY WINE

2¼ lb. (1 kg.) bilberries
9 oz. (250 g.) concentrated red grape juice
2¼ lb. (1 kg.) sugar
1 teaspoon tartaric acid
1 Campden tablet
1 teaspoon pectin-destroying enzyme
½ teaspoon grape tannin
5½ pints (3 l.) water
Burgundy yeast and nutrient

Pour the water into a bin and add the tartaric acid, the pectin-destroying enzyme and a crushed Campden tablet.

Crush the bilberries (if you are not putting them through a juice extractor) and drop them into the bin. Cover the bin and leave it in a warm place for 24 hours.

Proceed as for beetroot wine.

BLACKBERRY 'PORT'

3½ lb. (1.75 kg.) wild blackberries
9 oz. (250 g.) black currants
1 lb. 2 oz. (525 g.) raisins
2¾ lb. (1.3 kg.) sugar
1 Campden tablet
1 teaspoon pectin-destroying enzyme
6 pints (3½ l.) water
Port yeast and nutrient

Pour the water into a bin and add the pectin-destroying enzyme and a crushed Campden tablet.

Wash and crush the blackberries and black currants and proceed as for apple wine. But, since this is high-alcohol wine, add the sugar in small doses each time fermentation slows down.

Best results are obtained by using a hydrometer, but there is

also a good rule-of-thumb method. Put in half the total amount of sugar at first, half the remainder about 10 days later and the residue about 8 days after that.

When adding the extra sugar, extract a little of the wine and dissolve the sugar in it. Pour the solution back gently.

BLACK-CURRANT WINE

2¼ lb. (1 kg.) black currants
9 oz. (250 g.) raisins
2¼ lb. (1 kg.) sugar
1 Campden tablet
1 teaspoon pectin-destroying enzyme
7 pints (4 l.) water
Burgundy yeast and nutrient
Saccharin

Proceed as for apple wine, but since this is a sweet wine add saccharin to taste when fermentation is finished and the wine has been siphoned into a storage jar.

CARROT WINE

4½ lb. (2.25 kg.) diced carrot
9 oz. (250 g.) concentrated white grape juice
2¼ lb. (1 kg.) sugar
¾ oz. (20 g.) citric acid
7 pints (4 l.) water
Sauternes yeast and nutrient
Saccharin

Simmer the diced carrot until tender. When cool, strain the liquor into a bin.

Proceed as for beetroot wine, but since this is a sweet wine add

saccharin to taste as soon as fermentation is finished.

CELERY WINE

4½ lb. (2.25 kg.) chopped celery
9 oz. (250 g.) concentrated white grape juice
2¼ lb. (1 kg.) sugar
½ oz. (15 g.) citric acid
¼ teaspoon grape tannin
7 pints (4 l.) water
Chablis yeast and nutrient

Simmer the chopped celery until tender. When cool, strain the liquor into the bin and proceed as for beetroot wine.

CHERRY WINE

4½ lb. (2.25 kg.) assorted cherries
9 oz. (250 g.) sultanas
1¾ lb. (875 g.) sugar
1 teaspoon citric acid
½ teaspoon grape tannin
1 teaspoon pectin-destroying enzyme
1 Campden tablet
6 pints (3½ l.) water
Bordeaux yeast and nutrient
Saccharin

Pour the water into a bin and add the citric acid, the pectin-destroying enzyme and a crushed Campden tablet.

Wash the cherries, remove the stalks, put them into the bin and proceed as for apple wine. Since this is a sweet wine, add saccharin to taste when fermentation is finished.

CRAB-APPLE WINE

4½ lb. (2.25 kg.) crab apples
9 oz. (250 g.) sultanas
2¾ lb. (1.3 kg.) sugar
1 teaspoon citric acid
1 teaspoon pectin-destroying enzyme
1 Campden tablet
6 pints (3½ l.) water
Sauternes yeast and nutrient

Follow recipe for apple wine.

DAMSON WINE

4½ lb. (2.25 kg.) damsons
9 oz. (250 g.) raisins
2¼ lb. (1 kg.) sugar
1 teaspoon tartaric acid
½ teaspoon grape tannin
1 Campden tablet
1 teaspoon pectin-destroying enzyme
6 pints (3½ l.) water
Bordeaux yeast and nutrient

Apart from substituting tartaric acid for citric, and adding grape tannin, proceed as for apple wine.

Continued . . .

Wine recipes (continued)

ELDERBERRY 'PORT'

2¼ *lb. (1 kg.) elderberries*
9 *oz. (250 g.) black currants*
1 *lb. 2 oz. (525 g.) blackberries*
1 *lb. 2 oz. (525 g.) raisins*
2¾ *lb. (1.3 kg.) sugar*
1 *teaspoon tartaric acid*
1 *teaspoon pectin-destroying enzyme*
1 *Campden tablet*
6 *pints (3½ l.) water*
Port yeast and nutrient

Pour the water into a bin and add the tartaric acid, the pectin-destroying enzyme and a crushed Campden tablet.

Wash the elderberries, black currants and blackberries, mash them into a pulp and proceed as for apple wine. But since this is a high-alcohol wine, add the sugar in small doses as described for blackberry 'port'.

ELDERFLOWER WINE

1¾ *pints (1 l.) elderflower florets*
1 *lb. 2 oz. (525 g.) concentrated white grape juice*
1¾ *lb. (800 g.) sugar*
2 *teaspoons citric acid*
1 *Campden tablet*
7 *pints (4 l.) water*
Sauternes yeast and nutrient

Carefully remove the stalks, leaves and stems and discard them.

Place the florets in a bin, pour hot water over them and macerate with the back of a wooden spoon.

Add 2 teaspoons of citric acid and a crushed Campden tablet, cover the bin and leave it in a warm place. Macerate the florets again on each of the following 3 days, then press them and strain off the liquor. Pour the liquor into a fermentation jar and proceed as for apple wine.

GOOSEBERRY WINE

3½ *lb. (1.75 g.) gooseberries*
9 *oz. (250 g.) sultanas*
2 *lb. (900 g.) sugar*
1 *Campden tablet*
1 *teaspoon pectin-destroying enzyme*
6 *pints (3½ l.) water*
Hock yeast and nutrient

Pour the water into a bin and add the tartaric acid, the pectin-destroying enzyme and a crushed Campden tablet. Wash the gooseberries, crush them into a mash and proceed as for apple wine.

GRAPE WINE (RED)

18 *lb. (8 kg.) black grapes*
1 *teaspoon pectin-destroying enzyme*
1 *Campden tablet*
Pommard yeast

(No water required. English grapes may require some sugar to bring the specific gravity up to 1.090.)

Wash the grapes, drop them into a bin with the pectin-destroying enzyme and a crushed Campden tablet, and mash them into a pulp. Cover, and leave it in a warm place for 24 hours.

Activate the yeast, add it to the pulp, re-cover the bin and return it to a warm place for 8 or 10 days.

Press and strain the pulp and add the sugar if necessary. (To extract the gallon of grape juice required in this recipe, a wine press is essential.) Pour the must into a fermentation jar and proceed as for apple wine.

GRAPE WINE (WHITE)

18 *lb. (8 kg.) white grapes*
1 *teaspoon pectin-destroying enzyme*
1 *Campden tablet*
Hock yeast

(No water or sugar required.) Put the grapes through a juice extractor or press them to extract the juice. Pour the juice into a jar, add the pectin-destroying enzyme and a crushed Campden tablet, fit an airlock and leave it in a warm place for 24 hours.

Activate the yeast, add it to the juice, re-fit the airlock and place the jar in an even temperature until fermentation is complete. Rack, and add one Campden tablet.

HONEY WINE (MEAD)

3 *lb. (1.5 kg.) honey*
¾ *oz. (20 g.) citric acid*
1 *level teaspoon grape tannin*
7 *pints (4 l.) water*
Maury yeast and nutrient

Dissolve the honey in warm water, pour it into a fermentation jar and, when cool, add the acid, tannin, nutrient and yeast. Top up with cold water, fit an airlock to the jar and store it in a warm place until fermentation is complete.

MULBERRY WINE

2¼ *lb. (1 kg.) mulberries*
1 *lb. 2 oz. (525 g.) sultanas*
2¾ *lb. (1.3 kg.) sugar*
1 *teaspoon tartaric acid*
1 *teaspoon grape tannin*
1 *teaspoon pectin-destroying enzyme*
1 *Campden tablet*
6 *pints (3½ l.) water*
Port yeast and nutrient

Pour the water into a bin and add the tartaric acid, pectin-destroying enzyme, tannin and a crushed Campden tablet.

Wash the mulberries, mash into a pulp and proceed as for apple wine. But since this is a high-alcohol wine, add the sugar in small doses as described for blackberry 'port'.

PLUM WINE

4½ *lb. (2.25 kg.) 'Victoria' plums*
1 *lb. 2 oz. (525 g.) raisins*
2¾ *lb. (1.3 kg.) sugar*
1 *teaspoon citric acid*
1 *Campden tablet*
1 *teaspoon pectin-destroying enzyme*
½ *teaspoon grape tannin*
6 *pints (3½ l.) water*
Sherry yeast and nutrient

Pour the water into a bin, add the tannin, the citric acid, the pectin-destroying enzyme and a crushed Campden tablet, and proceed as for apple wine. But since this is a high-alcohol wine, add the sugar in small doses as described for blackberry 'port'.

RASPBERRY WINE

2¼ *lb. (1 kg.) raspberries*
1 *lb. 2 oz. (525 g.) sultanas*
2¼ *lb. (1 kg.) sugar*
1 *teaspoon pectin-destroying enzyme*
1 *Campden tablet*
6 *pints (3½ l.) water*
Port yeast and nutrient
Saccharin

Pour the water into a bin and add the pectin-destroying enzyme and a crushed Campden tablet.

Wash the raspberries, crush them into a mash and proceed as for apple wine. This is intended to be a sweet wine, so when fermentation is complete add saccharin to taste.

RHUBARB WINE

4½ *lb. (2.25 kg.) chopped rhubarb*
Thinly pared rind of 1 lemon
9 *oz. (250 g.) sultanas*
2½ *lb. (1.25 kg.) sugar*
1 *Campden tablet*
1 *teaspoon pectin-destroying enzyme*
6 *pints (3½ l.) water*
Graves yeast and nutrient

This wine should be made in May or early June.

Pour the water into a bin and add the pectin-destroying enzyme and a crushed Campden tablet.

Discard the leaves and feet of the rhubarb, wipe and chop the stems, drop them into the bin with the lemon rind, and proceed as for apple wine.

KEEPING POULTRY AND BEES

Producing eggs and honey in your garden

Poultry and bees bring a new dimension to garden food production and self-sufficiency. Both form the basis for fascinating hobbies, while really fresh eggs and home-produced honey provide a welcome change for your table, which the whole family can enjoy.

Both activities dovetail neatly with other forms of food-growing. Added to garden waste, poultry manure ensures plentiful supplies of rich compost to promote maximum vegetable yields. With a hive of bees to distribute the pollen from spring blossom, fruit crops are given the best possible start each year.

If either enterprise seems a little challenging for a

suburban garden, remember that these and other forms of garden husbandry were commonplace during and just after the war, when many foods were in short supply.

They faded from the scene only as plenty and prosperity returned and rationing came to an end.

Nowadays, the main incentives for home food-growing are to combat ever-rising prices and to enjoy fresh, natural produce instead of processed and packaged goods. Together, they provide a powerful argument for producing as wide a variety of food as possible from your garden.

Keeping poultry

Though 'keeping a few chickens' is generally regarded as the prerogative of country dwellers, they can, in fact, be kept in the smallest of town gardens.

Well-kept poultry units will neither smell unpleasant nor attract rats, and so long as you do not keep a cockerel – which is unnecessary, anyway – there will be no dawn chorus to annoy neighbours.

No licence is required to keep domestic poultry, nor is planning permission normally necessary when installing a small poultry house. All the same, before keeping them it would be wise to check your local by-laws and search your house deeds or rent agreement for any restrictions there may be on keeping livestock.

You can start poultry-keeping at any time of year, but perhaps the best plan is to buy your first batch of growing pullets during the summer. They will start laying in late summer or early autumn, and will have settled down to full egg production before winter.

Outlay and returns

Ever-rising costs make it difficult to present the beginner with exact costs and returns, though these can, of course, be checked at the time of buying. However, certain percentages do appear to remain fairly constant.

The most significant is that you should obtain fresh eggs at perhaps three-quarters of the price you would pay for them in a shop. This takes into account the cost of the birds and their feed, and allows for annual depreciation of housing and equipment. It takes into consideration, too, the value of the carcases, whether you sell them or eat them yourself.

Another bonus, often overlooked, is the manure that you will collect throughout the year. Added to the compost heaps, it will hasten the rotting of vegetable matter and make a real contribution to growing good crops.

This estimated cost assumes that you will be keeping a minimum of six pullets, each of which will eat about 100 lb. (45 kg.) of feed in a year, and give you in return about 21 dozen eggs. Once they begin laying, your flock should provide about two-and-a-half dozen eggs a week – which is ample for the average family.

One way of producing eggs even more cheaply is to keep 12 birds instead of six. Though your initial outlay will be higher, you will be able to sell surplus eggs to neighbours. The price obtained should pay most of the feed bills for the whole flock.

If you are intending to keep 12 birds, it is advisable to buy six at first and another half-dozen six months later. This will assure a continuous egg supply throughout the year.

Housing

Unless you have a spare building, housing is generally the largest single expense. However, a well-maintained unit should last for many years, so that annual depreciation is small.

If you are lucky enough to have a shed or similar outbuilding that could be converted, your outlay will be very much less.

Poultry housing does not have to be elaborate but it should at least provide dry, draught-free shelter for night-time roosting and for day-time use during bad weather. Failing this, the birds will be miserable and egg production will suffer.

In spite of this, poultry do not need coddling and it is essential to provide some ventilation even on cold winter nights. Lack of ventilation may lead to respiratory complaints, and the general health of the birds will certainly suffer.

Within the house you will have to provide nesting and perching space. Generally, too, the feeding and drinking vessels are placed under cover – for the convenience of the poultry-keeper, as well as for the comfort of the birds.

Even in town gardens it is essential to make the house fox-proof by fixing wire-netting across open windows and ensuring that doors can be securely latched at night.

Deep-litter houses This, if you are short of space, is probably the best way to keep poultry. No separate run is required, and a floor space of not less than 4 sq. ft (0.4 sq. m.) per bird is sufficient.

The birds will enjoy dry and relatively warm conditions, whatever the weather, yet are assured of abundant light and fresh air if you fit a netting-covered frame in the doorway during daylight hours.

Depending on its size, a garden shed with only a few minor adaptations would be quite suitable for six pullets.

The diagram shows a typical deep-litter house. Most of the floor is covered initially by a 12 in. (305 mm.) layer of chopped straw or wood shavings, or a mixture of the

DEEP-LITTER UNIT

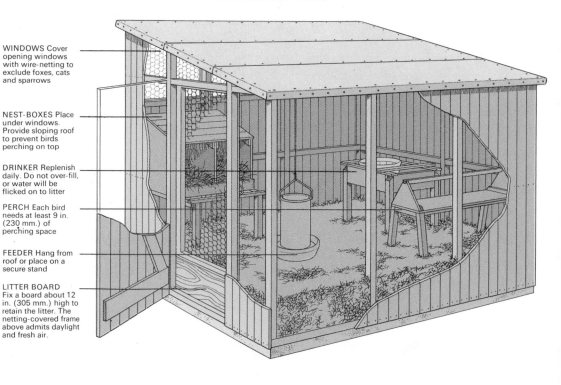

WINDOWS Cover opening windows with wire-netting to exclude foxes, cats and sparrows

NEST-BOXES Place under windows. Provide sloping roof to prevent birds perching on top

DRINKER Replenish daily. Do not over-fill, or water will be flicked on to litter

PERCH Each bird needs at least 9 in. (230 mm.) of perching space

FEEDER Hang from roof or place on a secure stand

LITTER BOARD Fix a board about 12 in. (305 mm.) high to retain the litter. The netting-covered frame above admits daylight and fresh air.

two. This will soon be broken down by the birds' droppings and constant scratchings to a dry, friable material ideally suited to the habits of poultry.

In winter, the litter helps to maintain the house temperature.

Build a perching frame 3 ft (1 m.) above floor level, allowing at least 9 in. (230 mm.) of perching space for each bird.

Fit a droppings board 9 in. (230 mm.) below the perch, and clean this weekly, so that droppings do not accumulate in one place on the litter.

Construct a screen door of wire-netting behind the main door of the shed. Leave this open during the day-time, except during the coldest weather, so that the birds get all the light and fresh air they need. If you close the main door on winter nights, be sure to leave a window open for ventilation.

Position the perching frame and droppings board away from the door so that the birds are not in a direct draught on nights when only the screen door is in position.

Ready-made houses and runs An alternative to the adapted deep-litter shed is to buy a purpose-built poultry house, either new or second-hand. For an average small garden, choose the type with a covered run linked to the house.

A linked house and run of this sort, suitable for six pullets, need be no larger than 10 ft (3 m.) long by 3 ft (1 m.) wide.

A run 4 ft (1.2 m.) high is suitable for heavy breeds (see Choosing your stock, p. 368), but allow 6 ft (1.8 m.) for light breeds.

It is an advantage to have the base of the house raised at least 12 in. (305 mm.) off the ground. This extends the area of the run and provides a place for dust-baths.

In a large garden, you may wish to provide a more extensive run where the birds can scratch around in the open. In this case allow at least 6 sq. yds (5 sq. m.) per bird, to prevent the soil from becoming muddy and infested with parasites. If possible provide two runs, each giving 3 sq. yds (2.5 sq. m.) per bird, so that they can be rested in turn.

However, hens often appear most contented – and lay the most eggs – in a compact house and covered run, or in a deep-litter house, where they are protected from the weather and have a dry floor to scratch about in. At all costs avoid a small run that is open to the wind and rain.

Free-range housing For would-be poultry-keepers who are fortunate enough to have a paddock or a substantial orchard, there remains the possibility of very simple housing in the form of a fold or ark. Such units can be bought new, but you may be able to purchase one second-hand at much less cost.

Housing of this type was formerly used by many commercial poultry-keepers, but most now favour a more intensive system. Unfortunately, many of the disused units have been left in the open to deteriorate, so check for rot before buying.

Poultry folds provide a sort of controlled free-range system. The fold – which includes a roosting and a nesting section – is moved to fresh grass each day. This provides interest and a little extra nourishment for the birds, but they are prevented from straying or falling prey to foxes.

Arks give little more than night-time shelter, together with a place for the pullets to lay their eggs.

Both systems require a good deal of land if the grass is not to suffer and to prevent a build-up of harmful parasites. For instance, for a fold you need sufficient grass to move the unit daily without occupying the same patch of ground more than once in about five weeks. If an ark or similar small house is used, a dozen pullets need up to a quarter of an acre.

In both cases the birds will probably lay fewer eggs than in a deep litter house but they will find a little of their own food. Put their rations in a weather-proof outdoor hopper. Ensure that birds housed in an ark are shut in at night.

Equipment

Apart from the house and run, nest-boxes, feeders and drinkers are the main items of equipment. They can be bought new or

READY-MADE HOUSE AND COVERED RUN

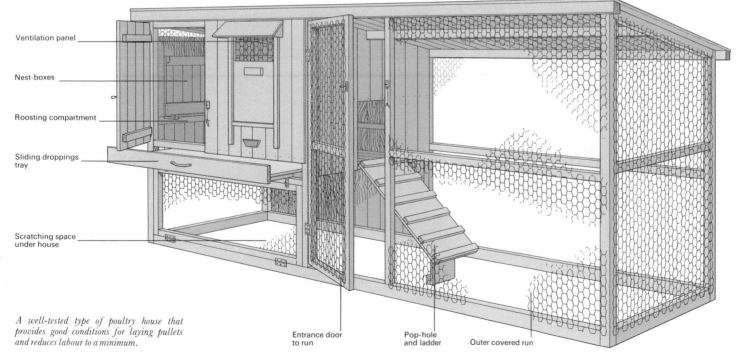

Ventilation panel

Nest-boxes

Roosting compartment

Sliding droppings tray

Scratching space under house

A well-tested type of poultry house that provides good conditions for laying pullets and reduces labour to a minimum.

Entrance door to run

Pop-hole and ladder

Outer covered run

second-hand, or you can make them yourself.

Nest-boxes A hen's instinct is to lay its eggs in the darkest part of the house. By providing boxes under the windows, you will prevent the eggs being laid in the litter, where they would get broken or lost.

If it is difficult to find a dark spot, hang heavy cloth, with slits cut in it, over the front of the boxes.

Put the boxes on a stand 18 in. (455 mm.) above the floor, with an alighting perch a few inches in front of the nests.

For six birds provide two nest-boxes, each measuring about 12 in. (305 mm.) wide, 15 in. (380 mm.) from front to back and 14 in. (355 mm.) high.

Fasten a 2½ in. (65 mm.) batten along the front to prevent the eggs rolling out.

Twelve birds will need three boxes of this size. Eggs may be broken if the pullets have insufficient nesting space.

Feeders Since feed accounts for 75% of the cost of producing an egg, wastage must be kept to a minimum. The best means of doing so is to provide your birds with the correct feeder.

An old washing-up bowl, for example, is not suitable. The hens will clamber into it and scatter the feed over the run.

There are several types of feeder available, and though you can make a suitable trough it will cost very little more to buy one. The feeder should be large enough to accommodate all your birds at the same time.

To calculate this, multiply the number of pullets by 4 in. (100 mm.) if you are providing a rectangular feeding trough. Thus, six pullets would need a double-sided trough at least 12 in. (305 mm.) long.

Rather less space is needed for tubular feeders.

Depending on design, feeders should be suspended or mounted at a level about 1 in. (25 mm.) above that of the birds' backs. This will cause them to stretch up to obtain their food, helping to reduce the amount of scattering.

If you are installing the trough type of feeder, buy or make one large enough to hold a day's feed for your birds without being more than a quarter full. The rim of the trough should be turned inwards for ½ in. (12 mm.) to provide an anti-waste lip.

Drinking vessel This is not nearly so critical as the feeder. In fact, a bucket with a brick at the bottom to prevent overturning is quite adequate, though there are both fount and trough vessels on the market.

Whatever type is used, wash and refill it with fresh water daily, allowing about 4 pints (2 l.) for six pullets. The water should be cool, so place it where it will be out of direct sunlight.

Lighting A valuable, but not essential, refinement is that of providing electric lighting to increase the output of eggs in winter. Starting with about three-quarters of an hour each evening in late September, increase this gradually to provide a 14 hour 'day' in midwinter.

Lighting ensures that pullets lay to their full potential. Without it, you will probably lose up to 60 eggs from each pullet during the winter, and this loss will be only partly made up during the following spring.

Package deals

Some rearers or agents offer a beginner's kit consisting of a house with perch and nest-box, run, feeder and drinking vessel, together with the number of pullets appropriate to the size of the house. For the newcomer, this is worth considering – especially as the price should be lower than when buying the items separately.

Choosing your stock

The best birds for garden egg production are the several cross-breeds and hybrids that combine the virtues of hardiness and docility with high egg yields. Rhode Island Reds crossed with Plymouth Rocks or Light Sussex possess these qualities. In addition, cross-bred birds of this type will lay the brown eggs so esteemed in the British egg-cup.

These medium-size and heavy breeds and crosses, in contrast to those derived from the more slender-bodied Leghorn, also provide a meaty carcase when their profitable egg-laying days are over – at the end of their first or second laying years.

Buy only from an established breeder, who will not only know the history of his birds but will also be able to supply much useful advice.

It is best to buy pullets when they are about 18 weeks old. By this time their rearing and vaccination programme will be complete, and they will begin laying within a few weeks. Though they cost more than younger birds, you are saved the cost of their feed during their non-productive months and the pullets are less liable to infection.

('Pullet,' incidentally, is the term used to describe a hen in its first laying season.)

Buy only free-range birds, or those that have been raised on deep-litter. Birds reared in cages tend to catch diseases when they are first put into a run or into a deep-litter house.

POULTRY HOUSING FOR PADDOCKS AND ORCHARDS

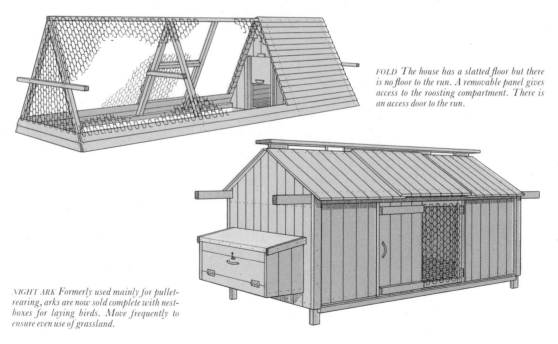

FOLD The house has a slatted floor but there is no floor to the run. A removable panel gives access to the roosting compartment. There is an access door to the run.

NIGHT ARK Formerly used mainly for pullet-rearing, arks are now sold complete with nest-boxes for laying birds. Move frequently to ensure even use of grassland.

Making a start

Prepare the house for the pullets a week or two before they are due to be delivered. If you are using a converted shed or a second-hand house, make sure that it is thoroughly cleaned and disinfected.

The best disinfectant is creosote, which will kill most bacteria and also lice and red mites.

Pay special attention to perches and nest-boxes. Red mites can live on in these places, awaiting new hosts for months or even years, so apply creosote to all cracks and crevices.

Once this is done, cover the floor with litter. For a deep-litter house the litter should be 9–12 in. (230–305 mm.) deep. Only a shallow layer is needed in a house with an attached run, and this need not be renewed once the birds are allowed outside after a day or two.

Deep-litter may be a mixture of chopped wheat straw, wood shavings, shredded paper and peat, though the latter is perhaps too expensive to be practical. Avoid barley straw, as the husks can cause irritation and swelling in the birds' beaks.

Line the nest-boxes with wood shavings or straw. Do not use hay; its warmth encourages lice and, if it gets wet, the eggs will be stained.

Settling in When ordering your birds, find out the brand of feed they were reared on so that, in their new surroundings, the food at least will be familiar. Put it in the house just before they arrive, and fill the water container, so that the pullets can be left to settle in without further disturbance.

Visit them in the evening to see if they have perched. Very likely they will not yet have discovered the perches, and for the first night or two you will have to put them on the bars yourself.

If you have provided an outside run, leave it until the second day before you open the pop-hole – the door between the house and the run. On the third day, when the birds are becoming accustomed to their new environment, you can move the drinking trough outside.

Make sure, however, that all the pullets are coming out into the run to drink.

Some birds take longer to settle down than others, but if, after three clear days, they still seem unhappy in their new home, contact your supplier and ask his advice.

Feeding

Present-day pullets are carefully bred to produce a certain number of eggs during their peak laying period in return for a certain outlay on feed. Quality and quantity of food are equally important.

No longer is it sensible to feed your birds on household scraps. To achieve maximum results, you must instead give them a proprietary brand of food in which protein, and all the other elements that contribute towards high egg production, have been blended scientifically.

This is available in two forms, layers' mash and pellets. Though both contain the same nutriments, pellets are not really to be recommended unless your birds are truly free-ranging.

If they are restricted to a house and run, they will consume their entire day's ration in half an hour. Having eaten their pellets they become bored, and may develop such habits as picking each others feathers, or egg-eating.

A dry layers' mash is a far better idea. Each bird will eat about 4½ oz. (130 g.) of this per day, and spend some four contented hours in doing so.

Multiply the ration by the number of pullets, add a little extra, and put this amount of mash into the feeder each day.

To save work, particularly if you have a tube feeder or a trough fitted with an anti-perching roller, you can put in several days' rations at once, topping-up as the mash is eaten.

When replenishing the trough, however, remember to mix the residue of the old ration with the new meal that you put in.

Extras and appetisers Once a day, preferably in mid-afternoon, scatter wheat – about 1 oz. (25 g.) for each bird – over the litter in the house or on the floor of the run. Searching and scratching for the grain, the birds will remain active until nightfall and will go to roost contented and with a full crop.

A few greens, such as the thinnings from your cabbage bed, also make a welcome addition to the birds' diet.

Tie these in bundles to the enclosing netting of the run, or from the roof of the deep-litter house, so that the pullets have to stretch up for them. If the greens are simply thrown into the run, they will soon become a trodden, befouled mess.

Calcium grit Egg-shells are largely composed of calcium, so for sound eggs it is essential that this element should be included in the diet.

Until a few years ago this was done by giving them limestone grit, or a grit composed of crushed sea-shells or egg-shells. Nowadays, the correct amount of calcium is generally included in layers' mash, and it is actually harmful to exceed this amount.

But check with your merchant when buying the feed that it does indeed contain calcium.

Stony grit As is well known, birds have no teeth. Instead, at least in the case of vegetable-eating birds, the food is taken into the gizzard – a muscular, horny-lined part of the digestive system. There, it is ground by the hard stone grit that the bird must swallow regularly if its food is to be processed adequately.

So it is with domestic poultry. If the birds are free-ranging, they will generally pick up enough grit for their needs during the course of the day, particularly if the land is stony.

But if they are confined you must provide them with regular supplies of granite or flint grit.

This may be bought from a seed merchant and given to your stock at a rate of 1 oz. (25 g.) for each bird per month. Scatter it among the litter rather than providing it in a trough where it will become dusty and spoiled.

General management

The principal routine jobs are providing food and water, cleaning out and, in due course, collecting the eggs. You can expect the first eggs when the pullets are about 23 weeks old if you buy the type of bird recommended on the opposite page.

In a deep-litter house, turn the litter over occasionally with a garden fork if it shows any signs of becoming compacted.

Weekly removal of droppings from beneath the perches is necessary. If the house has a run attached, fork the soil over every week, and replace the top 6 in. (150 mm.) with fresh garden soil at least twice a year. Even better, if you have space to spare, move the whole unit to fresh ground every week or two.

These are the necessary tasks, involving only a few hours throughout the year. But no time spent with your birds is wasted.

Give them, if possible, a few minutes each day, getting to know them, studying their individual characteristics, and watching for any signs that may occur of bullying, broodiness or illness.

Laying period Once pullets have begun to lay, they will continue to do so for the next 12 months – or for up to 15 months in the case of some cross-breeds – provided they have the right conditions and there is artificial lighting in the house during the winter. During this period, each bird will produce an average of five eggs a week.

After this, they will begin to moult. Until they grow new feathers, they will produce no eggs at all. During this time, keep them as free from stress as possible, feed them on a high-protein diet and, in winter, prolong the day with artificial light.

After six to eight weeks they will begin to lay once more, but in their second or subsequent seasons they will not be so productive as they were in their first. Neither will the internal quality of the eggs be quite so good, with a tendency for the whites to be thin and watery.

For this reason, many people regard old birds as uneconomic, and prefer to replace them with young birds. Certainly, a professional poultry-keeper would endorse this point of view, but whether you follow suit is up to you.

But do not get rid of just a few hens and mix new birds with the old. The earlier inhabitants of the house will resent the newcomers' presence, and will drive them away from food and water.

Getting rid of old stock

Killing, plucking and dressing their own birds is a task that many people do not wish to face, and in any case should not be attempted unless you have experience and can be sure of doing it humanely. Failing this, ask your local butcher, a poultry expert or even the RSPCA inspector if he will do it for you. A butcher may be interested in buying the carcases; or you can, of course, put them in your freezer for casseroling at a later date.

Holidays

There is not much difficulty in leaving your pullets for a week or two, provided you can persuade a neighbour to take over the routine tasks for you. Ask him to change the water each day, and top up the feeder every two or three days.

The eggs must be collected daily. No doubt you will tell him to keep these to repay his efforts.

Things that may go wrong

If you have bought your pullets at the right age, and from a reputable dealer, they will already have been vaccinated against most of the

diseases they are likely to catch, so that with a high standard of hygiene you are unlikely to have much trouble.

If a bird does seem to be off-colour, separate it from the others and put it in a warm place with food and water near by. If it does not improve in a day or so, make a note of the symptoms, such as the colour and size of the comb, whether the bird is perching or not and if it is off its feed, and ring the vet or the poultry supplier.

Sometimes the trouble may be due to a fault in management or housing rather than to disease. The essential thing is to spot as quickly as possible that all is not well, so that prompt remedial action can be taken.

Parasites Inspect your birds regularly, as parasites can cause a decline in egg production. If lice are present, they are usually seen running between the feathers below the vent. Dust the bird with a delousing powder.

Red mites are more persistent and harder to spot, since they do not live on the bird during the day. Instead, they live in cracks and crevices, often at the ends of the perches, and emerge only at night to suck the blood of their victims while they are roosting.

Remove the perches from time to time and inspect the sockets for signs of the mites. When active, they are bright red in colour and about the size of a pin-head; inactive, they are considerably smaller and usually grey.

In either event, dust the crevices with red-mite powder, which may be bought from your poultry supplier, or dab creosote regularly on the perch supports.

Cracked or soft-shelled eggs Pullets sometimes produce soft-shelled eggs at the very beginning of their laying period. This is because their reproductive systems have not yet settled down, and the trouble should cease within a week or so.

If it does not, contact your feed supplier or poultry breeder and ask for their advice. Soft-shelled, or very small eggs are also occasionally laid at the end of the season, just before the moult begins.

If you are constantly finding cracked eggs, the chances are that it is your fault, either because the nesting material is inadequate or because you are startling the birds with noisy or abrupt movements.

Always work quietly and smoothly, and tap on the door of the house before opening it. Ridiculous as it may seem, this does prevent panic – and broken eggs.

Feather loss If this occurs outside the normal moult period, it may be due to one of several causes. The most common takes place in autumn when, for some reason associated with the dwindling daylight hours, some birds lose their neck feathers.

This can be corrected by lengthening the day by using artificial light.

Fourteen hours of light is the period to aim for, gradually extending the time when the lamp is switched on, either in the morning or evening, as the days shorten. This will also promote egg production.

But the same symptoms may also occur through fear, lack of food or water, or bullying and feather-pulling by the birds'

companions. Whatever the reason, keep a watchful eye on any bird that is losing its plumage and, if possible, separate it from the others and keep it in a warm, dry place until the feathers start to grow again.

Broodiness This behavioural pattern, that induces hens to attempt to hatch their eggs, has been largely bred out of modern birds. This is for the very good reason, so far as poultry-keepers are concerned, that no eggs are laid while the period of broodiness lasts. But if it does occur it is necessary to act quickly.

The symptoms are easily recognised. A broody bird will, when approached, sit tight on the nest, fluff out its feathers and, after a squawk of warning, peck at any intruder. The tip of the comb assumes a purplish hue and the underside of the body is hot – both signs that the bird is running a temperature.

If forcibly removed from the nest, the bird will strut about for a few minutes and return as quickly as possible.

The best cure for a broody bird is to take it out of the house and put it in a cage or crate with plenty of ventilation through the floor and sides. Purpose-built broody units, often attached to the backs of poultry houses, have wire-netting floors. Leave the bird there for three or four days, with plenty of food and water, and it will soon return to normal.

As on all other occasions when returning single birds to the house after a prolonged absence, do so after the flock has settled down for the night. Otherwise its old companions may turn on it.

COOKING
with eggs

Lovers of good food appreciate that eggs play an integral part in most branches of cookery. Though they are often taken for granted, once you have a constant supply of fresh eggs from your own birds you will enjoy experimenting with the many and varied ways they can be used for feeding the family.

Sometimes called 'the complete meal in a shell', eggs are rich in protein but contain no sugar and very little carbohydrate. They are therefore particularly valuable for anyone on a calorie-controlled diet. They can be used in savoury or sweet dishes; to garnish, enrich, bind or glaze, and also as a raising agent.

With one or two eggs, it is possible to produce a satisfying meal in a few minutes.

Storing eggs

The ideal storage temperature is about 10°C (50°F). For this reason, if you keep eggs in a refrigerator, do not store them too near the ice box. Keep eggs well away from strong-smelling foods, as the shells are porous and the contents may become tainted.

Ideally, store eggs pointed end down. When required for use in baking, bring them into the kitchen an hour or so before they are needed.

Suitably prepared eggs will keep for nine to ten months in the freezer, so in times of glut it can be helpful to store some in this way. Pack them in sealed containers in quantities suited for everyday use in the kitchen.

To store whole eggs, beat them lightly and add ½ teaspoon of either sugar or salt to each egg. Place in a covered container, with a label showing the quantity, the date and whether they are sugared or salted.

Egg yolks or whites can be frozen separately, with ½ teaspoon of sugar or salt added for every two yolks or whites. Pack and label as for whole eggs.

Eggs left in their shells crack if stored in the freezer, and hard-boiled egg becomes 'rubbery'. (For methods of preserving whole eggs, see p. 348.)

Poaching, boiling and scrambling

Contrary to common practice, when poaching eggs it is unnecessary to add either vinegar or salt to the water.

To cook without an egg-poacher, pour a 1½ in. (40 mm.) depth of water into a shallow pan. Bring to the boil, then lower the heat until the water is barely simmering.

Crack an egg into a cup or saucer, hold this close to the water and slide the egg out. Cook it for 2 to 3 minutes, according to taste, then lift out with a perforated spoon.

Drain well before serving.

When poaching more than one egg, remove in the order that they went in. When poaching eggs for use in a recipe, cook until the white is just set, then lift out and place the cooked egg in cold water. This holds the egg at that stage until you are ready to use it in the recipe.

When boiling eggs, lower them into a pan of cold or simmering water to cover completely, and time from the moment the water comes to a gentle boil. If possible, have eggs at room temperature before boiling as this helps to prevent shells cracking while heating. Salt in the water helps to harden any escaping white if the shells do crack.

Avoid boiling the water too fast, as this sets the white hard before the yolk is ready.

Cool hard-boiled eggs as rapidly as possible by placing the pan under a cold tap. This prevents an ugly grey-black ring forming between the white and the yolk.

For scrambled eggs, it is usual to allow two eggs per person. Break them into a bowl, add seasoning and beat well to blend the yolks and whites.

Melt a little butter in a pan over medium heat. Pour in the beaten egg, then stir and lift as the egg starts to cook. Mix in 1 dessert-spoon of milk or cream, as this helps to cool the mixture and ensure that it cooks evenly. Too fierce a heat, or over-cooking, makes eggs 'rubbery'.

Remove the pan from the heat while some of the mixture is still liquid, stir well, then turn out and serve immediately.

Hot scrambled eggs, mixed with ingredients such as chopped cooked mushrooms, chopped prawns, flaked smoked fish or chutney, make a delicious filling for vol-au-vents or pastry cases. When cool, use scrambled eggs as a sandwich filling, adding chopped chives, cucumber, celery or beetroot. A little mayonnaise will help to bind the mixture.

Coddled eggs

Place the eggs in gently boiling water, then place a lid on the pan and switch off the heat. Allow about 6½ minutes for a small egg, and 9 minutes for a large egg.

Custards

Young children who dislike eggs cooked in the usual ways will often enjoy custards. To make a custard of pouring consistency, allow 3 eggs (or 2 whole eggs and 1 yolk), 1 pint (600 ml.) milk, 1 oz. (25 g.) sugar, and 1 teaspoon cornflour. A thicker custard, for use in trifles or other puddings, requires 4 eggs (or 2 whole eggs and 2 yolks), 1 pint milk, 1 oz. sugar, and 1 teaspoon cornflour. Follow the same method to make either type of custard.

Beat the eggs with the sugar and cornflour until smooth and well blended. Heat the milk and stir about half of it into the egg mixture. Pour the mixture back into the saucepan and cook over gentle heat until the mixture is creamy and will coat the back of a spoon.

Strain the custard into a bowl to remove any possible 'threads' of cooked white. If not to be eaten immediately, cover the surface of the custard with a circle of damp greaseproof paper to prevent a skin forming.

Baked custard requires 3 eggs (or 2 whole eggs and 1 yolk), 1 pint (600 ml.) milk, and 1 oz. (25 g.) sugar.

Beat the eggs and the sugar together, add the milk and strain into a buttered dish. Place the dish in a baking tin containing sufficient cold water to come half-way up the side of the custard dish. Bake at 170°C (325°F), or gas mark 3, for 45–50 minutes.

The water in the baking tin ensures slow, even cooking, and helps to produce a creamy texture without bubbles or separation. Adding extra yolks will produce a firmer custard – capable of holding its shape when cold – which can be turned out if wished.

All the above custards can be flavoured with a sprinkling of grated nutmeg, a little finely grated orange or lemon rind, or vanilla sugar.

Using eggs for coating

Beat 1 egg with 1 dessertspoon of milk. Dip the food in this mixture, taking care to coat it thoroughly, then roll it in flour, breadcrumbs or crushed cornflakes.

When used for shallow or deep-frying, the egg and crumb coating helps to keep the food moist.

Using eggs for binding

Beat 1 or more eggs as required and mix thoroughly with ingredients such as mashed potato and minced, cooked meats when making croquettes, rissoles and similar mixtures.

The egg cooks as heat penetrates the mixture, and holds the food together.

Using egg white as frosting

Lightly beat 1 egg white. Dip fruits such as grapes, cherries or currants in the egg white, roll them in caster sugar and leave to dry. Use frosted fruits for decorating cakes or cold sweets.

A useful egg wash or glaze can be made from 1 egg lightly whisked with ½ teaspoon salt or sugar, or 1 egg yolk whisked with 2 teaspoons water and ½ teaspoon salt or sugar. Brushed evenly over the surface, this glaze produces a shiny, golden finish on pastry, buns, scones and bread.

The glaze can also be brushed over the base of pastry cases before filling with liquid (as for a custard tart) to help prevent the liquid seeping through.

Mayonnaise

Mayonnaise that is freshly made and flavoured to your own taste makes a delicious change from bought types and is another good use for home-produced eggs. You will need:

2 egg yolks
½ teaspoon salt
Pinch each of pepper, dry mustard and caster sugar.
Either *1–2 tablespoons vinegar (preferably wine or cider vinegar)*
Or *1–2 tablespoons lemon juice*
½ pint (300 ml.) olive oil

Before making, keep the yolks and the oil at the same room temperature for an hour or two. Place the yolks and the seasoning in a bowl and add 1 dessertspoon of vinegar or lemon juice.

Whisk these ingredients together thoroughly.

Continue whisking, adding oil drop by drop at first, then in a fine steady stream until all the oil is used and the mixture thickens. Adjust the flavour by adding more vinegar or lemon juice to taste, and thin down with a little hot water if necessary.

If the mixture curdles, put another egg yolk in a clean bowl and gradually add the curdled mixture to it.

Mayonnaise does not freeze well, but should keep for up to a week in a closed jar in a refrigerator. It can be given additional flavourings, such as chopped cucumber, watercress, capers or gherkins.

Keeping bees

In a sense, honey is a product of the sun, for it is made from the nectar secreted by myriads of spring and summer flowers. Both nectar and pollen are collected by bees, the nectar in a honey sac – roughly corresponding to a bird's crop – while the pollen clings to the insect's legs and furry body.

The bee's honey sac contains enzymes that at once begin to break the nectar down into simpler, more easily digested sugars. When a worker bee returns to the hive, it regurgitates nectar and enzymes together into a cell of the honeycomb, which is later sealed over with wax provided by other worker bees within the hive.

The chemical process continues within the cell, finally converting the nectar into honey. The excess water in the cells is evaporated by squads of bees that stand just inside the entrance to the hive, fanning their wings to drive a constant airflow around the honeycombs.

Meanwhile, the pollen gathered by the foraging bee is packed into the comb cells for use by the nurse bees. By a glandular process, they convert it to bee milk for feeding to the larvae in the lower part of the hive.

So far as the bees are concerned, the honey stores they have so tirelessly accumulated have but one purpose: to provide a supply of high-energy food that will ensure the survival of the colony through the months when no flowers are available. What the bee-keeper hopes and works for is that the bees will gather and store much more honey than they need, so that in the late summer he will be able to remove this surplus for his own use.

This is made possible by providing the bees with a good, ready-made home, by exercising skilled care in their welfare and, if necessary, augmenting their winter stores with sugar.

Apart from the opportunity to harvest one of the finest and most wholesome of natural products, bee-keeping provides a hobby whose fascination never wanes. It requires little space and, properly managed, the bees will soon give you an excellent return on your initial outlay.

Bee-keeping is a skill that grows with the years and with experience of bee-handling. It is not possible here to do more than to suggest how to make a start.

Where to keep bees

Though bees are most generally envisaged as inhabitants of ancient country gardens, they can be kept with complete success in a much wider variety of habitats. Bees are indifferent to scenery; all they require is an environment in which suitable flowers grow.

Airports, railway embankments, town allotments, overgrown waste tips and quarries all support thriving bee colonies. There is even a bee-hive on the roof of a City of London office block; apparently the City squares and gardens supply sufficient pasture for its needs.

Conversely, some of our richest farmlands are now bee deserts; mile upon mile of wheat, sugar beet and other crops that yield no bee food at all. And careless spraying can decimate bee populations in rural areas.

However, almost any area within a couple of miles' flight of a lime avenue, heathery heath or a large orchard may be ideal for keeping bees. A fruit farmer may even pay you to keep your hive on his land during the blossom season.

A district of small gardens containing herbaceous borders, flowering trees and shrubs also provides excellent bee pasture. But if you intend to keep bees in such an area, there are several important points to be borne in mind.

The neighbouring gardens should be well-established, containing plenty of trees of medium height, as well as tall fences or hedges. These help to keep the bees' flight path high – a consideration that will be much appreciated by your neighbours. Recently built housing estates, or those with low fences and lately established plants, are not really suitable for bee-keeping.

For the same reason, you should screen your hives with a high fence, bushes or dense, climbing plants. These will force the bees high on their inward and outward journeys, and will save your neighbours' gardens from being constantly traversed by a stream of low-flying, purposeful insects.

For your own comfort, and that of your family, you should establish your hives at a reasonable distance – say 30 ft (9 m.) or more from the house. The site, which need be no more than a couple of yards square, should be dry and sheltered, but not deeply shaded.

Which direction the hives face does not particularly matter, though it is an advantage if they can be warmed by a little winter sunshine. Apart from that, if the bees have a good store of food, if the hives are dry and have good air circulation, they will survive the worst the British winter has to offer.

Bees require considerably less attention than other livestock. The chief tasks are good hive maintenance, the provision of additional combs and boxes as the colony expands in the summer, a regular search for embryo queens during the swarming season in June and July, and making sure that the bees have an adequate winter food supply.

Apart from this they may be left largely to their own devices until it is time for you to collect your share of the honey.

Handling bees

All authorities are agreed that bee-keeping is very much a matter of temperament. Bees react badly to rough or impatient handling, and are aware, in much the same way as dogs and horses, of your state of mind if you are afraid of them.

In time, most people can acquire the art of handling bees with gentleness and confidence; all the same, it would be a good idea to visit your local bee-keepers' association before going to the expense of buying a hive.

There, you will be able to discover if you and bees enjoy each other's company, as well as gaining much useful information and practical help.

A sympathetic understanding of bees and their way of life is not only a prerequisite of bee-keeping – it will also considerably lessen your chances of being stung.

Getting stung is a hazard that prospective bee-keepers will have to accept. No matter how skilfully you handle the creatures, or how good your protective clothing, sooner or later you will collect the odd sting or two.

The dangers of this, however, are much exaggerated. Fewer than one person in every thousand is really allergic to bee venom, and though a sting – most likely on the hand – will produce a sharp pain and some swelling, there will be no lasting damage.

It may also be some consolation to know that after a time, and several stings, antibodies develop in the blood of bee-keepers that go some way to lessen the effects of the venom.

Costs and equipment

If you buy new equipment the initial capital outlay in setting up as a bee-keeper is fairly high – say about £100 for a complete outfit, including the bees.

But here again your local association will give you advice, and may be able to suggest a source of good second-hand equipment.

In that case, you might be able to make a start for as little as £50. You will not have to replace your basic equipment for years, and your running costs – a few kilos of sugar and some new wax foundations for the combs – will be negligible.

Returns

The returns on your investment vary considerably. In the first year you may get enough honey for your table, but little more, since the bees are building up their stores and there will not be much surplus. After that, the results depend very much on the season and on the position of the hive.

In a good year, with plenty of flowers available, to obtain 100 lb. (45 kg.) of honey from a single hive is by no means unheard of, while in a poor season you may get very little or none at all.

However, taking an average over several years the amateur might reasonably expect to get 30 lb. (13.5 kg.) of honey from each of his hives.

The hive

Bees are still essentially wild creatures that are just as happy to build their nest in a hollow tree or in any other dry, weatherproof space of the right size, as in the most thoughtfully constructed hive. A man-made hive is entirely for the convenience of the bee-keeper, to enable him to remove the honeycombs with the minimum amount of disturbance to the bees.

There are several standard designs of hive available, of which the best, from the point of view of cost and efficiency, are the simple, single-walled types. All, however, are similar in that they consist of a series of rectangular wooden boxes, open top and bottom, standing one on top of the other. The lowest rests on a floor board containing the entrance hole, while the uppermost is roofed.

In each box there hangs a number of frames in which the combs are built. Those in the upper boxes – known as 'supers' – are used as honey stores, while the combs in the lower part of the hive form the brood nest in which the queen lays her eggs and the larvae are fed by the worker nurses.

It is usual to place a queen excluder between the lower and upper boxes; this is a perforated screen with holes large enough to allow the smaller workers to pass to and fro, but denying access to the bigger queen. This will prevent her laying eggs in the honey storage area.

A hive consisting of a deep box for the brood chamber, two or three supers (additional supers can be added as the bees fill the lower ones), a queen excluder, an inner cover and a roof is sufficient for the first year.

By the following summer, however, when your bees may swarm, it would be a good idea to obtain a second hive so that you are ready to house the new colony.

Equipment With the exception of a honey-extractor, all the items described here are essential for successful bee-keeping and are needed so frequently that they cannot be hired or borrowed. However, you may be able to buy second-hand equipment at considerably less cost.

Protective clothing The most important protection is a bee-veil, which is generally made of net or plastic. This is attached to a broad-brimmed hat to carry the veil clear of the face and the back of the neck, while the lower edge is fitted with tapes that tie around the chest.

Wear a zip-up jacket with close-fitting cuffs, and tuck your trouser bottoms into heavy socks. Your outfit should be reasonably clean, since bees are somewhat sensitive to dirt and smells.

Gauntlets are a matter of choice. Though they will protect your hands from possible stings, they make it difficult to perform delicate tasks. Since bees become incensed by rough handling, it is probably best, if you have the courage, to work with bare hands.

If you handle your bees with gentleness and confidence, you are unlikely to get stung. At least, not very often.

Bee-smoker This implement, consisting of a bellows with an attached funnel, is used to subdue bees when removing combs, or when opening the hive for any other reason. You may have to use it only occasionally; all the same, you should always have one standing by, ready-charged with materials, such as dry, rotten wood, rags or hessian which smoulder when lit.

The cool smoke will subdue the bees without doing them any permanent harm. There are two types of smoker available – straight-nosed and the more efficient bent-nosed.

Hive tool This is a steel, multipurpose instrument with a scraper at one end and a flat blade at the other. The tool is used as a lever to prise box sections apart and to scrape wax from the frames.

Feeder When you take honey from a hive you are removing part of the bees' winter food supply. If the colony is to survive the cold, flowerless months, this loss must be replaced by an allowance of sugar. This is supplied to the bees in a syrup contained in a feeder, of which there are several types.

Honey-extractor Working on the same principle as a spin drier, this machine extracts the honey from the comb by centrifugal force.

Sooner or later you will probably want to own one, but since it is an expensive item – another £60 or more on top of your original £100 – it might be better for the first year or so to see if you can borrow or hire one through your bee-keepers' association.

An alternative is to supply the bees with a number of small wooden boxes, called 'sections', rather than filling the supers with the larger frames from which the honey must be extracted. Once the bees have filled and sealed the sections, they are simply removed from the hive and served or sold,

SINGLE-WALLED 'NATIONAL' HIVE

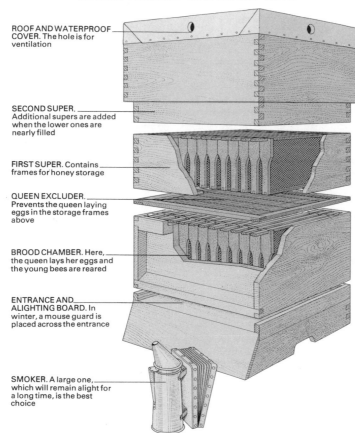

ROOF AND WATERPROOF COVER. The hole is for ventilation

SECOND SUPER. Additional supers are added when the lower ones are nearly filled

FIRST SUPER. Contains frames for honey storage

QUEEN EXCLUDER. Prevents the queen laying eggs in the storage frames above

BROOD CHAMBER. Here, the queen lays her eggs and the young bees are reared

ENTRANCE AND ALIGHTING BOARD. In winter, a mouse guard is placed across the entrance

SMOKER. A large one, which will remain alight for a long time, is the best choice

wax and all, as delicious, chewy 'honeycomb'.

But despite the apparent ease of this method, there are one or two snags. Bees are highly social creatures that do not like working in separate little boxes, and will do so only when there is an exceptionally heavy flow of nectar. Also, your total yield will certainly be less than if you had used the larger frames and extracted the honey in liquid form.

Building a colony

The simplest way is to buy an entire colony, or a nucleus, from a dealer. A colony consists of ten combs, a queen, a brood chamber, stores of honey and pollen and about 40,000 bees, while a nucleus combines the same elements on a smaller scale – say three or four combs with, of course, a much smaller number of bees.

Though many people do begin with a full colony, there are several disadvantages. In the first place, it is more expensive to buy a colony than a nucleus and, secondly, to open a hive containing 40,000 bees can be an awesome experience for the novice.

Starting with a colony is very much a matter of jumping in at the deep end; on the other hand, if you buy a nucleus, you and your bees can grow up together. You will have the satisfaction of watching the colony grow from small beginnings, and gain confidence in bee-handling as it does so.

But by far the most exciting – as well as the cheapest – method of starting your own apiary is to capture a swarm. There is, however, an element of chance involved, and you need sufficient leisure to stay within earshot of the telephone for a few days – ready to take immediate action.

The swarm

Depending on whether you want it to occur or not, this is either the most fascinating or the most infuriating moment of the bee-keeper's year.

Either way, there is little you can do to prevent it.

Swarming is essential not only to the survival of the bee species, but also to thousands of different kinds of plants as well. It is the means whereby the bee population spreads, carrying out its timeless, fortuitous function of plant pollination.

Swarming arises out of the complex social structure of the colony, in which food and activities are shared to a degree that makes it appear as though there were a common will, or even intelligence, devoted to the survival of the group.

No individual bee can exist on its own; therefore, if the species is to continue, there has to be a means of creating new colonies, and it is the instinct to do so that causes swarming.

This generally occurs in early summer. Through most of the year the queen lays eggs, steadily building up the population of the hive until it reaches a peak of some 60,000 individuals. This usually coincides with a period of fine weather and an ample supply of blossom.

However, the first sign of swarming is most often the appearance of young queen larvae within the hive. These are easily distinguished by the size and position of the cells they occupy – much larger than those of future worker bees, and hanging down vertically instead of being horizontal.

As the time approaches for the young queens to emerge from their cells, the hive becomes more and more agitated. Then, usually on a fine morning or early afternoon, there is a sudden and tremendous exodus.

Up to half the adult population, together with the reigning queen, takes to the air, leaving the remainder – together with the emergent queen – to take charge of the brood chamber, the larvae and the accumulated stores of honey.

The emigrants do not move very far at first. For a few minutes they circle, apparently aimlessly, emitting a low, booming note audible from a considerable distance.

They then settle on a nearby branch or fence, thousands of bees clinging to each other's legs in a solid cluster about the queen, while scouts are sent forth in all directions in search of a new home.

Capturing a swarm

How long the cluster will remain in this position is a matter of chance. It might be hours, or even as much as a day; on the other hand, they could be off in a few minutes to build a new home miles away.

Prompt action is necessary if the bee-keeper is not to lose a valuable percentage of his stock.

Curiously enough, despite their terrifying appearance, bees in this state are quite easily handled, and can be coaxed into a new hive or even a cardboard box without much difficulty.

If they are hanging from a low branch, they can be dislodged by shaking it or by striking the branch so that they fall into a container held underneath.

It is at this point that the beginner, if he is lucky, can make a real saving. Quite often, established bee-keepers are willing to part with a swarm. They probably have several other hives whose inhabitants are about to do the same thing, and their owners may not wish to increase their stock.

In this case, you may be able to buy your first colony for as little as £5.

Once again, it is best to consult your local bee-keepers' association, who may be able to put you in touch with a member with a swarm for sale.

Of course, there is no guarantee that his bees will swarm. What usually happens is that he lets you know when he sees the first signs – the presence of queen cells and the growing disquiet among his bees. You must then stand by for a few days, awaiting the telephone call telling you that swarming has begun.

Having collected the bees in a suitable box, they must then be introduced to your – and their – new hive. This should consist of a lower brood chamber, plus a queen excluder and one or two supers, ready-stocked with wax foundation frames for the creation of nursery cells and honey stores.

Remove the entrance block to the hive and place a board from the ground to the entrance. Upend the box over the foot of the board, and give it a sharp tap to dislodge the bees.

After a few minutes they will run up the slope and enter the hive. Once most of the bees are in, replace the entrance block leaving an entry hole about the width of your hand. Attach a syrup-filled feeder to the feeding hole, and keep it replenished for between a week and a fortnight to encourage comb-building.

Do not worry if the population drops during the first three weeks or so; it will soon build up again. The decrease is due to the fact that during this period there are no young bees to replace those that have died of old age.

Making a start

Bee-keeping is a highly skilled occupation whose fascination is never-ending. If you are cut out for it, you will soon discover that the more you know the more there remains to be learned about bee behaviour and society, about their methods of harvesting and comb construction, and even how the bee language works.

On the other hand, you may find that you remain apprehensive about stings and that your nervousness causes the bees to react unfavourably.

It is essential, therefore, to obtain as much information as you can before you begin.

While there are a great many books on bee-keeping, their advice is sometimes contradictory. No matter how well written, they cannot really tell you what it is like to handle bees.

So before you buy your first hive, join your local bee-keepers' association; the public library will tell you the address of the nearest one.

You will find that they will welcome newcomers to their art, give you much practical help and advice and, above all, give you the invaluable experience of handling bees yourself.

Index

Entries in bold type indicate
main entries in the Growing and
Cooking section

A

Acid soils 19
Adzuki beans 262
Alfalfa 262
Alkaline soils 19
American gooseberry mildew 286
Aminotriazole 37
Angelica 62
Anthracnose 286
Aphids 282
Apple canker 286
Apple sawfly 282
Apples
  bottling 311–12
  drying 344
  freezing 301, 306
  growing and pruning 62–69
  pests and diseases 69
  preparing and cooking 72
  spraying 69
  varieties.................63, 70–71
  recipes
    baked 74
    baked dumplings 73
    butter 325
    cake, Danish 72, 215
    charlotte 74
    cheese cake 306
    chutney 336–7
    crumble 72
    jam 318
    jelly 322
    marzipan 73, 137
    pickle 331, 333–4
    pie, Dutch 73, 137
    puffs 73, 215
    salad 73, 216
    sauce 339–40
    snow 72
    wine 362
    with meringue 72
Apples, Crab
  growing 74
  recipes
    jelly 322
    pickle 334
    wine 363
Apricots
  bottling 311–12
  drying 344
  freezing 301
  growing 40–41, 75
  preparing and cooking 76
  recipes
    butter 325
    chutney 336
    compôte 77, 215
    flan 77, 143
    jam 318–19
    mousse 76
    pasty 76
    pickle 334
    soufflé 76
Artichokes, Globe
  freezing 303
  growing 77–78
  preparing and cooking 79
  recipes
    à la Grecque 307
    cold stuffed 80
    in garlic dressing 79
    quiche 80
    vinaigrette 79
    with curry mayonnaise .79, 144
Artichokes, Jerusalem
  freezing 303
  growing 80–81
  preparing and cooking 81
  recipes
    sauté 81
    soup, creamed 81
    with onions 81
Asparagus
  freezing 303
  growing 82–83
  preparing and cooking 83
  recipes
    à la flamande 83
    boiled 83
    salad 84, 144
    soufflé 83
    soup 84
    vol-au-vents 307
Asparagus beetle 282
Asparagus peas 84
Aubergines
  freezing 303
  growing 85
  preparing and cooking 86
  recipes
    à la Grecque 86, 211
    moussaka 86
    salad 86

B

Bacterial canker 286
Balm 87
Basil 87–88
Bay 88–89
Bean seed fly 282
Bean sprouts: see **Sprouting seeds**
Beans, Broad
  freezing 303
  growing 89–90
  preparing and cooking 90
  recipes
    bean and bacon pot 307
    creamed, with bacon 91
    salad 90
    soup 90
    with butter 90, 135
Beans, French
  freezing 303
  growing 91–92
  preparing and cooking 92
  salting 347
  recipes
    and tomatoes....................93
    cheesy 92
    haricot bean casserole 93
    haricot bean salad 93, 216
    haricot beans and bacon 93
    pickle 331
    Provençale 92
    savoury 309
    with herbs..................93,141
Beans, Haricot: see **Beans, French**
Beans, Runner
  freezing 303
  growing 94–95
  preparing and cooking 95
  salting 347
  recipes
    au gratin 96
    baked, with mushrooms 96, 207
    in cream sauce 95
    sweet and sour 95
Beans, Soya 96–97
Bee-keeping 10, 372–4
Beetroot
  freezing 303
  growing 98–99
  preparing and cooking 99
  recipes
    and soured cream salad 99
    chutney 336
    pickle 332
    quick borsch.............99, 144
    relish 341
    Russian salad 99
    steaks 99
    wine 363
Benomyl 292
Bilberries
  gathering and using 351
  recipes
    jelly 322
    wine 363
Bindweed 38
Bioresmethrin 292
Birds
  protecting fruit 45–46
  protecting seedlings 31, 36
Bitter pit 286
Black bean aphid 282
Black currants:
  see **Currants, Black**
Black leg 286
Black root rot 286
Blackberries
  bottling 311–12
  freezing 301
  growing 40, 100–1
  preparing and cooking 101
  propagating 47
  recipes
    and apple pie 101, 209
    cheese 324
    chutney 337
    compôte 101
    flan 306
    fool 102
    jam 318
    jelly 322
    ketchup 340
    mousse 102, 137
    pickle 334
    syrup 328
    wine 363
    yoghourt shake 101
Black-currant gall mite 282
Black-currant leaf midge 282
Blackfly (aphids) 282
Blanching vegetables (before
  freezing)....................302–3
Blewits 354–5
Blossom end rot 286
Blotchy ripening 286
Blueberries
  freezing 301
  growing 12, 102–3
  preparing and cooking 103
  recipes
    American pancakes 103
    berry brulée 103
    cheese cake 103, 209
Bolting 286
Bonemeal 18–19
Borage 104
Borax 292
Bordeaux mixture 292
Borecole: see **Kale**
Boron deficiency 20, 286
Borsch 99
Bottling
  equipment 310
  fruit 310–13
Bouquet garni 346
Boysenberry 187
Broad beans: see **Beans, Broad**
Broccoli: see **Cauliflowers and
  broccoli**
**Broccoli, Sprouting and
  Calabrese**
  freezing 303
  growing 104–5
  preparing and cooking 105
  recipes
    au gratin 105, 135
    cheese puffs 106
    vinaigrette 105, 139
    with almonds 106
Bromophos 292
Broom 356
Brown rot 286
Brussels sprouts
  freezing 303
  growing 106–7
  preparing and cooking 107
  recipes
    and pork 107
    au gratin 307
    in the basket 108
    soup 107, 216
    with chestnuts 108, 213
    with mushrooms 108
    with nutmeg 107
Buckwheat 262
Bud-drop 287
Burnet 108–9
Bush trees 40–43

C

Cabbage aphids 282
Cabbage root fly 282
Cabbage whitefly 282
Cabbages
  Chinese 113
  freezing 303
  growing 109–11
  preparing and cooking 111
  recipes
    casserole 112
    coleslaw, with Roquefort
      dressing 111, 139

creamed 111
curried 112, 135
dolmas 112
pickle 330
red, braised 112
savoy, braised 111
soup 113, 139
stuffed 112, 213
Calabrese 104–5
Calcium nitrate 292
Calomel dust 292
Cane blight 287
Cane spot 287
Capillary irrigation for
  greenhouses 49
Capsicums : see **Peppers and
chillis**
Capsid bugs 282
Captan 292
Carbaryl 292
Cardoons 114–15
Carrot fly 282
Carrots
  freezing 304
  growing 115–16
  preparing and cooking 116
  recipes
    à la Vichy 117, 141
    honey-glazed 117
    juice 328
    mould 116
    pickle 332
    salad 117, 139
    summer casserole 117
    Turkish salad 116
    vinaigrette 117
    wine 363
Catch-crops 28
Caterpillars 282
Cauliflowers and broccoli
  freezing 304
  growing 118–19
  preparing and cooking 119
  recipes
    and bacon cheese 120
    and prawn salad 121
    in disguise 120
    pickle 330–2
    soufflés 120, 135
    soup 120, 216
    spiced 121
    with buttered crumbs 119
Celeriac
  freezing 304
  growing 121–2
  preparing and cooking 122
  recipes
    au gratin 123
    salad 123
    soup 122, 139
    steaks 122
    with mushroom stuffing ... 123

Celery
  freezing 304
  growing 123–5
  preparing and cooking 125
  recipes
    and leek casserole 307
    and lettuce salad 126
    braised 126
    cheese soufflés 125, 207
    pickle 332
    relish 341
    soup 125
    vinegar 342
    wine 363
    with ham and cheese 126
Celery fly 283
Ceps 355
Chalk soils 16
Chanterelle 355
Chards 78
Chelated compounds 292
Cherries
  bottling 311–12
  freezing 301
  growing 40–41, 126–8
  preparing and cooking 128
  recipes
    cocktail 128
    flan 128, 137, 306
    in red wine 128, 143
    jam 318
    pickle 334
    wine 363
    with Drambuie 128
Chervil 129
Cheshunt compound 292
Chestnut, Sweet 350
Chick peas : see **Sprouting seeds**
Chickweed
  controlling 39
  gathering and using 353
Chicory
  growing 130
  preparing and cooking 131
  recipes
    and egg salad 131
    and grapefruit salad ... 131, 216
    braised 131
    in ham cases 131, 213
    with lemon sauce 131
Chillis : see **Peppers and chillis**
Chinese bean sprouts 262
Chinese cabbages 113
Chives 132
Chlorosis 287
Chocolate spot 287
Chutneys
  equipment and methods 335–6
  recipes
    apple 336
    apple and red pepper 336
    apple and tomato 336

    apricot 336
    beetroot 336
    blackberry and apple 337
    cranberry and apple 337
    damson 337
    gooseberry 337
    Indian 337
    marrow and apple 337
    mixed fruit 337
    mixed fruit, Chinese style ... 337
    peach 338
    pear and ginger 338
    pear and lemon 338
    pepper 338
    plum 338
    pumpkin 338
    rhubarb 338
    tomato 338
Clay soils 15–16
Cloches, choosing and
  managing 54–56
  sowing under 31
Club root 287
Cob nuts : see **Nuts**
Codling moth 283
Colcannon 177
Coleslaw 111
Compost, Garden 17, 21
Compost, Sowing and potting 32–33
Containers (growing plants in) ... 13
Copper fungicide 292
Coral spot 287
Cordons 12, 40–43
Coriander 145
Corn salad 145–6
Couch grass 39
Courgettes : see **Marrows and
courgettes**
Crab apples : see **Apples, Crab**
Cranberries (chutney recipe) 337
Creeping buttercup 38
Creeping thistle 38
Creeping yellow cress 39
Cress : see **Land cress; Mustard
and cress; Watercress**
Crop rotation 26–27
Crown gall 287
Crown rot 287
Cucumber mosaic virus 287
Cucumbers
  growing 146–8
  preparing and cooking 149
  salting 347
  recipes
    and pepper salad 149
    baked 307
    braised 149
    casserole 150
    cold stuffed 150
    in dill dressing 149
    Indian salad 150
    pickle 331–3

    salad 150
    sauce 150
    soup, chilled 144, 149
    vinegar 342
Cultivators 15
Currants, Black
  bottling 311–12
  freezing 301
  growing 40, 151–2
  pests 282
  preparing and cooking 152
  propagating 47
  recipes
    and mint shake 137, 153
    butter 325
    jam 318
    jelly 322
    pudding 153, 215
    tart, American 152
    wine 363
Currants, Red
  bottling 311–12
  freezing 301
  growing 40, 153–5
  preparing and cooking 155
  propagating 47
  recipes
    boats 156
    compôte 155
    jam 318
    jelly 323
    mousse 156
    soup 155
    summer pudding 155
    with yoghourt 143, 155
Currants, White
  bottling 311–12
  freezing 301
  growing 40, 153–5
  preparing and cooking 155
  propagating 47
  recipe
    with yoghourt 155
Cuttings
  herbs 29
  soft fruits 47
Cutworms 283

D

Dalapon 37, 39
Damping off 287
Damsons
  bottling 311–12
  freezing 301
  growing 156
  preparing and cooking 157
  recipes
    and apple pie 157
    charlotte 157, 215
    cheese 325

    chutney 337
    jam 318
    pickle 334
    puffs 157
    sauce 339
    stewed 157
    wine 363
    with baked custard 157
Dandelions
  controlling 38
  gathering and using 353
Derris 292
Diazinon 292
Dibbers 15
Dichlobenil 37–39
Dichlofluanid 292
Dichlorvos 292
Die-back 287
Digging 22–24
Dill 158
Dimethoate 292
Dinocap 292
Diquat 37–39
Diseases
  control in greenhouses 51
  identification and control 286–91
DNOC 292
Docks 38
Double-digging 24
Downy mildew 288
Drainage 25
Dried blood 18–19
Drying
  fruit 343–4
  herbs 345–6
  vegetables 344–5
Dwarf beans : see **Beans, French**
Dwarf pyramids 40–43

E

Egg plant : see **Aubergines**
Eggs
  cooking with 370–1
  freezing 370
  home produced 365–71
  pickling 332
  preserving 348
Elderberries and elderflowers
  gathering and using 350
  recipes
    syrup 328
    wine 364
Endive
  growing 159
  preparing and cooking 160
  recipes
    and olive salad 160
    braised 160
Espaliers 11, 12, 40–43

F

F1 hybrids 30
Family trees 41
Fan-trained tree for fruit
   gardens 40–43
Farmyard manure 17, 19
Fat hen 352
Fences (growing
   fruit against) 11, 12, 27
Fenitrothion 292
Fennel 160
Fennel, Florence
   freezing 304
   growing 161
   preparing and cooking 161
   recipes
      à la martinez 144, 162
      buttered 161
      Italian salad 162
      with flambé mackerel 161
Fenugreek 262
Fertilisers and manures 17–20
Fig canker 288
Figs
   bottling 311–12
   freezing 302
   growing 162–3
   preparing and cooking 163
   recipes
      in brandy 163
      with orange juice 163, 209
Filberts: see **Nuts**
Finocchio: see **Fennel, Florence**
Fire blight 288
Fish-meal 18–19
Flea beetle 283
Florence fennel: see **Fennel,**
   Florence
Foliar feeding 19
Foot rot 288
Forks 14
Formaldehyde 292
Formothion 292
Frames 53–54
Freezing
   calendar 299
   freezer types 294–5
   fruit 300–2
   herbs 305
   techniques 294–8
   vegetables 302–5
   recipes (quick-frozen dishes)
      apple cheese cake 306
      artichokes à la Grecque 307
      asparagus vol-au-vents 307
      bean and bacon pot 307
      beetroot, savoury 309
      blackberry flan 306
      brussels sprouts au gratin ... 307

celery and leek casserole 307
cherry flan 306
courgettes Provençale 308
cucumber, baked 307
Eve's pudding 306
leeks Provençale 308
onions in white sauce 308
onion sauce basic 307
pancakes stuffed with
   mushrooms 308
pasta sauce 308
peach cream brulée 306
piperade 308
potato and cucumber pie ... 308
pumpkin soup 308
raspberry cream 306
raspberry jam, uncooked.... 307
ratatouille 308
strawberry ice cream 306
tomato Provençale 308
vegetable pie 309
vegetable soup 309
winter soup 309
French beans: see **Beans, French**
Frit fly 283
Fritted trace elements
   (fungicide) 292
Frost damage 288
Fruit buds 44
Fruit butters: see Fruit cheeses and
   butters
Fruit cages 45–46
Fruit cheeses and butters
   equipment and methods 323–4
   recipes
      apple butter 325
      apricot butter 325
      blackberry cheese 324
      black-currant butter 325
      damson cheese 325
      gooseberry butter 325
      marrow butter 325
      medlar cheese 325
      plum butter 325
      quince cheese 325
      rhubarb cheese 325
      tomato butter 325
Fruit crops
   calendar 277–80
   planning 10–13, 40–41
   planting and supporting 42–43
   propagating 47
   protecting 45–46
   pruning 43–45
   See also individual fruit entries
Fruit juice: see Syrups and juices
Fruit tree red spider mites 283
Fruits, wild 349–51
Fungi: see **Mushrooms**
Fungicides
   safety rules 281
   types of 292

G

Gages: see **Plums and gages**
Gamma-BHC 292
Gangrene 288
Garden hygiene 281
Garden lines 15
Garlic
   cooking with 164
   growing 164
   recipes
      bread 164, 216
      butter, tournedos with 165
      dressing 164
      soup with French sage 165
      spaghetti, Italian style 165
      vinegar 343
Gherkins
   growing 146–8
   recipe
      pickle 331
Glasshouse red spider mites 283
Glasshouse whitefly 283
Globe artichokes: see **Artichokes,**
   Globe
Glyphosate 37
Gooseberries
   bottling 311–12
   freezing 302
   growing 40, 165–5
   pests 286
   preparing and cooking 167
   propagating 47
   recipes
      butter 325
      chutney 337
      fool 143, 167
      jam 319
      jelly 322
      meringue 137, 168
      pickle 334
      sauce, savoury 167
      sauce, sweet 167
      stewed 167
      trifle 168
      wine 364
Gooseberry sawflies 283
Grapes
   drying 344
   freezing 302
   growing 168–72
   preparing and serving 172
   recipes
      and bananas................. 172
      and crisp Camembert 172
      in aspic 173
      in French dressing 173
      ketchup 340
      salad 173, 209
      wine 364
Greenback 288

Greenfly (aphids) 282
Greengages: see **Plums and gages**
Greenhouses
   cropping programme 52
   heating 50
   hygiene 51
   management 49–52
   shading 50
   siting and foundations 10, 49
   staging 51
   types 48–49, 51
Grey mould 288
Ground elder
   controlling............... : 39
   gathering and using 352
Groundsel 39
Growth buds 44

H

Hairy bitter cress 39
Halo blight 288
Hamburg parsley 223
Hardening off 34
Haricot beans: see **Beans, French**
Hazelnuts: see **Nuts**
Heeled cuttings 29
Heeling-in 42
Herbs
   calendar 277–80
   drying 345–6
   freezing 305
   planning beds and
      growing 10, 12–13, 28–29
   propagating 29
Hoes and hoeing.............. 14–15, 37
Honey production 272–4
   recipe
      wine 364
Honey fungus 288
Hoof and horn 18–19
Hop manure 18
Horseradish
   growing 173–4
   preparing and cooking 174
   recipes
      cream 174
      relish 341
      sauce 174
      vinegar 343
Horsetail 39
Hoses 15
Hyssop 174–5

I

Indian chutney 337
Inter-cropping 28

Iron deficiency 20
Irrigation 36

J

Jams
   equipment and methods .. 314–17
   recipes
      apple 318
      apple and date............... 318
      apple ginger 318
      apricot 318
      blackberry 318
      blackberry and apple 318
      blackberry and elderberry . 318
      black-currant 318
      cherry 318
      cherry and red-currant 318
      damson 318
      gooseberry 319
      greengage 319
      loganberry 319
      marrow and apricot 319
      marrow and ginger 319
      peach 319
      peach and pear 319
      plum 319
      quince 319
      raspberry 319
      rhubarb and ginger 320
      rose-petal 320
      strawberry 320
      whole strawberry............. 320
Jellies
   equipment and methods of
      making 320–2
   recipes
      apple 322
      bilberry 322
      blackberry 322
      blackberry and apple.......... 322
      black-currant 322
      crab-apple 322
      gooseberry 322
      loganberry 322
      quince 323
      red-currant 323
      rose-petal 323
      sloe and apple 323
      tomato 323
Jerusalem artichokes: see **Arti-**
   chokes, Jerusalem

K

Kale
   growing 175–6
   preparing and cooking 176
   recipes
      and potato cakes.............. 176

colcannon 177
creamed 176
soup................... 139, 176
timbale of............... 177, 213
Ketchups: see Sauces, ketchups and relishes
Kohl-rabi
freezing 304
growing 177
preparing and cooking 178
recipes
casserole 178
in Mornay sauce.............. 178
sugar-browned 178
with chives and parsley 178

L

Land cress...................... 179
Laterals.............................44
Lavender vinegar 343
Leaders 44
Leaf eelworm 283
Leaf spot 288
Leafhoppers 283
Leatherjackets 283
Lectin 92
Leeks
freezing 304
growing 179–80
preparing and cooking 180
recipes
and ham soufflé 182
braised 181
cheesy 181
chiffonade salad 182
crême vichyssoise 181
crisp-fried 181
French flan 182, 213
in papillotes 182
Provençale 307
soup........................... 181
Lentils 262
Lettuces
growing 183–5
preparing and serving 185
recipes
braised 141, 186
Florida salad 135, 185
Greek mixed salad 144, 185
low-calorie salad 186
soup................... 186, 211
Waldorf salad 186
with lemon dressing 186
with soured cream dressing 185
Levington compost 33
Light soils 16
Lime (testing for and adding) 19
Lime-sulphur 292
Liquid fertilisers 19
Loam soils 16

Loganberries
bottling 311–12
freezing 302
growing 40, 187
preparing and cooking 188
propagating 47
recipes
choux pastry with 143, 188
cream 188
ice cream 188
jam 319
jelly 322
mousse 188, 215
Lovage 189

M

Magnesium deficiency 20, 288
Magnesium sulphate 292
Malathion 292
Maneb 292
Manganese deficiency.......20, 289
Mangetout : see **Peas**
Manures and fertilisers 17–20
Marjoram 189–90
Marrows and courgettes
freezing 304
growing 190–1
preparing and cooking 192
recipes
baked 192, 207
butter 325
buttered 192
chutney 337
courgette salad 193
courgettes au gratin 193
courgettes Provençale 307
courgettes with pork,
   Spanish style 193
jam 319
pickle 331–2
purée 194
Sicilian caponata
   (courgettes) 193
soup........................... 192
stuffed rings 194
MCPA 37
Mead 364
Mealy bugs 284
Mecoprop 37–39
Medlars
growing 194
preparing and cooking 195
recipes
cheese 325
fool 195
Melons
freezing 302
growing 195–7
preparing and serving 197
recipes

basket, savoury................. 197
basket, sweet 197, 209
Italian style 198, 211
with Cointreau 198
with raspberries 198
Metaldehyde 292
Methocarb 292
Millipedes 284
Mineral deficiencies . 20, 286, 288–9
Mint
cooking with..................... 199
growing 198–9
recipes
and cucumber salad 199
sauce 199
vinegar 343
Mixed fruit chutney 337
Molybdenum deficiency 20
Morels 354
Mosaic 289
Moussaka 86
Mulberries
bottling 311–12
freezing 302
growing 199–200
preparing and cooking 200
recipes
baked 200
tansy 200
wine 364
Mulberry canker 289
Mulching 36
Mung beans 262
Muriate of potash 18–19
Mushroom compost 17
Mushroom diseases 289
Mushroom flies 284
Mushrooms
drying 344
freezing 304
growing 201
preparing and cooking 202
wild 354–5
recipes
and bacon omelette 202, 207
in soured cream 202, 213
ketchup 340
pancakes, stuffed with 307
pickle 332
soufflé 202
spread 202
Mustard and cress 203
Mustard pickle 333
Mustard relish 341

N

Nasturtium seeds (pickle recipe) 331
Neck rot 289
Nectarines
bottling 311–12

freezing 302
growing 225–7
preparing and serving 227
Nettles
controlling 39
gathering and using 352
recipe
syrup 328
New Zealand spinach : see **Spinach**
Nicotine 292
Nitrate of soda 18–19
Nitro-chalk 18–19
Nitrogen
deficiency symptoms 20
value of...........................17
Nodal cuttings 29
'No-digging' methods 22
Notching 44
Nut weevil 284
Nuts
growing 203–4
preparing and cooking 204
salting 347
sweet chestnut 350
recipes
hazelnut truffles 204
sugar-coated hazelnuts....... 204

O

Onion eelworm 284
Onion fly 284
Onions
drying 345
freezing 304
growing 217–19
preparing and cooking 219
sets 218
spring onions 218
recipes
dolmas 220
glazed 221
in white sauce 308
pickle 331
quiche 207, 220
sauce 220, 307
soup 220
stuffed 221
vinegar 343
with forcemeat 220

P

Papery bark 289
Paraquat 37–39
Parasol mushroom 354
Parsley
cooking with 222
growing 221–2
salting 347

recipes
butter sauce 222
dip............................. 222
maitre d'hôtel butter 222
Parsley, Hamburg............. 223
Parsnip canker 289
Parsnips
freezing 304
growing 223–4
preparing and cooking 224
recipes
fried 224
purée 224
Paths 10, 26–27
Patios (growing plants on).........13
Pea pests 284
Peach leaf curl 289
Peaches and nectarines
bottling 311–12
drying 344
freezing 302
growing 40, 225–7
preparing and serving 143, 227
propagating 47
recipes
and raspberry flan 228
chutney 338
compôte 228
crème brulée 306
curried 227
jam 319
melba 227
pickle 334
stuffed 143, 228
Pear leaf pests 284
Pears
bottling 311–12
drying 344
freezing 302
growing 40, 228–9
preparing and cooking 230
varieties................... 229–30
recipes
and peppers, with
   yoghourt 211, 231
chutney 338
cinnamon 215, 231
croûtes aux poires 209, 231
in wine sauce 230
jam 319
pickle 334
Peas
freezing 304
growing 231–3
preparing and cooking 233
salting 347
recipes
buttered mangetout............ 233
pease pudding 234
soup 234
summer vegetable
   cabaret 141, 233

Peat pots 33
Peat soils 16
Pectin 316
Peppers and chillis
  freezing 305
  growing 234–5
  preparing and cooking 235
  recipes
    and tuna fish salad 211, 235
    chutney 336, 338
    cocktail 235
    cold stuffed 207, 235
    ketchup 340
    relish 341
    vinegar 342
Permethrin 292
Pesticides
  safety rules 281
  types 292
Pests
  control in greenhouses 51
  identification and control .. 282–5
Petal blight 289
pH levels 19
Phenolic compound 292
Phosphates
  deficiency symptoms................. 20
  value of 17
Piccalilli 333
Pickles
  equipment and methods .. 328–30
  recipes
    apple 334
    apricot 334
    beetroot 332
    blackberry 334
    cabbage 330
    carrots 332
    cauliflower.............. 330, 332
    celery and cucumber 332
    cherries 334
    crab-apple 334
    cucumber 331
    damson 334
    eggs 332
    gherkins 331
    gooseberry 334
    marrows 332
    mixed 332
    mushroom 332
    mustard 333
    nasturtium seed 331
    onion, cauliflower and
      cucumber.................... 331
    onion, cauliflower, bean
      and marrow 331
    onion and apple 331
    onion and cucumber 331
    onions 331
    peach 334
    pears 334
    piccalilli 333

pimento 333
plum 334
sweet 333
sweet apple and cucumber . 333
tomato, green 333
tomato, red 333
walnuts 331
Pickling cabbages : see **Cabbages**
Pimento pickle 333
Pirimicarb 292
Pirimiphos methyl 292
Planning
  fruit gardens 10–13, 40–41
  herb gardens 10–13, 28–29
  kitchen gardens....... 10–13, 26–28
  soft fruit crops 27
Planting
  fruit trees and bushes 42–43
  vegetables.......................... 35–36
Plum sawfly 284
Plums and gages
  bottling 311–12
  drying 344
  freezing 302
  growing 40, 236–8
  preparing and cooking 238
  recipes
    Alsatian greengage tart 238
    butter 325
    chutney 338
    compôte of gages 238
    custard, baked................. 238
    in red wine 209, 238
    jam 319
    pickle 334
    wine 364
Potash
  deficiency 20
  value of 17
Potato blight 289
Potato cyst eelworm 284
Potatoes
  freezing 304
  growing 239–40
  preparing and cooking....... 240–1
  recipes
    baked 213, 241
    nests 207, 242
    pie, Bulgarian 241
    potato and cucumber pie ... 308
    soup 242
    salads 139, 141, 241
Poultry manure 18
Poultry-keeping 10, 365–71
Powdery mildew...................... 289
Powdery scab 289
Preserving
  bottling 309–13
  chutneys 335–8
  drying 343–6
  eggs 348
  freezing 294–308

fruit cheeses and butters 323–5
jams 314–20
jellies 320–3
pickles 328–34
salting 346–7
sauces, ketchups and
  relishes........................ 339–41
syrups and juices 326–8
vinegars 342–3
Pricking out 34
Primroses 356
Propachlor 37
Propagators 34–35
Pruning 43–45
See also individual fruit entries
Pumpkins and squashes
  growing 242
  preparing and cooking 243
  recipes
    chutney 338
    pie 209, 243
    soup 243, 308
Pyrethrum 292

Q

Quince
  freezing 302
  growing............................ 243–4
  preparing and cooking 244
  recipes
    and apple pie.................. 244
    cheese 325
    jam 319
    jelly 323
Quintozene 292

R

Radishes
  growing 244–5
  preparing and serving 245
  recipes
    mousse 245
Raised beds 13, 25
Rakes................................. 14
Rape kale : see **Kale**
Raspberries
  bottling 311–12
  freezing 302
  growing 40, 246–7
  preparing and cooking 247
  propagating........................ 47
  recipes
    cream 306
    cream, pancakes with 137, 248
    flan 143, 248
    ice cream 248
    jam 319
    jam, uncooked 307

tartlets, Bavarian................ 247
wine 364
with soured cream 247
Raspberry beetle 285
Ratatouille 308
Red cabbages : see **Cabbages**
Red currants : see **Currants, Red**
Red spider mites 283
Relishes : see Sauces, ketchups and
  relishes
Reversion 290
Rhubarb
  bottling 311–12
  freezing 302
  growing 248–9
  preparing and cooking 250
  recipes
    and banana fool........... 215, 250
    cheese 325
    chutney 338
    crumble 137, 250
    jam 320
    meringue 250
    mousse 251
    pie 251
    poached 250
    sauce 340
    wine 364
Ridge cucumbers : see **Cucumbers**
Ring culture 272–3
Root aphids 285
Root rot 290
Rose hips
  gathering and using 350
  recipe
    syrup 328
Rose petals
  recipes
    jelly 323
    preserve 320
    vinegar 343
Rosemary 251–2
Rotation of crops 26–27
Rowan berries 351
Runner beans : see **Beans, Runner**
Rust 290

S

Sage 252–3
Salad burnet 108–9
Salsify
  growing 253
  preparing and cooking 254
  recipes
    with cheese 135, 254
    with mousseline sauce 254
Salting
  equipment and method 346
  recipes
    beans 347

cucumbers 347
hazelnuts 347
parsley 347
peas 347
sauerkraut 347
Sandy soils 16
Sauces, ketchups and relishes
  equipment and methods 339
  recipes
    apple sauce..................... 339
    beetroot relish 341
    blackberry ketchup 340
    celery relish 341
    corn relish 341
    damson sauce 339
    grape ketchup 340
    green tomato sauce 340
    mushroom ketchup 340
    mustard relish 341
    pepper relish 341
    red tomato sauce 340
    rhubarb sauce 340
    tomato and apple sauce 340
    tomato and green pepper
      ketchup...................... 340
    tomato and horseradish
      relish 340
    tomato ketchup 340
    tomato relish 341
Sauerkraut 347
Savory 254–5
Savoy cabbages : see **Cabbages**
Scab 290
Scald 290
Scale insects 285
Sclerotinia disease 290
Scorzoneras 255
Screens 11–12
Seakale
  growing 256–7
  preparing and cooking 257–8
  recipes
    braised 258
    salad 257
    with egg sauce 258
Seakale beet : see **Spinach**
Seaweed 18
Secateurs 15, 43
Seedlings
  containers for 33
  hardening off 34
  pricking out 34
  protection from birds 31, 36
  thinning 32
  transplanting 35
Seeds
  containers for sowing 33
  F1 hybrids 30
  germination times 32
  home-saved 30
  life of 32
  pelleted 30–32

owing indoors and under
  glass 32–35
sowing outdoors 30–32
Self-blanching celery : see **Celery**
Sewage sludge 18
Shading
  greenhouses 50
  seedlings 35–36
Shaggy ink cap 354
Shallots 258
Shanking 290
Shepherd's purse 39
Shoddy 18
Shothole 290
Silver beet : see **Spinach**
Silver leaf 290
Simazine 37
Sloes
  gathering and using 351
  recipe
    jelly 323
Slugs and snails
  controlling 285, 292
Snails : see Slugs and snails
Soakaways 25
Sodium chlorate 37, 39
Sodium hypochlorite 292
Sodium molybdate 292
Soil types 15–17
Soil warming 53–54
Soil-borne diseases 290
Sorrel 352
Sow thistle 39
Sowing seeds : see Seeds
Soya beans 96–97
Space-saving ideas 13
Spades
  choosing 14
  using 22
Spent hops 18
Spinach
  freezing 305
  growing 259–60
  preparing and cooking 260
  recipes
    and anchovy quiche 260
    crisp buttered 135, 260
    mould 141, 260
    salad 211, 261
    soup 216, 261
Spinach beet : see **Spinach**
Split stone 290
Splitting 290
Spraing 291

Spray damage 291
Sprayers 292
Spring onions 218–19
Sprouting seeds
  cooking and serving 262
  growing 261–2
  recipes
    bean sprouts with mushrooms
      and chicken 263
    bean sprouts with
      noodles 139, 263
    mixed sprout salad 263
Spur blight 291
Spurs 44
Squashes : see **Pumpkins and
  squashes**
Stem and bulb eelworm 285
Stony pit 291
Strawberries
  alpine 265
  bottling 311–12
  freezing 302
  growing 263–5
  preparing and serving 265
  protecting 46
  wild strawberries 351
  recipes
    cream 143, 266
    ice cream 307
    jam 320
    meringue cake 266
    mousse 265
    trifle 266
Strawberry beetle 285
Strawberry mite 285
Strawberry pots and barrels 13
Successional crops 28
Sugar peas : see **Peas**
Sulphate of ammonia 18–19
Sulphate of potash 18–19
Sulphur 292
Summer pudding 155
Summer savory 254–5
Sunflowers : see **Sprouting seeds**
Superphosphate 18–19
Swedes
  growing 266–7
  preparing and cooking 267
  recipe
    with bacon 267
Sweet basil 87–88
Sweet chestnut 350
Sweet corn
  freezing 305

growing 267–8
preparing and cooking 268
  recipes
    and leek soup 211, 269
    creamed 269
    fritters 268
    relish 341
    toasts 213, 269
Sweet peppers : see **Peppers
  and chillis**
Sweet pickle 333
Swift moth 285
Swiss chard : see **Spinach**
Syrups and juices
  equipment and methods 326–7
  recipes
    blackberry syrup 328
    carrot juice 328
    elderberry syrup 328
    nettle syrup 328
    rose-hip syrup 328
    tomato juice 328

T

Tar oil 292
Tarragon
  cooking with 270
  growing 269–70
  recipe
    vinegar 343
Tecnazene 292
Thinning seedlings 32
Thiophanate-methyl 292
Thiram 292
Tip-layering 47
Tomato blight 291
Tomatoes
  bottling 311–12
  freezing 305
  growing 271–3
  preparing and cooking 273
  recipes
    butter 325
    chutney 336, 338
    jelly 323
    juice 328
    ketchup 340
    mould 273
    pickle 333
    Provençale 308
    relish 341
    sauce 274, 340

soup 211, 274
stuffed 141, 207, 274
Tools 14–15
Tortrix moths 285
Trace elements 17, 20, 292
Transplanting 35–36
Trichlorphon 292
Triticale 262
Trowels 15
Tumbleweed 37
Turnips
  freezing 305
  growing 274–5
  preparing and cooking 275
  recipes
    buttered 135, 275
    glazed 275

V

Vegetable crops
  calendar 277–80
  harvesting 36
  planning 10–13, 26–28
Veitchberry 187
Vinegars
  equipment and methods 342
  recipes
    celery 342
    chilli 342
    cucumber 342
    fruit 342
    garlic 343
    horseradish 343
    lavender 343
    mint 343
    onion 343
    rose-petal 343
    tarragon 343
    violet 343
Violet root rot 291
Violets
  gathering and crystallising 356
  recipe
    vinegar 343
Virus diseases 291

W

Walnuts
  recipe
    pickled 331

Wart disease 291
Watercress
  growing and serving 276
  recipe
    soup 276
Watering
  in greenhouses 49–50
  outdoors 36
Watering cans 15
Weeds and weedkillers 37–39
Welsh onions 219
Wheat 262
Wheelbarrows 15
Whiptail 291
White blister 291
White rot 291
Wild flowers 349, 356
Wild strawberries 351
Wine-making
  equipment and methods ... 358–62
  recipes
    apple 362
    beetroot 363
    bilberry 363
    blackberry 363
    black-currant 363
    carrot 363
    celery 363
    cherry 363
    crab-apple 363
    damson 363
    elderberry 364
    elderflower 364
    gooseberry 364
    grape 364
    honey (mead) 364
    mulberry 364
    plum 364
    raspberry 364
    rhubarb 364
Winter moth 285
Winter radish : see **Radishes**
Winter savory 254–5
Winter soup 309
Wire stem 291
Wireworm 285
Wood hedgehog 355
Wool shoddy 18
Woolly aphid 285

Z

Zineb 292

TYPESETTING Brown Knight & Truscott Limited, Tonbridge
SEPARATIONS Adroit Litho, Birmingham; Mullis Morgan Limited, London
PRINTING AND BINDING Hazell Watson & Viney Limited, Aylesbury